W9-CFF-339

Annual Review of

INFORMATION SCIENCE AND TECHNOLOGY

Annual Review of
INFORMATION SCIENCE AND TECHNOLOGY

Volume 36 • 2002

Blaise Cronin, Editor

Published on behalf of the
American Society for Information Science and Technology
by Information Today, Inc.

Information Today, Inc.
Medford, New Jersey

ISBN: 1-57387-131-1
ISSN: 0066-4200
CODEN: ARISBC
LC No. 66-25096

Published and distributed by
Information Today, Inc.
143 Old Marlton Pike
Medford, NJ 08055-8750

On behalf of

The American Society for Information Science and Technology
1320 Fenwick Lane, Suite 510
Silver Spring, MD 20910-3602, U.S.A.

LSL
REF
Z
699
.A1
A65
V. 36
2002

Information Today, Inc. Staff
Publisher: Thomas H. Hogan, Sr.
Editor-in-Chief: John B. Bryans
Managing Editor: Deborah R. Poulson
Copy Editor: Dorothy Pike
Production Manager: M. Heide Dengler
Cover Designer: Victoria Stover
Book Designers: Kara Mia Jalkowski,
  Lisa M. Boccadutre

ARIST Staff
Editor: Blaise Cronin
Associate Editor: Debora Shaw
Copy Editors: Shaun McMahon,
  Tamara Misenor McMahon
Indexer: Amy Novick

Table of Contents

SECTION I:
Communication and Collaboration

SECTION II:
Knowledge Discovery

v

SECTION III:
Intelligence and Strategy

SECTION IV:
Information Theory

SECTION V:
Technology and Service Delivery

Preface and Introduction

Blaise Cronin

This is the 36th volume of the *Annual Review of Information Science and Technology (ARIST)* and the first under my editorship. Readers who are new to *ARIST* and interested in its purpose and evolution may wish to visit the Web site hosted on the homepage of the American Society for Information Science and Technology (ASIST), the parent organization (http://www.asis. org/Publications/ARIST/index.html). For the last twenty-five years *ARIST* has been expertly edited by Professor Martha Williams, to whom we owe a very considerable debt. She has set an exacting benchmark for her successors.

A change in editorship is almost invariably accompanied by changes in the product, whether in terms of style, coverage, or design, or all of the foregoing. Connoisseurs of *ARIST* will quickly notice some of the initial changes, and not all of these, I imagine, will be greeted with unalloyed enthusiasm. Perhaps the most obvious breach with convention is the adoption of the APA (American Psychological Association) referencing style, a move welcomed rapturously, it must be said, by some contributing authors. Since the *Journal of the American Society for Information Science and Technology (JASIST)* uses this convention, and since *ARIST* and *JASIST* are stablemates with much in common, not least authors, readers, and topic coverage, there seems little reason for *ARIST* to persist with its rather baroque bibliographic practices: all the more so now that *JASIST*'s transatlantic peer, the *Journal of Documentation*, has announced its adoption of the APA referencing style. Additionally, I should note, authors are being granted some latitude in their interpretation of the APA rules.

I am also keen to move beyond the bibliographic review model and have authors inject more of their own voices into the text in an effort to overcome (and I am quoting here from Theodore D. Kemper's piece, *Toward Sociology as a Science, Maybe,* in the August 11, 2000 issue of the *Chronicle of Higher Education*) what the sociologist John Lofland of the University of California at Davis termed "analytic *interruptus,*" the failure of many review chapter authors to engage analytically with their subject matter. The aim, in other words, is to provide the reader with a balanced, though certainly not uncritical or characterless overview of current and emerging issues, a summary of recent work in the focal area, and a sense of the important research questions to be addressed. Other actual or imminent changes are sufficiently cosmetic or uncontentious as to be unremarkable, such as the inclusion of short biographical entries on our contributors—those who, ultimately, provide the volume's warrant. The nature of the index to the volume changes as well, covering the text of the reviews but not the bibliographic references. On the production side, there have also been a few changes. The practice of sending camera-ready copy to the publisher will be discontinued with the present volume: henceforth, the publisher, Information Today, Inc., will have ultimate responsibility for copyediting and proofing. For some time it has been the practice to publish *ARIST* late in the year, typically to coincide with the ASIST annual meeting in November. That practice changes with volume 36: Henceforth, *ARIST* will appear at the beginning of the calendar year.

Some things, however, will not change. *ARIST* has long been considered a landmark publication within the information science community. It provides the reader with analytical, authoritative, and accessible overviews of recent trends and significant developments. I fully intend to see that these three virtues are reaffirmed in the years ahead. The range of topics will vary considerably, reflecting the dynamism of the domain and the diversity of prevailing research, both theoretical and applied. My goal is to progressively broaden the coverage by increasing the number of chapters and reducing slightly the average length both of the text and bibliography. While *ARIST* will naturally continue to cover foundational topics associated with what I shall call classical information science, of which bibliometrics and information retrieval are notable staples, my intention is to expand its footprint, prudently and selectively, in an effort to connect more tightly with cognate academic and professional communities where the study of information phenomena, behaviors, and artifacts is also of central intellectual concern. Interest in information science, broadly defined, is growing apace, and the challenge for *ARIST* is to consolidate its leadership position by building on its pedigree and perceived authority. However, introversion or ideational xenophobia could eventually undermine *ARIST's* value and attractiveness to core constituencies. Thus, the principal challenge, as I see it, is to subtly reposition *ARIST* such that it neither abandons its heartland market nor fails to establish a credible presence in emerging areas of importance to the wider information science community.

In their elegant study, *Visualizing a Discipline*, published in the *Journal of the American Society for Information Science* (1998 v. *49*, pp. 327–355), Howard White and Katherine McCain mapped the intellectual boundaries of the discipline and identified a core population of information science scholars. They claimed that the "rich word 'information' has seduced some into characterizations of the field that are, to date, overgeneral." They went on to add that these "definitions would have *ASIS*-style information science dealing with employers' payrolls, a housewife's grocery receipts, *Nightline*, arrival and departure listings in airports, the Grand Ole Opry, and color-coded vial caps used by crack dealers." The problem with this exclusionary logic, even allowing for a degree of playful irony, is that it ignores the fact that insights, regularities, and proto-models pertaining to information generation and use are quite possibly instantiated in all of these cases and contexts, as Paul Solomon's chapter in the present volume should make clear. In fact, their comments echo in some regards those of Roy Harris in his recent review of George Steiner's *Grammars of Creation* published in the *Times Higher Education Supplement* (May 4, 2001, p. 27):

> Steiner ushers us into the library, the museum, the art gallery, the university, occasionally the academic conference. He never takes us into the kitchen, or the street, or the factory, or the football match. That, as a writer, is his prerogative. But then he cannot complain if at the end of his book we conclude that he was never interested in elucidating human creativity at all, but in celebrating the mystique of his threatened professional world, and lamenting its passing.

A further irony in all of this is that many of those listed in White and McCain's canonical group are not information scientists in the strict sense of the term; in fact, many of them were intellectual journeymen who fortuitously traversed the formative landscape of information science. Moreover, some of these scholars' most significant work might not have passed the White/McCain admissibility test. This is not a trivial semantic issue, nor a spat between latter-day schoolmen; rather it is a plea to recognize the need for ecumenism without, I should add, irresponsibly ceding turf or diminishing one's intellectual patrimony.

What, then, does repositioning *ARIST* entail? First, the gradual identification of activity domains that are currently underrepresented, and, second, drawing upon a larger and more heterogeneous pool of authors to reflect the range of perspectives and approaches in play. In all of this, of course, it will be critical to both preserve and augment the traditional values that have contributed to *ARIST*'s longevity. Volume 36 affords a sense of what I have in mind. We open with an expansive (so much for the Editor's suggested word cap) and imaginatively structured review of the sprawling literature on scholarly communication and bibliometrics, two areas that lie at the heart of classical information science. The authors, Christine Borgman and Jonathan Furner, are information science "insiders" (even though Christine's doctorate is in communication), but they reach outside to embrace the burgeoning research literature of cybermetrics, much of which, at first blush, might seem to lie beyond the information science pale. By way of contrast, I have invited a complete "outsider," Philip Davies, whose academic home is international and strategic studies, to introduce *ARIST* readers to the high-profile topic of information warfare and its correlatives. His wide-ranging chapter on intelligence, information technology, and information warfare brings a raft of new topics to the pages of *ARIST* for the first time. Yet, as he makes abundantly clear in his introduction and subsequent analysis, these topics are implicitly, if not always explicitly, connected to the day-to-day concerns of many ASIST members and to a growing band of researchers in the broadly defined information science domain. The admittedly simplistic insider/outsider dualism breaks down with Susan Herring, a sociolinguist (i.e., outsider) who recently made a strategic career shift into information science where she is arguably better positioned to apply her theoretical and methodological skills to communicative structures and discursive practices in computer-mediated environments. But would the kinds of conversations, interactions, and observations that are grist to her investigative mill pass muster with White and McCain? Possibly, but I certainly do not doubt the value of applying the formalisms of linguistics to novel communicative contexts and emergent information behaviors.

Another topic, which is indicative of the push into new territory, is "intellectual capital." As many readers will know, there is a considerable literature on information economics, much of it originating in mainstream economics, some of it in information science, but *ARIST* has not heretofore offered a systematic deconstruction of the concept of intellectual capital and the challenges associated with valuing and managing intangible assets. The chapter by Herbert Snyder and Jennifer Burek Pierce constitutes a highly commendable effort to relate the arcana of accounting to the praxis of information science.

Although this year's *ARIST* does not include a chapter with the ubiquitous words "knowledge management" in the title, many of the complex issues associated with the creation, codification, and communication of knowledge are addressed in nuanced fashion by Elisabeth Davenport and Hazel Hall. Their approach is to root knowledge management in organizational dynamics, and they pay special attention to the concept of "communities of practice," a salient term in the literature of business administration and organizational theory, but one that, thus far, has not been foregrounded in *ARIST*. Their chapter is notable for stressing the importance of the tacit and the informal, and also for debunking the all-too-common notion that virtual communities are somehow synonymous with communities of practice—a concept, by the way, that evokes fond memories of "invisibles colleges," another signature topic of the classical information science literature.

Several of the issues raised by Davenport and Hall relating to sociotechnical systems design find their echo in Thomas Finholt's extremely lucid exposition of collaboratories, another subject making its debut in *ARIST*. His review of much recent research shows clearly that normative expectations and behavioral factors play important roles in shaping scientists' use and assessment of the value of collaboratories. Several other chapters deal with subjects that have previously appeared in *ARIST*. Pierrette Bergeron and Christine Hiller's overview of trends and developments in competitive intelligence builds on earlier contributions dealing with environmental scanning and social intelligence, but this is the first time *ARIST* has devoted a chapter specifically to competitive intelligence, a topic of considerable interest to professional information managers in a wide variety of corporate and other settings.

While Paul Solomon's chapter on discovering information is another first, many of the underlying themes have been pebble-dashed across previous *ARIST* volumes. Solomon weaves together the dispersed literature on information seeking, sense making, and information encountering in an effort to demonstrate the importance of context. His goal is to illuminate the ways in which situational factors facilitate or inhibit the creation, discovery, and shaping of information. This leads him to introduce the idea of a sociotechnical systems design science, a theme that finds its echo in a number of other chapters (e.g., Davenport & Hall, Finholt). A different, more formalistic, take on information discovery is provided by Gerald Benoît, whose chapter on data mining is a solid synthesis of a fast-moving field, one that, as he notes in his introduction, has been treated previously in *ARIST*.

In the section on *Information Theory,* Ian Cornelius has crafted the kind of chapter that will appeal especially to those whom I have somewhat whimsically labeled as classical information scientists. It revisits several of the grandees of early information science, Bertram Brookes for instance, in a clear-headed effort to determine whether information science has a theory of information. But he also connects the reader with the work of outsiders, both old and new, such as Claude Shannon and Jon Barwise. Counterpointing Cornelius, we have a grounded analysis of social informatics by Steve Sawyer and Kristin Eschenfelder. This is not the first time "social informatics" has appeared in *ARIST*: An earlier chapter brought a social informatics perspective to bear on digital library design. However, the present authors range more widely and, more specifically, have attempted to answer a question that has been asked more than once: Just what is social informatics? Or, to put it another way, as the authors do here, what is not social informatics?

I have grouped the remaining two chapters under the rubric *Technology and Service Delivery*. The topic of digital libraries is set to become a perennial of *ARIST*, given the extraordinary growth in research and development activity, not just within the information science community, but in a number of other academic disciplines, most notably computer science. Indeed, digital libraries constitute the principal site, anthropologically speaking, where these two tribes meet and seek to forge a *lingua franca* to drive next-generation digital library provision. Edward Fox (computer science) and Shalini Urs (information science) have provided a well-structured conspectus of current research and development trends worldwide. Volume 36 concludes with another overview of trends in information technology and their effect on information provision, this time in the area of health care. The subject is not new to *ARIST*, but, as with digital libraries, this is a huge sphere of activity characterized by rapid and frequent innovation, a sense of which is well conveyed by the authors, Marie Russell and Michael Brittain.

In conclusion, these thirteen chapters constitute a modest initial effort to chart a slightly different course for *ARIST*. As I write this introduction, the contributors to volume 37 are beavering away on their chapters. If all goes according to plan, the 2003 *ARIST* will introduce several more novel topics and also a number of outsider authors who have not previously graced our pages.

Blaise Cronin
Editor

Acknowledgments

Bringing *ARIST* annually into the light of day, even after almost four decades, still requires considerable team effort and a little luck. Those who do most to lighten the editorial burden are the stalwart members of the Advisory Board and the many colleagues who act as manuscript reviewers, all of whose names appear immediately hereafter. Their efforts are warmly acknowledged. The bulk of the copyediting and bibliographic checking has been carried out by Tamara Misenor McMahon and Shaun McMahon, to whom I am most grateful. Amy Novick created the functional and informative index to the reviews. Last but not least, I wish to acknowledge the numerous contributions made by my associate editor, Debora Shaw, in helping bring Volume 36 to press expeditiously under somewhat unusual circumstances.

ARIST Advisory Board

Chapter Reviewers

Michael Buckland	Paul Kantor	Javed Mostafa
John Budd	Rob Kling	Christine Ogan
Keith Cogdill	Jane Klobas	John Prescott
Bonnie Cooper Carroll	Ray Larson	Ronald Rice
Elisabeth Davenport	Emile Levine	Alice Robbin
Susan Dumais	Leah Lievrouw	Howard Rosenbaum
Denham Grey	Robert Losee	Victor Rosenberg
Glynn Harmon	Peter Lyman	Diane Sonnenwald
Birger Hjørland	Anna McDaniel	John Walsh

Contributors

Gerald Benoît received his doctorate from the University of California at Los Angeles for an interdisciplinary study of systems design, combining critical theory and the philosophy of language to information systems design and use. His research focuses on language issues in information retrieval, with a special interest in visualization and end-user interpretation. Dr. Benoît is an assistant professor in the College of Communications and Information Studies at the University of Kentucky.

Pierrette Bergeron is an associate professor at the École de bibliothéconomie et des sciences de l'information (EBSI) of the Université de Montréal, Canada. Her research and teaching interests are in the areas of strategic information management, including competitive intelligence and knowledge management, information policy, organizational information use, and management of information services. She holds a Ph.D. in information transfer from Syracuse University.

Christine L. Borgman holds the Presidential Chair in Information Studies at the University of California, Los Angeles and is a Visiting Professor of Information Science at Loughborough University in England. Her teaching and research interests include digital libraries, human-computer interaction, information seeking behavior, electronic publishing, scholarly communication, bibliometrics, and information technology policy. Professor Borgman has published widely in the fields of information studies, computer science, and communication and has lectured or conducted research in more than twenty countries. She was a Fulbright Visiting Professor in Budapest, Hungary and a Scholar-in-Residence at the Rockefeller Foundation Center in Bellagio, Italy. She holds a B.A. in mathematics (Michigan State University), M.L.S. (Pittsburgh), and Ph.D. in communication (Stanford). She currently serves on the editorial boards of *Journal of the American Society for Information Science and Technology, Journal of Documentation, Journal of Computer-Mediated Communication, The Information Society,* and the *Journal of Digital Information.*

J. Michael Brittain has held senior academic appointments at the University of Loughborough in the U.K., the University of Adelaide in Australia, and, most recently, as Professor of Information Management in the School of Communications and Information Management at the Victoria University of Wellington, New Zealand. Dr. Brittain has published widely on the subjects of health informatics, education and training for health informatics, social science information provision, and information systems. Since returning to the U.K. at the beginning of 2001, he has worked as a consultant in the health informatics field.

Ian Cornelius is a member of the Department of Library and Information Studies at University College Dublin, Ireland. His current research interests include theories of information, information policy, and the theory of information studies. His teaching responsibilities include courses concerned with the general social and intellectual background of information, including information policy, information and society, and research methods. Dr. Cornelius has previously worked in universities in England, Scotland, Australia, and at Columbia University in New York. From 1993 to 1994 he was a visiting fellow in the Department of Social and Political Science in the European University Institute, Florence. His book *Meaning and Method in Information Studies* was published by Ablex in 1996.

Elisabeth Davenport is Professor of Information Management in the School of Computing at Napier University in Edinburgh, Scotland. She holds degrees in Greek and English Literature from Edinburgh University (1969; 1973), and an M.Sc. and Ph.D. in Information Science from Strathclyde University (1986; 1993). She has held academic appointments at Strathclyde University, Indiana University, and Queen Margaret University College. She has published widely and is a member of several editorial boards, including *The Information Society, Library Quarterly,* the *Annual Review of Information Science and Technology,* and the *Journal of Documentation.* Her current areas of research are knowledge management, classification in the workplace, digital genres, inter-organizational systems and small and medium-sized enterprises (SMEs), and social intelligence.

Philip H. J. Davies is an academic specialist on intelligence and security studies. He is the author of a number of articles on information warfare, intelligence history, and defense policy, as well as *The British Secret Services* (Transaction, 1996). At present Dr. Davies is completing an historical analysis of the British Secret Intelligence Service for Frank Cass Ltd., and is working on a comparative study of American and British intelligence institutions for Greenwood Press. He is Associate Professor of International and Strategic Studies at the University of Malaya in Malaysia.

Kristin Eschenfelder is an assistant professor at the University of Wisconsin-Madison School of Library and Information Studies. Her current research focuses on the social nature of large organizational Web information systems, their consequences for organizations and organizational work, and how we can improve the human and technical processes required to manage them. She also conducts research in the area of information policy, examining the mutual shaping of law and information and communications technologies use. Eschenfelder earned her doctorate in 2000 from the Syracuse University School of Information Studies, where she also completed an M.S. in telecommunications and network management. She earned a B.A. in Latin American studies from the College of William and Mary in 1992.

Thomas A. Finholt is Director of the Collaboratory for Research on Electronic Work and a senior associate research scientist at the University of Michigan's School of Information. He received his Ph.D. in social and decision sciences from Carnegie Mellon University and his B.A. in history from Swarthmore College. Dr. Finholt's past work has included investigation of the impact of computer-mediated communication on group performance, examination of the role played by online archives in geographically dispersed organizations, and description of social processes within online groups. Dr. Finholt's current research focuses on the social and organizational impact of collaboration technology. He is currently directing NSF-funded projects to develop and evaluate collaboratories in the earthquake engineering and space physics research communities and is a co-investigator on NIH-funded efforts to build collaboratories for HIV/AIDS research. Dr. Finholt is also leading a project, in cooperation with Bell Labs, to develop collaboratory technology for software engineering.

Edward A. Fox holds a Ph.D. and M.S. in computer science from Cornell University, and a B.S. from M.I.T. Since 1983 he has been at Virginia Tech, where he serves as Professor of Computer Science, directing its Internet Technology Innovation Center, Digital Library Research Laboratory, and the international Networked Digital Library of Theses and Dissertations. For the Association for Computing Machinery, he is co-editor-in-chief of the *Journal of Educational Resources in Computing*. He was General Chair for JCDL 2001 and Program Chair for ACM DL '99, DL '96, and SIGIR '95 meetings. He was lead guest editor for *Communications of the ACM* special issues July 1989, April 1991, April 1995, April 1998, and May 2001. He served from 1987 to 1995 as ACM SIGIR vice chair, and then chair. He has authored numerous publications and has served on many editorial boards in areas such as digital libraries, information storage and retrieval, hypertext/hypermedia/multimedia, and electronic publishing.

Jonathan Furner is Assistant Professor in the Department of Information Studies at the University of California, Los Angeles. He has a Ph.D. in information studies and an M.Sc. in information management from the University of Sheffield, and an M.A. in philosophy and social theory from the University of Cambridge. In his Ph.D. dissertation, he developed novel mathematical methods for characterizing and comparing hypertext structures; his current teaching and research interests span the fields of information retrieval, hypertext, bibliometrics, subject analysis, and the history, philosophy, and sociology of information studies. His work has appeared in the *Journal of the American Society for Information Science* and the *Journal of Documentation*, and he serves on the editorial boards of the *Journal of Information Science* and *Information Processing & Management*.

Hazel Hall is Senior Lecturer in Information Management at Napier University School of Computing in Edinburgh, Scotland. Her current research interests include online information services provision, business information sources and services, the education and training of information professionals, and the impact of these areas on knowledge management activity within organizations. As well as holding qualifications in information management, Hazel's background includes qualifications in French and Italian language and literature from the Universities of Birmingham, Nantes and Paris Sorbonne.

Susan C. Herring is Associate Professor of Information Science at Indiana University, Bloomington. Trained as a linguist (she holds an M.A. and Ph.D. in Linguistics from the University of California at Berkeley), Dr. Herring has since 1991 been applying linguistic methods to the study of computer-mediated communication (CMC) on the Internet. Her research interests include gender and online communication, interaction management, multi-modal CMC, and the effects of the Internet on global linguistic diversity and language change. She has published three edited collections, *Computer-Mediated Communication: Linguistic, Social and Cross-Cultural Perspectives* (Benjamins, 1996), *Computer-Mediated Discourse Analysis* (1997, special issue of the *Electronic Journal of Communication*), and *Textual Parameters in Older Languages* (Benjamins, 2000), as well as a number of articles and book chapters on CMC.

Christine A. Hiller has been an adjunct professor at the Université de Montréal's École de bibliothéconomie et des sciences de l'information (EBSI) for several years. She has taught courses in corporate information systems and competitive intelligence. Christine holds a master's degree in library and information studies from McGill University and has worked for more than ten years in the competitive intelligence field.

Jennifer Burek Pierce earned her Ph.D. in speech communication and her M.L.S. from Indiana University in 1999. Since then, she has worked as a consultant, a librarian, and also as a lecturer at the School of Library and Information Science at the Catholic University of America in Washington, DC. Her main research interest is in the ways women's organizations and magazines encouraged social and civic activism in the years following suffrage.

Marie Russell is a Research Fellow at the Health Services Research Center, Victoria University of Wellington, New Zealand, undertaking evaluations and research in health services. She worked formerly as a librarian, mainly in the nongovernment international aid and development sector. After completing her M.A. (Applied) in social science research in 1996 she worked as a freelance researcher and as a radio broadcaster, making human interest documentaries for New Zealand's National Radio. Her recent voluntary work concerns families and children's rights, and public library services.

Steve Sawyer is an associate professor in the newly formed School of Information Sciences and Technology at the Pennsylvania State University. He was a founding member of the faculty in 1999 and was named its Faculty Member of the Year in 2001. Steve holds affiliate appointments in Management Science and Information Systems, Labor Studies and Industrial Relations, and the Institute for Information Policy at Penn State. He continues his affiliation with Syracuse University where he is a member of the Center for Digital Commerce. Steve does social and organizational informatics research with a particular focus on studying how people work together and how they use information and communication technologies. Present research investigates how software development can be improved through attending to the social aspects of working together, studying how people adapt to working with large scale information systems implementations, and understanding IT-driven changes to work and organization.

Herbert W. Snyder received his Ph.D. from Syracuse University and taught at Indiana University before joining the faculty at Ft. Lewis College, Colorado. He has published in the areas of scholarly communication, financial management for libraries and information organizations, and white-collar crime in nonprofit organizations. Prior to entering academia, Dr. Snyder worked as an investigator for the New York State Department of Labor and as an intelligence analyst for the U.S. Army.

Paul Solomon earned a B.S. from Pennsylvania State University in business administration, an M.B.A. from the University of Washington, and M.L.S. and Ph.D. degrees from the University of Maryland. He also did graduate work in economics, statistics and operations research, information systems, and organization theory at the University of Pennsylvania. He held positions as statistician, operations research analyst, operations analyst, and program analyst in the private sector and with various agencies of the federal government before joining the faculty of the School of Information and Library Science, University of North Carolina at Chapel Hill in 1991, where he is currently Associate Professor and Associate Dean. He spent the 1996–97 academic year as Fulbright Professor at the Department of Information Studies, University of Tampere, Finland. His current research focuses on how people create information as they engage in work and life, and the influence of information structures on information-related behavior.

Shalini R. Urs is Professor and Chairperson of the Department of Library and Information Science, University of Mysore, India. She directs the Vidyanidhi: Indian Digital Library of Electronic Theses project. She is coordinating the creation of the *UNESCO International Guide for Electronic Theses and Dissertations*. Dr. Urs chaired the 4th International Conference of Asian Digital Libraries (ICADL) held in Bangalore, India in 2001. She is also one of the editors of the *ETD Source Book* to be published by Marcel Dekker. She was a Fulbright Research Scholar at Virginia Tech, USA for six months from August 2000 to February 2001. She was a British Council Scholar at the College of Librarianship, Wales, U.K. during 1981.

About the Editor

Blaise Cronin is the Rudy Professor of Information Science at Indiana University, Bloomington, where he has been Dean of the School of Library and Information Science since 1991. He is concurrently the Talis Information Visiting Professor of Information Science in the Department of Information and Communication at the Manchester Metropolitan University and also Visiting Professor in the School of Computing at Napier University, Edinburgh. From 1985 to 1991 he was Professor of Information Science and Head of the Department of Information Science at the Strathclyde University Business School in Glasgow.

Professor Cronin is the author of numerous research articles, monographs, technical reports, conference papers, and other publications. Much of his research focuses on scholarly communication, citation analysis, and cybermetrics—the intersection of information science and social studies of science. He has also published extensively on topics such as information warfare, information and knowledge management, marketing, and strategic intelligence. Professor Cronin was founding editor of the *Journal of Economic & Social Intelligence*, and sits on many editorial boards, including *Journal of Documentation*, *Scientometrics*, *Cybermetrics*, *Library Quarterly*, and *International Journal of Information Management*. He has considerable international experience, having taught, conducted research, or consulted in more than thirty countries: Clients have included the World Bank, Asian Development Bank, Unesco, Brazilian Ministry of Science & Technology, European Commission, British Council, Her Majesty's Treasury, Hewlett-Packard Ltd., British Library, Commonwealth Agricultural Bureaux, and Association for Information Management. Over the years, he has been a keynote or invited speaker at scores of conferences, nationally and internationally. Professor Cronin was a founding director of Crossaig, an electronic publishing start-up in Scotland, which was acquired in 1992 by ISI (Institute for Scientific Information) in Philadelphia. For six years he was a member of ISI's strategic advisory board.

Professor Cronin was educated at Trinity College Dublin (M.A.) and the Queen's University of Belfast (Ph.D., D.S.Sc.). In 1997, he was awarded the degree Doctor of Letters (D.Litt., *honoris causa*) by Queen Margaret University College, Edinburgh for his scholarly contributions to information science.

About the Associate Editor

Debora Shaw is an associate professor and associate dean at the School of Library and Information Science, Indiana University, Bloomington. Her research focuses on information organization, information seeking and use, and patterns of publication. Her work has been published in the *Journal of the American Society for Information Science*, the *Journal of Documentation*, *Online Review*, and *First Monday*, among others. She serves on the editorial boards of the *Journal of Educational Resources in Computing* and *Library and Information Science Research*.

Dr. Shaw served as President of the American Society for Information Science and Technology (1997), and has also served on the Society's Board of Directors. She has been affiliated with *ARIST* as both a chapter author and as indexer over the past fifteen years. Dr. Shaw received bachelor's and master's degrees from the University of Michigan and a Ph.D. from Indiana University. She was on the faculty at the University of Illinois before joining Indiana University.

Communication and Collaboration

CHAPTER 1

Scholarly Communication and Bibliometrics

Christine L. Borgman
Jonathan Furner
University of California, Los Angeles

Introduction

Why devote an *ARIST* chapter to scholarly communication and bibliometrics, and why now? Bibliometrics already is a frequently covered *ARIST* topic, with chapters such as that by White and McCain (1989) on bibliometrics generally, White and McCain (1997) on visualization of literatures, Wilson and Hood (2001) on informetric laws, and Tabah (2001) on literature dynamics. Similarly, scholarly communication has been addressed in other *ARIST* chapters such as Bishop and Star (1996) on social informatics and digital libraries, Schamber (1994) on relevance and information behavior, and many earlier chapters on information needs and uses. More than a decade ago, the first author addressed the intersection of scholarly communication and bibliometrics with a journal special issue and an edited book (Borgman, 1990; Borgman & Paisley, 1989), and she recently examined interim developments (Borgman, 2000a, 2000c). This review covers the decade (1990–2000) since the comprehensive 1990 volume, citing earlier works only when necessary to explain the foundation for recent developments.

Given the amount of attention these topics have received, what is new and exciting enough to warrant a full chapter in 2001? What is new is that electronic scholarly communication is reaching critical mass, and we are witnessing qualitative and quantitative changes in the ways scholars communicate with each other for informal conversations, for collaborating locally and over distances, for publishing and disseminating their work, and for constructing links between their work and that of others. Most readers of this chapter will be scholars and students who conduct research; write papers; submit their work to journals, conferences, and book publishers; search for new information resources; and read the work of other scholars. We expect that most readers conduct substantial portions of their scholarly activities online. Many will have their own Web sites where they post their work, and many will circulate their work to colleagues in electronic form, whether through direct distribution or through online preprint servers. The cycle of scholarly activities is blending into a continuous, looping flow, as people discuss, write, share, and seek information through networked information systems.

In technological terms, scholarly communication is being transformed through the use of personal and portable computers, electronic mail, word processing software, electronic publishing, digital libraries, the Internet, the World Wide Web, mobile phones, wireless networks, and other information technologies. But how much has human behavior really changed? How much has the infrastructure for scholarly communication changed? Are we witnessing a revolution in scholarly communication, or an evolution? Or a coevolution of technology and behavior? (Bishop & Star, 1996; Borgman, 2000b; Kling & McKim, 1999). And how do we determine what kinds of change are occurring?

Bibliometrics offers a powerful set of methods and measures for studying the structure and process of scholarly communication. Citation analysis, the best known of bibliometric approaches, has become more sophisticated, and the advent of networked information technologies has led to quantitative and qualitative advances in other bibliometric methods. More content is available online in digital libraries, and more of it is in full text (and in other media including still and moving images, sound, and numeric data). More connections exist between documents, both in the form of citations and in the form of active hyperlinks that allow an information seeker to move between related documents (Cronin, Snyder, Rosenbaum, Martinson, & Callahan, 1998; Harnad & Carr, 2000; Lynch, 1998). Bibliometrics is being applied in new ways, to ask new questions. Co-citation measures designed to identify relationships between print publications are being applied to frame the intellectual space of the Web (Larson, 1996). Similarly, impact factors, which were developed to assess the influence of a journal, an author, a laboratory, a university, or a country, are being applied to assess the influence of Web sites (Almind & Ingwersen, 1997; Ingwersen, 1998; Smith, 1999). In addition to bibliometrics, scientometrics, and informetrics, we now have "cybermetrics" (the title of an electronic journal) and "Webometrics" (Almind & Ingwersen, 1997). Citations are complemented by "sitations" (McKiernan, 1996; Rousseau, 1997).

Bibliometrics is now an accepted method in the sociology of science (J. R. Cole, 2000; Cronin & Atkins, 2000; Merton, 2000), especially by scholars whose inquiries are well served by quantitative methods and structural approaches. Others prefer more qualitative methods and more interpretive or constructivist approaches to the study of scholarly communication. Bibliometrics has gained popularity due to its complementarity to econometrics, social network analysis, and other quantitative approaches to modeling behavior (Diamond, 2000). Concerns such as the nature of "trust" have moved from sociology to electronic commerce, and may be modeled through bibliometrics (Davenport & Cronin, 2000). Documents are no longer viewed simply as stable artifacts of communication. Rather, documents can be malleable, mutable, and mobile (Bishop & Star, 1996), and can have a "social life" (Brown & Duguid, 1995, 2000). New genres of documents are emerging to take advantage of the special capabilities of electronic forms. Electronic publishing, while expanding rapidly, still consists of a wide range of unstable forms and genres (Kling & McKim, 1999; Schauder, 1994). As electronic publishing evolves, and perhaps stabilizes, we can employ bibliometrics to observe patterns and trends as they emerge. Bibliometrics can be applied to a broader array of behaviors and to a broader array of content than in the past, and thus more sophisticated methods and measures are required (Paisley, 1990). Indeed, a generation of scholars schooled in bibliometrics is developing innovative new methods to explore new research questions, and scholars schooled in other areas are contributing new methods and new questions. In sum, this is an ideal time to devote an *ARIST* chapter to scholarly communication and bibliometrics, and to draw yet more researchers' attention to fertile territory that is ripe for exploration.

Scope

The Communicative Activity of Scholarly Authors

Our use of the term "scholarly communication" in the title of this chapter is intended to signal that our primary interest is in the communicative activity of scholars. In other words, we are deliberately limiting ourselves to consideration (a) of a particular group of people, and (b) of a particular kind of goal-oriented activity. We also propose to take "scholars," in this context, strictly to refer to people directly engaged in the creation of original scholarly works—in other words, authors. Clearly, there are several other groups of people who may be characterized not only by their common engagement in scholarship but also by their shared propensity for communicative activity—groups such as peer reviewers, editors, indexers, information seekers, and readers. It may further be argued that the fundamental activity common to all these groups is the making of *relevance judgments*—i.e., the making of assessments of, or decisions about, the extent to which particular documents are deemed relevant, in particular situations, by the judge. Even once the limitation to authors is made, we may still distinguish between the various kinds of communication behavior exhibited by authors in their various capacities (a) as *writers* (i.e., choosers of occasions for writing; of genres to write in; of subjects, themes, and arguments to write about; and of sentences and words to write); (b) as *linkers* (choosers of documents to cite, acknowledge, or otherwise point, link, or refer to); (c) as *submitters* (choosers of journals or other sources to submit papers to); (d) as *collaborators* (choosers of coauthors to work with, or institutions to affiliate with); and so on.

Bibliometric Methods

Our second primary area of interest in this chapter is the bibliometric methods that may be used in the study of scholarly communication. One general method by which communicative activity may be explained, interpreted, or otherwise understood, is to consider the objects, agents, events, products, and contexts of such activity as entities to be counted, measured, or quantified. Numerical data may be collected about samples drawn from general populations of such entities; these data may be analyzed using statistical techniques; and conclusions drawn about the nature of the populations, and about the existence of certain causal processes. Of course, quantitative methods such as these are applied in many different disciplines, and in many cases the development and application of domain-specific quantitative methods has become a field of study in its own right: allied to psychology, for instance, we have psychometrics; economics has econometrics; biology, biometrics; sociology, sociometrics; and so on. Analogously, the field whose concern is with the measurement specifically of properties of *documents*, and of document-related processes, is known as bibliometrics (from the Greek *biblion*, "book"). Other related terms are "informetrics," "scientometrics," and "librametrics." All these may be distinguished by subtle shades of meaning; the interested reader is referred to Sengupta (1992) and Tague-Sutcliffe (1992) for clarifications.

In bibliometrics, as in the other fields mentioned, the derived measures or metrics are typically counts of the frequencies with which events of specified types are observed to occur, which (once expressed as ratios of the total number of observed events) may be considered as probabilities of occurrence. The probability distributions that are thus formed are known as the bibliometric distributions, and these form the basis of certain bibliometric "laws." Examples are the well-known Bradford, Lotka, and Zipf distributions, of journals, authors, and words, respectively. Many of these distributions may be distinguished from other common empirical distributions (such as the uniform and normal distributions) by an asymmetric skew and a long tail. Distributions of a similar nature have been observed in other fields (sociometrics, for instance) where the objects of interest are not documents, but other products of human activity. Much historical and current research is concerned with: (a) collecting data from ever larger and more representative samples in order to more accurately determine the parameters of the distributions from which the samples are drawn; (b) identifying commonalities among observed distributions (and, potentially, reduction to one or more general formulae of which individual distributions are special cases); and (c) hypothesizing as to the cause of such regularity, given the voluntary nature of the human actions that are being observed. (As indicated above, Wilson and Hood (2001) have recently covered this ground in their *ARIST* chapter on the informetric laws, and we do not intend to go further here.) Egghe and Rousseau (1990) provide a textbook of informetric methods; Diodato (1994) offers a dictionary of bibliometric terminology, and readers looking for authoritative definitions and discussion of the bibliometric distributions are directed to these sources.

A Typology of Research Studies

The focus of this chapter, then, is the knowledge of scholarly communicative behavior that bibliometric methods can provide. One of our primary purposes is to review the findings of those studies that use bibliometric methods in order to describe, explain, predict, and evaluate the communication behavior of scholars. Yet we may make a distinction between, on the one hand, *studies that use* bibliometric methods, and on the other, *studies of the use of* bibliometric methods. In effect, we have two (intricately interrelated) central topics: (a) the nature of scholars' communicative behavior (as explored bibliometrically); and (b) the theoretical basis for, design of, and evaluation of bibliometric methods (as applied in efforts to improve our understanding of scholarly communication behavior). Somewhat arbitrarily, we might label studies that lean toward either side of this distinction as "behavioral" and "methodological" studies, respectively, although in practice studies vary in the relative extents to which they represent advances either in our understanding of behavior or our understanding of method.

The distinctions we have already made are summarized, along with a few others, in Table 1.1, which offers a seven-facet scheme for the classification of studies of the kind reviewed in this chapter. Facet A expresses the distinction between writing, linking, submission, and collaboration as communicative activities to be examined; Facet B embodies the dichotomy of behavioral and methodological studies. As indicated in the Table, other significant variables are (Facet D) the level of *aggregation* at which behavior is being observed (person, group, domain, nation), and (Facet E) the extent to which *comparison* is made (across people, groups, domains, nations, or methods). We have organized the present chapter along the broad lines of Facet A, reviewing both behavioral and methodological studies under each heading of "Linking," "Writing," "Submission," and

Table 1.1 Seven-facet scheme for the classification of
bibliometrics studies of scholarly communication

A. BEHAVIOR	A1. Writing
	A2. Linking
	A3. Submission
	A4. Collaboration
B. ORIENTATION	B1. Behavioral
	B2. Methodological
C. GOAL	C1. Description
	C2. Explanation
	C3. Prediction
	C4. Evaluation
D. LEVEL OF AGGREGATION	D1. Person
	D2. Group
	D3. Domain
	D4. Nation
E. SCOPE	E1. Noncomparative
	E2. Comparative
F. EXTENT OF TRIANGULATION	F1. Single-method
	F2. Multi-method
G. FORMAT	G1. Research paper: empirical
	G2. Research paper: theoretical
	G3. Literature review
	G4. Reference work

"Collaboration." By dint, no doubt, of the special complexities and challenges it presents, however, the largest quantity of work continues to be done in the analysis of linking activity, and we have divided the section on "Linking" into subsections accordingly.

Linking or Citing?

The terms "link" and "linking" are commonly associated, in the scholarly, professional, and popular literatures alike, with hypertext in general, and the World Wide Web in particular. Historically, bibliometricians interested in the explicit expressions of connections between documents have preferred to talk about "citations" and "citing." These latter terms, and the area of study known as "citation analysis," have come to be used in a somewhat narrower sense, in which: (a) the documents being linked are typically scholarly papers published in academic journals; (b) the principal mode of distribution of the documents is in hard-copy format; (c) the links take the form of bibliographic references collected in lists at the end of citing documents; and (d) the links are identified by the authors of the citing documents. It is only relatively recently, with the emergence of Web-accessible databases of full-text scholarly papers whose citations are instantly navigable by readers, that researchers have begun in earnest to apply the well-established methods of citation analysis to the electronic environment. Given the prior and pervasive usage of "links" and "linking," we prefer to retain the distinction between citation analysis (in the narrower sense described above) and *link analysis* defined in a broader sense—to encompass all quantitative techniques in which inter-document connections are classified and counted with a view to the description, explanation, prediction, and evaluation of document-related phenomena. Our intention is to highlight the potential of using bibliometric techniques, not just in their traditional domains of application (i.e., networks of printed journal papers), but in the new digital environments that have developed over the last decade.

The methods of link analysis, then, are those employed in studies in which data are collected primarily in the form of counts of *links*—pointers to, references to, or citations of "target," "cited," or "later" documents made in the text of "origin," "source," "citing," or "earlier" documents. (The distinction between "later" and "earlier" documents is one that may only be made in the context of networks of printed papers, each of which exists in only one permanent version.) There are two general purposes for which link analyses may be conducted: contextualization and evaluation. In the following sections, we consider what we will from now on call *relational link analysis* and *evaluative link analysis* in turn. (The more obvious label—contextual link analysis—is unfortunately one that could lead to confusion with the particular technique of "citation context analysis" discussed in our section on theoretical and methodological citation studies.) A simple distinction may also be drawn between (a) relational and evaluative studies, in which quantitative link analysis is employed as a method for describing, evaluating, explaining, or predicting some aspect of human behavior other than the act of linking, and (b) studies in which the act of citing is itself the phenomenon to be understood (and which may not, strictly speaking, involve link analysis as defined above) (Snyder, Cronin, & Davenport, 1995). In a third section, we discuss studies of this latter type in which the *theoretical and methodological foundations* of link analysis are examined.

Relational Link Analysis

Relational link analysis is a means to set links in context. In relational studies, link counts are used as indicators of the level of connectedness, the strength of relationship, or the direction of flow, *between* documents, people, journals, groups, organizations, domains, or nations. Relational citation analysis is used to answer research questions of the type, "Who is *related to* whom?" On the basis of scores derived from link counts, we may produce maps, graphs, or networks of individuals positioned in a way that demonstrates their relatedness to one another. Such maps may then be used (a) to inform descriptions and explanations of the historical and contemporary structure and direction of communication in particular organizations, domains, or geographical areas, and to assist in the making of inductive predictions of future trends, and (b) in information retrieval (IR) systems, to assist information seekers in identifying probably relevant documents (i.e., those "nearest" or most closely related to an initial query).

The first of these applications—visualization of literatures—was recently the subject of a comprehensive review in *ARIST* (White & McCain, 1997), and we do not intend to retread that ground here. Similarly, we have decided to reserve an overview of the second application—IR—for a separate occasion, since the design and evaluation of IR systems is typically considered to be a field of inquiry distinct from that of scholarly communication. Note should perhaps be made, however, of a few studies (Chen & Carr, 1999; Ding, Chowdhury, & Foo, 1999; Small, 1999; White, 2000; White & McCain, 1998), published after White and McCain's (1997) review, that may serve as recent exemplars of work in co-citation analysis.

Evaluative Link Analysis

The more controversial of the purposes of link analysis is that of evaluation. In *evaluative link analysis*, link counts are used as indicators or measurements of the level of quality, importance, influence, or performance, of individual documents, people, journals, groups, domains (subject areas, fields, or disciplines), or nations. Evaluative link analysis is used to answer research questions of the type, "Whose research or influence is *better*, or has greater impact, than whose?" Ranked lists can be produced on the basis of scores derived from link counts, thus allowing direct comparison of the performance of one individual (or group) with that of another. Such rankings may then be used to inform policies and decisions about the distribution of resources and rewards such as funding, prizes, tenure, or purchase agreements.

The classic overview of this subfield was provided by Narin (1976); van Raan (1988) and Kostoff (1997) each have compiled useful handbooks; Garfield and Welljams-Dorof (1992a) make a succinct presentation of the ISI-sponsored viewpoint; several reviews have appeared more recently in the journal *Scientometrics* (Kostoff, 1996; Narin & Hamilton, 1996; van Raan, 1997); and van Raan (2000) summarizes the latest developments. An historical account of the development of evaluative bibliometrics in the U.S. is given by Narin, Hamilton, and Olivastro (2000). In the period under consideration in the present review (1990–2000), hundreds of published papers have reported evaluative citation analyses. It is not our intention to provide a comprehensive review of this work, as interest in most of these studies is limited to those working in the particular scholarly or professional communities whose artifacts are evaluated. For the sake of example, we make reference to a few evaluations that have been published in the core journals of library and information science (LIS); otherwise, our primary concern is with developments in method and measurement. In the next subsection, we describe a few of the more common measures. In the subsections following, we consider evaluations of documents, people, journals, groups, and nations, in turn.

Measures of Evaluation

The fundamental measure used in most evaluative studies is *citedness*—the number of times an individual x is cited, or the frequency of occurrence of citations whose target is x. A value for *citedness rate* (aka *normalized citedness* or *mean citedness*) may be calculated by dividing total citedness either by the number of years over which citation activity is observed, or by the number of years over which citation activity was possible (e.g., since a cited document's date of publication, or a cited author's date of entry to the field).

Since the late-1990s, and specifically with the application of citation-analytic techniques in second-generation Web search engines such as

Google (http://www.google.com), interest in measures of greater sophistication than raw citedness has resurfaced. In their original paper on the workings of Google, Brin and Page (1998) describe their PageRank formula for ranking individual Web pages on the basis not only of (a) the number of "citations" each page receives (i.e., the number of Web pages linking to the "cited" page), but also of (b) the PageRank of "citing" pages, and (c) the total number of "citations" (outgoing links) made in each "citing" page. In effect, the pages with the highest PageRanks are the ones that are most highly cited by those other pages that have high in-degree (many incoming links) but low out-degree (few outgoing links). Given an adjacency matrix in which the structure of the Web is represented by binary values indicating the presence or absence of a link between each pair of documents, the set of PageRanks corresponds to the principal eigenvector of the matrix when normalized by link-totals. Brin and Page (1998, p. 110) claim that, using an algorithm for calculating eigenvectors that is a standard procedure in linear algebra, "a PageRank for 26 million Web pages can be computed in a few hours on a medium-size workstation."

Kleinberg (1999) introduces a related idea that is currently implemented in IBM's experimental search engine, Clever (Chakrabarti et al., 1999). Kleinberg describes an iterative algorithm, similarly based on the derivation of principal eigenvectors from adjacency matrices, that assigns weights of *two* kinds to individual Web pages on the following reciprocal basis: if a given page "cites" many pages with high *authority*-weights, its *hub*-weight should be high; if a given page is "cited" by many pages with high *hub*-weights, its *authority*-weight should be high. The result is the identification of good hubs—pages that provide collections of links to many good authorities—as well as good authorities—pages that are pointed to by many good hubs and that are thus good candidates for the "best" (most probably relevant) sources of information about the topic of a given query.

The success of systems such as Google and Clever is reflected in the extent to which research in Web-based IR is currently dominated by attempts to implement link-analytic techniques at ever-increasing levels of sophistication. It should be recognized (in a manner that Brin and Page, for example, do not) that bibliometricians working on conventional citation analysis have, in their efforts to replace reliance on crude citation counts, produced similar formulations at earlier dates (see, for example, Pinski & Narin [1976])—and, moreover, that these echo the measures of relative "standing" of individuals in social networks first examined in the 1950s and '60s (Kleinberg, 1999). Doreian (1994) describes an iterative algorithm for calculating values for a measure of standing of documents in citation networks that predates current concerns with Web IR; but it remains the case that work of this kind has had little influence on the methods used in "traditional" citation-based evaluations of scholars and their products.

Evaluation of Documents

One simple kind of evaluative study is that which analyzes the counts of citations received by individual documents. In the first in a series of papers published in *Current Contents* in which he identifies and ranks the "most-cited papers of all time," Garfield (1990) lists those articles that attracted most citations from citing papers indexed by *Science Citation Index* (*SCI*) in the period 1945–88. About 175 million citations were analyzed; 33 million cited items were distinguished and ranked in order of the total number of citations received in the forty-four-year period; and the "citation classics" appearing at the top of this ranking were listed. The paper ranked at number one, published in the *Journal of Biological Chemistry* in 1951 and describing a method of protein determination, had received the remarkable number of 187,652 citations, for a mean of 4,938 citations per year since publication. This method of evaluating documents may also be used to identify "hot" (newly published and already highly cited) papers, and thus the "hot" research areas that provide their subject matter, by limiting both publication and citation "windows" to short, most-recent periods.

In the LIS domain, Brooks (2000) reports on a citation analysis of the twenty-eight papers that have won the annual "Best *JASIS* Paper Award" for "the outstanding paper published in the *Journal of the American Society for Information Science*" in each year between 1969 and 1996. Counts of citations received by these papers were compared with counts for a sample of other (nonaward-winning) *JASIS* papers, and the award winners were found to be cited at a significantly higher rate, supplying some evidence of a correlation between citation counts and peers' judgments of quality (echoing earlier correlative studies such as those reported in Bayer & Folger [1966] and Cole & Cole [1967]). It remains unclear, however, to what extent award winners have been cited on their own merits, without the citing author's knowledge of their "best paper" status.

Evaluation of People

ISI regularly publishes lists, not just of most-cited papers, but also of most-cited authors. Such lists have been used since the 1960s to forecast, with a fair degree of success, future Nobel prize winners (see, for example, Garfield & Welljams-Dorof [1992b]).

In the LIS domain, two articles published in *Library Quarterly* (Budd, 2000; Budd & Seavey, 1996) have extended a series of papers reporting evaluations of the scholarly productivity of U.S. faculty. Taking ISI's *Social Sciences Citation Index* as their source of data, the investigators produced lists both of individuals and of LIS programs, ranked both by productivity (number of publications authored) and citedness (number of citations received) in specified time periods (1981–92 and 1993–98, respectively). Normalized rankings of programs were produced by dividing the total score for each program by the number of faculty in that program; a composite ranking of programs was also derived by assigning scores corresponding to positions achieved in the separate productivity and citedness rankings; and this composite ranking was directly compared with that produced by the magazine *US News & World Report*, which is based not on publication nor citation counts, but on a survey of the opinions of faculty. No attempt was made, however, to combine productivity and citedness scores in a single measure of the performance of individuals in a manner such as that suggested by Sen, Pandalai, and Karanjai (1998).

In two smaller-scale studies, Bradley, Willett, and Wood (1992) and Cronin and Overfelt (1994a) have conducted citation analyses of faculty at the Department of Information Studies of the University of Sheffield and the School of Library and Information Science of Indiana University, respectively. The designers of studies such as these typically find themselves grappling with four questions, inter alia, that bear on methodological issues:

1. How should credit be allocated in the case of multi-authored works?
2. How should citedness scores be normalized to take into account the varying time-in-field of individual faculty?
3. Should author self-citations be included in citation counts, or should only "residual" (nonself-citing) citations be considered?
4. How may productivity (number of publications authored) and citedness scores be combined in order to produce a single measure of the performance of individuals?

With respect to the first of these issues, Harsanyi (1993) provides a comprehensive review both of numerous different aspects of the problem and of potential solutions. Following MacRoberts and MacRoberts (1987), Cronin and Overfelt (1994a) identify three different approaches: (a) "straight" counting, by which only the first author of an article receives credit for it; (b) "whole" counting, in which every author of an article receives credit for it; and (c) "adjusted" counting, in which each coauthor receives a fractional count. The straight counting approach seems to reintroduce the "first-author problem" for which the print and CD-ROM versions of ISI's citation indexes used to be criticized; in these versions of the indexes, cited items were listed under first authors only. Burrell and Rousseau (1995) further elucidate the implications of fractional counting; Egghe, Rousseau, and van Hooydonk (2000) describe three more complex methods of accrediting publications to authors that were not considered by Cronin and Overfelt.

Cronin and Overfelt found that rankings of faculty at Indiana were subject to significant change when decisions on the first two of these issues are varied. Referring to a general trend toward collaboration and coauthorship, they surmise that, since junior faculty are more likely than their senior colleagues to be coauthors, "straight" counting under-represents their impact. They conclude that adjusted counting is an "attractive" means of correcting for this distortion, and that normalized counting based on time-in-field is also more "equitable." Nevertheless, there seems to be little consensus in the literature as to how each of the four issues listed above should be dealt with; no standardized framework for the citation-based evaluation of individuals yet exists.

In a series of "influmetric" studies (see, for example, Cronin [1991], Cronin, McKenzie, & Rubio [1993], Cronin, McKenzie, & Stiffler [1992], and Cronin & Overfelt [1994a]) culminating in a monographic treatment (Cronin, 1995), Cronin and his coworkers have developed the notion that the published *acknowledgments* made by scholarly authors of the contributions of others may be similarly, perhaps even more directly, regarded as indicators of the extent of influence or impact of the acknowledged on the acknowledger. Cronin was able to employ bibliometric methods in analyzing counts of instances of acknowledgment in order to develop a typology of acknowledgments, to identify highly acknowledged authors in various disciplines, to characterize the frequency distributions of acknowledgments, and to describe acknowledgers' behavior. Future attempts to use acknowledgment statistics as an evaluative tool may be hamstrung, however, by the labor-intensive nature of the manual data gathering that is involved.

Evaluation of Journals

Counts of citations received by the articles published in specific journals can be used to rank journal titles. Harter (1998), for instance, uses citation counts to compare the impact of eight well-established electronic journals with that of competing titles that appear only in print form. Since 1976, ISI has published in its annual *Journal Citation Reports* lists of journals, classified by subject area, and ranked according to their "impact factor" (IF) (Garfield, 1973). ISI calculates values for a journal's IF by dividing (a) the number of citations received in the current year by papers published in the journal in the previous two years, by (b) the number of papers published in the journal in the previous two years. In effect, the IF is a measure of the number of citations received in a given year by the "average" paper in a given journal. Many other citation-based methods of ranking journals have been suggested in the literature. Nisonger (1999) reviews these in the context of a comprehensive overview of evaluations of the *Journal of the American Society for Information Science* (*JASIS*) in published analyses of LIS journals.

Van Leeuwen, Moed, and Reedijk (1999) summarize some of the criticisms that have been leveled at ISI's IF: (a) the accuracy of IF values may vary, often as a result of citations being counted in the numerator of the IF formula even though they are to theoretically "uncitable" works (e.g., letters and editorials) that are not counted in the denominator (see also Moed & van Leeuwen [1995]); (b) a journal's IF may be correlated (positively or negatively) with the proportion of its content that consists of reviews, letters, or notes; (c) other parameters of the distribution of citations received by a journal (e.g., the percentage of articles that are *uncited* in a given year) may provide very different indications of a journal's impact than the mean of that distribution; (d) the two-year citation "window" used in IF calculations may lead to systematic bias against journals in fields (specifically, many in the social sciences and humanities) where the maximum citedness of the average article is obtained more than two years after publication. Rousseau and van Hooydonk (1996) supply evidence to suggest that a journal's IF may be correlated at an even more basic level simply with the number of papers that the journal publishes; Roy, Roy, and Johnson (1983) were among the first to suggest the possible correlation of impact with number of papers.

Journal IFs are sometimes used, not simply as measures of the competitiveness of the journals themselves, but as convenient surrogates for citation counts for individual papers, especially in the evaluation of the output of individual authors for promotion or tenure decisions. If a given author has published an article in *JASIS*, for instance, it is easier to measure the worth of that particular article by finding *JASIS*'s current IF, than by conducting a search for all citations made to that article. (If the article is a very recently published one, of course, there will in any case be no citations to count.) But the use of journal IFs in this manner has been subject to regular criticism for reasons additional to those commonly invoked in general critiques of citation analysis. Seglen (1992) demonstrates clearly that the typical distribution of citation counts for the articles published in a given journal is not Gaussian (with counts distributed "normally" around a mean represented by the journal's IF), but highly skewed, with a few articles receiving much higher numbers of citations than the IF will indicate. Seglen concludes that the IF is thus not representative of individual articles, and should not be treated as such. Seglen (1994) reports on a study in which two groups of authors were compared—one group characterized by citation scores roughly twice the size of the other's, but both publishing in similar sets of journals. Analysis of the citation counts received by papers published in individual journals showed that the ratio between the highly cited and the less-cited groups' citation scores did not vary significantly from journal to journal. Seglen drew the conclusion that the likelihood of being cited does not increase with publication in a journal with a high IF; there is no "citation bonus" to be garnered from publishing in a high-impact journal. It remains to be explained, of course, how some journals have higher IFs than others: Seglen (1998) suggests that much of the variation stems from the nature of the research area that any given journal covers, and from the length or secondary status of articles typically published in a journal (long papers and review articles tend to receive more citations), as well as from the "quality" of the typical submission.

Álvarez and Pulgarín (1998) describe a statistical method based on quantum measurement, a technique derived from item response theory and Rasch probability, that may be used to normalize for the "field effects" highlighted by Seglen and many others. Álvarez and Pulgarín evaluate each single citation in library and information science, for instance, as being "equivalent" (in terms of its "diffusive" power) to 190 citations in biochemistry and molecular biology. Other attempts, more or less arbitrary, to normalize for field effects in the calculation of IFs are described by Sen (1999), van Leeuwen, Moed, and Reedijk (1999), and Vinkler (2000).

Evaluation of Groups and Organizations

The performance of individual scholars may be aggregated at the level of groups of various sizes. Research groups, departments, and entire universities and corporations may thus be evaluated in much the same way as that employed (e.g., by Bradley et al. [1992] and Cronin & Overfelt [1994a]—see above) to assess the performance of individuals (Russell & Rousseau, in press; van Raan, 1999). According to Garfield and Welljams-Dorof (1992a, p. 324), the value of using citation-based institutional rankings as science-and-technology (S&T) indicators is "obvious:" "... university administrators and corporate managers can compare their peers and competitors. Government and private funding sources can monitor the return on their S&T investment. And policymakers can identify relative strengths and weaknesses in strategically important S&T sectors."

Noyons, Moed, and Luwel (1999) describe their comparative evaluation of a Belgian research institute in micro-electronics, in which indicators of its own performance and that of its peer institutions were derived both from counts of citations received by publications written by members of those institutions, and from structural maps created using co-citation and co-word techniques. Vinkler (2000) summarizes the applicability of a range of metrics, varying in degree of sophistication, for evaluating the performance of research teams, differentiating "gross" indicators (e.g., raw counts of citations received) from "specific" indicators (e.g., number of citations per paper or per researcher), "distribution" indicators (e.g., proportion of total citations received by all research teams being compared), and "relative" indicators such as Vinkler's Relative Citation Rate (RCR)—the number of citations received, divided by the sum of the IFs of the journals where the cited papers were published. This last metric is an example of a measure that compares counts of observed citations with estimates of some "expected" citation score, and is similar to the categorical journal impact used by ISI in their "macro" journal studies (see Garfield (1975) for an early example of such a study). Van Hooydonk (1998) examines several alternative formulae of this nature, and Ingwersen, Larsen, and Wormell (2000) conduct a comparison of observed with expected (IF-based) scores in their evaluation of nine Danish research centers.

Evaluation of Nations

Moed, de Bruin, and van Leeuwen (1995) review bibliometric methods of assessing the research performance of entire nations. In his overview of "what citations tell us about Canadian research," Garfield (1993) demonstrates the range of indicators of national productivity that may be derived from citation data. The tables and figures published in this article indicate both recent trends in Canadian science (based on raw citation counts—total numbers of citations to Canadian papers in regularly spaced five-year windows—and on impact factors—average numbers of citations per paper published in these periods) and Canada's relative standing in the world (based on comparisons of these data with those for other nations). (Switzerland heads a listing of the twenty "highest-impact" nations for 1981–1990.) May (1997) and Rousseau and Rousseau (1998) refine methods of ranking countries by the supposed impact of their research output; Egghe, et al. (2000) consider some of the technical problems that arise over the attribution of publications written by cross-national collaborators.

The relatively low positions of Germany and France in May's rankings came as a surprise to many. In a provocatively titled piece, van Leeuwen, Moed, Tijssen, Visser, and van Raan (2000) respond to May's analysis by discussing "First evidence of serious language-bias in the use of citation analysis for the evaluation of national science systems." Van Leeuwen, et al. report their finding that the national impact factors of France and Germany (i.e., the average citedness of articles published by French and German authors in the most recent five-year period) would reach much higher levels if all cited articles written in languages other than English were eliminated from the analysis. This is because the impact factor of the average paper written in English—when calculated from *SCI* data—is higher than that of the average non-English paper. The implication is that this phenomenon, in turn, is a result of the combination of two factors: (a) the general tendency for authors to cite papers written in their own language (see, for example, Yitzhaki [1998]); and (b) the predominance of English-language journals among those that are published, and thus among those whose citing articles are indexed by *SCI*. Van Leeuwen et al. use their finding to criticize *SCI*'s indexing policy, but the "bias" seems to be less a fault of ISI, and more a reflection of the real-life practice of authors, publishers, readers, and citers. What seems to be needed is a more sophisticated method of normalizing impact-factor scores in order to "correct" for the outcomes of own-language citing behavior.

Theoretical Foundations of Link Analysis

Many studies take the act of linking itself to be the phenomenon to be described, evaluated, explained, or predicted. Studies of this type may conveniently be categorized as theoretical. The purpose of these is justification; i.e., establishing the validity and reliability (or invalidity and unreliability) of conducting link analyses of the kinds described above. Theoretical linking studies seek to answer research questions of the type, "*why* do people link?" The idea is that, if we can improve our understanding of the nature and role of links and the act of linking, we can correspondingly improve our understanding of whatever it is that link counts can be used to measure. Any justification of the use of quantitative link analysis in studies of the former type is typically couched—on those occasions where such justification is provided—in terms that derive from evidence supplied by theoretical studies, and in particular by answers to the question, "w*hy* does author *a* decide to link document *x* to document *y*?" Cronin (1984) provides the classic overview of theories of citation.

In some theoretical studies, the contents, contexts, or other characteristics of individual links are examined in order to determine their function, purpose, role, or meaning (such work is often called *citation content analysis* or *citation context analysis* [Small, 1982]); in others, the creators of links (viz., linkers) are observed or questioned in order to determine their motivations, intentions, or goals in linking (these are commonly known as *citer motivation* or *citer behavior* studies). The stated aim of such studies is typically the isolation of those factors, influences, reasons, criteria, or sometimes even "determinants" that lead (or that are perceived to lead) linkers to behave, judge, decide, act, and, thus, link in the ways that they do. Liu (1993) provides an overview of citation studies of this kind.

Defenses of Evaluative Link Analysis

Historically, the archetypal contribution of a given theoretical linking study has been a link typology; i.e., a scheme of categories, classes, or types of links. Garfield's oft-reproduced list of fifteen "major reasons" for citing, first presented in 1965 (Garfield, 1965), is a well-known scheme, but is rather more *prescriptive* of "when to cite" (this phrase is the title of Garfield's paper in *Library Quarterly* of 1996 [Garfield, 1996]) than *descriptive* of the actual motivations of citers in practice. The general prescription is that authors should use the opportunity to cite as a means of "acknowledging intellectual debts;" i.e., to give credit to those whose earlier work is, in one *relevant* way or another, *related* to that of the citer, and thus deserving of credit through citation. In this sense, Garfield's list is one of *criteria* by which the degree of relevance of the relationship between citing and cited work may be determined. The citer acting on the basis of Garfield's criteria would be selflessly serving the goals of scholarship.

That citers do, in practice and in general, act in this way is the primary component of a presumptive argument typically made (or implied) by the proponents of evaluative citation analysis, which runs as follows:

1. that the motivation or goal of the citer is to identify all and only *citation-worthy* works—works that "ought" to be cited in the citing work;
2. that the general result of citers' activities is such that (a) all works that ought to be cited in the citing work indeed are cited, and (b) all works that are cited indeed ought to be cited in the citing work; and
3. that the quality of a given citable work consists in its citation worthiness, and thus may be measured by citation counts.

Such an argument is typical of presentations of so-called "normative" theories of citing (the idea being that citers are, in effect, conditioned to follow the norms of science in general and the norms of citation practice in their chosen fields in particular), and is often associated with the writings of Merton (1973), Garfield (1979), and Price (1986).

Critiques of Evaluative Link Analysis

Defenders of evaluative citation analysis typically point to evidence of the correlation of citation counts with other measures of the quality of documents or their authors, such as publication productivity, peer ratings, and awards of grants and prizes (for two older but continuously well-cited examples of such defenses, see Bayer & Folger [1966] and Cole & Cole [1967]). Yet the plausibility of each part of the normative argument has regularly been denied, and much empirical evidence supporting its falsification has been marshaled by its detractors. Cole (2000) provides an historical synopsis of early resistance to the use of citations for evaluative purposes. Edge (1979) wrote an influential critical review; MacRoberts and MacRoberts began publishing a series of critiques in the mid-1980s (see, for example, MacRoberts & MacRoberts [1987, 1996]); Peritz (1992) offered a succinct summary of "problems of theory and method;" and recently Seglen has assumed the MacRoberts' mantle as perhaps the most prolific contributor to the critical viewpoint (see, for example, Seglen [1998]).

Fault is regularly found with certain technical aspects of the means by which ISI's citation indexes are compiled (see Seglen [1998] for a summary of such reliability issues), and citation analysis is sometimes seen to be invalidated by its specific reliance on these indexes. In their study of the citing literature of sociology, for instance, Cronin, Snyder, and Atkins (1997) found evidence to suggest that there are two distinct populations of highly cited scholars in sociology—one consisting of authors cited in the journal literature, another of authors cited in the monographic literature. Given the citation indexes' limited coverage of monographic citing material, the latter population may regularly go unrecognized.

Moreover, and more fundamentally, at least two of the basic assumptions made by the normative theorists may be tested by empirical means. First, it is suggested that the motivations and goals of citers are more numerous and complex than the normative argument supposes, and many may be characterized as personal, self-serving, or political (rather than as professional, scholarship-serving, or rational). Second, it is argued that, even by the normative theorists' own standards, not all works that "ought" to be cited are, and not all works that are cited "ought" to be. The validity of using citation counts in evaluative citation analysis rests on the truth of a hypothesis that does more than suggest simply that the probability of citation of an earlier document by a later one varies *partly* with the level of quality of the earlier document and partly with other variables; it proposes that the quality of the earlier document is *the most significant* factor affecting its citation count. Detractors of citation analysis point to evidence that the combined effect of other variables is sufficiently powerful and complex to rule out *any* such positive correlation between citation count and cited-document quality. Seglen (1998, p. 226) concludes that "... citation rates are determined by so many technical factors that it is doubtful whether pure scientific quality has any detectable effect at all ..." In practice, it is common both for low-quality work to be cited, and for high-quality work to go uncited. Even if it is conceded, as Seglen suggests we should, that citers are motivated less by considerations of quality and more by the mere fact that, in the course of any research project, certain documents (whatever their quality) are *used* (i.e., read) and certain others are not, we might still observe that it is also common both for material that is used to go uncited, and for material that is not used to be cited (White & Wang, 1997).

One of the primary aims of empirical studies of citation context/content and citer motivation has been to supply evidence to support or disprove one or more hypotheses of the following kind—that it is more likely that a given (earlier) document will be cited by another (later) one if either (a) the earlier document, or (b) the pair of documents, is characterized by a certain property.

Some of the properties that have been suggested as candidate factors influencing citation are identified in the following sections, accompanied by references to studies that have isolated such factors as being of particular significance. In the first section, we consider attributes of cited ("earlier") documents; in the second, we focus on attributes of document pairs.

Attributes of Cited Documents

1. *Quality of content*: The content of the earlier document is of a high quality (Shadish, Tolliver, Gray, & Sen Gupta, 1995).

2. *Gender of author*: The earlier document is written by a male author (Baldi, 1998).

3. *Number of authors*: The earlier document is written by a large number of coauthors (Rousseau, 1992b).

4. *Source*: The earlier document is a journal article (Baldi, 1998).

5. *Citedness*: The earlier document has been cited many times before. This is the so-called "Matthew" or "halo" effect identified by Merton (1968a), who quotes from the Gospel according to St. Matthew: "For unto every one that hath shall be given, and he shall have abundance; but from him that hath not shall be taken away from that which he hath."

6. *Subject*: The earlier document is a recent one on a "hot" topic. As Seglen (1998, p. 225) points out, the very choice, made by a researcher, of a topic on which to write "will determine, *a priori*, the probability of becoming highly cited."

7. *Approach*: The earlier document is a review of previous work or otherwise of a "secondary" nature.

8. *Field*: The earlier document is in a field of basic (rather than applied) research.

9. *Assimilation*: The earlier document does not cover material that is now so well understood that it has been "obliterated by incorporation" (Merton, 1968b).

Attributes of Citing/Cited Pairs

1. *Relatedness of content*: The content of the earlier document is relevantly related to that of the later document (White & Wang, 1997). In their study of the semantic relationships between citing and cited documents in a sample of document pairs drawn from three LIS journals, Harter, Nisonger, and Weng (1993, p. 543) found the subject similarity to be "typically very small."

2. *Field*: The field in which both documents are written is one characterized by high citation rates (i.e., has a high "citation potential"), whether due to: (a) (in a field in which citation practice is highly institutionalized) a high mean number of citations per citing document; (b) (in a highly productive field) a high mean number of citing documents written per citer; (c) (in a rapidly growing field) a high number of citers relative to the number of citable documents (Vinkler, 1996).

3. *Persuasiveness*: The earlier document is perceived by the author of the later document (a) to be supportive or justificatory of the ideas or arguments put forward in the later document, (b) to be written by an author whose name will lend authority to the later document, (c) to meet the expectations of the later document's audience (Case & Higgins, 2000).

4. *Availability*: The earlier document is available for examination by the author of the later one.

5. *Author self-citation*: The earlier document is written by the same author as the later one (see the next section below).

6. *Journal self-citation*: The earlier document is published in the journal to which the later document is to be submitted.

7. *Social citation*: The earlier document is written by a friend, colleague, co-author, mentor, or student of the author of the later one, or by an editor or a referee of the journal to which the later document is to be submitted.

8. *Language self-citation*: The earlier document is written in the same language as the later one (Yitzhaki, 1998).

9. *Nationality self-citation*: The earlier document is written by an author of the same nationality as that of the author of the later one (Herman, 1991).

10. *Time difference*: The earlier document is published not long before the later one.

Author Self-Citation

Author self-citation may be said to occur when at least one of the authors of a cited document is the same person as one of the authors of the citing document. The *author self-citation rate* of an individual may be calculated by dividing the number of self-citations by the total number of all citations made by the individual. In effect, this rate indicates the probability that any given citation, drawn randomly from the population originally sampled, will be a self-citation.

The very ubiquity of the phenomenon of self-citation is commonly thought to pose problems for those who would attest to the reliability of citation analysis for evaluative purposes. The assumption typically made is that authors guilty of "excessive" self-citing are doing so gratuitously, in order "to prove how clever they are" (Baird & Oppenheim, 1994, p. 7) or in an unashamed attempt specifically to raise their own citation counts. Yet it should be clear that there are many noble reasons for self-citing. "In some research papers, discussion of relevant information will include the author's previous work, and it is no less improper to exclude it out of modesty than to include a poor reference out of egotism." (Bonzi & Snyder, 1991, p. 245). Very often, adherence to one primary norm of citing—that which suggests that citations should be made to previous work on which the present work builds—would seem to *require* the author to self-cite. In fact, as a researcher publishes more and more, quite possibly in a specialized research area that she is making more and more her own, the more difficult it may become *not* to self-cite. In the case of multiauthored papers, a decision not to self-cite may even be seen as a disservice to coauthors. It might be argued, on these bases, that evaluative studies that deliberately ignore self-citations are unfairly penalizing scholars who tend to publish in new or unfashionable fields in which few others are working, as well as those who have built careers through systematic exploration of a particular topic with which their name is associated (but see White [2001] for a rather different perspective).

There will continue to be an interest, then, in comparisons of the self-citation practices (a) of individual authors, and (b) of whole disciplines. The research questions are: (a) do high author self-citation rates betray egotists whose infected citation counts are thus rendered inadmissible in evaluations of their performance or influence?; and (b) do author self-citation rates vary between disciplines, and (if so) what are the reasons for such variation? Partial answers to the latter part of the second question may be found in comparative examinations of authors' motivations to cite and to self-cite: Are the factors that combine to increase the probability of a self-citation different from those that are positively correlated with citation events in general?

In their study of the citations made in a sample of journal papers in library and information science (LIS), Dimitroff and Arlitsch (1995) found that any given article was more likely to contain at least one self-citation if it were a full-length research paper, if it addressed theoretical topics, if it were authored by faculty rather than practitioners, or if it had a large number of coauthors. Bonzi and Snyder (1991, p. 248) conducted a survey of authors' self-assessments of the functions of citations they had made; reasons that were more likely to be given for self-citations than for citations of other kinds were that "[The cited work is] earlier work on which current work builds," and that "[The purpose of the citation is to] establish [the cited work's] writer's authority in the field." In a follow-up study, Snyder and Bonzi (1998) analyzed citations made in six different disciplines, and found significant differences in the proportions of the total number of citations in each discipline that were self-citations: 15 percent in the physical sciences, 6 percent in the social sciences, and 3 percent in the humanities. Snyder and Bonzi (p. 435) suggest that the discrepancy may be partly due to "the more incremental nature of research in the physical sciences."

Quality, Popularity, Citation-Worthiness, and Credit-Worthiness

The third plank of the normative argument—that the quality of a work consists in its citation-worthiness, and thus may be measured by citation counts—also deserves attention. Evaluative citation analysis is sometimes impugned on the basis that "quality"—the characteristic that citation counts are used to measure—is not an attribute that may be evaluated objectively at all, but one whose values depend on the subjective opinions of individuals. Where, then, is the warrant (it is asked) for any attempt to reify such a property, whether through citation counts or indeed through any objective measure? We might choose to head off such an attack by carefully distinguishing between (a) individuals' judgments of quality (which are subjective), and (b) the evidence or records that such judgments have been made (which is normally objective, reliable, and easily gathered). It might be that, as evaluators, we are satisfied with our ability merely to determine the degree of consensus about the level of quality of documents. We might be happy, in other words, to measure (and to distribute resources on the basis of) what is, in effect, *popularity*.

A more intransigent problem arises, however, once we distinguish between (a) *citation-worthiness*, defined as a property perceived to inhere in the relationships between documents, and (b) *credit-worthiness* (cf. "quality"), defined as a property perceived to inhere in individual documents. In one sense, the distinction is unimportant: judgments as to the level of either kind of worthiness are subjective evaluations, made by individual people; and evidence of the occurrence of judgments of either kind is objective. In another respect, the distinction is crucial: Citations do not provide evidence of the making of judgments of credit-worthiness (i.e., judgments of quality); yet evaluative citation analysis proceeds as if they do.

The point (it might be argued) is that not all credit-worthy works happen to be *relevantly related* to other works. A given work may be perceived to be highly credit-worthy and thus of high quality—perhaps by virtue of its author exhibiting high levels of creativity or innovation in its subject matter or execution—and yet bear no relevant relation to any potentially citing work. Thus, no matter how credit-worthy such a work may be, its credit-worthiness will not be recognized in the form of citation events; no evidence of its credit-worthiness will be supplied by citation counts.

Trends in Link Analysis

In the search for explanations of linking practice, several trends may be identified that, in combination, distinguish work done in the period under consideration (1990–2000) from earlier studies. We distinguish below between, first, technological trends, and second, theoretical and methodological trends.

Technological Trends

One important group of related trends may be observed to stem directly from a shared recognition that technological developments have redefined the scope both of the arenas in which scholars' communication may take place, and of the contexts in which bibliometric techniques may usefully be applied. Prominent among these developments is the emergence of hypertext technology in general, and the rapid rise to its currently dominant state of the World Wide Web in particular.

Hypertext and Citation Analysis

Hypertext databases (of which the Web may be considered a vast, distributed example) and citation networks have the same formal structure. Each may be represented, at the same level of abstraction, as a directed graph, consisting of (a) a set of nodes (i.e., "pages" or documents), and (b) a set of ordered pairs of those nodes, each of which may be considered as a directed, inter-nodal link (i.e., a hyperlink or citation). This graph-theoretic formalization of structure has been documented and developed for various purposes on various occasions in the separate literatures of hypertext (see, e.g., Botafogo, Rivlin, & Shneiderman [1992] and Furner, Ellis, & Willett [1996]) and citation analysis (see, e.g., Doreian [1988] and Pinski & Narin [1976]). Seldom have the connections between these literatures been made explicit; but see Kleinberg, Kumar, Raghavan, Rajagopalan, and Tomkins (1999) for a recent exception.

The analogies that might profitably be drawn between hypertext and citation networks are not limited to observations about structure. For example, we might expect that researchers would be interested enough to ask in general—just as students of scholarly citation processes have asked with regard to the specific document types that are the preserve of the academic and scientific world—what motivations lead authors of hypertexts, or of electronic documents specifically created for the Web, to link nodes together in the manner that they do? On what criteria do linkers base their decisions to link or not to link? What are the factors that influence linkers' prioritization of such criteria? Kim (2000), reporting on a study of the hyperlinking motivations of fifteen authors of scholarly papers published in electronic form, concludes that linking behavior (much like traditional citing behavior?) is inherently multidimensional: Each individual link may be made for a variety of scholarly and non-scholarly ("social" and/or "technological") reasons. Cronin, et al. (1998) describe their derivation of a typology of "genres of invocation"—ways in which scholars are invoked (cited, acknowledged, linked to, pointed to, referred to, or simply "mentioned" in the manner studied by Beniger [1990]) on the Web—and suggest various means by which and purposes for which counts of invocations might be analyzed bibliometrically.

Digital Libraries and Open Archives

We are currently witnessing the construction of large-scale, full-text, distributed digital libraries of scholarly works (journal articles, technical reports, etc.) in which inter-document citations are rendered in active (actionable) form, so that readers may navigate among works, following citations at will, and enjoying the facility immediately to retrieve and view related material, just as Web surfers have long been able to take advantage of the hyperlinks created specifically for this purpose by the authors of Web pages. In 1999, a consortium of commercial publishers began to collaborate on the implementation of CrossRef (http://www.crossref.org), a technology that uses Digital Object Identifiers (DOIs) to identify the papers cited in the journals published by consortium members, and thus to enable the automatic creation of active hyperlinks between electronic versions of citing and cited papers (Atkins et al., 2000). Caplan and Arms (1999) reviewed the then current state-of-the-art of reference linking for journal articles; Atkins (1999) summarized the approach of ISI to reference linking in the *Web of Science* version of its citation indexes.

Effective use of commercial databases of hyperlinked journal articles is hampered by the "financial firewalls" that readers come up against when attempting to navigate beyond the corpus to which they or their institutions subscribe. Access to research archives maintained by academic rather than commercial institutions is typically more open. Such digital libraries are the results of the first steps taken toward realizing the dream of "the ideal online resource for scholars and scientists: all research papers in all fields, systematically interconnected, effortlessly accessible and rationally navigable from any researcher's desk worldwide" (Harnad & Carr, 2000, p. 630).

The most well established repository of research papers in electronic form, increasing in size by 25,000 papers a year, is the arXiv.org e-Print Archive (http://www.arXiv.org), formerly known as the LANL e-Print Archive (Ginsparg, 1994), and maintained at the Los Alamos National Laboratory (Los Alamos, New Mexico) as a digital library for physics, mathematics, computer science, and related disciplines. The provision of free, open, discipline-based access to e-prints—electronic preprint and reprints—is the response of many scholarly communities to the tactics of the commercial journal publishers, who are perceived to profit unreasonably from scholarly work (Harnad, 1990, 1999). The usefulness of arXiv.org, and other e-print archives like it (CogPrints [http://cogprints.soton.ac.uk], for example, in the cognitive sciences, and BioMed Central [http://www.biomedcentral.com] in the biomedical sciences), will be further enhanced by the implementation of techniques for automatically detecting the occurrence of citations within texts, and creating active hyperlinks on that basis (Hitchcock et al., 2000). Such techniques have been developed in a series of exploratory projects conducted in a variety of contexts, including the Open Journal project (Hitchcock et al., 1998), the Open Citation project (http://opcit.eprints.org) (aka OpCit) (Harnad & Carr, 2000), NEC's ResearchIndex (http://www.researchindex.org) (formerly CiteSeer) (Lawrence, Giles, & Bollacker, 1999), and Ex Libris' SFX (http://www.sfxit.com) framework for dynamic, context-sensitive linking (Van de Sompel & Hochstenbach, 1999a, 1999b). Interoperability among the various emerging "standards" for automated citation detection and link creation is one of the primary goals of the Sante Fe

Convention (Van de Sompel & Lagoze, 2000), developed by the Open Archives Initiative (http://www.openarchives.org); the citation detection process itself may be made easier through widespread adoption of a standard format specification such as the Scholarly Link Specification Framework (aka SLinkS) (http://www.openly.com/SLinkS). Doyle (2000) reviews some of the proposed solutions to the link-standardization problem.

The nature and extent of the benefits that will be enjoyed by information seekers using open, hyperlinked e-print archives are already becoming clear. The facilities to conduct keyword searches of full, digitized texts, and to navigate directly from one citing paper to another cited paper, will be supplemented by the provision of citation-based retrieval functionality, by which the searcher may identify documents whose relationship to a query is not necessarily one of adjacency or similarity of content, but of level of co-citation or bibliographic coupling. Documents in retrieval sets may further be ranked by citedness, by their qualities as "hubs" or "authorities" (Kleinberg, 1999, pp. 606–607), or by other, more reader-centered measures of popularity such as hit-rate or frequency of download. Such is the promise of "a universal citation database as a catalyst for reform in scholarly communication" (Cameron, 1997): New methods of retrieval are, in effect, new methods of communication.

A full discussion of the implications of link-based retrieval for the design of future IR systems is beyond the scope of the present review, but it is also clear that new measures of scholarly communication will soon be possible. For example, we will be able to determine both (a) the extent to which the mere availability of certain material either in general electronic form or in some specific proprietary format is an influence on the decisions of authors to cite or not to cite that material, and (b) the extent of correlation between the level of citedness of a document and the extent to which it is used. This is because we will be able to measure not only the mere existence of citations but also the frequency with which the hyperlinks representing those citations are activated, the time spent viewing cited works, and the frequency with which cited works are downloaded for future use. Ultimately, we will be able to compare these measurements with properties of citing texts, cited texts, and citing-cited pairs, in an effort to determine which of these properties have the most influence on decisions to view (retrieve), to use (read), and to save (for future use). Evaluative bibliometric analysis, just like bibliometric IR, will become reader-centered rather than writer-centered. Cronin (2001) reviews the kinds of opportunity provided to bibliometricians by the new, Web-based contexts, contents, and technologies.

At the time of writing, very little of the current digital library development work in open linking, cross-referencing, etc., involves the use of bibliometric (i.e., quantitative) methods. Studies in which some kind of link or citation analysis is applied with a view to improving our understanding of the ways in which open link structures are created or used are currently few and far between; nevertheless, reports of the ways in which these structures are being built are of definite relevance in the present context, in the sense that they are indicative of the kind of arena in which we might expect bibliometric methods to be applied in the future. The "usage-based analysis" of the Computing Research Repository (http://www.arxiv.org/archive/cs/intro.html) (aka CoRR, part of arXiv.org) reported by Carr, Hitchcock, Hall, and Harnad (2000) represents one small step in this direction.

Bibliometric Analyses of the World Wide Web

Counts of documents accessible via the Web, and related estimates of the Web's rate of growth, have been undertaken by various means since its inauguration (see, for example, Gray [1996]). The varying extent to which the entire population of Web documents is indexed by individual search engines, and the degree of overlap between those services' coverages, have subsequently become of particular interest to both developers and users (see, for example, Lawrence and Giles [1998]). The results of a study conducted by Albert, Jeong, and Barabasi (1999) suggest that the distance between any two Web documents is almost always less than twenty links. In other words, the Web is indeed huge, but it is also so highly connected that it may be viewed as a "small world," in the sense established by Milgram (1967), recently revisited in a high-profile paper by Watts and Strogatz (1998), and embedded in the popular imagination in the notions of "six degrees of separation" and "(Kevin) Bacon numbers" (Gladwell, 1999). A more detailed model of Web structure is provided by the "bow-tie" model (Broder et al., 2000), constructed through analysis of over 200 million pages and 1.5 billion links identified by AltaVista's Web crawler, which suggests that the Web consists of four main components, each of roughly the same size: a "strongly connected component" (SCC) at its heart; a set of pages (the "in" component) that link to the SCC, but that are not linked to by it; a set of pages (the "out" component) that are linked to by the SCC, but that do not link to it; and a set of pages ("tendrils") that neither link to, nor are linked to by, the SCC.

Larson (1996) was one of the earliest to consider the Web from an explicitly bibliometric point of view, in this case using the techniques of co-citation analysis and multidimensional scaling, in order to construct a two-dimensional map depicting the relationships among Web pages in the field of earth sciences. Larson's work may thus be considered part of the literature of relational citation analysis as defined earlier. Almind and Ingwersen (1997, p. 404) introduced the term "Webometrics" in reference to "research of all network-based communication using informetric or other quantitative measures," and described a Webometric case study of Web pages originating in Denmark, Sweden, and Norway. Almind and Ingwersen compared counts of Web pages with counts of research papers indexed in ISI's citation indexes, and found that Norway's relative "visibility" on the Web was better than might be predicted from the traditional citation data. Almind and Ingwersen were more concerned to identify the characteristics of the "typical" Web document (its size, the frequency of outgoing links, etc.) than they were to evaluate documents on the basis of counts of incoming links, and their study should be seen as a contribution to the literature on writers' productivity.

In a subsequent paper, Ingwersen (1998) developed the notion of the Web impact factor (Web-IF) as an indicator of the "relative attractiveness" of individual Web pages, institutional Web sites, and national Web presences. Values for the Web-IF of a given Web site or country are calculated by dividing the number of *pages pointing to* that site or country by the number of *pages in* that site or country. In Ingwersen's comparison of the four Nordic countries with the U.K., France, and Japan, Norway was found to have the highest Web-IF. Smith (1999) clarifies some methodological issues regarding the calculation and interpretation of Web-IF values; Snyder and Rosenbaum (1999) caution against using commercial search engines for data gathering in such bibliometric analyses of Web links, since their coverage is highly variable and their search functionality limited, poorly documented, and changeable. The inability of conventional search engines to access the so-called "dark," "deep," "gray," or "hidden" Web (Lyman & Varian, 2000)—that formed by pages created in real time, in on-the-fly responses to searchers' queries—is also a source of hindrance to bibliometricians seeking to model the Web's structural properties.

The first issue of *Cybermetrics*, an electronic journal devoted to scientometrics, informetrics, and bibliometrics, was published in 1997. In it, Rousseau (1997) used McKiernan's term "sitation" (McKiernan, 1996) to refer to any of a given Web site's incoming links; the neologism in the journal's title seems already to have enjoyed wider usage, whereas McKiernan's term has as yet failed to catch on. Rousseau's exploratory data—counts of sitations received by Web pages in the field of bibliometrics—indicated the possibility that a Lotka-like "power law" function (see Rousseau & Rousseau [1993] for an introductory presentation) may be used to model the empirical distribution of such counts. This conjecture has subsequently been confirmed by three analyses of massive Web document-sets (325 thousand, 40 million, and 200 million documents, respectively) (Barabasi & Albert, 1999; Broder et al., 2000; Kumar, Raghavan, Rajagopaian, & Tomkins, 1999). All three suggest that the distribution of in-degrees (where the in-degree of a document is the number of its incoming links) may be modeled by a power law function, such that the probability that a document has in-degree i is proportional to $1/i^x$, for some $x > 1$. Broder et al. perceive a fractal-like quality to such distributions, in that they occur at macroscopic levels (on the entire Web), microscopic levels (within single Web sites), and at all levels in between. Egghe (2000) provides a review of the challenges that the Web sets for bibliometric analyses.

Theoretical and Methodological Trends

A second, no less significant, group of related trends may be identified in the development of theoretical and methodological approaches to understanding linking behavior. A selection of such intellectual trends is summarized in the following subsections.

The Definitions of Concepts

Links are commonly conceptualized as representations of the relationships between documents. A conceptualization of this kind may be characterized as being *artifact oriented*, in that it is the citing/cited document pair (rather than the citing author) that is the dominant component of the definition, and studies that conceptualize links in these terms are typically more concerned with properties of documents rather than properties of people. Conversely, links may primarily be viewed either as the results of human actions, or as actions or events in themselves. The current trend is toward a *person-oriented* conceptualization, which allows the researcher to focus on the motivations, goals, and purposes of the citer, and on those aspects of the situation in which the citer finds herself—beyond observable properties of the citing/cited document pair—that may potentially have an influence on the citer's judgment and decision making. Cronin (2000), drawing on Wouters (1999), offers a sophisticated semiotic analysis of citations (viewed as signs) and citation behavior (viewed as symbolic practice) in which artifact-centered and person-centered orientations may potentially be reconciled.

The Goals of Inquiry

The inquirer into linking behavior may have a goal of any of several kinds. That goal may be simply to *describe* and classify the behavior observed; it may be further to *explain* the behavior, either by identifying a *causal* mechanism (which may or may not allow for prediction of future behavior) or by interpreting the *meaning* that the agents assign to their activity and to the context in which the activity takes place; alternatively, the goal may be to *evaluate* or even prescribe behavior on the basis of judgments as to its relative worth or utility. In the 1990–2000 period, there is evidence of a continuing trend toward explanatory studies, and away both from purely descriptive accounts of linking behavior and from prescriptions of best practice. Research questions are more commonly posed in the form, "*Why* does person *x* cite document *d* at time *t*?," rather than, "*What* (or *when*) does (or should) person *x* cite?" Data relating to questions of the latter type continue, of course, to be used frequently in evaluative and relational linking studies, whose goals are not to understand citing behavior *per se*, but to provide more general accounts of various scholarly communication processes.

In attempts to understand the motivations of linkers and thence to supply a theory of linking, at least two general explanatory approaches or orientations may be identified. One of these emphasizes the *purposes* of individual citations—i.e., the uses to which they are put by the citer or the functions that the citer intends for them to fulfill; the other focuses on the *criteria* that are used by citers in making decisions about the citation worthiness of individual citations. That we can make such a distinction is not to deny that among the criteria of the kind identified in studies taking the second approach are likely to be properties of cited documents (or of cited/citing pairs) that differentiate among candidates for particular purposes, and thus that it may on occasion be difficult (and unnecessary) to distinguish between purpose and criterion. Nevertheless, it is usually possible to contrast studies of the first kind— that are concerned more with citation *function*, with finding answers to questions of the form "Why does author *x* cite document *d* at time *t*?" in analyses of the *roles* that individual citations are understood to play for the citer, and with explaining the "when" of citing—with studies of the second kind—that are concerned more with citation *quality*, with find- ing answers in analyses of the *reasons* that citers have for choosing cer- tain citations rather than others, and with explaining the "what" of citing. The observed trend is for researchers increasingly to seek under- standing of criteria, quality, and reasons rather than of purposes, func- tion, and roles.

Citation Behavior as Relevance Behavior

At the most general level, much current intellectual development in citation studies is related to a tendency for research designers simply to take more seriously the notions that citer behavior, like relevance judges' behavior in general (Schamber, Eisenberg, & Nilan, 1990), is: (a) *individual and subjective*—in that different people, even when placed in otherwise similar situations and taking into account similar factors, will make different decisions; (b) *complex and multidimensional*—in that single decisions are often based on multiple factors, and multiple kinds of factors, simultaneously; and (c) *dynamic and situational*—in that, on different occasions or when placed in different situations, people take account of different factors and make different decisions.

Studies of relevance judges' behavior—i.e., studies of those decisions and actions of information seekers that are based on their judgments as to whether or not particular documents are deemed relevant in particular situations—are core to the subfield of library and information science that is devoted to understanding information-related behavior. Furthermore, the perception that there is an important analogy to be drawn between linking behavior and the making of relevance judgments has been expressed with increasing frequency. Harter (1992: pp. 612–613) puts it as follows: "An author who includes particular citations in his list of references is announcing to readers the historical relevance of these citations to the research; at some point in the research or writing process the author found each reference relevant. Relevance is the idea that connects IR to bibliometrics, and understanding it in one context should aid our understanding of it in the other." Studies of linking behavior may thus be explicitly positioned not simply as contributions to the general literature of information-related behavior, but specifically as close relatives of impressive recent work that has led to an improved understanding of the criteria used by information seekers when judging relevance. An implicit recognition is that the use of relevance judgments as grounds for subsequent decision making and action is not solely the preserve of information seekers; authors (not just as linkers, but also as writers, submitters, and collaborators), indexers, editors, and reviewers are all continuously engaged in action-guiding evaluations of the relevance of concepts, documents, and people.

Beyond Content/Context Analysis

We might imagine a primitive study of relevance behavior that involved the *researchers* assigning *information seekers'* relevance judgments to the *researchers'* predefined categories of reasons for making such judgments. Perhaps such categories would include "Topicality," "Currency," "Authority," and so on. What grounds would we have for making the assumption that the researchers' post hoc, hypothetical categorization accurately reflected the process of reasoning in which information seekers in fact engaged? Yet, this is precisely one assumption made by most contributors to the "cottage industry" of citation typology that was most active between 1965 and 1985. In work of this kind, categories are derived from analysis of either the content or the context of existing citations.

Interpretivism in Link Analysis

Since the mid-1980s, however, researchers have tended to take more care—both when identifying categories and when making assignments of individual citing actions to categories—to seek justification for doing so in the evidence gathered from direct questioning of the agents themselves. This development might be labeled the "*interpretivist*" trend in studies of citing behavior.

Reports of notable studies in which researchers have sought to elicit citers' opinions about their own citing activity have appeared in three recent articles. Shadish, et al. (1995) report on two related surveys of authors' perceptions of documents they have cited. In the first of these, they randomly sampled one citation from each of all 283 full-length articles published in 1985 in three top journals in psychology. The author of each article was asked (and 192 [68 percent] assented) to specify, on a five-point Likert scale, the degree to which they agreed with each of twenty-eight statements describing the cited document. Further, each author was asked to indicate the one attribute (of the twenty-eight) that was the "most important" in their decision to cite, and to answer nine "Yes/No" questions about "things that might have increased the likelihood that respondents would know about the reference" (such as whether or not they had ever "spoken directly or by phone" with the cited author). In their factor analysis of responses to the Likert items, Shadish et al. extracted a number of groups of moderately correlated factors; they then carried out a multiple regression analysis to test the relationship between degree of citedness and citing authors' perceptions of cited works—i.e., to determine which of the groups of factors was the best predictor of citation scores. Their results showed that a highly cited work is more likely than a less-cited work to be the following:

1. perceived as an "exemplar"—i.e., as a classic reference in a field, as a "concept marker," as a representative of a particular genre, as one of the earliest works in a field, as authored by a recognized authority, as generative of much novel work, or as especially resistant to falsification;

2. old;

3. perceived as "high quality;" and

4. perceived as a source of a method or a design feature.

Most significantly of all, however, a highly cited work is *less* likely than a less-cited work to be perceived as "creative." Shadish et al. (p. 485) posit the existence of high quality but poorly cited articles "that are creative in a way that does not fit into existing conceptual frameworks or into accepted social norms for scholarship in an area."

Shadish et al. were led from their findings to conclude that, although citation counts are correlated with perceptions of quality, quality is not the only factor that has an impact on citation counts, and other such factors are themselves not correlated with quality. Evidence is provided by the observations, firstly, that some work that is perceived as high quality (e.g., documents perceived to be "creative in a way that no one is ready to use") is not highly cited, and secondly, that some work that is highly cited (e.g., documents perceived to have "exemplar" status) is not perceived as high quality (Shadish et al., 1995, p. 495). As a result, it can never be possible, through examination of citation counts alone, to determine the level of quality of an individual document; and if citation counts continue to be used in university promotion decisions, the authors of "creative" works (for example) will find themselves to be at an immediate disadvantage.

Responding to calls for comparisons across disciplines, Case and Higgins (2000) set out to replicate Shadish et al.'s study, in a different discipline (communication studies) and using a slightly modified research design. Case and Higgins' analysis indicated that the two best predictors of citation counts were the citer's perception of the cited work as a "Classic" (i.e., in Shadish et al.'s terms, an exemplar), and the citer's having a "Social Reason" for citing (e.g., to demonstrate their familiarity with the important literature in the field, to cite a document published in a prestigious journal in the field, to appeal to the readers or reviewers of the journal in which the citing document is to be published, or to "establish the legitimacy" of the topic of the citing document). Case and Higgins take care to remind the reader (p. 642) that, as always, "results from one discipline may not be easily generalized to other disciplines;" but they tentatively conclude that one interpretation of their data might be to support the constructivist argument that citations are "largely used to persuade." Certainly, Case and Higgins's identification of the importance of "Social Reasons" for citers in the field of communication studies is striking.

In a landmark study, White and Wang (1997) conducted interviews in 1995 with twelve faculty and graduate students working in the field of agricultural economics. Interviewees were questioned about their decisions to cite (or not to cite) documents that were either those in fact cited by the interviewees in the final reports of the research projects on which they had been working, or those identified as potentially relevant references by searches carried out in 1992. (White and Wang's citation study was part of a larger, long-term study of researchers' use of documents in general.) In their content analysis of the interviews, White and Wang identified a total of 314 individual decisions to cite or not to cite and categorized each on the basis of (a) the citing author's judgment as to the *contribution* the cited document made to the citing paper and (b) the *criteria* used by the citing author in choosing to cite the cited document. White and Wang were also able to identify (c) a set of "metalevel" concerns, i.e., beliefs held by the citer about the role and function of citation practice, and about the criteria by which such practice might be evaluated, that sometimes had an impact on individual citing decisions. White and Wang noted that their scheme of categories of the ways in which cited documents contribute to citing documents (by providing, for example, definitions of concepts, justifications of arguments, data, methods, or analogies) bears close similarity to other schemes (such as that devised by Peritz [1983]) derived rationally rather than empirically; they also found that most of the criteria identified as being used in citation decisions were equivalent to those observed in their earlier study of the "document use decisions" (i.e., decisions to use or not to use documents retrieved in searches of bibliographic databases) made by interviewees in the early stages of their projects.

White and Wang concluded (p. 147) that "citing behavior is complex, multidimensional behavior" and summarized their findings roughly as follows. Firstly, the "topicality" and "content" of the cited document were the most commonly used criteria on which citation decisions were based, although numerous other criteria were used on multiple occasions. Secondly, the choice of criteria in a particular instance seemed to depend on the "frame of reference" or purpose prioritized by the citer at that instance (e.g., execution of the research project or of the immediate task, augmentation of the field, satisfaction of external judges). Thirdly, some "metalevel" beliefs influence citation decisions independently of considerations of the ways in which individual documents can be used: These include beliefs about the value (even the morality) of self-citing, of copy-citing (copying citations found in other citers' papers), of citing secondary sources, of citing articles from peripheral journals, and of citing to meet external judges' expectations. White and Wang suggest that it might be possible, on this basis, to identify particular styles or codes of citing, and that certain styles may be characteristic not just of individual citers but of disciplines.

Structuralism in Link Analysis

A concurrent development might be called the *"structuralist"* trend. This consists in the increasing interest in deriving explanatory models from sophisticated statistical analyses of the objective properties of both cited and citing documents, and of cited-citing document pairs. In studies designed from this perspective, citations (and noncitations alike) are considered as discrete events, each involving a pair (or dyad) of documents, one "potentially citing" (the origin, source, or "later," document) and one "potentially cited" (the target, destination, or "earlier," document). The decision taken by the author of a later document x to "cite" a particular earlier document y may be viewed as the result of an assessment that, in a given situation, the degree of relevance of the relationship between x and y exceeds a certain threshold, and, consequently, that this relationship should be explicitly represented in the form of a citation. From a graph-theoretic viewpoint, the universe of "potentially citing" and "potentially cited" documents may be regarded as a directed graph (Harary, Norman, & Cartwright, 1965), each of whose nodes represents a document, and each of whose links represents the occurrence of a positive citation event—i.e., an assessment made by the author of a later document x that the relationship between x and an earlier document y is sufficiently relevant for it to be expressed in the form of a citation.

Each pair of documents may be characterized by multiple attributes of the origin, of the target, and of the relationship between origin and target. These attributes may be treated as the *independent* variables, whose level of correlation with the *dependent* variable (whether or not that pair of documents is the object of a citation event) is to be assessed.

We may ask, for example, how much of an effect the nationality of the author of document y has on the probability that it will ever be cited (i.e., the probability that it will ever participate in a citation event); we may also distinguish this question from one that asks about the effect that the nationality of the author of document y has on the probability that it will be cited specifically *in document* x. Our conjecture might be not only that English-speaking authors are more likely to be cited, but also that this likelihood increases even further if the authors of the citing papers are themselves English-speaking. (For examples of studies of nationality and language self-citation, see Herman [1991] and Yitzhaki [1998], respectively.)

What are the kinds of attributes that we might hypothesize as having an effect on the likelihood that an author will link a given pair of documents in a citation event? Many different variables have been identified in the literature as candidate factors; some of these were specified in the lists in the previous section on "Critiques of Evaluative Link Analysis." Many studies have been carried out with the aim of determining the relative impact of these variables. An impressive recent addition is described by Baldi (1998), who sampled 100 documents from the 384 painstakingly identified by Hargens (1993) as the totality of literature published between 1965 and 1980 in the field of celestial masers, a subfield of astrophysics. Baldi constructed an adjacency matrix containing $(n^2-n)/2 = 4950$ binary values (where $n = 100$), each value of 0 or 1 representing an observation of the absence or presence, respectively, of a citation in later document i to earlier document j. Baldi went on to treat each of these observations as an event that could itself be described not only by the binary absence/presence property, but also by numerous properties of the later and earlier documents and of the relationship between them. Baldi's aim was to determine the impact of each of these latter properties (the independent variables), and of each of certain combinations of such properties, on the absence/presence property (the dependent variable). The properties that he found to have the most significant effect were the following (in order of strength):

1. gender of authors of cited document;
2. format of cited document;
3. shared subtopic;
4. number of authors of cited document;

5. quality of cited document (Baldi measures "quality" by the frequency with which the cited document is cited in the third and fourth years after its publication, excluding self-citations and the citation from the citing paper itself under consideration).

In other words, in the field of celestial masers, any given document j is more likely to be cited by any given document i if its authors are male, if it is not a book chapter, if it is about the same subtopic as the citing document, if it has many authors, or if it has already been cited many times.

Baldi also found that, with the crucial exception of the gender of the cited author, none of the properties commonly highlighted by proponents of "constructivist" theories of citing had a significant impact. He concluded (1998, p. 843), "… at least in the research area examined, one's position in the stratification structure of science is likely to be the result of the worth and usefulness of one's scientific contributions rather than the reverse, as social constructivists would have us believe." The implication of the first few words of Baldi's conclusion is clear: Further comparison of citing practices within different disciplines is necessary if we are to determine how far results such as these may be generalized. Baldi (1998, pp. 843–844) hypothesizes that properties of cited authors may have rather less impact in the natural sciences than they do in the social sciences, since the former are "more codified" and are characterized by "greater consensus over what constitutes quality work."

In an earlier study with similar aims and methods, Peters and van Raan (1994) identified the following factors as predictive of citation counts:

1. the identity of the cited author;
2. the size of the cited paper's bibliography (i.e., the number of citations made in the cited paper);
3. the language of the cited paper (English papers being cited three times more frequently than those written in French or German);
4. the impact (or "prestige") of the cited journal; and
5. the Price Index (Price, 1970) of the cited paper (i.e., the proportion of citations made in the cited paper that are to works published in the last five years).

Yet Peters and van Raan also concluded that all such predicting factors explained only 58 percent of the variance in citation counts. The implication is that other factors, perhaps less easy to operationalize and measure and hence not included in their study, must have considerable effect.

At a general level, the interpretivist and structuralist trends are oppositional, in that the former is characterized by an emphasis on the primacy of the citer's personal actions (influenced but not determined by context), whereas the latter consists of the renewal of interest in identifying probabilistic regularities and patterns that (as some might be tempted to say) "govern" human behavior. This should not be taken to imply, however, that a reconciliation is logically impossible, or even that evidence of both trends cannot be found simultaneously in single studies (see, e.g., White & Wang, 1997).

The Ethics of Citers

Another trend is the increasing level of interest in understanding what White and Wang (1997) call "metalevel concerns"—i.e., the beliefs, attitudes, and opinions about the function and value of citing in general that are held by citers themselves. The set of such beliefs held by an individual citer—her opinions as to when and what, in general, she should cite—could almost be construed as her philosophy or ethic of citing. A distinction might then be made between "normative" ethics, held by citers who cite in the ways that they think they "should" do so, and "egotistical" ethics, held by those who cite in the ways that they believe will most benefit their own personal goals. Prior to the time frame of the present article, Gilbert (1977) established the view of citing as an act of persuasion, by which the citer is concerned to convince the reader of the validity of the citer's own arguments; it is now commonplace for studies of citer motivation to distinguish a normative theory of citing from some version of a theory that attributes an egotistical attitude to the "average" citer. Baldi (1998), for instance, refers to the "social constructivist" view; Case and Higgins (2000) to a "persuasional" strategy. The citing ethic of an individual may simultaneously involve both normative and egotistical values, and it will always be difficult to categorize individual acts of citation as having been guided by one or the other. It is clear, nevertheless, that contemporary researchers are rather more willing than their fore-bears to account for such acts in egotistical terms.

General Theories of Citing

Echoing Cronin (1984), calls for a "theory of citing" have long been a regular feature of the bibliometric literature. In a discussion paper published in *Scientometrics* along with invited responses from such as Cronin (1998), Egghe (1998), and Kostoff (1998), Leydesdorff (1998, p. 5) rearticulates the plea ("Citation analysis calls for a theory of what is being analyzed; citation analysts consequently tend to be in need of theoretical legitimation"), and supplies a major contribution to the debate about the possibility and nature of a theory of this kind. Leydesdorff distinguishes between at least two things to be explained in any theory of citing: the citation per se, and citation analysis as an area of study. He sketches the histories both of citation practice (identifying shifts over time in the function and role of citations) and of citation analysis, positioning the latter in the framework provided by the interdisciplinary field of science and technology studies. He paints a rich portrait of the inherent complexity of citation practice, arguing that citation networks are dual layered (the result of interaction between first-order, social networks of authors and second-order networks of "communications" or texts). He uses this distinction to demonstrate that any individual cited-citing pair may be viewed as an author-author, text-text, author-text, or text-author relation, as well as either at a disaggregated (micro-) level or at various (macro-) levels of aggregation, and suggests a two-facet taxonomy of the functions of citations on this basis. He further concludes that social and cognitive perspectives on citation practice are equally necessary; that there thus exists a multiplicity of theories of citation; and that it remains "uncertain" whether a meta-theory reconciling the insights, for example, of qualitative and quantitative studies is attainable.

We may nevertheless identify an increasing tendency for researchers to take seriously certain notions that are made explicit in interpretivist accounts of citing behavior: Citers' own interpretations of the meanings and roles of citation-related phenomena both influence and are influenced by the social structure of the scholarly community, the citation researcher is as much a part of this community as the scholars whose behavior she is studying, and the very occurrence of citation-analytic activity affects the phenomena that it is supposedly measuring (Luukkonen, 1997; Woolgar, 1991). It is time, perhaps, for a *critical* theory of citing, that seeks not only to account for the mutual influence of social structures and citers' motivations, but that also leads the way for the researcher-citer to make a positive contribution to the development of a more equitable system of scholarly reward.

Writing, Submission, and Collaboration

Our focus in this chapter is on authors and on what can be learned about their scholarly communication behavior via bibliometric theory and method. Scholarly authors make relevance decisions throughout the cycle of their communication activities. The section above on "Linking" focuses on decisions to cite (i.e., to choose to create certain links between documents). Here the section on "Writing" focuses on decisions to write (i.e., to choose to create certain documents), the "Submission" section addresses decisions to submit documents to journals, and the "Collaboration" section focuses on decisions to work with other authors. All of these decisions (or the evidentiary records of decisions) may be viewed as events, and any study that involves the counting of such events may be viewed as a bibliometric study. Writing, submission, and collaboration are areas with great potential for bibliometric study, although we found less empirical research in these topics than expected. We summarize what we found, and suggest promising questions and methods for future research.

Writing

Writing is of interest because "a scholar makes his or her statement in the text, not in the reference list" (Paisley, 1990, p. 285). Authors' choices of words in the text and titles of their publications can be studied to address questions such as the content of their publications, trends within fields, and the transfer of ideas from one field to another. Authors' word choices also can be used for evaluative purposes, especially in combination with linking studies. Methods for bibliometric studies of writing (sometimes called *stylometrics*) are similar to those of content analysis, a well-established area of research in communication and in psychology.[1] Both approaches count words in the text and titles.

However, bibliometrics is concerned with *characteristics* of the text itself, while content analysis is concerned with the *meaning* of the text. Thus the two approaches are distinguished more by their purposes than by their methods (Paisley, 1990). Typical examples of content analysis include Evans and Davies (2000), who examined how males and females are portrayed in elementary school reading textbooks, and Lisovskaya and Karpov (1999), who analyzed how ideologies represented in Russian textbooks varied between communist and post-communist periods.

Research productivity is an area long studied by bibliometricians. The statistical distribution of research productivity has been postulated to follow Lotka's law, namely that a small number of authors account for a large portion of the work produced (Gupta & Karisiddippa, 1999; Gupta, Kumar, Syed, & Singh, 1996; Rousseau, 1992a, 1993; Wagner-Dobler & Berg, 1995). These and similar studies find that the empirical distribution fits Lotka's law to varying degrees. Various adjustments to the law are proposed for a better fit and issues of sampling and measurement are raised in these studies.

Paisley (1990) proposed that the demographics of authorship was a potentially fruitful area for bibliometric research, and indeed we find some subsequent work in this area. Meadows (1998) analyzes a wide range of demographic studies of authorship. Of particular interest are studies of differences in productivity and in type of publication by discipline. Disciplines vary by factors such as the number of authors per article (typically greater in the sciences than in social sciences and humanities) and the number of articles published (more per author in the sciences and medicine than in social sciences and technology). Bonzi (1992) found similar distributions by disciplines in one large research university. Bates (1998) analyzed productivity by type of publication within one discipline (library and information science) in the four most productive universities in that field. She found that individual publication patterns tend to follow the discipline orientation of authors within this multidisciplinary field. For example, humanities-oriented LIS authors tend to write books, while science and technology-oriented authors tend to write journal articles. Her data indicate that the ranking of authors and universities within a discipline varies considerably depending upon what forms of publications are included in the dataset. Studies that use journal citation data (which are the easiest to obtain) as a surrogate for all forms of publication yield much different results from those that include books or those that include book reviews in authorship counts. Although the studies reviewed by Meadows (1998) suggest that when counts are adjusted by weighting the effort involved in different types of publication (e.g., books, articles, patents), outputs are similar across fields. Scholars' choices of the form in which they write appear to influence their recognition (as reflected in citation counts) considerably.

Other demographic variables applied to writing productivity include gender (Gupta, Kumar, & Aggarwal, 1999), university (Budd, 1995, 1999), "career age" (Bonzi, 1992), and chronological age (Diamond, 2000). Comparisons based on these demographic variables tend to be anomalous. For example, writing output may increase with age, as scholars gain more funding and more collaborators. Conversely, productivity in writing output may decline with age. The latter result is usually attributed to an increase in administrative and other gate-keeping duties (reviewing, tenure and promotion committees, service in scholarly societies and academic governance, etc.) rather than to a decline in capacity (Diamond, 2000; Meadows, 1998). We also found a large number of evaluative studies of the productivity of individual departments and fields, often in combination with citation analyses; most tend to be narrow in focus and primarily of local interest.

Writing style is another area of potential interest for bibliometric study. Diamond and Levy (1994), responding to arguments that the field of economics "rewards obscurity and penalizes clarity" (Diamond, 2000, p. 329), analyzed texts with a grammar-checking program and compared the results to citations received. Their only significant finding was that passive voice was negatively related to citations received. Fortunately, they also found that the use of passive voice was decreasing over time.

We found a few other studies that fall on the boundaries of writing and other areas of interest. For example, although information seeking and use is outside the scope of the present chapter, some interesting work falls on the boundaries of information-seeking, writing, and citing. These are studies that ask questions about the relationship between the resources available to scholars to be cited and what those scholars choose to cite in their own writing (Harter, 1998; Harter & Kim, 1996; Jacobs, Woodfield, & Morris, 2000). Similarly, while decisions of what to cite fall within the linking category for the purposes of the present article, White (2001) analyzes citations made by authors as a characteristic of writing style. In an exploratory study of "citation identity" (the set of authors that an author cites), he selected four pairs of authors who work in similar areas. He found that citation identities are highly individualized, with authors having much different thresholds of what they consider acceptable numbers of citations per article and acceptable variety of citations over time. Some build all of their work on the same core set of cited authors, while others paint a broad sweep across topics and disciplines.

Several studies have employed bibliometrics to produce biographical sketches of authors. These studies fall somewhere between evaluative bibliometrics and studies of writing. White (2000) applies a wide range of citation and co-citation methods to characterize the writing and influence of Eugene Garfield, for example. Kalyane and Kademani (1997) produced a "scientometric portrait" of Barbara McClintock, who won the Nobel laureate in physiology.

Other research on scholarly productivity lies on the boundary with evaluative bibliometrics. Wouters (2000) comments that scholars' early objections to the development of citation indexes were founded on concerns that private knowledge about productivity and recognition would become public knowledge. Diamond (2000), an economist, argues that measures of writing and productivity can be used to allocate scarce resources within the academy. In analyzing the academic labor market, he reports on studies (published prior to the time frame of the present chapter), which consistently found that the number of citations received is correlated with salary. Thus authors have an economic incentive to write more, and especially to gain citations for their work (Cronin, 1996). As Diamond notes, citations vary more than salaries do, which suggests that intrinsic rewards may be driving writing behavior more than extrinsic ones.

The typical genres of scholarly publishing are partly artifacts of print publication. In a print world, journal articles are aggregated into journal issues and thence into volumes; conference papers are aggregated into proceedings volumes; and monographs are published as a whole (although they can be serialized, as was common in past centuries). In an electronic world, articles and papers are easily distributed individually because they need not be collected into convenient and economical packages for mailing, and monographs can be serialized online. Scholars may tend to write in smaller units when the technology and publication venues make it convenient to do so (Borgman, 2000b). Even in a print world, authors tend to decompose their prior written documents and use parts of them in later publications (Bishop, 1999; Covi, 1999; Rayward, 1994). Electronic publication allows individual chapters, sections, tables, and illustrations to be distributed. Similarly, electronic documents can be tightly coupled through hyperlinks, with a specific part of one paper linked to a specific part of another. Electronic publishing also offers the ability to update previous works, raising issues about when a revised document should be considered a variant on the previous version and when it should be considered a new document (Buckland, 1997). We have not encountered studies that employ bibliometrics to examine units of writing and how they may change from print to electronic forms, and we suggest that this may be a fruitful area of research.

Submission

Sometime before, during, or after writing a document for publication, authors make a conscious decision about where to submit it. Authors are making relevance judgments when selecting a journal, conference, book publisher, e-print server, or other publication venue. Bibliometric methods are of limited value for capturing the motivations for submission, because the methods are inherently unobtrusive. However, bibliometrics can be used to analyze the record of where authors chose to submit their work, to corroborate other evidence about submission decisions, and to test hypotheses about submission patterns.

Scholarly documents represent ideas that authors own, or at least ideas for which they claim some rights (van Raan, 2000). Authors wish to position their work so that it will reach its intended audience and will bring them recognition, whether in the form of citations, acknowledgments, scientific prizes, or tangible property rights (such as patents). In selecting the "best" venue to submit the work, authors may draw explicitly on bibliometric evaluations such as journal impact factors (discussed earlier under "Linking") or subjective opinions by colleagues on the most highly regarded journals, conferences, or publishers. Authors with sophisticated knowledge of how the literature in their field is controlled bibliographically can draw upon bibliometric indicators, directories that indicate where journals are indexed, and on a variety of other tools to position their work (Borgman, 1993, 2000b). Robinson (1991) proposes a bibliometric method specifically for determining which journal is most appropriate for a given article, providing examples for the field of economics.

A few studies are starting to examine authors' choices between print and electronic journals (Harter, 1998; Kling & McKim, 1999; Schauder, 1994; Youngen, 1998). Harnad (1995), Odlyzko (1995), Okerson and O'Donnell (1995), and others predicted that electronic publishing would soon replace the bulk of print publishing for scholarly journals. The number of electronic journals has grown substantially since their predictions, although many of the new entrants are electronic versions of established print journals (Kling & McKim, 1999). Data on comparative submission rates is difficult to obtain, due both to its proprietary nature and to the wide range of definitions of "electronic journal." Harter's (1998) data for 1995 on two of the most highly cited electronic-only journals showed that they published very small numbers of articles (four each for the *Online Journal of Current Clinical Trials* and *Psycoloquy*) compared to print journals in their fields (median number of articles 107 and 30, respectively), confirming anecdotal reports that electronic-only journals are not attracting large numbers of submissions. Online databases of "e-prints" and "preprints" such as the arXiv.org e-Print Archive (http://www.arXiv.org) attract large numbers of submissions in fields such as high-energy physics, mathematics, and computer science (Ginsparg, 1994; Youngen, 1998). However, e-print servers are not the equivalent of journals; they serve as a repository and distribution mechanism for published and unpublished documents. Authors can submit articles that have been accepted by journals, adding the publication data at the time of submission to the e-print server or later when the article is published (http://www.arxiv.org/help.faq). It is not yet clear whether electronic journals will supplant print journals, as originally predicted, or whether hybrid print and electronic forms will predominate. At present, it appears that electronic forms are favored for access and distribution, but print forms are favored as the permanent archival record of scholarship. Bibliometric studies of submission patterns to electronic-only, print-only, and hybrid journals will shed light on this important question.

The distribution of submissions is highly skewed, with a few top journals attracting large numbers of articles and many other journals attracting relatively few (S. Cole, 2000). Cole asks whether this is evidence of the economic efficiency of the journal system, such that journals with high rejection rates necessarily publish the best papers, and thus attract other good papers and citations. He reviews the many arguments for and against this proposition (most of which have to do with social, rather than bibliometric, variables), concluding that the system is not efficient. Rather, much of the distribution has to do with self-selection by authors, who know which of their own work is best and which papers to submit to what journals. Odlyzko (1998), who argues that electronic journal publishing is the most efficient and cost-effective solution to the spiraling costs of scholarly publication, also acknowledges the "perverse incentives" of authors to publish in prestigious journals regardless of journal prices.

Bibliometrics is not likely to shed much light on the motivations of authors for choosing where to submit their work, but it can provide evidence of what those choices are. Pierce (1999, p. 271), for example, uses bibliometrics to explore the behavior of "boundary crossing" authors. She identifies three forms of boundary crossing behavior: Borrowing theory or method from other fields, collaborating with coauthors from other fields, and placing one's work in the journals of other disciplines. The latter is potentially the most effective form of crossing disciplinary boundaries, and can be studied bibliometrically. She identified 199 articles in four core journals of political science and sociology where the first authors were affiliated with other disciplines. Citation analyses revealed that these articles received more citations from the disciplines in which they were published than from their home disciplines, and more citations from other disciplines than from either the home discipline or the discipline of publication; thus she judged the boundary crossing to be successful. Pierce (1999) concludes that scholars are more able to place their work across disciplines than has been assumed in other studies of journal submission patterns.

Most bibliometric studies of the distribution of authorship fall in the category of literature dynamics or visualizing literature, which were addressed in recent *ARIST* chapters by Tabah (2001) and White and McCain (1997). Wormell (1998) mapped the distribution of authorship by country of top library and information science journals as a means of determining who was submitting to what journals. She also examined relationships between the geographic distribution of authors, citations, and subscriptions to determine the geographic scope of influence of these journals.

Collaboration

Collaboration is a significant factor in scholarly productivity. Just as the format of publication (e.g., papers, articles, books) and number of publications vary by discipline, so do collaborations and coauthorships (Bordons & Gomez, 2000; Meadows, 1998). Solo research is the norm in some disciplines, particularly in the humanities, but also in mathematics, while collaborative research is typical of most scientific disciplines. Although coauthorship is often used as a convenient surrogate for collaboration (especially in bibliometric studies), it is but one aspect of collaboration. Bordons and Gomez (2000), in their extensive review of recent bibliometric research on collaboration, summarize multiple aspects of this complex relationship and the associated methodological risks. For example, scholars may work together on a project but publish their results separately, and thus not appear as coauthors despite their collaboration. Conversely, individuals such as heads of laboratories may be listed as coauthors by social convention, but may not have participated directly in the research reported. In other cases, scholars may have multiple concurrent affiliations or may be visitors in someone's lab. Depending upon how affiliations are listed on a paper, intra-institutional collaboration may appear to be multi-institutional or multinational, and vice versa. Bibliometric studies of collaboration usually require data on the names of individuals and their affiliations. The ISI citation databases are essentially the sole source for such information, which limits the scope of this type of research.

Bibliometric studies of collaboration generally conclude that the amount of collaboration between scholars (usually as evidenced by number of coauthors) is growing, and that the degree of collaboration continues to vary greatly by field (Arunachalam, 2000; Bordons & Gomez, 2000; Meadows, 1998; Pao, 1992; Russell, 2000). Reasons for the growth in collaboration are many. One is the increasing specialization within disciplines, such that multiple partners are often needed to tackle complex research problems. Another is economics, given the need to amortize expensive laboratory equipment, computers, data, and other resources across multiple researchers and projects. Yet another is sources of funding that encourage larger projects (Bordons & Gomez, 2000). Higher rates of collaboration are usually associated with higher productivity, although counts will vary based on the method of allocating authorship (one credit for each publication vs. partial credit based on number of authors, etc.).

Collaboration is a form of boundary crossing between disciplines (Qin, Lancaster, & Allen, 1997; Pierce, 1999), although determining disciplinary affiliations of authors is a complex exercise that influences the outcomes of such studies. Persson, Melin, and Kretschmer (Kretschmer, 1993, 1997; Persson & Beckman, 1995; Persson & Melin, 1996; Persson, Melin, Danell, & Kaludis, 1997) are among the authors who have explored coauthorship and collaboration across international boundaries and identified evidence of invisible colleges.

Studies of collaboration often are a form of evaluative citation analysis, as discussed earlier under linking. They can be used to assess the level of partnerships between countries and between laboratories, for example. Similarly, many studies of collaboration fall in the category of mapping literatures that is outside the scope of this review.

Conclusions

The circumstances of scholarly communication have changed radically in the decade covered by this review. A large and growing portion of scholars' communicative activities are conducted via computers and networks: interpersonal interaction with colleagues, searching for information, writing, submitting works for publication, reviewing, collaborating with colleagues, and the conduct of research itself. More of the content of scholarly publications is available online, whether published electronically, published concurrently in print and electronic forms, or published in print and later collected into digital libraries. Once online, documents can be linked electronically. Citations, acknowledgments, datasets, and other indicators of relationships between documents become active links whose paths can be followed through networks. Both the content and the links can be treated as indicators of scholarly communication, thus providing rich new data sources for bibliometric study. As scholarly communication evolves and as methods for studying it improve, opportunities become available for new theory, method, and topics of inquiry.

Our goal in this review was to identify the research areas, methods, and theories that have been explored at the intersection of scholarly communication and bibliometrics during the decade since the last major review and to identify which of these opportunities have yet to be pursued. We found even more activity in these areas than we could review, so narrowed our focus to the study of scholars as authors. We required that studies be concerned with what could be learned about scholarly communication via bibliometrics, including both studies that *use* bibliometrics and those that study the *use of* bibliometrics. Thus we excluded behavioral studies of other scholarly activities such as information searching and peer reviewing, as well as the large body of research that employs bibliometrics to map literatures but does not have an explicitly behavioral component. Even with these constraints, and without claiming to be comprehensive, we have reviewed studies reported in more than 200 publications. We found that some aspects of scholarly communication and bibliometrics have been addressed extensively, while others are only beginning to be explored.

The area that continues to receive the most attention, not surprisingly, is evaluative bibliometrics. Bibliometrics offers a wide range of methods and measures for evaluating scholarly productivity and for comparing the recognition of individuals, groups, fields, universities, nations, and other aggregates. Evaluative studies are based on assumptions, whether implicit or explicit, about how and why the authors of one work cite other works. We are finding that while the methods and measures for evaluative bibliometrics are becoming more sophisticated, the defenses and critiques of citation-related behavior also are becoming more sophisticated. Many of the implicit assumptions about scholars' choices of what to cite are being called into question. Similarly, the validity of some widely accepted measures is being questioned. At the same time, new theories and new methods are available for examining those assumptions and pursuing better ways of accounting for scholarly behavior.

Among the most promising developments are new theories of citation-related behavior and new bibliometric concepts, for example, viewing citation choices as judgments of relevance or of trust. Also of interest are studies of social networks in electronic environments and the explicit application of bibliometric methods to the study of the World Wide Web.

We found less activity than expected in bibliometric research on scholars' activities in writing, in submitting for publication, and in collaboration. Given that scholars actually make their claims in their texts rather than in their citations, and we now have direct access to their texts, this area seems ripe for bibliometric study. Some bibliometric research has been done on scholarly productivity across disciplines, boundary-crossing activities, choices in submitting to print and electronic journals, and other judgments concerning where scholars choose to place their work. We also found studies that challenged the use of coauthorship as a surrogate for collaboration, exploring other means of assessing scholars' behavior in working together.

Overall trends in scholarly communication and bibliometrics reflect larger trends in social science and technology research. Part of what we are seeing is a tension between structural and interpretive approaches and between quantitative and qualitative methods. Our review identified developments in theory and method on all of these fronts. We are seeing interesting new measures and models, and significant new interpretations of scholarly behavior. We view these developments as complementary, for each challenges the other. Models must be explained, and theories must be validated. Some of the territory reviewed has been deeply mined, while research in other areas has barely scratched the surface. A plethora of opportunities and challenges remains for those wishing to investigate this rich territory.

Acknowledgments

The authors wish to thank Nadia Caidi for literature searches and compilation of materials and Blaise Cronin, Eugene Garfield, and four anonymous reviewers for their insightful comments on an earlier draft.

Endnote

[1] A search of the PsycInfo database on the exact subject heading "content analysis," limited to publications of 1990 or later, in English, yielded more than 1200 records. Additional records were found in the ERIC and LISA databases, with some overlap in the three sets.

Bibliography

Albert, R., Jeong, H., & Barabasi, A.-L. (1999). Diameter of the World Wide Web. *Nature, 401*, 130–131.

Almind, T. C., & Ingwersen, P. (1997). Informetric analyses on the World Wide Web: Methodological approaches to "Webometrics." *Journal of Documentation, 53*, 404–426.

Álvarez, P., & Pulgarín, A. (1998). Equating research production in different scientific fields. *Information Processing & Management, 34*, 465–470.

Arunachalam, S. (2000). International collaboration in science: The case of India and China. In B. Cronin & H. B. Atkins (Eds.), *The web of knowledge: A Festschrift in honor of Eugene Garfield* (pp. 215–231). Medford, NJ: Information Today.

Atkins, H. (1999). The ISI Web of Science: Links and electronic journals: How links work today in the Web of Science, and the challenges posed by electronic journals. *D-Lib Magazine 5*(9). Retrieved February 20, 2001, from the World Wide Web: http://www.dlib.org/dlib/september99/atkins/09atkins.html

Atkins, H., Lyons, C., Ratner, H., Risher, C., Shillum, C., Sidman, D., & Stevens, A. (2000). Reference linking with DOIs: A case study. *D-Lib Magazine 6*(2). Retrieved February 20, 2001, from the World Wide Web: http://www.dlib.org/dlib/february00/02risher.html

Baird, L. M., & Oppenheim, C. (1994). Do citations matter? *Journal of Information Science, 20*, 2–15.

Baldi, S. (1998). Normative versus social constructivist processes in the allocation of citations: A network-analytic model. *American Sociological Review, 63*, 829–846.

Barabasi, A.-L., & Albert, R. (1999). Emergence of scaling in random networks. *Science, 286*, 509–512.

Bates, M. J. (1998). The role of publication type in the evaluation of LIS programs. *Library & Information Science Research, 20*, 187–198.

Bayer, A. E., & Folger, J. (1966). Some correlates of a citation measure of productivity in science. *Sociology of Education, 39*, 381–390.

Beniger, J. R. (1990). Identifying the important theorists of communication: Use of latent measures to test manifest assumptions in scholarly communication. In C. L. Borgman (Ed.), *Scholarly communication and bibliometrics* (pp. 254–280). Newbury Park, CA: Sage.

Bishop, A. P. (1999). Document structure and digital libraries: How researchers mobilize information in journal articles. *Information Processing & Management, 35,* 255–279.

Bishop, A. P., & Star, S. L. (1996). Social informatics of digital library use and infrastructure. *Annual Review of Information Science and Technology, 31,* 301–401.

Bonzi, S. (1992). Trends in research productivity among senior faculty. *Information Processing & Management, 28,* 111–120.

Bonzi, S., & Snyder, H. W. (1991). Motivations for citation: A comparison of self citation and citation to others. *Scientometrics, 21,* 245–254.

Bordons, M., & Gomez, I. (2000). Collaboration networks in science. In B. Cronin & H. B. Atkins (Eds.), *The web of knowledge: A Festschrift in honor of Eugene Garfield* (pp. 197–213). Medford, NJ: Information Today.

Borgman, C. L. (1989). Bibliometrics and scholarly communication: Editor's introduction. *Communication Research, 16,* 583–599.

Borgman, C. L. (Ed.). (1990). *Scholarly communication and bibliometrics.* Newbury Park, CA: Sage.

Borgman, C. L. (1993). Round in circles: The scholar as author and end-user in the electronic environment. In H. Woodward & S. Pilling (Eds.), *The international serials industry* (pp. 45–59). London: Gower.

Borgman, C. L. (2000a). Digital libraries and the continuum of scholarly communication. *Journal of Documentation, 56,* 412–430.

Borgman, C. L. (2000b). *From Gutenberg to the global information infrastructure: Access to information in the networked world.* Cambridge, MA: MIT Press.

Borgman, C. L. (2000c). Scholarly communication and bibliometrics revisited. In B. Cronin & H. B. Atkins (Eds.), *The web of knowledge: A Festschrift in honor of Eugene Garfield* (pp. 143–162). Medford, NJ: Information Today.

Borgman, C. L., & Paisley, W. (1989). Bibliometric methods for the study of scholarly communication: Preface. *Communication Research, 16,* 581–582.

Botafogo, R. A., Rivlin, E., & Shneiderman, B. (1992). Structural analysis of hypertexts: Identifying hierarchies and useful metrics. *ACM Transactions on Information Systems, 10,* 142–180.

Bradley, S. J., Willett, P., & Wood, F. E. (1992). A publication and citation analysis of the Department of Information Studies, University of Sheffield, 1980–1990. *Journal of Information Science, 18,* 225–232.

Brin, S., & Page, L. (1998). Anatomy of a large-scale hypertextual Web search engine. *Computer Networks and ISDN Systems, 30,* 107–117.

Broder, A., Kumar, R., Maghoul, F., Raghavan, P., Rajagopalan, S., Stata, R., Tomkins, A., & Wiener, J. (2000). Graph structure in the Web. In D. Bulterman (Ed.), *Proceedings of the 9th International World Wide Web Conference: The Web: The next generation* (Amsterdam, May 15–19, 2000). Amsterdam: Elsevier. Retrieved February 20, 2001, from the World Wide Web: http://www9.org/w9cdrom/160/160.html

Brooks, T. A. (2000). How good are the best papers of JASIS? *Journal of the American Society for Information Science, 51,* 485–486.

Brown, J. S., & Duguid, P. (1995). The social life of documents. *First Monday, 1*(1). Retrieved February 20, 2001, from the World Wide Web: http://www. firstmonday.dk/issues/issue1/documents/index.html

Brown, J. S., & Duguid, P. (2000). *The social life of information*. Boston, MA: Harvard Business School Press.

Buckland, M. (1997). What is a "document"? *Journal of the American Society for Information Science, 48*, 804–809.

Budd, J. M. (1995). Faculty publishing productivity: An institutional analysis and comparison with library and other measures. *College & Research Libraries, 56*, 547–554.

Budd, J. M. (1999). Increases in faculty publishing activity: An analysis of ARL and ACRL institutions. *College & Research Libraries, 60*, 308–315.

Budd, J. M. (2000). Scholarly productivity of U.S. LIS faculty: An update. *Library Quarterly, 70*, 230–245.

Budd, J. M., & Seavey, C. A. (1996). Productivity of U.S. library and information science faculty: The Hayes study revisited. *Library Quarterly, 66*, 1–20.

Burrell, Q., & Rousseau, R. (1995). Fractional counts for authorship attribution: A numerical study. *Journal of the American Society for Information Science, 46*, 97–102.

Cameron, R. D. (1997). A universal citation database as a catalyst for reform in scholarly communication. *First Monday, 2*(4). Retrieved February 20, 2001, from the World Wide Web: http://www.firstmonday.org/issues/issue2_4/cameron/index.html

Caplan, P., & Arms, W. Y. (1999). Reference linking for journal articles. *D-Lib Magazine, 5*(7/8). Retrieved February 20, 2001, from the World Wide Web: http://www.dlib.org/dlib/july99/caplan/07caplan.html

Carr, L., Hitchcock, S., Hall, W., & Harnad, S. (2000). A usage based analysis of CoRR. *ACM Journal of Computer Documentation, 24*, 54–59.

Case, D. O., & Higgins, G. M. (2000). How can we investigate citation behavior?: A study of reasons for citing literature in communication. *Journal of the American Society for Information Science, 51*, 635–645.

Chakrabarti, S., Dom, B. E., Kumar, S. R., Raghavan, P., Rajagopalan, S., Tomkins, A., Gibson, D., & Kleinberg, J. M. (1999). Mining the Web's link structure. *Computer, 32*, 60–67.

Chen, C., & Carr, L. (1999). Trailblazing the literature of hypertext: Author co-citation analysis (1989–1998). In K. Tochtermann, J. Westbomke, U. K. Wiil, & J. J. Leggett (Eds.), *Hypertext '99: Returning to our diverse roots: The 10th ACM Conference on Hypertext and Hypermedia* (Darmstadt, Germany, February 21-25, 1999) (pp. 51–60). New York: ACM Press.

Cole, J. R. (2000). A short history of the use of citations as a measure of the impact of scientific and scholarly work. In B. Cronin & H. B. Atkins (Eds.), *The web of knowledge: A Festschrift in honor of Eugene Garfield* (pp. 281–300). Medford, NJ: Information Today.

Cole, S. (2000). The role of journals in the growth of scientific knowledge. In B. Cronin & H. B. Atkins (Eds.), *The web of knowledge: A Festschrift in honor of Eugene Garfield* (pp. 143–162). Medford, NJ: Information Today.

Cole, S., & Cole, J. R. (1967). Scientific output and recognition: A study in the operation of the reward system in science. *American Sociological Review, 32*, 377–390.

Covi, L. M. (1999). Material mastery: Situating digital library use in university research practices. *Information Processing & Management, 35*, 293–316.

Cronin, B. (1984). *The citation process: The role and significance of citations in scientific communication.* London: Taylor Graham.

Cronin, B. (1991). Let the credits roll: The role of mentors and trusted assessors in disciplinary formation. *Journal of Documentation, 47*, 227–239.

Cronin, B. (1995). *The scholar's courtesy: The role of acknowledgement in the primary communication process.* London: Taylor Graham.

Cronin, B. (1996). Rates of return to citation. *Journal of Documentation, 52*, 188–197.

Cronin, B. (1998). Metatheorizing citation. *Scientometrics, 43*, 45–55.

Cronin, B. (2000). Semiotics and evaluative bibliometrics. *Journal of Documentation, 56*, 440–453.

Cronin, B. (2001). Bibliometrics and beyond: Some thoughts on Web-based citation analysis. *Journal of Information Science, 27*, 1–7.

Cronin, B., & Atkins, H. B. (2000). The scholar's spoor. In B. Cronin & H. B. Atkins (Eds.), *The web of knowledge: A Festschrift in honor of Eugene Garfield* (pp. 1–7). Medford, NJ: Information Today.

Cronin, B., McKenzie, G., & Rubio, L. (1993). The norms of acknowledgement in four humanities and social science disciplines. *Journal of Documentation, 49*, 29–43.

Cronin, B., McKenzie, G., & Stiffler, M. (1992). Patterns of acknowledgement. *Journal of Documentation, 48*, 107–122.

Cronin, B., & Overfelt, K. (1994a). Citation-based auditing of academic performance. *Journal of the American Society for Information Science, 45*, 61–72.

Cronin, B., & Overfelt, K. (1994b). The scholar's courtesy: A survey of acknowledgement behavior. *Journal of Documentation, 50*, 165–196.

Cronin, B., Snyder, H., & Atkins, H. (1997). Comparative citation rankings of authors in monographic and journal literature: A study of sociology. *Journal of Documentation, 53*, 263–273.

Cronin, B., Snyder, H. W., Rosenbaum, H., Martinson, A., & Callahan, E. (1998). Invoked on the Web. *Journal of the American Society for Information Science, 49*, 1319–1328.

Davenport, E., & Cronin, B. (2000). The citation network as a prototype for representing trust in virtual environments. In B. Cronin & H. B. Atkins (Eds.), *The web of knowledge: A Festschrift in honor of Eugene Garfield* (pp. 517–534). Medford, NJ: Information Today.

Diamond, A. M., Jr. (2000). The complementarity of scientometrics and economics. In B. Cronin & H. B. Atkins (Eds.), *The web of knowledge: a Festschrift in honor of Eugene Garfield* (pp. 321–336). Medford, NJ: Information Today.

Diamond, A. M., Jr., & Levy, D. M. (1994). The metrics of style: Adam Smith teaches efficient rhetoric. *Economic Inquiry, 32*, 138–145.

Dimitroff, A., & Arlitsch, K. (1995). Self-citations in the library and information science literature. *Journal of Documentation, 51*, 44–56.

Ding, Y., Chowdhury, G., & Foo, S. (1999). Mapping the intellectual structure of information retrieval studies: An author co-citation analysis, 1987–1997. *Journal of Information Science, 25*, 67–78.

Diodato, V. (1994). *Dictionary of bibliometrics*. New York: Haworth Press.

Doreian, P. (1988). Measuring the relative standing of disciplinary journals. *Information Processing & Management, 24*, 45–56.

Doreian, P. (1994). A measure of standing for citation networks within a wider environment. *Information Processing & Management, 30*, 21–31.

Doyle, M. (2000). Pragmatic citing and linking in electronic scholarly publishing. *Learned Publishing, 13*, 5–14.

Edge, D. O. (1979). Quantitative measures of communication in science: A critical review. *History of Science, 17*, 102–134.

Egghe, L. (1998). Mathematical theories of citation. *Scientometrics, 43*, 57–62.

Egghe, L. (2000). New informetric aspects of the Internet: Some reflections—many problems. *Journal of Information Science, 26*, 329–335.

Egghe, L., & Rousseau, R. (1990). *Introduction to informetrics: Quantitative methods in library, documentation and information science*. Amsterdam: Elsevier.

Egghe, L., Rousseau, R., & van Hooydonk, G. (2000). Methods for accrediting publications to authors or countries: Consequences for evaluation studies. *Journal of the American Society for Information Science, 51*, 145–157.

Evans, L., & Davies, K. (2000). No sissy boys here: A content analysis of the representation of masculinity in elementary school reading textbooks. *Sex Roles, 42*, 255–270.

Furner, J., Ellis, D., & Willett, P. (1996). The representation and comparison of hypertext structures using graphs. In M. Agosti & A. F. Smeaton (Eds.), *Information retrieval and hypertext* (pp. 75–96). Boston, MA: Kluwer.

Garfield, E. (1965). Can citation indexing be automated? In M. E. Stevens, V. E. Giuliano, & L. B. Heilprin (Eds.), *Statistical association methods for mechanized documentation: Symposium proceedings* (pp. 189–192). Washington, DC: National Bureau of Standards.

Garfield, E. (1973, August 15). The new ISI Journal Citation Reports should significantly affect the future course of scientific publication. *Current Contents, 33*, 5–6.

Garfield, E. (1975, May 19). Journal citation studies, 20: Agriculture journals and the agricultural literature. *Current Contents, 20*, 5–11.

Garfield, E. (1979). *Citation indexing: Its theory and application in science, technology, and humanities*. New York: John Wiley.

Garfield, E. (1990, February 12). The most-cited papers of all time, SCI 1945–1988, part 1A: The SCI top 100: Will the Lowry method ever be obliterated? *Current Contents, 7,* 3–14.

Garfield, E. (1993). What citations tell us about Canadian research. *Canadian Journal of Information and Library Science, 18,* 14–35.

Garfield, E. (1996). When to cite. *Library Quarterly, 66,* 449–458.

Garfield, E., & Welljams-Dorof, A. (1992a). Citation data: Their use as quantitative indicators for science and technology evaluation and policy-making. *Science and Public Policy, 19,* 321–327.

Garfield, E., & Welljams-Dorof, A. (1992b). Of Nobel class: A citation perspective on high impact research authors. *Theoretical Medicine, 13,* 117–135.

Gilbert, G. N. (1977). Referencing as persuasion. *Social Studies of Science, 7,* 113–122.

Ginsparg, P. (1994). First steps towards electronic research communication. *Computers in Physics, 8,* 390–396.

Gladwell, M. (1999, January 11). Six degrees of Lois Weisberg. *New Yorker, 74*(41), 52–63.

Gray, M. (1996, June 20). Internet statistics: Web growth, Internet growth. Cambridge, MA: Massachusetts Institute of Technology. Retrieved February 20, 2001, from the World Wide Web: http://www.mit.edu/people/mkgray/net

Gupta, B. M., & Karisiddippa, C. R. (1999). Collaboration and author productivity: A study with a new variable in Lotka's law. *Scientometrics, 44,* 129–134.

Gupta, B. M., Kumar, S., & Aggarwal, B. S. (1999). A comparison of productivity of male and female scientists of CSIR. *Scientometrics, 45,* 269–289.

Gupta, B. M., Kumar, S., Syed, S., & Singh, K. V. (1996). Distribution of productivity among authors in potato research, 1900-1980. *Library Science with a Slant to Documentation and Information Studies, 33,* 127–134.

Harary, F., Norman, R. Z., & Cartwright, D. (1965). *Structural models: An introduction to the theory of directed graphs.* New York: John Wiley.

Hargens, L. L. (1993). *Reference networks and scientific development: A comparative study* (NSF proposal, grant no. SBR-9223317). Columbus, OH: Department of Sociology, Ohio State University.

Harnad, S. (1990). Scholarly skywriting and the prepublication continuum of scientific inquiry. *Psychological Science, 1,* 342–343.

Harnad, S. (1995). The post-Gutenberg galaxy: How to get there from here. *The Information Society, 11,* 285–291.

Harnad, S. (1999). Free at last: The future of peer-reviewed journals. *D-Lib Magazine, 5*(12). Retrieved February 20, 2001, from the World Wide Web: http://www.dlib.org/dlib/december99/12harnad.html

Harnad, S., & Carr, L. (2000). Integrating, navigating, and analysing open Eprint archives through open citation linking (the OpCit project). *Current Science, 79,* 629–638.

Harsanyi, M. A. (1993). Multiple authors, multiple problems: Bibliometrics and the study of scholarly collaboration: A literature review. *Library & Information Science Research, 15,* 325–354.

Harter, S. P. (1992). Psychological relevance and information science. *Journal of the American Society for Information Science, 43*, 602–615.

Harter, S. P. (1998). Scholarly communication and electronic journals: An impact study. *Journal of the American Society for Information Science, 49*, 507–516.

Harter, S. P., & Kim, H. J. (1996). Accessing electronic journals and other e-publications: An empirical study. *College & Research Libraries, 57*, 440–456.

Harter, S. P., Nisonger, T. E., & Weng, A. (1993). Semantic relationships between cited and citing articles in library and information science journals. *Journal of the American Society for Information Science, 44*, 543–552.

Herman, I. L. (1991). Receptivity to foreign literature: A comparison of UK and US citing behavior in librarianship and information science. *Library & Information Science Research, 13*, 37–47.

Hitchcock, S., Carr, L., Hall, W., Harris, S., Probets, S., Evans, D., & Brailsford, D. (1998). Linking electronic journals: Lessons from the Open Journal project. *D-Lib Magazine, 4*(12). Retrieved February 20, 2001, from the World Wide Web: http://www.dlib.org/dlib/december98/12hitchcock.html

Hitchcock, S., Carr, L., Jiao, Z., Bergmark, D., Hall, W., Lagoze, C., & Harnad, S. (2000). Developing services for open eprint archives: Globalisation, integration and the impact of links. In R. K. Furuta (Ed.), *DL'00: Proceedings of the 5th ACM Conference on Digital Libraries* (San Antonio, TX, June 2-7, 2000) (pp. 143–151). New York: ACM Press.

Ingwersen, P. (1998). The calculation of Web impact factors. *Journal of Documentation, 54*, 236–243.

Ingwersen, P., Larsen, B., & Wormell, I. (2000). Applying diachronic citation analysis to research program evaluations. In B. Cronin & H. B. Atkins (Eds.), *The web of knowledge: A Festschrift in honor of Eugene Garfield* (pp. 373–387). Medford, NJ: Information Today.

Jacobs, N., Woodfield, J., & Morris, A. (2000). Using local citation data to relate the use of journal articles by academic researchers to the coverage of full-text document access systems. *Journal of Documentation, 56*, 563–581.

Kalyane, V. L., & Kademani, B. S. (1997). Scientometric portrait of Barbara McClintock: The Nobel laureate in physiology. *Kelpro Bulletin, 1*, 3–14.

Kim, H. J. (2000). Motivations for hyperlinking in scholarly electronic articles: A qualitative study. *Journal of the American Society for Information Science, 51*, 887–899.

Kleinberg, J. M. (1999). Authoritative sources in a hyperlinked environment. *Journal of the ACM, 46*, 604–632.

Kleinberg, J. M., Kumar, R., Raghavan, P., Rajagopalan, S., & Tomkins, A. S. (1999). The Web as a graph: Measurements, models, and methods. In T. Asano, H. Imai, D. T. Lee, S. Nakano, & T. Tokuyama (Eds.), *Computing and Combinatorics: 5th Annual International Conference, COCOON'99: Tokyo, Japan, July 1999: Proceedings*. Berlin: Springer. Retrieved February 20, 2001, from the World Wide Web: http://link.springer.de/link/service/series/0558/papers/1627/16270001.pdf

Kling, R., & McKim, G. (1999). Scholarly communication and the continuum of electronic publishing. *Journal of the American Society for Information Science, 50*, 890–906.

Kostoff, R. N. (1996). Performance measures for government-sponsored research: Overview and background. *Scientometrics, 36*, 281–292.

Kostoff, R. N. (1997). *The handbook of research impact assessment* (7th ed.). Springfield, VA: National Technical Information Service.

Kostoff, R. N. (1998). The use and misuse of citation analysis in research evaluation. *Scientometrics, 43*, 27–43.

Kretschmer, H. (1993). Measurement of social stratification: A contribution to the disput on the Ortega hypothesis. *Scientometrics, 26*, 97–113.

Kretschmer, H. (1997). Patterns of behavior in co-authorship networks of invisible colleges. *Scientometrics, 40*, 579–591.

Kumar, R., Raghavan, P., Rajagopalan, S., & Tomkins, A. (1999). Trawling the Web for emerging cyber-communities. In A. Mendelzon (Ed.), *Proceedings of the Eighth International World Wide Web Conference* (Toronto, Canada, May 11-14, 1999). Amsterdam: Elsevier. Retrieved February 20, 2001, from the World Wide Web: http://www8.org/w8-papers/4a-search-mining/trawling/trawling.html

Larson, R. R. (1996). Bibliometrics of the World Wide Web: An exploratory analysis of the intellectual structure of cyberspace. In S. Hardin (Ed.), *Global complexity: Information, chaos, and control: Proceedings of the 59th ASIS Annual Meeting* (Baltimore, MD, October 21–24, 1996) (pp. 71–78). Medford, NJ: Information Today.

Lawrence, S., & Giles, C. L. (1998). Searching the World Wide Web. *Science, 280*, 98–100.

Lawrence, S., Giles, C. L., & Bollacker, K. (1999). Digital libraries and autonomous citation indexing. *Computer, 32*, 67–71.

Leydesdorff, L. (1998). Theories of citation? *Scientometrics, 43*, 5–25.

Lisovskaya, E., & Karpov, V. (1999). New ideologies in postcommunist Russian textbooks. *Comparative Education Review, 43*, 522–543.

Liu, M. (1993). The complexities of citation practice: A review of citation studies. *Journal of Documentation, 49*, 370–408.

Luukkonen, T. (1997). Why has Latour's theory of citations been ignored by the bibliometric community?: Discussion of sociological interpretations of citation analysis. *Scientometrics, 38*, 27–37.

Lyman, P., & Varian, H. R. (2000). How much information? Internet [Online]. Berkeley, CA: School of Information Management and Systems, University of California, Berkeley. Retrieved February 20, 2001, from the World Wide Web: http://www.sims.berkeley.edu/how-much-info/internet.html

Lynch, C. A. (1998). Identifiers and their role in information applications. *Bulletin of the American Society for Information Science, 24*(2), 17–20.

MacRoberts, M. H., & MacRoberts, B. R. (1987). Problems of citation analysis: A critical review. *Journal of the American Society for Information Science, 40*, 342–349.

MacRoberts, M. H., & MacRoberts, B. R. (1996). Problems of citation analysis. *Scientometrics, 36,* 435–444.

May, R. M. (1997). The scientific wealth of nations. *Science, 275,* 793–796.

McKiernan, G. (1996). CitedSites(sm): Citation indexing of Web resources [Online]. Ames, IA: Iowa State University. Retrieved February 20, 2001, from the World Wide Web: http://www.public.iastate.edu/~CYBERSTACKS/Cited.htm

Meadows, A. J. (1998). *Communicating research.* San Diego, CA: Academic Press.

Merton, R. K. (1968a). The Matthew effect in science. *Science, 159,* 56–63.

Merton, R. K. (1968b). *Social theory and social structure.* New York: Free Press.

Merton, R. K. (1973). *The sociology of science: Theoretical and empirical investigations.* Chicago, IL: University of Chicago Press.

Merton, R. K. (2000). On the Garfield input to the sociology of science: A retrospective collage. In B. Cronin & H. B. Atkins (Eds.), *The web of knowledge: A Festschrift in honor of Eugene Garfield* (pp. 435–448). Medford, NJ: Information Today.

Milgram, S. (1967). The small world problem. *Psychology Today, 2,* 60–67.

Moed, H. F., de Bruin, R. E., & van Leeuwen, T. N. (1995). New bibliometric tools for the assessment of national research performance: Database description, overview of indicators and first applications. *Scientometrics, 33,* 381–422.

Moed, H. F., & van Leeuwen, T. N. (1995). Improving the accuracy of the Institute for Scientific Information's journal impact factors. *Journal of the American Society for Information Science, 46,* 461–467.

Moed, H. F., van Leeuwen, T. N., & Reedijk, J. (1999). Towards appropriate indicators of journal impact. *Scientometrics, 46,* 575–589.

Narin, F. (1976). *Evaluative bibliometrics: The use of publication and citation analysis in the evaluation of scientific activity.* Cherry Hill, NJ: Computer Horizons.

Narin, F., & Hamilton, K. S. (1996). Bibliometric performance measures. *Scientometrics, 36,* 293–310.

Narin, F., Hamilton, K. S., & Olivastro, D. (2000). The development of scientific indicators in the United States. In B. Cronin & H. B. Atkins (Eds.), *The web of knowledge: A Festschrift in honor of Eugene Garfield* (pp. 337–360). Medford, NJ: Information Today.

Nisonger, T. E. (1999). JASIS and library and information science journal rankings: A review and analysis of the last half-century. *Journal of the American Society for Information Science, 50,* 1004–1019.

Noyons, E. C. M., Moed, H. F., & Luwel, M. (1999). Combining mapping and citation analysis for evaluative bibliometric purposes: A bibliometric study. *Journal of the American Society for Information Science, 50,* 115–131.

Odlyzko, A. M. (1995). Tragic loss or good riddance?: The impending demise of traditional scholarly journals. *International Journal of Human-Computer Studies, 42,* 71–122.

Odlyzko, A. M. (1998). The economics of electronic journals. In R. Ekman & R. E. Quandt (Eds.), *Technology and scholarly communication* (pp. 380–393). Berkeley, CA: University of California Press.

Okerson, A. S., & O'Donnell, J. J. (Eds.). (1995). *Scholarly journals at the cross-roads: A subversive proposal for electronic publishing.* Washington, DC: Association of Research Libraries.

Paisley, W. (1990). The future of bibliometrics. In C. L. Borgman (Ed.), *Scholarly communication and bibliometrics* (pp. 281–299). Newbury Park, CA: Sage.

Pao, M. L. (1992). Global and local collaborators: A study of scientific collaboration. *Information Processing & Management, 28,* 99–109.

Peritz, B. C. (1983). A classification of citation roles for the social sciences and related fields. *Scientometrics, 5,* 303–312.

Peritz, B. C. (1992). On the objectives of citation analysis: Problems of theory and method. *Journal of the American Society for Information Science, 43,* 448–451.

Persson, O., & Beckmann, M. (1995). Locating the network of interacting authors in scientific specialties. *Scientometrics, 33,* 351–366.

Persson, O., & Melin, G. (1996). Equalization, growth and integration of science. *Scientometrics, 37,* 153–157.

Persson, O., Melin, G., Danell, R., & Kaloudis, A. (1997). Research collaboration at Nordic universities. *Scientometrics, 39,* 209–223.

Peters, H. F. P., & van Raan, A. F. J. (1994). On determinants of citation scores: A case study in chemical engineering. *Journal of the American Society for Information Science, 45,* 39–49.

Pierce, S. J. (1999). Boundary crossing in research literatures as a means of interdisciplinary information transfer. *Journal of the American Society for Information Science, 50,* 271–279.

Pinski, G., & Narin, F. (1976). Citation influence for journal aggregates of scientific publications: Theory, with application to the literature of physics. *Information Processing & Management, 12,* 297–312.

Price, D. J. de S. (1970). Citation measures of hard science, soft science, technology and nonscience. In C. E. Nelson & D. K. Pollock (Eds.), *Communication among scientists and engineers* (pp. 3–22). Lexington, MA: Heath.

Price, D. J. de S. (1986). *Little science, big science: and beyond.* New York: Columbia University Press.

Qin, J., Lancaster, F. W., & Allen, B. (1997). Types and levels of collaboration in interdisciplinary research in the sciences. *Journal of the American Society for Information Science, 48,* 893–916.

Rayward, W. B. (1994). Some schemes for restructuring and mobilising information in documents: A historical perspective. *Information Processing & Management, 30,* 163–175.

Robinson, M. D. (1991). Applied bibliometrics: Using citation analysis in the journal submission process. *Journal of the American Society for Information Science, 42,* 308–310.

Rousseau, R. (1992a). Breakdown of the robustness property of Lotka's Law: The case of adjusted counts for multiauthorship attribution. *Journal of the American Society for Information Science, 43,* 645–647.

Rousseau, R. (1992b). Why am I not cited or why are multi-authored papers more cited than others? [Letter]. *Journal of Documentation, 48,* 79–80.

Rousseau, R. (1993). A table for estimating the exponent in Lotka's Law. *Journal of Documentation, 49*, 409–412.

Rousseau, R. (1997). Sitations: An exploratory study. *Cybermetrics: International Journal of Scientometrics, Informetrics and Bibliometrics, 1*(1). Retrieved February 20, 2001, from the World Wide Web: http://www.cindoc.csic.es/cybermetrics/articles/v1i1p1.html

Rousseau, R., & Rousseau, S. (1993). Informetric distributions: A tutorial review. *Canadian Journal of Information and Library Science, 18*, 51–63.

Rousseau, R., & van Hooydonk, G. (1996). Journal production and journal impact factors. *Journal of the American Society for Information Science, 47*, 775–780.

Rousseau, S., & Rousseau, R. (1998). The scientific wealth of European nations: Taking effectiveness into account. *Scientometrics, 42*, 75–87.

Roy, R., Roy, N. R., & Johnson, G. G. (1983). Approximating total citation counts from 1st author counts and from total papers. *Scientometrics, 5*, 117–124.

Russell, J. M. (2000). Publication indicators in Latin America revisited. In B. Cronin & H. B. Atkins (Eds.), *The web of knowledge: A Festschrift in honor of Eugene Garfield* (pp. 233–250). Medford, NJ: Information Today.

Russell, J. M., & Rousseau, R. (in press). Bibliometrics and institutional evaluation. In K. Rosner (Ed.), *The encyclopedia of life support systems*. Oxford, England: UNESCO-EOLSS.

Schamber, L. (1994). Relevance and information behavior. *Annual Review of Information Science and Technology, 29*, 3–48.

Schamber, L., Eisenberg, M. B., & Nilan, M. S. (1990). A re-examination of relevance: Toward a dynamic, situational definition. *Information Processing & Management, 26*, 755–776.

Schauder, D. (1994). Electronic publishing of professional articles: Attitudes of academics and implications for the scholarly communication industry. *Journal of the American Society for Information Science, 45*, 73–100.

Seglen, P. O. (1992). The skewness of science. *Journal of the American Society for Information Science, 43*, 628–638.

Seglen, P. O. (1994). Causal relationship between article citedness and journal impact. *Journal of the American Society for Information Science, 45*, 1–11.

Seglen, P. O. (1998). Citation rates and journal impact factors are not suitable for evaluation of research. *Acta Orthopaedica Scandinavica, 69*, 224–229.

Sen, B. K. (1999). Symbols and formulas for a few bibliometric concepts. *Journal of Documentation, 55*, 325–334.

Sen, B. K., Pandalai, T. A., & Karanjai, A. (1998). Ranking of scientists: A new approach. *Journal of Documentation, 54*, 622–628.

Sengupta, I. N. (1992). Bibliometrics, informetrics, scientometrics and librametrics: An overview. *Libri, 42*, 75–98.

Shadish, W. R., Tolliver, D., Gray, M., & Sen Gupta, S. K. (1995). Author judgments about works they cite: Three studies from psychology journals. *Social Studies of Science, 25*, 477–498.

Small, H. (1982). Citation context analysis. In B. Dervin & M. Voigt (Eds.), *Progress in communication sciences: Volume 3* (pp. 287–310). Norwood, NJ: Ablex.

Small, H. (1999). Visualizing science by citation mapping. *Journal of the American Society for Information Science, 50,* 799–813.

Smith, A. G. (1999). A tale of two Web spaces: Comparing sites using Web impact factors. *Journal of Documentation, 55,* 577–592.

Snyder, H. W., & Bonzi, S. (1998). Patterns of self-citation across disciplines (1980–1989). *Journal of Information Science, 24,* 431–435.

Snyder, H. W., Cronin, B., & Davenport, E. (1995). What's the use of citation?: Citation analysis as a literature topic in selected disciplines of the social sciences. *Journal of Information Science, 21,* 75–85.

Snyder, H. W., & Rosenbaum, H. (1999). Can search engines be used as tools for Web-link analysis?: A critical review. *Journal of Documentation, 55,* 375–384.

Tabah, A. (2001). Literature dynamics: Studies on growth, diffusion, and epidemics. *Annual Review of Information Science and Technology, 34.*

Tague-Sutcliffe, J. (1992). An introduction to informetrics. *Information Processing & Management, 28,* 1–3.

Van de Sompel, H., & Hochstenbach, P. (1999a). Reference linking in a hybrid library environment, part 1: Frameworks for linking. *D-Lib Magazine, 5*(4). Retrieved February 20, 2001, from the World Wide Web: http://www.dlib.org/dlib/april99/van_de_sompel/04van_de_sompel-pt1.html

Van de Sompel, H., & Hochstenbach, P. (1999b). Reference linking in a hybrid library environment, part 2: SFX, a generic linking solution. *D-Lib Magazine, 5*(4). Retrieved February 20, 2001, from the World Wide Web: http://www.dlib.org/dlib/april99/van_de_sompel/04van_de_sompel-pt2.html

Van de Sompel, H., & Lagoze, C. (2000). The Sante Fe Convention of the Open Archives Initiative. *D-Lib Magazine, 6*(2). Retrieved February 20, 2001, from the World Wide Web: http://www.dlib.org/dlib/february00/vandesompel-oai/02vandesompel-oai.html

van Hooydonk, G. (1998). Standardizing relative impacts: Estimating the quality of research from citation counts. *Journal of the American Society for Information Science, 49,* 932–941.

van Leeuwen, T. N., Moed, H. F., & Reedijk, J. (1999). Critical comments on Institute for Scientific Information impact factors: A sample of inorganic molecular chemistry journals. *Journal of Information Science, 25,* 489–498.

van Leeuwen, T. N., Moed, H. F., Tijssen, R. J. W., Visser, M. S., & van Raan, A. F. J. (2000). First evidence of serious language-bias in the use of citation analysis for the evaluation of national science systems. *Research Evaluation, 9,* 155–156.

van Raan, A. F. J. (1988). *Handbook of quantitative studies of science and technology.* Amsterdam: Elsevier.

van Raan, A. F. J. (1997). Scientometrics: State of the art. *Scientometrics, 38,* 205–218.

van Raan, A. F. J. (1999). Advanced bibliometric methods for the evaluation of universities. *Scientometrics, 45*, 417–423.

van Raan, A. F. J. (2000). The Pandora's box of citation analysis: Measuring scientific excellence: The last evil? In B. Cronin & H. B. Atkins (Eds.), *The web of knowledge: A Festschrift in honor of Eugene Garfield* (pp. 301–319). Medford, NJ: Information Today.

Vinkler, P. (1996). Relationships between the rate of scientific development and citations: The chances for a citedness model. *Scientometrics, 35*, 375–386.

Vinkler, P. (2000). Evaluation of the publication activity of research teams by means of scientometric indicators. *Current Science, 79*, 602–612.

Wagner-Dobler, R., & Berg, J. (1995). The dependence of Lotka's Law on the selection of time periods in the development of scientific areas and authors. *Journal of Documentation, 51*, 28–43.

Watts, D. J., & Strogatz, S. H. (1998). Collective dynamics of "small-world" networks. *Nature, 393*, 440–442.

White, H. D. (2000). Toward ego-centered citation analysis. In B. Cronin & H. B. Atkins (Eds.), *The web of knowledge: A Festschrift in honor of Eugene Garfield* (pp. 475–496). Medford, NJ: Information Today.

White, H. D. (2001). Authors as citers over time. *Journal of the American Society for Information Science and Technology, 52*, 87–108.

White, H. D., & McCain, K. W. (1989). Bibliometrics. *Annual Review of Information Science and Technology, 24*, 119–186.

White, H. D., & McCain, K. W. (1997). Visualization of literatures. *Annual Review of Information Science and Technology, 32*, 99–168.

White, H. D., & McCain, K. W. (1998). Visualizing a discipline: An author co-citation analysis of information science, 1972–1995. *Journal of the American Society for Information Science, 49*, 327–355.

White, M. D., & Wang, P. (1997). A qualitative study of citing behavior: Contributions, criteria, and metalevel documentation concerns. *Library Quarterly, 67*, 122–154.

Wilson, C. S., & Hood, W. W. (2001). Informetric laws. *Annual Review of Information Science and Technology, 34*.

Woolgar, S. (1991). Beyond the citation debate: Towards a sociology of measurement technologies and their use in science policy. *Science and Public Policy, 18*, 319–326.

Wormell, I. (1998). Informetric analysis of the international impact of scientific journals: How "international" are the international journals? *Journal of Documentation, 54*, 584–605.

Wouters, P. (1999). *The citation culture*. Unpublished Ph.D. thesis, University of Amsterdam, Amsterdam.

Wouters, P. (2000). Garfield as alchemist. In B. Cronin, & H. B. Atkins (Eds.), *The web of knowledge: A Festschrift in honor of Eugene Garfield* (pp. 65–71). Medford, NJ: Information Today.

Yitzhaki, M. (1998). The "language preference" in sociology: Measures of "language self-citation," "relative own-language preference indicator," and "mutual use of languages." *Scientometrics, 41,* 243–254.

Youngen, G. K. (1998). Citation patterns to traditional and electronic pre-prints in the published literature. *College & Research Libraries, 59,* 448–456.

CHAPTER 2

Collaboratories

Thomas A. Finholt
University of Michigan

Introduction

Science is an inherently collaborative enterprise. This trend has accelerated over the past few decades. The Internet, in particular, has created new possibilities for the organization of joint scientific work, specifically among geographically separated collaborators. A notable instance of Internet-mediated science is the collaboratory, or laboratory without walls, in which scientists are connected to each other, to instruments, and to data, independent of time and location. This chapter explores past and current collaboratory efforts to identify factors that predict success and failure. The chapter concludes with an assessment of directions for future collaboratory development.

Historically, joint intellectual activity has depended on physical proximity. For example, the probability of person-to-person communication under traditional circumstances is strongly constrained by distance; diminishing to zero beyond thirty meters (Allen, 1977; Kraut, Egido, & Galegher, 1990). In terms of a particularly important kind of group intellectual activity, scientific collaboration, proximity has a direct effect on the quality and frequency of collaboration (Katz, 1994). Further, convenient access to scarce instruments provides an additional imperative for co-location in science (Hagstrom, 1965). In the high energy physics community, for instance, research activity is confined to a handful of labs worldwide (Traweek, 1992). Other scientific communities face similar limitations. The conventional response to these limitations has historically been residency, either permanent or temporary, at an instrument site. Therefore, in terms of the performance of joint intellectual work, sharing a common work setting has evolved as a critical tool to support both frequent interaction among collaborators and the use of unique facilities.

Despite the benefits of co-location, there are important individual and collective costs. Individual costs involve lost productivity associated with dislocation from a familiar environment, as when a scientist travels to a remote facility. On a collective scale, co-location inevitably involves exclusion and isolation from those who are located elsewhere. Some mechanisms, such as conferences and workshops, can attenuate this effect. For the most part, however, a shared physical space comes to define a shared intellectual space in which collaboration with those nearby is much more likely than with those who are distant, even after controlling for disciplinary differences (Kraut et al., 1990). Focusing on science, there are additional collective costs of co-location. Specifically, to the extent that co-location plays into competitive rivalries among research sites, cooperation may be undermined. For example, lack of cooperation can lead to redundant capacity, such as supporting several independent and underutilized instruments, rather than a single shared and fully utilized instrument. More important, barriers to interaction across sites may slow the integration of knowledge required to resolve research questions that exceed the capacity of single sites, or even single disciplines. The global AIDS epidemic, for example, is often cited as the kind of large research problem that requires unprecedented levels of cooperation from communities that have, in the past, worked independently (e.g., clinicians, bench scientists, activists, and policy makers).

Trends in the Organization of Scientific Work

The greatest transformation in the organization of scientific work has been the increased orientation toward large-scale projects, or "big science" (Weinberg, 1961). As noted in Price's (1963) landmark analysis, greater size and complexity of research tasks are reflected in a higher need for collaboration, at least when measured as the number of authors on publications. This trend toward collaboration is increasing and appears to be independent of discipline, as shown in recent analyses of authorship in biology (Zhang, 1997), information science (Lipetz, 1999), social science (Endersby, 1996), and political science (Fisher, Cobane, Vander Ven, & Cullen, 1998). Collaboration in science has become so well accepted that in 1997, the then chair of the National Science Board, Richard Zare, wrote in a *Science* editorial that future research progress would demand mechanisms to support mega-collaborations of the type required to solve critical global problems such as AIDS (Zare, 1997). In Zare's formulation, research activity would be organized as a form of "distributed intelligence" in which experience and knowledge held by scientists at one location could be easily shared and utilized by scientists elsewhere. Specifically, Zare (1997, p. 1047) described an era where "knowledge is available to anyone, located anywhere, at any time; and in which power, information, and control are moving from centralized systems to individuals." This model suggests a dramatic revision of the historical organization of science, away from "invisible colleges," where the bulk of new knowledge is created by a small core of elite researchers working among themselves (Crane, 1972; Price & Beaver, 1966)—such that 16 percent of practicing scientists account for about 50 percent of all publications (Price, 1986). By contrast, the notion of distributed intelligence suggests a mobilization of scientific effort—and a corresponding increase in research output and capacity—so that a larger fraction of the scientific workforce participates in the creation of new knowledge.

The notion of science as distributed intelligence relies heavily on information technology to overcome barriers of time and space. Specifically, studies of scientists and engineers at work suggest that the amount and quality of interaction with colleagues, particularly spontaneous and informal conversations, is an important predictor of productivity (Allen, 1977; Fox, 1983; Hagstrom, 1965; Kraut, et al., 1988; Kraut, et al., 1990; Menzel, 1962; Pelz & Andrews, 1966). Scientists who are remote from communities of elite and active researchers, then, are at a disadvantage in terms of initiating contact with leading investigators that can lead to deeper collaborations. Therefore, the introduction of tools, such as electronic mail, that facilitate easier communication between scientists at nonelite institutions and those at elite institutions could produce increased involvement by nonelite scientists in cutting-edge research. This outcome is one possibility predicted by the "peripherality hypothesis" (Sproull & Kiesler, 1991, p. 95). According to this hypothesis, the introduction of electronic communication may produce universal benefits, differential benefits for those who are relatively advantaged, or differential benefits for those who are relatively disadvatanged (as in the previous scenario comparing nonelite and elite scientists). For example, a number of studies in business settings have shown how employees of global firms use computer-mediated communication to overcome barriers of remote geographic location (Constant, Sproull, & Kiesler, 1996; Finholt, Sproull, & Kiesler, in press; Kraut & Attewell, 1997). In these cases, electronic mail, bulletin boards, and mailing lists allowed peripheral employees to have the same access to important activities and information flows as centrally located employees, such as those at headquarters sites.

Evidence from a small number of studies appears to support the idea that electronic mail and other computer-mediated communications do enhance scientific productivity (Bishop, 1994; Bruce, 1994; Cohen, 1996; Hesse, Sproull, Kiesler, & Walsh, 1993; Walsh & Roselle, 1999), and that computer networks seem to support larger and more dispersed collaborations (Orlikowski & Yates, 1994; Raefeli, Sudweeks, Konstan, & Mabry, 1998; Walsh & Roselle, 1999). However, there is weaker evidence with respect to differential benefits for nonelite scientists. For example, in a survey study of 399 scientists in experimental biology, mathematics, physics, and sociology, Walsh and Maloney (in press) found slight evidence that electronic mail use was differentially benefiting peripheral scientists relative to core scientists. That is, e-mail use was universally associated with higher productivity, but not in a way that changed the status of peripheral scientists compared to core scientists. Similarly, Cohen (1996) found little support for the equalizing effect of e-mail use among a sample of academic researchers.

One speculation with respect to the absence of a peripherality effect revolves around features of the Internet that grant people discretion regarding selection of communication partners. That is, proponents of the distributed intelligence concept believe that mechanisms like the Internet will break down barriers among disciplines and institutions by allowing people to act on preferences to associate with others who are different. However, Van Alstyne and Brynjolfsson (1996) argue that if preferences run counter to this expectation, people may choose to associate and communicate mostly with similar others (i.e., because this requires less effort). In this case, then, use of the Internet will produce increased balkanization rather than increased diversification. Under the balkanization scenario, scientists will interact and collaborate more with geographically distributed scientists, but these distant collaborators will be highly similar on critical dimensions (e.g., status, training, methodology preference).

The Collaboratory Concept

Studies cited in the preceding section suggest that, at least on preliminary examination, electronic communication alone may not be enough to enable a broader range of collaboration in science. This broader collaboration refers both to increased interaction independent of location, as well as the reduction of status barriers, such that distinctions between elite and nonelite scientists become less significant. However, electronic communication, combined with better access to critical instruments and data, may produce differential benefits. That is, while communication is unquestionably important in fostering and sustaining successful scientific collaborations, joint research work also requires access to specialized equipment and unique data sets. This suggests that a true test of the peripherality hypothesis in science requires elaboration of additional network capabilities; particularly applications that enhance sharing of data and data visualizations, and applications that allow remote use of important instruments and facilities.

One mechanism to achieve enhanced access to data and instruments is the "collaboratory." First proposed by visionary scientists and computer scientists in the late eighties, a collaboratory is "a center without walls, in which researchers can perform their research without regard to physical location—interacting with colleagues, accessing instrumentation, sharing data and computational resources, and accessing information in digital libraries" (Wulf, 1989, p. 19). The term "collaboratory" is a hybrid of collaborate and laboratory. Hence, elaborations of the collaboratory concept stress the simultaneous need to solve problems of control and operation of instrumentation over the Internet, of access and distribution of data sets, and of convenient and flexible interaction with colleagues. Development of computing technology to support collaboratories has not been guided by a grand plan. Rather, systems have emerged through a combination of prodding by visionaries, appropriation of technology designed for other purposes, and the availability of low-cost, high-performance personal computers.

Early proponents of scientific computing anticipated some of the functions of the collaboratory. For example, Vannevar Bush (1945) explored how computers might be used to help scientists keep pace with the explosion of scientific knowledge. He imagined a machine, called the "memex," that would allow scientists to access and retrieve data and results from a vast array of scientific publications. Pioneers such as Douglas Engelbart wrote in the sixties about the use of computing to support intellectual work, and built prototype systems for computer-supported meetings (Engelbart, 1963). The initial practical step on the path to collaboratories occurred with the opening of the first wide area computer network in 1969, called the ARPAnet after the Advanced Research Projects Agency of the U.S. Department of Defense, which sponsored the development of the network. Although originally designed to share scarce computing resources, the most important function of the ARPAnet, ultimately, was its support for electronic mail between researchers in computer science and artificial intelligence (Newell & Sproull, 1982). Throughout the seventies and eighties, networking technologies developed further, culminating in the creation of the Internet in 1985; thus creating the first worldwide community of online users (Lynch & Preston, 1990).

The collaboratory idea appeared as scientists recognized the potential represented by expanding national and international computer networks. The first explicit discussion of collaboratories occurred at a National Science Foundation (NSF)-sponsored workshop in 1989 convened by Joshua Lederberg and Keith Uncapher. This workshop gave the collaboratory concept visibility within the NSF and other relevant national scientific communities. The report of the workshop outlined a number of specific research priorities, including enabling infrastructure to support collaboratories; construction of collaboratory test beds in various scientific disciplines; and studies of the process of collaboration and the use of these test beds by scientists (Lederberg & Uncapher, 1989). One outcome of the 1989 workshop was a series of further workshops in

1993 sponsored by the Computer Science and Telecommunications Board of the National Research Council (NRC) to explore the feasibility and utility of collaboratories for three disciplines: molecular biology, physical oceanography, and space physics. These fields were chosen for their heterogeneity in size, style of research, technical sophistication, and traditional sources of support. An important result of this activity was the NRC's report *National Collaboratories: Applying Information Technology for Scientific Research* (National Research Council, 1993). The report called for substantial support to develop, refine, and evaluate the collaboratory concept in realistic settings. The impact of these, and other prototype collaboratories, is discussed at length later in this chapter.

Four broad changes since the earliest days of the ARPAnet have created conditions conducive to collaboratory development. First, when the ARPAnet appeared, its bandwidth was limited and network use was restricted to institutions with ARPA projects. Today, even the smallest institutions and the most peripheral scientists can have network connections. Second, in the early days, network connections were scarce. Today, through the proliferation of personal computing and local area networks, network connections are ubiquitous. Third, early user applications had command line interfaces. Today, most software products have intuitive, graphical interfaces that allow users to perform sophisticated actions without learning obscure command sequences. Finally, while early network use was confined to a small community of computer scientists, contemporary users represent a broad spectrum of scientific disciplines as well as a mass audience from business and the general public.

At a more specific level, nearly two decades of technology evolution have led to a rich variety of computer and network tools for the support of collaborative work. Combinations of these existing tools, with elaboration of some new tools, form the core capabilities that constitute a collaboratory. As shown in Figure 2.1, derived from Atkins (1993), these capabilities can be defined as technology to link people with people, technology to link people with information, and technology to link people with facilities. Examples of people-to-people technologies include familiar applications, such as electronic mail, and tools for data conferencing, such as Microsoft NetMeeting. Technologies to link people with information, including the World Wide Web and digital libraries, have recently experienced tremendous growth in sophistication and use (for a

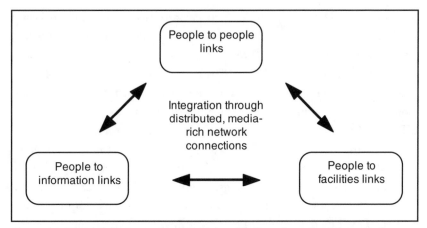

Figure 2.1 The collaboratory concept: Using distributed, media-rich network connections to link people to each other, to facilities, and to information

more detailed survey of digital libraries see the chapter by Edward Fox and Shalini Urs in this volume as well as the special issue of *Communications of the ACM*, April 1995, edited by Fox, Akscyn, Furuta, and Leggett). Finally, technologies to link people to facilities include data viewers that display the current modes and status of remote instruments as well as services that provide scientifically critical data. An early effort along these lines was the MOS Implementation System, which allowed very large scale integrated chip designers to access remote fabrication facilities (Lewicki, Cohen, Losleben, & Trotter, 1984).

Collaboratory Experiences

The previous sections have described broad scientific and technological trends that have led to collaboratory development. This section offers a chronological description of notable operational collaboratories, covering the period from 1980 to 2000. The focus here is on those collaboratory efforts that have been or are in use by practicing scientists and that have produced accounts of this use. Table 2.1 summarizes key features of the collaboratory efforts described below.

SCIENCEnet, 1980s

SCIENCEnet was a proprietary network service initiated in 1980 to meet the unique information and communication needs of the

Table 2.1 Descriptive characteristics of U.S. collaboratory efforts, 1992–2000

Project Title	Start Date	Sponsor	Total Budget	Target Community	Peak use	Total Use	Relevant Studies
Worm Community System	1990	NSF	$1,741,141	c. elegans researchers	NA	NA	Star94
UARC	1992	NSF	$4,455,329	Space physicists	54	163	Finholt97
CoVis	1992	NSF	$4,794,633	K-12 students	NA	NA	Fishmann00
CMDA	1994	NSF/NIH	$2,273,321	Electron Microscopy	NA	NA	Hadida-Hassan99
Remote Experimental Environment	1995	DOE	NA	Fusion researchers	NA	NA	Caspar98
EMSL Collaboratory	1995	DOE	NA	NMR users	5	17	Bair99
Chickscope	1996	U. of Ill.	NA	Microscopy, K-12 students	30	900	Bruce97
MMC Collaboratory	1997	DOE/NIST	$10,890,000	Electron Microscopy	NA	NA	Zaluzec98
Diesel Combustion Collaboratory	1997	DOE	$7,155,000	Diesel combustion	NA	NA	Pancerella99
Great Lakes Regional CFAR	1998	NIH	$814,088	AIDS researchers	25	86	Teasley01
SPARC	1998	NSF	$2,440,000	Space physicists	34	215	Olson00
BioCoRE	1998	NIH	$1,225,000	Structural biologists	NA	NA	Bhandarkar99
Nano-Manipulator	1998	NIH	$1,225,000	Remote use of AFM	NA	NA	Sonnenwald01
Bugscope	1999	NSF	$447,751	Microscopy, K-16 students	30	1500	Potter00

oceanography community. In return for a monthly fee, SCIENCEnet subscribers obtained access to colleagues and to data. For example, SCIENCEnet supported project-oriented mailing lists used to coordinate activity among scientists in multiple locations. In addition, SCIENCEnet provided infrastructure for the storage and transport of large data sets. A critical feature of SCIENCEnet was its global coverage, which permitted logins from forty-five countries and the Antarctic, as well as via satellite link from research vessels. SCIENCEnet was particularly well suited to the needs of oceanographers, who frequently collaborate to coordinate data gathering across remote locations, or who monitor arrays of automatic sensors, such as buoys moored in the ocean or sensors installed on polar ice caps.

Hesse et al. (1993) conducted a systematic analysis of SCIENCEnet use and the relationship of usage to scientific outcomes. Data came from a 1988 survey of 338 SCIENCEnet users. Respondents were stratified by category of use, where frequent users had greater than median levels of use and infrequent users had below median levels of use. Scientists were also classified according to location (inland versus coastal), seniority, and disciplinary affiliation (physical oceanography—the target audience for SCIENCEnet—versus other). Outcomes included scientific productivity, measured as publications; professional recognition; and social integration, measured as the extent of each respondent's social network. Results showed that frequent SCIENCEnet users were more active, productive scientists. As compared with infrequent users, they worked at more prestigious institutions, received more professional recognition, published more, and knew more oceanographers. Controlling for category of use, network usage was still positively related to publications, recognition, and social integration. Further, for inland scientists, use of SCIENCEnet helped to overcome the disadvantage of a noncoastal location, at least in terms of publications. Perhaps the most interesting observation from Hesse et al.'s study was the finding that SCIENCEnet users reported that SCIENCEnet's operators were very sensitive to the special needs of oceanographers—and therefore worked hard to make the system as useful and invisible as possible, in order to allow users to maximize their focus on conducting research.

Worm Community System, 1990–1996

The Worm Community System (WCS) was initiated by Bruce Schatz (1991) and others in 1990 to meet the needs of biologists studying *c. elegans*, a tiny nematode with desirable scientific properties, such as transparent skin and the ability to be frozen and unfrozen for shipping between labs. At the time WCS was built, the community of scientists studying *c. elegans* included 1,400 researchers at over 100 labs. The WCS consisted of a set of hypertext-linked resources, which was a novel architecture at a time before widespread use of the World Wide Web. The WCS included graphics of the *c. elegans* physical structure; a genetic map; formal and informal research notes (including a newsletter called the *Worm Breeder's Gazette*); directory services; a thesaurus; and a database called *acedb*. Star and Ruhleder (1994) described use of the WCS, based on observations of and interviews with over 100 researchers at twenty-five labs over a three-year period, 1991–1994. They found that, while respondents described WCS as easy to use and relevant to *c. elegans* research, "most have not signed on; many have chosen instead to use Gopher [an Internet-based document search and retrieval protocol developed by Alberti, Anklesaria, Lindner, McCahill, & Torrey (1992)] and other simpler net utilities with less technical functionality" (Star & Ruhleder, 1994, pp. 254–255). This finding was disappointing for the WCS developers, particularly given the efforts by the WCS team to ensure adequate feedback from the user community during the development of WCS.

Star and Ruhleder identified several factors in the nonuse of the WCS. At a high level, a key problem was that the target audience of biologists had to master relatively complex system installations (e.g., choosing the proper X-windows version) within alien computing environments (e.g., Unix workstations). Lower-level problems included information barriers ("where do I download the WCS system from?"), unforeseen consequences (e.g., the difficulty of maintaining a unique operating system, such as Unix, among mostly Macintosh computers), and political/cultural issues ("What is the appropriate trade-off between private and public information?"). Specifically, in terms of political/cultural factors, many post-docs were reluctant to share ideas or data via WCS, or similar mechanisms, for fear of being anticipated, or scooped, by others. Star and Ruhleder summarized researchers' experience with the WCS in terms of Bateson's (1972) "double bind" concept—whereby actions, with respect to the WCS, were often contradictory. For example, users were torn between the power of the WCS versus the inconvenience of learning new systems and leaving familiar work environments (i.e., most work was performed from a desktop machine, while WCS-related work had to be done from a special workstation).

Upper Atmospheric Research Collaboratory, 1992–1999

The Upper Atmospheric Research Collaboratory (UARC) was initiated in 1993 to serve the needs of a distributed community of space physicists who were users of instruments located at a National Science Foundation-funded observatory located above the Arctic Circle on the west coast of

Greenland. Space physics focuses on the interaction between the Earth's atmosphere and magnetosphere and the sun. The best-known phenomena studied by space physicists are the northern and southern lights, or the photon emissions associated with charged particles in the ionosphere. The goal of UARC was to provide real-time control of remote instruments used to study these and other upper atmospheric events. In addition, UARC was intended to support communication among geographically distributed colleagues about shared real-time data and to provide access to archived data. Finally, UARC was intended to demonstrate the utility of "user-centered" design, in which the system evolved through rich interactions between computer scientists, space physicists, and behavioral scientists—with the latter playing a critical role in determining system requirements and evaluating the system in use (Finholt & Olson, 1997; McDaniel, Olson, & Olson, 1994). The original UARC implementation, which was operational from 1992 to 1998, was built in NeXTStep, and required either a NeXT workstation or a workstation configured with the NeXTStep operating system. A later version, based on Java applets, was operational from 1995 to 1998, and could be run on any operating system with a Java-compatible Web browser.

Olson et al. (1998) provide a summary of experiences with the UARC system. During the NeXTStep era, UARC succeeded in providing real-time output from instruments in Greenland, notably an incoherent scatter radar, to a small number of users in Europe and in North America. For the most part, during this early period, UARC was used as a tool for the collective viewing of live data and for discussion of the data. Typically, scientists would organize activity in small groups around focal observing intervals, called "campaigns," much as they did pre-UARC— except that UARC eliminated the need to travel to the Greenland observatory. A key finding related to early UARC use was the observation that the collaboratory expanded the pool of participants in data gathering sessions, compared with traditional sessions, but the additional participants tended to be relatively passive (McDaniel, Olson, & Magee, 1996). That is, in the collaboratory setting, greater ease of access to research activity provided an opportunity for more people to watch—and to increase their level of participation as needed. Finholt, Lewis, & Mott (1995) found that this feature of UARC supported educational use, to the extent that novice space physicists could "lurk" in the collaboratory and observe experienced scientists at work, much as Lave and Wenger (1991) have described novice workers doing in shared physical settings.

Increased use of the World Wide Web within the space physics community, starting around 1994, influenced a redesign of UARC. The second generation system abandoned the NeXTStep environment, which, because it required a separate workstation or special modifications to existing workstations, had become a barrier to adoption. The second generation version of UARC also introduced a more scalable data distribution approach. These changes enabled dramatic new kinds of collaboratory use. First, interest in global-scale phenomena forced expansion from the original Greenland site to the entire chain of incoherent scatter radars—now including observatories in Norway, Massachusetts, Puerto Rico, and Peru. Scientists also demanded output from spacecraft, including imaging satellites in polar orbit as well as satellites monitoring the solar wind and the surface of the sun. Second, scientists who focused on computational models of the upper atmosphere wanted to view their simulated data side-by-side with observational data—and to discuss differences in real time with experts in interpretation of the observational data. Finally, scientists discovered that tools developed for real-time data gathering and visualization could be easily adapted for viewing archival data. This produced a need for "retrospective" campaigns in which the collaboratory was used to view a significant data interval (e.g., a solar sub-storm) from several corroborating instruments (e.g., radar, satellite, computational models, and so forth). Later UARC campaigns, as a result of these changes, had a different character and involved many more scientists and institutions. For example, in April 1997, more than fifty scientists from twenty labs logged into UARC over a four-day period coinciding with a coronal mass ejection.

While the evolution from the NeXTStep-based system to a Java-based system did result in the new kinds of use described above, there were still many problems. The goal of the redesign was to produce a UARC system that would be free of the orphaned NeXTStep environment and would run on the heterogeneous mix of machines and operating systems used in the space physics community. The reality was that the change to Java coincided with rapid evolution of the Java language, such that the initial Java applet version of UARC ran on beta versions of a limited set of Web browsers—and then on only some operating systems. Users were forced to download updated browsers frequently; in some cases the UARC choice was not the main browser in use at a site (e.g., Sun's HotJava browser versus more popular programs). The cost in extra effort for users severely undermined confidence in the UARC system and tarnished otherwise successful efforts to increase the scale and scope of the collaboratory.

Environmental Molecular Sciences Laboratory Collaboratory, 1993–Present

The Environmental Molecular Sciences Laboratory (EMSL) Collaboratory was initiated in 1993 at the Pacific Northwest National Laboratory (Bair, 1999; Kouzes, Myers, & Wulf, 1996). The collaboratory capability was developed in parallel with creation of the EMSL's physical facility—a collection of instruments and expertise focused on environmental molecular science. Environmental molecular science, in this case, refers to a molecular-level understanding of the physical, chemical, and biological processes that underlie remediation of contaminated soils and groundwater, processing and disposal of stored waste materials, and human health and ecological effects of exposure to pollutants. The EMSL facility consists of data resources (notably a 20 terabyte robotic tape archive), magnetic resonance instruments, and mass spectrometers. Key elements of the collaboratory include applications to support remote operation of the magnetic resonance and mass spectrometer instruments, as well as an electronic notebook for instrument users to record and retrieve data. In addition, collaboratory users have access to a set of generic collaboration tools, including whiteboards, chat rooms, audio and video conferencing, and application sharing (i.e., remote viewing of a shared screen image). As of 1999, the EMSL Collaboratory had gone through three generations of development, with the current system implemented as a Java application.

Schur et al. (1998) summarize user experiences in the EMSL Collaboratory. Schur et al. focused on the 200 researchers targeted as potential users of the collaboratory. They conducted interviews with scientists prior to collaboratory use and then observed collaboratory use by a geographically dispersed research team. Researchers contrasted their current practices with a desired ideal, using a standard paradigm of two to five researchers engaged with an eight-hour experimental run. Respondents said that under current practices, disproportionate amounts of time and attention were sunk into preparation for experiments and reporting of experimental results. Collaboration with colleagues occurred mostly around transitions, such as moving from experimental preparation to actually conducting an experiment, and not when needed the most. By contrast, researchers wished to devote the bulk of their time and attention to analysis and interpretation of experimental results, while streamlining preparation and reporting activities. Throughout all experimental activities, they wanted continuous access to colleagues for consultation and discussion, but on an as-needed basis.

Observations of scientists in the collaboratory concentrated on a team conducting a protein structure analysis using a Nuclear Magnetic Resonance (NMR) spectrometer and on a team of intelligence analysts working on detection of nuclear material for purposes of detecting nonproliferation treaty violations. The observational studies produced a number of key findings. First, scientists co-located with research instruments worried that the collaboratory would reduce them to instrument technicians—doing the bidding of remote scientists at the expense of their own work. In fact, collaboratory use produced sufficient efficiencies such that the local scientists actually had more time to pursue their own projects. Second, much as scientists wished, collaboratory use did allow them to focus more on analysis and less on details of data collection and transmission (e.g., faxes, file transfers, and e-mail). Third, with experience, collaboratory users moved from using collaborative tools in traditional ways, such as one person presenting to others as in a telelecture, to novel techniques focused more on application sharing and data conferencing (even forgoing video-mediated interaction in favor of data conferencing). Finally, audio and shared cursor movements, such as with telepointers, proved much more important and useful than video in the collaboratory for signaling the beginning and end of tasks, and for avoiding interruptions and talking over others when speaking.

K-12 Collaboratories

A significant potential use of collaboratories is to introduce elementary and secondary school students to authentic research practices, such as the CoVis project's efforts (1992–1998) to build electronic notebooks to support access and analysis by student teams to the same kinds of data used by practicing scientists (Edelson, Pea, & Gomez, 1996; Fishman, 2000), or through access to previously exotic research instruments. Good examples of this latter strategy include classroom use of electron microscopes at the Argonne National Laboratory (Zaluzec, 1998) and the nanoManipulator at the University of North Carolina described in detail with the other National Institutes of Health collaboratories, below (Jones, Superfine, & Taylor, 1999); undergraduate access to nuclear magnetic resonance spectrometers at the Pacific Northwest National Laboratory (Myers, Chonacky, Dunning, & Leber, 1997); and two prototypes that emerged from the World Wide Laboratory (WWL) project at the University of Illinois. The overall goal of the WWL effort has been to provide remote and automated access to imaging instrumentation, such as electron microscopes and nuclear magnetic resonance imaging (MRI) spectrometers, for teams of geographically distributed researchers (Carragher & Potter, 1999). The project has produced a number of Web-based applications for controlling instruments and viewing data displays, aimed at research scientists. An interesting consequence of the Web-based tool development, however, was the realization that with these new tools, access to various high-powered imaging instruments was now available to anyone with an Internet connection and a Web browser.

This realization led to a proposal to use WWL tools in a prototype effort to allow students in kindergarten through high school classrooms to remotely track the development of a chicken embryo using MRI facilities at the University of Illinois' Beckman Institute. This experiment, called Chickscope (1995–1998), involved students from ten classrooms, their teachers, and instrument operators at the University of Illinois during the spring of 1996 (Bruce et al., 1997). Eight of the classrooms were in Champaign-Urbana, one was in a nearby rural county, and one was in South Carolina. The project had two goals: (a) determine the impact of Internet access to high-powered scientific instrumentation for science instruction in the K-12 environment; and (b) test interactive control of the MRI instrument under diverse and adverse conditions (e.g., low bandwidth connections). In addition to remote control of the MRI instrument, Chickscope users also had an archive of images, a chat room, and a special chat area for input from MRI experts. Over the course of the twenty-one-day incubation period, each classroom was granted two twenty-minute observation sessions per week. At the end of the experiment, students and teachers reported that access to the MRI was useful—but required some effort to learn how to interpret the MRI images. Everyone was excited to have an additional modality for learning about chicken embryonic development. Finally, teachers reported that the use of Chickscope had a number of beneficial learning outcomes, including increased ability to compare and contrast data, and improved 3-D spatial reasoning (e.g., required to make sense of the planar sections captured by the MRI field of view as it "sliced" through the egg).

Bugscope (1999–present), a successor project to Chickscope, builds on the earlier project's success by reducing costs, such as instrument time and operator effort, while expanding participation (Potter et al., 2000). The focus of Bugscope is the use of an environmental scanning electron microscope (ESEM) to view insects. An ESEM is a special kind of electron microscope that allows specimens to be viewed in their natural state, i.e., without a conductive coating. Classrooms submit proposals for studies they wish to perform, and approved projects are given microscope time to analyze their samples. In contrast to Chickscope, classrooms receive only one hour of viewing time, but multiple classrooms can participate in a session. As of February, 2000, thirty classrooms involving 1,000 students all over the country had used Bugscope. This expansion was achieved while also reducing costs and demands on instrument time. Bugscope users have been enthusiastic in their support for the facility and there are currently over 100 proposals for new Bugscope projects.

DOE 2000 Collaboratories

The EMSL Collaboratory, described above, is one of several collaboratory test beds funded by the Department of Energy under the DOE 2000 initiative. Other projects include the Diesel Combustion Collaboratory (1997–2000) (Pancerella, Rahn, & Yang, 1999); the Materials Microcharacterization Collaboratory (MCC, 1997–2000) (Zaluzec, 1997, 1998); and the Remote Experiment Environment (REE, 1994–1997), a collaboratory to support observation and participation in magnetic fusion energy research involving the DIII-D tokamak experiment (Caspar et al., 1998; McHarg, Caspar, Davis, & Greenwood, 1999). A tokamak is a machine for creating a toroidally shaped magnetic confinement field used to contain the plasma, or very high-temperature gases, required to achieve a fusion reaction. Fusion is a kind of nuclear reaction in which two light atomic nuclei combine to form another element with the release of energy. The DIII-D tokamak experiment refers to a specific machine, the largest tokamak in the U.S., located at General Atomics in San Diego, California. REE merits extra attention because of the effort to document users' experiences in this collaboratory.

Because operation of the DIII-D tokamak is expensive, scientists must work together in the planning and operation of experimental runs. Within the REE, remote scientists can view data, interact with colleagues at the tokamak site and elsewhere, and observe—via video and audio—activity at the experiment control center. A test use of the REE involved a number of experiments controlled from Lawrence Livermore National Laboratory, in Livermore, California, using the DIII-D tokamak (Bly, Keith, & Henline, 1997). Over the course of the experimental runs, scientists at the two locations were able to coordinate their efforts to accomplish a successful experiment. Reactions to the collaboratory-style experiment varied. Remote participants were enthusiastic about their increased access to activity at the DIII-D tokamak, while local participants sometimes resented the intrusion of the "outsiders." Remote participants also felt excluded from key cues—such as warning lights and alarms—that were available to local participants.

Engineering Collaboratories

Many of the early collaboratory projects, summarized above, had to produce applications from scratch. Recently, software producers have identified a market for collaboration tools, such as application sharing and presence awareness, and have released a number of products—some of which have become immediately successful; for example, Mirabilis' ICQ (Mirabilis was acquired by America Online, or AOL), AOL's Instant Messenger, and Microsoft's NetMeeting. The cost of these tools, free for download in many cases, combined with their ease of use, has led to wide experimentation in business settings. The most pressing need for collaborative technology is often in engineering contexts in which engineers must confer over drawings and other visual data. While use of tools like NetMeeting, which allows data conferencing over images and output from applications, has grown dramatically, there are very few systematic studies of NetMeeting use. Two exceptions include recent analyses of NetMeeting use in aerospace engineering (Mark, Grudin, & Poltrock, 1999) and in software engineering (Finholt, Rocco, Bree, Jain, & Herbsleb, 1998).

Both studies focused on use with geographically distributed teams of engineers, where NetMeeting was used along with conventional telephone-based audio conferencing. In the aerospace case, principal findings included overdependence on a small number of technically savvy users; awkward organization of conversational turn taking; high overhead associated with initiating data conferences; restrictive models of use (e.g., only broadcasting briefing slides and not collaborating over joint work); multitasking by data conference participants; and problems of awareness (e.g., not knowing who was who, and not knowing who was present at remote locations). For the software engineers, principal findings included observation of difficulties reconciling different screen resolutions when sharing screens; awkward organization of turn taking—particularly when transferring control over a shared application; the importance of highly motivated NetMeeting "champions" in getting groups over initial learning curves; and the need to run NetMeeting in the background to allow spontaneous data conferencing sessions.

National Institutes of Health Collaboratories

The National Institutes of Health (NIH) have recently launched two significant collaboratory initiatives. The National Center for Research Resources (NCRR) made a series of collaboratory supplement awards to research resource awardees during the period 1998–2002. These supplements were designed to take existing, shared resources, such as instruments and supercomputer simulations, and enhance access to these resources via the addition of network-based collaboration tools. NCRR collaboratory awards included support for work on structural biology via the BioCoRE, or Biological Collaborative Research Environment (Bhandarkar et al., 1999); advanced microscopy via the CMDA, or Collaboratory for Microscopic Digital Anatomy (Hadida-Hassan et al., 1999; Young et al., 1996); and the "nanoManipulator," a mechanism for remotely steering the head of an atomic force microscope (AFM)—allowing direct manipulation of nanoscale materials (Sonnenwald, Bergquist, Maglaughlin, Kupstats-Soo, & Whitton, 2001; Jones, et al., 1999).

In a parallel effort, the National Cancer Institute is funding a virtual Center for AIDS Research (CFAR) spanning four midwestern universities: Northwestern, Minnesota, Wisconsin, and Michigan. The Great Lakes Regional Center for AIDS Research (GLRCFAR, 1998–2002) combines complementary expertise across the sites in a way that none of the sites, alone, could match. Further, the GLRCFAR is notable because it represents the first attempt to build a collaboratory employing only off-the-shelf components. While the GLRCFAR was initiated in 1998, collaboratory use has already become routinized (Teasley, 2001; Teasley & Jain, 2000). For example, CFAR participants log in twice a month for a collaboratory-based seminar series, using PlaceWare. PlaceWare is a Web-based tool that simulates a virtual lecture hall, based loosely on the LambdaMOO system developed at Xerox Palo Alto Research Center (Curtis, 1997). MOOs (multi-user dungeon [MUD] object-oriented) were originally conceived as a virtual space used for text-based adventure games (derived from Dungeons and Dragons, hence the dungeon reference) but since expanded to cover implementations like PlaceWare, and also other scientific MUDs and MOOS (e.g., Churchill & Bly, 1999; Glusman, 1995; Van Buren, Curtis, Nichols, & Brundage, 1994). In addition to PlaceWare lectures, GLRCFAR scientists regularly confer via NetMeeting, both to write clinical protocols and proposals, and also to view live output from remote instruments (e.g., electron microscope images of patient tissues). Finally, the GLRCFAR is the virtual home for documents and data relevant to joint work across the four-member institutions.

Space Physics and Aeronomy Research Collaboratory, 1998–2001

The Space Physics and Aeronomy Research Collaboratory (SPARC) is a successor project to UARC. As a follow-on effort, SPARC has been able to focus on expanding and improving UARC. From an implementation perspective, SPARC is designed as a "thin client" application. This means that users access all features of the collaboratory through a conventional Web browser, rather than through specialized software, as in both generations of UARC. For example, in UARC, the initial NeXTStep system was a barrier to use because the technology was exotic and the subsequent Java applet system was too unstable to win user confidence. With

SPARC, the interface is familiar—anyone who uses a Web browser can get started—and demands on local workstations involve only display of conventional Web elements, such as standard graphics formats (e.g., JPEG or GIF). A critical operational difference between UARC and SPARC is that SPARC facilities are available continuously, while UARC's were available only during campaign intervals. Finally, SPARC represents a reorientation of the collaboratory to post-hoc data exploration and analysis, termed an electronic workshop, as opposed to real-time data collection, which was the main emphasis in UARC. SPARC still supports real-time data gathering, but scientists found a greater need for retrospective, group investigation of data and visualizations from intervals of known value and interest.

The Collaboratory Challenge

In 1993, William Wulf wrote about the "collaboratory opportunity." He noted that the configuration of technologies, needs, and practices were then coming into alignment to make virtual labs possible. In some ways, developments since the early nineties have exceeded Wulf's projections. For example, the explosion in Internet use, driven by the World Wide Web, has had an impact on science just as it has on other spheres of human activity. Yet, by comparison with the breakout success of the Web (Schatz & Hardin, 1994), collaboratory use has been confined to a much smaller number of users. Even within the space of scientific applications on the Web, collaboratories have been dwarfed by digital libraries and knowledge bases, such as the Los Alamos preprint server (Ginsparg, 1994), GenBank (Ouellette, 1998), and the Protein Data Bank (PDB) (Berman, et al., 2000). For example, considering only the PDB, this resource receives an average of between 60,000 and 100,000 hits per day and currently stores 12,592 different structures (Research Collaboratory for Structural Bioinformatics, 2000). It is important to consider whether the relatively modest size and growth of collaboratories, compared to systems like the PDB, reflect a failure of the original collaboratory vision. Rather than failure, the experience with collaboratories, to date, indicates the enormous difficulties of supporting complex group work in virtual settings. Overcoming these difficulties represents the great challenge for the next stage of collaboratory development and use. Meeting this challenge involves both extracting lessons learned from previous collaboratory efforts and solving a number of critical problems at the tricky intersection of technology with individual and group behavior.

Meeting the Challenge: Lessons Learned

A number of tentative conclusions can be drawn from observation of collaboratories in use. It is helpful to start by examining the impact of collaboratory use on the organization and output of work, specifically the work of scientists—since most collaboratories have been targeted at scientific applications. Across the examples described earlier, it is clear that collaboratories have changed the number and type of participants in scientific work. For example, from the UARC and SPARC cases, relaxing of the constraints on travel to Greenland and other remote observatory sites has expanded the number of potential participants in research tasks, such as data collection. In addition, participants are more diverse, both in terms of experience and expertise. The earlier examples also suggest that collaboratories can increase the pace and efficiency of some scientific tasks. For instance, in the case of the Great Lakes Regional Center for AIDS Research, scientists reported that the use of collaboratory tools dramatically reduced the time required to produce a clinical protocol from weeks to hours. Similarly, among space physicists, monitoring conditions via SPARC has allowed them to use scarce instrument time more effectively by activating instruments only under optimal conditions, and not according to a predetermined schedule.

It is less clear that collaboratories have qualitatively changed scientific work, but there is some suggestive evidence. Specifically, use of collaboratory tools forces reflection on resources, such as data, which may have previously been unshared, that become shared. In one community of brain researchers, this realization produced a formal covenant, signed by scientists as a condition of use of the collaboratory, that specified how community data were to be used. This covenant paid particular attention to protecting the interests of younger researchers to prevent senior researchers from anticipating, or "scooping," their results. Along the same lines, space physicists using UARC and SPARC articulated "rules of the road" describing how public data were to be used, including rights of first publication and mechanisms for sharing credit, such as to instrument owners. In terms of scientific output, collaboratories seem to produce at least two kinds of changes. First, it becomes much easier to combine theoretical visualizations with visualizations of observational data. This helps bridge the gulf that exists in many fields between theoreticians and experimentalists. The capacity to blur the distinction between computational and physical simulations, for example, is a centerpiece of the National Science Foundation's George E. Brown Jr. Network for Earthquake Engineering Simulation (NEES). Within NEES, collaboratory tools will allow researchers to combine distributed physical simulation facilities, such as shaking tables and centrifuges, with computational simulations to produce complex real-time models of entire structures, or even entire built complexes such as cities. Second, collaboratories seem to produce a larger field of view. Among space physicists, for example, the ability to view hundreds of instruments worldwide encourages a more global orientation.

To summarize, experience to date with collaboratories suggests:

1. use does not need to be constant to provide value (general purpose tool vs. specialized instrument analogy);
2. systems that are easily integrated into existing work environments are more readily adopted (stand-alone application vs. browser accessible);
3. some domains of activity are more naturally inclined toward collaboration (data collection vs. contemplation and idea formation);
4. long-distance collaboration creates new expectations for participants, including altered roles (e.g., operators who must be more responsive, students who guide faculty, senior investigators who must accommodate less experienced participants).

Meeting the Challenge: Solving Critical Problems

Perhaps the most significant barrier to both the design and use of collaboratories is that most group practices and routines assume a shared space. For example, studies of distributed cognition show that people inventively exploit features of the social and physical world as resources for accomplishing tasks, and thereby reduce their reliance on mental symbolic manipulations (Hutchins, 1995; Pea, 1993). An illustration of this phenomenon is the use, by naval navigators, of the "three-scale nomogram," or a predrawn chart where the multiplication, addition, and division required to compute speed from distance traveled per unit time are represented as complementary logarithmic scales (Hutchins, 1990, p. 201). Changing the circumstances for collaboration, as in collaboratories, may undermine the effectiveness of the collaborative process by introducing new demands due to loss of a common physical setting. One critical new demand in the virtual context is that workers must be explicit about information that is normally tacit when co-located.

For example, scientists seated together at a workstation can unambiguously reference features in a data visualization simply by pointing. In a virtual setting, the same scientists must first ensure that they have each produced the same visualization and then ensure that a specific feature referenced by one is the same feature viewed by the other (e.g., through a specific coordinate system or through reference to unmistakable landmarks). In this scenario, the loss of tacit cues in the virtual setting may mean a greater risk of losing common ground (Clark & Brennan, 1991), where common ground is the shared cognitive understanding that allows collaborators to successfully coordinate their effort to accomplish joint work. At a minimum, then, collaboratory collaborations may require more effort, in terms of communicating the additional information required to achieve common ground. A challenge for collaboratory developers is producing tools and applications that compensate for the absence of a shared setting, such as through so-called WISIWYS (What I See Is What You See) interfaces. For instance, in both UARC and SPARC, research has focused on mechanisms for data display and data transport to ensure that what one scientist sees can be seen by other scientists (Hall, Mathur, Jahanian, Prakash, & Rasmussen, 1996; Lee, Prakash, Jaeger, & Wu, 1996).

Given the significance of co-location, and more importantly, the long development of human practices and behaviors contingent on co-location, it is not surprising that attempts to organize activity in virtual settings have proven difficult. This is the main point Olson and Olson (2001) make in arguing that "distance matters." Based on laboratory experiments and empirical observations in the field, Olson and Teasley (1996) conclude that for some tasks, co-location is still essential. Specifically, when tasks are tightly coupled; that is, dependent on frequent interaction and feedback among collaborators, contemporary communication technologies—such as e-mail, video and audio conferencing, and groupware (e.g., Lotus Notes)—do not provide an adequate substitute for co-location. In part, this failure is attributed to inadequate design and poor infrastructure. For example, accurate gaze detection is a key way that humans impute additional meaning in conversations. Yet, most video conferencing applications offer weak support for this kind of fine-grained detail.

Overcoming the difficulties inherent in virtual interaction, then, is partially a matter of elaborating designs and technologies that make virtual settings more like physical settings. Yet, even if successful designs and technologies are identified, there remain critical barriers to successful virtual collaboration. Olson, Finholt, & Teasley (2000) characterize these additional barriers in terms of collaboration readiness and collaboration technology readiness (see also Olson & Olson, 2001; Sonnenwald, 2000; Sonnenwald & Pierce, 1995). Collaboration readiness refers to the extent that potential collaborators are motivated to work with each other. In terms of collaboratory introduction, success seems to require a positive orientation toward collaboration, either as a result of incentives or as a result of normative practice. For example, in the Great Lakes Regional CFAR case, funding from the CFAR was directly tied to willingness to collaborate, as measured by acceptance and use of collaboration tools. This coercive approach worked to bring otherwise reluctant scientists to use PlaceWare, NetMeeting, and so forth, resulting in sufficient critical mass to motivate continued use of these tools. In the case of UARC, initial participants in the collaboratory were selected based on pre-existing collaborations. Additionally, space physics, as a field, has a history of highly collaborative research.

Collaboration technology readiness refers both to the presence of sufficient technology infrastructure, and to the availability of local technology expertise, both explicit and implicit. For example, Olson et al. (2000, p. 12) describe a progression from applications that require minimum training, such as e-mail, to technologies that require greater investment, such as data conferencing tools. Attempts to leapfrog steps in this progression can produce frustration and resistance. Similarly, attempts to implement sophisticated applications, such as desktop video conferencing, will have a higher probability of success when underlying infrastructure is adequate—in this case, access to high bandwidth network connections. In terms of collaboratory development, important lessons can be drawn from the difficulties described earlier with respect to the evolution of UARC from a NeXTStep-based system to a Java-based system. That is, apparent technological advantages, such as the purported universality of Java code, needed to be weighed against the equally important factors of familiarity and reliability.

Future Collaboratory Development

Laboratories emerged as physical settings designed to house rare and expensive instruments, as well as the scientists using the instruments. The forms of social organization that grew out of this arrangement depended heavily on co-location. Today, the evolution of information technology suggests a form of collaboration without proximity. Specifically, the goal of collaboratory development is the creation of "laboratories without walls." This concluding section explores the consequences for scientific practice and for scientific communities when collaboration becomes independent of physical location.

As noted earlier, in discussion of the peripherality hypothesis, a hope for collaboratory elaboration and use is that improved access to important but scarce instruments and data, combined with easy communication among researchers will diminish the barriers of status, time, and space that hamper scientific progress. However, it is important to note that powerful forces will continue to exist that will move collaboratories in the direction of exclusivity and selection that have characterized the historic organization of science. First, the availability of a means for contact between two scientists does not guarantee that contact will occur. For instance, science in the virtual realm may be just as likely as traditional science to be typified by strict enforcement of boundaries defining invisible colleges. In an examination of an early system that supported network-mediated communication among scientists, Hiltz and Turoff (1993) found that elite scientists using the system were more likely to receive messages than nonelite scientists, but that elite scientists were more likely to ignore the messages they received, particularly when those messages were sent by nonelite scientists. Second, economic considerations dictate that some scientific data and results will always be secured from widespread access. In chemistry, the bulk of practicing chemists are employed in private firms. These firms have proprietary interests in the products of their employees, specifically intellectual property such as patentable compounds and processes. As a result, chemists as a group use public computer networks less than other scientific disciplines that are dominated by academic practitioners (Walsh & Bayma, 1996). Third, scientific collaborations appear to require face-to-face contact, at least initially, suggesting that conferences and invited meetings will continue to function as critical filters on scientific participation. In a study of interpersonal communication networks among computer scientists, Carley and Wendt (1991) found that face-to-face contact was critical in starting a scientific relationship. While the computer scientists used e-mail to maintain existing collaborations, none of the identified collaborative relationships started via e-mail.

Collaboratory advocates envision the ultimate withering away of physical laboratories. However, it seems more realistic to suggest that collaboratory use will augment, but not replace, proximity as a tool for fostering scientific collaboration. Further, the benefits of collaboratory use may differ depending upon the status and experience of collaboratory users. Opportunities and gains seem most obvious for graduate and undergraduate students and nonelite scientists, since these are often the members of the scientific community least able to travel and meet other scientists. Collaboratories may represent a mechanism for accelerating students' immersion into important networks. For example, through UARC, space physics graduate students were able to participate in experiments during their first year, while in the past this did not occur until the third or fourth year. For elite scientists, collaboratories may offer more imposition than benefit. Specifically, if collaboratory sessions become opportunities for nonelite scientists and students to bombard these senior investigators with questions or demands, the senior scientists may respond by withdrawing their participation (and rely on traditional means for continuing collaborations). Finally, for nonelite scientists, collaboratories may provide broader access to some resources, such as instrument time, and may deliver access to elite scientists (although still at the discretion of the elite scientists). Most importantly, nonelites may use collaboratories to foster links with one another, which could be both valuable and damaging (viz., the balkanization outcome described by Van Alstyne and Brynjolfsson [1996]—in which the Internet may reinforce connections among those who are similar vs. creation of more diverse links). From the perspective of creating an intellectual community, the collaboratory may fill a critical niche, particularly for scientists at smaller institutions where they may have few local colleagues. However, if the concentration of nonelites is taken as an indication of the secondary status of a community, collaboratories may become the home for scientists who are marginalized in their larger, more traditional scientific communities. An instance of this may be the phenomenon of "e-journals," which are numerous on the Web (Odlyzko, 1999), yet continue to have a clearly inferior status relative to traditional journals.

In summary, the emergence of collaboratories represents an important convergence of computing technology with scientific practice. Collaboratories, by themselves, will not produce changes in science. However, at this early stage in their development, it may be possible to anticipate openings for change afforded by collaboratories and be prepared to exploit these openings. This means that those in the scientific community, and beyond, should actively explore how collaboratories can be used to expand participation in science, rather than accepting collaboratories and other new technologies as extensions of the status quo.

Bibliography

Alberti, B., Anklesaria, F., Lindner, P., McCahill, M., & Torrey, D. (1992). The Internet gopher protocol: A distributed document and search retrieval protocol [Machine-readable data file]. Microcomputer and Workstation Networks Center (Producer). University of Minnesota Gopher Server (Distributor).

Allen, T. J. (1977). *Managing the flow of technology*. Cambridge, MA: MIT Press.

Anklesaria, F., McCahill, M., Lindner, P., Johnson, D., Torrey, D., & Albert, B. (1993). The Internet Gopher Protocol (a distributed document search and retrieval protocol). RFC 1436.

Atkins, D. E. (1993, December). *Overview of the Upper Atmospheric Research Collaboratory*. Paper presented at the Upper Atmospheric Research Collaboratory Workshop, Menlo Park, CA.

Bair, R. A. (1999). Collaboratories: Building electronic scientific communities. In T. H. Dunning (Chair), *Impact of advances in computing and communications technologies on chemical science and technology: Report of a workshop* (pp. 125–140). Washington, DC: National Academy Press.

Bateson, G. (1972). *Steps to an ecology of mind*. New York: Ballantine.

Berman, H. M., Westbrook, J., Feng, Z., Gilliland, G., Bhat, T. N., Weissig, H., Shindyalov, I. N., & Bourne, P. E. (2000). The protein data bank. *Nucleic Acids Research, 28,* 235–242.

Bhandarkar, M., Budescu, G., Humphrey, W. F., Izaguirre, J. A., Izrailev, S., Kale, L. V., Losztin, D., Molnar, F., Phillips, J. C., & Schulten, K. (1999). BioCoRE: A collaboratory for structural biology. In A. G. Bruzzone, A. Uchrmacher, & E. H. Page (Eds.), *Proceedings of the SCS International Conference on Web-Based Modeling and Simulation* (pp. 242–251). San Francisco, CA: Society for Computer Simulation International.

Bishop, A. P. (1994). The role of computer networks in aerospace engineering. *Library Trends, 42,* 694–729.

Bly, S., Keith, K. M., & Henline, P. A. (1997). *The work of scientists and the building of collaboratories.* General Atomics Report #GA-A22619.

Bruce, B. C., Carragher, B. O., Damon, B. M., Dawson, M. J., Eurell, J. A., Gregory, C. D., Lauterbur, P. C., Marjanovic, M. M., Mason-Fossum, B., Morris, H. D., Potter, C. S., & Thakkar, U. (1997). Chickscope: An interactive MRI classroom curriculum innovation for K-12. *Computers and Education Journal, 29* (2), 73–87.

Bruce, H. (1994). Internet services and academic work: An Australian perspective. *Internet Research, 4,* 24–34.

Bush, V. (1945). As we may think. *The Atlantic Monthly, 176,* 101–108.

Carley, K., & Wendt, K. (1991). Electronic mail and scientific communication: A study of the SOAR extended research group. *Knowledge: Creation, Diffusion, Utilization, 12,* 406–440.

Carragher, B., & Potter, C. S. (1999). The world wide laboratory: Remote and automated access to imaging instrumentation. In T. H. Dunning (Chair), *Impact of advances in computing and communications technologies on chemical science and technology: Report of a workshop* (pp. 141–153). Washington, DC: National Academy Press.

Caspar, T. A., Meyer, W. M., Moller, J. M., Henline, P., Keith, K., McHarg, B., Davis, S., & Greenwood, D. (1998). Collaboratory operations in magnetic fusion research. *ACM Interactions, 5* (3), 56–64.

Churchill, E. F., & Bly, S. (1999). It's all in the words: Supporting work activities with lightweight tools. In S. Hayne (Ed.), *Proceedings of the International ACM SIGGROUP Conference on Supporting Group Work, Group '99* (pp. 40–49). New York: ACM Press.

Clark, H. H., & Brennan, S. E. (1991). Grounding in communication. In L. B. Resnick, J. M. Levine, & S. D. Teasley (Eds.), *Perspectives on socially-shared cognition* (pp. 127–149). Washington, DC: American Psychological Association.

Cohen, J. (1996). Computer mediated communication and publication productivity among faculty. *Internet Research, 6* (2-3), 41–63.

Constant, D., Sproull, L. S., & Kiesler, S. B. (1996). The kindness of strangers: The usefulness of electronic weak ties for technical advice. *Organizational Science, 7,* 199–135.

Crane, D. (1972). *Invisible colleges*. Chicago: University of Chicago Press.

Curtis, P. (1997). Mudding: Social phenomena in text-based virtual realities. In S. Kiesler (Ed.), *Culture of the Internet*, (pp. 121–142). Mahwah, NJ: Lawrence Erlbaum Associates.

Edelson, D. C., Pea, R. D., & Gomez, L. M. (1996). The collaboratory notebook. *Communications of the ACM, 39* (4), 32–33.

Endersby, J. W. (1996). Collaborative research in the social sciences: Multiple authorship and publication credit. *Social Science Quarterly, 77,* 375–392.

Engelbart, D. C. (1963). A conceptual framework for the augmentation of man's intellect. In P. D. Howerton & D. C. Weeks (Eds.) *Vistas in information handling, 1* (pp. 1–29). Washington, DC: Spartan Books.

Finholt, T. A., Lewis, S. A., & Mott, W. H. (1995). Distance learning in the Upper Atmospheric Research Collaboratory. Unpublished manuscript. Collaboratory for Research on Electronic Work, The University of Michigan, Ann Arbor, MI.

Finholt, T. A., & Olson, G. M. (1997). From laboratories to collaboratories: A new organizational form for scientific collaboration. *Psychological Science, 8,* 28–36.

Finholt, T. A., Rocco, E., Bree, D., Jain, N., & Herbsleb, J. (1998). NotMeeting: A field trial of NetMeeting in a geographically distributed organization. *SIGGROUP Bulletin, 21* (1), 66–69.

Finholt, T. A., Sproull, L., & Kiesler, S. (in press). Outsiders on the inside: Sharing know-how across space and time. In P. Hinds & S. Kiesler (Eds.), *Distributed work*. Cambridge, MA: MIT Press.

Fisher, B. S., Cobane, C. T., Vander Ven, T. M., & Cullen, F. T. (1998). How many authors does it take to publish an article? Trends and patterns in political science. *PS-Political Science and Politics, 31,* 847–856.

Fishman, B. (2000). How activity fosters CMS tool use in classrooms: Reinventing innovations in local contexts. *Journal of Interactive Learning, 11* (1), 3–27.

Fox, E. A., Akscyn, R. M., Furuta, R. K., & Leggett, J. J. (Eds.). (1995). Digital libraries [Special issue]. *Communications of the ACM, 38* (4).

Fox, M. F. (1983). Publication productivity among scientists. *Social Studies of Science, 13,* 285–305.

Ginsparg, P. (1994). First steps toward electronic research communication. *Computers in Physics, 8,* 390–396.

Glusman, G. (1995). *BioMOO's purpose*. Retrieved February 1, 2001, from the World Wide Web: http://bioinformatics.weizmann.ac.il:70/0/biomoo/purpose

Gomez, L., Fishman, B., & Pea, R. (1998). The CoVis project: Building a large-scale science education testbed. *Interactive Learning Environments, 6* (1–2), 59–92.

Hadida-Hassan, M., Young, S. J., Peltier, S. T., Wong, M., Lamont, S., & Ellisman, M. H. (1999). Web-based telemicroscopy. *Journal of Structural Biology, 125,* 235–245.

Hagstrom, W. O. (1965). *Scientific community*. New York: Basic Books.

Hall, R. W., Mathur, A. G., Jahanian, F., Prakash, A., & Rasmussen, C. (1996). Corona: A communication service for scalable, reliable group collaboration systems. In M. S. Ackerman (Ed.), *Proceedings of the ACM 1996 Conference on Computer-Supported Cooperative Work* (pp. 140–149). New York: ACM Press.

Hesse, B. W., Sproull, L. S., Keisler, S. B., & Walsh, J. P. (1993). Returns to science: Computer networks in oceanography. *Communications of the ACM, 36* (8), 90–101.

Hiltz, S. R, & Turoff, M. (1993). *The network nation: Human communication via computer* (Rev. ed.). Cambridge, MA: MIT Press.

Hutchins, E. (1990). The technology of team navigation. In J. Galegher, R. E. Kraut, & C. Egido (Eds.), *Intellectual teamwork: Social and technological foundations of cooperative work* (pp. 191–220). Hillsdale, NJ: Lawrence Erlbaum Associates.

Hutchins, E. (1995). *Cognition in the wild.* Cambridge, MA: MIT Press.

Jones, M. G., Superfine, R., & Taylor, R. (1999). Virtual viruses. *Science Teacher, 66* (7), 48–50.

Katz, J. S. (1994). Geographical proximity and scientific collaboration. *Scientometrics, 31* (1), 31–43.

Kouzes, R. T., Myers, J. D., & Wulf, W. A. (1996). Collaboratories: Doing science on the Internet. *IEEE Computer, 29* (8), 40–46.

Kraut, R. E., & Attewell, P. (1997). Media use in a global corporation: Electronic mail and organizational knowledge. In S. B. Kiesler (Ed.), *Culture of the Internet* (pp. 323–342). Mahwah, NJ: Lawrence Erlbaum Associates.

Kraut, R. E., Egido, C., & Galegher, J. (1990). Patterns of contact and communication in scientific research collaboration. In R. Kraut, C. Egido, & J. Galegher (Eds.), *Intellectual teamwork: Social and technological foundations of cooperative work*, (pp. 149–171). Hillsdale, NJ: Lawrence Erlbaum Associates.

Kraut, R. E., Galegher, J., & Egido, C. (1988). Relationships and tasks in scientific collaboration. *Human-Computer Interaction, 3,* 31–58.

Lave, J., & Wenger, E. (1991). *Situated learning: Legitimate peripheral participation.* New York: Cambridge University Press.

Lederberg, J., & Uncapher, K. (1989). *Towards a national collaboratory: Report of an invitational workshop at the Rockefeller University, March 17–18.* Washington, DC: National Science Foundation, Directorate for Computer and Information Science Engineering.

Lee, J. H., Prakash, A., Jaeger, T., & Wu, G. (1996). Supporting multi-user, multi-applet workspaces in CBE. In M. S. Ackerman (Ed.), *Proceedings of the ACM 1996 Conference on Computer Supported Cooperative Work* (pp. 344–353). New York: ACM Press.

Lewicki, G., Cohen, D., Losleben, P., & Trotter, D. (1984). MOSIS: Present and future. In P. Penfield (Ed.), *Advanced research in VSLI* (pp. 124–128). Dedham, MA: Artech House, Inc.

Lipetz, B. A. (1999). Aspects of JASIS authorship through five decades. *Journal of the American Socieity for Information Science, 50,* 994–1003.

Lynch, C., & Preston, C. (1990). Internet access to information resources. *Annual Review of Information Science and Technology, 25,* 263–312.

Mark, G., Grudin, J., & Poltrock, S. E. (1999). Meeting at the desktop: An empirical study of virtually collocated teams. In S. Bødker, M. Kyng, & K. Schmidt (Eds.), *Proceedings of the Sixth European Conference on Computer Supported Cooperative Work* (pp. 159–178). Dordrecht, NL: Kluwer Academic.

McDaniel, S. E., Olson, G. M., & Magee, J. (1996). Identifying and analyzing multiple threads in computer-mediated and face-to-face communication. In M. S. Ackerman (Ed.), *Proceedings of the ACM 1996 Conference on Computer Supported Cooperative Work* (pp. 39–47). New York: ACM Press.

McDaniel, S. E., Olson, G. M., & Olson, J. S. (1994). Methods in search of methodology: Combining HCI and object orientation. In B. Adelson, S. T. Dumais, & J. R. Olson (Eds.), *Proceedings of CHI '94 Conference on Human Factors and Computing Systems* (pp. 145–151). New York: ACM Press.

McHarg, B. B., Casper, T. A., Davis, S., & Greenwood, D. (1999). Tools for remote collaboration on the DIII-D national fusion facility. *Fusion Engineering and Design, 43,* 343–355.

Menzel, H. (1962). Planned and unplanned scientific communication. In B. Barber & W. Hirsch (Eds.), *The sociology of science* (pp. 417–441). Glencoe, IL: Free Press.

Myers, J. D., Chonacky, N., Dunning, T., & Leber, E. (1997). Collaboratories: Bringing national laboratories into the undergraduate classroom and laboratory. *Council on Undergraduate Research Quarterly, 17,* 116–120.

National Research Council (1993). *National collaboratories: Applying information technology for scientific research.* Washington, DC: National Academy Press.

Newell, A., & Sproull, R. F. (1982). Computer networks: Prospects for scientists. *Science, 215,* 843–852.

Odlyzko, A. (1999). The economics of electronic journals. In R. Ekman & R. Quandt (Eds.), *Technology and scholarly communication* (pp. 380–393). Berkeley, CA: University of California Press.

Olson, G. M., Atkins, D. E., Clauer, R., Finholt, T. A., Jahanian, F., Killeen, T. L., Prakash, A., & Weymouth, T. (1998). The Upper Atmospheric Research Collaboratory (UARC). *ACM Interactions, 5* (4), 48–55.

Olson, G. M., Finholt, T. A., & Teasley, S. D. (2000). Behavioral aspects of collaboratories. In S. H. Koslow & M. F. Huerta (Eds.), *Electronic collaboration in science* (pp. 1–14). Mahwah, NJ: Lawrence Erlbaum Associates.

Olson, G. M., & Olson, J. S. (2001). Distance matters. *Human Computer Interaction, 15,* 139–179.

Olson, J. S., & Teasley, S. D. (1996). Groupware in the wild: Lessons learned from a year of virtual collocation. In M. S. Ackerman (Ed.), *Proceedings of the ACM 1996 Conference on Computer Supported Cooperative Work* (pp. 419–427). New York: ACM Press.

Orlikowski, W. J., & Yates, J. (1994). Genre repertoire: The structuring of communicative practices in organizations. *Administrative Science Quarterly, 39,* 541–574.

Ouellette, B. F. (1998). The GenBank sequence database. *Methods of Biochemistry Analysis, 39,* 16–45.

Pancerella, C. M., Rahn, L. A., & Yang, C. L. (1999, November). *The Diesel Combustion Collaboratory: Combustion researchers collaborating over the Internet.* Paper presented at SC99, ACM/IEEE Conference on High Performance Networking and Computing. Portland, OR.

Pea, R. D. (1993). Practices of distributed intelligence and designs for education. In G. Salomon (Ed.), *Distributed cognitions: Psychological and educational considerations* (pp. 47–87). Cambridge: Cambridge University Press.

Pelz, D. C., & Andrews, F. M. (1966). *Scientists in organizations.* New York: John Wiley.

Potter, C. S., Carragher, B. O., Carroll, L., Conway, C., Grosser, B., Hanlon, J., Kisseberth, N., Robinson, S., Stone, D., Thakkar, U., & Weber, D. (2000). Bugscope: A sustainable microscope project for K-12. In B. Fishman & S. O'Connor-Divelbiss (Eds.) *Fourth International Conference on the Learning Sciences* (pp. 376–383). Mahwah, NJ: Lawrence Erlbaum Associates.

Price, D. J. de S. (1963). *Little science, big science.* New York: Columbia University Press.

Price, D. J. de S. (1986). *Little science, big science...and beyond.* New York: Columbia University Press.

Price, D. J. de S., & Beaver, D. D. (1966). Collaboration in an invisible college. *American Psychologist, 21,* 1011–1018.

Raefeli, M. S., Sudweeks, F., Konstan, J., & Mabry, E. (1998). ProjectH overview: A collaborative quantitative study of computer-mediated communication. In F. Sudweeks, M. McLaughlin, & M. S. Rafaeli (Eds.), *Network and netplay: Virtual groups on the Internet* (pp. 265–282). Cambridge, MA: MIT Press.

Research Collaboratory for Structural Bioinformatics (2000). *Protein Data Bank Annual Report, 1999–2000.* New Brunswick, NJ: Rutgers University.

Schatz, B. (1991–1992). Building an electronic community system. *Journal of Mangement Information Systems, 8* (3), 87–101.

Schatz, B. R., & Hardin, J. B. (1994). NCSA Mosaic and the World Wide Web: Global hypermedia protocols for the Internet. *Science, 265,* 895–901.

Schur, A., Keating, K. A., Payne, D. A., Valdez, T., Yates, K. R., & Myers, J. D. (1998). Collaborative suites for experiment-oriented scientific research. *ACM Interactions, 3* (5), 40–47.

Sonnenwald, D. H. (1995). Contested collaboration: A descriptive model of intergroup communication in information system design. *Information Processing & Management, 31,* 859–877.

Sonnenwald, D. H., Bergquist, R., Maglaughlin, K. A., Kupstats-Soo, E., & Whitton, M. (2001). Designing to support collaborative scientific research across distances: The nanoManipulator example. In E. Churchill, D.

Snowdon, & A. Munro (Eds.), *Collaborative Virtual Environments* (pp. 202–224). London: Springer Verlag.

Sonnenwald, D. H., & Pierce, L. (2000). Information behavior in dynamic group work contexts: Interwoven situational awareness, dense social networks and contested collaboration in command and control. *Information Processing & Management, 36,* 461–479.

Sproull, L. S., & Kiesler, S. B. (1991). *Connections: New ways of working in the networked organization.* Cambridge, MA: MIT Press.

Star, S. L., & Ruhleder, K. (1994). Steps toward an ecology of infrastructure: Complex problems in design and access for large-scale collaborative systems. In R. K. Furuta & C. Neuwirth (Eds.), *Proceedings of the Conference on Computer Supported Cooperative Work* (pp. 253–264). New York: ACM Press.

Teasley, S. D. (2001, February). Yours, mine and ours: Sharing data in geographically distributed collaborations. In B. Jasny & P. J. Hines (Chairs), *Staying afloat in a sea of data.* Symposium conducted at the 167th National Meeting of the American Association for the Advancement of Science, San Francisco, CA.

Teasely, S. D., & Jain, N. (2000). Scientists together working apart: The CFAR collaboratory. Unpublished manuscript. Collaboratory for Research on Electronic Work, The University of Michigan, Ann Arbor, MI.

Traweek, S. (1992). *Beamtimes and lifetimes: The world of high energy physics.* Cambridge, MA: Harvard University Press.

Van Alstyne, M., & Brynjolfsson, E. (1996). Could the Internet balkanize science? *Science, 274,* 1479–1480.

Van Buren, D., Curtis, P., Nichols, D. A., & Brundage, M. (1994, September). *The AstroVR collaboratory: An on-line multi-user environment for research in astrophysics.* Paper presented at the Fourth Annual Conference on Astronomical Data Analysis Software and Systems, Baltimore, MD.

Walsh, J. P., & Bayma, T. (1996). Computer networks and scientific work. *Social Studies of Science, 26,* 661–703.

Walsh, J. P., & Maloney, N. (in press). Scientific productivity, new communication technology and inequality: Does CMC narrow the gap? In P. Hinds & S. Kiesler (Eds.), *Distributed work.* Cambridge, MA: MIT Press.

Walsh, J. P., & Roselle, A. (1999). Computer networks and the virtual college. *Encyclopedia of Library and Information Science, 65,* 22–42.

Weinberg, A. (1961). Impact of large-scale science on the United States. *Science, 134,* 161–164.

Wulf, W. A. (1989). The national collaboratory—a white paper. In J. Lederberg & K. Uncaphar, *Towards a National Collaboratory: Report of an invitational workshop at the Rockefeller University, March 17–18* (Appendix A). Washington, DC: National Science Foundation, Directorate for Computer and Information Science Engineering.

Wulf, W. A. (1993). The collaboratory opportunity. *Science, 261,* 854–855.

Young, S. J., Fan, G. G. Y., Hessler, D., Lamont, S., Elvins, T. T., Hadida-Hassan, M., Hanyzewski, G. A., Durking, J. W., Hubbard, P., Kindlmann, G., Wong, E.,

Greenberg, D., Karin, S., & Ellisman, M. H. (1996). Implementing a collaboratory for microscopic digital anatomy. *International Journal of Supercomputer Applications and High Performance Computing, 10,* 170–181.

Zaluzec, N. (1997, October). *Interactive collaboratories for microscopy and microanalysis.* Paper presented at the Multinational Conference on Electron Microscopy-97, Portoroz, Slovenia.

Zaluzec, N. (1998). The telepresence microscopy collaboratory. *Teleconference, 17* (9), 17–20.

Zare, R. N. (1997). Knowledge and distributed intelligence. *Science, 275,* 1047.

Zhang, H. Q. (1997). More authors, more institutions, and more funding sources: Hot papers in biology from 1991 to 1993. *Journal of the American Society for Information Science, 48,* 662–666.

CHAPTER 3

Computer-Mediated Communication on the Internet

Susan C. Herring
Indiana University

Introduction

In his 1986 *ARIST* review of computer-mediated communication (CMC) systems, Steinfield (1986) identified a number of gaps in the literature on CMC that he hoped would be filled by future research. Noting that most early CMC work focused on experimental or case studies in organizational contexts (e.g., Rice, 1980), Steinfield called for (1) studies that paid closer attention to the effects of system design features on CMC, (2) empirical research in real-world, rather than laboratory settings, (3) research on CMC use in nontraditional settings, such as on electronic bulletin boards, (4) longitudinal research to capture long-term impacts of CMC, and (5) studies addressing the privacy implications of using CMC as research data.

In the intervening years, researchers have made progress toward filling these gaps, as well as in analyzing new CMC-related phenomena, as part of an explosion in CMC research triggered by the popular expansion of the Internet in the late 1980s and 1990s. (The Internet is not mentioned in Steinfield's review.) The Internet brought millions of people online, and what they did mostly was communicate, in the process generating large amounts of authentic usage data in a variety of modes (e.g., e-mail, listservs, newsgroups, chat, MUDs [Multi-User

Dungeons/Dimensions]) and social contexts (professional, political, recreational, commercial, etc.). Archives of Internet—and earlier, ARPANET (Advanced Research Projects Agency Network)—messages posted to discussion groups are available for the past twenty-five years, making longitudinal studies of Internet use possible. And as more and more researchers have succumbed to the lure of easily accessible Internet data, CMC research ethics has become a topic of increasingly frequent debate.

In addition to providing a test bed for earlier theories and observations about CMC, the Internet increasingly *defines* CMC by providing the context within which many, if not most, CMC applications operate. Over the past fifteen years, the Internet has incorporated into its web of interconnected telecommunications local area networks (LANs) and intranets, as well as wide area networks (WANs) that previously operated semi-independently, such as ARPANET, Bitnet and Usenet. This incorporation came about not through imperialistic spread so much as through groups, organizations, and institutions voluntarily linking to the Internet in order to be able to access its vast information and communication resources. Thus any discussion of CMC today must necessarily reference the Internet.

Albeit a recent phenomenon, CMC on the Internet has already generated a vast, interdisciplinary research literature, a complete coverage of which is beyond the scope of a single review chapter. For other recent reviews of CMC, see Wellman et al. (1996), who survey research on what they call "Computer Supported Social Networks" (CSSNs), and Rice & Gattiker (2000), who take as their object "Computer-Mediated Communication and Information Systems" (CISs). Substantial review sections are also included in Walther (1996), of experimental and organizational CMC research, and Soukup (2000), of early research, empirical Internet research, and critical CMC scholarship.

This review, in keeping with the desiderata outlined by Steinfield (1986), focuses on empirical research on naturally occurring online communication in noninstitutional and nonorganizational contexts from the late 1980s to the present. Such communication arguably best reflects the organic potential of the Internet itself, as a large, geographically dispersed, interconnected, and relatively unstructured medium, to shape human interaction. The general phenomena of interest within this perspective includes the effects of the Internet on language and communication, on interpersonal relations, and on group dynamics, as well as the emergence of social structures and norms, and macro-societal impacts of Internet communication. The research methods commonly employed to address these phenomena are drawn mostly from language-related disciplines, such as communication, linguistics, and rhetoric, and from the social sciences.

Much of the available research on Internet communication concerns text-based CMC, in which a sender types a message that is transmitted via networked computers and read as text on the recipient's (or recipients') computer screen(s). CMC of this type, which was all that was generally available until the mid-1990s, is interactive and reciprocal, in that recipients can reply in the same manner in which the message was sent. Also reviewed are interactive uses of multimodal CMC—text combined with two-dimensional or three-dimensional graphics, video and/or audio—including communication via the World Wide Web, which combines interaction with features of broadcast media. Nonreciprocally interactive mass media and commercial uses of the Web, however, are excluded from this review.

The body of the chapter is organized into three principal sections. The first section, following immediately below, introduces a classification of CMC types in terms of mode, and reviews the history and characteristics of nine CMC modes on the Internet: e-mail, listservs, Usenet, split-screen talk protocols, chat, MUDs, the World Wide Web, audio- and video-based CMC, and graphical virtual reality (VR) environments. The second section evaluates what Internet CMC research can tell us in relation to claims about CMC—most focusing on its technologically imposed limitations—made on the basis of pre-Internet research. The third section identifies new communicative phenomena enabled by the Internet and surveys research into the opportunities and challenges they raise. The chapter concludes by identifying directions for future CMC research.

Modes of CMC

Perhaps the most important cumulative finding of Internet research over the past fifteen years is that computer-mediated communication varies according to the technologies on which it is based, and according to its contexts of use. Thus synchronous CMC (e.g., real-time chat) differs systematically from asynchronous CMC (e.g., e-mail, in which sender and receiver need not be logged on at the same time) in message length, complexity, formality, and interactivity—due, in part, to temporal constraints on message production and processing (Condon & Čech, forthcoming; Ko, 1996). Other system features that influence communication include the granularity of message transmission (message-by-message, as opposed to character-by-character; Cherny, 1999), buffer size, the availability of multiple channels of communication, and default settings regarding the quoting of previous messages (Severinson-Eklundh & Macdonald, 1994).

At the same time, contextual factors associated with the situation of use can cause system-based generalizations to break down. Differences in user demographics, including age, gender, race, and level of education, can result in different communication styles and content, even among users of the same CMC system (Burkhalter, 1999; Herring, in press a). Such differences may cut across technological boundaries, as, for example, gender differences in verbal aggression, which are characteristic of both synchronous and asynchronous CMC (Herring, in press b). Additionally, purpose and topic of communication cause recreational chat, for instance, to differ in coherence and tone from pedagogical chat (Herring & Nix, 1997). Other situational variables found to influence online communication include participant structure (e.g., the number of participants, and whether the communication is public or private; Baym, 1995), social network density (Paolillo, 2001; Wellman, 1997), and language choice (Paolillo, 1996).

These findings suggest that CMC types could be identified for the purposes of study and comparison on the basis of individual technical and contextual variables, e.g., synchronous vs. asynchronous, recreational vs. pedagogical, male vs. female, or as a combination of such variables. In fact, most observation-based Internet research of the sort reviewed in this chapter (in contrast to experimental CMC research) does not classify its object of study purely by abstracting out its variable dimensions, but rather (or additionally) situates it within a popularly recognizable (named) *mode*. A mode is a genre of CMC that combines messaging protocols and the social and cultural practices that have evolved around their use (Herring, in press a; Murray, 1988), although the "cultures of use" of newer CMC technologies may be emergent or latent. Thus social MUDs are a mode distinct from Internet Relay Chat, in that each has its own history and norms (Cherny, 1999) even though both are forms of synchronous CMC used predominantly by young people for recreational purposes. CMC mode thus provides a cultural context within which observations about online communication can be interpreted. The following subsections review the major CMC modes currently in use on the Internet—their historical origins, their system design features, their typical contexts of use, and a representative sampling of issues that have been researched in relation to each. Examples of communication are provided for newer or less common modes with which some readers may be unfamiliar.

The emergence of CMC modes is closely tied to the history of the Internet itself. For the purposes of this review, the Internet is defined broadly to include its predecessor the ARPANET (see historical overview in Lynch and Preston, 1990), the Usenet (which developed alongside the ARPANET/Internet but was eventually subsumed by it; see Hauben and Hauben, 1997), and the World Wide Web (see Berners-Lee, 1996, for its genesis and subsequent development). Internet history has been chronicled in numerous books, articles, and Web sites that focus variously on the development of computer networking technology and infrastructure (Leiner et al., 1997; Salus 1995), its human inventors and the contexts in which they worked (Hafner & Lyon, 1996), and the genesis of specific modes of CMC such as bulletin board systems (Rheingold, 1993) and MUDs (Reid, 1994). The key events in this history can be situated along a time line as in Figure 3.1. For a more detailed timeline of the development of the Internet, see Dodge & Kitchin (2000).

In what follows, each mode is presented in the approximate chronological order in which the technology on which it is based first appeared.

E-Mail

In the 1960s, a computer professional using a time-sharing system could leave text messages on the system for another user to read when he later logged on (Licklider, Taylor, & Herbert, 1968). The first electronic mail or "e-mail" message to be transmitted between two networked computers was sent in 1972, by engineer Ray Tomlinson as a test of the SNDMSG protocol he was developing (Hafner & Lyon, 1996,

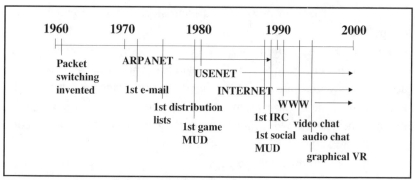

Figure 3.1 The co-evolution of the Internet and CMC

p. 191). By 1973, e-mail had become the most popular use of the U.S. defense-funded ARPANET, to the surprise of its inventors, who had intended the network primarily as a vehicle for the transmission of data and computer programs (Rheingold, 1993; but see Licklider et al., 1968, who foresaw the potential of computer networks to enhance human-to-human communication). Person-to-person e-mail remains one of the most popular uses of CMC on the Internet today (Baron, 2000; Hoffman, Kalsbeek, & Novak, 1996).

E-mail is text-based, asynchronous, and involves message-by-message transmission. A distinctive feature of the e-mail message that dates back to the early 1970s is its header, containing "to," "from," and "subject" lines as well as routing information (Hafner & Lyon, 1996). The presence of the header causes an e-mail message to resemble a written memorandum structurally, although a comparative study conducted by Cho (forthcoming) found that private e-mail messages in an academic workplace setting were stylistically different from memoranda: more informal and nonstandard in their use of spelling and punctuation. E-mail messages also share structural features with letters: they often include epistolary formulae such as greetings (e.g., "Hi"), closings (e.g., "Best,") and signatures (Cho, forthcoming; Herring, 1996b), and, like a letter, tend to display a three-part structure (opening–message body–closing; Condon & Čech, forthcoming; Herring, 1996b). These features can reveal personal information about the sender and receiver, making e-mail less anonymous than other (i.e., synchronous) textual modes of CMC (Danet, 1998; Donath, 1999).

The asynchronous nature of e-mail allows users to take time to compose and edit their messages, and the casual informality of some users' e-mails is counterbalanced by the existence of e-mail messages that are carefully edited, formal, and linguistically complex (Herring, 1998a). Asynchronicity also means that users can communicate at their temporal convenience, without the requirement that message recipients be logged on. These features, together with a text-only interface that allows users to manage their self-presentation to a greater extent than face-to-face or telephone communication, account in part for e-mail's enduring and widespread popularity for both personal and professional communication (Sproull & Kiesler, 1991; Walther, 1996).

Relatively few studies have been carried out on private e-mail exchanges, due, perhaps, to the ethical issues involved in accessing and studying them. Some exceptions are Cho (forthcoming) on the informality of e-mail messages in comparison to memoranda in a workplace setting; Rowe (forthcoming) on the evolution of a private e-mail style between adult sisters, and Severinson-Eklundh (forthcoming; Severinson-Eklundh & Macdonald, 1994) on the practice of "quoting" parts of messages in e-mail responses. Anecdotal evidence suggests that women send longer and more frequent private e-mails than men, and that geographically dispersed family members who use e-mail communicate more frequently and more openly with one another than they did before e-mail (Cohen, 2001).

Listserv Discussion Lists

Discussion lists—also called distribution lists and mailing lists—distribute e-mail messages posted to a listserver (or *listserv*) to a list of subscribers. One of the earliest discussion lists, MsgGroup, was started in 1975 by ARPA personnel to share information about the development of electronic messaging protocols, and continued to function with the same moderator, Einar Stefferud, until 1986 (Hafner & Lyon, 1996). Another early discussion list that started around the same time was sf [science fiction]-lovers (Hafner & Lyon, 1996). The late 1980s and early 1990s saw an explosion of listserv discussion lists devoted to more-or-less intellectual topics, reflecting the interests of the primary users of the Internet at that time, people affiliated with universities. In the mid-1990s the range of topics widened, although listserv lists still tend to attract an academic and professional readership.

Discussion lists, like e-mail, are textual and asynchronous, the primary difference being that in the former, messages are distributed via a listserver to multiple participants as the default. A listserver also maintains a list of subscribers, and can archive messages and other textual resources and make them accessible to subscribers on demand (Millen, 2000). Moderated discussion lists, in which messages are filtered through a person (or persons) who approves them for distribution, offer the possibility for control over message tone and content (Korenman & Wyatt, 1996). For subscribers, electing to receive a day's worth of messages in a single-message "digest" is a means for managing the high message volume generated on some lists (Sproull & Kiesler, 1991).

The culture of discussion lists on the Internet has been influenced by their professional and academic origins. Research has found that discussions tend to focus on information exchange (queries and responses), although debate of issues, including contentious debate, is not uncommon (Herring, 1996b; Hert, 1997; Mabrey, 1997). The tendency for group asynchronous discussions on the Internet to degenerate into polarized disagreement has been attributed variously to the depersonalizing effects of the text-only medium (Kiesler, Siegel, & McGuire, 1984; Kim & Raja, 1990), to male-gendered communicative practices (Herring, 1994), and to reduced social accountability resulting from the fact that, in contrast to private e-mail, participants in Internet discussions are often not previously acquainted and may never meet face to face (Friedman, Kahn, & Howe, 2000). Despite this tendency toward contentiousness, discussion groups are sometimes characterized as "virtual communities," especially when their members have a pre-existing basis for interacting, such as geographical proximity (e.g., residence in the San Francisco Bay Area, in the case of The WELL; Rheingold, 1993) or professional affinity (women in computer science, in the case of Systers-L; Camp, 1996). This latter perspective emphasizes the positive nonmaterial resources—such as support, advice, and information—that are shared in online groups (Preece, 2000; Wellman & Gulia, 1999).

Because of open membership policies and the availability of public message archives, discussion lists are easily accessible to researchers interested in group computer-mediated communication. In addition to the topics mentioned above, studies have investigated the functional content of messages (Herring, 1996b; Rafaeli & Sudweeks, 1997); patterns of posting over time (Millen, 2000); group dynamics (Hert, 1997; Korenman & Wyatt, 1996); "netiquette" (Herring, 1994, 1996a); "lurking," or reading messages without posting (Nonnecke & Preece, 2000); topic decay (Lambiase, forthcoming), and the effects of gender on participation (Hall, 1996; Herring, 1993, 1996a, in press b; Herring, Johnson, & DiBenedetto, 1992, 1995; Selfe & Meyer, 1991; Sierpe, 2000). A diachronic study identified changes in formality and politeness over an eleven-year period in an early discussion list (Herring, 1998a).

Usenet Newsgroups

Originally intended as a populist alternative to the government-supported ARPANET, which was then available only at a few elite universities, Usenet news was developed in 1979 by three graduate students at Duke University and the University of North Carolina. The name Usenet was meant to represent "Unix Users Network"; instead of packet switching and TCP/IP, Usenet made use of the Unix-to-Unix Copy Program (UUCP) file sharing protocol (Rheingold, 1993). The first four Usenet nodes were established in 1980, and by 1988 had expanded to 11,000 (Hauben & Hauben, 1997); in 1999, posting to Usenet was the third largest activity on the Internet, after e-mail and browsing the Web (Smith, 1999).

Usenet is an asynchronous bulletin board system in which e-mail messages are posted to a publicly available site; users access the messages via a newsreader client (or, since the mid-1990s, a Web browser), which allows them to view messages either in the temporal sequence in which they were posted, or grouped into "threads" according to subject line. Communication takes place within "newsgroups," which are organized into hierarchies by topic and named with identifiers in order of increasing specificity (e.g., comp.sys.mac, soc.culture.jewish, alt.sex.fetish.spanking). In 1999, Smith estimated that there were 79,000 newsgroups worldwide. To create linkage among messages in what is otherwise a vast and potentially fragmented communication space, users frequently cross-post messages to other newsgroups (Smith, 1999) and "quote" portions of other messages (Baym, 1995; Hodsdon, forthcoming; Severinson-Eklundh, forthcoming).

Social accountability is low on Usenet. Unlike listserv lists, which maintain records of subscribers' names and e-mail addresses, unmoderated Usenet newsgroups have no means of monitoring who reads or posts to them. Reduced social accountability, combined with the libertarian value on uncensored speech that Usenet inherited from the hacker culture of its early developers and users (Pfaffenberger, 1996), often gives rise to "flaming," or hostile message content (Ebben, 1994; Kim & Raja, 1990; Spertus, 1997; Sutton, 1994). Other antisocial behaviors common on Usenet include "spamming," or sending the same message multiple times (Marvin, 1995), and "trolling," or pretending to ask a naïve question in order to provoke flaming (Donath, 1999; trollfaq, http://www.altairiv.demon.co.uk/afaq/posts/trollfaq.html). In 1992, 95 percent of Usenet users were estimated to be male (Sproull, quoted in Kramarae & Taylor, 1993); today, although male and female Web users in the United States have reached numerical parity (Rickert & Sacharow, 2000), males still make up a majority of Usenet posters.

Usenet messages are publicly accessible, and organizations such as Dejanews have been archiving Usenet postings in searchable databases since 1995. With the recent purchase of Dejanews by Google, the nature of these archives is changing; for example, users may now delete their Usenet posts from Dejanews. The ready availability of data has made Usenet a popular focus of CMC research. In addition to the studies mentioned above, research has investigated participation patterns in very large-scale conversations (Jones & Rafaeli, 2000; Sack, 2000; Smith, 1999); community formation (Baym, 1995; MacKinnon, 1995; McLaughlin, Osborne, & Smith, 1995); identity, authenticity, and deception (Burkhalter, 1999; Donath, 1999); differences between new and experienced participants (Weber, forthcoming); use of languages other than English (Paolillo, 1996, 2000); support groups (King & Moreggi, 1998; Sharf, 1999); and hate speech (Hodsdon, forthcoming; Zickmund, 1997).

Split-Screen Protocols: Talk, Phone, and ICQ

The earliest synchronous protocol, UNIX "talk," was available in the 1970s alongside e-mail (Hafner & Lyon, 1996). However, it was felt by the ARPANET developers on MsgGroup (see "Discussion Lists" earlier) to be less useful for multiparty conferencing than e-mail, and was not developed for the Internet until years later. "Talk" and the similar VAX "phone" utility are synchronous protocols in which two (or in the case of "phone," up to three) users logged on to a UNIX or VAX system at the same time can "talk" via text. Each user's monitor screen splits horizontally into two or three sections, and their messages appear character-by-character, scrolling independently within each section. In the mid-1990s, this concept was incorporated as an option into the ICQ ("I Seek You") Internet communication network developed by Mirabilis Ltd. in Israel. Although talk and phone are limited to UNIX and VAX users who know of their existence, ICQ has become widely popular; in 1999, over 11 million people were using ICQ on a daily basis (Zastrow, 1999). This figure includes all ICQ activity, not just chatting. ICQ also has paging and file transmission features (Zastrow, 1999). The official ICQ Web site (http://www.icq.com/icqtour/rendezvous.html) listed the total number of users as of November 2000 as over 82 million.

Split-screen protocols differ from other forms of CMC currently available in using character-by-character transmission, rather than message-by-message transmission, as is the case for e-mail (Cherny, 1999, terms this distinction "two-way" vs. "one-way" transmission). Character-by-character (two-way) transmission has consequences for interaction management: Users often anticipate how another's sentence will end, and begin typing before the other finishes, resulting in a high incidence of overlap and more efficient communication (in the sense of requiring fewer words) overall (Anderson, Beard, & Walther, forthcoming; Woodburn, Proctor, Arnott, & Newell, 1991). McGrath (1990) claims that two-way CMC systems render turn-taking "irrelevant." A second feature of such systems that shapes communication is their use of a split-screen interface; this limits the number of participants because of the space required for each scrolling window. Such interfaces are difficult to log and archive (Herring, 1999a), making communication in this mode ephemeral. The screen capture in Figure 3.2 shows the messages produced by two users after approximately five minutes of conversation, but does not preserve the temporal sequence of the messages. ICQ allows users to save logs of their chats, but the logs follow a one-way transmission format, with turns following one another in sequence, and no overlap indicated.

The ephemerality of split-screen conversations combined with their mostly private, one-to-one nature makes them less amenable to study than public, more persistent forms of CMC. No naturalistic

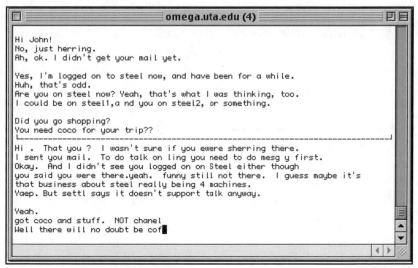

Figure 3.2 An example of UNIX "talk"

(i.e., nonexperimental) studies of use of talk, phone, or ICQ were available to the author at the time of this review.

Chat

The first chat program, Internet Relay Chat (IRC), was written in Finland in 1988 by Jarkko Oikarinen, a student at the University of Oahu, to enable synchronous communication among multiple participants (Pioch, 1997). The IRC chat protocol was later adapted for use by Internet service providers such as AmericaOnline (AOL), and on Web sites, where it is known as "Web chat." More recent Web-based chat programs make use of color and graphics in addition to text. Over the past decade, chat has become popular on a global scale, especially among younger users (Danet, Ruedenberg-Wright, & Rosenbaum-Tamari, 1997).

Chat is synchronous and involves message-by-message (one-way) transmission. Users connect to a chat site, join "channels" (on IRC) or "rooms" (on AOL), and communicate by typing typically brief (one-line) messages, which are transmitted in their entirety when the user presses the "send" key. Messages are displayed to everyone in the room or channel in the temporal order in which they are received, with the user's nickname appended automatically before each message (Figure 3.3).

Users can scroll back to read earlier messages within a limited buffer, making chat less ephemeral than split-screen protocols, although sessions are not automatically logged. Perhaps one of the most striking features of chat conversations is that they often initially appear chaotic. When multiple participants are involved, messages can scroll quickly up and off the screen. Further, chat systems disrupt patterns of turn taking, due to the tendency of overlapping exchanges to cause an initiating message and its response to become separated by irrelevant messages (Herring, 1999a). However, the same features that render chat fragmented and chaotic also make it popular. Loosened turn-taking fosters playfulness (Danet et al., 1997; Herring, 1999a), and simultaneous multiple conversations foster enhanced interpersonal—what Walther (1996) terms "hyperpersonal"—interactivity (Herring, 1999a).

The culture of chat rooms, although varying according to purpose, is typically sociable, playful, and disinhibited. Much chat content is phatic, indeed banal, and chat conversations tend to be stylistically informal (Werry, 1996). Topics decay quickly, making unstructured chat unconducive to extended, focused discussion (Herring & Nix, 1997), although users who chat together on a regular basis can develop strategies for maintaining coherence (Herring, 1999a; Schlager, Fusco, & Schank, in press). The requirement on most public chat sites that each user select a nickname (effectively, a pseudonym) creates an environment conducive to play, flirting, and other activities for which the user may wish to avoid being held socially accountable (Bechar-Israeli, 1995; Danet, 1998).

As a very popular and publicly-accessible CMC mode, chat has attracted the attention of a number of Internet researchers. A commonly described feature of chat (and synchronous CMC in general) is the use of abbreviations (e.g., lol "laughing out loud"), nonstandard spellings, and ASCII graphics (Ferrara, Brunner, & Whittemore, 1991; Livia, forthcoming; Murray, 1990; Reid, 1991; Werry, 1996; Wilkins, 1991). Many researchers point to typographic and orthographic innovations as evidence of users' attempts to compensate for the lack of vocal, facial, and gestural cues in text-only CMC (Daft & Lengel, 1984; Herring, in press a; Kiesler et al., 1984; Reid, 1991). Other aspects of group chat that have been researched include choice of nickname (Bechar-Israeli, 1995), influence of social network ties (Paolillo, 2001), community formation (Liu, 1999), expression of gender identity

<Kayleigh> wulf you never told me you were a man, im shocked

*** Signoff: d{0_o}b (Off to Hell!)

<hippygirl> hi all

<aOK-88> I demand Fax SEX NOW!!!!!!!

*** csyen has left channel #chatzone

*** | PseudO | (xxxx@xxx##.xxxx.xxx) has joined channel #chatzone

<wulferina> lol

<^ducky> you wouldnt know what sex is would you aOK

*** snacks has left channel #chatzone

*** PhoneSex- (XxxxxXxx@xxxx.xxx.xxx) has joined channel #chatzone

*** DelilA has left channel #chatzone

<MARY-J> Hello frod.

*** fartmunch (xxXX@xxx.xx-xxxx.xxx) has joined channel #chatzone

<smoothman> hello hippygirl

Figure 3.3. An example of Internet Relay Chat

(Herring, 1998b; Rodino, 1997; Soukup, 1999), and sexual harassment (Herring, 1999b). Figure 3.3 shows an example of Internet Relay Chat from the EFNet channel #chatzone.

Private Chat

From the outset, IRC allowed users to chat privately. They could use the "/msg" command for occasional private comments, or open a person-to-person dcc (direct client-to-client) connection (Pioch, 1997), enabling backchannel communication to take place in parallel with public group chat. Alternatively, two or more users could create a private channel for extended, independent chat. Similar features are available on MUDs (see below) under the command names "whisper" and "page;" MUD users can also create private rooms (Cherny, 1995, 1999).

However, the versions of chat popularized on AOL and on some Web sites do not preserve these private messaging features. To fill the gap, AOL implemented "instant messaging" (IM), a synchronous means of exchanging short text messages with others logged on to AOL at the same time. IM has a feature, shared by ICQ, that makes it highly popular: a user can designate a list of people with whom she is potentially interested in communicating, and the system will inform her when any of those people are logged on to the system, and hence potentially available for interaction. IRC has this feature as well, via the "/notify" command (Pioch, 1997). Instant messaging protocols have since been developed for other systems; one of the most widely used is included with the Microsoft Outlook mail software (CyberAtlas, 2001). In 2000, IBM employees sent over one million instant messages a day to each other (Dean, 2001), and the number of instant messaging users worldwide is predicted to reach 180 million by 2004 (CyberAtlas, 2001). Accordingly, the culture of private chat has evolved from primarily social uses among teenagers, to workplace use (Dean, 2001).

Privacy issues surround the study of person-to-person communication, and instant messaging is a relatively recent phenomenon; as a consequence, little research is available that investigates private chat. McRae (1996) interviewed participants on a social MUD about virtual sex, most of which takes place through private conversation. Cogdill, Fanderclai, Kilborn, and Williams (2001) captured text logs from the perspective of a single user on an educational MUD, and analyzed the interplay of private backchanneling with public classroom activities. According to anecdotal report, instant messaging is becoming the preferred mode of CMC in some workplaces (Dean, 2001), its purported advantages over e-mail being "contact management and the ability to configure different levels of availability" (Scevak, 2001, online).

Multi-User Dimensions (MUDs)

MUDs are multi-user virtual reality environments in which users can navigate a textual representation of a spatial environment and engage in synchronous chat with other participants logged on to the MUD. In some user-extensible MUDs, users also have the option to interact with programmed objects, create new objects, and extend the environment itself. The first MUD, created in 1979 and 1980 by Roy Trubshaw and Richard Bartle, students at the University of Essex in England, was a role-playing adventure game modeled on earlier single-player online games such as "Rogue" and the popular group face-to-face game "Dungeons and Dragons" (Cherny, 1999; Reid, 1994; Rheingold, 1993).

The acronym MUD originally meant "Multi-User Dungeons," but was reinterpreted to mean "Multi-User Dimensions" with the rise in popularity of social MUDs in the late 1980s and early 1990s. MOOs (MUDs, Object Oriented) date to 1991 and represent an advance in MUD programming; today most MUDs are technically MOOs (Cherny, 1999). Access to MUDs is via telnet or one of a number of MUD clients currently downloadable for free from the World Wide Web. Although still somewhat limited to users in the know, adventure MUDs such as EverQuest and Ultima Online enjoy a growing popularity on the Internet (Kolbert, 2001), alongside social MUDs such as LambdaMOO (Curtis, 1992), and educational MUDs such as MediaMOO (Bruckman & Resnick, 1995) and LinguaMOO (Haynes & Holmevik, 1997).

MUDs resemble IRC and other chat systems in their communicative affordances, making available a similar range of textual communication commands (Cherny, 1995, 1999), and often exhibiting overlapping exchanges, abbreviation, and language play (Cherny, 1999; Kendall, 1996). At the same time, MUDs also preserve some game-like features from their origin as adventure role-playing games. By convention, users take on pseudonyms and describe their "characters" in nonrealistic terms. They also navigate through a virtual playing field defined in terms of a geographical metaphor (e.g., a house, a university, a fantasy landscape; Anders, 1999; Giese, 1998), and accrue power and influence, e.g., "wizard" status, the longer they "play" (Cherny, 1999; Reid, 1994). These features, which are present to some extent in all three major MUD genres (educational MUDs generally do not allow students to attain wizard status), encourage playful behavior (Cherny, 1999; Danet, 1998), including the collaborative enactment of narrative fantasies (Kolko, 1995) and experimentation with gender identity (Bruckman, 1993; Danet, 1998; McRae, 1996). The geographical metaphor also symbolically defines the boundaries of interaction within a MUD, leading to a possibly greater perception of groupness or virtual community than in other text-based modes of group CMC (Cherny, 1999; Reid, 1994). This perception, combined with the user-extensible nature of social MUD environments, leads users to commit time and energy to MUDs, reinforcing the users' sense of belonging, and sometimes leading them to resent the presence of outsiders whose commitment to the MUD is perceived to be weaker than theirs (Cherny, 1999).

Access to MUDs may be limited formally (one must have a registered "character" in order to carry out a full range of possible behaviors) and informally (guests and newcomers may be treated with suspicion). Despite these potential obstacles to participation, and despite (or perhaps because of) their relatively restricted, "exotic" status, MUDs have attracted the attention of many Internet researchers with interests in, among other topics, antisocial behaviors and sanctions against them (Dibbell, 1993; Reid, 1994); systems of MUD governance (Curtis, 1992; Kolko & Reid, 1998); power hierarchies (Cherny, 1999; Reid, 1998); gender switching (Bruckman, 1993; Danet, 1998; McRae, 1996); virtual sex (Deuel, 1996; McRae, 1996); community social activities, including online weddings (Jacobson, 1996; Turkle, 1995); and psychological issues such as escapism and MUD addiction (Turkle, 1995).

Figure 3.4 displays a sample of a session from a MUD (HoloMUCK) that includes navigation and the use of the "page" command. The "You" in line 8 refers to the user; other players see the name of his character, Kilian.

The World Wide Web

The World Wide Web, conceptualized in 1989 by British scientist Tim Berners-Lee of the CERN (European Organization for Nuclear Research) in Geneva, was implemented on the Internet in 1991.

---

w

You head west...

Main Street (800W)

This once-desolate section of Main Street is looking busier these days.

To the north, at 800 W. Main St., stands the Red Dragon Inn.

[Obvious exits: north, w, e]

page dex= are u free tomorrow between 8 Your pager vibrates slightly. and 10..am??

You page, " are u free tomorrow between 8 and 10..am??" to Dex.

01) Dex pages: "no, not till tomorrow night"

Time> Tue Oct 31 19:54:33 1995

Figure 3.4. An example of MUD Communication (Anders, 1999, pp. 139–140)

Berners-Lee's goal, influenced by Bush's (1945) proposal for the "memex" machine and Nelson's (1967) ideas about "hypertext," was to create a shared information space through which large numbers of people and machines could communicate via associative links (Berners-Lee, 1996). However, it was not until the introduction of the Mosaic graphical Web browser in 1993 that the Web became widely accessible. The cessation of National Science Foundation funding for the Internet backbone in 1995, and the subsequent increase in commercial involvement with the Internet, gave further impetus to the development of the Web, primarily as a marketing medium (Goggin, 2000; McChesney, 2000). Commercial uses currently dominate the Web; according to a recent estimate, at the end of 1999 there were about five million Web sites, some containing up to 100,000 pages, of which 54.7 percent were in the .com domain, as compared to only 6.7 percent with the .edu suffix (Cybermetrics, 2000). In response, in part, to the number and heterogeneity of .com sites, in November 2000 new domain names were approved that added categories such as .info and .biz (Associated Press, 2000). Web browsing is currently the "killer ap" of the Internet, rivaling e-mail in popularity (Pastore, 2000).

In one sense, the Web subsumes and integrates all other CMC modes, making it a "meta" mode (Soukup, 2000; Wakeford, 2000). It can link to chat interfaces, discussion lists, Usenet newsgroups, and e-mail—in addition to Web pages written in Hyper-Text Mark-up Language (HTML)—because of its hypertextual nature (but see Jackson, 1997, who argues that the Web is not hypertextual in a strict sense). The Web also links different communication media (text, graphics, audio, and video), thereby subsuming multimedia CMC applications as well (O'Sullivan, 1999). Viewed from this perspective, the range of characteristics associated with Web communication is very broad. In another sense, we may consider the practices of writing HTML documents, creating links between documents, and navigating the interconnected space defined by those links to be unique to the Web, and describe them alongside other CMC modes.

Surprisingly, given its popularity, the Web has been relatively little studied as an interpersonal communication medium. There appear to be two reasons for this: (1) Web-based communication is less interactive than e-mail, discussion groups, or chat, causing some researchers initially not to consider it a mode of CMC (Wakeford, 2000); and (2) the Web communicates meaning and structure through nontextual means, for which CMC researchers traditionally lack methods of analysis (Soukup, 2000). However, some researchers have explicitly addressed the extent to which the Web is an interactive, as opposed to a broadcast or mass, medium (Hoffman & Novak, 1995; O'Sullivan, 1999). Authoring and reading a Web page are asymmetrical activities in which the reader interacts with a machine—the page is not affected by the act of being read, nor does it respond. At the same time, the reader has the option to react by creating his own Web page that critiques or comments on the author's page (e.g., Coste, 2000), or by providing feedback via e-mail or other means to the author, who could choose to change his page in response. Moreover, Web sites may incorporate opportunities for direct interaction between users and sites, ranging from information boxes to be filled in, to the possibility of entering content directly onto the site, to intelligent interfaces that "learn" and "remember" visitors' preferences from visit to visit (O'Sullivan, 1999). In these respects, the Web is clearly more interactive than traditional mass media. A second theme is the communication structures created by the web of links themselves, which, as Jackson (1997) points out, involves selection and thus can serve different agendas by focusing users' attention in particular ways. Related to this is the nature of users' navigational choices, and the meanings created by following different paths through a network of links. Other topics researched include the genre conventions of personal home pages (Cheung, 2000), the characteristics of Web sites that cause "fascination" (Smit, 2000), or a "flow" experience for viewers (Hoffman & Novak, 1995), and Web communities (Mallapragada, 2000; Pullen, 2000).

Audio and Video

The World Wide Web enabled the incorporation of sound and moving images into Web pages. In a parallel development to the Web, members of the Cornell University Information Technology Department launched CUseeMe, the first Internet audio and video conferencing software, in 1993 (Dorcey, 1995; Meloan, 1995). CUseeMe combined text-based chat with one-way audio and video transmission, the latter requiring only an inexpensive videocam placed atop each transmitter's computer. Because the CUseeMe program was free and used standard Internet bandwidth, it caught on quickly, despite the low quality of its transmissions: the small black and white video image was grainy and jerky, the sound frequently broke up, and sound and video were not synchronized (Meloan, 1995; Sloan, 1997). Since being taken over commercially in 1998, CUseeMe (along with Microsoft NetMeeting and other Internet conferencing programs) has taken advantage of the increasing bandwidth of the Internet to improve audio and video transmission (which now includes color and two-way transmission) and added group conferencing, application sharing, and whiteboard features (http://www.cuseeme.com).

A related development was the introduction in 1995 of free telephony via the Internet (www.pulver.com). As in the case of video chat, voice calls over the Internet are of lower quality than traditional telephony, being subject to delays, distortion, and break-up of the data stream, but they are inexpensive, requiring only standard sound software and an Internet connection (Hill, Ozer, & Mace, 1996). A number of products has been developed, including Internet Phone, Netscape CoolTalk, and Netspeak WebPhone, all of which allow multiple calls to be conferenced. While currently limited in use, calls made over IP-based networks are predicted to account for 35 percent of all telephone network traffic by the year 2002 (Berat, 1996).

Despite the fact that both involve point-to-point (one-to-one) transmission, video- and audio-based modes of CMC have given rise to communities of users on the Internet. CUseeMe servers (or *reflectors*) list names of persons interested in videochatting with strangers (Sloan, 1997), and individuals maintain Web sites with screen shots of CUseeMe friends with whom they videochat on a regular basis (www.cheznims.com). According to Sloan (1997), video conferencing bridges distance and builds relationships, due to the greater richness of the channel compared to plain text (see also Neal, 1997; Walther, 1999). Similarly, Internet telephony companies maintain lists at their servers of interest groups—"chat rooms" organized by topic (e.g., programming enthusiasts, sex groups)—where users can initiate and accept conversation. According to Hill, Ozer, and Mace (1996, online), some Internet phone communities "resemble the rough-and-tumble world of Usenet newsgroups."

Because of their one-to-one nature and low degree of persistence, little information exists at present about the nature of communication in

Figure 3.5 A video image on CUseeMe (Chou, 1999)

audio and video chat, apart from anecdotal reports. One suggestive study (Yates & Graddol, 1996) compared CUseeMe, IRC, telephone, and face-to-face conversation, and found that CUseeMe users talked more about themselves and their physical appearance than did conversants in any other mode.

Graphical Virtual Reality (VR) Environments

Graphical virtual reality environments, introduced to the Internet in the mid-1990s, trace their genesis to developments in networked multi-participant computer gaming—e.g., George Lucas' graphical Habitat environment that ran on Commodore 64 computers in the mid- to late-1980s (Mauz, 2000)—and nonimmersive (desktop) virtual reality simu-lation (Robertson, Card, & Mackinlay, 1993). Expanding the concept of group chat protocols such as IRC and MUDs, the first graphical VR envi-ronments were designed to combine text-based chat with graphics depicting a physical backdrop or space, such as a room in a house or an outdoor scene. An early prototype of the Palace, in fact, made use of an IRC client (Bumgardner, 1994). Users—represented by graphical icons or *avatars*—navigate through a virtual space using the mouse or computer keyboard, exploring, interacting with the environment, and, if they have permission, building in it. Two of the earliest and best-known such environments are the Palace (two-dimensional graphics), developed by Jim Bumgardner for Time-Warner corporation in 1994 and opened to the public in November 1995, and AlphaWorld (later ActiveWorlds, using three-dimensional graphics), developed by Ron Britvich for Knowledge Adventure Worlds (later Worlds, Inc.) and released publicly in June 1995. Both environments have attracted and maintained active communities of users up to the present, despite difficulties that have arisen due to internal struggles (Scannell, 1999; Suler, 1996), as well as to changes in ownership and technical support (Eep2, 2000; Suler, 1996). The Palace is currently owned by Communities.com (http://www.communities.com), and Active Worlds by ActiveWorlds.com (http://www.activeworlds.com).

Graphical VR environments make the metaphor of physicality in text-based MUDs literal and explicit. Members, or *citizens*, "own property," and issues of territoriality may arise in interaction, as, for example, when a gang of disruptive users began vandalizing others' buildings in the first year of AlphaWorld's existence (Rookie's AlphaWorld Report, http://www.geocities.com/CapitolHill/2333/rookie.html), or when users of a different system, WorldsAway, began to socialize in their private apartments rather than hanging out in disorderly public places (Scannell, 1999).

The requirement that users take on physical representations of bodies, or avatars, has communicative consequences as well. In the Palace, avatars and backdrops are brightly colored and deliberately cartoonish (the default avatar is a disembodied smiley face [Bumgardner, 1994]), and users can create their own, giving rise to collections of avatars, some humorous, some menacing, some sexy, that a user can "wear" depending on her mood and the nature of the interaction (Suler, 1996). (The similarity to cartoons is reinforced by the fact that users' words appear as typed text over their avatars' heads, as well as in a line-by-line chat window (in the case of ActiveWorlds) below the graphics screen. In the Palace, users' words are further enclosed in cartoonlike speech and thought bubbles.) A WorldsAway avatar can exchange heads with another avatar as a way to express a personal relationship

(Scannell, 1999). In contrast, ActiveWorlds avatars, at least in the U.S., favor realism: humanlike forms can perform automated movements such as dance or fight, and express emotions such as anger and joy through body movement (McClellan, 1996). According to the chairman and founder of Worlds, Inc., Dave Gobel, Americans are more "buttoned-down" in their taste for realism in 3D VR than are the Japanese, who prefer fantasy (Steinhardt, n.d.). In an experimental prototype, Vilhjálmsson (1997) has taken realism to its logical extreme by designing avatars with facial features that modulate to correspond to words typed, or to indicate subtle social meanings such as "recognition" of another avatar. As embodied representations, avatars also have a field of "personal space," which can be violated by having another avatar located too close; Krikorian, Lee, Chock, and Harms (2000) found that relative distance between avatars in the Palace corresponds to differing degrees of personal liking. As Naper (2001) points out for a Norwegian ActiveWorld, visual design, perspective, location, and movement are semiotic signs that contribute meaning, and thus must be analyzed as part of computer-mediated communication.

Most studies to date of graphical chat environments have been ethnographic. Suler (1996) provides a first-person account of Palace history in its first year, including social tensions within the community based on new-old member status, wizard-nonwizard status, and problems raised by anonymity and an increasing user population. Scannell (1999) interviewed regular users about social practices in the Palace, WorldsAway (Dreamscape), and ActiveWorlds, pointing out tensions between individual and group interests that were also present in the 19th-century settlement of the American West. Another focus is community and the spontaneous social structures that evolve as groups of strangers share virtual space over a period of time. These structures include a police force and a community newspaper in ActiveWorlds (McClellan, 1996), and a social event organizing committee at the Palace (Suler, 1996). Overall, graphical VR environments appear to intensify many of the same social dynamics that have previously been observed in MUDs. Figure 3.6 shows a screen capture of an educational 3D graphical environment that makes use of the Active Worlds platform (used with permission from Katy Börner).

Figure 3.6 **An example of a 3D graphical environment**

Early Claims About CMC Revisted

The bulk of the research surveyed in the previous section investigated spontaneous communication in culturally contextualized Internet modes. In contrast, much early CMC research based its claims on experiments in what Walther (1996) calls "zero-history groups," groups of people who have never interacted before (and who are unlikely to interact again in the future), and who thus lack a shared CMC cultural context. Other influential early CMC studies were speculative in nature, basing their claims on predictive studies of managers' media choices (Walther, 1999), and/or reasoning deductively from the characteristics of the medium (Steinfield, 1986), rather than making empirical observations (but see Hiltz and Turoff [1978], who made early observations about CMC use via a computer conferencing system). Most of this early research (with the exception of Hiltz and Turoff) focused on the ways in which CMC systems allegedly restricted or limited human communication relative to face-to-face communication. What does Internet communication tell us about the issues raised in previous CMC research and about CMC in general? This section considers the findings of observational Internet-based research in relation to three earlier claims, extending the claims as generalizations and evaluating the extent to which the Internet evidence supports or refutes them.

Appropriate Uses

An influential early model for the interpretation of CMC was the theory of information richness proposed by Daft and Lengel (1984, 1986). According to this view, "lean" media such as text-based CMC, which make use of a single channel of communication, are best suited for straightforward, concrete tasks (such as scheduling), while rich, multiple channel media such as face-to-face speech are preferred for complex and ambiguous tasks (such as negotiation). The text-only nature of CMC further makes it low in "social presence" (Short, Williams & Christie, 1976; Spears & Lea, 1992), making it better suited for the transmission of factual, impersonal information than for relational communication.

It is difficult to address these claims directly, because nonexperimental research that considers the relationship between task and medium choice is rare (but see the ethnographic research of Murray, 1988 on computer professionals at IBM; and Perry, Fruchter, and Spinelli, 2001). However, indirect evidence can be brought to bear from Internet research. The overall content of communication on the Internet includes a high frequency of relational communication. This was first noted by Rice and Love (1987); in a study of socio-emotional content in a medical discussion list on CompuServ, they found that over 60 percent of messages contained such content, even though the participants were medical professionals and the topic of the group was serious. More extreme counter evidence can be adduced from the widespread popularity of recreational chat environments (discussed earlier), friendships and marriages initiated through CMC (Jacobson, 1996; Lea & Spears, 1995; Parks & Floyd, 1996), and the perceived usefulness of CMC by many people for maintaining contact with distant friends and family (Hampton & Wellman, 1999). Even academic discussion lists contain more opinions and emotional debate than facts (Herring, 1996b). Thus, if the Internet has revealed one thing clearly, it is that CMC is not restricted to task-oriented, factual exchanges—the overall trend is in the opposite direction. Users are able to adapt to the text-only nature of the medium to express social and personal meanings, intimately and sometimes eloquently, as letter writers and authors of literary texts have done for centuries, suggesting that typed text is not in and of itself inherently impoverished.

Yet stating that relational communication occurs frequently does not exclude the possibility that such communication may be relatively more difficult or less successful in CMC. Here the evidence from the Internet is mixed: Miscommunication has been claimed to be common in CMC, especially with regard to the expression of affect (hence, the alleged need to use emoticons to express what one "really means" [Rivera, Cooke, & Bauhs, 1996]). Nevertheless, some users feel more comfortable communicating intimately via CMC, and prefer it to face-to-face interaction, in which they might not have such conversations at all (for example, with estranged family members). Thus the potential for misunderstanding caused by reduced social cues in CMC is offset, for some users, by the advantages of the editable text-only medium, which allows for greater reflection, distance, and control over impression management (Walther, 1996, 1999).

Conversely, stating that exchange of information is not the primary activity on the Internet is not the same as stating that information exchange is not facilitated by the medium. Indeed, the evidence suggests that the Internet promotes the exchange of information, as it also promotes interpersonal communication (Burnett, 2000; Wellman et al., 1996). At the same time, there is reason to question, in a general sense, the quality of information available on the Internet. The difficulty of verifying the reliability of a source (Donath, 1999; Fallis, 2000), and the lack of quality control on information posted, for example, on a newsgroup or the World Wide Web, means that for some users the ease and convenience of the Internet may be overridden by concerns about quality and reliability. In short, while it seems intuitively correct that medium choice is sensitive to the nature of the task, other considerations also play a role where CMC is concerned, including those related to properties of the medium other than its text-only nature.

One such property is temporal synchronicity. Synchronous (real-time) CMC fosters significantly different communication behaviors from asynchronous CMC; synchronous messages tend to be shorter, less syntactically complex, more limited in vocabulary, more playful, and contain more phatic social communication (Danet et al., 1997; Ko, 1996; Werry, 1996) than asynchronous messages, which tend to be longer, more edited, more multifunctional, and more linguistically complex (Condon & Čech, forthcoming; Herring, 1999a). In keeping with these differences—which arise because of differences in temporal constraints on message production in the two CMC types—synchronous CMC appears to be better suited for social interaction and asynchronous CMC for more complex discussion and problem solving. Indeed, these respective strengths are reflected in the most common uses of synchronous and synchronous CMC on the Internet.

It is not clear, however, how this difference reflects information richness, if at all. Arguing from the observed effects, information richness theory seems to suggest that synchronous CMC is "richer" than asynchronous CMC, and has greater social presence, because it is better suited for relational communication. This characterization is inconsistent, however, with the claim that greater social presence enables more complex interactions, in that synchronous CMC enables less complex interactions than asynchronous CMC. That is, synchronous CMC is both simple and highly relational. Thus the synchronicity distinction reveals that task complexity and the richness/social presence of a medium are not necessarily interrelated, contrary to the claim of information richness theory. Overall, the information richness and social presence models, at least as originally formulated, appear to make more incorrect than correct predictions about communication on the Internet. (See Rice & Gattiker [2000] for a somewhat different perspective on this topic.)

Social Effects

Another highly influential early CMC theory is what is known as the cues-filtered-out view (Kiesler et al., 1984; Kiesler, Zubrow, Moses, &

Geller, 1985; Sproull & Kiesler, 1991). According to this view, CMC is characterized by a relative lack of physical and social cues, again due to its text-only nature, and this has consequences for social behavior. Kiesler and her colleagues conducted a number of experimental studies comparing CMC with face-to-face interaction, and found that subjects were more disinhibited and more polarized in arguments when using CMC. They interpreted this to mean that the lack of cues as to the identity of the addressee has a depersonalizing effect, causing users to forget that they are communicating with other human beings. They also proposed that CMC is more anonymous, and therefore more egalitarian, than face-to-face communication, in that cues to people's social status, gender, age, race, physical ability, etc., are absent (see also Barlow, 1996; Graddol & Swann, 1989).

On the face of it, the frequent recurrence of flaming and antisocial, aggressive behaviors in group environments on the Internet appears to support the claim that CMC causes disinhibition and polarization. Moreover, such behaviors tend to be reported most frequently in contexts where anonymity is high and social accountability is low, such as on Usenet (Kim & Raja, 1990; Pfaffenberger, 1996), MUDs (Dibbell, 1993; Reid, 1994), and the Palace in the early days before visitors were assigned registration numbers (Suler, 1996). In a longitudinal study of an early discussion list, Herring (1998a) found an increase in violations of politeness over time, raising the possible interpretation that the medium was to blame.

However, the claim that the computer medium necessarily causes boorish behavior has been challenged in Internet research. Lea, O'Shea, Fung, and Spears (1992) and Rafaeli and Sudweeks (1997) find that flaming is not a statistically predominant behavior in discussion groups, and indeed there are Internet environments in which it is almost completely absent. Moreover, Herring (1994, 1996a) finds that there is a gender component to flaming; it is carried out mostly by males, who also express a more tolerant attitude toward it than do females. In contrast, females tend to be polite and supportive; Hall (1996) suggests that asynchronous CMC exaggerates these behaviors relative to face-to-face communication. The cues-filtered-out model does not explain why anonymity and depersonalization should affect males differently from females, nor indeed why some users behave badly on a regular basis while others never do. A more nuanced view is required, one that takes into consideration variables such as degree of anonymity, user demographics, topic, and purpose of communication (Baym, 1995; Herring, in press a).

The claim that gender, age, race, etc., are invisible in CMC also receives *prima facie* support from some Internet research. Cases of deception involving aspects of identity are not uncommon (Bell & La Rue, 1995; Bruckman, 1993; Donath, 1999; Turkle, 1995; van Gelder, 1990). At the same time, gender differences have been found in participation and discourse style (Hall, 1996; Herring, 1993, 1996a, 1998b; Savicki, Lingenfelter, & Kelley, 1997; for an overview, see Herring, in press b), and racial identity is also signaled discursively (Burkhalter, 1999; Jacobs-Huey, forthcoming). In general, most people interact in their real-life identities online, even if they choose an anonymous identifier, due in part to the difficulty of convincingly maintaining an identity that is foreign to their real-life experiences (Curtis, 1992; Cherny, 1999; Herring, 1998b). This is especially true in asynchronous discussion lists, where people wishing to enhance their reputations as experts on a given topic must sign their messages in order to receive recognition for their contributions (Donath, 1999). In short, the available evidence suggests that most users do not take advantage of the potential for anonymity that the Internet affords, with the result that some information about user identity is usually available, although the amount of personal detail available varies according to the circumstances and CMC mode. For example, an e-mail message typically conveys considerable information in its header (e-mail address, name, organization, date and time, route the message followed, etc.) and may contain a signature file with fax, phone number, URL to sender's Web page, and other details as well (Donath, 1999). In contrast, IRC messages reveal only senders' (nick)names, although a command allows others to view their e-mail addresses and the names of the servers from which they are logged on.

It follows that if users are not anonymous, differential status may attach to them, and communication will not necessarily be egalitarian and nonhierarchical. In asynchronous group discussion, a minority of users tends to dominate in amount of posting (Herring, 1993, forthcoming; Hert, 1997), with the majority lurking, or reading without contributing (Nonnecke & Preece, 2000). In one intriguing study, Selfe and Meyer (1991) found that the highest status members of an academic discussion list (male professors) continued to dominate the discussion even during a two-week period when identifiers were stripped from messages as an experiment in anonymity. This suggests that what encourages high rates of participation are factors such as self-confidence and perceived entitlement, rather than anonymity *per se*. Participation rates are more balanced in synchronous CMC modes such as IRC and MUDs, where lurkers are more visible, and the cost involved in sending a message is lower (Herring, 1998b). However, such systems often have hierarchy built in, in the form of roles such as "operator" on IRC (Paolillo, 2001) and "wizard" on MUDs (Reid, 1994; Suler, 1996), who have the power to limit other people's use of the system. Finally, virtual groups sometimes empower individuals from among their ranks by electing them to governance positions, thereby institutionalizing status differences (Kolko & Reid, 1998; MacKinnon, 1995). In addition to status differences based on real-world rank, gender, and role within the virtual community, status is also associated with experience in an online forum, with inexperienced users ("newbies") enjoying fewer rights and sometimes receiving less respectful treatment than experienced users (Naper, 2001; Suler, 1996; Weber, forthcoming).

At the same time, the Internet clearly provides greater opportunities for some people to be heard than would otherwise be the case. Individuals and groups who would not otherwise have access to public media or be taken seriously are able to express themselves on the Internet, including minorities of all types, as well as antisocial elements. Indeed, it is difficult to prevent those with Internet access from posting whatever they like, short of removing their access privileges, and even then they usually have alternative ways to gain access (Dibbell, 1993). The question of whether this is a desirable or undesirable characteristic of Internet communication is controversial. (See "Freedom of Expression" in the next section.)

Effects on Language and Communication

A final early prediction is that communicating via computers affects the nature of language and communication itself. Thus Baron (1984) speculated that CMC could reduce the expressive potential of human language, leading to a more homogeneous, affectless, structurally simpler, and less socially nuanced style of communication over time. Baron's view was based in part on the observation that text-based CMC lacks the prosodic and nonverbal cues, such as intonation, voice quality, and facial expression, which contribute to the expression of (especially, social) meaning.

Baron's claim involves two parts, one having to do with linguistic complexity and the other with expressiveness. Some writers have observed that e-mail language is structurally simpler than traditional forms of writing, made up of shorter, grammatically less complex sentences, and containing more sentence fragments and typographical errors (Hale, 1996). In partial support of this view, Cho (forthcoming) found e-mail messages to contain fewer passive constructions (such as "the book was written by a young author") and to rank higher than written memoranda on an ease of readability scale. However, e-mail messages posted to professional discussion lists tend to be linguistically sophisticated, making use of complex grammar and containing few errors (Herring, 1998a). This suggests that factors such as level of user education and purpose for communication condition language complexity in asynchronous CMC. In contrast, synchronous CMC is structurally limited: In a study comparing informal spoken conversation, formal written documents, and communication in a synchronous chat system, Ko (1996) found the CMC to be simpler even than spontaneous speech in terms of range of vocabulary used and measures of word and sentence length. We may add to this the observation that chat exhibits abbreviation to a greater extent than e-mail (or speech). Unlike users of e-mail, chat users are under pressure to type at a conversational pace; the cost of speed of production appears to be linguistic complexity.

There is no evidence from Internet research that CMC is stylistically homogeneous. On the contrary, as the above suggests, a great deal of linguistic variation exists, even within a single mode such as e-mail. There is also variation across modes; Cherny (1999) presents evidence that language use in a social MUD follows conventions that differ from those for IRC, even though both are synchronous, recreational chat modes. Nonetheless, conventions do form (such as the abbreviations "u" and "r" for "you" and "are"), and are learned by new users, leading to the possibility that, over time, users converge toward a common usage, and thus, that something like a monolithic chat or e-mail style could eventually emerge. Here, again, there is evidence to suggest the contrary:

Experienced, core users tend to diverge from the norms of the group (Herring, 1998a; Paolillo, 2001), perhaps to distinguish themselves from the crowd. At the same time, at least for professional e-mail, prescriptive norms of use are starting to emerge, as attested by the growing number of e-mail style guides (e.g., Booher, 2001; Hale, 1996). Nonetheless, given that users send e-mail for a variety of purposes, it seems likely that stylistic variety will continue to exist.

Expressivity was touched on briefly earlier, in the discussion of relational communication, where it was observed that social meanings appear to be conveyed effectively through CMC. Users achieve this in part through creative uses of language, such as novel spellings, repeated punctuation, and ASCII graphics designed to convey attitude, nonspeech sounds, and facial expressions (Cho, forthcoming; Livia, forthcoming; Werry, 1996). This is especially common in synchronous chat, despite the fact that expressive language often requires extra keystrokes, and thereby goes against the principle of economy of effort that otherwise conditions chat language. Overall, it appears that CMC is less expressive than face-to-face communication, but more expressive than standard, edited written language. Yates and Graddol (1996) suggest that speech is an overly rich medium that generates inappropriate meanings (through gesture, facial expression, tone of voice, etc.) that must constantly be cancelled. Viewed from this perspective, CMC allows users to express more precisely what they mean, without the interference of unintended physical cues (see also Walther [1999]).

Each of the sets of predictions considered above assumes that communicative consequences follow necessarily from the properties of CMC systems. The evidence from the past fifteen years of Internet research does not support a strong technologically deterministic view, at least as regards the effects of text-only CMC systems. Situational factors can (and regularly do) override the predispositions of the medium, and users can adapt the medium to their communicative needs, just as with communication in other media.

Current Issues in CMC Research

In contrast with early CMC research that focused on the limitations of the medium for accomplishing traditional communicative ends, recent research tends to focus on new forms of communication enabled by the Internet. This trend corresponds to a shift in thinking about computer networking in terms of its intended, first-order effects—e.g., to facilitate the transfer of information among geographically dispersed participants—to a growing recognition of its (largely unintended) second-order effects, including its larger societal impacts, as has also occurred in the past with communication technologies such as the telephone (see Sproull & Kiesler, 1991). (The telephone was originally intended to transmit live concerts and public lectures to distant listeners. Only later was its usefulness for interpersonal communication recognized [Sproull & Kiesler, 1991].) The early days of the Internet were characterized by considerable hype and projection, both utopian and dystopian, concerning such notions as democracy, hierarchy, and social behavior. This section presents in overview some of the secondary effects of Internet communication currently represented in the research literature, identifying opportunities and challenges raised by each.

Freedom of Expression

Historically, the culture of the Internet has been shaped by the libertarian philosophy of the mostly young, white, upper-middle-class American males who created it and who made the protocols and software to support CMC available for free (Pfaffenberger, 1996; Turkle, 1988). Along with free software, the creators of the Internet placed a high value on free information exchange, which they believed could come about only with complete freedom of speech. Moreover, they believed that the Internet structurally encouraged free speech, by "routing around censorship" (Barlow, 1996, online). The open nature of Internet communication means that individuals and groups who might otherwise not have an opportunity to make themselves heard can present their views in a public forum, resulting in a diversity of viewpoints being represented online.

However, unconstrained speech in Internet forums has brought with it numerous challenges, including a low "signal-to-noise-ratio" (i.e., more low-quality than high-quality communication) and the difficulty of controlling antisocial CMC behaviors such as spamming (Marvin, 1995), flaming (Kim & Raja, 1990), hate speech (Glassman, 2000; Zickmund, 1997), and sexual harassment (Bell & La Rue, 1995; Dibbell, 1993;

Ferganchick-Neufang, 1998; Herring, 1999b). These behaviors not only harm individuals, but can also be disruptive to online groups (Reid, 1994; Suler, 1996). Accordingly, some propose that the right of the individual to say anything in an online forum should, under certain circumstances, be constrained in the interest of the common good (Ess, 1996). Solutions that have been proposed in response to the challenges inherent in enforcing restrictions on online communication include technical means such as filters (Spertus, 1996, 1997) and social means such as public censure (McLaughlin et al., 1995; Spertus, 1996).

Community

The 1990s saw the introduction of the term "virtual community" to describe groups of people who communicate primarily—and in some cases exclusively—via the Internet (Rheingold, 1993; Wellman & Gulia, 1999). Some Internet observers suggest that online group communication fills a void left by the decline of face-to-face communities in contemporary urban societies (Barlow, 1995; Rheingold, 1993), although others (S. Jones, 1995; Wellman, 1997) caution against romanticizing a notion of face-to-face community that may never actually have existed. In addition, debate centers around the definition of "community" itself: Is any online group a community, or is community something that arises only under certain conditions? Most CMC scholars support the latter view, pointing to processes of community formation involving, for example, key (often disruptive) incidents leading to the articulation of norms, sanctions, and in some cases, the constitution of systems of governance (Dibbell, 1993; MacKinnon, 1995; McLaughlin et al., 1995; Reid, 1994). Others see evidence of community in linguistic practice; for example, in insider language use (Baym, 1995; Cherny, 1999). Yet other researchers focus on the self-reports of people who experience a sense of engagement and belonging in an online group (Rheingold, 1993; Scannell, 1999), even when they themselves do not participate (Nonnecke & Preece, 2000).

In contrast, others point to the ephemerality of Internet group membership and the low degree of commitment required to participate as evidence that exclusively computer-mediated groups foster pseudocommunity at best (Beniger, 1987; S. Jones, 1995). Consistent with this view, a growing body of evidence points to off-line interaction as a requisite for sustainable online community (Hampton & Wellman, 1999); Virnoche and

Marx (1997) label such forms virtual extensions (of real intermittent communities). Wellman and Gulia (1999) claim that, much as in the "real world," the Net fosters multiple, partial, specialized communities in which social ties are intermittent and varying in strength. Such hybrid communities may combine the best of both worlds: the "interactive broadcasting" capabilities of CMC, with the advantages of face-to-face communication for interpersonal identification, authentication, and accountability (Etzioni, 1999). Others, focusing on the similarities between the two, claim that both the Net and the "real world" foster multiple, partial, specialized communities in which social ties are intermittent and varying in strength (Wellman & Gulia, 1999).

Personal Impacts

More and more people are spending time online, and CMC is coming to replace other leisure-time activities (Pew Internet and American Life Project, 2000). Participation in CMC has been claimed to be psychologically beneficial, allowing for self-expression (Deuel, 1996), experimentation with identity (Bruckman, 1993; Danet, 1998), and meaningful relationship formation (Lea & Spears, 1995; Parks & Floyd, 1996). Individuals who spend a lot of time online generally have more, not fewer, social contacts, and e-mail may foster more open communication with friends and family than would otherwise take place (Hampton & Wellman, 1999; Wellman, 1997). Generalizations should be made with caution, however, since perceptions of the benefits of Internet communication vary according to age, social class, and ethnic background (Kraut, Scherlis, Mukhopadhyaya, Manning, & Kiesler, 1996).

At the same time, some writers warn that heavy use of CMC can lead to addiction, alienation from face-to-face relationships, and depression (Griffiths, 1998; Stoll, 1995). These claims find support in a self-report study of 169 subjects during their first year or two online (Kraut, Kiesler, Mukhopadhyaya, Scherlis, & Patterson, 1998). However, others suggest that CMC overuse is a symptom, rather than a cause, of these conditions (King, 1996a; Turkle, 1995), and that participation in CMC has no negative psychological impacts for most users. Information overload is another risk associated with Internet use (Chao, 1995, cited in Wellman & Gulia, 1999; Sproull & Kiesler, 1991).

Trust and Deception

On the Internet, an individual can connect easily with multiple sources for information and interaction. Moreover, people are often willing to assist strangers online, perhaps because the risks and costs of intervention are perceived to be lower than they are offline (Wellman & Gulia, 1999). However, in order to engage in safe, meaningful interaction, one must trust that one's interlocutor is generally truthful and sincere. Deception is easy to carry out in a mediated environment such as the Internet, in that hard physical evidence is generally lacking to confirm that someone is who and what they claim to be (Bell & La Rue, 1995; Donath, 1999; van Gelder, 1990). Virtual reality environments, whether text-based or graphical, may further increase vulnerability to deception, in that they require users to suspend disbelief in order to interact with their virtual surroundings (Anders, 1999). Even in CMC environments where identity play is common, participants may feel deceived when they discover that the "woman" they have befriended is really a man (McRae, 1996). The adverse consequences of gullibility can range from minor (in the case of identity play and trolls (Donath [1999]) to potentially serious (in the case of scams and stalkers [D'Amico, 1997; Federal Trade Commission, 2000]).

Trust may be enhanced in online forums through face-to-face contact (Diani, 2000). Olson and Olson (2000, p. 42) summarize the findings of experimental research on trust and communication medium as follows: "In the lab, face-to-face interaction promotes the greatest trust, followed by the telephone, then text-chat, then e-mail, until with e-mail, test subjects behave mostly in a self-serving way." Other means for enhancing trust include having (known) participants vouch for unknown participants as a criterion for membership (Levien, 2000), and discouraging anonymous communication (Perrole, 1991). However, anonymity can also be a legitimate means to protect a participant's privacy (Donath, 1999; Friedman, Kahn, & Howe, 2000); a challenge is to foster social accountability without sacrificing privacy protections.

Privacy

Many people reveal personal information in online interaction, an observation variously attributed to the medium's inherent tendency to foster disinhibition (Kiesler et al., 1984), naïve users' perceptions that group CMC is private (King, 1996b), or a sense that one's words will not be noticed in the vast data flow, especially when posted to an obscure newsgroup or chat room.

However, the reality is that most types of computer-mediated messages leave a persistent trace, which enables them to be archived and traced back to the system that mailed them. E-mail messages can also be intercepted or misdirected (Meeks, 1999). Moreover, most Internet groups are technically accessible by people other than the intended members of the group, who may use them for purposes ranging from benign to malevolent. Thus a user should consider when it is appropriate to self-disclose and when it is prudent to be cautious in online interaction (Friedman et al., 2000).

The persistence of electronic communication, in combination with the ease with which it can be observed invisibly, also makes the Internet a powerful vehicle for surveillance and tracking. The U.S. government's proposed Carnivore/DCS1000 system would monitor electronic communication through Internet service providers for purposes of law enforcement (Kerr, 2000), and commercial Web sites place "cookies" on users' computers to track their Web usage patterns for marketing purposes (Berghel, 2001). As awareness of these practices grows, Internet users increasingly report feeling concerned about threats to their privacy (Pew Internet and American Life Project, 2000).

Internet Research Ethics

The Internet is an unprecedented boon to the scientific study of communication and related social processes. Data from authentic interactions of a wide variety of types are available for analysis without the presence of the researcher biasing the data collection process (Herring, 1996c). Moreover, the persistent nature of textual CMC encourages reflection and study, such that even people who would not have undertaken empirical research before are now drawn to Internet research.

At the same time, the very ease of data collection on the Internet raises ethical concerns. Participants may not be aware that their words are being collected and studied. Moreover, even when their identities are masked through the use of pseudonyms, it may be possible to link their words with their (online) identities by searching archives such as Dejanews (in the case of postings to Usenet). Further, inexperienced researchers may engage in ethically dubious data collection practices, putting CMC users at risk of harm (Frankel & Siang, 1999).

Currently there is considerable debate about appropriate ethical practice in Internet CMC research. For a balanced exposition of the issues, see Mann and Stewart (2000). Some researchers advocate obtaining informed consent from subjects prior to conducting any CMC research (Frankel & Siang, 1999), regardless of whether researcher intervention is involved. Others recommend asking permission to quote particular messages prior to including them in presentations or publications (Sharf, 1999), and/or masking all identifying information about the users and the groups (King, 1996b). However, informed consent poses practical problems due to the shifting membership of Internet groups, and could have a chilling effect on critical research (Herring, 1996c). The challenge is to strike a balance between allowing researchers to carry out quality CMC research, and protecting users from potential harm. A further issue concerns whether users have a right to privacy when posting to discussion groups and chat rooms, even if the research places them at no risk of harm. Underlying the debate are questions concerning the definition of "harm," and how the traditional public-private distinction should be applied to CMC (Herring, 1996c; King, 1996b).

Very Large Scale Conversations

Another affordance of the Internet is the extent to which it makes possible, on a heretofore unprecedented scale, simultaneous conversations among large numbers of people. These "very large scale conversations" (Sack, 2000) offer ready access to the combined expertise of many people, and enable efficient one-to-many as well as many-to-many communication (Sproull & Kiesler, 1991).

Large-scale online conversations also raise new challenges. Coherence is difficult to maintain, in that conversation management (turn taking, exchange tracking, topic maintenance) tends to be fragmented in multiparticipant groups (Herring, 1999a, forthcoming). In the absence of a strong moderator, computer-mediated groups tend toward disagreement and polarization, making consensus among large numbers of participants difficult to achieve (Sudweeks & Rafaeli, 1996), except on noncontroversial, status quo maintaining topics (Diani, 2000). The constraints on large online groups—their optimal size (Jones & Rafaeli, 2000), their natural life cycles (Lambiase, forthcoming)—also need to be understood, in order to maximize group viability. Finally, there is a need to analyze how reputation is achieved and influence exerted in large computer-mediated groups (Donath, 1999; MacKinnon, 1995).

E-Democracy

From the beginning, enthusiasts have seen in the Internet a potential means to increase the involvement of ordinary people in the democratic process. Åström (2001) distinguishes among "thin" democracy (the elite competing for citizens' votes, e.g., through campaigning), "quick" democracy (direct citizen input into decision making, without the intermediary of elected representatives), and "strong" democracy (an active citizenry informed by public deliberation of issues), asserting that the Internet can, and should, facilitate each type. Others distinguish status quo maintaining from novel or transformative political communication on the Internet, valuing the latter over the former (Becker, 2000; Lax, 2000).

However, while examples of political uses of the Internet abound (e.g., Knudson, 1998; Lax, 2000; Ogan, 1993; Stubbs, 1998), some researchers doubt its transformative power. Diani (2000) claims that online groups are unlikely to generate sufficient trust to motivate radical social movements without extensive face-to-face interaction. A more serious reservation is that elite ruling groups are better positioned than ordinary people to exploit Internet technology to further their ends (Diani, 2000). Others question the "strong democracy" premise that exchanging information in open debate will necessarily lead to a more involved or informed citizenry, citing the lack of interest of the ordinary citizen in political processes, and the uneven accessibility of online information (Åström, 2001; Lax, 2000). To this could be added the often dubious quality of public online discussions (see earlier discussion of freedom of speech and very large scale conversations).

Globalization

From its origins in the United States, the Internet has, since the 1990s, been spreading to other countries at a seemingly relentless pace

(Petrazzini & Kibati, 1999). Globalization is welcomed by humanists who embrace the potential of an interconnected "global village" to promote information exchange and cross-cultural understanding (Ess, 2001; Hawisher & Selfe, 2000), as well as by capitalists eager to access foreign markets (Global Reach, http://www.glreach.com). However, while there is a general sense that the Internet will bring about important changes on a global scale, its likely impacts are as yet little understood.

One question concerns the extent to which current inequalities in access will eventually level out. Less than 4 percent of the world's population now has Internet access, and fewer than 50 percent have telephone access (Gauntlett, 2000a). Moreover, the majority of Internet traffic is still routed through North America (Petrazzini & Kibati, 1999; Yates, 1996), and in 2000, 87 percent of all Web pages were written in English, even though native speakers of English accounted for only about 7 percent of the world's population (Cybermetrics, 2000). Some scholars fear that Internet communication will spread the cultural values and the language of its dominant, and historically prior, group of users—North American English speakers—at the expense of smaller, politically and economically weaker groups (Buszard-Welcher, 2000; Mattelart, 1996; Nunberg, 2000; Yates, 1996). In the meantime, speakers of different languages are coming increasingly in contact (if only by encountering Web sites in foreign languages), creating a rising demand for automated, online translation (Silberman, 2000).

Another challenge raised by globalization is determining legal jurisdiction over information and communication on the Internet. King (1999) points out that local community standards (for example, with respect to pornography and hate speech) tend to be supplanted by the lowest common denominator (i.e., whatever is legal anywhere in the world is effectively available everywhere through the Net). At the same time, the research literature contains a growing number of examples of peoples, including minority groups, adapting and regulating Internet technology for their own purposes (e.g., Arnold & Plymire, 2000; Hongladarom, 2001).

Commercialization

Since the end of U.S. National Science Foundation funding of the Internet backbone in 1995, the costs of operating the Internet have increasingly been taken up by commercial interests (for a critique, see McChesney, 2000). E-commerce is now the dominant use of the Web (Cybermetrics, 2000), and access to CMC is increasingly via commercial Internet service providers and Web browsers, which intersperse e-mail and chat interfaces with advertising (Goggin, 2000). The commercialization of the Internet—and especially the Web—has undeniably expanded its reach and potential (Goggin, 2000). Moreover, advocates of commercialization argue that it encourages small businesses and fosters competition, making new and better products available to consumers at lower prices; in addition, online shopping offers convenience. Finally, the ability to handle business transactions electronically (such as purchasing airline tickets) eliminates middlemen, resulting, theoretically, in savings passed on to consumers (McChesney, 2000). Some see in these developments the potential for large media and corporate monopolies to be crushed, consistent with the democratic potential of the Internet itself (Barlow and Negroponte, cited in McChesney, 2000).

Most Internet scholars who have written on the topic, however, consider commercialization a regrettable (if inevitable) development, one more likely to reinforce the ownership and control of media by large corporate interests than to promote online democracy. McChesney (2000) points out that, rather than encouraging competition, corporations engage in mergers and other activities to create monopolies. Monopolies tend to distribute mainstream, mass media content, resulting in a depoliticization of online culture (see also Brown, 2000). Moreover, the prevalence of advertising on the Web leads to the development of increasingly manipulative technologies such as interactive banners and pop-up ads, which potentially interfere with CMC, especially when attached to search engines and servers (Goggin, 2000). A major challenge for the future will be to preserve a commerce-free public sphere on the Internet, alongside the growing number of commercial initiatives.

Second-order technology effects are like the ripples that spread outward when a pebble is tossed into a pond, continuing to spread for some time in ever-widening circles (Sproull & Kiesler, 1991). The Internet is still new enough that its wider impacts are only starting to be felt. The evidence available thus far suggests that neither utopian nor exclusively dystopian scenarios will likely come about in the foreseeable future; Internet communication raises both opportunities and dangers. Rather than, "Will the Internet ultimately prove beneficial or detrimental to human society?," the most important questions for the future, which current research is already starting to address, are, "Who will benefit, who will be harmed, in what ways?"

Directions for Future Study

Internet research is still in its infancy. More questions have been raised than have yet been definitively answered, and new CMC technologies are emerging faster than researchers can describe them, let alone investigate their natural use. Among the emergent technologies that cry out for future study is wireless Web access via mobile phones and handheld devices (J. Jones, 2000). Future research also urgently needs to address multimodal CMC technologies (Soukup, 2000). At the same time, researchers should not prematurely abandon the older, text-based modes, for textual CMC will continue to be important (Walther, 1999).

To date, Internet CMC research has had a text bias. This was appropriate in the early days of the Internet, when most CMC was text only, but the situation is rapidly changing as increased bandwidth makes high-quality audio, video, and graphics easier to transmit and hence more common. Methods need to be developed for analyzing the meaning communicated by visual layout and graphic design in Web pages (Schmid-Isler, 2000; Soukup, 2000). Video and graphical VR environments additionally require methods for analyzing dynamic spatial relations (Krikorian, Lee, Chock, & Harms, 2000), perspective, gesture, and movement—not just as design issues, but as channels of communication. Moreover, the phenomenon of multimodality itself has yet to be systematically addressed: How do different channels of communication interact to construct rich, multilevel meanings? One of the goals of such study should be to identify the advantages and limitations of different channels for different uses (Lombard & Ditton, 1997; Neal, 1997; Walther, 1999).

Internet CMC research currently also has an interactive bias; that is, it focuses mostly on CMC media that enable reciprocal and symmetrical interaction. While it is currently fashionable to talk about the "interactivity" of the World Wide Web (see, e.g., O'Sullivan, 1999), Web pages are not symmetrically interactive (Jackson, 1997). However, as the Web increasingly subsumes other CMC modes, this distinction is becoming blurred. Some researchers are starting to focus on the Web as a communication medium in its own right (Coste, 2000; Gauntlett, 2000b; Herman & Swiss, 2000; Mitra & Cohen, 1999), but much more needs to be done. This includes developing methods for analyzing (1) the multimodal text (textual dimension), (2) patterns of available links (spatial dimension), (3) users' navigational trajectories (temporal dimension), and (4) the patterns of human-human interaction grounded in Web sites (social dimension).

Internet CMC research also tends to display a group bias. Many studies have analyzed data from discussion groups, chat rooms, and MUDs, for the practical reason that such data are easily accessible; in this sense, the Internet provides us with an unprecedented opportunity to study group processes (Korenman & Wyatt, 1996; Sudweeks & Rafaeli, 1996). However, we cannot assume that the findings for large Internet groups will necessarily scale to small groups or one-to-one communication. Research is needed that systematically investigates the effects of number of participants on communicative phenomena such as amount of participation, turn taking, coherence, politeness, sociability, influence, and power dynamics. Given their enormous popularity, much more research is needed on one-to-one e-mail and instant messaging and how each varies according to characteristics of users and communicative purposes.

As CMC practices evolve at a rapid rate, it is imperative that we preserve records of their evolution. This is being done by default for much asynchronous group CMC (and no doubt some private e-mail collections), for which the technology requires the user actively to delete messages or else they will remain. Capitalizing on this persistence, asynchronous messages have been collected since 1975 in public archives and databases, where with foresight and good management they will remain for purposes of future study. However, the situation is very different for synchronous CMC, which disappears unless the user actively intervenes to log it. Only sparse corpora of chat exist from the early 1990s, and no serious longitudinal study of chat has yet been attempted. As digital data storage capacities increase, CMC researchers should make preserving and analyzing extended samples of synchronous CMC a high priority.

Finally, the Internet has often been represented in CMC research as though it were a self-contained environment, a "virtual" world apart from "real life." Phenomena such as online communities and identity play have made it tempting to do this, especially in the early days when a relatively small percentage of the population had access to the exotic "cyberspace" realm. Such a fiction can no longer be maintained; today Internet use is increasingly a part of everyday routine for large numbers of people around the world. How is CMC integrated into the complex whole of people's communicative activities? When do they choose to communicate via the Internet and when face-to-face, by telephone, fax, etc.; and how does choice of modality affect the communication (Murray, 1988)? Comparative studies of face-to-face conversation and CMC, telephone conversation and CMC, and Short Message Service (SMS) via cell phones and CMC over the Internet—preferably involving the same individuals—are needed to address the ubiquitous claims that "CMC causes people to do X more/less that they would otherwise do in modality Y." In all such studies, of course, different modes of CMC also need to be distinguished.

In conclusion, much work remains, even though we know a great deal more about CMC now than we did fifteen years ago. It has been said that Internet years are like dog years—one Internet year is equivalent to seven pre-Internet years in terms of the amount of change that takes place. If that is so, then we have already experienced in the past fifteen years more than a century's worth of change—longer than the average human life span. And many of us are not yet old, meaning that we can look forward to more change (and more learning) in the future. One of the great promises of CMC research, with all its interdisciplinary diversity, is that it will eventually reveal to us the underlying principles, the systematic dimensions of variation, that can account for the relationship between features of communication media and human communication more generally.

Bibliography

Anders, P. (1999). *Envisioning cyberspace: Designing 3D electronic spaces*. New York: McGraw-Hill.

Anderson, J. F., Beard, F. K., & Walther, J. B. (forthcoming). The local management of computer-mediated conversation. In S. Herring (Ed.), *Computer-mediated conversation*.

Arnold, A. L., & Plymire, D. C. (2000). The Cherokee Indians and the Internet. In D. Gauntlett (Ed.), *Web.studies: Rewiring media studies for the digital age* (pp. 186-193). London: Arnold.

Associated Press. (2000, November 16). New domain names approved. *CNN.com*. Retrieved June 15, 2001, from the World Wide Web: http://www.cnn.com/2000/TECH/computing/11/16/internet.names.ap

Åström, J. (2001). Should democracy online be quick, strong, or thin? *Communications of the ACM, 44*(1), 49–51.

Barlow, J. P. (1995). Is there a there in cyberspace? *Utne Reader, 68*. Retrieved June 15, 2001 from the World Wide Web: http://www.eff.org/pub/Publications/John_Perry_Barlow/HTML/utne_community.html

Barlow, J. P. (1996). Declaration of the independence of cyberspace. Retrieved June 15, 2001 from the World Wide Web: http://www/eff/org/pub/Censorship/Internet_censorship_bills/barlow_0296.declaration

Baron, N. S. (1984). Computer mediated communication as a force in language change. *Visible Language, 18* (2), 118–141.

Baron, N. S. (2000). *Alphabet to e-mail: How written English evolved and where it's heading*. London: Routledge.

Baym, N. (1995). The emergence of community in computer-mediated communication. In S. Jones (Ed.), *Cybersociety: Computer-mediated communication and community* (pp. 138–163). Thousand Oaks, CA: Sage.

Bechar-Israeli, H. (1995). From <Bonehead> to <cLoNehEAd>: Nicknames, play and identity on Internet Relay Chat. *Journal of Computer-Mediated Communication, 1* (2). Retrieved June 15, 2001 from the World Wide Web: http://www.ascusc.org/jcmc/vol1/issue2

Becker, T. (2000). Rating the impact of new technologies on democracy. *Communications of the ACM, 44*(1), 39–43.

Bell, V. & de La Rue, D. (1995). Gender harassment on the Internet. Retrieved June 15, 2001 from the World Wide Web: http://www.gsu.edu/~lawppw/lawand.papers/harass.html

Beninger, J. (1987). Personalization of the mass media and the growth of pseudo-community. *Communication Research, 14*(3), 25–34.

Berat, J. (1996, May 20). Sorting out Internet telephony. *ZDNet Anchor Desk*. Retrieved June 15, 2001 from the World Wide Web: http://www.zdnet.com/anchordesk/story/story_2113.html

Berghel, H. (2001). Caustic cookies. *Communications of the ACM, 44*(5), 19–22.

Berners-Lee, T. (1996). The World Wide Web: Past, present and future. Retrieved June 15, 2001 from the World Wide Web: http://www.w3.org/People/Berners-Lee/1996/ppf.html

Booher, D. (2001). *E-Writing: 21st century tools for effective communication*. New York: Pocket Books.

Brown, J. (2000, August 25). What happened to the women's Web? *Salon*. Retrieved June 15, 2001 from the World Wide Web: http://www.salon.com/tech/feature/2000/08/25/womens_web.html

Bruckman, A. S. (1993). Gender swapping in cyberspace. *Proceedings of INET '93*. Retrieved June 15, 2001 via anonymous ftp from media.mit.edu in pub/MediaMOO/papers.gender-swapping

Bruckman, A. S., & Resnick, M. (1995). The MediaMOO project: Constructionism and professional community. *Convergence, 1*(1), 94–109.

Bumgardner, J. (1994). A little Palace history. Retrieved June 15, 2001 from the World Wide Web: http://www.jbum.com/jbum/history

Burkhalter, B. (1999). Reading race online. In M. Smith & P. Kollock (Eds.), *Communities in cyberspace* (pp. 60–75). London: Routledge.

Burnett, G. (2000). Information exchange in virtual communities: A typology. *Information Research, 5*(4). Retrieved June 15, 2001 from the World Wide Web: http://www.shef.ac.uk/~is/publications/infres/paper82a.html

Bush, V. (1945). As we may think. *Atlantic Monthly, 176,* 101–108.

Buszard-Welcher, L. (2000). Can the Web help save my language? Retrieved June 15, 2001 from the World Wide Web: http://www.potawatomilang.org/Reference/endlgsweb4.htm

Camp, L. J. (1996). We are geeks, and we are not guys: The Systers mailing list. (with A. Borg). In L. Cherny & E. R. Weise (Eds.), *Wired_women: Gender and new realities in cyberspace* (114–125). Seattle, WA: Seal Press.

Chao, J. (1995, June 20). Net loss: The pioneers move on. *Toronto Globe and Mail*, p. A13.

Cherny, L. (1995). The modal complexity of speech events in a social MUD. *Electronic Journal of Communication / La revue électronique de communication, 5*(4). Retrieved June 15, 2001 from the World Wide Web: http://www.cios.org/www/ejc/v5n495.htm

Cherny, L. (1999). *Conversation and community: Chat in a virtual world*. Stanford, CA: Center for the Study of Language and Information.

Cheung, C. (2000). A home on the Web: Presentations of self on personal homepages. In D. Gauntlett (Ed.), *Web.studies: Rewiring media studies for the digital age* (pp. 43–51). London: Arnold.

Cho, N. (forthcoming). Linguistic features of electronic mail. In S. Herring (Ed.), *Computer-mediated conversation*.

Chou, C. C. (1999, January). Computer-mediated communication systems for synchronous online learning. Paper Presented at the Pan-Pacific Distance Learning Association Annual Conference. Retrieved June 15, 2001 from the World Wide Web: http://www2.hawaii.edu/~cchou/ppdla99/index.htm

Cogdill, S., Fanderclai, T. L., Kilborn, J., & Williams, M. G. (2001) Backchannel: Whispering in digital conversation. *Proceedings of the 34th Hawaii International Conference on System Sciences*. Retrieved June 15, 2001 from the World Wide Web: http://www.hic.ss.hawaii.edu/HICSS_34/PDFs/DDPTC03.pdf

Cohen, J. (2001, May 17). He-mails, she-mails: Where sender meets gender. *The New York Times*, pp. D1, D9.

Condon, S. L., & Čech, C. G. (1996). Discourse management strategies in face-to-face and computer-mediated decision making interactions. *Electronic Journal of Communication, 6*(3). Retrieved June 15, 2001 from the World Wide Web: http://www.cios.org/www/ejc/v6n396.htm

Condon, S. L., & Čech, C. G. (forthcoming). Discourse management in three modalities. In S. Herring (Ed.), *Computer-mediated conversation.*

Coste, R. (2000). Fighting speech with speech: David Duke, the Anti-Defamation League, online bookstores, and hate filters. *Proceedings of the 33rd Hawaii International Conference on System Sciences.* Retrieved June 15, 2001 from the World Wide Web: http://dlib.computer.org/conferen/hicss/0493/pdf/04933012.pdf

Curtis, P. (1992). Mudding: Social phenomena in text-based virtual realities. *Proceedings of DIAC92.* Retrieved June 15, 2001 from the World Wide Web: ftp://ftp.lambda.moo.mud.org/pub/MOO/papers/DIAC92.ps

CyberAtlas. (2001, May 1). Hardware: Evolution of instant messaging increases stakes for Microsoft, AOL. Retrieved June 15, 2001 from the World Wide Web: http://cyberatlas.internet.com/big_picture/hardware/article/0,,5921_756111, 00.html

Cybermetrics. (2000). Measuring the Internet. *Cybermetrics: International Journal of Scientometrics, Informetrics and Bibliometrics, 4.* Retrieved June 15, 2001 from the World Wide Web: http://www.cindoc.csic.es/cybermetrics/links22.html

Daft, R. L., & Lengel, R. H. (1984). Information richness: A new approach to managerial behavior and organization design. *Research in Organizational Behavior, 6,* 191–233.

Daft, R. L., & Lengel, R. H. (1986). Organizational informational requirements, media richness and structural design. *Management Science, 32,* 554–571.

D'Amico, M. (1997). *The law vs. online stalking.* Retrieved June 15, 2001 from the World Wide Web: http://www.madcapps.com/Writings/cybsersta.htm

Danet, B. (1998). Text as mask: Gender and identity on the Internet. In S. Jones (Ed.), *CyberSociety 2.0: Revisiting computer mediated communication and community* (pp. 129–158). Thousand Oaks, CA: Sage.

Danet, B., Ruedenberg-Wright, L., & Rosenbaum-Tamari, Y. (1997). Hmmm ... where's that smoke coming from? Writing, play and performance on Internet Relay Chat. In S. Rafaeli, F. Sudweeks, & M. McLaughlin (Eds.), *Network and netplay: Virtual groups on the Internet* (pp. 41–76). Cambridge, MA: AAAI/MIT Press.

Dean, K. (2001, January 25). Instant messaging grows up. *Wired News.* Retrieved June 15, 2001 from the World Wide Web: http://www.wired.com/news/print/0,1294,33736,00.html

Deuel, N. (1996). Our passionate response to virtual reality. In S. Herring (Ed.), *Computer-mediated communication: Linguistic, social and cross-cultural perspectives* (pp. 129–146). Amsterdam: John Benjamins.

Diani, M. (2000). Social movement networks virtual and real. *Information, Communication & Society, 3,* 386–401.

Dibbell, J. (1993, December 21). A rape in cyberspace, or how an evil clown, a Haitian trickster spirit, two wizards, and a cast of dozens turned a database into a society. *Village Voice*, pp. 36–42.

Dodge, M., & Kitchin, R. (2000). *Mapping cyberspace.* London: Routledge. [Internet timeline can also be found at http://www.mappingcyberspace.com/gallery/figure1_1.html]

Donath, J. (1999). Identity and deception in the virtual community. In M. Smith & P. Kollock (Eds.), *Communities in cyberspace* (pp. 29–59). London: Routledge.

Dorcey, T. (1995). The CU-SeeMe desktop videoconferencing software. *ConneXions, 9*(3), 42–45.

Ebben, M. M. (1994). *Women on the net: An exploratory study of gender dynamics on the soc.women computer network.* Unpublished doctoral dissertation, University of Illinois at Urbana Champaign.

Eep2. (2000). Active Worlds history. Retrieved June 15, 2001 from the World Wide Web: http://tnic.com/eep/aw/history.html

Ess, C. (1996). Beyond false dilemmas: Men and women on the net—a plea for democracy and understanding. *Computer-Mediated Communication Magazine, 3*(1). Retrieved June 15, 2001 from the World Wide Web: http://www.december.com/cmc/mag/1996/jan/ess.html

Ess, C. (2001). What's culture got to do with it? Cultural collisions in the electronic global village, creative interferences, and the rise of culturally-mediated computing. In C. Ess & F. Sudweeks (Eds.), *Culture, technology, communication: Towards an intercultural global village* (pp. 1–30). Albany, NY: SUNY Press.

Etzioni, A. (1999). Face-to-face and computer-mediated communities, a comparative analysis. *The Information Society, 15*, 241–248.

Fallis, D. (2000). Veritistic social epistemology and information science. *Social Epistemology, 14*, 305–316.

Federal Trade Commission. (2000). Law enforcers target "top 10" online scams. Retrieved June 15, 2001 from the World Wide Web: http://www.ftc.gov/opa/2000/10/topten.htm

Ferganchick-Neufang, J. (1998). Virtual harassment: Women and online education. *First Monday, 3*(2). Retrieved June 15, 2001 from the World Wide Web: http://www.firstmonday.dk/issues/issue3_2/fergan/

Ferrara, K., Brunner, H., & Whittemore, G. (1991). Interactive written discourse as an emergent register. *Written Communication, 8*(1), 8–34.

Frankel, M. S., & Siang, S. (1999). *Ethical and legal aspects of human subjects research on the Internet* [Workshop report]. American Association for the Advancement of Science. Retrieved June 15, 2001 from the World Wide Web: http://www.aaas.org/spp/dspp/sfrl/projects/intres/main.htm

Friedman, B., Kahn, P., & Howe, D. (2000). Trust online. *Communications of the ACM, 43* (12), 34–40.

Gauntlett, D. (2000a). The future: Faster, smaller, more, more, more. In D. Gauntlett (Ed.), *Web.studies: Rewiring media studies for the digital age* (pp. 212–217). London: Arnold.

Gauntlett, D. (Ed.). (2000b). *Web.studies: Rewiring media studies for the digital age*. London: Arnold.

Giese, M. (1998). Constructing a virtual geography: Narrative of space in a text-based environment. *Journal of Communication Inquiry, 22* (2), 152–176.

Glassman, E. (2000). Cyber hate: The discourse of intolerance in the new Europe. In L. Lengel (Ed.), *Culture @nd technology in the new Europe: Civic discourse in transformation in post-communist nations* (pp. 145–164). Stamford, CT: Ablex.

Goggin, G. (2000). Pay per browse? The Web's commercial futures. In D. Gauntlett (Ed.), *Web.studies: Rewiring media studies for the digital age* (pp. 103–112). London: Arnold.

Graddol. D., & Swann, J. (1989). *Gender voices*. Oxford: Basil Blackwell.

Griffiths, M. (1998). Internet addiction: Does it really exist? In J. Gackenbach (Ed.), *Psychology and the Internet: Intrapersonal, interpersonal, and transpersonal implications* (pp. 61–75). San Diego, CA: Academic Press.

Hafner, K., & Lyon, M. (1996). *Where wizards stay up late: The origins of the Internet*. New York: Simon & Schuster.

Hale, C. (Ed.). (1996). *Wired style: Principles of English usage in the digital age*. San Francisco: HardWired.

Hall, K. (1996). Cyberfeminism. In S. Herring (Ed.), *Computer-mediated communication: Linguistic, social and cross-cultural perspectives* (pp. 147–170). Amsterdam: John Benjamins.

Hampton, K. N., & Wellman, B. (1999). Netville online and offline. *American Behavioral Scientist, 43,* 475–492.

Hauben, M., & Hauben, R. (1997). *Netizens: On the history and impact of Usenet and the Internet*. Los Alamitos, CA: IEEE Computer Society.

Hawisher, G., & Selfe, C. (2000). Introduction: Testing the claims. In G. E. Hawisher & C. L. Selfe (Eds.), *Global literacies and the World-Wide Web* (pp. 1–18). New York: Routledge.

Haynes, C., & Holmevik, J. R. (Eds). (1997). *High wired: On the design, use, and theory of educational MOOs*. Ann Arbor, MI: University of Michigan Press.

Herman, A., & Swiss, T. (Eds.). (2000). *The World Wide Web and contemporary cultural theory*. New York: Routledge.

Herring, S. C. (1993). Gender and democracy in computer-mediated communication. *Electronic Journal of Communication, 3* (2). Retrieved June 15, 2001, from the World Wide Web: http://www.cios.org/www/ejc/v3n293.htm

Herring, S. C. (1994). Politeness in computer culture: Why women thank and men flame. In M. Bucholtz, A. Liang, L. Sutton, & C. Hines (Eds.), *Cultural performances: Proceedings of the Third Berkeley Women and Language Conference* (pp. 278–94). Berkeley, CA: Berkeley Women and Language Group.

Herring, S. C. (1996a). Posting in a different voice: Gender and ethics in computer-mediated communication. In C. Ess (Ed.), *Philosophical perspectives on computer-mediated communication* (pp. 115–145). Albany, NY: SUNY Press.

Herring, S. C. (1996b). Two variants of an electronic message schema. In S. Herring (Ed.), *Computer-mediated communication: Linguistic, social and cross-cultural perspectives* (pp. 81–106). Amsterdam: John Benjamins.

Herring, S. C. (1996c). Linguistic and critical research on computer-mediated communication: Some ethical and scholarly considerations. *The Information Society, 12*(2), 153–168.

Herring, S. C. (1998a). Le style du courrier électronique: variabilité et changement. *Terminogramme, 84–85,* 9–16.

Herring, S. C. (1998b, September 25). *Virtual gender performances.* Talk presented to Discourse Studies Program, Texas A&M University, College Station.

Herring, S. C. (1999a). Interactional coherence in CMC. *Journal of Computer-Mediated Communication, 4*(4). Retrieved June 15, 2001, from the World Wide Web: http://www.ascusc.org/jcmc/vol4/issue4

Herring, S. C. (1999b). The rhetorical dynamics of gender harassment on-line. *The Information Society, 15*(3), 151–167.

Herring, S. C. (in press a). Computer-mediated discourse. In D. Tannen, D. Schiffrin, & H. Hamilton (Eds.), *Handbook of discourse analysis.* Oxford: Blackwell.

Herring, S. C. (in press b). Gender and power in online communication. In J. Holmes & M. Meyerhoff (Eds.), *Handbook of language and gender.* Oxford: Blackwell.

Herring, S. C. (forthcoming). Who's got the floor in computer-mediated conversation? Edelsky's gender patterns revisited. In S. Herring (Ed.), *Computer-mediated conversation.*

Herring, S. C., Johnson, D. A., & DiBenedetto, T. (1992). Participation in electronic discourse in a "feminist" field. In K. Hall, M. Bucholtz, & B. Moonwomon (Eds.), *Locating power: The Proceedings of the Second Berkeley Women and Language Conference* (pp. 250–262). Berkeley, CA: Berkeley Women and Language Group.

Herring, S. C., Johnson, D. A., & DiBenedetto, T. (1995). "This discussion is going too far!" Male resistance to female participation on the Internet. In M. Bucholtz & K. Hall (Eds.), *Gender articulated: Language and the socially constructed self* (pp. 67–96). London: Routledge.

Herring, S. C., & Nix, C. G. (1997, March). *Is "serious chat" an oxymoron? Academic vs. social uses of Internet Relay Chat.* Paper presented at the meeting of the American Association of Applied Linguistics, Orlando, FL.

Hert, P. (1997). Social dynamics of an on-line scholarly debate. *The Information Society, 13,* 329–360.

Hill, J., Ozer, J., & Mace, T. (1996, October 8). Real-time communication. *PC Magazine, 15* (17). Retrieved June 15, 2001, from the World Wide Web: http://www.zdnet.com/pcmag/issues/1517/pcmg0023.htm

Hiltz, R. S., & Turoff, M. (1978). *The network nation: Human communication via computer.* New York: Addison-Wesley.

Hodsdon, C. B. (forthcoming). Conversations within conversations: Intertextuality in racially antagonistic dialogue on Usenet. In S. Herring (Ed.), *Computer-mediated conversation.*

Hoffman, D. L., Kalsbeek, W. D., & Novak, T. P. (1996). Internet and Web use in the U.S. *Communications of the ACM, 39* (12), 36–46.

Hoffman, D. L., & Novak, T. P. (1995). *Marketing in hypermedia computer-mediated environments: Conceptual foundations.* Retrieved June 15, 2001, from the World Wide Web: http://www2000.ogsm.vanderbilt.edu/cmepaper.revision.july11.1995/cmepaper.html

Hongladarom, S. (2001). Global culture, local cultures, and the Internet: The Thai example. In C. Ess (Ed.), *Culture, technology, communication: Towards an intercultural global village* (pp. 307–324). Albany, NY: SUNY Press.

Jackson, M. (1997). Assessing the structure of communication on the World Wide Web. *Journal of Computer-Mediated Communication, 3* (1). Retrieved June 15, 2001, from the World Wide Web: http:www.ascusc.org/jcmc/vol3/issue1/jackson.html

Jacobs-Huey, L. (forthcoming). ...BTW, how do YOU wear your hair? Identity, knowledge and authority in an electronic speech community. In S. Herring (Ed.), *Computer-mediated conversation.*

Jacobson, D. (1996). Contexts and cues in cyberspace: The pragmatics of naming in text-based virtual realities. *Journal of Anthropological Research, 52,* 461–481.

Jones, J. (2000, April 28). A brief history of wireless. *ZDNet.* Retrieved June 15, 2001, from the World Wide Web: http://icq.zdnet.com/special/stories/wireless/0,10676,2557092,00.html

Jones, Q., & Rafaeli, S. (2000). What do virtual "tells" tell? Placing cybersociety research into a hierarchy of social explanation. *Proceedings of the 33rd Hawaii International Conference on System Sciences.* Retrieved June 15, 2001 from the World Wide Web: http://dlib.computer.org/conferen/hicss/0493/pdf/04931011.pdf

Jones, S. (1995). Understanding community in the information age. In S. Jones (Ed.), *Cybersociety: Computer-mediated communication and community* (pp. 10–35). Thousand Oaks, CA: Sage.

Jones, S. (Ed.). (1999). *Doing Internet research: Critical issues and methods for examining the net.* Thousand Oaks, CA: Sage.

Kendall, L. (1996). MUDder? I hardly know 'er! Adventures of a feminist MUDder. In L. Cherny & E. R. Weise (Eds.), *Wired_women: Gender and new realities in cyberspace* (pp. 207–223). Seattle, WA: Seal Press.

Kerr, D. M. (2000, September 6). Statement for the record of Donald M. Kerr, Assistant Director, Laboratory Division, Federal Bureau of Investigation on Carnivore diagnostic tool. Retrieved June 15, 2001 from the World Wide Web: http://www.fbi.gov/congress/congress00/kerr090600.htm

Kiesler, S., Siegel, J., & McGuire, T. W. (1984). Social psychological aspects of computer-mediated communication. *American Psychologist, 39,* 1123–1134.

Kiesler, S., Zubrow, D., Moses, A. M., & Geller, V. (1985). Affect in computer-mediated communication: An experiment in synchronous terminal-to-terminal discussion. *Human Computer Interaction, 1,* 77–104.

Kim, M-S., & Raja, N. S. (1990). Verbal aggression and self-disclosure on computer bulletin boards. Washington, DC: ERIC Clearinghouse on Languages and Linguistics. (ERIC Document No. ED334620).

King, S. (1996a). Is the Internet addictive, or are addicts using the Internet? Retrieved June 15, 2001, from the World Wide Web: http://www.concentric.net/~Astorm/iad.html

King, S. (1996b). Researching Internet communities: Proposed ethical guidelines for the reporting of results. *The Information Society, 12,* 119–127.

King, S. (1999). Internet gambling and pornography: Illustrative examples of the psychological consequences of communication anarchy. *CyberPsychology & Behavior, 2* (3), 175–193.

King, S., & Moreggi, D. (1998). Internet therapy and self-help groups—The pros and cons. In J. Gackenbach (Ed.), *Psychology and the Internet* (pp. 77–109). London: Academic.

Knudson, J. (1998). Rebellion in Chiapas: Insurrection by Internet and public relations. *Media, Culture, and Society, 20,* 507–518.

Ko, K.-K. (1996). Structural characteristics of computer-mediated language: A comparative analysis of InterChange discourse. *Electronic Journal of Communication, 6*(3). Retrieved June 15, 2001, from the World Wide Web: http://www.cios.org/www/ejc/v6n396.htm

Kolbert, E. (2001, May 28). Pimps and dragons: How an online world survived a social breakdown. *The New Yorker, 77*(13), 88–98.

Kolko, B. (1995). Building a world with words: The narrative reality of virtual communities. *Works and Days, 13*(1/2), 105–126. Retrieved June 15, 2001, from the World Wide Web: http://acorn.grove.iup.edu/en/workdays/toc.html

Kolko, B., & Reid, E. (1998). Dissolution and fragmentation: Problems in online communities. In S. Jones (Ed.), *Cybersociety 2.0: Revisiting computer mediated communication and community* (pp. 212–229). Thousand Oaks, CA: Sage.

Korenman, J., & Wyatt, N. (1996). Group dynamics in an e-mail forum. In S. Herring (Ed.), *Computer-mediated communication: Linguistic, social and cross-cultural perspectives* (pp. 225–242). Amsterdam: John Benjamins.

Kramarae, C., & Taylor, H. J. (1993). Women and men on electronic networks: A conversation or a monologue? In H. J. Taylor, C. Kramarae, & M. Ebben (Eds.), *Women, information technology, and scholarship* (pp. 52-61). Urbana, IL: Center for Advanced Study.

Kraut, R., Patterson, M., Lundmark, V., Kiesler, S., Mukhopadhyay, T., & Scherlis, W. (1998). Internet paradox: A social technology that reduces social involvement and psychological well-being. *American Psychologist, 53,* 1017–1031.

Kraut, R., Scherlis, W., Mukhopadhyaya, T., Manning, J., & Kiesler, S. (1996). The HomeNet field trial of residential Internet services. *Communications of the ACM, 39* (12), 55–63.

Krikorian, D., Lee, J.-S., Chock, T. M., & Harms, C. (2000). Isn't that spatial? Distance and communication in a 2-D virtual environment. *Journal of Computer-Mediated Communication, 5*(4). Retrieved June 15, 2001, from the World Wide Web: http://www.ascusc.org/jcmc/vol5/issue4/krikorian.html

Lambiase, J. J. (forthcoming). Hanging by a thread: Topic development and death in an electronic discussion of the Oklahoma City bombing. In S. Herring (Ed.), *Computer-mediated conversation.*

Lax, S. (2000). The Internet and democracy. In D. Gauntlett (Ed.), *Web.studies: Rewiring media studies for the digital age* (pp.159–169). London: Arnold.

Lea, M., O'Shea, T., Fung, P., & Spears, R. (1992). "Flaming" in computer-mediated communication: Observations, explanations, implications. In M. Lea (Ed.), *Contexts of computer-mediated communication* (pp. 89-112). New York: Harvester Wheatsheaf.

Lea, M., & Spears, R. (1995). Love at first byte? Building personal relationships over computer networks. In J. T. Wood & S. Duck (Eds.), *Understudied relationships: Off the beaten track* (pp. 197-233). Thousand Oaks, CA: Sage.

Leiner, B. M., Cerf, V. G., Clark, D. D., Kahn, R. E., Kleinrock, L., Lynch, D. C., Postel. J., Roberts, L. G., & Wolff, S. S. (1997). The past and future history of the Internet. *Communications of the ACM, 40* (2), 102–108.

Levien, R. (2000). Advogato's trust metric. Retrieved June 15, 2001, from the World Wide Web: http://www.advogato.org/trust-metric.html

Licklider, J. C. R., Taylor, R. W., & Herbert, E. (1968). The computer as a communication device. *Science and Technology, 76,* 21–31.

Liu, G. Z. (1999). Virtual community presence in Internet Relay Chatting. *Journal of Computer-Mediated Communication, 5*(1). Retrieved June 15, 2001, from the World Wide Web: http://www.ascusc.org/jcmc/vol5/issue1/liu.html

Livia, A. (forthcoming). BSR ES TU F? Brevity and expressivity on the French Minitel. In S. Herring (Ed.), *Computer-mediated conversation.*

Lombard, M., & Ditton, T. (1997). At the heart of it all: The concept of presence. *Journal of Computer-Mediated Communication, 3*(2). Retrieved June 15, 2001, from the World Wide Web: http://www.ascusc.org/jcmc/vol3/issue2/lombard.html

Lynch, C. A. & Preston, C. M. (1990). Internet access to information resources. *Annual Review of Information Science and Technology, 25,* 263–312.

Mabrey, E. A. (1997). Frames and flames: The structure of argumentative messages on the net. In S. Rafaeli, F. Sudweeks, & M. McLaughlin (Eds.), *Network and netplay: Virtual groups on the Internet* (pp. 13–26). Cambridge, MA: AAAI/MIT Press.

MacKinnon, R. C. (1995). Searching for the Leviathan in Usenet. In S. Jones (Ed.), *Cybersociety: Computer-mediated communication and community* (pp. 112–137). Thousand Oaks, CA: Sage.

Mallapragada, M. (2000). The Indian diaspora in the USA and around the Web. In D. Gauntlett (Ed.), *Web.studies: Rewiring media studies for the digital age* (pp. 179–185). London: Arnold.

Mann, C., & Stewart, F. (2000). *Internet communication and qualitative research: A handbook for researching online.* Thousand Oaks, CA: Sage.

Marvin, L.-E. (1995). Spoof, spam and lag. *Journal of Computer-Mediated Communication, 1* (2). Retrieved June 15, 2001, from the World Wide Web: http://www.ascusc.org/jcmc/vol1/issue2 /marvin.html

Mattelart, A. (1996, October). Les enjeux de la globalisation des réseaux. *Internet: L'extase et l'effroi* [special issue of *Le Monde Diplomatique*], 10–14.

Mauz. (2000). Mauz's Active Worlds pages: History. Retrieved June 15, 2001, from the World Wide Web: http://tnic.com/mauz/awhistory.html

McChesney, R. (2000). So much for the magic of technology and the free market: The World Wide Web and the corporate media system. In A. Herman & T. Swiss (Eds.), *The World Wide Web and contemporary cultural theory* (pp. 5–35). New York: Routledge.

McClellan, J. (1996). Alpha World: Police pages. Retrieved June 15, 2001, from the World Wide Web: http://binky.paragon.co.uk/it/issue19/Alpha/Alpha.html

McGrath, J. E. (1990). Time matters in groups. In J. Galegher, R. E. Kraut, & C. Egido (Eds.), *Intellectual teamwork: Social and technical foundations of cooperative work* (pp. 23–61). Hillsdale, NJ: Lawrence Erlbaum.

McLaughlin, M. L., Osborne, K. K., & Smith, C. B. (1995). Standards of conduct on Usenet. In S. Jones (Ed.), *Cybersociety: Computer-mediated communication and community* (pp. 90–111). Thousand Oaks, CA: Sage.

McRae, S. (1996). Coming apart at the seams: Sex, text and the virtual body. In L. Cherny & E. Weise (Eds.), *Wired_women: Gender and new realities in cyberspace* (pp. 242–263). Seattle: Seal Press.

Meeks, B. (1999). The privacy hoax. *Communications of the ACM, 42*(2), 17–19.

Meloan, S. (1995). CU-SeeMe. *Urban Desires, 1.6.* Retrieved June 15, 2001, from the World Wide Web: http://desires.com/1.6/Toys/Cuseeme/cuseeme.html

Millen, D. (2000). Community portals and collective goods: Conversation archives as an information resource. *Proceedings of the 33rd Hawaii International Conference on System Sciences.* Retrieved June 15, 2001 from the World Wide Web: http://dlib.computer.org/conferen/hicss/0493/pdf/04933030.pdf

Mitra, A., & Cohen, E. (1999). Analyzing the Web: Directions and challenges. In S. Jones (Ed.), *Doing Internet research: Critical issues and methods for examining the net* (pp. 179–202). Thousand Oaks, CA: Sage.

Murray, D. E. (1988). The context of oral and written language: A framework for mode and medium switching. *Language in Society, 17,* 351–373.

Murray, D. E. (1990). CmC. *English Today, 23,* 42–46.

Naper, I. (2001). System features of an inhabited 3D virtual environment supporting multimodality in communication. *Proceedings of the 34th Hawaii International Conference on System Sciences.* Retrieved June 15, 2001 from the World Wide Web: http://www.hic.ss.hawaii.edu/HICSS_34/PDFs/ DDPTC10.pdf

Neal, L. (1997). *Virtual classrooms and communities.* Paper presented at the Group'97 Conference of the Association for Computing Machinery. Phoenix, AZ. Retrieved June 15, 2001, from the World Wide Web: http://www3.ncsu. edu/dox/NBE/neal/nealtitle.htm

Nelson, T. (1967). Getting it out of our system. In G. Schechter (Ed.), *Information retrieval: A critical review.* Washington, DC: Thompson Books.

Nonnecke, B., & Preece, J. (2000). Persistence and lurkers in discussion lists: A pilot study. *Proceedings of the 33rd Hawaii International Conference on System Sciences.* Retrieved June 15, 2001 from the World Wide Web: http://dlib.computer.org/conferen/hicss/0493/pdf/04933031.pdf

Nunberg, G. (2000). Will the Internet always speak English? *The American Prospect, 11*(10). Retrieved June 15, 2001, from the World Wide Web: http://www.prospect.org/print/V11/10/nunberg-g.html

Ogan, C. (1993). Listserver communication during the Gulf War: What kind of medium is the electronic bulletin board? *Journal of Broadcasting and Electronic Media, 37,* 177–196.

Olson, J. S., & Olson, G. M. (2000). i2i trust in e-commerce. *Communications of the ACM, 43* (12), 41–44.

O'Sullivan, P. B. (1999). "Personal broadcasting:" Theoretical implications of the Web. Retrieved June 15, 2001, from the World Wide Web: http://www.ilstu. edu/~posull/PersBroad.htm

Paolillo, J. C. (1996). Language choice on soc.culture.punjab. *Electronic Journal of Communication, 6*(3). Retrieved June 15, 2001, from the World Wide Web: http://www.cios.org/www/ejc/v6n396.htm

Paolillo, J. C. (2000). Visualizing Usenet: A factor-analytic approach. *Proceedings of the 33rd Hawaii International Conference on System Sciences.* Retrieved June 15, 2001 from the World Wide Web: http://dlib.computer.org/conferen/ hicss/0493/pdf/04933033.pdf

Paolillo, J. C. (2001). Language variation on Internet Relay Chat: A social network approach. *Journal of Sociolinguistics, 5*(2), 180–213.

Parks, M., & Floyd, K. (1996). Making friends in cyberspace. *Journal of Communication, 46*(1), 80–97.

Pastore, M. (2000, May 12). Women use Web to change social landscape. *CyberAtlas.* Retrieved June 15, 2001, from the World Wide Web: http:// cyberatlas.internet.com/big_picture/demographics.html

Perrole, J. A. (1991). Conversations and trust in computer interfaces. In C. Dunlop & R. Kling (Eds.), *Computerization and controversy* (pp. 350–363). Boston: Academic Press.

Perry, M. J., Fruchter, R., & Spinelli, G. (2001). Spaces, traces and networked design. *Proceedings of the 34th Hawaii International Conference on System Sciences.* Retrieved June 15, 2001 from the World Wide Web: http://www.hic. ss.hawaii.edu/HICSS_34/PDFs/DDPTC08.pdf

Petrazzini, B., & Kibati, M. (1999). The Internet in developing countries. *Communications of the ACM, 42*(6), 31–36.

Pew Internet and American Life Project. (2000). Trust and privacy online: Why Americans want to rewrite the rules. Retrieved June 15, 2001, from the World Wide Web: http://www.pewinternet.org/reports/toc.asp?Report=19

Pfaffenberger, B. (1996). "If I want it, it's OK:" Usenet and the (outer) limits of free speech. *The Information Society, 12,* 365–386.

Pioch, N. (1997). A short IRC primer. Retrieved June 15, 2001, from the World Wide Web: http://www.irchelp.org/irchelp/ircprimer.html

Preece, J. (2000). *Online communities: Designing usability, supporting sociability*. Chichester, U.K.: John Wiley.

Pullen, K. (2000). I-love-Xena.com: Creating on-line fan communities. In D. Gauntlett (Ed.), *Web.studies: Rewiring media studies for the digital age* (pp. 52–61). London: Arnold.

Rafaeli, S., & Sudweeks, F. (1997). Networked interactivity. *Journal of Computer-Mediated Communication, 2*(4). Retrieved June 15, 2001, from the World Wide Web: http://www.ascusc.org/jcmc/vol2/issue4

Reid, E. M. (1991). *Electropolis: Communication and community on Internet Relay Chat*. Unpublished senior honours thesis, University of Melbourne, Australia. Retrieved June 15, 2001, from the World Wide Web: http://www.crosswinds.net/~aluluei/electropolis.htm

Reid, E. M. (1994). *Cultural formations in text-based virtual realities*. Unpublished master's thesis, University of Melbourne, Australia. Retrieved June 15, 2001, from the World Wide Web: http://home.earthlink.net/~aluluei/cult-form.htm

Reid, E. M. (1998). Hierarchy and power: Social control in cyberspace. In M. Smith & P. Kollock (Eds.), *Communities in cyberspace* (pp. 107–133). London: Routledge.

Rheingold, H. (1993). *The virtual community: Homesteading on the electronic frontier*. Reading, MA: Addison-Wesley. Retrieved June 15, 2001, from the World Wide Web: http://www.rheingold.com/vc/book

Rice, R. E. (1980). The impacts of computer-mediated organizational and interpersonal communication. *Annual Review of Information Science and Technology, 15,* 221–250.

Rice, R. E., & Gattiker, U. E. (2000). New media and organizational structuring. In F. Jablin & L. Putnam (Eds.), *The new handbook of organizational communication* (pp. 544–581). Thousand Oaks, CA: Sage.

Rice, R. E., & Love, G. (1987). Electronic emotion: Socioemotional content in a computer-mediated network. *Communication Research, 14,* 85–108.

Rickert, A., & Sacharow, A. (2000). *It's a woman's World Wide Web*. Media Metrix and Jupiter Communications report. Retrieved June 15, 2001, from the World Wide Web: http://www.mediametrix.com/data/MMXI-JUP-WWWW.pdf

Rivera, K., Cooke, N. J., & Bauhs, J. A. (1996). The effects of emotional icons on remote communication. *Human Factors in Computing Systems: CHI '96 Conference Proceedings*. Retrieved June 15, 2001, from the World Wide Web:

http://www.uni-paderborn.de/StaffWeb/chi96/E1Pub/WWW/chi96www/intpost/ Rivera/rk_txt.htm

Robertson, G. G., Card, S. K., & Mackinlay, J. D. (1993). Nonimmersive virtual reality. *Computer, 26,* 81–83.

Rodino, M. (1997). Breaking out of binaries: Reconceptualizing gender and its relationship to language in computer-mediated communication. *Journal of Computer-Mediated Communication, 3*(3). Retrieved June 15, 2001, from the World Wide Web: http://www.ascusc.org/jcmc/vol3/issue3/rodino.html

Rowe, C. (forthcoming). Genesis and evolution of an e-mail driven sibling code. In S. Herring (Ed.), *Computer-mediated conversation.*

Sack, W. (2000). Discourse diagrams: Interface design for very large-scale conversations. *Proceedings of the 33rd Hawaii International Conference on System Sciences.* Retrieved June 15, 2001 from the World Wide Web: http://dlib.computer.org/conferen/hicss/0493/pdf/04933034.pdf

Salus, P. (1995). *Casting the net: From ARPANET to Internet and beyond.* Reading, MA: Addison-Wesley.

Savicki, V., Lingenfelter, D., & Kelley, M. (1997). Gender language style and group composition in Internet discussion groups. *Journal of Computer-Mediated Communication, 2* (3). Retrieved June 15, 2001, from the World Wide Web: http://www.ascusc.org/jcmc/vol2/issue3

Scannell, B. (1999). Life on the border: Cyberspace and the frontier in historical perspective. Retrieved June 15, 2001, from the World Wide Web: http://www.kether.com/thesis/context.html

Scevak, N. (2001, April 27). Is wireless instant messaging the future of communication? *InternetNews.* Retrieved June 15, 2001, from the World Wide Web: http://www.internetnews.com/intl-news/article/0,,6_753901,00.html

Schlager, M. S., Fusco, J., & Schank, P. (in press). Evolution of an on-line education community of practice. In K. A. Renninger & W. Shumar (Eds.), *Building virtual communities: Learning and change in cyberspace.* New York: Cambridge University Press.

Schmid-Isler, S. (2000). The language of digital genres: A semiotic investigation of style and iconology on the World Wide Web. *Proceedings of the 33rd Hawaii International Conference on System Sciences.* Retrieved June 15, 2001 from the World Wide Web: http://dlib.computer.org/conferen/hicss/0493/pdf

Selfe, C. L., & Meyer, P. R. (1991). Testing claims for on-line conferences. *Written Communication, 8*(2), 163–192.

Severinson-Eklundh, K. (forthcoming). To quote or not to quote: Setting the context for computer-mediated dialogues. In S. Herring (Ed.), *Computer-mediated conversation.*

Severinson-Eklundh, K., & Macdonald, C. (1994). The use of quoting to preserve context in electronic mail dialogues. *IEEE Transactions on Professional Communication, 37*(4), 197–202.

Sharf, B. F. (1999). Beyond netiquette: the ethics of doing naturalistic discourse research on the Internet. In S. Jones (Ed.), *Doing Internet research: Critical issues and methods for examining the net* (pp. 243–256). Thousand Oaks, CA: Sage.

Short, J., Williams, E., & Christie, B. (1976). *The social psychology of telecommunications*. London: Wiley.

Sierpe, E. (2000). Gender and technological practices in electronic discussion lists: An examination of JESSE, the library/information science education forum. *Library & Information Science Research, 22*, 273–289.

Silberman, S. (2000). Talking to strangers. *Wired 8.05*. Retrieved June 15, 2001, from the World Wide Web: http://www.wired.com/wired/archive/8.05/translation.html?11=1&topic

Sloan, B. (1997, February). Using CUSeeMe to keep in touch: A glimpse into the future for remote communication in the built environment. *Habitat, 3*. Retrieved June 15, 2001, from the World Wide Web: http://ctiweb.cf.ac.uk/HABITAT/HABITAT3/cuseeme.html

Smit, C. R. (2000). Fascination: The modern allure of the Internet. In D. Gauntlett (Ed.), *Web.studies: Rewiring media studies for the digital age* (pp. 130–136). London: Arnold.

Smith, M. A. (1999). Invisible crowds in cyberspace: Mapping the social structure of Usenet. In M. Smith & P. Kollock (Eds.), *Communities in cyberspace*. London: Routledge.

Soukup, C. (1999). The gendered interactional patterns of computer-mediated chatrooms: A critical ethnographic study. *The Information Society, 15*, 169–176.

Soukup, C. (2000). Building a theory of multi-media CMC. *New Media & Society, 2*, 407–425.

Spears, R., & Lea, M. (1992). Social influence and the influence of the "social" in computer-mediated communication. In M. Lea (Ed.), *Contexts of computer-mediated communication* (pp. 30–65). London: Harvester Wheatsheaf.

Spertus, E. (1996). Social and technical means for fighting online harassment. Retrieved June 15, 2001, from the World Wide Web: http://www.ai.mit.edu/people/ellens/Gender/gk

Spertus, E. (1997). Smokey: Automatic recognition of hostile messages. *Proceedings of the Ninth Innovative Applications of Artificial Intelligence Conference*. Retrieved June 15, 2001, from the World Wide Web: http://www.ai.mit.edu/people/ellens/smokey.ps

Sproull, L., & Kiesler, S. (1986). Reducing social context cues: Electronic mail in organizational communication. *Management Science, 32*, 1492–1512.

Sproull, L., & Kiesler, S. (1991). *Connections: New ways of working in the networked organization*. Cambridge, MA: MIT Press.

Steinfield, C. W. (1986). Computer-mediated communication systems. *Annual Review of Information Science and Technology, 21*, 167–202.

Steinhardt, S. (n.d.). An interview with Dave Gobel, chairman and founder of Worlds Inc. *Online Magazine*. Retrieved June 15, 2001, from the World Wide Web: http://www.online-magazine.com/gobel1.htm

Stoll, C. (1995). *Silicon snake oil: Second thoughts on the information highway.* New York: Doubleday.

Stubbs, P. (1998). Conflict and cooperation in the virtual community: E-mail and the wars of the Yugoslav succession. *Sociological Research Online, 3*(3). Retrieved June 15, 2001, from the World Wide Web: http://www.socresonline. org.uk/socresonline/3/3/7.html

Sudweeks, F., & Rafaeli, S. (1996). How do you get a hundred strangers to agree? Computer mediated communication and collaboration. In T. Harrison & T. Stephens (Eds.), *Computer networking and scholarly communication in the twenty-first-century university* (pp. 115–136). Albany, NY: SUNY Press.

Suler, J. (1996). *The Psychology of Cyberspace.* Retrieved June 15, 2001, from the World Wide Web: http://www.rider.edu/users/suler/psycyber/psycyber.html

Sutton, L. (1994). Using Usenet: Gender, power, and silence in electronic discourse. In S. Gahl, A. Dolbey, & C. Johnson (Eds.), *Proceedings of the 20th Annual Meeting of the Berkeley Linguistics Society* (pp. 506–520). Berkeley, CA: Berkeley Linguistics Society.

Turkle, S. (1988). Computational reticence: Why women fear the intimate machine. In C. Kramarae (Ed.), *Technology and women's voices: Keeping in touch* (pp. 41–61). London: Routledge & Kegan Paul.

Turkle, S. (1995). *Life on the screen: Identity in the age of the Internet.* New York: Simon & Schuster.

van Gelder, L. (1990). The strange case of the electronic lover. In G. Gumpert & S. L. Fish (Eds.), *Talking to strangers: Mediated therapeutic communication* (pp. 128–142). Norwood, NJ: Ablex.

Vilhjálmsson, H. H. (1997). *Autonomous communicative behaviors in avatars.* Unpublished master's thesis, Massachusetts Institute of Technology, Cambridge. Retrieved June 15, 2001, from the World Wide Web: http://hannes.www.media.edu/people/hannes/msthesis /a_interface.html

Virnoche, M., & Marx, G. (1997). "Only connect"—E.M. Forster in an age of electronic communication: Computer-mediated association and community networks. *Sociological Inquiry, 67,* 85–100.

Wakeford, N. (2000). New media, new methodologies: Studying the Web. In D. Gauntlett (Ed.), *Web.studies: Rewiring media studies for the digital age* (pp. 31–41). London: Arnold.

Walther, J. (1996). Computer-mediated communication: Impersonal, interpersonal and hyperpersonal interaction. *Communication Research, 23*(1), 3–43

Walther, J. (1999). Visual cues and computer-mediated communication: Don't look before you leap. Retrieved June 15, 2001, from the World Wide Web: http://www.rensselaer.edu/~walthj/ica99.html

Weber, H. L. (forthcoming). Missed cues: How disputes can socialize virtual newcomers. In S. Herring (Ed.), *Computer-mediated conversation.*

Wellman, B. (1997). An electronic group is virtually a social network. In S. Kiesler (Ed.), *Culture of the Internet* (pp. 179–204). Mahwah, NJ: Lawrence Erlbaum.

Wellman, B., & Gulia, M. (1999). Net surfers don't ride alone: Virtual communities as communities. In M. Smith & P. Kollock (Eds.), *Communities in cyberspace* (pp. 167–194). London: Routledge.

Wellman, B., Salaff, J., Dimitrova, D., Garton, L., Gulia, M., & Haythornwaite, C. (1996). Computer networks as social networks: Collaborative work, telework and virtual community. *Annual Review of Sociology, 22,* 212–238.

Werry, C. C. (1996). Linguistic and interactional features of Internet Relay Chat. In S. Herring (Ed.), *Computer-mediated communication: Linguistic, social and cross-cultural perspectives* (pp. 47–63). Amsterdam: John Benjamins.

Wilkins, H. (1991). Computer talk: Long-distance conversations by computer. *Written Communication, 8*(1), 56–78.

Woodburn, R., Proctor, R., Arnott, J. L., & Newell, A. F. (1991). A study of conversational turn-taking in a communication aid for the disabled. *Proceedings of HCI 91: People and Computers, 4,* 359–371.

Yates, S. J. (1996). English in cyberspace. In S. Goodman & D. Graddol (Eds.), *Redesigning English: New texts, new identities* (pp. 106–140). London: Routledge.

Yates, S. J., & Graddol, D. (1996, July). "I read this chat is heavy:" The discursive construction of identity in CMC. Paper presented at the 5th International Pragmatics Conference, Mexico City.

Zastrow, J. (1999). ICQ for info pros. *Database, 22*(3), 36–38.

Zickmund, S. (1997). Approaching the radical other: The discursive culture of cyberhate. In S. Jones (Ed.), *Virtual culture: Identity and communication in cybersociety* (pp. 185–205). Thousand Oaks, CA: Sage.

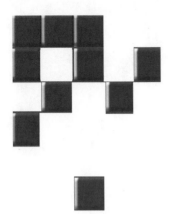

Knowledge Discovery

CHAPTER 4

Organizational Knowledge and Communities of Practice

Elisabeth Davenport
Hazel Hall
Napier University, Edinburgh

Introduction

A community of practice has recently been defined as "a flexible group of professionals, informally bound by common interests, who interact through interdependent tasks guided by a common purpose thereby embodying a store of common knowledge" (Jubert, 1999, p. 166). The association of communities of practice with the production of collective knowledge has long been recognized, and they have been objects of study for a number of decades in the context of professional communication, particularly communication in science (Abbott, 1988; Bazerman & Paradis, 1991). Recently, however, they have been invoked in the domain of organization studies as sites where people learn and share insights. If, as Stinchcombe suggests, an organization is "a set of stable social relations, deliberately created, with the explicit intention of continuously accomplishing some specific goals or purposes" (Stinchcombe, 1965, p. 142), where does this "flexible" and "embodied" source of knowledge fit? Can communities of practice be harnessed, engineered, and managed like other organizational groups, or does their strength lie in the fact that they operate outside the stable and persistent social relations that characterize the organization?

171

The current "state of the notion" reveals a number of tensions. Brown and Duguid (1993, p. 187) point out that "the community of practice is by no means necessarily harmonious, nor is it necessarily a face-to-face or contiguous grouping." The community of practice, as we understand it, denotes the level of the social world at which a particular practice is common and coordinated, at which generic understandings are created and shared, and negotiation is conducted. This is the locus at which it is possible to explore the social and physical context in which artifacts are used, to understand the roles objects play internally and across boundaries. If, as Bowker and Star (1999) suggest, the concepts that drive institutions are political products, we should not be surprised to find that communities of practice are described, defined, and justified in a number of different ways. For epistemologists, communities of practice are a means of exploring concepts of social or collective knowledge. For managers interested in performance, they offer an opportunity to derive templates or frameworks for the creation of organizational knowledge at a number of levels (the workgroup, the firm, the sector) in the interest of improved productivity. For designers, they provide case studies of interactions with artifacts and infrastructures in a range of off-line and online contexts.

Our review of the literature takes account of these different approaches in covering a number of topics: contributing domains; current (corporate) manifestations; motivations and infrastructures; tools for analyzing communities of practice; and analytic case studies.

Contributing Domains

We have identified three domains that contribute to current concepts of communities of practice. The first is studies of situated learning (and situated action). The second is studies of distributed cognition (or the interplay of people, artifacts, and context in problem solving at different levels). The third is communication studies, specifically a linguistic tradition that explores social networks by means of discourse analysis and conversation analysis (see, for example, Cohen & Sproull, 1996; Engeström & Middleton, 1997). In each of these domains, knowledge can be described as "corporate," that is, embodied in the work of the collective and expressed (implicitly or explicitly) in the interactions of participants who share tasks.

Situated Learning and Situated Action

We start our review of origins with "situated learning," as it provides examples of "primitives." By "primitives" we mean examples of practice in physical communities: midwives, butchers, flutemakers. We would contrast these with "complexes," that is, examples of practice in virtual worlds. Seminal texts by Lave (1988, 1991) and Lave and Wenger (1991) demonstrate that learning is grounded in context and artifacts, and that context, in most situations, is a community in which participants must learn how to handle the tasks and artifacts that are handed to them. This is achieved gradually, as a novice moves from a condition of peripheral participation to full membership. Educationists trying to model the classroom process (where learner and pedagogue seek to establish comparable understandings of each one's expectations of the other) have drawn heavily on Lave and Wenger's work. Fleming, for example, states that situated learning draws on the "ordinary, everyday, finely detailed methodic practices of participants to an activity in specific settings" (Fleming, 1994, p. 525). Learning, in this context, means being able to participate appropriately in the settings "where the subject or discipline is being done" (Fleming, 1994, p. 526). Fleming suggests that situated learning can be engineered by deconstructing the process through a number of analytic steps. The first is to identify how sequences of activities are assembled and constructed in the specific settings in which they are used ("structural anatomy"). The next step is to try to understand how methodic practices are used on a given occasion ("functional anatomy"). This step is followed by an exploration of how the "machinery" supports these activities and practices; by asking how descriptions, facts, and processes work together to produce what participants in the learning dialogue recognize as an explanation of the phenomenon in question. Gherardi, Nicolini, and Odella (1998) describe a "situated curriculum" for organizational learning based on Lave's work, taking construction site managers as a case in point.

Lave's work is cited as a major source of inspiration by Brown and Duguid (2000). In 1991, they themselves suggested that a "communities of practice" framework could account for organizational learning (Brown & Duguid, 1991). A number of micro-level empirical studies at Xerox PARC have demonstrated the importance of communities of practice as a locus of problem solving in ad hoc unforeseen contingencies where micro-level adaptations may lead to design modifications in company products. Chaiklin and Lave (1993, p. 14) describe this as "the skilled improvisations, organized in orderly ways, that are designed to maintain openness to the possibilities that the materials at hand present." The photocopier is the specific object of attention in seminal case studies of Xerox engineers (Orr, 1987, 1990) and office workers (Suchman, 1986). A number of different social interactions (dialogues and narrative exchange) that validate innovation at different levels of organization are brought into play in these scenarios, which are repeated at different levels of organization. Situated action has provided a useful theoretical framework for analyzing innovative micro-level responses to organizational blockages and breakdowns in other contexts, such as students offering each other peer assistance in libraries (Twidale & Nichols, 1996) or insurance firm help-desk operators handling novel procedural requests (Ackerman & Halverson, 1999). Typically such work is invisible. It is the "articulation" work that gets things done at the local level and allows managers to perceive the contours of the workplace as smoother than they are when examined in detail. There has been much discussion in the "organizational memory" literature of how such local innovations pervade the organization and how their authors achieve recognition (Gerson & Star, 1986, p. 258).

Brown and Duguid (1998, 2000) draw on Nonaka and Takeuchi's (1995) account (the SECI [Socialization, Externalization, Combination, and Internalization] model) of the interplay of tacit and explicit knowledge in communities of practice. Nonaka and Takeuchi use the term "ba" to describe a multivalent space, where social and individual, tacit and explicit knowledge contribute to emergent innovation. This model of knowledge creation draws its strength from the many parables and case studies (Nonaka 1991; Nonaka & Konno, 1998; Nonaka, Umemoto & Sasaki, 1998; von Krogh, Ichijo & Nonaka, 2000) that show how the concept of "ba" can guide and explain innovation.

Distributed Cognition

Lave's 1991 chapter "Situating learning in communities of practice" appeared in an edited volume by Resnick, Levine, and Teasley (1991), which brought together a number of strands of enquiry relevant to communities of practice. The same volume contains a paper by Hutchins, where he takes "tentative steps towards a framework for thinking about cognitive phenomena at the level of groups" (Hutchins, 1991, p. 305) by offering a formal model of "confirmation bias," the propensity to discount evidence that runs counter to an already formed interpretation. In several exemplary studies (e.g., Hutchins 1995a, 1995b, 1996; Hutchins & Klausen, 1997) of small close operating environments (a bridge of a ship; a cockpit), he presents both a methodology for and an explanation of distributed cognition, or the division of knowledge across people and artifacts as communal tasks are completed in an environment that is more or less familiar. Weick and Roberts (1993) offer a comparable account of flight deck "heedful interrelating." Similar observations can be found in the literature on cockpit resource management (e.g., Ginnett, 1993). Recent work in this area has been undertaken in the interests of designers. Wright, Pocock, and Fields (1988) have explored the information that pilots share when changing shifts and its implication for the design of automated cockpits. A number of studies have explored the use of paper strips in flight control rooms (e.g., Mackay, 1999) again in the context of proposed automation of the tasks that characterize this specialist community. In each of these cases, each member of the team understands an artifact in the light of the activities of those around him or her. Knowledge of how to proceed is cumulative: Each activity is validated by that which follows. Weick (1995, 1996) offers a rich account of how this happens in his account of the "substance" of organizational sense making.

Greenberg and Dickelman (2000, p. 18) offer an analytic review of studies of distributed cognition as a "foundation for performance support." Their interest is in "environments that enable people to complete work with a minimum of training or learning in advance of doing a task." They draw heavily on the work of Salomon (1993a, p. 19) to support their claim that "supporting performance on the job in a computer-mediated environment" fosters knowledge acquisition and "turns knowledge into action" more effectively than training in advance. They advocate a focus on activity analysis, with due attention paid to transformations in representation as tasks and outcomes migrate across different levels (Nardi, 1996). They cite Nardi's "person with tool" as an important unit of analysis. A specific example of distributed cognition in a community of practice is provided by Yanow and Cook (Cook & Yanow, 1993; Yanow, 2000), who describe the construction of flutes by a group of craftsmen. The artifact (the flute) emerges from a sequence of activities performed by specialist artisans, each of whom contributes unique expertise, which is only valuable as part of the collective process of construction. Each contribution is validated by the feel of the product as it passes from hand to hand. Cumulating knowledge is embedded in the product, which embodies the knowledge of the group. A more complicated community is discussed by Perry (1998), who has analyzed a group of civil engineers on a construction site using distributed cognition as an explanatory framework.

Discourse Analysis and Conversation Analysis

In each of these cases, knowledge emerges in a space where those involved—the interactors—are physically present, where tangible artifacts and human actors intersect, and where tacit knowledge is manifest in action. What about more complicated cases where there are multiple media in play (physical artifacts, documents that support their development, visual and audio recordings that mediate interaction) or where members of a community are dispersed? These are, of course, the conditions that characterize many professional communities, which may be distinguished from other communities of practice by their reliance on explicit knowledge as well as tacit knowledge: a corpus of cumulated experience which becomes, in itself, a key artifact in community activity (Kaufer & Carley, 1993). A comprehensive and carefully structured corpus is a useful scaffold for situated learners. In many cases, however, domain documentation cumulates in an ad hoc fashion, and finding one's way becomes an important component of apprenticeship. The paths that are used will reflect the practice of the domain community, as much as formal architectures (Bishop, 1999; Covi, 1999; Davenport & Cronin, 1998; Elliott & Kling, 1997; Erdelez & Doty, 1999).

What Covi (1999) calls "material mastery" is an important component of "professional capital," or "habitus," a concept explored by Bourdieu (1990) in his exploration of the "logic of practice." Lave (1988) paraphrases "habitus" as "meaning made body," as Bourdieu is making the claim that "much of the generative basis of practice is inscribed in the person in the form of dispositions" (Lave, 1988 p. 181). In many academic and professional communities, "dispositions" are shaped by texts, and apprenticeship or situated learning can be undertaken to a greater or lesser extent by cumulative insight into how to read the range of materials that support work in a given professional domain (Bazerman & Paradis, 1991). A number of studies have demonstrated that the making of a graduate involves a number of reading stages (Bhatia, 1994; Swales, 1990). In this way individuals learn how to behave as members of a professional group, and thus sustain and reproduce the knowledge of the collective. Emergent professional communities will struggle to have their codified, or explicit, knowledge accepted. In this context, the case of the nursing profession has been discussed in a number of fora; most fully by Bowker and Star (1999, pp. 229–254). In large collectives where members are remote from each other, matters of whom to trust arise, and different collectives have derived different mechanisms to handle these issues: regulation, audit, peer assessment, and recommender systems. Many of these mechanisms operate by means of established documentary and communicative genres. In the section that follows, we review studies of genres and communities of practice.

Genre Analysis

Historically, certain genres of documentation have been associated with the recurring activities that characterize communities of practice: process manuals, articles of association, contracts, the inventory, records of property transfers, and daybooks. Although such forms show local diversity, they are recognizable within epistemological trading zones (Berkenkotter, 1995) as performing or enacting similar functions; in other words, they function as codes of conduct. They are not totally fixed, however; as new habits emerge and are endorsed by a community of practice, they, in turn, become encoded, and join the repertoire of knowledge of how to behave. Where practice changes (as it does in cases where new technologies are introduced into an organization, which may trigger a community of practice), new genres are likely to emerge as practitioners adapt to new circumstances and establish fresh routines. In such cases, genres articulate tacit knowledge; acting as bridges between uncodified "walk-arounds" and codified knowledge; or in Brown and Duguid's terms (1998), "non-canonical" and "canonical" knowledge (also see Nonaka & Konno, 1998).

Much of our understanding of genres and their role in communities of practice is due to a body of work by Yates, Orlikowski, and their colleagues over the past decade. A broad definition of genres is offered in their groundbreaking paper (Yates & Orlikowski, 1992) in which they identify three characteristic elements: a recurrent situation, substance ("social motives ... themes ... topics"), and form (structural features, communication medium, and symbolism). Genres are enacted through rules, which associate appropriate elements of form and substance with certain recurrent situations. To engage with a genre is to "implicitly or explicitly draw on genre rules," and also to "reinforce and sustain the legitimacy of those rules" (Yates & Orlikowski, 1992, pp. 301–302). Genres exist at different levels of abstraction, and will be defined differently "in different cultures and at different times" (Yates & Orlikowsi, 1992, p. 303). What is interesting about genres is their dual status as (1) an articulation of what has emerged as appropriate behavior (their role as a categorizing device), and (2) as a prescription for activity in a community of practice (their role as a regulatory device). Genres are thus, say Yates and Orlikowski, structurational devices.

In subsequent work (Orlikowski & Yates, 1994; Yates, Orlikowski, & Rennecker, 1997), they develop the concept of a genre repertoire, which can account for interactive behavior in both off-line and online communities. A genre repertoire is "largely implicit, and rooted in members' prior experiences of working and interacting. Once established, a genre repertoire serves as a powerful social template for shaping how, why, and with what effort members of a community interact to get their work done" (Orlikowski & Yates, 1994, p. 541). Davenport (1999) draws on this work in micro studies of information and communication technologies in households, and of a small networked enterprise. She presents digital genres as instances of self-organizing social coding devices: as new habits emerge and are endorsed by a community of practice, they in turn become encoded, and join the repertoire of knowledge of how to behave (also see Davenport & Rosenbaum, 2000).

Brown and Duguid (1994) offer a rich review of genres and their role in communities of practice. Genres, they claim, are a fundamental feature of group cognition: People "read" an artifact against or in the context of its "type," and that is how they acquire an understanding of it. The "types" in these readings are "genres." They evolve locally and continually in practice, and are limited to particular organizations or institutions to the extent that "old-timers" can usually recognize organizational newcomers by their generic transgressions. Because genres are coupled with context, they carry many cues about the environment—the equivalent of a portable context. The social or communal context of genres is ignored at the designer's peril. Brown and Duguid cite the persistent failure of attempts to have the public adopt customized electronic newspapers as a case in point; none of these has offered the flexible affordance of the paper version. Because they are flexible and can evolve, genres are a highly appropriate form for the articulation of practice.

Conversational genres play as important a role in community formation as documentary genres, and studies of business genres have focused as much on the former as on the latter. (Bargiela-Chiappini & Nickerson, 1999; Boden, 1994; Loos, 1999). Genre can be an important component of framing (Tannen, 1995), or the setting up and fulfillment of expectations (in the case of Tannen's study, expectations about the storyline of a movie). Much business communication can be analyzed as a form of conversation, where knowledge of turn-taking, or appropriate response, is important (Goodwin, 1995). Conversation, defined broadly in this way, is a medium for organizational knowledge, as it is inherently collective or heteroglossic (it is not acceptable to talk to oneself), and it generates a social artifact (a contract, for example) that emerges as each participant in the practice takes part. Turn-taking is analogous to the passing of the baton or the sequential handling of an artifact that contributes to a collective outcome. In the case of conversation, this may be a completed transaction, or a negotiated solution to a problem. Learning how to handle conversation is an important part of participation in communities of practice, both online and off-line (Schlegoff, 1991). Erickson (1999) provides a pertinent case study of an online community that is learning to compose limericks, and we return to this topic in the section on online communities of practice.

Communities of Practice at Work

Discussions and case studies of communities of practice in the workplace fall into two classes: those written from a performative perspective and those written from an interpretive or constructivist perspective (Contu & Wilmott, 2000). The most complete recent account of communities of practice is provided by Wenger (1998, 2000a, 2000b; Wenger & Snyder, 2000), whose first engagement with the topic was as coauthor of the seminal interpretive text on situated learning (Lave & Wenger, 1991). Wenger's current work, however, has been criticized for its performative approach:

> We encounter an (unacknowledged) shift or slippage from an earlier representation of learning as praxis fashioned within a discourse of critique to a formulation of learning as technology conceived within a discourse of regulation and performance.
>
> (Contu & Wilmott, 2000, p. 272–273)

Fox (2000) criticizes Wenger's recent account of communities of practice for failure to address adequately issues of power in the workplace. In the section that follows, we review both approaches, starting with the performative perspective.

The Performative Perspective

Wenger's (1998, p. 4) monograph offers a comprehensive account of communities of practice. They are, he suggests, groups whose members are bound by their participation in a "valued enterprise," such as "singing in tune," "discovering scientific facts," or "fixing a machine." To participate competently in such an enterprise is to show knowledge of the area involved, and learning in a community of practice is the evolving ability to have meaningful experiences. An important component of this is community identity, which allows members of the group to share their personal histories and experiences of change. Identity, says

Wenger, allows communities to reflect on the complex relations that define them and it involves activities like categorization, association, and differentiation (Wenger, 1998, p. 13). The theme of identity is developed at length in a later chapter, "Modes of belonging" (Wenger, 1998, pp. 172–187). Wenger (1998, pp. 58–59) develops his theme in a sustained case study of an insurance claims office, and covers ground similar to that discussed in studies of distributed cognition, using the terms "reification" and "participation" to describe the "interplay" of humans and artifacts.

Communities of practice are distinguished from other groupings by mutual engagement, joint enterprise (that implies a regime of mutual accountability), a shared repertoire (that both articulates shared experience and records its history), and the emergence of meaning in practice. Wenger discusses the artifacts that constitute this repertoire at some length, and acknowledges the importance of genres in this context. He restricts his use of the term to traditional documentary sources, explaining in an endnote that he begs to differ from those who use the term to describe "anything that is both collective and tacit" (Wenger, 1998, p. 288). Communities of practice are ambivalent as, like any community, they are contained within boundaries, but their boundaries are areas where connections with others may be made. Wenger discusses what happens at the edges of community at length, and we review his comments in the section on infrastructure later in this chapter. He emphasizes that communities of practice are local phenomena, and offers a checklist of features that might allow an observer to say that a particular group was such a community (Wenger, 1998, pp. 122–123). But the "localness" of a community of practice must not result in isolation: "It is incumbent on a learning community to deal with its position in various communities and economies with respect to various enterprises, styles and discourses. It must seek the reconfigurations necessary to make its learning empowering locally and in other relevant contexts" (Wenger, 1998, p. 220).

In a subsequent article, Wenger and Snyder (2000) discuss the significance of the community of practice as an organizational form that is informal, driven by the desire to share expertise, sets its own agenda, finds its own "shape," and is sustained by the interest and passion of participants. Communities of practice are not goal driven (unlike teams and projects), nor are they necessarily deadline driven. Freedom from such constraints makes them, in some circumstances, environments that are more hospitable to sharing and synergy than conventional competing organizational subgroups. In the latter, commitment to knowledge sharing may be conditioned by existing institutional incentive schemes that may offer little or no obvious reward to those who are asked to participate in knowledge management initiatives. What communities of practice offer is a chance to span departmental or other legacy organizational boundaries, which may not allow insight to emerge when a functional unit runs into difficulties.

Wenger and Snyder (2000) support their case with a series of checklists that shows how communities of practice differ from other groups, and where they may have an impact on organizational performance. (A comparable "cookbook" approach is to be found in Dixon, 2000.) They offer "tips" on identifying potential candidates, and on the appropriate infrastructure to allow such groups to achieve community of practice status, supported with case studies of new technology development, fixing software bugs, and leveraging knowledge in a newly expanded organization. We revisit some of these later in the section on motivation. In a subsequent review of "Communities of practice and social learning systems" (Wenger, 2000b, p. 243), the checklist is extended into a series of tables that covers "community dimensions," "boundary dimensions," and "identity dimensions." Wenger concludes with a fractal model of community: "More generally, if a community is large, it is a good idea to structure it in layers, as a 'fractal' of embedded sub-communities.... With such a fractal structure, by belonging to your own sub-community, you experience in a local and direct way your belonging to a much broader community." He cites cases of groups in Shell Oil and DaimlerChrysler.

As we note above, Xerox has fostered the community of practice as an organizational form that has been a source of innovation for a number of years. The company has developed a distinctive philosophy and managerial approach heavily influenced by Nonaka's SECI model, which provides a framework to manage the oscillation and intertwining of tacit and explicit knowledge. As also noted above, Nonaka sees middle managers as the knowledge managers in any organization. A recent case study from Xerox (Storck & Hill, 2000) describes a community of practice that links middle managers from a number of functional groups working on innovative solutions to a specific long-term problem. Jubert's (1999) account of communities of practice in Siemens reveals a more formal arrangement, where, as in the case of Shell described by Wenger (2000a), managers select group members and foster participation on the basis of observations of prior competence. Hamel (2000), in contrast, in a study of a radical community of practice in IBM, describes what is almost an underground group, reminiscent of earlier descriptions of "skunkworks," or design groups who are given freedom to work outside established corporate structures.

Many of the perspectivist studies are uncritical, with a focus on "how to do it good," rather than on identifying what factors in communities of practice might work in what ways. Two exceptions to this trend within the performative, or managerialist, tradition are provided in the papers by Lam (2000) and the monograph by Baumard (1999), both of which deal overtly with the subject of tacit knowledge. The first is an ambitious attempt to place our understanding of both tacit and explicit knowledge in the context of micro- and macro-level institutionalism; critiquing the Western emphasis on explicit knowledge and its associated reward structures. The second offers sustained and detailed case studies of four very different organizations—Qantas, Indigo, Indosuez, Pechiney—demonstrating that the effects of participation in relevant communities of practice are highly specific to the domains involved.

The Interpretive Approach

The interpretive approach has its roots in design work, and several of the case studies that we reference below were undertaken as human-computer interaction (HCI) work. These studies aim to provide an explanation of communities of practice, rather than a template or blueprint for exploitation. Such work exploits a number of ethnographic methods and frameworks: activity theory, actor network theory, discourse, and conversation analysis. The first of these can provide a comprehensive account as it embraces concepts of activity, action, operations, community, artifact, and rules (Kuutti, 1996). Although there are studies at the level of the firm that use these methods to analyze the interactions of different internal communities (the accounts of Schlumberger by

Bowker [1994], and the Salk laboratory by Latour and Woolgar [1979]), we focus here on micro-level local studies. In some fields (engineering, journalism, high-energy physics), a portfolio of such work is emerging, which may provide an opportunity for deep and informative empirical analysis of communities of practice in these sectors. Such a corpus has emerged in the Danish National Research Laboratory, where a series of studies has explored multiple aspects of engineering practice (e.g., Hertzum & Pejtersen, 2000; Pejtersen & Albrechtsen, 2000). These draw heavily on the methods of cognitive systems engineering (Rasmussen, Pejtersen, & Goodstein, 1994, pp. 68–69), which emphasize detailed understanding of work domain activities by means of systematic means-ends analysis, focusing on "prototypical tasks, situations based on domain characteristics, and typical decision tasks."

A number of recent studies of engineering communities draws on distributed cognition, actor network theory, and activity theory. As we indicate earlier, Fox (2000) criticizes current thinking on communities of practice for failing to address adequately social dynamics; and suggests that actor network theory may allow a more realistic exploratory framework. An example of this political approach is provided by Suchman's (2000) account of the processes of alignment that allow diverse engineers (from different communities of practice) to work together to build a bridge. Activity theory offers a further analytic framework that is hospitable to political analysis. Blackler and his colleagues (Blackler, Crump, & McDonald, 1999, 2000) use the approach because it elicits inconsistencies, paradoxes, and tensions, which may offer opportunities for organizational learning. Engeström (2000) suggests that the framework is applied at too high a level in their study of organizational change in a high-tech manufacturing firm, and provides a reanalysis of the case focusing more specifically on the description of activities, tasks, and operations.

The journalism community has been analyzed in a number of ethnographic studies (e.g., Fabritius, 1998; Macaulay, 1999). Macaulay (1999), using activity theory and taking a national newspaper as her context, demonstrates that the "source" (a complex entity) is the unifying artifact in this community, where different colleagues must work together to validate the information that feeds into the creation of a news item. Baumard (1999) explores the case of the editor of a highly specialized newsletter that handles competitor intelligence, and shows how individual decision making both shapes and is shaped by the sources in the domain.

Motivation

Discussions of motivation to participate in communities of practice fall into two broad classes, underpinned respectively by a market philosophy (Sawyer, Eschenfelder, & Heckman, 2000) and a philosophy of care. Beer and Nohria (2000) make a comparable distinction between "e" (economic value) and "o" (organizational capability) worldviews. Those motivated by a market philosophy are likely to participate on the basis of a calculus of reciprocal benefit, described by some analysts in terms of game theory (Axelrod, 1997). Reciprocity may be direct, or indirect, where "acts of kindness are returned not by recipients, but by third parties" (Nowak & Sigmund, 2000, p. 819). This has been described as "image scoring" by Wedekind and Milinski (2000). Similar motivations have been described in analyses of situational trust in team formation; that is trust based on the assessment of risk involved in accepting the collaboration, the perceived benefit of the proposed exchange, the perceived competence of the partner, and the moral significance of the exchange (Lewicki & Bunker, 1996). How these may operate in the online world (and how they might be compressed) is an issue to be explored in the discussion of online communities of practice later in the chapter. It may be that computer agents will operate using such calculations. We can see such a calculus at work in a number of prescriptive studies of community formation.

Factors that motivate people to codify and share knowledge for the benefit of others have been identified as a priority area for knowledge research (Holsthouse, 1998, p. 277). Such research can respond to corporate goals identified by earlier studies of knowledge management and organizational learning. Cohen (1998, p. 27), for example, refers to 100 knowledge projects, most of which had as one of their three main aims that of developing "a knowledge-intensive culture by encouraging and aggregating behaviors such as knowledge sharing (as opposed to hoarding) and proactively seeking and offering knowledge." Since innovation driven by knowledge creation is achieved by groups, there is a "need to examine more closely both tacit knowing and creativity as they are expressed by members of groups—singly and collectively" (Leonard & Sensiper, 1998, p. 115).

Willingness to share anything usually depends on reciprocity. Nowak and Sigmund (2000) identify two types of reciprocity: (1) direct—two individuals associate long enough for each to play roles of receiver and giver of favors; (2) indirect—third parties donate favors without the expectation of a return from the receiver. Third party donors, while not anticipating immediate compensation for favors granted, tend to anticipate repayment at a later date in the form of a favor from another third party. There must be an exchange at some point, otherwise donors will withdraw their participation: They will not support free riders (Dyer & Nobeoka, 2000, p. 349).

Reward and Recognition as Factors in Motivation

Samitt (1999, p. 50) argues that "Knowledge management strategies need to be linked to people by building reward and recognition programs to encourage employees to share best practices, strategies, and ideas." Others support this view; for example:

> knowledge management initiatives should incorporate effective change management focussed on ... the "What's in it for me?" question. You can't force people to learn or share precious knowledge. You have to motivate them, even seduce them, show them the importance and reward their sharing activities. Develop an appropriate reward system and incentive scheme to get the message across that knowledge and learning are crucial to the sustainability of the business.
>
> (van der Spek & Kingma, 2000, p. 27)

An organization might explicitly offer to repay individuals who engage in knowledge sharing activity in the form of a "hard" tangible benefit, such as enhanced pay. At the other end of the scale, employees are rewarded in more subtle ways, for example, in enjoying the personal satisfaction of holding membership in a thriving knowledge-sharing community. Since "knowledge can only be volunteered ... [and] cannot be conscripted" (Snowden, 2000, p. 9), individuals and teams decide whether any reward offered matches the value of knowledge sharing: "People's time and energy are limited and they will choose to do what they believe will give them a worthwhile return on those scarce resources" (Cohen, 1998, p. 31). Some rewards are more appropriate for individuals than for groups and vice versa. Those identified in the literature are outlined here. Though much of the literature focuses on individuals, there are some examples of incentives that are targeted at the building of community.

Economic Rewards

Perhaps the most obvious explicit reward systems are those that involve economic incentives such as increased pay or bonuses in the forms of cash or stock options. Beer and Nohria (2000), for example, demonstrate how straightforward economic incentives offered to individuals encouraged organizational change at Scott Paper in the 1990s. They state that "proponents of this system argue that financial incentives guarantee that employees' interests match stockholders' interests" (Beer & Nohria, 2000, p. 137).

Systems for awarding economic rewards for knowledge sharing are not necessarily tied to financial indicators such as increased revenue or stock values. Beer and Nohria (2000) highlight companies that work on commitment-based contracts with their employees. Such incentives might include a skills-based pay system and shared rewards in order to pull all workers into a shared community of purpose. The idea is that individuals are motivated through commitment, and pay is used as a fair exchange.

Access to Information and Knowledge as Reward: Social Capital

Another tangible reward of participating in knowledge-sharing ventures is access to the information and knowledge shared by the other partners, or the creation and management of social capital (Lesser & Prusak, 2000). There is "the expectation ... that one will get valuable knowledge in return for giving it ... you need to contribute knowledge to become part of the knowledge networks on which your success depends" (Cohen, 1998, p. 31). This is illustrated well in the case study of the motor parts manufacturers where "any production-related knowledge that Toyota or a supplier possesses (cost, quality, inventory management, etc.) is viewed as accessible to virtually any member of the network (with perhaps the exception of a direct competitor) because it is, in effect, the property of the network" (Dyer & Nobeoka, 2000, p. 358.) and "suppliers are motivated to participate because they quickly learn that participating in the collective learning processes is vastly superior to trying to isolate their proprietary knowledge" (Dyer & Nobeoka, 2000, p. 351). The price paid is a limited ability to protect proprietary production knowledge, which is deemed acceptable since "intellectual property rights reside at the network, rather than the firm, level" (Dyer & Nobeoka, 2000, p. 358). "Free riding" is prevented through established rules that forbid suppliers access to Toyota's knowledge until they explicitly agree to share their knowledge (Dyer & Nobeoka, 2000, p. 351).

Career Advancement/Security Rewards

Career advancement can be tied to various factors, including the extent to which individuals hoard or share their expertise. Von Krogh (1998) describes one scenario:

> When organizational members' futures with the company are dependent on the expertise they demonstrate, and not on the extent to which they actually help others, individuals will attempt to build up and defend their own hegemonies of knowledge ... In this competitive context, sharing more knowledge than necessary will lead to reduced power and influence. The individual will not be motivated to make his knowledge explicit or shareable unless there are clear transactions that would make this favorable. He will judge the knowledge sharing as a transaction, knowledge shared being based on expected returns.
>
> (von Krogh, 1998, p. 140)

It is argued, therefore, that career advancement should become an explicit reward for knowledge sharing. In providing this incentive to staff, firms reward an individual performance, as well as the act of helping other colleagues to perform well. This is already the case in a number of firms. For example, at McKinsey and Andersen Consulting (now Accenture), partnerships are awarded on the basis of votes cast to individuals by their colleagues, which in turn are dependent more on the degree to which individuals have cooperated in the workplace than on their ability to compete (Hargadon, 1998, p. 225).

The guarantee of future work also motivates people and organizations to operate in particular ways. For example, in the study of the inter-firm network of motor component suppliers membership of the supplier association for a number of firms was sought "primarily to demonstrate ... commitment to Toyota in the hopes that Toyota would reward them with more business" (Dyer & Nobeoka, 2000, p. 363).

Enhanced Reputation as Reward

Nowak and Sigmund (2000) explain that a human obsession with reputation and status lies behind an important "soft" reward for knowledge sharing—acknowledgment from our peers: "we feel cheated when our good deeds go unnoticed, and refrain from bad deeds lest they become known" (Nowak & Sigmund, 2000, p. 819). This is borne out in the literature. Hargadon (1998), for example, quotes an engineer at the design firm IDEO who describes the benefits of spreading about knowledge and skills as higher visibility and winning the reputation of being an attractive work colleague. Similarly, at Unilever, flattery worked when pulling staff together for project work: "the compliment of being invited to participate in ... workshops, and after that being involved in global strategic projects [on the basis of an established reputation], was perceived as immensely rewarding" (von Krogh, 1998, p. 147). Tiegland (2000, p. 173) describes a similar phenomenon in the context of a community of programmers: "programmers were under a form of social pressure from their external community to help fellow members solve their difficult problems, often attempting to 'show off' in front of the others." At times, high performance in the external community of practice jeopardized performance in the internal community of the workplace. If conditions do not protect reputation, for example, when injustices such as idea stealing are tolerated, people are more likely to "establish their hegemonies of knowledge and protect their turf" (von Krogh, 1998, p. 142); and knowledge sharing activity is diminished. Judge, Fryxell, and Dooley (2000) found that reputation is one of the most important factors in motivation in high performance corporate R & D environments.

Reputation building can be perceived as a long-term project. Individuals who recognize this are more likely to be knowledge sharers from the outset. This is illustrated in studies by Erdelez (2000) and Rioux (2000), who explore "shared encountering" of information for others. Some people simply gain pleasure as a result of demonstrating their own altruistic and prosocial behavior. Others enjoy seeing the positive results of their efforts:

> At McKinsey, the Rapid Response Team emerged to satisfy the need to maintain interactive problem solving by promising to link anyone facing a problem with others who might have useful, related knowledge—within 24 hours. They accomplished this feat by maintaining the human connection, and the individuals involved took pride in knowing who knew what in the organization and in their ability to find the right people to solve each problem.
>
> (Hargadon, 1998, p. 222)

Personal satisfaction, then, can motivate individuals to share their knowledge.

Creating Environments for Participation in Communities of Practice

Organizations can set up a range of incentives instead of, or in addition to, reward schemes to encourage knowledge sharing. These include making knowledge sharing part of the job of each individual within the firm, encouraging employees to work in groups as communities, allowing experimentation and risk taking in the workplace, and providing tools for these activities. Unlike the earlier examples, they do not rely on reciprocity. Aspects of each of these types of incentives are discussed below.

It is argued that knowledge sharing is more likely to be encouraged in employees who know that this is a requirement of their jobs (Davenport &

Klahr, 1998, p. 207). Von Krogh (1998, p. 144) suggests that there should be two sets of responsibilities for the individual: "the responsibility to acquire expertise; and the responsibility to make your help accessible to those who need it as your expertise grows." Where other incentives such as reward schemes are not in place, assigning specific responsibilities to particular individuals is more likely to encourage knowledge sharing than simply expecting people to make contributions as part of a general team effort. This was demonstrated at Citibank: "Citibank developed a technical marvel of a database but initially failed to create incentives for people to enter information into it. But when the company assigned employees the responsibility of finding and entering those practices, then they began to get entered" (O'Dell & Jackson Grayson, 1998, p. 164).

Time spent in working hours on knowledge sharing activity should be regarded as entirely legitimate (Davenport & Klahr, 1998, p. 207). Time should be set aside specifically for people to learn, share, and help one another: "unless capturing and sharing information are built into work processes, sharing will not happen" (O'Dell & Jackson Grayson, 1998, p. 157).

Knowledge sharing can be formalized into a key employee role through activities such as training and systematic project debriefings (von Krogh, 1998, p. 145). Leading by example can also have an impact: "managers should, on a modest level, review information behavior by addressing individuals and key groups, and senior executives need to concentrate on setting good examples of behavior" (Davenport, 1997, p. 101). Mentoring and assisting should be highly regarded, otherwise "rational people may be unlikely to surrender the power they gain from being an important knowledge source—especially since sharing tacit knowledge requires time devoted to personal contact" (Leonard & Sensiper, 1998, p. 123).

For those operating in communities, then, the incentives for knowledge sharing are less concrete than the output of the reward systems described earlier in this chapter. The incentives to share knowledge are identified as the carrot of the continued vitality of the community and relationships between partners, and the stick of obligation to other group members. Perhaps the most important incentives, however, are those that the participants would probably not even recognize as incentives, but rather as conditions that make knowledge transfer simple to achieve, i.e., the environment that supports social interaction among members. These incentives are examined in further detail below.

Participants understand that the viability of their community depends on their commitment to it. This is "embodied in the willingness of individuals to share information and knowledge with other members of the community" (Merali, 2000, p. 81). If no contributions are made, the results are drastic: The community will not live. However, each contribution to knowledge sharing increases not only common knowledge, but also the trust among community members. As trust increases, more participants become willing to share and so further contributions will be made. Dyer and Nobeoka (2000, p. 352) note that this mutual causality applies equally to group identity, "both a cause, and a consequence, of collective learning processes." Thus, a further incentive to contribute in a community is the expectation of stronger relationships with partners and access to higher quality knowledge in the future.

The debate in the literature as to how far a community should extend is pertinent to the question of vitality. In the case of online communities, it is argued that there must be controls on membership so that expertise is not diluted by those of marginal use to the community as a whole (Snowden, 2000, p. 13). However, those at the margins, such as lurkers on a listserv, can later become integrated into the main group, bringing fresh ideas: "People learn by taking a position on the periphery of skilled practice and being allowed ... to move slowly into the community and the practice involved" (Brown & Duguid, 1998, p. 107).

Communities vary in their ability to foster knowledge-sharing activity. Von Krogh (1998) identifies environments of "care" as being most conducive to knowledge sharing. Here, "the goal of learning shifts from obtaining 'maximum grip' to reaching 'maximum leverage' on others' knowledge ... [There is] a mutual intent to help others to optimize their task performance, and, therefore, to share knowledge" (von Krogh, 1998, p. 141). Individuals are less likely to regret "giving it away" when such an incentive exists.

Sometimes the disincentive of not sharing knowledge is stronger than any incentive offered to encourage sharing. In the community setting, each originator of high-quality knowledge recognizes the threshold at which it makes sense to publish. This is determined, to an extent, by peer pressure: "I codify at the point where the socialization pressure of the ecology forces me to volunteer my knowledge" (Snowden, 2000, p. 16). Community members who are meshed together in relationships of codependency reach this point sooner than those who have been grouped according to similar status and interest. Communities belonging to this second group "are more susceptible to rivalries that (sic) those of co-dependency and knowledge exchange is frequently inhibited as a result" (Snowden, 1998, p. 14).

In any environment, knowledge sharing depends upon social interaction. It is argued that the easier it is for individuals to interact, the more likely that interactions will take place. Ease of social interaction can be achieved by using these techniques:

- Clear rules on the operation of the community: For this reason the Toyota network publishes clear rules for the community participants (Dyer & Nobeoka, 2000, p. 364).

- Shared language: O'Dell and Jackson Grayson (1998, p. 165) demonstrate how this can be achieved through the use of a common framework for classifying information that enables "diverse units to talk to each other more effectively about their business problems."

- Social events: When individuals enjoy social relationships with their colleagues they find it easier to share knowledge on serious issues (von Krogh, 1998, p. 145). The Toyota suppliers association, for example, has a PR/sports committee to encourage friendships (Dyer & Nobeoka, 2000, p. 353).

- Collocation of staff: Physical co-location makes it possible for individuals to communicate easily with one another (Allen, 1984). It is recognized that electronic virtual communities are essential in some disciplines, for example, biotechnology, where multiple authorship of research papers is common; and it is technically possible for people to telecommute from just about anywhere. However, "experience suggests that knowledge workers still want and need to work and live in close proximity ... the clustering of high-tech work in the Silicon Valley and the Northeast [provides] evidence that face-to-face relationships are still the only truly effective way to transfer tacit knowledge" (Cohen, 1998, p. 37). Certain knowledge-transfer activities that rely on factors such as observation or awareness of body language cannot be undertaken remotely (Holsthouse, 1998, pp. 277–278). This would, for instance, apply to brainstorming (Leonard & Sensiper, 1998, pp. 118) or in cases where there is potential for misunderstanding (O'Dell & Jackson Grayson, 1998, p. 157).

The philosophy of care, in contrast, relies on mutual regard, rather than the expectation of mutual benefit.

Infrastructure

The importance of adequate infrastructure is stressed by Wenger and Snyder (2000, pp. 144–145). The kinds of support that they outline are, in some ways, a blueprint for an organizational memory system, conceived in terms of the eclectic specification ("from storage to active remembering") offered by Bannon and Kuutti (1996). Such a specification may address some of the challenges identified in the work of earlier analysts of organizational memory (e.g., Stein, 1995), who present tacit knowledge as a major impediment to the design of fully comprehensive memory systems. "Active remembering" has inspired a number of case studies, which capture the local interplay of knowledge and memory as work unfolds when participants are not present together (Ackerman & Halverson, 1999; Decortis, Noirfalise & Pecheux, 1998; Sauvagnac & Falzon, 1998). Much of our discussion of infrastructure covers issues that are pertinent to this. Although some analysts (e.g., Newell, Scarborough, Swan, & Hislop, 2000) distinguish technological and cultural infrastructure at most, we offer a more detailed taxonomy based on work by Star and Ruhleder (1994) that may provide a better measure of the kinds of support that may be required. This involves:

- technologies for communication and representation
- "boundary objects" that are instantiated by such information and communication technologies and that may be shared by members of a group and across groups
- "social infrastructure," or the networks that are brought into play to establish, maintain or enhance position or status

• "discursive infrastructure," the genres, or shaping stories that allow managers and other participants in practice to make sense of interactions

Technologies for Communication and Representation

A number of technologies to support group interaction and computer-supported cooperative work exist, and we give examples in a later section on online communities of practice. The focus in this section is on intranets, and on the claims that have been made about their role in fostering shared or collective knowledge in communities of practice.

Individuals are motivated to act when (a) it is easy to do so (Snowden, 2000, p. 10) and (b) the usefulness of acting is obvious. The provision of a suitable technological infrastructure, such as an intranet (Brown & Duguid, 1998, p. 98) for knowledge creation and sharing is important for this.

Brown and Duguid (1998, p. 105) are critical of new technology that is ostensibly meant to help knowledge management efforts when in fact it simply "attends primarily to individuals and the explicit information that passes between them." They argue that tools for information sharing need to be integrated into communities and should match the levels of formality operated in the communities they serve:

> The local informality found within communities differs from levels of explicitness and formality often demanded between communities … The demands for formality demanded by technologies can disrupt more productive informal relations … Technologies thus have to include different degrees of formality and trust … if new technologies ask people to negotiate all their social interrelations like their banking relations, they will leave little room for the informal, the tacit, and the socially embedded—which is where know-how lies and important work gets done.
>
> (Brown & Duguid, 1998, p. 105)

If employers expect workers—especially those working across distributed organizations—to use corporate intranets and e-mail systems as "places" for informal discussion, then the design of the systems needs to reflect this:

> This choice between formality and informality will have repercussions in the design of complex technologies. But it also has implications on the implementation of such things as corporate intranets and mail systems. Increasingly work-places seek to control the sorts of interactions and exchanges these are used for. Yet these systems in many ways replace the coffee pot and the water cooler as the site of informal but highly important knowledge diffusion. Limiting their infor-mality is likely to limit their importance.
>
> (Brown & Duguid, 1998, p. 106)

Kransdorff (2000, p. 78) points out that "individuals are generally bet-ter speakers than they are writers." Facilities that allow input to shared information systems that replicate patterns of speech would be expected to attract greater participation than those that require users to spend time reformatting ideas before submitting them to an electronic knowl-edge base. This point may explain the disappointment of those who experience initial high levels of interest in new knowledge management systems but later discover that "implementation efforts often fall victim to a 'build it and they will come' approach" (Ruggles, 1998, p. 84). At the Chevron Corporation, the company "started by creating an internal elec-tronic database and expected people to enter their practices and contact others with intriguing solutions. The company experienced good access initially, but then usage began to trail off" (O'Dell & Jackson Grayson, 1998, p.164).

Even if it is possible to motivate everyone to share knowledge through the provision of state-of-the-art technological tools, it is argued that some types of knowledge are unsuitable for electronic storage and retrieval. O'Dell and Jackson Grayson (1998, p. 164) suggest that "really important and useful information for improvement is too complex to put online. At Chevron this is recognized. Here the database is meant to enhance and support existing knowledge sharing mechanisms on best practice. AMP use the database as a pointer with basic information on the system and follow-up encouraged through named individuals cited on the system."

Rather than encourage people to share information, systems may encourage people to impede such practices. It has been suggested that in some circumstances workers might actually sabotage knowledge management systems over fears of job security. When discussing the building of knowledge bases of customer support information it is noted that "support analysts may question the wisdom of furnishing their knowledge for a system if they believe that the system may someday replace their own jobs" (Davenport & Klahr, 1998, p. 206).

Intranets implemented without due preparation and analysis (Lamb, 1999; Scheepers & Darmsgaard, 1997) are not likely to improve organizational performance. Newell et al. (2000) describe such a case in a study of a European bank, where inadequate incentives led to lack of input. This point is corroborated in Orlikowski's (1993) analogous study of a failed Lotus Notes implementation where an existing incentive scheme made no provision for use of the novel technology (also see Schultze & Boland, 1997). These issues are also discussed in an earlier *ARIST* chapter by Davenport and McKim (1995). In a recent discussion of the knowledge management concept, Swan and Scarborough (2001), suggest that an "episodic" model (the "episodes" are agenda setting, selecting, implementing, and routinization) is appropriate. "Community" is associated with the selection and implementation phases, and they warn against relying solely on intranets as a sharing mechanism.

Representation

A key problem is mutual understanding within and across local regimes (Star, 1995). In face-to-face "primitive" communities like that of the flutemakers described earlier, representation of collective knowledge is not an issue. Where members of groups are dispersed in space or time (across a site, for example, or in cases where they are members of different workshifts), representation may be a critical issue. It may be equally critical where trans-domain understanding is at stake. Salomon (1993b) states that there can be no distributed cognition without individual cognition, and that many cognitions are not distributed. The representation of individual and group understanding may be an important feature of the reciprocal interplay between them.

Recent work on the mapping of argumentation is relevant to this problem. Eden and his colleagues (Eden & Spender, 1998) have worked for a number of years on software applications modeling arguments that support decisions. The current version is marketed as "Decision Explorer," which can produce what are called "idiographic causal maps" (Eden & Ackerman, 1998). Bood (1998) compares a number of approaches to argumentation mapping, drawing on earlier work by Huff (1988). Raeithel and Velichkovsky (1996), working within an activity theory framework, offer a review of a number of representational approaches (repertory grid included) that may help those who analyze collaboration in groups.

Two further bodies of work on formal representation are pertinent. The first considers ontologies (for example, Vickery, 1997); specifically enterprise ontology work (Uschold, King, Moralee, & Zorigios, 1999) that seeks to model the diverse activities of a given domain and the capabilities and other resources to support them (Kingston & MacIntosh, 2000). The models are presented as formal hierarchies, though the terms linked in this way may be annotated with textual unstructured descriptions. Such structures are, in effect, thesauri, suggests Soergel (1999), who has designed a generic thesaurus that might equally serve as an ontology (Soergel, 1998). By capturing dimensions of expertise—e.g., role, capability, competence and project history—these richly faceted structures can help managers identify members of teams who, jointly, embody the collective knowledge that is required to achieve a given project objective. An alternative approach is to consider documents as surrogates for expertise; specifically the generic documents that imply collective understanding in different domains (Davenport & Rosenbaum, 2000). Pejtersen and Albrechtsen (2000) have recently presented a framework for "ecological" classification that covers dimensions of human expertise and documentation.

The second domain that can enhance representation of individual and group interaction is a body of work on XML (Extensible Markup Language) and e-commerce. This suggests that metadata may offer a consistent notation to capture local knowledge at different levels of aggregation, and thus contribute to improved interaction within domains (Attipoe, 1999). Bryan (1998) points out that XML is flexible enough to be able to describe any logical text structure, whether it be a form memo, letter, report, book, encyclopedia, dictionary, or database, and suggests that emerging Business Object Libraries like Common Business Language (CBL) or Biztalk will accelerate the adoption of XML as an e-commerce standard. Glushko, Tenenbaum, and Meltzes (1999) explain the design rationale for the CBL: based on an extensible public collection of generic business interface definitions, it tells potential trading partners what online services a company offers and what documents to use for those services. The library's strength lies in the fact that it is easier to interconnect companies in terms of the documents they exchange, as they already largely agree on these. Services are, in effect, defined by the documents they accept and produce. The responsibility for document definition will lie with communities of practice: Early adopting communities are mathematicians, genealogists, and chemists (Green, 1999). Strong proponents of XML predict it will allow online businesses to build on one another's published content and services to create innovative virtual companies, markets, and trading communities; these can be leveraged by "comparison-shopping" agents, which can exploit the affordance of XML to rapidly configure appropriate resources (Glushko et al., 1999; Maes, Guttman, & Moukas, 1999). Recent developments in voice-based XML (VoxML [Voice Markup Language]) may overcome reluctance by practitioners to keyboard texts into appropriate systems.

Indexing of specifications and classifications based on the categories used by participants has been proposed in a number of domains. Keiichi, Voss, Juhnke, and Kreifelts (1998) describe a concept indexing system that generates categories on the fly, using annotations made by domain specialists as they read professional literature. Hubar and Gillaspy (1998) discuss the development of an AIDS scheme that uses the terminology of patients and their helpers. In such cases, the development of an endogenous classification will have political consequences—an issue explored in depth by Bowker and Star (1999), who draw many of their examples from the world of nursing classification. Albrechtsen and Jacob (1998) have reviewed the development of endogenous schemes in different contexts (e.g., AIDS, nursing), in a study of "dialogic" or "heteroglossic" classification (also see Jacob & Albrechtsen, 1998). These terms denote an eclectic scheme, and have none of the implications in terms of turn-taking that a conversation analyst, for example, might invoke. Jacob and Shaw (1998) provide a comprehensive review of socio-cognitive perspectives to representation in an earlier *ARIST* volume.

Boundary Infrastructure

Where such schemes are designed to support inter-domain understanding, they may be considered "boundary objects" (Albrechtsen & Jacob, 1998). The term was introduced in 1989 by Star and Greisemer (1989), who proposed that a class of objects provides common ground for different social actors to work together. Boundary objects may be artifacts, texts, prescriptions, classification systems, or indexes, and are, to some extent, protean: "plastic enough to adapt to local needs, and the constraints of the several parties employing them, yet robust enough to maintain common identity across sites" (Star & Greisemer, 1989, p. 393). Individuals may also be part of boundary infrastructure, where they contribute to the diffusion of knowledge across and between communities (the traditional gatekeeper role). One approach is to foster a specific organizational role, "the broker." This role within the firm is treated in depth by Wenger (2000b, pp. 235–236), who classifies brokers into three types: "boundary spanners" (comparable to Berkenkotter's [1995] "key informants," trusted authorities in a number of fields), "roamers," and "outposts." The role of brokers is explored at the level of the firm (and of inter-organizational knowledge sharing) by Hargadon (1998). As we note above, Nonaka and Konno (1998) suggest that the role of the broker is essential to the innovative interplay of tacit and explicit knowledge. Such brokering is assigned to middle managers in the "ba" model, the group most likely to be lost in re-engineering initiatives.

In addition to boundary objects and brokers, Wenger proposes that boundary interactions are an important feature of the diffusion process, and that these can be managed or harnessed in the interests of innovation (Wenger, 2000b, pp. 236–238). He offers examples of simple mechanisms (online and off-line): sabbaticals, visits, seminars, and, at the periphery, help desks, FAQ lists, "visiting rooms," and fairs. At a more formal level, organizations may foster cross-disciplinary projects.

Social Infrastructure

By "social infrastructure," we refer to networks of contacts (online and off-line), and what is transferred by means of these networks. As we indicate above, levels of diffusion may depend on the social capital established in professional and working networks, although the efficacy of different types of network may vary across sectors, or even across groups within firms. The nature of the bonds and relationships that link members of communities of practice can be explored with the help of a body of work on social networks (Garton, Haythornthwaite, & Wellman, 1998; Haythornthwaite, 1996, 1999). These suggest that participants in networks operate with a portfolio of relationships, whose density varies according to their purpose in belonging to the network (Wellman & Gulia, 1999).

Studies of the role of weak and strong ties in fostering innovation have been inconclusive. (Lam [2000] offers a skeptical analysis of different types of institutional networks and their respective innovation potentials.) Some communities of practice appear to draw their strength from the weak ties that link participants (Granovetter, 1973). In such cases, less intense networks are more wide-ranging, and thus offer more cross-fertilizing power. Intensity of relationship in communities of practice may be linked to a time frame. Lewicki and Bunker (1996) suggest that interpersonal trust develops as a three phase process, which moves from surface interaction to intimacy over time. Ties are likely to be strong where members of a community practice have bonded in apprenticeships (traditional situated learning) in closed communities like the print shop (von Krogh, et al. [2000] "high care" knowledge environments); and although such ties may reinforce the knowledge of the community, they are unlikely to foster innovation. Wenger and Snyder (2000) describe such a high care social infrastructure in the case of an officially endorsed community of practice at American Management Systems. Participants must contribute one knowledge development project a year. In return, their participation is "paid for by their business units, which fund their annual projects, cover their attendance at workshops, and send them to an annual conference that brings together all the company's communities of practice" (Wenger & Snyder, 2000, p. 144).

Discursive/Narrative Infrastructure

If, as Wenger suggests, stories or narratives are a critical component of identity in communities of practice, how, then, may the creation and recording of stories be supported? Undertaking the eliciting, capture, and analysis of stories is not a trivial task. A review of work in this area is provided by Boyce (1996), and Clayman and Maynard (1995) provide an account of methodologies. Deuten and Rip (2000, p. 69), for example, claim that "agency appears only in, and through, narrative," and that understanding the constitutive role of narrative in an organization is a fundamental managerial competence. By analyzing what they call narrative infrastructure (the "rails along which multiactor and multilevel processes gain thrust and direction") in a case study of product innovation in a biotechnology firm, they show "how actually, over time, attribution and typicifaction in stories, and the implied stories contained in interactions link up, and an overall plot emerges." They thus identify a narrative infrastructure that enables, as well as constrains, further actions. A linear storyline reduces complexity: "a variety of accounts, formal and informal, technical and social, strategic and operational, for internal and external purposes" (Deuten & Rip, 2000, pp. 70–71). One can inquire how these accounts evolve along the "journey of innovation," and why they can become more linear over time. As Callon (1991) has pointed out, linearity fixes events—the linear narrative is irreversible, and is thus an extremely useful managerial tool. Suchman and Trigg (1993, p. 177) provide an account of "pseudo-narratives" in an AI community that "are constructed for the specific purpose of reconstructing common sense knowledge as something that can be transparently read off of the particular technical representations to hand." A comparable (and much cited) account of narrative in an office supply firm is offered by Boje (1991).

Narrative Infrastructure and Working Memory

In explaining how coherence can emerge in a multiactor, multilevel process, without any one actor specifically being responsible (a form of organizational knowledge), Deuten and Rip (2000, p. 72) stress that narration, rather than text, must be the focus of attention. This is because "narration occurs in interactions, informs and shapes them, and makes action into something memorable." This proposition is consistent with Bannon and Kuutti's (1996) presentation of the concept of active remembering, mentioned above. Deuten and Rip (2000) invoke Schön's (1983) observation that naming a situation or a problem as something recognizable mobilizes resources from past experience. Such observations are consistent with other analyses of organizational memory that have moved away from a repository approach (Stein, 1995) to an exploration of how an archive may intersect with understanding that emerges in activity (Ackerman & MacDonald, 1996; Cross & Baird, 2000; Morison, 1997). Writing with a design focus, Marshall, Shipman, and McCall (2000) present community memory as a cyclical process that involves seeding, evolution, and reseeding, and they describe interfaces that allow capture of insight on the fly. As we note above, comparable accounts of the emergence of memory in narrative transformations are offered by Sauvagnac and Falzon (1998), in a case study of medical diagnosis, the outcome of a process of team observations and transformations reflected in an evolving record as it migrates across different specialist groups. This is one of a number of studies of medical matters based on the theme of "good organizational reasons for bad records." (See, for example, Bowker and Star, 1999.) Where markers of the transformation are available (in the form of annotations in the paper record, for example), the resulting history can afford a more detailed understanding in cases of "handover" or "changeover" where documentation is a critical boundary object (Decortis et al., 1998). Many attempts to formalize medical records have been less successful than anticipated, because of lack of annotation. Current design work on annotating electronic documents may overcome the problem (Churchill, Trevor, Bly, Nelson, & Cubranic, 2000).

We can see similarities between narrative infrastructure or "the evolving aggregation of actors/narratives in their material and social setting, that enables and constrains the possible stories, actions, and interactions by actors" (Deuten & Rip, 2000, p. 74) and Wenger's shared repertoires that contribute to shared identity in communities of practice. Another pertinent concept is the "industry recipe," which Tsoukas (1996) develops in his discussion of organizations as sites of distributed knowledge. An industry recipe is a discourse developed over time within a particular industry. The recipe is learned within the context of discursive practices; it reflects the tacit knowledge of those involved in practice, and can offer guidance to managers faced with the problem of what Tsoukas describes as the tension between expectation, (personal) dispositions, and interactive situations. How a manager understands a recipe is always influenced by immediate circumstances and local agendas. Tsoukas describes organizational knowledge as distributed because it is always incomplete (those involved cannot know all that they need to know), and always spread across contexts and organizational members. The key to coordinated action, he maintains, is not an overview from the top, but that those "lower down" find more and more ways of getting connected and interrelating the knowledge that each one has (Tsoukas, 1996, p. 22). We can see similarities between "industry recipes" and Alexandrian pattern libraries of the sort described by Falconer (1999) and Bayle et al. (1998). The patterns are more or less formal representations of responses to recurrent problems in social space, and can be used in situated design work. We discuss some novel, local representations of this sort in the next section.

Online Communities of Practice

In this section, we consider the contentious case of online communities of practice. Not all online communities are communities of practice. As Lutters and Ackerman (1997) point out: "It is assuredly premature to attribute community to the full range of Net life" (p. 41). They proffer the term "collectivity" to describe the "full range of communities, clubs, groups, gangs, church associations, building societies, skidrow hotels, and so on that will exist in the Net" (p. 41). Davenport and Hall (2001) suggest that if communities of practice are indeed sites for organizational learning, it may be possible to define them in terms of a framework. They provide a tentative model taking distributed cognition, situated learning, situated action, and social infrastructure as quasi-normative characteristics that distinguish online communities of practice from their material or hybrid counterparts, and use this to evaluate three empirical projects (Davenport & Hall, 2001).

Teigland (2000, p. 171) observes that online communities "exhibit many of the characteristics of material communities of practice—reciprocity, identity, and so on—but the individuals involved have never typically met, and they work through what is by definition a codified exchange of information, which goes against other aspects of the theory." They, thus, fail to exhibit the defining characteristics of face-to-face interaction and tacit knowledge. Teigland suggests that current defining criteria may need to be revised. Secondly, an online community of practice may be ephemeral (Wolf, 1997), and the knowledge created may be lost where innovative local practice is uncoupled from an organization that might use it, unless infrastructure, which can sustain what may be learned, is in place. The world of software design has provided some of the most compelling examples of online communities to date. Sawnhey and Pirandelli (2000) discuss this sector in terms of "communities of creation," and offer a taxonomy that covers open, closed, and gated communities. Sun MicroSystems' Community Source License (SCSL) is presented as an exemplary partially open system that has "specific rules for membership, a sponsor, and a system for managing intellectual property rights that allows members to benefit from the intellectual property they help to create" (Sawnhey & Pirandelli, 2000, p. 42). These authors conclude that the creativity of such communities will be strongest where the infrastructure includes mechanisms for rewards, but rewards at the level of the community, rather than of the individual (by means, for example, of a license that allows members to mutually exploit the innovations that they have contributed to—a form of monetized social capital).

Design work contexts other than the software industry also provide examples of online communities of practice. Yates and Sumner (1997) offer two case studies that support the proposition that genres act as stabilizers that counteract centripetal and centrifugal tension in groups supported by computer-mediated communication (CMC). In the first study, they use techniques from conversation analysis to show how micro-genres emerge in a discussion list, not strictly a community of practice. The second case, however, is a study of a cross-disciplinary design community, and the reworking of community genres by one of the designers, in a response to a less than optimal previous genre repertoire. "As the community recognized common breakdowns in the design process, they improved their representations to overcome these breakdowns. The outcome was a progression toward well-defined design representations that made explicit significant objects and their relationships" (Yates & Sumner, 1997).

Hildreth and Kimble (1999) describe the development of a planning document (an amalgam of multiple "soft knowledge" inputs from different teams) in a transcontinental project, focusing on the document's role as an infrastructural boundary object in a community of practice. The document "bounded" internal differences (national and cultural) and acted as a "collaborative catalyst" (Hildreth & Kimble, 1999, p. 23). Although the planning document could be most fully interpreted by "old timers" who were familiar with the knowledge of previous generations embedded in the artifact, Hildreth and Kimble comment on its usefulness in situated learning. Nonnecke and Preece (1999) have studied lurkers on online discussion lists, a practice that appears to be a form of legitimate peripheral participation.

Online communities raise a number of issues related to "intricacies of design" (Mynatt, Adler, Ito, & O'Day, 1997) in terms of providing cues and markers for participants. Social and conversational rhythm (Erickson, 1997) is an important factor in community cohesion, and designers must accommodate the complicated management of markers for participants whose activity bridges virtual and physical space. Help for "newbies" who must learn to find their way is an important component of situated learning in such communities. Although many online communities exist to allow their members to inhabit alternative personae (Turkle, 1996), real life (RL) identity matters in most organizational interactions, and information on the presentation of the self should be provided. Reed (2001), in an analysis of the process of making conversation on a Web-list, shows how ignorant behavior by a newcomer can provoke strong negative reactions. The projects described by Mynatt and her group lie outside the commercial context. These were undertaken at Xerox PARC and elsewhere (Mynatt et al., 1997). Bobrow (1997), the codesigner of one of these (Pueblo), summarizes the project as shifting from 2D (the text message) to 3C (community, coordination, collaboration). Designing for 3C is not a trivial matter. Even within a focused and small group, differences will arise over issues like privacy or connection management (Dourish, 1997; Kendall, 1999): "patterns of homogeneity and individuality, and the tension between them, present challenges for design that are both subtle and critical" (Dourish, 1997, p. 39). Such issues are managed by protocols and codes in the world of MOOs (MUD, Object Oriented): Naper (2001) presents an analysis of interaction in the virtual fantasy world of Patagonia (rendered in the Active Worlds platform), whose actors might be justly described as members of a community of practice. Holmström and Jakobsson (2001) discuss the affordances of different media in a case study of Active Worlds as a platform to design learning communities.

Online communities also test the concept of social capital, or as Lesser (2000, p. 4) describes it, "the wealth (or benefit) that exists because of an individual's social relationships." This concept emerged outside the context of organizational practice (see, for example, Blanchard & Horan, 2000), but is now invoked by workplace analysts (e.g., Coleman, 2000). Social capital implies accumulation over time. Such accumulation may be observed where online communities persist (for example, Internet groups that consolidate peer-to-peer interactions in sectors like health care) because they represent solutions to long-term or persistent problems. Other online communities are less stable. Web shoppers, for example, present an interesting challenge to the community of practice framework, as the communities of practice involved are highly specific (e.g., eBay), and, in some cases, extremely short-lived. However, the practices that have been identified in the other case studies as conducive to the creation of knowledge in communities of practice can be observed here (McWilliam, 2000). These include:

- accelerated apprenticeship
- micro-level situated action that solves ad hoc problems
- boundary objects in the form of novel representations and forms (new genres like the Web-Ring, for example)
- social infrastructure in the form of recommender systems
- track records (Wexelblat, 1999; Wexelblat & Maes, 1999)
- brokers who can partner those with shared tastes or partner consumers and products; they can capture and disseminate the insights that consumers provide either across communities of practice, or to vendors and designers (Maes et al., 1999), blurring the boundaries of demand and supply in an increasingly intimate form of product or service codevelopment (Cronin & Davenport, 2001)

In a speculative article on the real value of online communities in the context of e-commerce, Armstrong and Hagel (2000) identify four types (communities of transaction, of interest, of fantasy, and of relationship) that can meet multiple social and commercial needs; commercial success is likely to be associated with companies that can satisfy such needs with products that embody most or all of these types of community. These authors suggest that moderators or sysops in this context are, in effect, conversation managers. The problem of capturing insight from what are in several instances floating communities (they are not tied to a formal institution) is, in some cases, already being solved by the emergence of brokers who will scavenge the Web for intellectual commodities (McVeigh, 2000). Strong proponents of computer agents consider their remit in terms of this type of role (Marsh & Meech, 2000). Where the consumer community of practice is broken down into component parts in this way, we see the apparent emergence of demand chain management, with the elements of the creation and diffusion of consumer insight commodified by different brokers. This raises issues of property rights and privacy. As Kollock (1999) points out, the Web blurs the distinction between public and private goods.

If online community is manifest as a long conversation (Erickson, 1997), what kind of infrastructure may capture the patterns of exchange? Technologies exist that support the spaces where such data may be captured (Internet Relay Chat, newsgroups, and electronic meeting systems); and recent work has demonstrated that interfaces based on visualizations of interaction analysis can offer rapid insight into the group process. Examples may be found in the work of Donath, Karahalios, and Viegas (1999) on the visualization of threads in online conversations; visualizations of turn-taking in the work of, among others, Millen and Dray (1999); and recent work of Erickson and his colleagues on participation in conversation circles (Erickson, Smith, Kellogg, Laff, & Richards, 1999).

At a more formal level, the formation of insight in online communities of practice may be supported by a structured database environment, like Lotus Teambuilder (Yates & Sumner, 1997), which builds on the concept of genre systems (nested sets of genres that capture typical interactions), or the shared-notetaking environment described by Landay and Davis (1999). Visualization may contribute to the success of such systems, and

Greene, Marchionini, Plaisant, and Shneiderman (2000) describe an interface that provides multiple points of view to support complex document management. A further example of more structured support is GSweb (Romano, Nunamaker, Briggs, & Vogel, 1998), a Web version of a complex groupware system with over ten years of development history behind it. A predecessor product designed by the group, GroupSystems, drew on standard genres for decision making (brainstorming, ranking, voting), supplemented over the years by dialogue boxes, e-mail, and other relevant digital genres. The GSweb prototype develops the idea of a collaborative portfolio further, combining tools that categorize and converge on key issues (translation tools, in other words) with tools that can offer a process overview (coordination). The principal representation device is the folder, nested and structured and accessed in Windows sequences. In addition, GSweb, like its predecessor GroupSystems, provides "tools for thought"—categorizer, outliner, commenter, and voter. Categorizer may be agent-based. Group outliner may produce an ontology for any given community whose work is embodied in the GSweb application. It is not yet clear to what extent such infrastructures may compensate for intuitive understanding of categories and cues that characterizes effective face-to-face interaction. As we note above, some analysts (e.g., Swan & Scarborough, 2001) are skeptical that information and communication technologies, per se, can contribute to community formation.

Conclusion

There is a growing recognition among analysts that the interplay of tacit and explicit knowledge is a critical factor in organizational learning, and a primary task of managers is the conversion of (tacit) human capital into (explicit) structural capital (Edvinsson, 1997). Together, these constitute an organization's intellectual capital (see the chapter by Snyder and Buerk Pierce in this volume), and social capital is an important component of this (Nahapiet & Ghoshal, 2000). Communities of practice, as we indicate at the start of this chapter, have been identified as the site where this alchemy can occur. From a performative perspective, they provide a means of constructing "recipes" for knowledge development: it is a matter of putting certain structures in place (an intranet, for example, and an appropriate incentive structure) and allocating personnel to communities, where they will work together and make insights available in appropriate knowledge bases. From a constructivist perspective, communities of practice, like other socio-technical systems, provide useful explanatory frames to study the development of collective knowledge (Kling, McKim, Fortuna, & King, [2000] offer the alternative term "socio-technical interaction networks"). In research terms, however, their status is ambivalent: The performative approach has not been supported by systematic inquiry, and the effectiveness of the constructivist approach at a level beyond the local case study has not been established.

In what ways, then, is the topic of "organizational learning and communities of practice" relevant to *ARIST*? From a technology point of view, communities of practice are a useful locus of design for a range of applications that support social interaction, and have raised a number of research issues, such as appropriate mix of online and face-to-face interaction, or the effectiveness of tools to represent diverse points of view or visualize different actors in a group. From an information science perspective, communities of practice are an appropriate focus for efforts to address a number of challenges. The first is how to accommodate organizational (as distinct from individual) design, an issue that has not been addressed to any great extent in information science research (however see Elliott & Kling, 1997; Kling & Elliott, 1994; Kling & Lamb, 1996; Lyman, 1999). With the notable exception of work on bibliometrics (specifically citation indexing and citation mapping) library and information science has focused in individual retrieval of individual documents (for more detail on citation and the representation of collective knowledge see the chapter by Borgmann and Furner in this volume). As this chapter demonstrates, an emerging body of work presented at the ISIC (Information Seeking in Context) series of conferences (Vakkari, Savolainen, & Dervin, 1997; Wilson & Allen, 1998) has attempted to address information seeking in context. As we note here, within this corpus, several studies consider context in terms of distributed cognition (e.g., Erdelez, 2000; Perry, 1998; Rioux, 2000).

The second challenge is how to support interactive work that brings multiple and diverse artifacts together. This problem is of growing concern in digital library research. In 1995, Marshall and her colleagues linked the concept of large-scale information resources for communities of practice to the concept of community memory, or "the open ended set of collective knowledge and shared understandings developed and maintained by the group." Her team explored ways to support electronic communities by means of artifacts in the same medium—"discourse, collected materials, answers to frequently asked questions, evaluations of these materials ... or sources ... as well as marginalia and annotations, alternative organizations of materials, filters and well-tuned queries" (Marshall et al., 2000, pp. 227–228). Comparable digital libraries work has been reported by Bishop, Neumann, Star, and Merkel (2000) who have identified issues for digital library design in recent discussions of "assemblages" (the artifacts, knowledge, practices, and community influences that shape library use) and infrastructure. They introduce the concept of document streams to describe material in digital libraries, where the distinction between genres, documents, and document surrogates may be blurred, and where new document structures are likely to emerge (Solomon [1998] has used the term "information mosaic" in a comparable context). In such a context, the role of boundary spanner may be crucial: Murphy (2001), for example, has recently presented two vignettes of engineers in the aerospace industry, who act as transformers of information across artifacts in online and face-to-face mode, and whose tacit knowledge contributes to the effective use of fragmented explicit resources. In attempting to place their work, Murphy found a community of practice approach helpful, because she was able to interpret their role as broker or boundary worker of the sort described by Wenger.

A third challenge to information science that can be explored in studies of communities of practice is how to address the accumulation and management of social capital. Inter-community sharing of knowledge in digital environments raises issues of legitimacy, credibility, and authority that are different from those in traditional environments. This area is explored in detail by Van House in an extended case study (Schiff, Van House, & Butler, 1997; Van House, 2001) of environmental planning that addresses all three of the challenges outlined above. The community in this case was composed of diverse organizations, whose understanding of a heterogeneous collection of materials supported by a digital library varied greatly. The most problematic issue in this case study was the creation and maintenance of social capital. Respondents expressed concern about de-contextualization, or inappropriate use of data produced by one community by those outside it, and about the opportunity costs of "productizing" their knowledge, or cleaning data, and creating documentation and metadata. Respondents were also worried about the credibility of the data, and conflicts of interest between computer experts and content specialists (Van House, in press). One way to overcome such tensions, as we suggest here, is to make the digital library, itself, the focus of a community of practice that can address such issues as they arise.

We conclude that the topic can be aligned with a number of studies in the information science domain that focuses on the ecology and ethology of the workplace (e.g., Bishop, Buttenfield, & Van House, 2001; Bishop & Star, 1996; Davenport & Cronin, 1998; Lyman, 1999; Lynch 1999; Nardi & O'Day, 1999; Sonnenwald, 1998). There is a shared perception among those who work on such studies that practice and resources mutually shape each other in the workplace. The community of practice is a compelling unit of analysis because it (1) allows socio-technical interactions to be observed at a number of different organizational levels, and (2) serves as a boundary object that pulls together insights from a number of disciplines in the interests of improved design.

Bibliography

Abbott, A. (1988). *The system of professions: An essay on the division of expert labor*. Chicago: University of Chicago Press.

Ackerman, M., & Halverson, C. (1999). Organizational memory: Processes, boundary objects, and trajectories. In R. Sprague (Ed.), *Proceedings of the 32nd Annual Hawaii International Conference on System Sciences* (CD ROM). Los Alamitos, CA: IEEE.

Ackerman, M. S., & McDonald, D. W. (1996). Answer Garden 2: Merging organizational memory with collaborative help. Retrieved February 5, 2001, from the World Wide Web: http://www.ics.uci.edu/~ackerman/pub/96b22/cscw96.ag2.html

Albrechtsen, H., & Jacob, E. (1998). The dynamics of classification systems as boundary objects for cooperation in the electronic library. *Library Trends, 47,* 293–312.

Allen, T. J. (1984). *Managing the flow of technology*. Cambridge, MA: MIT Press.

Armstrong, A., & Hagel, J. (2000). The real value of online communities. In E. L. Lesser, M. A. Fontaine, & J. A. Slusher (Eds.), *Knowledge and communities* (pp. 85–95). Oxford: Butterworth-Heinemann.

Attipoe, A. (1999). Knowledge structuring for corporate memory. *Markup Languages: Theory and Practice, 1*(4), 27–36.

Axelrod, R. (1997). *The complexity of cooperation*. Princeton, NJ: Princeton University Press.

Bannon, L., & Kuutti, K. (1996). Shifting perspectives on organizational memory: From storage to active remembering. In R. Sprague (Ed.), *Proceedings of the 29th Annual Hawaii International Conference on Systems Sciences* (pp. 156–167). Los Alamitos, CA: IEEE.

Bargiela-Chiapinni, F., & Nickerson, C. (1999). Business writing as social action. In F. Bargiela-Chiapinni & C. Nickerson (Eds.), *Writing business: Genres, media and discourses* (pp. 1–32). London: Longman.

Baumard, P. (1999). *Tacit knowledge in organizations*. London: Sage.

Bayle, E., Bellamy, R., Casady, G., Erickson, T., Fincher, S., Grinter, B., Gross, B., Lehder, D., Marmolin, H., Moore, B., Potts, C., Skousen, G., & Thomas, J. (1998). Putting it all together: Towards a pattern language for interaction design. Summary report of the CHI'97 Workshop. *SIGCHI Bulletin, 30*(1), 17–23.

Bazerman, C., & Paradis, J. (1991). *Textual dynamics of the professions*. Madison, WI: University of Wisconsin Press.

Beer, M., & Nohria, N. (2000). Cracking the code of change. *Harvard Business Review, 78*(3) 133–139.

Berkenkotter, C. (1995). Theoretical issues surrounding interdisciplinary interpenetration. *Social Epistemology, 9*(2), 175–187.

Bhatia, V. (1994). Approaches to genre analysis. In V. Bhatia (Ed.), *Analysing genre: Language use in professional settings* (pp. 13–41). London: Longman.

Bishop, A. (1999). Document structure and digital libraries: How researchers mobilize information in journal articles. *Information Processing & Management, 35*, 255–279.

Bishop, A., Buttenfield, B. B., & Van House, N. (Eds.) (in press). *Digital library use: Social practice in design and evaluation*. Cambridge, MA: MIT Press.

Bishop, A., Neumann, L., Star, S., & Merkel, C. (2000). Digital libraries: Situating use in changing information infrastructure. *Journal of the American Society for Information Science, 51*, 394–413.

Bishop, A., & Star, S. L. (1996). Social informatics of digital library use and infrastructure. *Annual Review of Information Science and Technology, 31*, 301–402.

Blackler, F., Crump, N., & McDonald, S. (1999). Managing experts and competing through innovation: An activity theoretical analysis. *Organization, 6*, 5–31.

Blackler, F., Crump, N., & McDonald, S. (2000). Organizing processes in complex activity networks. *Organization, 7*, 277–300.

Blanchard, A., & Horan, T. (2000). Virtual communities and social capital. In E. L. Lesser (Ed.), *Knowledge management and social capital* (pp. 159–178). Oxford: Butterworth-Heinemann.

Bobrow, D. (1997). 3C or not 3C, that is the question. *SIGGROUP Bulletin, 18*(1), 33–35.

Boden, D. (1994). *The business of talk*. London: Polity Press.

Boje, D. (1991). The storytelling organization: A study of story performance in an office supply firm. *Administrative Science Quarterly, 36*(1), 106–126.

Bood, R. (1998). Charting organizational learning: A comparison of multiple mapping techniques. In C. Eden & J.-C. Spender (Eds.), *Managerial and organizational cognition: Theory, methods, research* (pp. 210–230). London: Sage.

Bourdieu, P. (1990). *The logic of practice.* Stanford, CA: Stanford University Press.

Bowker, G. (1994). *Science on the run: Information management and industrial geophysics at Schlumberger, 1920–1940.* Cambridge, MA: MIT Press.

Bowker, G., & Star, S. (1999). *Sorting things out: Classification and its consequences.* Cambridge, MA: MIT Press.

Boyce, M. (1996). Organizational story and storytelling: A critical review. *Journal of Organizational Change Management, 9*(5). Retrieved February 5, 2001, from the World Wide Web: http://newton.uor.edu/FacultyFolder/MBoyce/5CRITICA.HTM

Brown, J., & Duguid, P. (1991). Organizational learning and communities-of-practice: Toward a unified view of working, learning and innovation. *Organization Science, 2*(1), 40–57.

Brown, J., & Duguid, P. (1993). Rethinking the border in design: An exploration of central and peripheral relations in practice. In S. Yelavich (Ed.), *The edge of the millennium: An international critique of architecture, urban planning, product and communication design.* New York: Whitney Library of Design.

Brown, J., & Duguid, P. (1994). Borderline issues: Social and managerial aspects of design. *Human-Computer Interaction, 9*(1), 3–36.

Brown, J., & Duguid, P. (1998). Organizing knowledge. *California Management Review, 40*(3), 90-111.

Brown, J., & Duguid, P. (2000). *The social life of information.* Boston: Harvard Business School Press.

Bryan, M. (1998). An introduction to the extensible markup language (XML). *Bulletin of the American Society for Information Science, 25*(1), 11–14.

Callon, M. (1991). Techno-economic networks and irreversibility. In J. Law (Ed.), *A sociology of monsters? Essays on power, technology and domination* (pp. 132–161). London: Routledge.

Chaiklin, S., & Lave, J. (1993). *Understanding practice: Perspectives on activity and context.* Cambridge: Cambridge University Press.

Churchill, E., Trevor, J., Bly, S., Nelson, L., & Cubranic, D. (2000). Anchored conversations: Chatting in the context of a document. *Proceedings of the CHI 2000 Conference on Human Factors in Computing Systems* (pp. 454–461). New York: ACM Press.

Clayman, S., & Maynard, D. (1995). Ethnomethodology and conversation analysis. In P. Ten Have & G. Psathas (Eds.), *Situated order: Studies in the social organization of talk and embodied activities* (pp. 1–30). Lanham, MD: University Press of America.

Cohen, D. (1998). Towards a knowledge context: Report on the first annual U.C. Berkeley Forum on Knowledge and the Firm. *California Management Review, 40*(3), 22–39.

Cohen, M. D., & Sproull, L. S. (Eds.). (1996). *Organizational learning.* London: Sage.

Coleman, J. S. (2000). Social capital in the creation of human capital. In E. L. Lesser (Ed.), *Knowledge and social capital* (pp. 17–41). Oxford: Butterworth-Heinemann.

Contu, A., & Willmott, H. (2000). Comment on Wenger and Yanow, Knowing in practice: A "delicate flower" in the organizational learning field. *Organization, 7,* 269–276.

Cook, S., & Yanow, D. (1993). Culture and organizational learning. *Journal of Management Inquiry, 2,* 373–390.

Covi, L. (1999). Material mastery: Situating digital library use in university research practices. *Information Processing & Management, 35,* 293–316.

Cronin, B., & Davenport, E. (2001). E-rogenous zones: Positioning pornography in the digital economy. *The Information Society, 17*(1), 33–48.

Cross, R., & Baird, L. (2000). Technology is not enough: Improving performance by building organizational memory. *Sloan Management Review, 41*(2), 69–78.

Davenport, E. (1999). Implicit orders: Documentary genres and organizational practice. In H. Albrechtsen (Ed.), *Proceedings of the 10th SIGCR classification workshop* (pp. 45–64). Silver Spring, MD: American Society for Information Science.

Davenport, E., & Cronin, B. (1998). Texts at work: Some thoughts on "just for you" service in the context of domain expertise. *Journal of Education for Library and Information Science, 39,* 264–274.

Davenport, E., & Hall, H. (2001). New knowledge and micro-level online organization: Communities of practice as a development framework. In R. Sprague (Ed.), *Proceedings of the 34th Annual Hawaii International Conference on Systems Sciences* (CD-ROM). Los Alamitos, CA: IEEE.

Davenport, E., & McKim, G. (1995). Groupware. *Annual Review of Information Science and Technology, 30,* 115–159.

Davenport, E., & Rosenbaum, H. (2000). A system for organizing situational knowledge in the workplace that is based on the shape of documents. In C. Beghtol, L. Howarth, & N. Williamson (Eds.), *Dynamism and stability in knowledge organization. Proceedings of the Sixth International ISKO Conference. Advances in Knowledge Organization* (pp. 352–358). Wurzburg: Ergon Verlag.

Davenport, T. H. (1997). *Information ecology: Mastering the information environment.* New York: Oxford University Press.

Davenport, T. H., & Klahr, P. (1998). Managing customer support knowledge. *California Management Review, 40*(3), 195–208.

Decortis, F., Noirfalise, S., & Pecheux, V. (1998). Distributed representations and collective memories in nuclear power plant shift changeover. In P. Marti & S.

Bagnara (Eds.), *Designing Collective Memories. Proceedings of the 7th Travail Humain Workshop* (11 pages). Paris: Le Travail Humain.

Deuten, J., & Rip, A. (2000). Narrative infrastructure in product creation processes. *Organization, 7,* 69–93.

Dixon, N. M. (2000). *Common knowledge: How companies thrive by sharing what they know.* Boston: Harvard Business School Press.

Donath, J., Karahalios, K., & Viegas, F. (1999). Vizualising conversation. In R. Sprague (Ed.), *Proceedings of the 32nd Annual Hawaii International Conference on Systems Sciences* (CD ROM). Los Alamitos, CA: IEEE.

Dourish, P. (1997). Different strokes for different folks: Privacy norms in three media spaces. *SIGGROUP Bulletin, 18*(1), 36–38.

Dyer, J., & Nobeoka, K. (2000). Creating and managing a high-performance knowledge-sharing network: The Toyota case. *Strategic Management Journal, 21,* 345–367.

Eden, C., & Ackerman, M. (1998). Analyzing and comparing idiographic causal maps. In C. Eden & J.-C. Spender (Eds.), *Managerial and organizational cognition: Theory, methods, research* (pp. 192–209). London: Sage.

Eden, C., & Spender, J.-C. (1998). *Managerial and organizational cognition: Theory, methods, research.* London: Sage.

Edvinsson, L. (1997). Developing intellectual capital at Skandia. *Long Range Planning, 30,* 366–373.

Elliott, M., & Kling, R. (1997). Professional use of digital libraries in organizations: Case study of legal research in civil and criminal courts. *Journal of the American Society for Information Science, 48,* 1023–1035.

Engeström, Y. (2000). Comment on Blacker et al., Activity theory and the social construction of knowledge: A story of four umpires. *Organization, 7,* 301–310.

Engeström, Y., & Middleton, D. (Eds.). (1997). *Cognition and communication at work.* Cambridge: Cambridge University Press.

Erdelez, S. (2000). Towards understanding information encountering on the Web. In D. Kraft (Ed.), *Proceedings of 63rd Annual Meeting of the American Society for Information Science* (pp. 363–371). Medford, NJ: Information Today, Inc.

Erdelez, S., & Doty, P. (1999). Adapting knowledge management to a heterogeneous information environment: A case study of county judges and clerks in rural Texas courts. In L. Woods (Ed.), *Proceedings of the 62nd Annual Meeting of the American Society for Information Science* (pp. 135–145). Medford, NJ: Information Today, Inc.

Erickson, T. (1997). Social interaction on the net: Virtual community or participatory genre? In J. Nunamaker & R. Sprague (Eds.), *Proceedings of the 30th Annual Hawaii International Conference on Systems Sciences* (pp. 23–30). Los Alamitos, CA: IEEE.

Erickson, T. (1999). Rhyme and punishment. In R. Sprague (Ed.), *Proceedings of the 32nd Annual Hawaii International Conference on Systems Sciences* (CD ROM). Los Alamitos, CA: IEEE.

Erickson, T., Smith, D., Kellogg, W., Laff, M., & Richards, J. (1999). Socially translucent systems: Social proxies, persistent conversation and the design of

"Babble." In M. Williams (Ed.), *Proceedings of the CHI 1999 Conference on Human Factors in Computing Systems: The CHI is the limit* (pp. 72–79). New York: ACM Press.

Fabritius, H. (1998). Triangulation as a multi-perspective strategy in a qualitative study of information seeking behaviour in journalists. In T. Wilson & D. Allen (Eds.), *Exploring the contexts of information behaviour: Proceedings of the Second International Conference on Research in Information Needs, Seeking and Use in Different Contexts* (pp. 406–419). London: Taylor Graham.

Falconer, J. (1999). The business pattern: A new tool for organizational knowledge capture and reuse. In L. Woods (Ed.), *Proceedings of the 62nd Annual Meeting of the American Society for Information Science* (pp. 313–330). Medford, NJ: Information Today, Inc.

Fleming, W. (1994). Methodography: The study of student learning as situated action. In G. Gibbs (Ed.), *Learning approaches evaluation and strategy: Improving student learning through assessment and evaluation* (pp. 525–544). Oxford: Oxford Brookes University.

Fox, S. (2000). Communities of practice, Foucault and actor-network theory. *Journal of Management Studies, 37,* 853–867.

Garton, L., Haythornthwaite, C., & Wellman, B. (1998). Studying online social networks. In S. Jones (Ed.), *Doing Internet research: Critical issues and methods for examining the Net* (pp. 75–106). London: Sage.

Gerson, E., & Star, S. (1986). Analyzing due process in the workplace. *ACM Transactions on Office Systems, 4*(3), 257–270.

Gherardi, I. S., Nicolini, D., & Odella, F. (1998). Toward a social understanding of how people learn in organizations: The notion of shared curriculum. *Management Learning, 29,* 273–298.

Ginnett, R. (1993). Crews as groups: Their formation and their leadership. In B. Wiener, B. Kanki, & R. Helmreich (Eds.), *Cockpit resource management.* New York: Academic Press.

Glushko, R., Tenenbaum, J., & Meltzes, B. (1999). An XML framework for agent-based e-commerce. *Communications of the ACM, 42*(3), 106–114.

Goodwin, M. (1995). Assembling a response: Setting and collaboratively constructed work talk. In P. Ten Have & G. Psathas (Eds.), *Situated order: Studies in the social organization of talk and embodied activities* (pp. 173–186). Lanham, MD: University Press of America.

Granovetter, M. (1973). The strength of weak ties. *American Journal of Sociology, 78,* 1360–1380.

Green, D. (1999). The evolution of Web searching. In B. McKenna (Ed.), *Proceedings of the 23rd International Online Meeting 1999* (pp. 251–258). Hinksey Hill, U.K.: Learned Information Ltd.

Greenberg, J., & Dickelman, G. (2000). Distributed cognition: A foundation for performance support. *Performance Improvement, 39*(6), 18–22.

Greene, S., Marchionini, G., Plaisant, C., & Shneiderman, B. (2000). Previews and overviews in digital libraries: Designing surrogates to support visual information seeking. *Journal of the American Society for Information Science, 51,* 380–393.

Hamel, G. (2000). Waking up IBM: How a gang of unlikely rebels transformed Big Blue. *Harvard Business Review, 78*(4), 137–146.

Hargadon, A. (1998). Firms as knowledge brokers: Lessons in pursuing continuous innovation. *California Management Review, 40*(3), 209–227.

Haythornthwaite, C. (1996). Social network analysis: An approach and technique for the study of information exchange. *Library & Information Science Research, 18,* 323–342.

Haythornthwaite, C. (1999). Collaborative work networks among distributed learners. In R. Sprague (Ed.), *Proceedings of the 32nd Annual Hawaii International Conference on System Sciences* (CD ROM). Los Alamitos, CA: IEEE.

Hertzum, M., & Pejtersen, A. (2000). Information seeking practices of engineers: Searching for documents as well as people. *Information Processing & Management, 36,* 761–778.

Hildreth, P., & Kimble, C. (1999). Communities of practice in the distributed international environment. In B. Fields & P. Wright (Eds.), *Design for collaboration: Communities constructing technology.* York: Department of Computer Science, University of York.

Holmström, H. & Jakobsson, M. (2001). Using models in virtual design. In R. Sprague (Ed.), *Proceedings of the 34th Annual Hawaii International Conference on Systems Sciences* (CD-ROM). Los Alamitos, CA: IEEE.

Holsthouse, D. (1998). Knowledge research issues. *California Management Review, 40*(3), 277–280.

Huber, J., & Gillaspy, M. (1998). Social constructs and disease: Implications for controlled vocabulary for HIV/AIDS. *Library Trends, 47,* 190–208.

Huff, A. (1988). *Mapping strategic thought.* Chichester: John Wiley.

Hutchins, E. (1991). The social organization of distributed cognition. In L. Resnick, J. M. Levine, & S. D. Teasley (Eds.), *Perspectives on socially shared cognition* (pp. 284–307). Washington, DC: American Psychological Association.

Hutchins, E. (1993). Learning to navigate. In S. Chaiklin & J. Lave (Eds.), *Understanding practice: Perspectives on activity and context* (pp. 35–63). Cambridge: Cambridge University Press.

Hutchins, E. (1995a). *Cognition in the wild.* Cambridge, MA: MIT Press.

Hutchins, E. (1995b). How a cockpit remembers its speeds. *Cognitive Science, 19*(3), 265–288.

Hutchins, E. (1996). Organizing work by adaptation. In M. D. Cohen & L. S. Sproull (Eds.), *Organizational learning* (pp. 20–57). London: Sage.

Hutchins, E., & Klausen, T. (1997). Distributed cognition in an airline cockpit. In E. Engeström & D. Middleton (Eds.), *Cognition and communication at work* (pp. 15–34). Cambridge: Cambridge University Press.

Jacob, E., & Albrechtsen, H. (1998). When essence becomes function: Post-structuralist implications for an ecological theory of organizational classification systems. In T. Wilson & D. Allen (Eds.), *Exploring the contexts of information behaviour: Proceedings of the Second International Conference on Research in Information Needs, Seeking and Use in Different Contexts* (pp. 519–534). London: Taylor Graham.

Jacob, E., & Shaw, D. (1998). Socognitive perspectives on representation. *Annual Review of Information Science and Technology, 33,* 131–186.

Jones, M. (1997). Successful corporate communities: All communities are not the same. *SIGGROUP Bulletin, 18*(2), 31–32.

Jubert, A. (1999). Developing an infrastructure for communities of practice. In B. McKenna (Ed.), *Proceedings of the 19th International Online Meeting* (pp. 165–168). Hinksey Hill, U.K.: Learned Information.

Judge, W. Q., Fryxell, G. E., & Dooley, R. S. (2000). The new task of R&D management: Creating goal-directed communities for innovation. In E. L. Lesser, M. A. Fontaine, & J. A. Slusher (Eds.), *Knowledge and communities* (pp. 37–51). Oxford: Butterworth-Heinemann.

Kaufer, D., & Carley, K. (1993). *Communication at a distance: The influence of print on sociocultural organization and change.* Hillsdale, NJ: Lawrence Erlbaum.

Keiichi, N., Voss, A., Juhnke, M., & Kreifelts, T. (1998). Concept index: Capturing emergent community knowledge from documents. *Designing collective memories. Proceedings of the 7th Travail Humain Workshop* (10 pages). Paris: Le Travail Humain.

Kendall, L. (1999). Recontextualizing "cyberspace": Methodological considerations for on-line research. In S. Jones (Ed.), *Doing Internet research: Critical issues and methods for examining the Net* (pp. 57–74). London: Sage.

Kingston, J., & Macintosh, A. (2000). Knowledge management through multiperspective modelling: Representing and distributing organisational memory. *Knowledge Based Systems Journal, 13*(2/3), 121–131.

Kling, R., & Elliott, M. (1994). Digital library design for organizational usability. *SIGOIS Bulletin, 15*(2), 59–70.

Kling, R., & Lamb, R. (1996). Analyzing alternative visions of electronic publishing and digital libraries. In R. Peek & G. Newby (Eds.), *Scholarly publishing: The electronic frontier* (pp. 17–54). Cambridge, MA: MIT Press.

Kling, R., McKim, G., Fortuna, J., & King, A. (2000). *A bit more to IT: Scientific multiple media communication forums as socio-technical interaction networks (working paper).* Retrieved November 16, 2000, from the World Wide Web: http://www.slis.indiana.edu/SCIT/a-bit-more-to-it.pdf

Kollock, P. (1999). Economies of online cooperation: Gift and public goods in cyberspace. In M. Smith & P. Kollock (Eds.), *Communities in cyberspace* (pp. 220–239). London: Routledge.

Kransdorff, A. (2000). Knowledge management's role in experiential learning. In S. Rock (Ed.), *Liberating knowledge* (pp. 73–79). London: IBM/CBI.

Kuutti, K. (1996). Activity theory as a potential framework for human-computer interaction research. In B. Nardi (Ed.), *Context as consciousness: Activity theory and human-computer interaction* (pp. 17–44). Cambridge, MA: MIT Press.

Lam, A. (2000). Tacit knowledge, organizational learning and societal institutions: An integrated framework. *Organization Studies, 21,* 487–513.

Lamb, R. (1999). Using intranets: Preliminary results from a socio-technical field study. In R. Sprague (Ed.), *Proceedings of the 32nd Annual Hawaii International Conference on System Sciences* (CD ROM). Los Alamitos, CA: IEEE.

Landay, J., & Davis, R. (1999). Making sharing pervasive: Ubiquitous computing for shared note taking. *IBM Systems Journal, 38,* 531–550.

Latour, B., & Woolgar, S. (1979). *Laboratory life: The social construction of scientific facts.* Beverley Hills, CA: Sage.

Lave, J. (1988). *Cognition in practice: Mind, mathematics, and culture in everyday life.* New York: Cambridge University Press.

Lave, J. (1991). Situated learning in communities of practice. In L. Resnick, J. M. Levine, & S. D. Teasley (Eds.), *Perspectives on socially shared cognition* (pp. 63–82). Washington, DC: American Psychological Association.

Lave, J., & Wenger, E. (1991). *Situated learning: Legitimate peripheral participation.* Cambridge: Cambridge University Press.

Leonard, D., & Sensiper, S. (1998). The role of tacit knowledge in group innovation. *California Management Review, 40*(3), 112–132.

Lesser, E. (2000). Leveraging social capital in organizations. In E. L. Lesser (Ed.), *Knowledge and social capital: Foundations and applications* (pp. 3–16). Oxford: Butterworth-Heinemann.

Lesser, E. L., & Prusak, L. (2000). Communities of practice, social capital and organizational knowledge. In E. L. Lesser, M. A. Fontaine, & J. A. Slusher (Eds.), *Knowledge and communities* (pp. 123–131). Oxford: Butterworth-Heinemann.

Lesser, E. L., Fontaine, M. A., & Slusher, J. A. (Eds.). (2000). *Knowledge and communities.* Oxford: Butterworth-Heinemann.

Lewicki, R., & Bunker, B. (1996). Developing and maintaining trust in working relationships. In R. Kramer & T. Tyler (Eds.), *Trust in organizations* (pp. 114–139). London: Sage.

Loos, I. (1999). Intertextual networks in organisations: The use of written and oral business discourse in relation to context. In F. Bargiela-Chiapinni & C. R. Nickerson (Eds.), *Writing business: Genres, media and discourses* (pp. 315–332). London: Longman.

Lutters, W., & Ackerman, M. (1997). A collectivity in electronic social space. *SIGGROUP Bulletin, 18*(1), 41–43.

Lyman, P. (1999). Designing libraries to be learning communities. In S. Criddle, L. Dempsey, & R. Heseltine (Eds.), *Information landscapes for a learning society: Networking and the future of libraries 3* (pp. 75–87). London: Library Association.

Lynch, C. (1999). Civilising the information ecology. In S. Criddle, L. Dempsey, & R. Heseltine (Eds.), *Information landscapes for a learning society: Networking and the future of libraries 3* (pp. 257–267). London: Library Association.

Macaulay, C. (1999). Inscribing the palimpsest: Information sources in the newsroom. In K. Buckner (Ed.), *Esprit i3 workshop on ethnographic studies in real and virtual environments: Inhabited information spaces and connected communities* (pp. 42–52). Edinburgh: Queen Margaret College.

Mackay, W. (1999). Is paper safer? The role of paper flight strips in air traffic control. *ACM Transactions on Computer-Human Interaction, 6,* 316–340.

Maes, P., Guttman, R., & Moukas, A. (1999). Agents that buy and sell. *Communications of the ACM, 42*(3), 81–91.

Marsh, S., & Meech, J. (2000). Trust in design. In G. Szillus & T. Turner (Eds.), *CHI '00 extended abstracts* (pp. 45–46). New York: ACM Press.

Marshall, C. C., Shipman, F. M., & McCall, R. (2000). Making large-scale information resources serve communities of practice. In E. L. Lesser, M. A. Fontaine, & J. A. Slusher (Eds.), *Knowledge and communities* (pp. 225–247). Oxford: Butterworth-Heinemann.

McVeigh, T. (2000, March 26). Mind virus could give us the shopping bug. *Observer,* p. 7.

McWilliam, G. (2000). Building stronger brands through online communities. *Sloan Management Review, 41*(3), 43–54.

Merali, Y. (2000). Self-organising communities. In S. Rock (Ed.), *Liberating knowledge* (pp. 80–87). London: IBM/CBI.

Millen, D., & Dray, S. (1999). Information sharing in an online community of journalists. In K. Buckner (Ed.), *Esprit i3 workshop on ethnographic studies in real and virtual environments: Inhabited information spaces and connected communities* (pp. 53–60). Edinburgh: Queen Margaret College.

Morrison, J. (1997). Organizational memory information systems: Characteristics and development strategies. In J. Nunamaker & R. Sprague (Eds.), *Proceedings of the 13th Annual Hawaii International Conference on System Sciences* (pp. 300–309). Los Alamitos, CA: IEEE.

Murphy, L. (2001). Digital documents in organizational communities of practice: A first look. In R. Sprague (Ed.), *Proceedings of the 34th Annual Hawaii International Conference on Systems Sciences* (CD-ROM). Los Alamitos, CA: IEEE.

Mynatt, E., Adler, A., Ito, M., & O'Day, V. (1997). Design for network communities. *CHI '97 Conference Proceedings on Human Factors in Computing Systems* (pp. 210–217). New York: ACM Press.

Nahapiet, J., & Ghoshal, S. (2000). Social capital, intellectual capital and the organizational advantage. In E. L. Lesser (Ed.), *Knowledge and social capital* (pp. 119–157). Oxford: Butterworth-Heinemann.

Naper, I. (2001). System features of an inhabited 3D virtual environment supporting multimodality in communication. In R. Sprague (Ed.), *Proceedings of the 34th Annual Hawaii International Conference on Systems Sciences* (CD-ROM). Los Alamitos, CA: IEEE.

Nardi, B. (Ed.). (1996). *Context and consciousness: Activity theory and human-computer interaction.* Cambridge, MA: MIT Press.

Nardi, B., & O'Day, V. (1999). *Information ecologies: Using technology with heart.* Cambridge, MA: MIT Press.

Newell, S., Scarborough, H., Swan, J., & Hislop, D. (2000). Intranets and knowledge management: De-centred technologies and the limits of technological discourse. In C. Prichard, R. Hull, M. Chumer, & H. Willmott (Eds.), *Managing knowledge: Critical investigations of work and learning* (pp. 88–106). Basingstoke, U.K.: Macmillan.

Nonaka, I. (1991). The knowledge-creating company. *Harvard Business Review, 69*(6), 14–37.

Nonaka, I., & Konno, N. (1998). The concept of "Ba": Building a foundation for knowledge creation. *California Management Review, 40*(3), 40–54.

Nonaka, I., & Takeuchi, H. (1995). *The knowledge creating company.* New York: Oxford University Press.

Nonaka, I., Umemoto, K., & Sasaki, K. (1998). Three tales of knowledge creating companies. In G. Von Krogh, J. Roos, & D. Kleine (Eds.), *Knowing in firms: Understanding, managing and measuring knowledge* (pp. 146–172). London: Sage.

Nonnecke, B., & Preece, J. (1999). Shedding light on lurkers in online communities. In K. Buckner (Ed.), *Esprit i3 workshop on ethnographic studies in real and virtual environments: Inhabited information spaces and connected communities* (pp. 123–128). Edinburgh: Queen Margaret College.

Nowak, M., & Sigmund, K. (2000, 5 May). Shrewd investments. *Science, 288,* 819–820.

O'Dell, C., & Jackson Grayson, C. (1998). If only we knew what we know: Identification and transfer of internal best practices. *California Management Review, 40*(3), 154–174.

Orlikowski, W. (1993). Learning from Notes: Organizational issues in groupware implementation. *The Information Society, 9*(3), 237–250.

Orlikowski, W., & Yates, J. (1994). Genre repertoire: The structuring of communicative practices in organizations. *Administrative Science Quarterly, 39,* 541–574.

Orr, J. (1987, June). Narratives at work: Story telling as cooperative diagnostic activity. *Field Service Manager,* 47–60.

Orr, J. (1990). Sharing knowledge, celebrating identity: Community memory in a service culture. In D. Middleton & D. Edwards (Eds.), *Collective remembering* (pp. 168–169). London: Sage.

Pejtersen, A., & Albrechtsen, H. (2000). Ecological work based classification schemes. In C. Beghtol, L. Howarth, & N. Williamson (Eds.), *Dynamism and stability in knowledge organization. Proceedings of the Sixth International ISKO Conference: Advances in Knowledge Organization* (pp. 97–110). Wurzburg: Ergon Verlag.

Perry, M. (1998). Process, representation and taskworld: Distributed cognition and the organisation of information. In T. Wilson & D. Allen (Eds.), *Exploring the contexts of information behaviour: Proceedings of the Second International*

Conference on Research in Information Needs, Seeking and Use in Different Contexts (pp. 552–567). London: Taylor Graham.

Raeithel, A., & Velichkovsky, B. (1996). Joint attention and co-construction: New ways to foster user-designer collaboration. In B. Nardi (Ed.), *Context and consciousness: Activity theory and human-computer interaction* (pp. 199–231). Cambridge, MA: MIT Press.

Rasmussen, J., Pejtersen, A., & Goodstein, L. (1994). *Cognitive systems engineering*. New York: John Wiley.

Reed, D. (2001) "Making conversation:" Sequential integrity and the local management of interaction on Internet newsgroups. In R. Sprague (Ed.), *Proceedings of the 34th Annual Hawaii International Conference on Systems Sciences* (CD-ROM). Los Alamitos, CA: IEEE.

Resnick, L., Levine, J. M., & Teasley, S. D. (1991). *Perspectives on socially shared cognition*. Washington, DC: American Psychological Association.

Rioux, K. (2000). Sharing information for others on the World Wide Web: A preliminary examination. *Proceedings of the 63rd Annual Meeting of the American Society for Information Science, 68–77.*

Romano, N., Nunamaker, J., Briggs, R., & Vogel, D. (1998). Architecture, design and development of an HTML/JavaScript Web-based group support system. *Journal of the American Society for Information Science, 49*, 649–667.

Ruggles, R. (1998). The state of the notion: Knowledge management in practice. *California Management Review, 40*(3), 80–89.

Salomon, G. (Ed.). (1993a). *Distributed cognitions*. New York: Cambridge University Press.

Salomon, G. (1993b). No distribution without individual's cognition: A dynamic interactional view. In G. Salomon (Ed.), *Distributed cognitions* (pp. 111–138). New York: Cambridge University Press.

Samitt, M. K. (1999). Knowledge management in a corporate environment: An annotated bibliography. *Business and Finance Bulletin, 110*, 39–50.

Sauvagnac, C., & Falzon, P. (1998). Memorizing decisions: From the report to organizational knowledge. In P. Marti & S. Bagnara (Eds.), *Designing Collective Memories. Proceedings of the 7th Travail Humain Workshop* (8 pages). Paris: Le Travail Humain.

Sawhney, M., & Pirandelli, E. (2000). Communities of creation. *California Management Review, 42*(4), 24–54.

Sawyer, S., Eschenfelder, K., & Heckman, R. (2000). Knowledge markets: Cooperation among distributed technical specialists. In T. Srikantaiah & M. Koenig (Eds.), *Knowledge management for the information professional* (pp. 181–204). Medford, NJ: Information Today, Inc.

Scheepers, R., & Damsgaard, J. (1997). Using Internet technology within the organization: A structurationalist analysis of intranets, *Proceedings of Group 97, Phoenix Arizona* (pp. 9–18). New York: ACM Press.

Schiff, L., Van House, N., & Butler, M. (1997). Understanding complex information environments: A social analysis of watershed planning. In R. Allen & E.

Rasmussen (Eds.), *Proceedings of the 2nd ACM International Conference on Digital Libraries* (pp. 161–168). New York: ACM Press.

Schlegoff, E. (1991). Conversation analysis and socially shared cognition. In L. Resnick, J. M. Levine, & S. D. Teasley (Eds.), *Perspectives on socially shared cognition* (pp. 150–171). Washington, DC: American Psychological Association.

Schön, D. (1983). Reflective practice in the science-based professions. In D. Schön (Ed.), *The reflective practitioner* (pp. 168-203). New York: Basic Books.

Schultze, U., & Boland, R. (1997). Hard and soft information genres: An analysis of two Notes databases. In J. Nunamaker & R. Sprague (Eds.), *Proceedings of the 30th Annual Hawaii International Conference on System Sciences* (pp. 40–49). Los Alamitos, CA: IEEE.

Snowden, D. (1998). A framework for creating an acceptable programme. In S. Rock (Ed.), *Knowledge management: A real business guide* (pp. 7–17). London: CBI/IBM.

Snowden, D. (2000). Liberating knowledge. In S. Rock (Ed.), *Liberating knowledge* (pp. 6–19). London: IBM/CBI.

Soergel, D. (1998). *Design of an integrated information structure interface. A unified framework for indexing and searching in database, expert, information retrieval and hypermedia systems.* (Unpublished internal paper): College of Library and Information Services, University of Maryland.

Soergel, D. (1999). The rise of ontologies or the re-invention of classification. *Journal of the American Society for Information Science, 50,* 1119–1120.

Solomon, P. (1998). Information mosaics: Patterns of action that structure. In T. Wilson & D. Allen (Eds.), *Exploring the contexts of information behaviour: Proceedings of the Second International Conference on Research in Information Needs, Seeking and Use in Different Contexts* (pp. 150–175). London: Taylor Graham.

Sonnenwald, D. (1998). Perspectives of human information behaviour: Contexts, situations, social networks and information horizons. In T. Wilson & D. Allen (Eds.), *Exploring the contexts of information behaviour: Proceedings of the Second International Conference on Research in Information Needs, Seeking and Use in Different Contexts* (pp. 176–190). London: Taylor Graham.

Star, S. (1995). The politics of formal representations: Wizards, gurus and organizational complexity. In S. Star (Ed.), *Ecologies of knowledge: Work and politics in science and technology.* Albany, NY: State University of New York Press.

Star, S., & Griesemer, J. (1989). Institutional ecology, "translations" and boundary objects: Amateurs and professionals in Berkeley's Museum of Vertebrate Zoology. *Social Studies of Science, 19,* 387–420.

Star, S., & Ruhlehder, K. (1994). Steps towards an ecology of infrastructure: Complex problems in design and access for large-scale collaborative systems. In R. Furuta & C. Neuwirth (Eds.), *CSCW '94: Proceedings of the Conference on Computer-Supported Cooperative Work* (pp. 253–264). New York: ACM Press.

Stein, E. (1995). Organizational memory: Review of concepts and recommendations for management. *International Journal of Information Management,* *15*(2), 17–32.

Stinchcombe, A. (1965). Social structure and environment. In J. March (Ed.), *The handbook of organizations* (pp. 142–193). Berkeley, CA: University of California Press.

Storck, J., & Hill, P. (2000). Knowledge diffusion through "strategic communities." *Sloan Management Review, 41*(2), 63–74.

Suchman, L. (1986). *Plans and situated actions: The problem of human-machine communication.* Cambridge: Cambridge University Press.

Suchman, L. (2000). Organizing alignment: A case of bridge-building. *Organization, 7,* 311–327.

Suchman, L., & Trigg, R. (1993). Artificial intelligence as craftwork. In S. Chaiklin & J. Lave (Eds.), *Understanding practice: Perspectives on activity and context* (pp. 144–178). Cambridge: Cambridge University Press.

Swales, J. (1990). *Genre analysis: English in academic and research setting.* Cambridge: Cambridge University Press.

Swan, J., & Scarbrough, H. (2001). Knowledge, purpose, and process: Linking knowledge management and innovation. In R. Sprague (Ed.), *Proceedings of the 34th Annual Hawaii International Conference on Systems Sciences* (CD-ROM). Los Alamitos, CA: IEEE.

Tannen, D. (1995). What's in a frame? Surface evidence for underlying expectations. In G. Psathas (Ed.), *Conversation analysis: The study of talk-in-interaction* (pp.138–181). Thousand Oaks, CA: Sage.

Teigland, R. (2000). Communities of practice at an Internet firm: Netovation vs. on-time performance. In E. L. Lesser, M. A. Fontaine, & J. A. Slusher (Eds.), *Knowledge and communities* (pp. 151–178). Oxford: Butterworth-Heinemann.

Tsoukas, H. (1996). The firm as a distributed knowledge system: A constructionist approach. *Strategic Management Journal 17*(special issue), 11–25.

Turkle, S. (1996). *Life on the screen.* Cambridge, MA: MIT Press.

Twidale, M., & Nichols, D. (1996). Collaborative browsing and visualisation of the search process. *Aslib Proceedings, 48*(7/8), 177–182.

Uschold, M., King, M., Moralee, S., & Zorgios, V. (1999). The enterprise ontology. *Knowledge Engineering Review, 13*(1), 31–89.

Vakkari, P., Savolainen, R., & Dervin, B. (1997). *Information seeking in context.* London: Taylor Graham.

van der Spek, R., & Kingma, J. (2000). Achieving successful knowledge management initiatives. In S. Rock (Ed.), *Liberating knowledge* (pp. 20–30). London: IBM/CBI.

Van House, N. (in press). Digital libraries and collaborative knowledge construction. In A. Bishop, B. B. Buttenfield, & N. Van House (Eds*). Digital library use: Social practice in design and evaluation.* Cambridge, MA: MIT Press.

Vickery, B. (1997). Ontologies. *Journal of Information Science, 23,* 277–286.

von Krogh, G. (1998). Care in knowledge creation. *California Management Review, 40*(3), 133–153.

von Krogh, G., Ichijo, K., & Nonaka, I. (2000). *Enabling knowledge creation: How to unlock the mystery of tacit knowledge and release the power of innovation.* Oxford: Oxford University Press.

Wedekind, C., & Milinski, M. (2000). Cooperation through image scoring in humans. *Science, 288,* 850–852.

Weick, K. (1995). The substance of sense making. In K. Weick (Ed.), *Sensemaking in organizations* (pp. 106–131). Thousand Oaks, CA: Sage.

Weick, K. (1996). The non-traditional quality of organizational learning. In M. D. Cohen & L. S. Sproull (Eds.), *Organizational learning* (pp. 163–174). London: Sage.

Weick, K., & Roberts, K. (1993). Collective mind in organizations: Heedful inter-relating on flight decks. *Administrative Science Quarterly, 38,* 357–381.

Wellman, B., & Gulia, M. (1999). Virtual communities as communities: Net surfers don't ride alone. In M. Smith & P. Kollock (Eds.), *Communities in cyberspace* (pp. 167–194). London: Routledge.

Wenger, E. (1998). *Communities of practice: Learning, meaning and identity.* New York: Cambridge University Press.

Wenger, E. (2000a). Communities of practice: The key to knowledge strategy. In E. L. Lesser, M. A. Fontaine, & J. A. Slusher (Eds.), *Knowledge and communities* (pp. 3–20). Oxford: Butterworth-Heinemann.

Wenger, E. (2000b). Communities of practices and social learning systems. *Organization, 7*(2), 225–246.

Wenger, E., & Snyder, W. (2000). Communities of practice: The organizational frontier. *Harvard Business Review, 78*(1), 139–145.

Wexelblat, A. (1999). History-based tools for navigation. In R. Sprague (Ed.), *Proceedings of the 32nd Annual Hawaii International Conference on System Sciences* (CD ROM). Los Alamitos, CA: IEEE.

Wexelblat, A., & Maes, P. (1999). Footprints: History-rich tools for information foraging. *Proceedings of the CHI '99 Conference on Human Factors in Computing Systems: The CHI is the limit* (pp. 270–277). New York: ACM Press.

Wilson, T., & Allen, D. (Eds.). (1998). *Exploring the contexts of information behaviour: Proceedings of the Second International Conference on Research in Information Needs, Seeking and Use in Different Contexts.* London: Taylor Graham.

Wolf, C. (1997). Transient coooperating communities. *SIGGROUP Bulletin, 18*(1), 47–49.

Wright, P., Pocock, S., & Fields, B. (1988). The prescription and practice of work on the flight deck. In P. Wright & B. Fields (Eds.), *Understanding work and designing artefacts* (seven pages). York: Department of Computer Science, University of York.

Yanow, D. (2000). Seeing organizational learning: A "cultural" view. *Organization, 7,* 247–268.

Yates, J., & Orlikowski, W. (1992). Genres of organizational communication: A structurational approach to studying communication and media. *Academy of Management Review, 17*(2), 299–326.

Yates, J., Orlikowski, W., & Rennecker, J. (1997). Collaborative genres for collaboration: Genre systems in digital media. In J. Nunamaker & R. Sprague (Eds.), *Proceedings of the 30th Annual Hawaii International Conference on System Sciences* (pp. 50–59). Los Alamitos, CA: IEEE.

Yates, S., & Sumner, T. (1997). Digital genres and the new burden of fixity. In J. Nunamaker & R. Sprague (Eds.), *Proceedings of the 30th Annual Hawaii International Conference on System Science.* (pp. 3–12). Los Alamitos, CA: IEEE.

CHAPTER 5

Discovering Information in Context

Paul Solomon
University of North Carolina at Chapel Hill

Introduction and Overview

This chapter has three purposes: to illuminate the ways in which people discover, shape, or create information as part of their lives and work; to consider how the resources and rules of people's situations facilitate or limit discovery of information; and to introduce the idea of a sociotechnical systems design science that is founded in part on understanding the discovery of information in context. In addressing these purposes the chapter focuses on both theoretical and research works in information studies and related fields that shed light on information as something that is embedded in the fabric of people's lives and work. Thus, the *discovery of information* view presented here characterizes information as being constructed through involvement in life's activities, problems, tasks, and social and technological structures, as opposed to being independent and context free. Given this process view, discovering information entails engagement, reflection, learning, and action—all the behaviors that research subjects often speak of as making sense—above and beyond the traditional focus of the information studies field: seeking without consideration of connections across time.

The chapter, thus, offers a reconceptualization and refocusing of the work of information studies from wondering why people use or do not use information institutions, systems, or sources toward considering what information is to people, how *stuff* ends up becoming information, and how information so discovered influences further action. The idea is that through such an understanding in context, a foundation will be set for designing collections (content and contexts), organizational schemes (representations and classifications), retrieval mechanisms, and displays that fit the problems and tasks of life and work. The hope is that this idea of fit might lead to the creation of systems that, through their flexibility, accommodate people at various stages in their discovery of information.

This view examines, in a positive way, such questions as why people do not use information systems when, in the eyes of information professionals, these systems are what people should be using. The aim is to develop an understanding of the difference between what information professionals label as information—the representations of objects or objects themselves that are contained in, for example, databases and libraries—and what becomes information as people move through life and interact socially as they discover what they need to know to function. Another way of labeling this distinction is with the anthropologist's *emic*—the perspective of the outsider—and *etic*—the perspective of the insider (Sandstrom & Sandstrom, 1995). This distinction is made to highlight similarity and difference in order to inform design.

Given the constraints of space and limits on number of references, there was no attempt to be exhaustive in selecting the literature employed here to elucidate the view of discovering information in context. There is a tendency to cite the recent and draw on work from related disciplines. Most attention is given to material that explores the nature of discovering information in context through social (or sociotechnical) studies of information.

This is a significantly different approach from that taken by Proper and Bruza (1999), for instance, whose consideration of *information discovery* is logic-based and represents a burgeoning literature emphasizing resource discovery on the Web. One purpose of resource discovery and other approaches that fall under the rubric of information discovery is to support individuals' shaping or making of information as they interact with information systems and technology. The insights gained from research that explores what information means to people in the context of their lives and work may inform information discovery and assist in information system design. Therefore, a portion of this chapter explores approaches that show promise in helping people discover information in context. Taken together, the social studies of information and the systems that support exploration and learning move toward the integration of research involving people and systems called for by Saracevic (1999).

There are no previous reviews (*ARIST* or otherwise) that explicitly focus on discovering information in context in the manner of this chapter. Nevertheless, there are several reviews that provide a foundation for the view presented here. These include the work by Faibisoff and Ely (1976), which surveyed studies of *information needs* and, in the spirit of the time, built upon the research to offer generalizations about information needs and guidelines for the design of information systems. This taking of stock is, perhaps, most significant in that it leads to a realization that such generalizations and principles seldom stand alone, but require the addition of context in order to produce products that support the discovery of information within situations and for particular tasks.

Dervin and Nilan's (1986) review addresses this issue, in part, by calling for a paradigm shift from a focus on system to a focus on user. By understanding situations, gaps, and use, it may be that we can understand what information means to people in context and provide information structures that support the interactions of situation, gap, and use. This work also focuses attention on the process involved in this interaction, which is labeled sense making. Katzer and Fletcher (1992) focus on managers and what constitutes information in managerial situations, where the information that (management) information systems provide and the information that managers use are often incongruent. McKinnon and Bruns (1992) and Auster and Choo (1993) provide reviews related to the Katzer and Fletcher work that focus on internal operations and environmental scanning, respectively. Palmquist (1992) highlights the influence or shaping effect of technology on individuals. Sugar (1995) brings people and systems together in his review. Pettigrew, Fidel, and Bruce (in press) review conceptual frameworks employed in, or resulting from, studies of information behavior.

Additional sources of theory and research relating to this review include the proceedings of the Information Seeking in Context conferences (Vakkari, Savolainen, & Dervin, 1997; Wilson & Allen, 1999), and the special issue of *Information Processing & Management* (1999, 35[6]) on information seeking in context.

Discovering information in context is an in-the-world idea; thus, one way you can make sense of the process of information discovery is to reflect on what becomes information for you as you read on. You might also consider how you shape what turns out to be information to you in your own way as a reflection of your own interests and concerns. This adventure begins with a consideration of some of the theoretical and conceptual views underlying the discovery of information in context. This is followed by explorations of such discovery in terms of process, structure, contexts, methods, and design.

Foundations

The previous section referred to some works that contributed to a conceptualization of individuals' discovery of information as they move through life in terms of structure, process, systems in interaction, and other people. This section adds the contributing theoretical view of *structuration* as well as the recent contributions of several continuing research streams.

Structuration

As discovery of information is viewed as a learning process—although it could also be a particular act within the process—it is useful to recognize that a system of activity functions through the interaction of structure and process. Therefore, ideas about the constitution of socio-technical systems seem basic to identifying and understanding the constituents of information discovery (e.g., making sense, reflection, thinking, learning, engagement). Structures of various sorts exist to focus attention and in doing so sometimes facilitate, inhibit, or prohibit actions. Thus, information systems focus attention on a particular sphere of activity, allow some tasks to be performed, prohibit others, and through these capacities exercise power (Introna, 1997). The act of structuring, then, limits our attention and view of situations.

Anthony Giddens' (1984) structuration theory and Luhmann's (1995) theory of autopoietic systems both provide similar general templates for considering the interaction of structure (resources and rules in Giddens' terms) and action. Structuration theory, in particular, recognizes the duality of structure and action, where structure encourages certain kinds of actions and prohibits others. The resulting actions reinforce, adapt, or change the facilitating structure.

Orlikowski (1992) uses Giddens' structuration theory to focus explicit attention on technology as a structure: resources and rules. Her field study, a software consulting firm, illustrates how the separate development and operation of a technological system led to its inability to fully fit the operational environment. This is an empirical expression of what Luhmann (1995) conveys in his treatise on the self-referential nature of social systems (autopoiesis): The structure of the system and the kinds of actions the system recognizes or permits cut the system off from other systems through, for instance, a lack of congruence of terminology or fit with the activities of other systems. Attempts to overcome these self-limiting effects of self-referential systems by incorporating the structures of other self-referential systems result in increased system complexity, which further limits a system's ability to meet the needs of other systems. This is also an expression of the challenge that we face in gaining an understanding of how people discover information in context and using that understanding to support systems design.

Barreau's (in press) study of a commercial off-the-shelf software package to support transactions (e.g., ordering, payments) in the publishing industry illustrates this autopoietic characteristic of systems. In each of the three organizational cases studied, the software did not quite fit and the organizations involved *made do* by forgoing desired functions or creating their own supporting systems, which resulted in a less-than-seamless integration. Bailey's (2000) analysis of nursing work in relation to an effort to implement a computerized patient record also illustrates how technological structures that are imposed on a task environment (labor and delivery) may not fit with the primary task at hand (patient care) as hospitals try to find ways of meeting secondary (e.g., regulatory, insurance) requirements for information. The lessons learned—both direct and indirect—from such intensive studies of information systems in action provide rich fodder for both general information system improvements and more specific information management structures in context.

What to Call the Processes and Actions of People as they Discover Information

One of the continuing struggles within the field of information studies has been the question of how to conceptualize, for the purpose of informing system design, people and the social and technological structures that promote and inhibit access to that which becomes information. There has been a tendency to focus on the individual's encounter with information systems—often bibliographic. This individual focus has led us to use such terms as *information seeking* and *information behavior* as we struggle to conceptualize the special nature of the interaction of human and system. These terms are, themselves, contentious for various reasons as evidenced by the December 1999 discussion thread on the JESSE listserv (http://listserv.utk.edu/cgi-bin/wa?A1=ind 9912&L=jesse). The view taken here of discovering information in context aims at adding social and temporal dimensions to our conceptual models and thinking. This review, therefore, turns to several continuing or emerging streams of research that contribute to the theoretical bases of the discussion.

Life in the Round

Chatman's (1996, 1999) studies of the information worlds of participants in a job training program, janitors, retired women, and women in prison has led her to develop a *theory of life in the round*, where context shapes inhabitants' definitions of what information is as well as appropriate ways of seeking and using it. Chatman's (1999) notion of *roundness* captures the difference between a focus on *just* information seeking, which expresses an ideal developed for scientists and engineers and applies it to all groups, and discovering information in context, which takes notice of the roundness created by the interaction of people, technology, and social structure. Chatman's (1996) concepts of *secrecy, deception, risk taking*, and *situational relevance*, when taken together, provide a basis for explaining why people cut themselves off from relevant information sources because the use of those sources may influence what happens in the future in a negative way—as was the case for an elderly woman who was afraid to discuss her dizziness with others for fear that she would lose her independence and end up in a nursing home.

Savolainen's (1995) concepts of *mastery of life* and *way of life* add to the picture by focusing attention on, respectively, the ways by which people maintain orderliness in their lives and balance work and leisure. Solomon (1999) uses the concept of *rounding* to consider from several different perspectives (i.e., work planning, college students' use of the Web, and travel planning) the recurrent patterns of action that structure how people discover information in order to understand what leads someone to break such a pattern.

Overall, this rounding work provides insights into how the social and the individual interact to shape the discovery of information.

Making Sense and Information Search as Processes

A primary contributor to understanding the discovery of information in context is the sense-making theory and associated sense-making methodology of Dervin (1999a). This work is important because it focuses attention on situations, information gaps, and the actions that people take to bridge these gaps. This integrated theoretical and methodological approach, thus, highlights people's actions and, consequently, emphasizes *verbings* (acts) over *nounings* (states) in understanding people's making of sense. The early descriptions (cf. Dervin & Nilan, 1986) of the theory and supporting sense-making research tend to emphasize individual sense making. More recently Dervin (1999a) has confronted the social and temporal aspects of sense making. She has also elaborated a theory of design based on sense-making theory that ties design to the possibility of helping people in designing, shaping, and creating information as a support to their making of sense (Dervin, 1999b).

Kuhlthau's (1993a, 1993b, 1997, 1999) *information search process* work is an examination of the ways in which people discover information through a constructive process of learning involving feelings, thoughts, and actions intertwined in a nonlinear progression. There are two significant results of this work that have contributed to an understanding of how people discover information in context. The first is the use of the research findings in developing a normative process model to guide the design of information services and training. This model simplifies the complex, nonlinear behavior of people during the information search into an idealized set of stages (i.e., task initiation, topic selection, prefocus exploration, focus formulation, information collection, search closure, writing) that require different sorts of actions while producing different kinds of feelings and thoughts. The second result is the recognition that, whatever stage the information search is in, it is influenced by what came before, and, in turn, influences what comes next.

Weick (1995) developed a social framework for understanding sense making in organizations. This framework, in particular, specifies sense making as being (1) grounded in the organization's construction of its *identity*, (2) an organization's ties to its past (*retrospect*), (3) what an organization does to enact its environment (*enactment*), (4) the nature of *social* interaction within the organization, (5) the emphasis within organizational life on production versus adaptation (*ongoing*), (6) the cues (or what constitutes information) employed by the organization (*extracted cues*), and (7) the organization's norms for interpreting cues (*plausibility*).

Building on the work of Dervin, Kuhlthau, Weick and others, Solomon (1997b, 1997c, 1997d) explores people's information-related behavior over three years of a work planning process in a government agency. This exploration explicitly considers the influence of perspective in understanding what information is in context by viewing the happenings from personal, social, and temporal perspectives. The study also provides insights into the reality of information discovery as a grounded process in which people talk about making sense of their situation and discover information as they engage in work.

Overall, the theoretical and research work related to how people make sense of their situations and construct (or discover) information has focused on social and dynamic, as well as individual, aspects of this process. It has also been exploring the implications of theory and research findings for practice.

Information Encountering

Erdelez (1995, 1997, 2000) has labeled people's accidental discovery of information as *information encountering*. This term is employed to make a distinction with information seeking, which is seen as a form of information acquisition that is focused on specific needs, sources, and tasks. Erdelez's research in academic and Web environments has led to the identification of the following functional components of information encountering: *noticing, stopping, examining, storing, using,* and *returning*. Ross (1999, reading for pleasure), Savolainen, (1995, everyday life information seeking), and Williamson (1998, older adults) have also studied this "by chance" encountering of information during the course of activities that do not involve direct information seeking. This work taken together suggests a general pattern of behavior by which people discover information as they make sense of what they encounter. This process is apparently a variable one, because much depends on motivations, interests, and connections with life and work. Also, this phenomenon of discovery as people encounter or come into contact with *stuff* of various sorts seems robust in situations both directed—in the vein of information seeking—and undirected—in the vein of reading books for pleasure or of attending to the daily news program or paper.

Reflecting, Thinking, Learning, and Knowing

In the *more, more, more* and *faster, faster, faster* mode of many technology-driven information societies (Davis & Meyer, 1998), consideration of the need for support of reflection, thinking, and learning in the design of socio-technical systems is often lost. Reflection and thinking are not visible and are, consequently, seen by some as the wasting of time. Schön (1983) provides a compelling set of examples of the importance of *reflection in practice* in the development of professional expertise. Using the vehicle of the teamwork involved in the navigation of a naval ship, Hutchins (1995) provides a comprehensive analysis from a cognitive anthropological perspective of cognition in context. A major emphasis of this work is on individual, team, and organizational learning, which together illustrate how individual, social, organizational, and task factors interact to produce learning and change not only in the performance of the navigation task, but also in the broader organizational culture.

After analyzing studies of the impact of new technologies on organizational learning and knowledge management, Blackler (1995) suggests that knowledge is the result of the active process of knowing, which is something that people do as a natural part of their being. Knowing is *mediated* by resources and rules. Knowing is *situated* by time period and task. It is *provisional* in that it is tested and perhaps reconstructed. It is *pragmatic* in that it is goal oriented. Finally, knowing is *contested* through the interactions of daily life and work. Thus, we are left with dimensions of a process of information discovery that is influenced by the characteristics of the structures in place.

Cole's (1997, 1998) study of information acquisition by history doctoral students illustrates the *in between-ness* in which people often find themselves when they are engaged in activities that result in information discovery. Cole found that his subjects were often *unconscious-unfocused* about what they were looking for because they were in the middle of trying to put the puzzle of their research together. Thus, we may do a disservice to people when we design systems that emphasize finality instead of providing support for reflection, thinking, and learning as options. Limberg's (1998, 1999) study of school children in Sweden adds the additional insight to the reflection, thinking, learning, and knowing in information discovery of a requirement for a substantive basis of content knowledge to support this process.

The review now turns to key aspects of information discovery—structure, process, and context—that were introduced in the preceding discussion.

Structure as a Facilitator/Inhibitor in Discovering Information

It is the purpose of this section to highlight the influence of structures of various kinds upon the process of discovering information. In particular, this section focuses on what research tells us about the role of resources and rules in enabling or preventing information discovery.

Tasks

Vakkari (1999) reviews studies of problem-solving tasks and concludes that the body of research does not have much to say about how variations in the problem situation influence search and relevance assessment behavior. He goes on to explore a variety of factors that may influence what can happen during the course of people's discovery of information. These factors include the task and its complexity, the nature of the problems (e.g., structured, unstructured) that the task supports (directly or indirectly), and prior knowledge (or experience) relating to the task. Finally, he highlights research findings that shed light on tasks and information types (e.g., Byström, 1999; Byström & Järvelin, 1995; Kuhlthau, 1993a), tasks and search strategies (e.g., Ellis & Haugan, 1997), and tasks and relevance criteria (Wang, 1997).

In addition to complexity, Marchionini (1995) adds specificity of the goal or motivation, volume and timing of answer, and time-to-completion as other task-related factors. Particularly in work-related situations, the task is a fundamental force that influences how and why people select sources, discover information in sources, evaluate information so discovered in relation to the task, and gain new insights related to completion of the task. As the task is a force for focusing attention, it also limits what workers attend to.

Communicative Structures

A wide range of social, technological, and socio-technical structures has arisen to support communication. These extend from the traditional approaches of face-to-face conversation, telephone calls, and meetings to real-time chat sessions, discussion forums, and e-mail. Each of these has a range of advantages and disadvantages. Solomon (1997c) considers how the variety of such structures extant in the organization influences communication related to work planning. From the standpoint of discovering information in context, these mechanisms provide situations for possibly obtaining direct access to information in response to a request. It is also possible that the initial request will lead to an interaction among parties to the communicative event that helps all involved discover or learn something they would not have learned with a direct response. Thus, another function of these mechanisms is to provide a context of interaction for gaining insights from others regarding the situation at hand.

Meetings

The *meeting* is one event in particular that gets much bad press in the literature of organizational life. Schwartzman's (1989) study of meetings as communicative events provides numerous examples of situations that lead to negative feelings about meetings (e.g., domination by a few participants, lack of resolution of issues). It also provides considerable evidence of processes that are employed during meetings such as *storytelling*, *explaining*, *arguing*, and *focusing* (consensus building) that make meetings one of the primary forums for information discovery, creation, and learning in organizations.

Texts

There is something about the shape and structure of texts that people learn to employ as an aid in focusing attention on critical elements as they use a text. This structuring is perhaps clearest in certain disciplinary text types (e.g., the psychological experiment or the clinical drug trial), but it is also something that is learned in elementary school as children, for instance, are taught how to write a letter, book report, or other text format. Imagine trying to read a research report that is just plain text with no headings to mark segments of a text. Cues provided by the headings and other markers in texts aid readers in discovering information. Researchers (e.g., Toms, Campbell, & Blades, 1999; Vaughan & Dillon, 1998) have begun to exploit text structure and shape in the design and use of new text forms, such as digital documents. Digital formats allow a variety of formatting possibilities, including adaptive texts that can be formatted at the command of their users (Hars, 2000), and possibly annotation and feedback to authors to gain some of the benefits of more interactive oral communication formats.

Terminology, Classification Schemes, and Category Structures

While many of the structures (e.g., categorizations, index languages, representations, metadata, displays) created by information professionals are designed to aid in access, discovery, and retrieval, they often fail in one or more of these functions. Thus, research in this area assists in our understanding of the role of such structures in facilitating the discovery of information as well as in supporting such discovery in practice.

Haas and Hert (in press) have been exploring the use of terminology both from the point of view of U.S. government statistical agencies (e.g., the Bureau of Labor Statistics) and the terms employed by users of their statistical products. There is great variety on both fronts, which leads to the challenge of understanding and communicating the definitions underlying the statistical terminology employed by the producers as well as communicating the interests of the users of these statistics to possibly make the contents available in forms and formats that would facilitate their discovery as information.

Bowker and Star (1999) provide an essay on the consequences of terminological and classification infrastructure decisions by institutions in nursing—nursing intervention classification—and medicine—international classification of diseases—among others. They argue that the development of flexible classifications, which incorporate a record of their evolution, is key for meeting the variety of uses of such classifications. Solomon (2000) considers the tension between stability and change that is evident in Bowker and Star's analysis of the classifications that they studied.

These studies discuss only a small sample of structural elements that may influence how people discover information. There are many others. Pettigrew (1999), for instance, documents the various elements that limit discovery possibilities in a foot clinic for the elderly. These structures include: the physical environment (building layout, weather), clinic activities (waiting and treatment processes), the nurse's situation (knowledge of local resources and patient, workload), and the patient's situation (personal circumstances, ability and desire to interact).

Information Discovery as Process

This section focuses on what research tells us about how the discovery of information unfolds over time. Kuhlthau's (1993a, 1993b, 1999) information search process model has served as a foundation for most of the subsequent research that attempts to either (1) sequence or classify process stages or (2) relate a particular stage to nature, form, or quality of information that comes into play.

Sequencing and Classifying Information-Related Behaviors in Tasks

Algon's (1999) study of project teams in the drug development process of a large pharmaceutical firm and Cole's (1997) study of doctoral students in history have both added to our understanding of the sequencing of the discovery process. Algon mapped the relationship of tasks within the drug development process, the form of interaction (with people, ideas or information, or things), and information-related behaviors such as *absorbing, conceptualizing, manipulating, organizing, seeking, providing*, and *verbalizing*. Overall, she found that the type of task and the information-related behaviors applied were related.

Cole focused on patterns of cognitive activity in his study as a basis for specifying five stages in history doctoral students' discovery process. These stages include (1) the *opening*, where some anomaly or conflict with previous knowledge raises a question for further investigation; (2) *puzzling over* or *representational activity*, where the nature of the anomaly is considered and theories or speculations are offered; (3) *searching for corroborating evidence*, where support for possible explanations is sought; (4) *closing*, where the matter has been satisfactorily resolved; and (5) *moving on*, where the previous information process sets the stage for further activity. In this last, the learning that took place during stages 1 through 4 enables new insight and understanding.

This sort of work, which maps either the physical progress or cognitive aspects of a task, is important because it provides a context for understanding where, when, why, and how information comes into play in the task. This understanding, in turn, may provide insight into how such activity could be supported.

Specifying the Relation of Information Attributes to Task or Process Steps

The few studies that take a process view in considering how what is or becomes information changes with the phase or stage of a task or process seem to cluster in three areas: selecting documents, learning a skill, and completing a work task.

Document Selection

A series of studies by Wang and White (1995), Wang (1997), and Wang and Soergel (1998) considers the changes in criteria and term use of agricultural economics graduate students and faculty as they decided whether to read and then cite a particular work. Wang and Soergel (1998), in particular, bring this series of research reports together into a model of document selection that lists key information elements of documents (e.g., title, author, date), criteria for evaluating the acceptability of a document on the basis of its information elements (e.g., topicality, quality, novelty), and values (e.g., social, emotional, functional) that come into play in the ultimate decision to accept, reject, or hold on to a document for reading.

Tang and Solomon (1998) studied the relevance judgment process of a graduate student by focusing on two stages of (1) document selection using retrieved bibliographic records, and (2) document evaluation using the full texts of items selected as possibly relevant on the basis of their bibliographic representations. During the first stage (document selection), the subject followed a three step process of (1) a slow, measured interaction with the retrieved items on a general topical basis to see what was in the retrieved set by indicating that a document was relevant, not relevant, or possibly relevant; (2) the sudden discovery or realization as a result of the interaction with the bibliographic records of specific criteria that were important to her; and (3) the quick re-evaluation with some well-formed criteria (e.g., recency of publication, document type, topical relevance). The second stage evaluation was more content-based, showing that the learning that had taken place during the subject's interactions with the texts and the more detailed exposition of the full texts enabled the subject to move to a more sophisticated level of application of criteria.

Tang (1999) followed up on the previous study by comparing and contrasting a laboratory experiment (using undergraduates enrolled in an introductory psychology class) and a naturalistic study (using advanced psychology graduate students enrolled in a meta-analysis class) that again used a two-staged document selection process to understand how relevance judgment criteria changed from stage one to two. Again, there were substantial differences among the criteria employed at the two stages and the sophistication of their use, though those differences varied among the two subject groups in reflection of the tasks at hand (prepare an outline of a presentation versus write up the results of their meta-analyses) and differences in their depth of knowledge. The findings suggest various possibilities for assisting people during document selection through criteria filters that would be available during the document selection process.

Learning Process

Moving beyond the world of information retrieval, Bergeron and Nilan (1991) focused on sources used by people learning to use a word processing program. In doing so, their interest involved understanding how the learning that took place influenced access to information about the software. Among other things, their findings suggest that the lack of fit of various printed and online help sources (prepared by experts) with the needs of the novice learners may have driven them to seek interactions with people, including fellow learners, who were able to help through direct interaction.

Work Process

Garber and Grunes (1992) offer a remarkable look at art directors' processes of discovering information as they searched for and selected images for advertisements. In specifying the process, the authors developed a model that highlighted information-intensive subtasks (i.e., creating the initial concept, preparing compositions, finding photos) in which the art directors naturally employed different sorts of strategies to get what they needed. For example, initially the art directors formulated an artistic concept—a general sense of what the layout is trying to do—and an image concept—the sorts of images that might fulfill the artistic concept. The task process that accompanied this activity started with a general overview of the type of image along with the criteria or restrictions that the art director had in mind. This set the stage for viewing some images that, on the surface, met the initial requirements. As each image was viewed, additional criteria or restrictions were added, or a previous criterion or restriction was altered. This interaction with candidate images was a critical part of the process of selecting images to assess their relevance to the theme of the advertisement. Based on this sort of evidence, the authors developed a prototype system to support image selection that allows its users to search for similar images—ones that meet the basic criteria—or explore alternative images—ones that are contrasts (e.g., a picture of a woman or child if a man is the starting point).

Research efforts that inform our understanding of information discovery from a process point of view are rare, but offer the potential for better understanding how interaction influences human behavior.

Contexts of Information Discovery

This section explores the situational dimension by very selectively considering research relating to information discovery across a variety of contexts. The research on everyday life by Chatman (1996, 1999) and Savolainen (1995) has already been mentioned. The specific context research offered here includes work life, searching the Web, and collaboration.

Work Life

Wenger's (1998) essay on communities of practice develops a social theory of learning that is based on the concepts of *practice, meaning, community, learning, locality,* and *boundary.* The theory brings these concepts together to show how they enable (or do not enable) the development of a community of practice that supports the discovery of information through situated learning and situated action. Nardi and O'Day's (1999) work on information ecologies recognizes the importance of fit between technologies and the people, situations, and tasks that they serve. Both of these works are helpful in that they begin to identify what it is about people working together to accomplish some end that is amenable to design.

Architects

Cohill (1993) studied architects at work by focusing on the information that they created, sought, and employed during the life of an architectural design project. While his motivation for doing this was to develop software to support design, what he found was that there was less need for design support than for support on business functions as the generation, coordination, and use of project management information often overwhelmed the design element of the project. Ultimately, he sketched a design for a small set of information-related tools that focused on the management aspects of a design project.

Nurses/Physicians in Clinical Situations

Several studies have either directly or indirectly illuminated the process of information discovery as medical personnel interact with patients and other staff to either diagnose illness, participate in patient care, or contribute to student or staff training. Forsythe, Buchanan, Osheroff, and Miller (1992) studied information situations in the clinical settings of teaching hospitals. In analyzing these situations they found that it was often impossible to separate the information from the context, as knowledge of the situation was critical for understanding the information problem. The character of information varied considerably across situations and was defined during the interaction. Timpka and Arborelius (1990) studied the nature of information in telephone interactions between nurses and patients. They found a mismatch between the diagnostic emphasis of the nurses in their requests for information from patients and the needs of patients for empathetic support during an illness. Bailey (2000) explored how nurses discover information in connection with the implementation of a computerized patient record. Her work provides insights into what constitutes information for the nurse during the labor and delivery process in contrast to what is collected in the computerized patient record.

Public Defenders

Hara (2000) studied public defenders in two counties—one large and one small—as she tried to understand the forces that contributed to the development of a community of practice. In particular, she identified the ways in which these two very different groups developed shared meaning, employed informal networks, developed and maintained a supportive culture of trust, and engaged in knowledge building. In the smaller county, there was evidence of scaffolding to support people at early stages in their careers, whereas the larger county housed new and established attorneys in different locations because of space issues. This spatial separation led to a lack of mentoring for the newer attorneys. The attorneys in the larger county also had heavier caseloads. The attorneys in the smaller county seemed more willing to share personal experiences and various supportive acts were in evidence (e.g., showing up for a difficult trial to offer moral support and feedback). There was also evidence of sharing of insights regarding the appropriateness of sources of information and the sorts of information that would be needed to develop an argument for a given case. The use of information technology was also explored. The attorneys' use of the public defenders' listserv in the larger county was similar to the attorneys' reliance upon each other for support in the smaller county.

Securities Analysts

Baldwin and Rice (1997) studied the influence of individual characteristics (e.g., age, gender) and institutional resources (e.g., staff, budget size) on use of information sources and outcomes. They found no statistically significant influence attributed to personal characteristics, but concluded that institutional resources did influence information sources and communication channels, as well as outcomes. While these are interesting findings, the link between the structuring effects of institutional resources, sources, and outcomes is not presented. It is also not clear exactly what information is to these analysts, or how information is discovered in the environmental monitoring that is a major component of the analysts' work.

Kuhlthau's (1997) study of one analyst is informative as an indicator of the nature of the analyst's work—routine monitoring resulting in reports providing information to clients with a high certainty of what is being reported, and more complex reports with considerable uncertainty as to future events—and the strategies employed to discover the information needed for both types of products. While written sources are consulted, the analyst needs to be ahead of what merely appears in print so that his research focuses on personal sources and statistics at the company level. Information for this analyst is confined to what is happening in the present, or likely to happen in the near future.

Searching on the Web

Choo, Detlor, and Turnbull (1999) develop a model of information seeking on the Web based on the external information seeking practices of knowledge workers. This model relates environmental scanning modes of *undirected* and *directed viewing*, and *informal* and *formal search* with the information seeking behaviors of *starting, chaining, browsing, differentiation, monitoring*, and *extracting* (Ellis & Haugin, 1997) to array specific discovery behaviors (e.g., following links on initial pages as a form of undirected viewing and chaining). In addition to being helpful in analyzing how people discover information, the arraying of specific discovery behaviors by sequence of actions focuses attention on modes and functions that might be worthy of design attention.

Fidel, et al. (1999) studied the Web searching practices of eight high school students in connection with a horticulture class. The students' searches were focused on finding information needed to complete an assignment. The students' searching moves were rapid as they skimmed pages relying on cues provided by pictures and other graphical elements to decide if a page would be likely to have the needed information. Also, students would go back a few pages or go to the start screen when they became lost. They were also quick to ask for help from all present. While the authors' original purpose in the study was to improve Web page design, they suggest other needs, including training not only in Web searching but also in the subject area. Both background knowledge and searching skills come together in the search process, especially where there was little stopping for reflection or thinking. Web search pages might better support such learners by suggesting links to authoritative sites (e.g., encyclopedias) and offering structures to guide the search. Also, the students' dependence on graphics as a tool for judging the applicability of a page suggests the importance of graphics as a design element.

Crossing Boundaries

The crossing of boundaries during collaboration provides a natural social interface for people to discover information. Yet, there are many collaborative situations in which such communication is inhibited rather than facilitated. The studies referred to here try to understand the nature of information transfer and discovery in collaboration.

Sonnenwald and Pierce (2000) studied collaboration during a simulated battlefield exercise. Three characteristics of the ways the participants discovered information emerged as influencing the success of the exercise: (1) *interwoven situational awareness*—shared (and often incomplete) understandings of the situation as it is unfolding, (2) dense social networks—recurrent interactions among participants, and (3) *contested collaboration*—the arguments that either stand in the way of progress or help people to understand the nature of the rapidly changing situation. These findings highlight some of the mechanisms within a collaborative situation that influence outcomes. Sonnenwald (1996) highlights roles at the *organizational, task, discipline,* and *personal* levels that support the discovery of information by negotiating, filtering, and transferring knowledge across boundaries.

Overall, contextual comparisons are useful in pointing to those patterns of behavior that appear again and again across contexts, as well as those that vary with the structures of particular domains or nature of the tasks performed. For instance, depth of knowledge is critical across contexts. In contrast, the nature and purposes of tasks tend to be variable across contexts, as are the characteristics of the structures that facilitate or inhibit task performance.

Methods for Studying Information Discovery

Much of the cited research has the common methodological element of intensive study of people interacting with other people and/or technology in the context of a task or problem. Many of the studies employ naturalistic approaches that incorporate sustained data collection and analysis over time (e.g., ethnography). Others create realistic environments for research purposes (e.g., experiments). Many collect both quantitative and qualitative data. While these research reports have far-ranging purposes, they all illuminate how people discover information in the context of life and work and, in the process, provide insights that could be employed in the design of systems that support interaction with the information resources necessary for discovery.

This section pursues two questions: (1) from a design point of view, what do our data collection methods need to capture to support design, and (2) what methodological strategies are emerging to support the discovery of information about how people discover information?

Orienting Data Collection and Analysis to Support Design

Bates's (1986) design model provides some clues for data collection. While her model was initially proposed in connection with subject access in online catalogs, it has also been used as a foundation for research design. The model highlights *variety* (of terminology employed in queries and object descriptions), *uncertainty* (of what the next query will be or how objects are described), and *complexity* (of docking and use of an information system) as key matters to be considered in design. The model, thus, provides a starting point for orienting data collection and analysis. If we can map the nature of variety, uncertainty, and complexity in a particular situation, we will have gone a long way toward understanding what information is to people with respect to particular tasks. Kuhlthau (1993b) elaborates on uncertainty and applies her conceptualizations to a security analyst (Kuhlthau, 1997).

When taken literally, use of variety, uncertainty, and complexity in the orientation of data collection has a certain biasing effect. Yoon and Nilan (1999) point out that people understand what they do not know through the lens of what they do know. An implication is that, in mapping variety, uncertainty, and complexity, we need to understand what is predictable, certain, and easy to use. Yoon and Nilan also add topic and comment as orthogonal considerations as people develop meaning through their discovery of information. *Topic* is seen as a first step in focusing; *comment* establishes context for topic. Comment as a process within the discovery of information may, in turn, lead to refinement in topic as a result of the learning about what information is that results from commenting.

Another design issue is the management of change that results from such processes as commenting, arguing, learning, and sense making during the course of discovering information. *Time* and *timing* are key related issues. Kuhlthau (1993a) highlights the dynamic aspects of discovery through her *information search process* model. Solomon (1997a) considers cycling and changes in organizational life and the influence of timing of actions on outcomes as limiting what is available in formal information systems, as well as what becomes information during performance of a task.

This suggests that methods to illuminate the discovery of information need to address *variety/consistency*, *uncertainty/certainty*, *complexity/ease of use*, *topic/comment*, and *time and timing*, along with specific *contextual factors* related to the purpose of research or design support.

Discovering How People Discover Information

The second question is addressed by highlighting some of the many approaches that aid in the investigation of learning, understanding, and meaning development as a basis for discovering what constitutes information in context.

Activity Theory

Activity theory is theoretical in that it aims at an account of knowing and doing in some situation. It is methodological in that it provides a framework for viewing a situation. It is analytical in that it focuses attention on certain elements, such as agent, object, and community, and their interactions, including instruments, rules, and roles (Blackler, 1995). As it emphasizes interactions to fit some task such as judging (Engeström, 1996), activity theory focuses attention on the struggles that agents, objects, and community go through to specify or shape what information is. Data collection includes specifying the characteristics of elements and mapping their interactions (or lack thereof). Analysis focuses on what makes sense (i.e., smooth flow of events) or not (i.e., anomalies, conflicts), and how and why repairs and revisions are made.

Contextual Inquiry for Contextual Design

Contextual inquiry (Beyer & Holtblatt, 1998) consists of a range of structured data collection (e.g., interviews, observations) and analysis tools (e.g., activity sequence, information flow) that provide some of the specific insights of, for instance, ethnographic methods, in a much abbreviated time frame. The models developed during analysis are, in turn, used to generate design requirements. Coble, Maffitt, Orland, and Kahn (1996) summarize the use of contextual inquiry to discover what information is for physicians and how the primary care services provided by physicians might be supported by a clinical workstation.

Discourse Analysis

Intensive analysis of texts—oral or written—is another approach that is increasingly coming into use as a mechanism for understanding the nature and form of both the interactions (human-human, human-computer, human-text) and the products of those interactions that are evidence of information discovery. Solomon (1997a) provides a series of analytical conceptualizations that are drawn from the literature on language for special purposes, conversational analysis, and discourse processes. These analytical conceptualizations are used to illustrate what constitutes information in information seeking conversations.

Tuominen and Savolainen (1997) outline an approach for studying information use as a process of social construction that focuses on discursive evidence. Use of this approach shows how information is constructed in the arguing, commenting, and discussing of work and life. Tuominen (1997) illustrates the approach in a study of the interactions of people seeking information in libraries. Findings include the specification of what seem to be problem-centered strategies (e.g., inside-the-head, misunderstanding) that attack the biases of either user-centered or system-centered approaches. Talja, Heinisuo, Pispa, Luukkainen, and Järvelin (1997) employ discourse analysis to address the issues of variety and uncertainty in the design of a Web-based regional information service in Finland. That is, the authors use discourse analysis to identify the variety of starting points of potential users of the system, the kinds of terms used to describe what people are looking for (e.g., family restaurants, exotic restaurants), and the classifications that these potential users employ as a basis for design.

Phenomenographical Analysis

Phenomenographical analysis (Marton & Booth, 1997) aids in the exploration of how people experience, understand, or think about the phenomena that they encounter in the world. This exploration has two dimensions: what people experience, and how they experience it. Data collection is typical of other ethnography-related methods, with analysis to categorize thoughts, feelings, and actions in relation to the focus of the study. Limberg (1998, 1999) recently employed this approach in information studies, comparing variation in learning outcomes with variation in students' information seeking and use. She found that learning was shaped by how these students saw what they were doing: finding facts to support a position, balancing 'facts' in order to choose the 'right' side of the argument, or scrutinizing and analyzing in order to learn about the topic to develop a considered and defensible position.

This chapter has so far emphasized a view of information as being discovered, shaped, and created by people in the context of their lives and work. This might be seen as the front-end work of knowing enough about variety/consistency, uncertainty/certainty, complexity/ease of use, topic/comment, time and timing, and contextual factors to advance the design of interactions that support discovery. This section has suggested the sorts of information that might inform design and considered several recent approaches specifically related to information studies concerns. The next section highlights some of the key matters needing attention in the design of interaction for information discovery.

Designing to Support Discovering Information in Context

The rise of the World Wide Web has been a force for the development of tools to support the discovery of information. The enormous scope and scale of the Web creates a tremendous need, from the system end, for interaction approaches that help people narrow down, focus in, and specify what is of likely interest. The term *information discovery* (along with such related terms as *resource discovery*) has been employed on the system end to describe the architectures (e.g., representations, classifications, and displays) needed to help people explore the Web. Lynch (1995) provides an overview of resource discovery issues in a networked world. Desai (1997) explores the indexing and metadata needs of discovery in digital libraries. Earlier Carroll and Rosson (1987) provided a thoughtful analysis of production and assimilation biases of people as active users of information systems, including a variety of strategies for designing interactions that support task performance and discovery or learning.

Designing interactions that provide for discovery requires support for (1) social awareness and navigation, as people become increasingly connected in dispersed networks, and (2) learning, as people shape or redefine what information is during the process of interaction. Brown and Duguid (2000, pp. 173–174) capture the spirit of this challenge in various ways—particularly in Duguid's anecdote of a medical historian's sniffing of letters for the aroma of vinegar in his quest to document outbreaks of cholera.

There is also the fundamental problem of scale. For instance, Arms (2000) considers information discovery in the context of automated digital libraries. His approach emphasizes existing tools (e.g., the search engine Google), which employ the inherent characteristics (e.g., number of incoming links) of the resource (e.g., Web pages) to provide the searcher with an ordered list of information to be discovered. While there are benefits to this approach, it does have limitations: A recent query produced about 834,000 items retrieved in response to a search on "information discovery." Work on clustering (Zamir & Etzioni, 1998) or classifying (Chen & Dumais, 2000) Web search results would contribute to information discovery by providing an overview of possibilities.

Can we translate an understanding of how people discover information as a process into information or resource discovery tools that support this process? The remainder of this section points to some advances in the areas of support of creativity, social navigation, and visualization.

Creativity Support

Creativity and support for innovation seem to be major impetus for, and potential outcomes of, discovery as a natural process. Ford (1999) speculates on how traditional information retrieval systems might be transformed to support divergent as well as convergent thinking. His speculation leads to the suggestion of combining higher-order knowledge representations and parallel and fuzzy pattern matching techniques as a design direction. As serendipity is a major force for creativity, it seems that offering the opportunity to see relationships through both high levels of abstraction, using case-based reasoning or argumentation, and relatively broad subject domain categorizations, using text summarization or term clustering, may be fruitful.

Shneiderman (2000) focuses on the capacities that interfaces need to support creativity. He lists four areas for interface support: helping people (1) *collect* existing work to support basic learning; (2) interact with others as they *relate* what they know with others (i.e., peers, mentors); (3) explore as they think or *create*; and (4) share the results of their efforts (*donate*). He sketches the sorts of tools that might be incorporated in interfaces to promote creativity by supporting (1) searching, filtering, and browsing; (2) collaboration; (3) visualization of data and processes; (4) seeing relationships and thinking about them; (5) what-if analysis of possible solutions; (6) composing; (7) reviewing previous activity; and (8) dissemination.

Themes for design attention that emerge from Ford's and Shneiderman's suggestions for design to support creativity as well as from research relating to discovery as a process include social navigation and flexible visualization.

Social Navigation

Social navigation is key to the phenomenon of interaction. That is, social navigation recognizes that the structure of the experience contributes to what people get out of an interaction. It also recognizes that information about other people and their activities may contribute to the interaction. The literature on computer-supported cooperative work is important to the consideration of social navigation. Overviews of technological developments can be found in the annual proceedings of the ACM conferences on Computer Supported Cooperative Work and Supporting Group Work. Here, attention is given to some recent work that informs design for social navigation.

Munro, Hook, and Benyon (1999) present a collection of fourteen articles on social navigation from a 1998 workshop in Sweden. This is a rich source of conceptualizations of how to support social navigation, of research on how social navigation influences the performance of work, and of examples of technologies that support social navigation.

Davenport (1999) provides a brief summary and analysis of efforts by a group of researchers in Edinburgh, Scotland, to conceptualize a social browser (Partner Lenses—PaLs) to mobilize the expertise within a community as well as provide a vehicle for observing and promoting social interactions. One of the outcomes of the work so far has been the realization of a need for multiple layers, including an *information retrieval* layer to support the finding of partners, a *social* layer to capture attributes of interactions (e.g., courtesy, responsiveness), and a *trust* layer to develop a sense of trust among partners. Trust is increasingly being recognized as an important issue in the social aspects of discovery (Iivonen & Huotari, 2000).

Erickson and Kellogg's (2000) work on social translucence adds three dimensions—*visibility*, *awareness*, and *accountability*—to Davenport's social browser requirements. While there is seemingly some overlap between the two sets, Erickson and Kellogg seem to get beyond technologies that impose barriers and move toward those that provide windows for sharing, creating, and focusing for the purposes at hand.

Flexible Visualization

The wide range of current design work on flexible visualization can be glimpsed through conference proceedings of the ACM's Special Interest Groups on Computer Human Interaction and Information Retrieval. The focus here is on recent efforts to facilitate discovery by putting control in the hands of people. Greene, Marchionini, Plaisant, and Shneiderman (2000) present a framework for the design of displays to support information discovery. Previews and overviews of individual objects (or object collections, e.g., the human body, images, or a medical history) serve as the entry point. These allow the user of the system to develop an overview of the system contents as well as to see how objects are related, displayed, and acted on. This framework has considerable potential in situations in which there is structured data (or unstructured data that is amenable to automatic structuring) to provide flexible interaction enabling people to discover information and perhaps gain knowledge.

Hars (2000) provides a model of an adaptive document that can actually be experienced in the HTML version of the article. The article does a number of things: (1) it introduces a range of knowledge infrastructures available on the Web (e.g., preprint archive, digital library, collaboratory), (2) it ties those infrastructures to modes of scientific interaction (e.g., reading, editing, commenting), and (3) it considers how texts might be structured to allow dynamic adaptation for individual readers at different stages of their interaction with the text. Such an adaptive mechanism would be a useful option as texts become available in full-text form, but where particular pieces of the text (e.g., abstract, methods, references) are needed at different stages of a discovery process.

Nardi and O'Day's (1996) work provides some interesting insights into the possibility of empowering people's discovery of information through the use of intelligent agents. They began their thinking about intelligent agents by studying human agents (e.g., reference librarians) and, in the process, came up with the ideas of (1) focusing software agents on particular purposes, (2) enabling evolution-friendly agents, (3) providing for cooperation between agents, users, and experts, and (4) using agents to add what they find to information bases. All of these ideas contribute to the design of diverse information ecologies that support a wide range of collaborative interactions. Such information ecologies would meet the requirements for social navigation and flexible visualization.

Davenport and Cronin (1998) extend Nardi and O'Day's work by considering a variety of *just-for-you* service views that contribute to the training and practice of information professionals. These include user needs, relevance studies, indexing and classification, professionalism, and the digital environment. While their analysis focuses on developing connections among these varied views in the curriculum, their work also suggests that, regardless of whether clients, customers, or patrons know the details of just how the pieces fit together to create the whole, researchers, faculty, and professionals need to provide the flexibility to help people shape their own discovery processes.

Conclusion

This review has considered information as something that is constructed by people in their interactions with other people, technology, and structures as they move through life and work. It also draws attention to the power, in turn, of people, systems, and institutions to shape what information is. The idea is that by understanding something of the consistency/variety, certainty/uncertainty, and ease of use/complexity of information construction, we will be able to develop theory and sociotechnical designs that provide users with increased ability to explore, shape, reflect, and learn.

A general design implication is the need to provide flexibility in selecting, ordering, and viewing. Key to this is the design of representations that allows such flexibility, which can be informed by gaining a more holistic understanding of how information is constituted in task situations. This is not to say that gaining insight into information discovery is easy or using that insight to influence design is trivial. Nevertheless, the hope is that such an evidence-based approach will result in designs that fit people's tasks and problems and help them shape their own discovery processes rather than stand in the way.

Acknowledgments

Many thanks to the anonymous reviewers whose comments have substantially improved this review.

Bibliography

Algon, J. (1999). *The effect of task on information-related behaviors of individuals in a work-group environment.* Unpublished doctoral dissertation, Rutgers University. (University Microfilms No. 9918306).

Arms, W. Y. (2000). Automated digital libraries: How effectively can computers be used for the skilled tasks of professional librarianship? *D-Lib Magazine, 6.* Retrieved January 20, 2001, from the World Wide Web: http://www.dlib. org/dlib/july00/arms/07arms.html

Auster, E., & Choo, C. W. (1993). Environmental scanning by CEOs in two Canadian industries. *Journal of the American Society for Information Science, 44,* 194–203.

Bailey, D. W. (2000). *Nurse work and the computerized patient record.* Unpublished doctoral dissertation, University of North Carolina at Chapel Hill.

Baldwin, N. S., & Rice, R. E. (1997). Information-seeking behavior of securities analysts: Individual and institutional influences, information sources and channels, and outcomes. *Journal of the American Society for Information Science, 48,* 674–693.

Barreau, D. (in press). Making do: Adapting transactional systems to organizational needs. *Library & Information Science Research.*

Bates, M. J. (1986). Subject access in online catalogs: A design model. *Journal of the American Society for Information Science, 37,* 357–376.

Bergeron, P., & Nilan, M. S. (1991). Users' information needs in the process of learning word-processing: A user-based approach looking at source use. *Canadian Journal of Information and Library Science, 16*(2), 13–27.

Beyer, H., & Holtblatt, K. (1998). *Contextual design: Defining customer-centered systems.* San Francisco: Morgan Kaufmann.

Blackler, F. (1995). Knowledge, knowledge work and organizations: An overview and interpretation. *Organization Studies, 16,* 1021–1046.

Bowker, G. C., & Star, S. L. (1999). *Sorting things out: Classification and its consequences.* Cambridge, MA: MIT Press.

Brown, J. S., & Duguid, P. (2000). *The social life of information.* Boston: Harvard Business School Press.

Byström, K. (1999). *Task complexity, information types and information sources* (Acta Universitatis Tamperensis No. 688). Tampere, Finland: University of Tampere.

Byström, K., & Järvelin, K. (1995). Task complexity affects information seeking and use. *Information Processing & Management, 31,* 191–213.

Carroll, J. M., & Rosson, M. B. (1987). Paradox of the active user. In J. M. Carroll (Ed.), *Interfacing thought: Cognitive aspects of human-computer interaction* (pp. 80–111). Cambridge, MA: MIT Press.

Chatman, E. A. (1996). The impoverished life-world of outsiders. *Journal of the American Society for Information Science, 47,* 193–206.

Chatman, E. A. (1999). A theory of life in the round. *Journal of the American Society for Information Science, 50,* 207–217.

Chen, H., & Dumais, S. (2000). Bringing order to the Web: Automatically categorizing search results. In T. Turner & S. Pemberton (Eds.), *Proceedings of the CHI conference on human factors in computing system* (pp. 145–152). New York: ACM.

Choo, C. W., Detlor, B., & Turnbull, D. (1999). Information seeking on the Web: An integrated model of browsing and searching. *Proceedings of the ASIS Annual Meeting, 36,* 3–16.

Coble, J. M., Maffitt, J. S., Orland, M. J., & Kahn, M. G. (1996). Using contextual inquiry to discover physicians' true needs. In D. Wixon & J. Ramey (Eds.), *Field methods casebook for software design* (pp. 229–248). New York: John Wiley.

Cohill, A. M. (1993). Patternmakers and toolbuilders: The design of information structures in the professional practice of architecture (Doctoral dissertation, Virginia Polytechnic Institute and State University, 1993). *Dissertation Abstracts International, 54*(05A), 1569 (University Microfilms International No. AAG9323766).

Cole, C. (1997). Information as process: The difference between corroborating evidence and "information" in humanistic research domains. *Information Processing & Management, 33,* 55–67.

Cole, C. (1998). Information acquisition in history Ph.D. students: Inferencing and the formation of knowledge structures. *Library Quarterly, 68,* 33–54.

Davenport, E. (1999). Matching partners: Tools for social browsing that take people as texts. *Canadian Journal of Information and Library Science, 24,* 1–16.

Davenport, E., & Cronin, B. (1998). Texts at work: Some thoughts on "just for you" service in the context of domain expertise. *Journal of Education for Library and Information Science, 39*(4), 264–274.

Davis, S., & Meyer, C. (1998). *Blur: The speed of change in the connected economy.* Reading, MA: Addison-Wesley.

Dervin, B. (1999a). On studying information seeking methodologically: The implications of connecting metatheory to method. *Information Processing & Management, 35,* 727–750.

Dervin, B. (1999b). Chaos, order, and sense-making: A proposed theory for information design. In R. Jacobson (Ed.), *Information design* (pp. 35–57). Cambridge, MA: MIT Press.

Dervin, B., & Nilan, M. (1986). Information needs and uses. *Annual Review of Information Science and Technology, 21,* 3–33.

Desai, B. C. (1997). Supporting discovery in digital libraries. *Journal of the American Society for Information Science, 48,* 190–204.

Ellis, D., & Haugan, M. (1997). Modelling the information seeking patterns of engineers and research scientists in an industrial environment. *Journal of Documentation, 53,* 384–403.

Engeström, Y. (1996). The tensions of judging: Handling cases of driving under the influence of alcohol in Finland and California. In Y. Engeström & D. Middleton (Eds.), *Cognition and communication at work* (pp. 199–232). New York: Cambridge University Press.

Erdelez, S. (1995). Information encountering: An exploration beyond information seeking (Doctoral dissertation, Syracuse University, 1995). *Dissertation Abstracts International, 57*(06A), 2246 (University Microfilms International No. AAG9633003).

Erdelez, S. (1997). Information encountering: A conceptual framework for accidental information discovery. In P. Vakkari, R. Savolainen, & B. Dervin (Eds.), *Information seeking in context: Proceedings of an international conference on research in information needs, seeking and use in different contexts* (pp. 412–421). London: Taylor Graham.

Erdelez, S. (2000). Towards understanding information encountering on the Web. *Proceedings of the ASIS Annual Meeting, 37,* 363–371.

Erickson, T., & Kellogg, W. A. (2000). Social translucence: An approach to designing systems that support social processes. *ACM Transaction on Computer-Human Interaction, 7*(1), 59–83.

Faibisoff, S. G., & Ely, D. P. (1976). Information and information needs. *Information Reports and Bibliographies, 5,* 2–16.

Fidel, R., Davies, R. K., Douglass, M. H., Holder, J. K., Hopkins, C. J., Kushner, E. J., Miyagishima, B. K., & Toney, C. D. (1999). A visit to the information mall: Web searching behavior of high school students. *Journal of the American Society for Information Science, 50,* 24–37.

Ford, N. (1999). Information retrieval and creativity: Towards support for the original thinker. *Journal of Documentation, 55,* 528–542.

Forsythe, D. E., Buchanan, B. G., Osheroff, J. A., & Miller, R. A. (1992). Expanding the concept of medical information: An observational study of physicians' information needs. *Computers and Biomedical Research, 25,* 181–200.

Garber, S. R., & Grunes, M. B. (1992). The art of search: A study of art directors. *Human Factors in Computing Systems: CHI '92 Conference Proceedings,* 157–163.

Giddens, A. (1984). *The constitution of society: Outline of the theory of structuration.* Berkeley, CA: University of California Press.

Greene, S., Marchionini, G., Plaisant, C., & Shneiderman, B. (2000). Previews and overviews in digital libraries: Designing surrogates to support visual information seeking. *Journal of the American Society for Information Science, 51,* 380–393.

Haas, S. W., & Hert, C. A. (In press). Terminology development and organization in multi-community environments: The case of statistical information. *Advances in Classification Research.*

Hara, N. (2000). *Social construction of knowledge in professional communities of practice: Tales in courtrooms.* Unpublished doctoral dissertation, Indiana University, Bloomington.

Hars, A. (2000). Web based knowledge infrastructures for the sciences: An adaptive document. *Communications of the Association for Information Systems, 4,* 1–34. Retrieved January 20, 2001, from the World Wide Web: http://cais.isworld.org/articles/default.asp?vol=4&art=1

Hutchins, E. (1995). *Cognition in the wild.* Cambridge, MA: MIT Press.

Introna, L. D. (1997). *Management, information and power.* London: Macmillan.

Iivonen, M., & Huotari, M. (2000). The impact of trust on the practice of knowledge management. *Proceedings of the ASIS Annual Meeting, 37,* 421–429.

Katzer, J., & Fletcher, P. T. (1992). The information environment of managers. *Annual Review of Information Science and Technology, 27,* 227–263.

Kuhlthau, C. C. (1993a). *Seeking meaning: A process approach to library and information services.* Norwood, NJ: Ablex.

Kuhlthau, C. C. (1993b). A principle of uncertainty for information seeking. *Journal of Documentation, 49,* 339–355.

Kuhlthau, C. C. (1997). The influence of uncertainty on the information seeking behavior of a securities analyst. In P. Vakkari, R. Savolainen, & B. Dervin (Eds.), *Information seeking in context* (pp. 268–274). London: Taylor Graham.

Kuhlthau, C. C. (1999). Investigating patterns in information seeking: Concepts in context. In T. Wilson & D. K. Allen (Eds.), *Exploring the contexts of information behaviour: Proceedings of the second international conference on information needs, seeking and use in different contexts* (pp. 10–20). London: Taylor Graham.

Landauer, T. K. (1995). *The trouble with computers: Usefulness, usability, and productivity.* Cambridge, MA: MIT Press.

Limberg, L. (1998). *Att söka information för att lära: En studie av samspel mellan informationssökning och lärande.* Borås, Sweden: VALFRID.

Limberg, L. (1999). Experiencing information seeking and learning: A study of the interaction between two phenomena. *Information Research, 5.* Retrieved January 20, 2001, from the World Wide Web: http://www.shef.ac.uk/~is/publications/infres/paper68.html

Luhmann, N. (1995). *Social systems.* Stanford, CA: Stanford University Press.

Lynch, C. (1995). Networked information resource discovery: An overview of current issues. *IEEE Journal on Selected Areas of Communications, 13,* 1505–1522.

Marchionini, G. (1995). *Information seeking in electronic environments.* New York: Cambridge University Press.Marton, F., & Booth, S. (1997). *Learning and awareness.* Mahwah, NJ: Lawrence Erlbaum Associates.

McKinnon, S. M., & Bruns, W. J., Jr. (1992). *The information mosaic.* Boston, MA: Harvard Business School Press.

Munro, A. J., Hook, K., & Benyon, D. (1999). *Social navigation of information space.* London: Springer.

Nardi, B. A., & O'Day, V. (1996). Intelligent agents: What we learned at the library. *Libri, 46,* 59–88.

Nardi, B. A., & O'Day, V. L. (1999). *Information ecologies: Using technology with heart.* Cambridge, MA: MIT Press.

Orlikowski, W. J. (1992). The duality of technology: Rethinking the concept of technology in organizations. *Organization Science, 3,* 398–427.

Palmquist, R. A. (1992). The impact of information technology on the individual. *Annual Review of Information Science and Technology, 27,* 3–42.

Pettigrew, K. E. (1999). Waiting for chiropody: Contextual results from an ethnographic study of the information behavior among attendees at community clinics. *Information Processing & Management, 35,* 801–817.

Pettigrew, K. E., Fidel, R., & Bruce, H. (in press). Conceptual frameworks in information behavior. *Annual Review of Information Science and Technology, 35.*

Proper, H. A., & Bruza, P. D. (1999). What is information discovery about? *Journal of the American Society for Information Science, 50,* 737–750.

Ross, C. S. (1999). Finding without seeking: The information encounter in the context of reading for pleasure. *Information Processing & Management, 35,* 783–799.

Sandstrom, A. R., & Sandstrom, P. E. (1995). The use and misuse of anthropological methods in library and information science research. *Library Quarterly, 65,* 161–199.

Saracevic, T. (1999). Information science. *Journal of the American Society for Information Science, 50,* 1051–1063.

Savolainen, R. (1995). Everyday life information seeking: Approaching information seeking in the context of "way of life." *Library & Information Science Research, 17,* 259–294.

Schön, D. A. (1983). *The reflective practitioner.* New York: Basic Books.

Schwartzman, H. B. (1989). *The meeting: Gatherings in organizations and communities.* New York: Plenum.

Shneiderman, B. (2000). Creating creativity: User interfaces for supporting innovation. *ACM Transactions on Computer-Human Interaction, 7*(1), 114–138.

Solomon, P. (1997a). Conversation in information-seeking contexts: A test of an analytical framework. *Library & Information Science Research, 19,* 217–247.

Solomon, P. (1997b). Discovering information behavior in sense making. I. Time and timing. *Journal of the American Society for Information Science, 48,* 1097–1108.

Solomon, P. (1997c). Discovering information behavior in sense making. II. The social. *Journal of the American Society for Information Science, 48,* 1109–1126.

Solomon, P. (1997d). Discovering information behavior in sense making. III. The person. *Journal of the American Society for Information Science, 48,* 1127–1138.

Solomon, P. (1999). Information mosaics: Patterns of action that structure. In T. D. Wilson & D. K. Allen (Eds.), *Exploring the contexts of information behaviour:*

Proceedings of the second international conference on information needs, seeking and use in different contexts (pp. 150–175). London: Taylor Graham.

Solomon, P. (2000). Exploring structuration in knowledge organization: Implications for managing the tension between stability and dynamism. *Advances in Knowledge Organization, 7,* 254–260.

Sonnenwald, D. H. (1996). Communication roles that support collaboration during the design process. *Design Studies, 17,* 277–301.

Sonnenwald, D. H., & Pierce, L. G. (2000). Information behavior in dynamic group work contexts: Interwoven situational awareness, dense social networks and contested collaboration in command and control. *Information Processing & Management, 36,* 461–479.

Sugar, W. (1995). User-centered perspective of information retrieval research and analysis methods. *Annual Review of Information Science and Technology, 30,* 77–109.

Talja, S., Heinisuo, R., Pispa, K., Luukkainen, S., & Järvelin, K. (1997). Discourse analysis in the development of a regional information system (pp. 109–128). In: *LIS research and professional practice: Proceedings of the 2nd British-Nordic Conference on Library and Information Studies.* London: Taylor Graham. Retrieved January 20, 2001, from the World Wide Web: http://www.info.uta.fi/informaatio/helmi/bailer

Tang, R. (1999). *Use of relevance criteria across stages of document evaluation: A micro level and macro level analysis.* Unpublished doctoral dissertation, University of North Carolina at Chapel Hill. (University Microfilms International # 9954723).

Tang, R., & Solomon, P. (1998). Towards an understanding of the dynamics of relevance judgment: An analysis of one person's search behavior. *Information Processing & Management, 34,* 237–256.

Timpka, T., & Arborelius, E. (1990). The primary-care nurse's dilemmas: A study of knowledge use and need during telephone consultations. *Journal of Advanced Nursing, 15,* 1457–1465.

Toms, E. G., Campbell, D. G., & Blades, R. (1999). Does genre define the shape of information? The role of form and function in user interaction with digital documents. *Proceedings of the ASIS Annual Meeting, 36,* 693–704.

Tuominen, K. (1997). User-centered discourse: An analysis of the subject positions of the user and the librarian. *Library Quarterly, 67,* 350–371.

Tuominen, K., & Savolainen, R. (1997). A social constructionist approach to the study of information use as discursive action. In P. Vakkari, R. Savolainen, & B. Dervin (Eds.), *Information seeking in context: Proceedings of an international conference on research in information needs, seeking and use in different contexts* (pp. 81–96). London: Taylor Graham.

Vakkari, P. (1999). Task complexity, problem structure and information actions: Integrating studies on information seeking and retrieval. *Information Processing & Management, 35,* 819–837.

Vakkari, P., Savolainen, R., & Dervin, B. (Eds.). (1997). *Information seeking in context: Proceedings of an international conference on research in information needs, seeking and use in different contexts* (pp. 412–421). London: Taylor Graham.

Vaughan, M. W., & Dillon, A. (1998). The role of genre in shaping our understanding of digital documents. *Proceedings of the ASIS Annual Meeting, 35,* 559–565.

Wang, P. (1997). Users' information needs at different stages of a research project: A cognitive view. In P. Vakkari, R. Savolainen, & B. Dervin (Eds.), *Information seeking in context: Proceedings of an international conference on research in information needs, seeking and use in different contexts* (pp. 307–318). London: Taylor Graham.

Wang, P., & Soergel, D. (1998). A cognitive model of document use during a research project. Study 1. Document selection. *Journal of the American Society for Information Science, 49,* 115–133.

Wang, P., & White, M. D. (1995). Document use during a research project: A longitudinal study. *Proceedings of the ASIS Annual Meeting, 32,* 181–188.

Weick, K. E. (1995). *Sensemaking in organizations.* Thousand Oaks, CA: Sage.

Wenger, E. (1998). *Communities of practice.* Cambridge, UK: Cambridge University Press.

Williamson, K. (1998). Discovered by chance: The role of incidental information acquisition in an ecological model of information use. *Library and Information Science Research, 20,* 23–40.

Wilson, T., & Allen, D. K. (Eds.). (1999). *Exploring the contexts of information behaviour: Proceedings of the second international conference on information needs, seeking and use in different contexts* (pp. 10–20). London: Taylor Graham.

Yoon, K., & Nilan, M. S. (1999). Toward a reconceptualization of information seeking research: Focus on the exchange of meaning. *Information Processing & Management, 35,* 871–890.

Zamir, O., & Etzioni, O. (1998). Web document clustering: A feasibility demonstration. In W. B. Croft (Ed.), *Proceedings of the Annual International ACM SIGIR Conference on Research and Development in Information Retrieval,* 46–54. New York: ACM.

CHAPTER 6

Data Mining

Gerald Benoît
University of Kentucky

Introduction

Data mining (DM) is a multistaged process of extracting previously unanticipated knowledge from large databases, and applying the results to decision making. Data mining tools detect patterns from the data and infer associations and rules from them. The extracted information may then be applied to prediction or classification models by identifying relations within the data records or between databases. Those patterns and rules can then guide decision making and forecast the effects of those decisions.

However, this definition may be applied equally to "knowledge discovery in databases" (KDD). Indeed, in the recent literature of DM and KDD, a source of confusion has emerged, making it difficult to determine the exact parameters of both. KDD is sometimes viewed as the broader discipline, of which data mining is merely a component—specifically pattern extraction, evaluation, and cleansing methods (Raghavan, Deogun, & Sever, 1998, p. 397). Thurasingham (1999, p. 2) remarked that "knowledge discovery," "pattern discovery," "data dredging," "information extraction," and "knowledge mining" are all employed as synonyms for DM. Trybula, in his *ARIST* chapter on text mining, observed that the "existing work [in KDD] is confusing because the terminology is inconsistent and poorly defined. Because terms are misapplied even among researchers, it is doubtful that the general public can be expected to understand the topic" (Trybula, 1999, p. 3). Today the terms are often used interchangeably or without distinction, which, as Reinartz (1999, p. 2) notes, results in a labyrinth.

This review takes the perspective that KDD is the larger view of the entire process, with DM emphasizing the cleaning, warehousing, mining, and interactive visualization of knowledge discovery in databases. Following Brachman et al., (1996, p. 42), DM in this chapter is considered to be the core function of KDD, whose techniques are used for verification "in which the system is limited to verifying a user's hypothesis," as well as for discovery, in which the system finds new, interesting patterns. Thus, the term includes the specific processes, computer technology, and algorithms for converting very large databases of structured, semistructured and full-text sources, into practical, validated knowledge to achieve some user or application-specific goal. Figure 6.1 demonstrates the KDD/DM relationship.

Perhaps because of the confusion surrounding the term, DM itself has evolved into an almost independent activity; from one professional meeting in 1995 to over ten in 1998 (Piatetsky-Shapiro, 1998). This evolution has sparked considerable investigation into the future of DM (Beeri & Buneman, 1999; Grossman, Kasif, Moore, Rocke, & Ullman, 1999; Gunopulos & Rastogi, 2000; Madria, Bhowmick, Ng, & Lim, 1999; Raghavan, Deogun, & Sever, 1998), and research by many academic disciplines on specific DM activities. The impetus comes primarily from the increased volume of data, an expanded user base, and responses by researchers to opportunities in computer technology. For example, in the past decade scientific computing (Fayyad, Haussler, & Stolorz, 1996), such as genomic, geospatial, and medical research, commonly amasses exceptionally large (10^8-10^{12} bytes) volumes of high dimensional data (10^2-10^4 data fields) (Ho, 2000). Such volume cannot be processed efficiently by most computer environments (Grossman et al., 1999). Therefore, questions arise regarding how to scale and integrate computer systems (Guo & Grossman, 1999; Nahm & Mooney, 2000; Sarawagi, Thomas, & Agrawal, 1998), manage the volume, and adjust DM algorithms to work efficiently on different system architectures. The volume of mineable data also surpasses human capacity to extract meaningful patterns without aid.

DM's evolution is also pressured by a shift in user population from statisticians to individual and domain-specific miners (Ankerst et al., 2000;

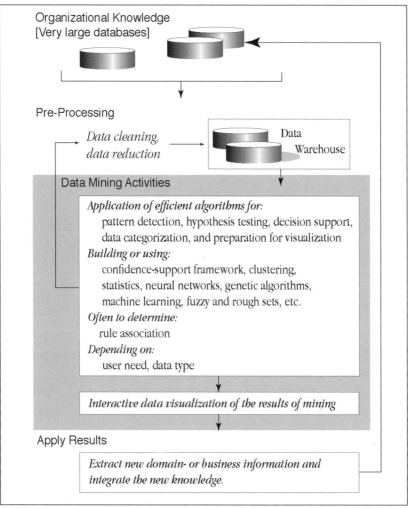

Figure 6.1 Knowledge discovery in databases

Baralis & Psaila, 1999). Traditionally, a subject specialist works with a data analyst in mining closed stores of historical data, suitable to structured, homogeneous databases (Agrawal et al., 1993; Savasere, Omiecinski & Navathe, 1995; Toivonen, 1996). Today, end-users are increasingly found to be domain specialists working without an analyst. These specialists may mine structured databases as well as weakly typed, tagged, and full-text sources. The emerging form of mixed-format mining (Mitchell, 1999) overlaps some natural language processing, information retrieval (Robertson & Gaizauskas, 1997), and Internet-based records, which further confuses DM's activities in relation to text mining and information extraction (Wilks, Slator, & Guthrie, 1996).

Given these developments, this review identifies four critical challenges to DM's future: data issues, algorithm design, the end-user, and computer architecture. Being an interdisciplinary approach to automating pattern discovery, data mining looks for answers from allied research: machine learning (Langley, Iba, & Thompson, 1990; Michalski, Bratko, & Kubat, 1998; Mitchell, 1999; Weiss & Kulikowski, 1991), artificial intelligence, database design, decision science, high-performance computing (Freitas, 1998; Stolorz & Musick, 1998), inductive logic programming (Thuraisingham, 1999), fuzzy logic (Loshin, 2000; Pedrycz & Smith, 1999), statistics (Bock & Diday, 2000; Glymour, Madigan, Pregibon, & Smyth, 1996), and hybrid investigations.

Scope and Limitations

Readers of *ARIST* are familiar with some of the main DM methods applied to structured data (Trybula, 1997) and text mining (Trybula, 1999). It is assumed that the reader is familiar with issues in information science, but may not be aware of the variety and depth of activities from other fields that overlap with DM. This chapter defines and discusses data mining processes in some detail, perhaps more than is typical in a review article, in order to demonstrate the novelty and currency of some techniques applied to DM problems. The extended introduction to DM processes should sensitize the reader to the many methods that are described in the literature and suggest why research is pursued in cognate fields. Naturally, the breadth of research, practice, and problems facing DM makes an exhaustive review of all work and all areas inadvisable. Some important topics, such as continuous vs. discrete data, the handling of missing values, and over-fitting of data, can be considered only briefly. Other issues, such as Kohonan artificial neural networks (Goodacre, 2000), deformable Markov model templates (Ge & Smyth, 2000), mining high-speed data streams (Domingos & Hulten, 2000), vector machines (DeCoste & Wagstaff, 2000), and temporal (Bettini, 2000) and geospatial information data mining (Hyland, Clifton, & Holland, 1999), must be left aside entirely. Nevertheless, this chapter offers a synoptic review of the major challenges facing DM and the research responses as well.

Works from artificial intelligence, machine learning, statistics, database theory, professional computing journals, and subject-specific work applying DM methods, such as medicine, were examined. The formats of the materials primarily include English language monographs, serials, conference proceedings, online library catalogs, and the Internet. This chapter first offers a synoptic view of DM practice in order to contextualize the challenges and responses. It then discusses specific issues related to data, algorithm design, end-users, and data mining architectures including the Internet and related text-mining activities.

Data Mining Processes

Readers interested in general overviews on DM are fortunate to have the following recently published monographs in print: Adriaans and Zantinge (1997), Berry and Linoff (1997, 2000), Berson and Smith (1997), Bigus (1996, 1998), Bramer (1999), Cabena et al. (1998), Cios, Pedrycz, and Swiniarski (1998), Devlin (1996), Groth (1998, 2000), Han and Kamber (2000), Inmon (1996), Kennedy (1997), Pyle (1999), Reinartz (1999), Thuraisingham (1999), Weiss and Indurkhya (1998), Westphal and Blaxton (1998), and Witten and Frank (2000). Regarding the Internet, Ho (2000) provides a thorough introduction to the field.

If our information needs were satisfied only by the discovery of known entities as a result of querying structured databases, then there would be no need for mining the data. The purpose of data mining is to explore databases for the unknown by exposing patterns in the data that are novel (or "determining their interestingness" [Freitas, 1999, p. 309]), supporting these patterns through statistical evidence, and presenting these results to the user via a graphic interface that facilitates investigation and interpretation to guide or support actions. To achieve these goals, DM relies on sophisticated mathematical and statistical models, as well as substantial computing power, to help users convert algorithmic behavior to human-understandable rules for action. For example, a pharmaceutical company develops a new drug that it wants to market. With no information about the potential market, the company turns to sales records, as evidence of past purchasing behavior, to discover which clients might be interested in the new product. Such data may be stored in a relational database, but standard SQL queries are unproductive. The firm may query the database for "which distributors in the Boston area purchased beta blockers?" but not "which distributors in the Boston area are likely to purchase this new drug and why?" DM assists in the automated discovery of patterns and may establish association rules to be interpreted by the end-user: "if a company distributes beta blocker x and has sales of over $\$y$ per year in the Boston area, the likelihood of that company purchasing the new drug is $z\%$."

This same firm may have a research arm that generates technical reports, clinical trial data, and other nonstructured records. Searching these types of flat files and weakly typed sources is not possible with SQL queries and full-text retrieval methods may not be useful because the researchers do not have a query to answer (or hypothesis to test). Here DM techniques are applied to discover patterns and suggest to the researchers a basis for further investigation.

The Mining of Data

Brachman and Anand (1996, p. 44) note that there is no systematized DM methodology, although major steps can be identified:

- Getting to know the data and the task: this stage is more significant than it sounds, especially when the data is to be pulled from multiple sources and when the analysis will not be done by the business user
- Acquisition: bringing the data into the appropriate environment for analysis
- Integration and checking: confirming the expected form and broad contents of the data and integrating the data into tools as required
- Data cleaning: looking for obvious flaws in the data and removing them, and removing records with errors or insignificant outliers
- Model and hypothesis development: simple exploration of the data through passive techniques and elaboration by deriving new data attributes where necessary; selection of an appropriate model in which to do analysis; and development of initial hypotheses to test

- Data mining: application of the core discovery procedures to reveal patterns and new knowledge or to explore hypotheses developed prior to this step
- Testing and verification: assessing the discovered knowledge, including testing predictive models on test sets and analyzing segmentation
- Interpretation and use: integration with existing domain knowledge, which may confirm, deny, or challenge the newly discovered patterns

Typically a subject specialist, working with a data analyst, refines the problem to be resolved. In what is termed *verification-driven*, or *top-down*, *data mining* (Berry & Linoff, 2000), this may be pursued by posing a standard query—e.g., what are the sales in Chicago for 2001? The result of these SQL queries generates a kind of cross-tabs report based on the predetermined structure of the database. The next step is to run appropriate machine learning algorithms (Langley & Simon, 1995; Mitchell, 1999), or combinations of algorithms. This step may entail repeatedly altering the selection and representation of data. For instance, the miner may segment the data based on an hypothesis that a set of properties (e.g., median age, income, and ZIP Code) form an appropriate group for a direct mail campaign and alter the selection of properties if nothing interpretable is generated.

Alternatively, the miner may not have an hypothesis (Nakhaeizadeh, Reinartz, & Wirth, 1997) and so asks the system to create one (called *predictive*, *discovery-driven*, or *bottom-up data mining* [Berry & Linoff, 2000; Weiss & Indurkhya, 1998]), such as "do sales for beta blockers in the Chicago area outpace those in the Los Angeles area?" The DM system either proves or disproves it through statistical regression. But to achieve this end, the data must have been previously selected and cleaned; and the granularity of each data type determined (Cabena et al., 1998). For instance, does the "Chicago area" include the geographic limits of that city or all markets served from Chicago area ZIP Codes? Will a distributor's sales be represented by a category (e.g., $1–$2 million sales/annum) or a value (e.g., $1,400,000).

In both situations, a DM application may first classify or cluster (Jain, Murty, & Flynn, 1999) the data, through some artificial intelligence algorithms (of which artificial neural networks are the most common), into a self-organizing map from which cause-effect association rules can be established. For instance, by clustering credit card purchasing histories of high-fashion clothing during a six-month period, it is possible to determine which customers are likely to purchase related adult luxury products. By altering the underlying statistical model, it is also possible to have neural networks build nonlinear predictive models. An example of this is determining which graduate school marketing campaign is likely to draw which types of applicants, regardless of the candidates' past academic performance.

The generated association rules also include probabilities. In Date's example (2000, p. 722) of a customer buying shoes, the association rule suggests that socks will be purchased, too—e.g., for all transactions tx (shoes $\in tx \rightarrow$ socks $\in tx$) where "shoes $\in tx$" is the rule antecedent and "socks $\in tx$" is the rule consequent, and tx ranges over all sales transactions, the probability of both purchases occurring in the same sale is x percent.

Association rules provide the user with two additional statistics: support and confidence. Support is the fraction of the population that satisfies the rule; confidence is that set of the population in which the antecedent and consequent are satisfied. In Date's socks and shoes example, the population is 4, the support is 50 percent and the confidence is 66.6 percent. The end-user is fairly confident in interpreting the association as "if a customer buys shoes, he is likely to buy socks as well, though not necessarily in the same transaction." The decision-making knowledge (or heuristic) of the domain specialist helps to avoid derived correlations that, for a specific data mining activity, may be useless. These include the "known but trivial" (people who buy shoes will buy socks), "chance" (the shoes and a shirt were on the same sale), "unknown but trivial" (brown shoes were purchased with black ones).

Association rules may be time-dependent or sequential. To illustrate, the purchases of a customer base may be grouped into sales periods (e.g., the "Spring Sale," "Summer White Sale," "Pre-School Fall Sale") and sequential algorithms may determine that if children's beach wear is purchased in the Spring Sale, there is an 80 percent chance that school clothing will be purchased during the Fall sale.

Besides association and sequencing, other main processes include classification and clustering, which are performed by specific computing algorithms. These techniques can be grouped based on how they treat the data: those that correlate or find relationships among the records (e.g., neural networks, link-analysis), those that partition the data (e.g., decision trees and rules, example-based nearest-neighbor classification, case-based reasoning, decision trellises [Frasconi, Gori, & Soda, 1999]), those that record deviations (deviation detection [Arning, 1996], nonlinear regression), and others (inductive logic, hybrid multistrategy techniques, such as combining rule-induction and case-based reasoning [Coenen, Swinnen, Vanhoof, & Wets, 2000]).

Finally, to profit from data mining activities, the human analyst, a domain expert, must be able to interpret the results of the model in a manner appropriate for that field—e.g., "each industry has evolved salient and customary ways of presenting analyses. The data mining output has to fit into this framework to be readily absorbed and accepted by the people who will use the results" (IBM, 1999, online). The results of the calculations are visualized on-screen, displaying complex multidimensional data; often in three-dimensional renderings. Such visualization software is intended to give the user a mental framework for interpreting the data (see Keim, 1999 for a comprehensive review of visualization techniques).

The basic DM processes described above incorporate several assumptions regarding the size and quality of the data, the knowledge of the end-user, and the computing environment. These assumptions cannot be taken for granted as DM evolves.

Data

All data mining activities are founded on the properties and representations of the data. As DM tools have no built-in semantic model of the data (Moxon, 1996; Spaccapietra & Maryanski, 1997), users must take necessary precautions to ensure that the data are "cleansed" or in a state that minimizes errors based on the data. Addressing the issue of missing values (Ragel & Crémilleux, 1999), inconsistent, noisy, and redundant data are part of the data cleaning process. In situations in which the nuisance data cannot be eliminated or probabilistically determined, DM requires more sophisticated statistical strategies to compensate by identifying variables and dependencies. However, data that are mined using compensating mathematical methods risk over-fitting the data to the model; that is, by accidentally selecting the best parameters for one particular model.

Thus, preparing data for mining entails a certain amount of risk, and so must be carefully performed.

Miners must determine record usability (Wright, 1996) and preprocess data to a fixed form, such as binary (Tsukimoto, 1999) or ordered variables. However, there are times when data may not be mapped to a standard form, such as a situation whereby data miners process free text where replicated fields may be missed. Similarly, many DM methods are designed around ordered numerical values and cannot easily process categorical data. Users who attempt to standardize their data through any number of methods (normalization, decimal scaling, standard deviation normalization, and data smoothing) may be able to improve feature selection, but accidentally introduce new errors (Liu & Motoda, 1998a, 1998b). For instance, when measures are small, neural networks often train well; but if not normalized, distance measures for nearest-neighbor calculations outweigh those features. Moreover, the miner must ensure that the normalization applied to the training set is also applied to mined data. Some methods, such as neural networks and regression trees, have smoothers implicit in their representation, and perform well for prediction. Smoothing also may reduce the search space by converting continuous features to discrete ones covering a fixed range of values.

This section discusses some approaches to mining of continuous, missing, and reduced data sets.

Continuous variables are often discretized (Dougherty, Kohavi, & Sahami, 1995; Fayyad & Irani, 1993; Zhong & Ohsuga, 1994), although this may result in a loss of information value. In the pharmaceutical company example, the marketing group may convert the volume of sales into discrete groups of "high" and "low" volume. This may help the sales force conceptualize the question, but, conversely, may degrade the DM process. In neural networks, for instance, input parameters that are not scaled or coded appropriately affect learning ability. The simplest method is to divide the range into equal-width units. Miners must be aware of the risk of losing information about the relationship between preassigned classes and interval boundaries when discretizing (Ching, Wong, & Chan, 1995).

One solution to missing data is to predict the values from other data. Such surrogate techniques, for instance using decision trees, are possible, but the answer is not simple. Some missing values may be null, but they may also be inapplicable to the task. This situation arises when heterogeneous databases are mined, because the relational model requires all types in a relation to have the same number of attributes (Deogun, Raghavan, & Sever, 1995). For example, in selecting a patient group for possible inclusion in a clinical trial, some missing data attributes may be estimated based on other examples for which the value is known. In growing a decision tree, the miner assigns a common value to a missing attribute, calculated from the entire set or projected from other members within a cluster. The missing data may also be assigned a probability of all possible values and then re-estimated based on the observed frequencies of other values within the training set (Quinlan, 1986, 1993).

Similar to the case of continuous values, missing data in neural networks are difficult to detect and prevent the network from converging. This, as Ho (2000, p. 48) notes, is a situation in which both domain expert and analyst should work together, and most DM applications fail to provide more interactive opportunities for users.

Another avenue toward resolving missing data, or addressing uncertainty by prediction, comes from fuzzy sets and rough sets (Deogun, Raghavan, Sarkar, & Sever, 1996; Lin & Cercone, 1997; Lingras & Yao, 1998; Raghavan, Sever, & Deogun, 1994). Rough sets expose hidden deterministic rules in databases, and can be expanded to extract probabilistic rules (Luba & Lasocki, 1994). The generalized rough set model can be applied where data are missing, or when users provide a range for the data. This addresses a great challenge for DM. Zhong, Skowron, and Ohsuga (1999) outline the interaction between rough sets, data mining, and granular soft computing. Finally, Hirota and Pedrycz (1999) outline the potential of fuzzy computing for data mining. Chiang, Chow, and Wang (2000) examine fuzzy sets for time-dependent linguistic systems—something that might first suggest using hidden Markov models.

Another data-centered technique to improve computer efficiency minimizes the size of the data set before processing. Data reduction is performed to reduce the size of the search space or to remove fields that detract from the efficiency of the mining algorithm (Agrawal, Mannila, Srikant, Toivonen, & Inkeri Verkamo, 1996); or contribute only marginally. Reducing the data requires the careful, validated selection of properties that are redundant (and therefore detract from effectiveness or information gain [Furtado & Madeira, 1999]) or cause the new data to be mined to become unrecognizable when compared to the training set.

One method is *feature selection*, a pre-pruning, inductive learning process. Feature selection improves both computation speed and the quality of classification (Deogun et al., 1995; Kira & Rendell, 1992).

Users may wish to select the "best" features of their data when there is a large number of features, or when calculating standard errors is computationally intensive. Simplification improves computer time, but users may tend to select the features to best suit their model (Elder, 2000), instead of working more with the data as a whole. For example, in decision tree learning, methods are developed that stop the tree's growth earlier, before it reaches the point where it perfectly classifies the data set. Approaches that allow the tree to over-fit the data and then prune the resulting rule set have also been developed (Ho, 2000). The latter case may be preferable because the rule set is more easily interpretable to the end-user.

Additionally, smaller sets increase the system's ability to test hypotheses. If the smaller set yields good results, it may be possible to bypass other tests on the entire dataset. Inexperienced miners may actually mistake good-looking sets for valid results and skip confirmatory tests (Elder, 2000). A reduction method based on smaller sets, on the other hand, can and should be subjected to confirmatory algorithms because the set can then be efficiently manipulated. This also suggests that small sets may be appropriate for distributed systems, which can later take the aggregate for a final output (Provost & Kolluri, 1999).

Data reduction techniques vary depending on the learning algorithm. For example, when reducing data for neural networks, the inputs must be fitted to a range, usually 0–1. The transformation choice will affect the training of the system. Inappropriate reduction introduces outliers, which in turn skew distributions, and consequently cause the network to perform poorly. Caruana and Freitag (1994) demonstrate a system that outperforms on the subset compared to the full set. This suggests that subsets can generate information about optimal values for testing against the entire dataset.

Algorithms

Algorithm design stressing computational efficiency (Joshi, 2000; Joshi, Han, Karypis, & Kumar, 2000) has become a critical issue in DM for several reasons. One is that most "first-generation algorithms" (Mitchell, 1999, p. 30) assume certain properties of the data, such as the ability to fit into a single computer's memory (Grossman et al., 1998) or deal only with numeric and symbolic data (Mitchell, 1999, p. 3). Another reason is the difficulty of learning rules for extremely large databases (Agrawal et al., 1993; Gray, Bosworth, Layman, & Pirahesh, 1995; Mitchell, 1999). DM algorithms also assume that the data have been carefully prepared before being subjected to largely automated rule production systems, minimizing the human end-user's interactive role (Fayyad, 1998). To illustrate, algorithms designed for small search spaces may generate spurious associations when applied to large, distributed, or parallel sources (Imasaki, 2000), which might then be handled more effectively if the user's knowledge were incorporated at key stages (Mitchell, 1999; Talavera & Bejar, 1999). The task in algorithm design is, thus, how to accommodate diverse sources of data, increases in the number of records, and attributes per observation; derive rule sets used to analyze the collection; and increase the user's participation. Some of the developments are outlined below.

Agent-based approaches (Mattox, 1998) are software applications programmed to investigate and collect data on their own. These intelligent agents prowl the Internet relying on user profiles (Joshi, 1999; Joshi, Joshi, Yesha, & Krishnapuram, 1999), user-supplied information about the subject (e.g., medical data, Kargupta, Hamzaoglu, & Stafford, 1997a), and document types of interest. PADMA (Kargupta, Hamzaoglu, Stafford, Hanagandi, & Buescher, 1996), Harvest, ParaSite (Spertus, 1997), OCCAM, and FAQ-Finder systems are examples. More interactive agents, such as the Internet shopping tool ShopBot, interact with and learn from unfamiliar information sources.

Association or *rule induction* procedures originally came from the retail industry. Examples such as analyzing customers' account portfolios to express item affinities in terms of confidence-rated rules have been adapted to many situations. Indeed, a most active area in DM research is improving the efficiency and removing redundancy of association and classification rules. Association rule production is not efficient with continuous classes, or in cases where there are many intervals in the data (Fayyad & Irani, 1993). In response, fuzzy techniques (Kuok, Fu, & Wong,

1998) improve predictions, but degrade the end-user's ability to comprehend the generated rules.

Ankerst et al. (2000) examine ways of improving the user's participation in semiautomatic classification. Some efficiency-oriented research examines the influence on processing speed versus set size (Shen, Shen, & Chen, 1999) and set type (Pasquier, Bastide, Taouil, & Lakhal, 1999b). Other work considers the impact of the data type on rule production. Data types include numeric (Fukuda, Morimoto, Shinichi, & Takeshi, 1999) and quantitative (Hong, Kuo, & Chi, 1999). Liu, Hsu, and Ma (1998) generalize association rules to classify high dimensional data.

Clustering, often the first step in DM, divides database records with many shared attributes into smaller segments, or clusters. DM systems automatically identify distinguishing characteristics and assign records to an n-dimensional space. It is common in demographic-based market analysis. In image databases, "clustering can be used to detect interesting spatial patterns and support content based retrievals of images and videos using low-level features such as texture, color histogram, shape descriptions, etc." (Aggarwal & Yu, 1999, p. 14). Good clustering techniques maximize the cluster membership while minimizing accidental membership, by applying either supervised or unsupervised artificial intelligence techniques.

The algorithms used in clustering must examine all data points, determine potential clustering features, and refine cluster membership, or "classifier generation and classifier application" (Reinartz, 1999, p. 32). As the size of the database grows, the likelihood of outliers also grows, requiring some means, such as feature selection or pruning (Kohavi & Sommerfield, 1995), of removing irrelevant dimensions. A popular technique is k-$means$ (Zaki & Ho, 2000, p.12), which randomly picks k data points as cluster centers and assigns new points to clusters in terms of squared error or Euclidean distance. The challenge, as Farnstrom, Lewis, and Elkan (2000) note, is scaling k-$means$ clustering. Through multiple additive regression, scaled k-$means$ clustering offers secondary validation and may be applied to parallel and distributed DM environments. For large data sets, Joshi et al. (2000) describe a method of creating "candidate k-itemsets," minimized frequent itemsets such as those used in market-based analysis. In a similar vein, Jagadish, Madar, and Ng (1999) suggest using "fascicles" to create association rules with small sets of entities that share a great number of properties, rather than seeking larger sets of items with less commonality.

Classification of data is arguably the most important component of data mining (Reinartz, 1999), and is the most commonly applied technique (Moxon, 1996). Classification employs a set of predetermined examples to develop a model to categorize a population of records to predefine the similarity of neighbors before machine learning techniques are employed (Datta, 1997; Wilson & Martinez, 1997). Typical uses are fraud detection (Bonchi, Giannoti, Mainetto, & Pedreschi, 1999) and credit risk applications. Classification employs some form of supervised learning method such as decision trees, neural networks, DNF rules, Bayesian classifiers (Langley et al., 1990), or genetic algorithms (Fu, 1999) to predict the membership of new records.

Another typical technique is the use of nearest neighbor classifiers, which utilize a training set to measure the similarity (or distance function) of all tuples and then attempt an analysis on the test data. Variations include k nearest neighbors (which classify each record based on a combination of classes of k records that are most similar to it in the data set), weighted voting of nearest neighbors (Cost & Salzberg, 1993), and edited nearest neighbors (Dasarathy, 1991). Mining of heterogeneous sources requires updated distance measurement functions (Wilson & Martinez, 1997).

Decision trees are a popular top-down approach to classification that divides the data set into leaf and node divisions (a recursive partitioning approach [Zaki & Ho, 2000]) until the entire set has been analyzed (Reinartz, 1999). Growing the tree usually employs CART (classification and regression) and CHAID (chi squared automatic interaction detection) techniques. Each interval node in the tree represents a decision on an attribute, which splits the database into two or more children. Decision trees are popular because they process both qualitative and quantitative data in an efficient and accurate manner. For qualitative attributes, the set of outcomes is the set of different values in the respective attribute domain; quantitative attributes rely upon a specific threshold value that is assigned by the user to generate different branches. This greedy search over the entire search space for all possible trees is very intense computationally and, in light of the huge size of databases, becoming impossible to perform. There are other related techniques that seek the "best" test attribute. These include nearest neighbor classifiers, which handle only a few hundred tuples; entropy; and information gain (these techniques are mentioned in passing for completeness' sake, but cannot be adequately addressed here).

Note that other techniques are useful as well. Each of the following is supported by an extensive body of literature, too vast to include in this review. These techniques, however, are important in DM. Extremely popular in business and classification (Smith & Gupta, 2000), *artificial neural networks* are nonlinear predictive models that learn from a prepared data set and are then applied to new, larger sets. Zhang and Zhang (1999) describe a novel approach based on a geometrical interpretation of the McCulloch-Pitts neural model. *Genetic algorithms* (GAs), like neural networks, are based on biological functions. GAs work by incorporating mutation and natural selection, and have been applied in scalable data mining (Kargupta, Riva Sanseverino, Johnson, & Agrawal, 1998). An offspring of genetic-based mining, genetic programming, is also employed (Wong, 2000). *Sequence-based* analysis is time-dependent, such as the case in which the purchase of one item might predict subsequent purchases. *Graphic models* and *hierarchical probabilistic representations* are directed graph, generalized Markov and hidden Markov models. These techniques are usually employed in conjunction with others, among them case-based reasoning, fuzzy logic, fractal-based transforms, lattice, and rough sets (Lin & Cercone, 1997).

Software applications implement the algorithms. The computing platform that stores, manipulates, examines, and presents the data must be sufficiently powerful or be provided with efficiently designed software. This is an important issue in DM because iterative data analyses often involve considerable computing overhead and complex, interactive visualization (Savasere et al., 1995).

The software used in data mining may be categorized based on the application's operation (Simoudis, 1995): generic, single task; generic, multitask; and application specific.

Generic, single-task applications emphasize classification (decision trees, neural networks, example-based, rule-discovery). These applications require significant pre- and postprocessing by the user, typically a developer who integrates these approaches as part of a complete application.

Generic, multitask systems support a variety of discovery tasks; typically combining several classification techniques, query/retrieval, clustering, and visualization. Multitask DM systems are designed primarily for users who understand data manipulation. See www.kdnuggets.com for a complete list of software applications.

Application-specific tools, on the other hand, are employed by domain specialists—people trained in a field, such as bioinformatics (Bourne, 2000), but who know little about the process of analysis. Such miners, therefore, rely more heavily upon the software to validate patterns detected in the data and to guide in the interpretation of results.

Users

The users of data mining were traditionally people who worked within a subject domain, such as business, and were assisted by trained statistical analysts. In spite of complex visualization tools to represent the results of mining, interpretation of association rules may still overwhelm the end-user. Independent application of DM techniques introduces new user-centered concerns. For instance, some algorithms confuse the end-user because they do not map easily to human terms (such as "if-then" rules) or may not use the original data's named attributes (Moxon, 1996).

DM supports the end-user by automating hypothesis discovery and testing as much as possible. Recently, however, researchers and applications developers have felt that the purpose of data mining is better served by integrating more of the user's knowledge and heuristics through the interface (Moxon, 1996). Many methods are not interactive and therefore cannot incorporate the user's prior knowledge, except in simple ways in which the domain knowledge of the user could improve the choice of algorithm and interpretation of results. This suggests work in graphic representations and natural language generation to improve the understandability of data mining results.

Grossman et al. (1999) note that the explosion of digital data has outpaced the ability of domain-specific users to process it. They suggest that the number of doctorates awarded in statistics has remained constant while the need for statistical analysts has grown; forcing subject specialists to depend more upon the software's guidance. The increased use of data mining technology by nondata analysts and the need for more human-oriented interactivity (queries and display) should spawn research in improving the user interface, casual browsing, and developing techniques to manage the metadata required for data mining.

Elder (2000) outlines ten concerns of the inexperienced applications-oriented data miner: lack of data, lack of training, reliance on a single technique, asking the "wrong" question of the data, listening only to the data, accepting over-fitted data, discounting the difficult cases, premature extrapolation, improper sampling, and searching too much for an interpretable answer. For example, inexperienced data miners may believe the first presentation of results and not see that variables in the data may accidentally "lift" the conclusions; that is, exert a causality that distorts the true behavior of the data. An experienced miner, or more sophisticated applications, on the other hand, may bundle several techniques for greater validation and present a multifaceted analysis.

Brachman et al. (1996, p. 44) also sound the insufficient training alarm: "Graduates of business schools are familiar with verification-driven analysis techniques, occasionally with predictive modeling, but rarely with other discovery techniques." Because of this, users may opt for tools that support models with which the user is comfortable. New data miners may also ignore the problems associated with missing data. Although in some domains, such as finance (Kovalerchuk, 2000), data warehousing minimizes the impact of dirty data, a particularly significant concern for users who emphasize interactive queries. New users are also subject to formulating poor or inappropriate hypotheses, and are faced, as a result, with an overabundance of patterns (Brachman et al., 1996, p. 44).

Domain-Specific Applications

Domain-specific data mining now plays a broader, more influential role because of the dearth of analysts and the expanded interest in applying DM techniques to serve domain-specific knowledge needs. Fountain, Dietterich, and Sudyka (2000), for example, turn integrated circuit tests into a method for optimizing VLSI design. Gavrilov, Anguelov, Indyk, and Motwani (2000) use stock market data to determine which evaluative measures are best for that field.

Astronomy, for example, employs time-dependent and image data (Ng & Huang, 1999). Astronomers formerly relied on visual inspection of photographs to find new phenomena; DM applications for this field are tailored to classify properties unique to astronomy (e.g., brightness, area, and morphology). Work on defining the best models for astronomy is underway (Schade et al., 2000). An attempt to apply some of these models to digital surveys of the skies is currently being undertaken (Odewahn, 1999). Brown and Mielke (2000) demonstrate the relationship of statistical mining with visualization for atmospheric sciences.

The biological sciences, medicine (Luvrac, Keravnou, & Blaz, 1996), and chemistry (Hemmer & Gasteiger, 2000) are particularly interested in adopting DM techniques. The trend within medical data mining is to focus on specific diseases or on processing the particular data objects generated in medical practice. An example of this is term domain distribution for medical text mining (Goldman, Chu, Parker, & Goldman, 1999). Hsu, Lee, Liu, and Ling's work (2000) on diabetic patients, the work of Pendharkar, Rodger, Yaverbaum, Herman, and Benner (1999) on breast cancer, and the efforts of Holmes, Durbin, and Winston (2000) in epidemiology are representative.

The nature, complexity, and volume of the data—such as genome expressions and sequence data—make biology a natural domain for exploitation by data mining techniques. Brazma (1999, ¶1) describes a yeast problem that suggests to the reader just how much computerized efforts have influenced the thinking of scientists:

> First genomic scale data about gene expression have recently started to become available in addition to complete genome sequence data and annotations. For instance DeRisi et al. have measured relative changes in the expression levels of almost all yeast genes during the diauxic shift at seven time points at two-hour intervals. The amounts of such data will be increasing rapidly, thus providing researchers with new challenges of finding ways to transform this data into knowledge, on one hand, while opening new possibilities of pure in silico studies of various aspects of genome functioning, on the other hand.

Genomic sequencing and mapping research have generated many Web-based databases. Along with other online sources, there is untapped potential in mining these systems for gene identification, cellular function, and relationships to diseases. Indeed, through scaled algorithms, it is possible to compare entire genomes. Other biological DM is highly specific. King, Karwath, Clare, and Dehaspe (2000) demonstrate the predictive uses of DM in biotechnology; Zweiger (1999) explains using biotechnical information to generate new metadata. Some work is underway to integrate DM full-text biomedical sources and link the results to Web-based database sites, such as SwissProt and GratefulMed, with interactive visualization (Stapley & Benoît, 2000; Benoît & Andrews, 2000). Advances in medical research on the Internet (genomic and other diseases, cellular function, drug data) and locally housed full-text holdings notwithstanding, the discovery of the relationships between these data sources remains largely unexplored.

Data Mining Architecture

Trends in incorporating increasingly large databases and the integration of DM into nonbusiness endeavors suggest that data mining is moving away from back-end technical offices with trained analysts to the front office or lab computer, and with consequences for computer system architecture (Nestorov & Tsur, 1999; Skillicorn, 1999; de Sousa, Mattoso, & Ebecken, 1999). More powerful networked desktop and micro computers suggest opportunities to resolve DM problems with distributed, parallel, and client/server architectures. For example, as Moxon (1996, ¶9) notes, although multiprocessing systems able to compute over 10,000 transactions per second are routine, "low-end four- and eight-way Pentium-based SMPs (symmetric multiprocessing) and the commoditization of clustering technology promise to make this high transaction-rate technology more affordable and easier to integrate into business." Newer network architectures, such as SMP workstations, MPP (massively parallel processing) (Kargupta & Chan, 2000), high-performance workstation clusters, and distributed DM are promising paths. The hardware-oriented responses may be based on high-performance computers, such as the ACSys Project (Williams et al., 1999), or networks of high-performance workstations.

In addition, the Internet, as a form of distributed computing, encourages mining of mixed media and heterogeneous databases, and introduces concerns associated with distributed processing. As Grossman et al. (1999, p. 5) state, the next generation Internet will increase throughput to "OC-3 (155

Mbytes/second) and higher, more than 100 times faster than the connectivity provided by current networks." This will affect scientific research, such as the Human Genome Project and space exploration data (Zaki & Ho, 2000), which, in days, generate petabytes (Fayyad, Haussler, & Stolorz, 1996) of high dimension data and which make databases increasingly available via the Internet. This section examines architecture-centered responses to very large data sets, through distributed, parallel, and client/server methods.

Distributed data mining partitioning the data store and computing load across a network is one avenue to handling very large datasets (Chattratichat et al., 1999). The JAM (Stolfo, Prodromidis, & Chan, 1997) and BODHI (Kargupta, Hamzaoglu, & Stafford, 1997a) models are examples that use local learning techniques to build the model at each site, and then integrate the models at a centralized location. Distributing data across a network for DM purposes requires tight integration of the communication protocols and the workstations (e.g., Id-Vis [Subramonian & Parthasarathy, 1998] and the Papyrus system [Grossman et al., 1998]). Distributed DM is not limited to high-performance computers. Shintani and Kitsuregawa (2000) describe how to generalize association rule mining on large-scale clusters of personal computers. This approach to load balancing combines the power of interconnected PCs in a computer network that a large, data-rich organization might have.

Integrating distributed data for mining (Lavington, Dewhurt, Wilkins, & Freitas, 1999; Sarawagi et al., 1998) resolves memory and storage issues, but introduces new problems. The heterogeneity of the data may increase (El-Khatib, Williams, MacKinnon, & Marwick, 2000), requiring more attention to the data cleaning stage and addressing local data variance. On the other hand, awareness of the data structure of distributed databases, or the metadata of tables in distributed systems, can be mined to generate a new information source from which patterns across the structure of databases might be established (Tsechansky, Pliskin, Rabinowitz, & Porath, 1999).

Alternatively, mining may be performed on parallel architectures. Mining in parallel inherits many local database issues, such as the preparation of a good data mart and indexes, and also requires careful choice of model. For example, allocating data in parallel systems risks skewing the results and may occasion shifting data across the network, a situation that is not always feasible due to limited network bandwidth, security concerns, and scalability problems (Kargupta & Chan, 2000). The basic approach to parallelization is the partitioning of data, processing, and queries. One method assigns parts of the programming to different processors. This type of "inter-model parallelism" increases execution without reducing throughput (Small & Edelstein, 2000), such as might be found in a neural net application on which different nodes or hidden layers run simultaneously on each processor. Alternatively "intra-model parallelism" distributes the load among processors and then recombines the results for a solution or conclusion. In all parallel data mining (PDM), some means of inter-node communication is needed to coordinate the independent activities.

Parallelization of data mining also raises some data modeling questions (Agrawal & Shafer, 1996; Parthasarathy, Zaki, & Li, 1998). For example, even with good data distribution, parallel data mining algorithms must reduce I/O to minimize competition for shared system buses (Brown, 2000). Brin, Motwani, and Silverstein (1997, p. 265), for instance, propose a method for "large itemset generation to reduce the number of passes over the transaction database by counting some $(k + 1)$-itemsets in parallel with counting k-itemsets."

Queries, too, may be parsed and relayed to individual CPUs (this process is called "inter-query parallelism") or parts of the query distributed ("intra-query parallelism"). The actual data mining may be performed through "partitioned parallelism," with individual threads processing subsets of the data. Data may be partitioned by "approximate concepts" (partitioned by rows), or "partial concepts" (partition by columns) (Skillicorn, 1999; see also Zhong & Ohsuga [1994]).

Algorithms require adjustment to work in parallel. Those designed to work on one system may fail on parallel systems unless refitted to be aware of dependencies or time-sequential data. For instance, Quinlan's decision tree algorithm C4.5 (Quinlan, 1993, 1986) has been adapted for parallel computing, PC4.5 (Li, 1997). Glymour et al. (1996) explore the similarities and differences between data mining and statistics and suggest opportunities, such as applying linear algebra, to solve problems of parallel algorithms.

The standard sequential algorithm for parallel DM is Apriori (Agrawal et al., 1993; Agrawal & Srikant, 1994). Apriori assumes that patterns in the data are short. This may not be the case in large databases. In an example in which the longest itemset is 40, 2^{40} subsets would be generated

(Aggarwal & Yu, 1999, p. 16), each of which needs to be validated against the database. The problem of size requires some type of solution, such as "look-ahead" techniques to locate long patterns before processing (Bayardo, 1998). Other algorithms, such as *count distribution*, minimize communications overhead and have been tested in 32-node configurations. The Eclat system has been shown to obtain speeds of as much as eleven times faster than count distribution. PDM is not perfected, however. Even the best algorithms will suffer from load-balancing problems when run in MPP-type environments.

Internet and Data Mining

As the Internet matures, it will play an increasingly important and diverse role in data mining. The Internet has already influenced DM itself in the sense that all Web sites and accessible back-end databases offer a tremendous collection to be mined (Florescu, Levy, & Mendelzon, 1998). Today it is used primarily to deliver text, weakly typed documents, and mixed media, but offers great potential for association analysis by mining the Web site content, document structure, site relations, and user behavior. Because of the text orientation of most Web documents, Web mining is closely linked to text mining and information retrieval. However, the Internet also delivers images and sound, and allows the user to access structured databases in a client/server (Fong, 1997) environment, which means mining the Internet is made especially difficult because of the heterogeneity of formats, questions of document structure, and the lack of quality control. For instance, a single research Web site may host published technical reports, lab notes, structured databases of unknown quality, chat and e-mail archives, and other nontextual source data. The use of Internet-specific techniques, such as creating documents with HTML, CSS, and XML tags, provides some semantic framework that can be analyzed. Wong and Fu (2000) suggest parsing Web documents to form associations among text data. Joshi et al. (1999) perceive stores of Web documents as a mine for analyzing the behavior of the user for system optimization or to profile the user for mass-personalization (Joshi, 1999). This "Webhousing" (Mattison, 1999) or Web-based analysis (Greening, 2000; Kimball, 1999; Kimball & Merz, 2000; Paliouras, Papaheodorou, Karkaletsis, Spyropolous, & Tzitziras, 1999; Pinter & Tsur, 1999; Pravica, 2000a, 2000b; Smith, 1999; Winter, 1999) is expected to influence the way

Web sites and business decisions are planned. In fact, Webhousing already influences issues of mass commercialization, such as how commercial graphics are selected for real-time Web-based advertising, or as part of e-commerce (Meña, 1999), and market modeling (Loshin, 2000; Auditore, 1999; Chou & Chou, 1999). Mining the Internet for clickstreams and combining use behavior with commercial personal database information is controversial. The literature suggests that this alters the relationship between marketing and customers (Biafore, 1999; Gardner, 1996) and raises privacy issues (Agrawal & Srikant, 2000; Berry, 1999b; Meña, 1999).

As the Internet gradually came to be incorporated as a mine, it is not surprising that the early views were database-biased. SQL was extended to create Web-oriented query languages. One, WebSQL (Mendelzon, Milhaila, & Milo, 1997), combines structured queries based on the hyperlinks of the documents, and content analysis based on information retrieval techniques (Frakes & Baeza-Yates, 1992). Other database-oriented methods have appeared: WebSite (Beeri et al., 1998), WebOQL (Arocena, Mendelzon, & Mihaila, 1997) and WebLog (Lakshmanan, Sadri, & Subramanian, 1996). Similarly, programs such as TSIMMIS (Chawathe et al., 1994) correlate data extracted from heterogeneous and semistructured sources to create a database representation of the information. As will be discussed below, text mining and information extraction turn to mining data from the semistructured sources on the Internet.

Some applications, like the ARANEUS system, focus on Internet-unique phenomena, such as hyperlinks (Merialdo, Atzeni, & Mecca, 1997). Others call for a Web-wide schema for metadata mining (Khosla, Kuhn, & Soparkar, 1996) and, responding to the dynamic nature of Web sites, incremental integration of schema for individual sites (Chen & Rundensteiner, 1999), or mining SGML's derivatives (XML, HTML, ODA [Thurisingham, 1999]).

Application of data mining to Web-based data has also influenced DM theory (Beeri & Buneman, 1999; Chaudhuri, 1998; Chen, Han, & Yu, 1996; Cooley, Mobasher, & Srivsatava, 1997; Dasarathy, 2000). Traditionally, DM required a large, closed, historically oriented database, optionally supported by data warehouses and data marts. Web-based data mining introduces the notion of the "clickstream" (Kimball & Merz, 2000). A clickstream is the trail of mouse and hyperlink actions taken by an end-user. These actions are recorded into a transaction log that is parsed almost continuously, with analysis sent to the administrator in near-real time. The immediacy of data gathering and the volume of Internet-based data traffic raise questions of data granularity (Pedrycz & Smith, 1999) and algorithms for time series. Client/server transactions offer interesting research possibilities into artificial intelligence and belief systems (Xiang & Chu, 1999), the nature of implicit facts in rule construction (Chou & Chou, 1999), and the categorization of data (Bleyberg, 1999).

Data mining as a management information system or Webmaster practice has evolved also to integrate Web-based methods, such as discovering document structures from Web pages (Ahonen, Mannila, & Nikunen, 1994), Java code (Bose & Sugumaran, 1999; Witten & Frank, 2000) and *n*-tier client/server architecture (Chattratichat et al., 1999).

The architecture of digital libraries (DLs) is often thought of as part of the Internet. DLs are digitized information distributed across several sites, and may consist of text, images, voice, and video (see the chapter by Fox and Urs in the present volume). Grossman (1996) notes that DLs, while text-oriented, also include tabular data; he suggests that mathematical methods can be applied to DLs. For example, tabular data describing "new homes in a region to the number of violent crimes per 100,000 count" (Grossman 1996, p. 2) might be mined fruitfully for prediction, classification, clustering, and anomalies.

Moreover, DLs often have keywords or other attributes. This suggests concept clustering (Grossman, 1996) by term or latent semantic indexing (Jiang, Berry, Donato, Ostouchov, & Grady, 1999), or association queries for attribute-based associations (Abiteboul, 1997).

Data Mining and Text Mining

DM combined with the Internet's current emphasis on textual data questions the relationship between data mining and text mining (Ahonen et al., 1997). Text mining (TM) is a fairly independent research domain with its own literature (Trybula, 1999). It is related to digital libraries, information retrieval, and computational linguistics (Lee & Yang, 2000) in the sense that it aims to discover knowledge from semistructured or unstructured text in text collections. Hearst (1999, ¶5), however, interprets data mining, text data mining, and information retrieval as different phenomena, because "the goal of data mining is to discover or derive new information from data, finding patterns across data sets, and/or separating signal from noise," while information retrieval is "query-centric," and text data mining is closer to corpus-based computational linguistics and exploratory data analysis (EDA). A large store of Web-based semi- and unstructured documents may be thought of as much as a data warehouse as the highly structured database that is typical of DM. Text documents can be used for data discovery and analysis and, when prepared, can be used for predictive purposes using regression, forecasting techniques, CHAID, decision trees and neural networks, and so on, just as DM does (Mattison, 1999); text mining, therefore, is included here.

Text mining (TM), like information retrieval (IR), may utilize any number of text tokenization and manipulation algorithms, such as singular value decomposition (Tan, Blau, Harp, & Goldman, 2000) and latent semantic indexing. Like data mining, TM requires techniques to analyze data and extract relationships from large collections of "weakly typed" (Beeri et al., 1998), usually local area network or Web-based documents. For a chapter-length treatment of text mining, see Trybula (1999).

Web-based data are difficult to process because the sections are often poorly identified. Similarly, there are often many sources of data on a topic, but locations differ, making Web-based text mining a distributed computing and redundant data challenge. Reminiscent of data mining's need for cleansed data, Web documents may only be partial, and there are no guarantees that the documents do not contain complementary, similar, or contradictory data (Beeri et al., 1998). This suggests that data integration from Web sources will be difficult (Atzeni, Mendelzon, & Mecca, 1999). Compounding the difficulty of integration is a text mine of mixed script, multilingual documents (Lee & Yang, 2000).

Advances in text mining algorithms alleviate some of these concerns. Using Reuters newswire sources, researchers (Feldman, Dagan, & Hirsch, 1998; Feldman, Klosgen, & Zilberstein, 1997; Feldman et al., 1999), for instance, analyze text category labels to find unexpected patterns among text articles. As the following will demonstrate, there are many similarities between evolving DM and Web-based text and data mining.

Three approaches to Web-based TM include mining the metadata (the data about the documents), such as performing knowledge discovery operations on labels associated with documents (Feldman et al., 2000); itemsets (groups of named entities that commonly occurred together; Hafaz,

Deogun, & Raghavan, 1999); and word-level mining. Mining the terms in text corpuses is aimed at automatic concept creation (Feldman et al., 1998), topic identification (Clifton & Couley, 2000), and discovering phrases and word co-occurrence (Ahonen et al., 1997). Others, such as Kryskiewicz (2000) and Pasquier, Bastide, Taouil, and Lakhal (1999a) describe a method of discovering frequent closed itemsets for association rules. Holt and Chung (2000) expand on this by minimizing the search space through inverted hashing and pruning. Makris, Tsakalidis, and Vassiliadis (2000) apply these techniques specifically to Net-based searching and filtering for e-commerce.

It is interesting to note that text mining brings researchers closer to computational linguistics, as it tends to be highly focused on natural language elements in texts (Knight, 1999). This means TM applications (Church & Rau, 1995) discover knowledge through automating content summarization (Kan & McKeown, 1999), content searching, document categorization, and lexical, grammatical, semantic, and linguistic analysis (Mattison, 1999). Standard DM techniques, such as self-organizing maps (Honkela, Kaski, Lagus, & Kohonen, 1996; Kaski, Honkela, Lagus, & Kohonen, 1996; Kohonen, 1998), can therefore be adjusted to integrate linguistic information from the texts in the form of self-organizing *semantic* maps (Ritter & Kohonen, 1989) as a preprocessing stage for documents. Once prepared, the text documents can be subjected to other DM techniques such as clustering and automatic extraction of rules.

The semistructured format of Web-based text documents, while presenting interesting opportunities such as semantic network analysis (Papadimitriou, 1999), has questionable usefulness in expanding the use of text mining for knowledge discovery (Beeri & Buneman, 1999; Lenzerini, 1999). Without a "common data model" of semistructured data or a common schema model, it will be difficult to develop Web and text-oriented DM models to develop translation and integration systems to support user tasks such as query formulation and system query decomposition (Beeri & Milo, 1999).

Data Mining and Information Extraction

Another form of mining that merges textual and structured databases is *information extraction* (IE). The function of IE, write Gaizauskas and Wilks (1998, p. 17), is "to extract information about a pre-specified set of entities, relations or events from natural language texts and to record this information in structured representations called templates." Unlike text mining and information retrieval, both of which may extract terms from free text and establish relationships between them (Baeza-Yates & Ribeiro-Nero, 1999) primarily to answer a query, IE is a complementary technique that populates a structured information source (the template), which is then analyzed using conventional queries or DM methods to generate rules (Soderland, 1999). Text mining involves applying data mining techniques to unstructured text. IE "is a form of shallow text understanding that locates specific pieces of data in natural language documents, transforming unstructured text into a structured database" (Nahm & Mooney, 2000, p. 627). Unlike IR, IE must maintain linguistic information about the extracted text: "'Carnegie hired Mellon' is not the same as 'Mellon hired Carnegie' which differs again from 'Mellon was hired by Carnegie'" (Gaizauskas & Wilks, 1998, p. 18).

IE was originally related to story comprehension and message understanding, based on the communications theory notion of scripts (Schank & Abelson, 1977), in which the role played by participants provided a predictive structure. IE quickly became associated with newswire analysis and online news (Jacobs & Rau, 1990) for business trend analysis.

Finally, IE's relationship with other knowledge extraction fields is not yet settled. Wilks et al. (1996) perceive IE as the next step beyond document retrieval while Robertson and Gaizauskas (1997) foresee a union of the two. IE has found special acceptance when applied to domain-specific documents in fields such as medicine (Lehnert, Soderland, Aronow, Feng, & Shmueli, 1994) and law (Pietrosanti & Graziadio, 1997).

Summary and Conclusions

This chapter presented a synoptic view of DM's recent evolution, as evidenced by the literature published between 1997 and 2000. This review follows the lead of several independent assessments in identifying four grand challenges: data-centered issues, data mining architecture, algorithm design, and the user. Within the framework of those four themes, the review presented a sample of specific research questions and activities, along with a brief description of the associated data mining process in order to guide readers in understanding the application of those activities. The conclusion one draws is that DM has reached a level of maturity; expanding its role in business (see Bergeron and Hiller's chapter in this volume) and other areas such as science.

Nevertheless, DM is at a crossroads. DM's unfolding results in a field too broad to be easily analyzed; the level of sophistication of constitutive research is advanced by several disciplines. As a result, DM's purview is not clearly defined by researchers or users, signaling that DM is at a crucial stage. Increasingly, DM responds to pressures arising from its growth by adopting cognate research, such as investigations into the efficiency of very large databases. In the same vein, DM practice moves to integrate mixed media formats; and to influence, and be influenced by, explorations in text mining, information extraction, and multimedia databases.

The review concludes that critical challenges remain in many areas of DM, including fundamentals of DM theory and the physical components of DM practice, the particulars of networked mining environments, and data reduction techniques. Additionally, DM practice is stressed by greater participation of independent miners who work without the aid of statistical analysts. These movements suggest opportunities for specifically designed interactive interfaces (Nguyen, Ho, & Himodaira, 2000) and query support (Konopnicki & Shmueli, 1999) suitable to DM's increased access to local, distributed, and heterogeneous information resources. Moreover, increased professional activities, such as the European Symposia (Zytkow & Quafafou, 1998; Zytkow & Rauch, 1999), may help stabilize DM's boundaries. Whatever DM's future may be, the question put to DM investigators is whether more robust, more powerful algorithms that are computationally efficient and able to return results to the user that are both interpretable and valid can be provided.

Bibliography

Abiteboul, S. (1997). *Object database support for digital libraries*. Retrieved March 1, 2001, from the World Wide Web: http://rocq.inria.fr/~abitebou/pub/dl97.ps

Adriaans, P. D., & Zantinge, D. (1997). *Data mining*. Reading, MA: Addison-Wesley.

Aggarwal, C. C., & Yu, P. S. (1999). Data mining techniques for associations, clustering and classification. In N. Zhong & L. Zhou (Eds.), *Methodologies for Knowledge Discovery and Data Mining, PAKDD-99* (pp. 13–23). Berlin: Springer.

Agrawal, R., & Shafer, J. C. (1996). Parallel mining of association rules: Design, implementation and experience. IBM Research Report RJ 10004. *IEEE Transactions on Knowledge and Data Engineering, 8,* 962–969.

Agrawal, R., & Srikant, R. (2000). Privacy-preserving data mining. In W. Chen, J. F. Naughton & P. A. Bernstein (Eds.), *Proceedings of the ACM-SIGMOD 2000 Conference on Management of Data. SIGMOD Record 29,* 439–450.

Agrawal, R., & Srikant, R. (1994). Fast algorithms for mining association rules. In M. Jarke & C. Zaniolo (Eds.), *Proceedings of the 20th International Conference on Very Large Data Bases, VLDB'94* (pp. 487–499). San Francisco: Morgan Kaufmann.

Agrawal, R., Imielinski, T., & Swami, A. (1993). Database mining: A performance perspective. *IEEE Transactions on Knowledge Data Engineering, 5,* 914–925.

Agrawal, R., Mannila, H., Srikant, R., Toivonen, H., & Inkeri Verkamo, A. (1996). Fast discovery of association rules. In U. M. Fayyad, G. Piatetsky-Shapiro, P. Smyth & R. Uthurusamy (Eds.), *Advances in knowledge discovery and data mining.* Menlo Park, CA: AAAI Press.

Ahonen, H., Heinonen, O., Klemettinen, M., & Inkeri Verkamo, A. (1997). *Applying data mining techniques in text analysis. (Report C-1997-23).* Helsinki: University of Helsinki, Dept. of Computer Science. Retrieved March 1, 2001, from the World Wide Web: http://www.cs.helsinki.fi/u/hahonen/publications.html

Ahonen, H., Mannila, H., & Nikunen, E. (1994). Generating grammars for SGML tagged texts lacking DTD. In M. Murata & H. Gallaire (Eds.), *Proceedings of the Workshop on Principles of Document Processing (PODP) '94.* Darmstadt. Retrieved March 1, 2001, from the World Wide Web: http://www.cs.helsinki .fi/u/hahonen/ahonen_podp94.ps

Ankerst, M., Ester, M., & Kriegel, H.-P. (2000). Towards an effective cooperation of the user and the computer for classification. *Proceedings of the Sixth ACM SIGKDD International Conference on Knowledge Discovery and Data Mining, KDD 2000* (pp. 179–188). New York: ACM Press.

Arning, A. R. (1996). A linear method for deviation detection in large databases. *Proceedings of the 2nd International Conference on Knowledge Discovery and Data Mining* (pp. 164–169). Menlo Park, CA: AAAI Press.

Arocena, G., Mendelzon, A., & Mihaila, G. (1997). Applications of a Web query language. In G. O. Arocena, A. O. Mendelzon, & G. A. Mihaila (Eds.), Proceedings of the 6th International WWW Conference. Retrieved March 1, 2001, from the World Wide Web: http://www.scope.gmd.de/info/www6/technical/paper267/paper267.html

Atzeni, P., Mendelzon, A., & Mecca, G. (Eds.). (1999). The World Wide Web and databases: EDBT Workshop, WebDB'98. New York: Springer.

Baeza-Yates, R., & Ribeiro-Nero, B. (1999). *Modern information retrieval.* New York: ACM Press.

Baralis, E., & Psaila, G. (1999). Incremental refinement of mining queries. In M. Mohania, & A. M. Tjoa (Eds.), *Data warehousing and knowledge discovery* (pp. 173–182). Berlin: Springer.

Bayardo, R. J. (1998). Efficiently mining long patterns from databases. In L. M. Haas & A. Tiwary (Eds.), *SIGMOD 1998, Proceedings of the ACM SIGMOD International Conference on Management of Data* (pp. 85–93). New York: ACM Press.

Beeri, C., & Buneman, P. (Eds.). (1999). *Database Theory—ICDT '99.* (Lecture notes in computer science 1540). Berlin: Springer.

Beeri, C., Elber, G., Milo, T., Sagio, Y., Shmueli, O., Tishby, N., Kogan, Y., Konopnicki, D., Mogilevski, P., & Slonim, N. (1998). WebSite—a tool suite for harnessing Web data. In P. Atzeni, A. Mendelzon, & G. Mecca (Eds.), *International Workshop on World Wide Web and Databases, WebDB* (pp. 152–171). Berlin: Springer.

Beeri, C., & Milo, T. (1999). Schemas for interpretation and translation of structured and semistructured data. In C. Beeri & P. Buneman (Eds.), *Database Theory—ICDT'99* (pp. 296–313). Berlin: Springer.

Benoît, G., & Andrews, J. E. (2000). Data discretization for novel resource discovery in large medical data sets. *Proceedings of the AMIA Annual Symposium,* (pp. 61–65). Bethesda, MD: American Medical Association. Retrieved March 1, 2001, from the World Wide Web: http://www.amia.org/pubs/symposia/D200636.pdf

Berry, M. J. A. (1999a). Mining the wallet. *Decision Support 2*(9). Retrieved March 1, 2001, from the World Wide Web: http://www.intelligententerprise.com/992206/decision.shtml

Berry, M. J. A. (1999b). The privacy backlash. *Intelligent Enterprise, 2*(15). Retrieved March 1, 2001, from the World Wide Web: http://www.intelligententerprise.com/992610/decision.shtml

Berry, M. J. A., & Linoff, G. (1997). *Data mining techniques for marketing, sales, and customer support.* New York: Wiley.

Berry, M. J. A., & Linoff, G. (2000). *Mastering data mining: The art and science of customer relationship management.* New York: Wiley.

Berson, A., & Smith, S. J. (1997). *Data warehousing, data mining, and OLAP.* New York: McGraw-Hill.

Berson, A., Smith, S., & Thearling, K. (2000). *Building data mining applications for CRM.* New York: McGraw-Hill.

Bettini, C. (2000). *Time granularities in databases, data mining, and temporal reasoning.* Berlin: Springer.

Biafore, S. (1999). Predictive solutions bring more power to decision makers. *Health Management Technology, 20*(10). Retrieved March 1, 2001, from the World Wide Web: http://healthmgttech.com

Bigus, J. P. (1996). *Data mining with neural networks: Solving business problems— from application development to decision support.* New York: McGraw-Hill.

Bigus, J. P., & Bigus, J. (1998). *Constructing intelligent agents with Java: A programmer's guide to smarter applications.* New York: Wiley.

Bleyberg, M. Z. (1999). Preserving text categorization through translation. *IEEE SMC'99 Conference Proceedings. International Conference on Systems, Man, and Cybernetics.* (pp. 912–917). Piscataway, NJ: IEEE.

Bock, H.-H., & Diday, E. (Eds.). (2000). *Analysis of symbolic data: Exploratory methods for extracting statistical information from complex data.* New York: Springer.

Bonchi, F., Giannoti, F., Mainetto, G., & Pedreschi, D. (1999). Using data mining techniques in fiscal fraud detection. In M. K. Mohania & A. Min Tjoa (Eds.), *Data warehousing and knowledge discovery, DaWaK'99.* (Lecture notes in computer science 1676) (pp. 369–376). Berlin: Springer.

Bose, R., & Sugumaran, V. (1999). Application of intelligent agent technology for managerial data analysis and mining. *Data Base for Advances in Information*

Systems, 30(1), 77–94. Retrieved March 1, 2001, from the World Wide Web: http://www.cis.gsu.edu/~dbase/

Bourne, P. E. (2000). Bioinformatics meets data mining: Time to dance? *Trends in Biotechnology, 18,* 228–230.

Brachman, R., & Anand, T. (1996). The process of knowledge discovery in databases: A human-centered approach. In U. M. Fayyad, G. Piatetsky-Shapiro, P. Smyth, & R. Uthurusamy (Eds.), *Advances in knowledge discovery and data mining* (pp. 35–57). Cambridge, MA: AAAI Press/MIT Press.

Brachman, R. J., Khabaza, T., Kloesgen, W., Piatetsky-Shapiro, G., & Simoudis, E. (1996). Mining business databases. *Communications of the ACM, 39*(11), 42–48.

Bramer, M. A. (Ed.) (1999). *Knowledge discovery and data mining.* London: Institution of Electrical Engineers.

Brazma, A. (1999). Mining the yeast genome expression and sequence data. *Bioinformer, 4.* Retrieved March 1, 2001, from the World Wide Web: http://bioinformer. ebi.ac.uk/newsletter/archives/4/lead_article.html

Brin, S., Motwani, R., & Silverstein, C. (1997). Beyond market baskets: Generalizing association rules to correlations. *Proceedings of the ACM-SIGMOD 1997 Conference on Management of Data, 265–276.*

Brown, A. D. (2000). *High-bandwidth, low-latency, and scalable storage systems.* Retrieved March 1, 2001, from the World Wide Web: http://www.pdl.cs.cmu .edu/NASD

Brown, T. J., & Mielke, P. W. (2000). *Statistical mining and data visualization in atmospheric sciences.* Boston: Kluwer.

Cabena, P., Hadjinian, P., Stadler, R., Verhees, J., & Zanasi, A. (1998). *Discovering data mining: From concept to implementation.* Upper Saddle River, NJ: Prentice-Hall.

Caruana, R., & Freitag, D. (1994). *Greedy attribute selection.* In W. W. Cohen & H. Hirsh (Eds.), *Machine Learning: Proceedings of the Eleventh International Conference* (pp. 28–36). San Francisco: Morgan Kaufmann.

Chattratichat, J., Darlington, J., Guo, Y., Hedvall, S., Köler, M., & Syed, J. (1999). An architecture for distributed enterprise data mining. *HPCN Europe, 1999,* 573–582.

Chaudhuri, S. (1998). Data mining and database systems: Where is the intersection? *Bulletin of the Technical Committee on Data Engineering, 21*(1), 4–8.

Chaudhuri, S., & Madigan, D. (Eds.) (1999). *The 5th ACM SIGKDD International Conference on Knowledge Discovery and Data Mining—KDD-99.* New York: ACM Press.

Chawathe, S., Garcia-Molina, H., Hammer, J., Ireland, K., Papakonstantinou, Y., Ullman, J., & Widom, J. (1994). The Tsimmis Project: Integration of heterogeneous information sources. *Proceedings of the 100th Anniversary Meeting of the Information Processing Society of Japan.* (pp. 7–18). Tokyo: Information Processing Society.

Chen, L., & Rundensteiner, E. A. (1999). *Aggregation path index for incremental Web view maintenance*. Retrieved March 1, 2001, from the World Wide Web: http://wpi.edu/pub/techreports/9933.ps.gz

Chen, M.-S., Han, J., & Yu, P. S. (1996). Data mining: An overview from a database perspective. *IEEE Transactions on Knowledge and Data Engineering, 8,* 866-883. Retrieved March 1, 2001, from the World Wide Web: http://db.cs.sfu.ca/sections/publication/kdd/kdd.html

Chiang, D.-A., Chow, L. R., & Wang, Y.-F. (2000, June). Mining time series data by a fuzzy linguistic summary system. *Fuzzy Sets and Systems, 112,* 419–432.

Ching, J., Wong, A., & Chan, K. (1995). Class-dependent discretization for inductive learning from continuous and mixed mode data. *IEEE Transactions on Knowledge and Data Engineering, 17,* 641–651.

Chou, D. C., & Chou, A. Y. (1999). A manager's guide to data mining. *Information Systems Management, 16*(14), 33–42.

Church, K. W., & Rau, L. F. (1995). Commercial applications of natural language processing. *Communications of the ACM, 38*(11), 71–79.

Cios, K., Pedrycz, W., & Swiniarski, R. (1998). *Data mining methods for knowledge discovery*. Boston: Kluwer.

Clifton, C., & Couley, R. (2000) TopCat: Data mining for topic identification in a text corpus. In M. J. Zaki & C.-T. Ho (Eds.), *Large-scale parallel data mining* (pp. 174–183). Berlin: Springer.

Coenen, F., Swinnen, G., Vanhoof, K., & Wets, G. (2000). The improvement of response modeling: Combining rule-induction and case-based reasoning. *Expert Systems with Applications, 18,* 307–313.

Cooley, R., Mobasher, B., & Srivastava, J. (1997). Web mining: Information and pattern discovery on the World Wide Web. *Proceedings of the 9th IEEE International Conference on Tools with Artificial Intelligence, ICTAI'97.* Menlo Park, CA: IEEE.

Cost, S., & Salzberg, S. (1993). A weighted nearest neighbor algorithm for learning with symbolic features. *Machine Learning, 10,* 37–78.

Dasarathy, B. V. (1991). *Nearest neighbor (NN) norms: NN pattern classification techniques*. Los Alamitos, CA: IEEE.

Dasarathy, B. V. (2000). *Data mining and knowledge discovery: Theory, tools, and technology II*. Bellingham, WA: SPIE (International Society for Optical Engineering).

Date, C. J. (2000). *An introduction to database systems*. (7th ed.). Reading, MA: Addison-Wesley.

Datta, P. (1997). Applying clustering to the classification problem. *Proceedings of the 14th National Conference on Artificial Intelligence* (pp. 82–87). Menlo Park, CA: AAAI Press.

de Sousa, M. S. R., Mattoso, M., & Ebecken, N. F. F. (1999). Mining a large database with a parallel database server. *Intelligent Data Analysis, 3,* 437–451.

DeCoste, D., & Wagstaff, K. (2000). Alpha seeding for support vector machines. *Proceedings of the Sixth ACM SIGKDD International Conference on Knowledge Discovery and Data Mining* (pp. 345–349). New York: ACM Press.

Deogun, J. S., Raghavan, V. V., Sarkar, A., & Sever, H. (1996). Data mining. Trends in research and development. In T. Y. Lin, & N. Cercone (Eds.), *Rough sets and data mining: Analysis of imprecise data* (pp. 9–46). Boston: Kluwer.

Deogun, J. S., Raghavan, V. V., & Sever, H. (1995). Exploiting upper approximations in the rough set methodology. In U. Fayyad, & R. Uthurusamy (Eds.), *First International Conference on Knowledge Discovery and Data Mining* (pp. 69–74). Berlin: Springer.

Devlin, B., (1996). *Data warehouse, from architecture to implementation*. Reading, MA: Addison-Wesley.

Domingos, P., & Hulten. G. (2000). Mining high-speed data streams. *Proceedings of the Sixth ACM SIGKDD International Conference on Knowledge Discovery and Data Mining* (pp. 71-80). New York: ACM Press. Retrieved March 1, 2001, from the World Wide Web: http://www.kric.ac.kr:8080/pubs/contents/proceedings/ai/347090

Dougherty, N., Kohavi, R., & Sahami, M. (1995). Supervised and unsupervised discretization of continuous features. In A. Prieditis & S. Russell (Eds.), *Machine Learning: Proceedings of the Twelfth International Conference* (pp. 194–202). San Francisco: Morgan Kaufmann.

El-Khatib, H. T., Williams, M. H., MacKinnon, L. M., & Marwick, D. H. (2000). A framework and test-suite for assessing approaches to resolving heterogeneity in distributed databases. *Information and Software Technology, 42,* 505–515.

Elder, J. F. (2000). *Top 10 data mining mistakes*. Retrieved March 1, 2001, from the World Wide Web: http://www.datamininglab.com

Farnstrom, F., Lewis, J., & Elkan, C. (2000). Scalability for clustering algorithms revisited. *SIGKDD Explorations, 2*(1), 51–57.

Fayyad, U. (1998). Mining databases: towards algorithms for knowledge discovery. *Bulletin of the Technical Committee on Data Engineering, 21*(1). Retrieved March 1, 2001, from the World Wide Web: http://www.research.microsoft.com/research/db/debull/98mar/fayyad6.ps

Fayyad, U., Haussler, D., & Stolorz, P. (1996). Mining scientific data. *Communications of the ACM, 39*(11), 51–57.

Fayyad, U., Piatetsky-Shapiro, G., & Smyth, P. (1996). From data mining to knowledge discovery: An overview. *Advances in knowledge discovery and data mining.* Menlo Park, CA: AAAI Press/MIT.

Fayyad, U., Piatetsky-Shapiro, G., & Smyth, P. (1996). Knowledge discovery and data mining: Toward a unifying framework. In *Proceedings of the Second International Conference on Knowledge Discovery and Data Mining KDD-96* (pp. 82–88). Menlo Park, CA: AAAI Press.

Fayyad, U., & Uthurusamy, R. (1999). Data mining and knowledge discovery in data bases: Introduction to the special issue. *Communications of the ACM, 39*(11), 24–26.

Fayyad, U. M., & Irani, K. B. (1993). Multi-interval discretization of continuous attributes for classification learning. In R. Bajcsy (Ed.), *Proceedings of the 13th International Joint Conference on Artificial Intelligence* (pp. 1022–1027). San Francisco: Morgan Kauffman.

Feldman, R., Aumann, Y., Fresko, M., Liphstat, O., Rosenfeld, B., & Schler, Y. (1999). Text mining via information extraction. In M. J. Zaki & C.-T. Ho (Eds.), *Large-scale parallel data mining* (pp. 165–173). Berlin: Springer.

Feldman, R., Dagan, I., & Hirsch, H. (1998). Mining text using keyword distributions. *Journal of Intelligent Information Systems, 10,* 281–300.

Feldman, R., Klosgen, W., Zilberstein, A. (1997). Visualization techniques to explore data mining results for document collections. In D. Heckerman, H. Mannila, D. Pregibon, & R. Uthurusamy (Eds.), *Proceedings of the Third International Conference on Knowledge Discovery and Data Mining, KDD 97* (pp. 16–23). Menlo Park, CA: AAAI Press.

Florescu, D., Levy, D., & Mendelzon, A. (1998). Database techniques for the World-Wide Web: A survey. *SIGMOD Record, 27*(3), 59–74.

Fong, J. (Ed.) (1997). *Data mining, data warehousing & client/server databases: Proceedings of the 8th International Database Workshop.* New York: Springer.

Fountain, T., Dietterich, T., & Sudyka, B. (2000). Mining IC test data to optimize VLSI testing. *Proceedings of the Sixth ACM SIGKDD International Conference on Knowledge Discovery and Data Mining, KDD 2000* (pp. 18–25). New York: ACM Press.

Frakes, W. B., & Baeza-Yates, R. (Eds.). (1992). *Information retrieval: Data structures & algorithms.* Englewood Cliffs, NJ: Prentice-Hall.

Franstrom, F., Lewis, J., & Elkan, C. (2000). Scalability for cluster algorithm revisited. *SIGKDD Exploration, 2*(1), 51–57.

Frasconi, P., Gori, M., & Soda, G. (1999). Data categorization using decision trellises. *IEEE Transactions on Knowledge and Data Engineering, 11,* 697–712.

Freitas, A. A. (1998). *Mining very large databases with parallel processing.* Boston: Kluwer.

Freitas, A. A. (1999). On rule interestingness measures. *Knowledge-Based Systems, 12,* 309–315.

Fu, Z. (1999). Dimensionality optimization by heuristic greedy learning vs. genetic algorithms in knowledge discovery and data mining. *Intelligent Data Analysis, 3,* 211–225.

Fukuda, T., Morimoto, Y., Shinichi, M., & Takeshi, T. (1999). Mining optimized association rules for numeric attributes. *Journal of Computer and System Sciences, 58*(1), 1–12.

Furtado, P., & Madeira, H. (1999). Analysis of accuracy of data reduction techniques. In M. K. Mohania & A. Min Tjoa (Eds.), *Data Warehousing and Knowledge Discovery, First International Conference, DaWaK '99* (pp. 377–388). New York: Springer.

Gaizauskas, R., & Wilks, Y. (1998). Information extraction: Beyond document retrieval. *Computational Linguistics and Chinese Language Processing, 3*(2), 17–60.

Gardner, C., (1996). *IBM Data Mining Technology.* Retrieved March 1, 2001, from the World Wide Web: http://booksrv2.raleigh.ibm.com/cgi-bin/bookmgr/bookmgr.exe/NOFRAMES/datamine/CCONTENTS

Gavrilov, M., Anguelov, D., Indyu, P., & Motwani, R. (2000). Mining the stock market: Which measure is best? *Proceedings of the Sixth ACM SIG KDD International Conference on Knowledge Discovery and Data Mining, KDD 2000* (pp. 487–496). New York: ACM Press.

Ge, X., & Smyth, P. (2000). Deformable Markov model templates for time-series pattern matching. *Proceedings of the Sixth ACM SIGKDD International Conference on Knowledge Discovery and Data Mining, KDD 2000* (pp. 81–90). Menlo Park: AAAI.

Glymour, C., & Cooper, G. F. (1999). *Computation, causation, and discovery*. Menlo Park, CA: AAAI Press.

Glymour, C., Madigan, D., Pregibon, D., & Smyth, P. (1996). Statistical inference and data mining. *Communications of the ACM, 39*(11), 35–41.

Goldman, J. A., Chu, W. W., Parker, D.S., & Goldman, R. M. (1999). Term domain distribution analysis: A data mining tool for text databases. *Methods of Information in Medicine, 38,* 96–101.

Goodacre, R. (2000). *Kohonan artificial neural networks*. Retrieved March 1, 2001, from the World Wide Web: http://gepasi.dbs.aber.ac.uk/roy/koho/kohonen.html

Gray, J., Bosworth, A., Layman, A., & Pirahesh, H. (1995). *Data cube: A relational aggregation operator generalizing group-by, cross-tab, and sub-totals.* (Microsoft Technical Report MSR-TR-95-22). Redmond, WA: Microsoft.

Greening, D. R. (2000). Data mining on the Web. *Web Techniques, 5*(1). Retrieved March 1, 2001, from the World Wide Web: http://www.webtechniques.com/archives/2000/01/greening

Grossman, R., Kasif, S., Moore, R., Rocke, D., & Ullman, J. (1999). *Data mining research: Opportunities and challenges. A report of three NSF workshops on mining large, massive, and distributed data.* Retrieved from the World Wide Web March 1, 2001: http://www.ncdm.uic.edu/M3D-final-report.htm

Grossman, R. L. (1996). Data mining challenges for digital libraries. *ACM Computing Surveys, 28*(4es). Retrieved March 1, 2001, from the World Wide Web: http://www.acm.org/pubs/citations/journals/surveys/1996-28-4es/a108-grossman

Grossman, R. L., Baily, S., Kasif, S., Mon, D., Ramu, A., & Malhi, B. (1998). The preliminary design of Papyrus: A system for high performance, distributed data mining over clusters, meta-clusters and super-clusters. In P. Chan & H. Kargupta (Eds.), *Proceedings of the KDD-98 Workshop on Distributed Data Mining* (pp. 37–43). Menlo Park: AAAI. Retrieved March 1, 2001, from the World Wide Web: http://www.lac.uic.edu/~grossman/papers/kdd-98-ddm.pdf

Groth, R. (1998). *Data mining: A hands-on approach for business professionals.* Upper Saddle River, NJ: Prentice-Hall.

Groth, R. (2000). *Data mining: Building competitive advantage*. Upper Saddle River, NJ: Prentice-Hall.

Gunopulos, D., & Rastogi, R. (2000). Workshop report: 2000 ACM SIGMOD Workshop on Research Issues in Data Mining and Knowledge Discovery. *SIGKDD Explorations, 2*(1), 83–84.

Guo, Y., & Grossman, R. (1999). *High performance data mining: Scaling algorithms, applications, and systems*. Boston: Kluwer.

Hafaz, A., Deogun, J., & Raghavan, V. V. (1999). The item-set tree: A data structure for data mining. In M. Mohania & A. M. Tjoa (Eds.), *Data warehousing and knowledge discovery* (pp. 183–192). Berlin: Springer.

Han, J., & Kamber, M. (2000). *Data mining: Concepts and techniques.* San Francisco: Morgan Kaufmann.

Hearst, M. (1999). Untangling text data mining. In *Proceedings of ACL'99.* Retrieved March 1, 2001, from the World Wide Web: http://www.sims.berkeley.edu/~hearst/papers/acl99/acl99-tdm.html

Hemmer, M. C., & Gasteiger, J. (2000). *Data mining in chemistry.* Retrieved March 1, 2001, from the World Wide Web: http://www.terena.nl/tnc2000/proceedings/10B/10b5.html

Hirota, K., & Pedrycz, W. (1999). Fuzzy computing for data mining. *Proceedings of the IEEE, 87,* 1575–1600.

Ho, T. B. (2000). *Introduction to knowledge discovery and data mining.* Retrieved March 1, 2001, from the World Wide Web: http://203.162.7.85/unescocourse/knowledge/AllChapters.doc

Holmes, J. H., Durbin, D. R., & Winston, F. K. (2000). The learning classifier system: An evolutionary computational approach to knowledge discovery in epidemiologic surveillance. *Artificial Intelligence in Medicine, 19,* 53–74.

Holsheimer, M., Kersten, M., Mannila, H., & Toivonen, H. (1995). A perspective on databases and data mining. In *First International Conference on Knowledge Discovery and Data Mining* (pp. 150–155). Menlo Park, CA: AAAI Press.

Holt, J. D., & Chung, S. M. (2000). Mining of association rules in text databases using inverted hashing and pruning. In Y. Kambayashi, M. Mohania, & A. M. Tjoa (Eds.), *Data mining and knowledge discovery* (Lecture notes in computer science 1874) (pp. 290–300). Berlin: Springer.

Hong, T.-P., Kuo, C.-S., & Chi, S.-C. (1999). Mining association rules from quantitative data. *Intelligent Data Analysis, 3,* 363–376.

Honkela, T., Kaski, S., Lagus, K., & Kohonen, T. (1996). *Newsgroup exploration with WEBSOM method and browsing interface.* (Technical Report A32). Helsinki: University of Technology, Laboratory of Computer and Information Science.

Hsu, W., Lee, M. L., Liu, B., & Ling, T. W. (2000). Exploration mining in diabetic patients databases: Findings and conclusions. *Proceedings of the Sixth ACM SIGKDD International Conference on Knowledge Discovery and Data Mining, KDD 2000,* 430–436.

Hurwitz Group. (1997). The changing role of data warehousing. *ENT, 11*(2). Retrieved March 1, 2001, from the World Wide Web: http://www.entmag.com/papers/hurwitz.htm

Hyland, R., Clifton, C., & Holland, R. E. (1999). *GeoNODE: Visualising news in geospatial contexts.* Retrieved March 1, 2001, from the World Wide Web: http://www.mitre.org/resources/centers/it/g061/geonode/AFCEA_GeoNODE_paper.html

IBM (1999). *Data mining: Extending the information warehouse framework.* Retrieved March 1, 2001, from the World Wide Web: http://www.almaden.ibm.com/cs/quest/papers/whitepaper.html#data-mining

Imasaki, K. (2000). *A survey of parallel data mining.* Retrieved March 1, 2001, from the World Wide Web: http://www.scs.carleton.ca/~kimasaki/DataMining/summary.htm

Imielinski, T., & Virmani, A. (1999). MSQL: A query language for database mining. *Data Mining and Knowledge Discovery, 3,* 373–408.

Imielinski, T., Virmani, A., & Abdulghani, A. (1999). DMajor—application programming interface for database mining. *Data Mining and Knowledge Discovery, 3,* 347–372.

Inmon, W. H. (1996). *Building the data warehouse.* (2nd ed.). New York: Wiley.

Jacobs, P. S., & Rau, L. F. (1990). SCISOR: extracting information from on-line news. *Communications of the ACM, 33*(11), 88–97.

Jagadish, H. V., Madar, J., & Ng, R. T. (1999). Semantic compression and pattern extraction with fascicles. In M. P. Atkinson, M. E. Orlowska, P. Valduriez, S. B. Zdonik, & M. L. Brodie (Eds.), *VLDB'99 Proceedings of the 25th International Conference on Very Large Data Bases* (pp. 186–198). San Francisco: Morgan Kauffman.

Jagadish, H. V., & Ng, R. T. (2000). Incompleteness in data mining. *ACM SIGMOD Workshop on Research Issues in Data Mining and Knowledge Discovery,* 1–10.

Jain, A. K., Murty, M. N., & Flynn, P. J. (1999). Data clustering: A review. *ACM Computing Surveys, 31,* 264–323.

Jiang, J., Berry, M., Donato, J. M., Ostouchov, G., & Grady, N. W. (1999). Mining consumer product data via latent semantic indexing. *Intelligent Data Analysis, 3,* 377–398.

Joshi, J. (1999). *Mining server logs for user profiles.* Retrieved March 1, 2001, from the World Wide Web: http://www.cs.umbc.edu/~ajoshi/web-mine/tr1.ps.gz

Joshi, K. P. (2000). *Analysis of data mining algorithms.* Retrieved March 1, 2001, from the World Wide Web: http://userpages.umbc.edu/~kjoshi1/data-mine/proj_rpt.htm

Joshi, K. P., Joshi, A., Yesha, Y., & Krishnapuram, R. (1999). Warehousing and mining Web logs. In *Proceedings of the Second International Workshop on Web Information and Data Management* (pp. 63–68). Menlo Park, CA: AAAI Press. Retrieved March 1, 2001, from the World Wide Web: http://www.acm.org/pubs/citations/proceedings/cikm/319759/p63-joshi

Joshi, M. V., Han, E.-H., Karypis, G., & Kumar, V. (2000). Efficient parallel algorithms for mining associations. In M. J. Zaki & C.-T. Ho (Eds.), *Large-scale parallel data mining* (pp. 83–126). Berlin: Springer.

Ju, P. (1997). *Databases on the Web: Designing and programming for network access.* New York: M&T Books.

Kan, M.-Y., & McKeown, K. R. (1999). *Information extraction and summarization: Domain independence through focus types.* Retrieved March 1, 2001, from the World Wide Web: http://www.cs.columbia.edu/~min/papers/sds/sds.html

Kargupta, H. & Chan, P. (2000). *Advances in distributed and parallel knowledge discovery.* Menlo Park, CA: AAAI Press.

Kargupta, H., Hamzaoglu, I., & Stafford, B. (1997a). Scalable, distributed data mining using an agent based architecture. In D. Heckerman, H. Mannila, & D. Pregibon (Eds.), *Proceedings of the Third International Conference on Knowledge Discovery and Data Mining, KDD-97* (pp. 211–214). Menlo Park, CA: AAAI Press. Retrieved March 1, 2001, from the World Wide Web: http://diadic1.eecs.wsu.edu/pubs.html

Kargupta, H., Hamzaoglu, I., & Stafford, B. (1997b). Web based parallel/distributed medical data mining using software agents. *1997 Fall Symposium, American*

Medical Informatics Association. Retrieved March 1, 2001, from the World Wide Web: http://www.eecs.wsu.edu/~hillol/pubs/padmaMed.ps

Kargupta, H., Hamzaoglu, I., Stafford, B., Hanagandi, V., & Buescher, K. (1996). PADMA: Parallel data mining agents for scalable text classification. In *Proceedings of the High Performance Computing on the Information Superhighway HPC-Asia '97* (pp. 290-295). Los Alamitos, CA: IEEE.

Kargupta, H., Riva Sanseverino, E., Johnson, E., & Agrawal, S. (1998). The genetic algorithm, linkage learning, and scalable data mining. In H. Cartwright (Ed.), *Intelligent data analysis in science: A handbook*. Oxford: Oxford University Press.

Kaski, S., Honkela, T., Lagus, K., & Kohonen, T. (1996). *Newsgroup extraction with websom method and browsing interface*. Retrieved March 1, 2001, from the World Wide Web: http://websom.hut.fi/websom/doc/websom.ps.gz

Keim, D. A. (1999). *Visual techniques for exploring databases*. (Tutorial Notes). Retrieved March 1, 2001, from the World Wide Web: http://www.dbs.informatik. uni-muenchen.de/~daniel/publication.html

Kennedy, R. L. (1997). *Solving data mining problems through pattern recognition*. Upper Saddle River, NJ: Prentice Hall.

Khosla, I., Kuhn, B., & Soparkar, N. (1996). Database searching using information mining. *Proceedings of the 1996 ACM-SIGMOD International Conference on the Management of Data*. New York: ACM Press.

Kimball, R. (1999, Dec. 7). The matrix. *Intelligent Enterprise, 2*(17). Retrieved March 1, 2001, from the World Wide Web: http://www.intelligententerprise.com

Kimball, R., & Merz, R. (2000). *The data webhouse toolkit*. New York: Wiley.

King, R. D., Karwath, A., Clare, A., & Dehaspe, L. (2000). Genome scale prediction of protein functional class from sequence using data mining. In S. R. Ramakrishnan (Ed.), *The Sixth International Conference on Knowledge Discovery and Data Mining, KDD 2000* (pp. 384–389). New York: ACM Press.

Kira, K., & Rendell, L. A. (1992). The feature selection problem: Traditional methods and a new algorithm. *Proceedings of the 10th National Conference on Artificial Intelligence, 129–134*.

Knight, K. (1999). Mining online text. *Communications of the ACM, 42*(11), 58–61.

Kohavi, R., & Sommerfield, D. (1995). Feature subset selection using the wrapper method: Overfitting and dynamic search space topology. In U. M. Fayyad & R. Uthurusamy (Eds.), *Knowledge Discovery and Data Mining (KDD-95) Proceedings* (pp. 192–197). Menlo Park, CA: AAAI Press.

Kohonen, T. (1998). Self-organization of very large document collections: State of the art. In L. Niklasson, M. Boden, & T. Ziemke, (Eds.), *Proceedings of ICANN98, the 8th International Conference on Artificial Neural Networks* (vol. 1, pp. 65–74). London: Springer.

Konopnicki, R., & Shmueli, O. (1999). WWW exploration queries. In R. Y. Pinter & S. Tsur, (Eds.), *Next Generation Information Technologies and Systems. 4th International Workshop, NGITS'99* (pp. 20–39). (Lecture Notes in Computer Science 1649). Berlin: Springer.

Kovalerchuk, B. (2000). *Data mining in finance: Advances in relational and hybrid methods*. Boston: Kluwer.

Kryszkiewicz, M. (2000). Mining around association and representation rules. In J. Stuller, J. Pokorny, B. Thalheim, & Y. Masunaga (Eds.), *Current issues in databases and information systems* (pp. 117–127). Berlin: Springer.

Kuok, C. M., Fu, A., & Wong, M. H. (1998). Mining fuzzy association rules in databases. *ACM SIGMOD, 27*(1), 1–12.

Lakshmanan, L., Sadri, F., & Subramanian, I. N. (1996). A declarative language for querying and restructuring the Web. *Proceedings of the 6th International Workshop on Research Issues in Data Engineering: Interoperability of Nontraditional Database Systems (RIDE-NDS'96)* (pp. 12–21). Menlo Park, CA: IEEE.

Langley, P., & Simon, H. A. (1995). Applications of machine learning and rule induction. *Communications of the ACM, 38*(11), 55–64.

Langley, P., Iba, W., & Thompson, K. (1990). An analysis of Bayesian classifiers. *Proceedings of the 8th National on Artificial Intelligence (AAAI-90)* (pp. 223–228). Cambridge, MA: MIT Press.

Lattig, M. (1998, November 8). The latest data warehouse buzz may be a bust. *InfoWorld, 21*(45). Retrieved March 1, 2001, from the World Wide Web: http://www.inquiry.com/pubs/infoworld/vol21/issue45/E03-45.asp

Lavington, S., Dewhurst, N., Wilkins, E., & Freitas, A. A. (1999, June). Interfacing knowledge discovery algorithms to large database management systems. *Information and Software Technology, 41,* 605–617.

Lavrac, N. (Ed.). (1997). *Intelligent data analysis in medicine and pharmacology*. Boston: Kluwer.

Lee, C.-H., & Yang, H.-C. (2000). Towards multilingual information discovery through a SOM based text mining approach. In A.-H. Tan & P. Yu (Eds.), *PRICAI 2000 Proceedings of the International Workshop on Text and Web Mining* (pp. 80–87). Retrieved March 1, 2001, from the World Wide Web: http://textmining.krdl.org.sg/PRICAI2000/TWMproceedings.html

Lehnert, W., Soderland, S., Aronow, D., Feng, F., & Shmueli, O. (1994). An inductive text classification for medical applications. *Journal for Experimental and Theoretical Artificial Intelligence, 7*(1), 49–80. Retrieved March 1, 2001, from the World Wide Web: http://www-nlp.cs.umass.edu/ciir-pubs/scamc_st.pdf

Lenzerini, M. (1999). Description logics and their relationship with databases. In C. Beeri & P. Buneman, (Eds.), *Proceedings of the International Conference on Database Theory ICDT '99* (pp. 32–38). Berlin: Springer.

Li, B. (1997). *Parallel C4.5 (PC4.5)*. Retrieved March 1, 2001, from the World Wide Web: http://www.cs.nyu.edu/~binli/pc4.5

Liao, W. (1999). *Data mining on the Internet*. Retrieved March 1, 2001, from the World Wide Web: http://www.mcs.kent.edu/~wliao

Lin, T. Y., & Cercone, N. (1997). *Rough sets and data mining: Analysis of imprecise data*. Boston: Kluwer.

Lingras, P. J., & Yao, Y. Y. (1998). Data mining using roughness theory. *Journal of the American Society for Information Science, 49*, 415–422.

Liu, B., Hsu, W., & Ma, Y. (1998). Integrating classification and association rule mining. In R. Agrawal & P. Stolorz (Eds.), *Proceedings of the Fourth International*

Conference on Knowledge Discovery and Data Mining (pp. 80–86). Menlo Park, CA: AAAI.

Liu, H., & Motoda, H. (1998a). *Feature extraction, construction and selection: A data mining perspective.* Boston: Kluwer.

Liu, H., & Motoda, H. (1998b). *Feature selection for knowledge discovery and data mining.* Boston: Kluwer.

Loshin, D. (2000). Value-added data: Merge ahead. *Intelligent Enterprise, 3*(3), 46–51.

Luba, T., & Lasocki, R. (1994). On unknown attribute values in functional dependencies. *Proceedings of the International Workshop on Rough Sets and Soft Computing* (pp. 490–497). Los Alamitos, CA: IEEE.

Luvrac, N., Keravnou, E. T., & Blaz, Z. (1996). *Intelligent data analysis in medicine and pharmacology.* Boston: Kluwer.

Madria, S. K., Bhowmick, S. S., Ng, W.-K., & Lim. E. P. (1999). Research issues in Web data mining. In M. Mohania & A. M. Tjoa (Eds.), *Data warehousing and knowledge discovery* (pp. 303–312). Berlin: Springer.

Makris, C., Tsakalidis, A. K., & Vassiliadis, B. (2000). Towards intelligent information retrieval engines: A multi-agent approach. In J. Stuller, J. Pokorny, B. Thalheim, & Y. Masunaga (Eds.), *East-European Conference on Advances in Databases and Information Systems Held Jointly with International Conference on Database Systems for Advanced Applications ADBIS-DASFAA* (pp. 157–170). Berlin: Springer.

Mattison, R. (1999). *Web warehousing and knowledge management.* New York: McGraw-Hill.

Mattox, D. (1998). Software agents for data management. In B. Thuraisingham (Ed.), *Handbook of data management.* New York: Auerbach.

Meña, J. (1999). *Data mining your Website.* Boston: Digital Press.

Mendelzon, A. O., Mihaila, G. A., & Milo, T. (1997). Querying the World Wide Web. *International Journal on Digital Libraries, 1*(1), 54–67.

Merialdo, P., Atzeni, P., & Mecca, G. (1997). Semistructured and structured data in the Web: Going back and forth. In W. Chen, J. F. Naughton, & P. A. Bernstein (Eds.), *Proceedings of the Workshop on the Management of Semistructured Data ACM SIGMOD '97. SIGMOD Record, 29*(2) 1–9.

Michalski, R. S., Bratko, I., & Kubat, M. (1998). *Machine learning and data mining.* New York: Wiley.

Mitchell, T. M. (1999). Machine learning and data mining. *Communications of the ACM, 42*(11), 30–36.

Mobasher, B., Jain, N., Han, E., & Srivastava, J. (1996). *Web mining: Pattern discovery from World Wide Web transactions.* (Technical Report TR-96050). Minneapolis, MN: University of Minnesota, Department of Computer Science.

Mohania, M., & Tjoa, A. M. (Eds.) (1999). *Data warehousing and knowledge discovery, DaWaK'99.* Berlin: Springer.

Moxon, B. (1996, August) Defining data mining. *DBMS Online.* Retrieved March 1, 2001, from the World Wide Web: http://www.dbmsmag.com/9608d53.html

Nahm, U. Y., & Mooney, R. J. (2000). A mutually beneficial integration of data mining and information extraction. *Proceedings of the Seventeenth National Conference on Artificial Intelligence (AAAI-2000)*, 627–632.

Nakhaeizadeh, G., Reinartz, T., & Wirth, R. (1997). Wissensentdeckung in Datenbanken und Data Mining: Ein Überblick. In G. Nakhaeizadeh (Ed.), *Data Mining: Theoretische Aspekte und Anwendungen* (pp. 1–33). Heidelberg: Physica.

Nestorov, S., & Tsur, S. (1999). Integrating data mining with relational DBMS: A tightly-coupled approach. In R. Y. Pinter & S. Tsur, (Eds.), *Next Generation Information Technologies and Systems, 4th International Workshop, NGITS'99* (pp. 295–311). Berlin: Springer.

Ng, M. K., & Huang, Z. (1999). Data-mining massive time series astronomical data: Challenges, problems and solutions. *Information and Software Technology, 41,* 545–556.

Nguyen, T. D., Ho, T. B., & Himodaira, H. (2000). Interactive visualization in mining large decision trees. In T. Terano, H. Liu, & A. L. P. Chen (Eds.), *Pacific-Asia Conference on Knowledge Discovery and Data Mining, PAKDD 2000* (pp. 345–348). Berlin: Springer.

Odewahn, S. (1999). *Science efforts underway with DPOSS.* Retrieved March 1, 2001, from the World Wide Web: http://www.astro.caltech.edu/~sco/sco1/dposs/science.html

Paliouras, G., Papatheodorous, C., Karkaletsis, V., Spyropoulos, C., & Tzitziras, P. (1999). From Web usage statistics to Web usage analysis. In *IEEE SMC'99 Conference Proceedings. International Conference on Systems, Man, and Cybernetics* (vol. 2, pp. 159–164). Piscataway, NJ: IEEE.

Papadimitriou, C. H. (1999). Novel computational approaches to information retrieval and data mining. In C. Beeri & P. Buneman, (Eds.), *Database Theory ICDT '99* (p. 31). Berlin: Springer.

Parthasarathy, S., Zaki, M., & Li, W. (1998). Memory placement techniques for parallel association mining. In *Fourth International Conference on Knowledge Discovery in Databases* (pp. 304–308). New York: Springer.

Pasquier, N., Bastide, Y., Taouil, R., & Lakhal, L. (1999b). Discovery of frequent closed itemsets for association rules. In C. Beeri & P. Buneman, (Eds.), *Database Theory ICDT '99* (pp. 398–416). Berlin: Springer.

Pasquier, N., Bastide, Y., Taouil, R., & Lakhal, L. (1999a). Efficient mining of association rules using closed itemset lattices. *Information Systems, 24*(1), 25–46.

Pedrycz, W., & Smith, M. H. (1999). Linguistic selectors and their optimization. *IEEE SMC'99 Conference Proceedings. International Conference on Systems, Man, and Cybernetics.* (pp. 906–911). Piscataway, NJ: IEEE.

Pendharkar, P. C., Rodger, J. A., Yaverbaum, G. J., Herman, H., & Benner, M. (1999). Association, statistical, mathematical and neural approaches for mining breast cancer patients. *Expert Systems with Applications, 17,* 223–232.

Piatetsky-Shapiro, G. (1998). *Data mining and knowledge discovery tools: The next generation.* Boston: Knowledge Stream. Retrieved March 1, 2001, from the World Wide Web: http://www.kdnuggets.com/gpspubs/dama-nextgen-98/sld001.htm

Pietrosanti, E., & Graziadio, B. (1997). Artificial intelligence and legal text management: Tools and techniquees for intelligent document processing and retrieval. In *Natural language processing: Extracting information for business needs* (pp. 277–291). London: Unicom Seminars.

Pinter, R. Y., & Tsur, S., (Eds.) (1999). *Next Generation Information Technologies and Systems. 4th International Workshop, NGITS' 99.* (Lecture Notes in Computer Science, 1649). Berlin: Springer.

Pravica, D. (2000a, January) "Who do you want to know today?" *Computing Canada, 26*(1). Retrieved September 1, 2000, from the World Wide Web: http://www.plesman.com/Archives/cc/2000/Jan/2601/cc260115a.html

Pravica, D. (2000b, March 17). Tracking the transactions is key to results – because all e-commerce relationships are mediated by computing applications, it's possible to develop data for every Web-based transaction. *Computing Canada.* Retrieved March 1, 2001, from the World Wide Web: http://www.findarticles .com/m0CGC/6_26/61888010/p1/article.jhtml

Provost, F. J., & Kolluri, V. (1999). A survey of methods for scaling up inductive learning algorithms. *Data Mining and Knowledge Discovery Journal, 3,* 131–169.

Pyle, D. (1999). *Data preparation for data mining.* San Francisco: Morgan Kaufmann.

Quinlan, J. R. (1993). *Q4.5 programs for machine learning.* San Francisco: Morgan Kaufmann.

Quinlan, J. R. (1986). Induction of decision trees. *Machine Learning, 1*(1), 81–106.

Ragel, A., & Crémilleux, B. (1999). MVC—a preprocessing method to deal with missing values. *Knowledge-Based Systems, 12,* 285–291.

Raghavan, V. V., Doegun, J. S., & Sever, H. (1998). Introduction to the special issue on data mining. *Journal of the American Society for Information Science, 49,* 397–402.

Raghavan, V. V., Sever, H., & Doegun, J. S. (1994). A system architecture for database mining applications. In W. P. Ziarco (Ed.), *Rough sets, fuzzy sets and knowledge discovery* (pp. 82–89). Berlin: Springer.

Reinartz, T. (1999). *Focusing solutions for data mining: Analytical studies and experimental results in real-world domains.* (Lecture notes in artificial intelligence 1623). Berlin: Springer.

Ritter, H., & Kohonen, T. (1989). Self-organizing semantic maps. *Biological Cybernetics, 61,* 241–254.

Robertson, A. M., & Gaizauskas, R. (1997). On the marriage of information retrieval and information extraction. In J. Furner & D. J. Harper (Eds.), *Proceedings of the 19th Annual BCS-IRSG Colloquium on IR Research* (pp. 60–67). London: British Computer Society. Retrieved March 1, 2001, from the World Wide Web: http://lorca.compapp.dcu.ie/BCS_IRSG-97/sand1.html

Sarawagi, S., Thomas, S., & Agrawal, R. (1998). Integrating association rule mining with relational database systems: Alternatives and implications. *SIGMOD'98,* 343–354. Retrieved March 1, 2001, from the World Wide Web: http:// dev.acm.org/pubs/contents/proceedings/mod/276304

Savasere, A., Omiecinski, E., & Navathe, S. B. (1995). An efficient algorithm for mining association rules in large databases. In U. Dayal, P. M. D. Gray, & S. Nishio (Eds.), *Proceedings of 21st International Conference on Very Large Data Bases VLDB95* (pp. 432–444). San Francisco: Morgan Kaufmann.

Schade, D., Dowler, P., Zingle, R., Durand, D., Gaudet, S., Hill, N., Jaeger, S., & Bohlender, D. (2000). A data mining model for astronomy. In N. Manset, C.

Veillet, & D. Crabtree (Eds.), *ASP Conference Series, Vol. 216, Astronomical Data Analysis Software and Systems IX* (p. 25). San Francisco: ASP.

Schank, R. C., & Abelson, R. P. (1977). *Scripts, plans, goals, and understanding.* Hillsdale, NJ: Lawrence Erlbaum.

Shen, L., Shen, H., & Cheng, L. (1999). New algorithms for efficient mining of association rules. *Information Sciences, 118,* 251–268.

Shintani, T., & Kitsuregawa, M. (2000). Parallel generalized association rule mining on large scale PC cluster. In M. J. Zaki & C.-T. Ho (Eds.), *Large-scale parallel data mining* (pp. 145–160). Berlin: Springer.

Simon, A. R. (1997). *Data warehouse for dummies.* Foster City, CA: IDG.

Simoudis, E. (1995). *Reality check for datamining.* IBM Almaden Research Center. Retrieved March 1, 2001, from the World Wide Web: http://www.almaden. ibm.com/stss/papers/reality

Skillicorn, D. (1999). Strategies for parallel data mining. *IEEE Concurrency, 7(4),* 25–35.

Small, R. D., & Edelstein, H. (2000). *Scalable data mining.* Retrieved March 1, 2001, from the World Wide Web: http://www.twocrows.com/whitep.htm

Smith, G., (1999, Dec. 13). Improved information retrieval. *Information Week.* Retrieved March 1, 2001, from the World Wide Web: http://www.informationweek.com

Smith, K. A., & Gupta, J. N. D. (2000). Neural networks in business: Techniques and applications for the operations researcher. *Computers & Operations Research, 27,* 1023–1044.

Soderland, S. (1999). Learning information extraction rules for semistructured and free-text. *Machine Learning, 34,* 1–44.

Spaccapietra, S., & Maryanski, F. (Eds.) (1997). *Data mining and reverse engineering: Searching for semantics.* New York: Chapman & Hall.

Spertus, E. (1997). *ParaSite: Mining structural information on the Web.* Retrieved March 1, 2001, from the World Wide Web: http://www.mills.edu/ACAD_INFO/ MCS/SPERTUS/Parasite/parasite.html

Stapley, B., & Benoît, G. (2000). BioBibliometrics: Information retrieval and visualization from co-occurrences of gene names in Medline abstracts. *Pacific Symposium on Biocomputing, 5,* 526–537. Retrieved March 1, 2001, from the World Wide Web: http://www-smi.stanford.edu/projects/helix/psb-online

Stolfo, S., Prodromidis, A. L., & Chan, P. K. (1997). JAM: Java agents for meta-learning over distributed databases. In *Proceedings of the Third International Conference on Knowledge Discovery and Data Mining* (pp. 74–81). Menlo Park, CA: AAAI Press.

Stolorz, P., & Musick, R. (1998). *Scalable high performance computing for knowledge discovery and data mining.* Boston: Kluwer.

Subramonian, R., & Parthasarathy, S. (1998). A framework for distributed data mining. In R. Agrawal & P. Stolorz (Eds.), *Proceedings of the Workshop on Distributed Data Mining, KDD98,* 23.

Talavera, L., & Bejar, J. (1999). Integrating declarative knowledge in hierarchical clustering tasks. *Advances in Intelligent Data Analysis. Third International Symposium, IDA-99* (pp. 211–22). (Lecture Notes in Computer Science 1642). Berlin: Springer.

Tan, P.-N., Blau, H., Harp, S., & Goldman, R. (2000). Textual data mining of service center call records. *Knowledge Discovery in Databases, 2000.* Retrieved March 1, 2001, from the World Wide Web: http://www-users.cs.umn.edu/~ptan/public.html

Terano, T., Liu, H., & Chen, A. L. P. (Eds.) (2000). *Pacific-Asia Conference on Knowledge Discovery and Data Mining, PAKDD 2000.* New York: Springer.

Thuraisingham, B. (1999). *Data mining: Technologies, techniques, tools, and trends.* Boca Raton, FL: CRC.

Toivonen, H. (1996). Sampling large databases for association rules. In T. M. Vijayaraman, A. P. Buchmann, C. Mohan, & N. L. Sarda (Eds.), *VLDB'96 Proceedings of the 22nd International Conference on Very Large Databases* (pp. 134–145). San Francisco: Morgan Kaufmann.

Trybula, W. J. (1997). Data mining and knowledge discovery. *Annual Review of Information Science and Technology, 32,* 197–229.

Trybula, W. J. (1999). Text Mining. *Annual Review of Information Science and Technology, 34,* 385–420.

Tsechansky, M. S., Pliskin, N., Rabinowitz, G., & Porath, A. (1999). Mining relational patterns from multiple relational tables. *Decision Support Systems, 27,* 117–195.

Tsukimoto, H. (1999). Rule extraction from prediction models. In N. Zhong & L. Zhou (Eds.), *Methodologies for knowledge discovery and data mining, PAKDD-99* (pp. 34–43). Berlin: Springer.

Weiss, S. M., & Indurkhya, N. (1998). *Predictive data mining: A practical guide.* San Francisco: Morgan Kaufmann.

Weiss, S. M., & Kulikowski, C. A. (1991). *Computer systems that learn.* San Mateo, CA: Morgan Kaufmann.

Westphal, C. R., & Blaxton, T. (1998). *Data mining solutions: Methods and tools for solving real-world problems.* New York: Wiley.

Wilks, Y. A., Slator, B. M., & Guthrie, L. (1996). *Electric Words: Dictionaries, computers, and meaning.* Cambridge, MA: MIT Press.

Williams, G., Atlas, I., Bakin, S., Christen, P., Hegland, M., Marquez, A., Milne, P., Nagappan, R., & Roberts, S. (1999). Large-scale parallel and distributed data mining. (Lecture notes in computer science, 1759). Berlin: Springer.

Wilson, D. R., & Martinez, T. R. (1997). Improved heterogeneous distance functions. *Journal of Artificial Intelligence Research, 6,* 1–34.

Winter, R. (1999). The E-Scalability Challenge. *Intelligent Enterprise, 2*(18). Retrieved March 1, 2001, from the World Wide Web: http://www.intelligententerprise.com/992112/scalable.shtml

Witten, I. H., & Frank, E. (2000). *Data mining: Practical machine learning tools and techniques with Java implementations.* San Francisco: Morgan Kaufmann.

Wong, M. L. (2000). *Data mining using grammar-based genetic programming and applications.* Boston: Kluwer.

Wong, W.-C., & Fu, A. W.-C. (2000). *Incremental document clustering for Web page classification.* Retrieved March 1, 2001, from the World Wide Web: http://www.cs.cuhk.hk/~adafu/Pub/IS2000.ps

Wright, P. (1996). Knowledge discovery preprocessing: Determining record usability. In U. M. Fayyad, G. Piatetsky-Shaprio, & P. Smyth (Eds.), *From data mining to knowledge discovery: An overview. Advances in Knowledge Discovery* (pp. 10–11). Menlo Park, CA: AAAI Press/MIT Press.

Xiang, Y, & Chu, T. (1999). Parallel learning of belief networks in large and difficult domains. *Data Mining and Knowledge Discovery* (vol. 3, pp. 315–339). Boston: Kluwer Academic.

Yang, J., Parekh, R., Honavar, V., & Dobbs, D. (1999). Data-driven theory refinement algorithms for bioinformatics. In *IEE-INNS Proceedings of the International Joint Conference on Neural Networks*. Retrieved March 1, 2001, from the World Wide Web: http://www.cs.iastate.edu/~parekh/papers/ijcnn99.ps

Zaki, M. J., & Ho, C.-T. (2000). *Large-scale parallel data mining*. New York: Springer.

Zhang, L., & Zhang, B. (1999). Neural network based classifiers for a vast amount of data. In N. Zhong, & L. Zhou (Eds.), *Methodologies for knowledge discovery and data mining, PAKDD-99.* (pp. 238-246). Berlin: Springer.

Zhong, N., & Ohsuga, S. (1994). Discovering concept clusters by decomposing databases. *Data & Knowledge Engineering, 12,* 223–244.

Zhong, N., Skowron, A., & Ohsuga, S. (1999). *New directions in rough sets, data mining, and granular-soft computing, RSFDGrC'99.* Berlin: Springer.

Zweiger, G. (1999). Knowledge discovery in gene-expression-microassay data: Mining the information output of the genome. *Trends in Biotechnology, 17,* 429–436.

Zytkow, J. M., & Quafafou, M. (Eds.) (1998). *Principles of Data Mining and Knowledge Discovery: Second European Symposium, PKDD '98.* Berlin: Springer.

Zytkow, J. M., & Rauch, J. (Eds.) (1999). *Principles of data mining and knowledge discovery: Third European Conference, PKDD '99.* Berlin: Springer.

Intelligence
and Strategy

CHAPTER 7

Intelligence, Information Technology, and Information Warfare

Philip H. J. Davies
University of Malaya

Introduction

This chapter, the first of its kind to appear in an *ARIST* volume, addresses the general state-of-the-art of intelligence and information warfare in the context of national security, provides a general background on these topics, and then reviews the status of clandestine collection in the subareas of hacking; human agent collection; signal interception; covert action; counterintelligence; and overall tasking, dissemination, and analysis. Although these topics are relatively esoteric to many or most information professionals, it is indeed difficult to find any topic in information science and technology not relevant to intelligence, information warfare, and national security, or conversely. Previous *ARIST* coverage in the broad areas of planning for information systems and services, basic techniques and technologies, or applications is relevant. In particular, earlier chapters on content analysis (1966–68 and 1987 volumes), information needs and uses, and national information policy (various volumes from 1966–82) provide a few examples, among many, that are more closely relevant. Indeed, intelligence in its many forms is essentially about the acquisition, interpretation, collation, assessment, and exploitation of information. Intelligence services are historically major innovators in information technology. From the

Colossus computer developed by the wartime British Government Code and Cipher School (GC&CS) to attack German machine codes to the use of commercial Cray supercomputers for cryptography by its successor Government Communications Headquarters (GCHQ) and its allies, the intelligence services have always been major information technology innovators and consumers. And, of course, communications and information security are essential concerns to these institutions which, in turn, play an increasingly central role in the development of information security in both public and private spheres. Hence, the topics of intelligence, information warfare, and national security in particular serve to extend the scope and depth of information science and technology in general.

Seventeen years ago, historians David Dilks and Christopher Andrew (1984) could confidently declare that the role and impact of national intelligence services constituted the "missing dimension" of diplomatic history. While this may no longer be the case (Robertson, 1987a), it can certainly be said that they remain the missing dimension of the so-called Revolution in Military Affairs (RMA); specifically the subfield thereof generally known as information warfare. There is a sense afoot, particularly in American quarters, that the emergence of the new information and communication technologies (ICTs) is radically transforming the way in which warfare is conducted, although this sense of discontinuity is not necessarily shared by British and European commentators (Badsey, 1999). In most cases this involves the use of ICTs, for example in battlefield communications or "smart weapons." One subclass of RMA thinking is directed specifically toward the use of ICTs as weapons (or windows of vulnerability) in their own rights. This is not to say intelligence *as such* is absent from discussions of RMA and information warfare. Martin Libicki (1995, p. 19) in his *What Is Information Warfare?* has postulated a form of information warfare he calls "intelligence-based warfare" (IBW), which

> occurs when intelligence is fed directly into operations (notably, targeting and battle damage assessment) rather than used as an input for overall command and control.... As sensors grow more acute and reliable, as they proliferate in type and number, and as they become capable of feeding fire-control systems in real time and near-real time, the task of developing, maintaining and exploiting systems that sense

the battlespace, assess its composition, and send the results to shooters assumes increasing importance for tomorrow's militaries.

This concept of intelligence, however, has more to do with the short-term, rapid turnaround varieties of tactical and operational intelligence in the battlefield than the work and product of national intelligence communities. But what about the slower and steadier work of predominantly civilian and policy-oriented national intelligence services? The problem addressed in this chapter is not the intelligence components of information warfare, but the implications of ICTs and information warfare for the work of national, central intelligence agencies and their communities.

The absence of national intelligence services in such an area of policy debate is surprising since intelligence is, as just observed, all about *information*. There is still some debate about what constitutes information warfare as such (see, for example, Libicki, 1995; Rathmell, 2000), depending on whether one defines it broadly as any and all conflict in which information is the central factor, or narrowly as conflict prosecuted primarily through the use of new-generation ICTs. Where the study of intelligence services and communities is concerned, the broad definition would cast the subject in terms of deception, propaganda, and related methods, which are hardly new at all. But such key features of the new ICTs as digital information and communications systems, global satellite communications, the Internet, and so forth, *are* new, and so it must be the narrow definition of information warfare that is relevant here. The Cold War, that intelligence war *par excellence*, may now be a welcome decade past, but intelligence remains a sphere of vital importance to national security. And while intelligence may now have more to do with counter-terrorism and international trade negotiations than counting nuclear weapons, in many respects that shift of emphasis means that it has more day-to-day relevance to the welfare and personal safety of the citizen in the street than in the days when it was concerned with the higher mathematics of the balance of terror. ICTs also have a centrality and an immediate, day-to-day relevance to the welfare and security of that same citizen in the street that they did not have a decade or so ago. As a result, some sort of critical evaluation of the consequences of the new ICTs for intelligence (and necessarily vice versa) is of ever more acute importance and necessity.

Information and Intelligence

Intellectual schemata designed to describe intelligence date at least to the late 1940s in American literature (Wark, 1987), but have entered the academic lexicon of other countries in only the last twenty-five years or so. In the popular imagination, intelligence, like information warfare, somehow manages to be both arcane and melodramatic. As always, the actual circumstances are a great deal more prosaic, and so are the analytical tools used to describe and to try to manage the intelligence world. Intelligence is essentially part and parcel with the workings of modern government. Peter Gill (1994), for example, has sought at some length to make the case for its recognition as a core state function, while the present author has striven to recast discussion of the subject in the slow-and-steady terms of public administration (Davies, 2000). Intelligence is not a universally standardized term, however. A well-established American definition of intelligence has been given as the "product resulting from the collection, evaluation, analysis, integration, and interpretation of all available information which concerns one or more aspects of foreign nations or of areas of operation which is immediately or potentially significant for planning" (Richelson, 1989, p. 1). Therefore, the analysis of intelligence is basic to the idea of intelligence, and information is considered an input to intelligence. As a consequence, one generally finds that American intelligence organizations such as the Central Intelligence Agency (CIA), the Defense Intelligence Agency, and State Department Bureau of Intelligence and National Research undertake the analysis of intelligence as well as its collection (Richelson, 2000).

By contrast, British officials, during briefings to U.K. academics, are prone to intone the mantra "intelligence is about secrets, not mysteries"; or as one leading British scholar in the field has put it, intelligence is "the secret collection of someone else's secrets" (Robertson, 1987b, pp. 46–47). As former Director of Requirements for the British Secret Intelligence Service (SIS), the late Nicholas Elliott (1993, p. 23), phrased it, the function of a secret service "is to find out by clandestine means what the overt organs of government cannot find out by overt means." That secret information is then fed to various departments and ministries of state such as the Foreign and Commonwealth Office, the Ministry of Defence, and the Cabinet Office, who then incorporate it into their own analysis and decision-making processes. Former Foreign and Commonwealth official Reginald Hibbert has elaborated upon this still further. According to Hibbert (1990, p. 113), "The Foreign Office is itself a huge assessment machine…. With its elaborate organisation of over 60 departments, some geographical in scope and some functional, it constitutes a capacious and versatile digestive system fed by the massive intake of information [composed of] the 50 percent or so overt, the 10 percent or so privileged, the 20 or 25 percent confidential, and the 10 percent secret." As a result, in British parlance, intelligence is but one variety of information contributing to what former senior U.K. intelligence official Michael Herman (1996) has described as governmental assessment and analysis.

Given the emphasis on assessment in the U.S. approach to intelligence, it is unsurprising that intelligence-oriented discussions of information warfare have tended to emphasize the analytical activity of threat assessment. Apart from Wynn Schwartau's (1996, p. 68) off-the-cuff observation that "spies are the original information warriors," attention has generally been paid to dealing with the threat from ICTs rather than the potential use of ICTs. In 1996, the Director of Central Intelligence (DCI) briefed Congress that the protection of national information systems was an emerging global security consideration, as part of his World Wide Threat Assessment Brief (reproduced in Schwartau, 1996). A similar analysis appeared in the unclassified edition of the CIA's intelligence studies journal *Studies in Intelligence*. L. Scott Johnson (1997) developed what he termed a functional model of information warfare, which essentially elaborated that most persistent theme in American information warfare literature: the "electronic Pearl Harbor." Johnson's functional model is concerned solely with U.S. vulnerability to information attack at the levels of information systems as such, information systems management, and decision making and policy. In this sense, intelligence-oriented examination of information warfare has, in the first place, added very little to the alarmist scenario-building of writers like Schwartau (1996) and Arquilla (1998); while in the second place, it has talked very little about intelligence itself. Martin Libicki (1995, p.19) explicitly coupled the notion of information warfare to intelligence collection. But even here, his notion of intelligence-based warfare, "when intelligence is fed directly into operations (notably, targeting and battle damage assessment) rather than used as an input for overall command and control," is concerned more with the short-term, rapid turnaround varieties of tactical and operational intelligence on the battlefield than with the work and product of national intelligence communities. With such an emphasis on threat assessment, the general public approaches information warfare in terms of *threat* rather than *opportunity*, while from the point of view of the intelligence community, it is at least as much opportunity as it is threat. To be sure, there have been many efforts to develop conventional defense service-oriented policies on offensive information warfare (see, for example, U.S. Joint Chiefs of Staff, 1998), but covertly implemented information warfare is as different from conventional military information warfare as the resistance cells and partisan support teams of the 1939–45 Special Operations Executive (SOE) and Special Air Service (SAS) were from the conventional armed forces of their day. Michael L. Brown has, perhaps, moved discussion furthest in the desired direction, at least at a conceptual level, in his three classes of information warfare. According to Brown (1996, p. 47), Type I information warfare consists of "managing the enemy's perceptions through deception operations, psychological operations … and a variety of other techniques." Type I is the most familiar form, then, and the type least particular to the new ICTs, as deception and *psyops* (psychological operations) are among the oldest and most established features of war. Type II information warfare, however, consists of "denying, destroying, degrading or distorting the enemy's information flows in order to break down his organizations and his ability to coordinate operations" (Brown 1996, p. 47); in other words, command, communications, control, computing, and intelligence attack (C4I). But Type III information warfare "gathers intelligence by exploiting the enemy's use of information systems," taking us directly into the spheres of ICTs, and of "secretly acquiring other people's secrets" (Brown, 1996, p. 47).

There is, however, a great deal of variability in how one identifies the constituent features of national intelligence systems. As early as 1949, one-time Office of Strategic Services analyst and future senior Central Intelligence Agency official Sherman Kent developed a taxonomical model of what constitutes intelligence; coining, in the process, an assortment of archetypal aphorisms such as "intelligence is information" and "intelligence is organization" (Kent, 1949). Perhaps the most exhaustive approach is the "elements of intelligence scheme" developed by the

Consortium for the Study of Intelligence (Godson, 1979, 1980a, 1980b, 1981, 1982, 1986a, 1986b). Under this scheme, the work of national intelligence communities consists of four chief elements: covert or clandestine intelligence collection, covert action, counterintelligence, and intelligence analysis and estimates. Former Deputy Chief of the British Secret Intelligence Service, John Bruce Lockhart (1987), has also suggested adding a fifth element, intelligence requirements—again reflective of the British emphasis on intelligence information designed to fill in the blanks, rather than policy-oriented analysis, which sometimes seems designed to tell policy makers what to think.

Clandestine collection is broadly divided into intelligence from human sources (HUMINT) and from technical sources (TECHINT), although many of these techniques shade into the nonsecret as well. HUMINT covers a number of overt and covert methods, and includes debriefing refugees, prisoners of war, escapees, and travelers returning from abroad, as well as handling or "running" penetration agents. TECHINT can be broken down chiefly into imagery intelligence (IMINT), typically overhead reconnaissance and surveillance by aircraft and satellites, and signals intelligence (SIGINT). SIGINT, in turn, consists of monitoring communications (COMINT) and noncommunicative signals such as radar and telemetry (electronic intelligence or ELINT). Covert action has two major subdivisions: paramilitary special operations, and purely political work known in U.S. jargon as covert action and in British as special political action. Often special operations may be used in conjunction with political actions, such as the mid-1950s coup in Guatemala (Phillips, 1977; Schlesinger & Kinzer, 1983). Counterintelligence is the process of detecting, monitoring, and intercepting hostile covert collection and covert action. It can be divided into purely defensive work, also called counterintelligence, and offensive penetration of hostile intelligence agencies—counter-espionage. Intelligence analysis is the process of evaluating raw intelligence information in terms of policy and decision-making needs to produce assessments or "finished" intelligence that can guide decision makers. Analysis, in turn, is divisible into single-source assessments, where a particular type of information is needed, and the pooling of information from all available intelligence types, overt and covert, or "all-source" analysis. Of course, one must somehow link the collection of information to the process of analysis and policy; and for this reason Lockhart (1987) has argued that the institutional mechanisms by which the users of intelligence articulate their needs to intelligence suppliers are at least as important to the intelligence process, hence the need for requirements or tasking to feature in the model.

Roughly speaking, these various elements can be laid out along the lines of an internal governmental market for intelligence, with collection, covert action, and counterintelligence on the supply, or producer, side. Analysis is a little ambiguous, as sometimes it is undertaken by producers (in the U.S.) and sometimes by consumers (in the U.K.), but agency tasking and incorporating intelligence into policy and operations lie firmly on the consumer side. This relationship can be represented as a cycle—the "intelligence cycle"—in which consumers examine their information needs and task the operational agencies. Information is collected and, in the American model, assessed, and then disseminated to consumers. They then re-evaluate their needs, revise their requirements, and re-task the agencies (e.g., Herman, 1996; Laqueur, 1985; for a differing view of the intelligence cycle see Treholt-Wilson, 1999). Unsurprisingly, at certain levels in the British system the last two steps are reversed, with raw information being disseminated to consumers who undertake their own analysis (Herman, 1995; Hibbert, 1990), and then re-task the agencies on that basis. The intelligence cycle is something of a Platonic ideal, as several commentators have noted that it rarely works out in practice; the overall process being more amorphous, a matter of continuous, running dialog. The new ICTs, and thereby the risks of information warfare as narrowly defined herein, have profoundly affected aspects of all four, or, if we accept Lockhart's suggestion, five elements of intelligence and the workings of the producer-consumer relationship. The remainder of this discussion will examine them in turn.

Clandestine Collection

As will become apparent, most information warfare discussion deals with methods and dangers more relevant to covert action, but the implications for covert collection are no less important. The impact of ICTs and their attendant risks appears to center on two main issues. The first is that ICTs have created an entirely new class of collection operation that has very little precedent and does not fit neatly into the existing categories of intelligence. That new form of espionage is clandestine access to information systems, a form of cybernetic penetration operation that could be referred to conveniently (although not elegantly) as "HACKINT," intelligence acquired by hacking into networked information systems (Davies, 1999). The second issue is the recurrent debate about the relative importance and roles of human and technical intelligence methods. This debate becomes particularly acute where the respective values of HUMINT and SIGINT to covert collection in the information revolution are being discussed.

HACKINT

As a general rule, commentators in the field tend to assume that the first major incident of clandestine cybernetic penetration was the so-called "Hannover hacker" incident (see, for example, Stoll, 1991). In this case, a group of West German computer aficionados, the Chaos Computer Club, led by one Markus Hess, systematically sought to attack and penetrate U.S. Department of Defense networked computers during the early 1980s. These actions were undertaken at the behest of, and supported by, the now defunct Soviet secret service, the KGB (*Komitet Gosudarstevennoye Besopasnostiye*, the Committee for State Security). This was hardly the first instance of clandestine penetration of computer systems, although it was certainly a very early case of a network-based attack.

Earlier operations against computers when stand-alone mainframes were the norm tended to require direct, physical access. An early such operation (although unlikely to prove the first if ever a comprehensive history of IT-based espionage becomes possible) was operation HAM, mounted by the Royal Canadian Mounted Police Security Service (RCMP/SS) during the 1970s. Relatively little attention has been paid to this incident, partly because it was in the very early days of computer-based intelligence, and partly because very little has been published on it, the official account in a subsequent Royal Commission enquiry being heavily redacted (one blank page in the report of the Commission of Inquiry Concerning Certain Activities of the Royal Canadian Mounted Police [1981]), and probably not least because it took place in Canada with reference to Canadian domestic politics rather than the global cut and thrust of the Cold War.

Operation HAM attacked the mainframe computer of a separatist group in the French-speaking province of Québec in 1973. The RCMP had learned that the separatist political, party the *Parti Québécois* (PQ), had computerized its membership lists; operation HAM involved the clandestine duplication of the relevant computer tapes (this was 1973). The reason for such on operation was concern that the PQ was receiving money from foreign countries to support its political agenda. There were also fears that radical elements were infiltrating the party (the October 1970 terrorist crisis was still fresh in people's minds, as well as the risk of Soviet-influenced operations) and there was a real possibility that federal civil servants with access-sensitive compartmented information (SCI) had been leaking that information to the PQ. HAM consisted of months of surveillance of the PQ headquarters premises; and then one night a clandestine entry team slipped in, removed the tapes (leaving blank dummy tapes in their place should someone walk into the office during the night), duplicated them and returned them before the start of the business day. Although HAM was an operational success, it failed miserably in terms of analytical production and dissemination because of a problem that would continue to nag computer-based intelligence operations for the next two decades or more. Investigative journalist John Sawatsky (1980, p. 247) noted, in his account of the affair, that "the Security Service did not know what to do with the information once it had possession. The Force lacked expertise to make assessments. The printout material ... was stored and seldom looked at.... On July 19, 1975 ... the HAM material was burned in an RCMP incinerator." Simply put, the Force simply was not sufficiently computer literate to process and interpret the reams of raw information it had acquired. HAM fell afoul of a combination of limited computer literacy and that *bête noire* of technical operations, information overload. Sawatsky (1980, p. 247) concludes, damningly, "despite its technical superiority the operation was a flop."

Network-based attacks on computer systems are, however, a newer and far different phenomenon in the lexicon of intelligence. HAM was really no different from inter-war German *Abwehr* agent Cicero secretly opening the safe of the British Ambassador in Rome and inspecting its contents (Andrew, 1987; Bazna, 1962; Moyzisch, 1952). Hacking into networked systems offers an entirely new form of clandestine collection that does not fit any of the established conventional "INTs." It is also potentially highly productive at a singularly low operational cost compared with agent running, signal interception, or satellite imagery. By one estimate, Markus Hess' group penetrated fifty military computers at the Pentagon, various defense contractors, the Los Alamos National Laboratory, Argonne National Laboratory, the Air Force Space Systems Division, and various U.S. military bases around the world (Madsen, 1993). Perhaps the most distinctive feature of this effort was the very low grade of information acquired. Stoll (1991), the astronomer-turned-sysop who pursued Hess down the telephone lines to Germany, found U.S. federal agencies deeply uninterested in pursuing Hess on the grounds that none of the systems attacked held classified or secret information. Indeed, a report by the U.S. General Accounting Office (GAO) estimated that Pentagon systems had been attacked roughly 250,000 times during 1995, with some 160,000 successful penetrations resulting (Brock, 1996). The GAO investigation was brought about by a penetration by a British 16-year-old hacker calling himself the "Datastream Cowboy," acting in concert with a figure using the e-mail handle "Kuji," whom U.S. authorities suspected of being a foreign intelligence officer. Just as with the case of the Hannover Hacker, however, the Pentagon took the reports calmly, noting that no systems handling classified or secret information had been compromised (Walker, 1996). In the event, Kuji and the Datastream Cowboy turned out to be far less sinister than U.S. defense officials expected—two British adolescents determined to find evidence of X-files-reminiscent conspiracies and aliens (Campbell, 1997). HACKINT has been a growth area of intelligence service activity for quite some time. Even in its relatively early days there was evidence from a source in Moscow's State Committee for Scientific Research run by the French security service, their *Direction de la sécurité territoriale*, that as much as 2.4 percent of the Soviet Union's total (and massive) foreign collection effort was cybernetic penetration (Madsen, 1993). Since then, virtually every major intelligence service has begun to mine this vein systematically.

One must be careful not to exaggerate the potential of clandestine cybernetic penetration. Despite the hype surrounding the Hannover Hacker incident, or the daunting numbers in the 1996 GAO report, the vast majority of systems penetrated did not hold highly classified SCI. This, certainly, was the basis of the Pentagon's seemingly complacent reaction to the GAO report; moreover, really sensitive computers in national defense and intelligence community centers, and networked systems like IntelNet, are uniformly either stand-alone systems or isolated from global cyberspace by one-way gates. However, during much of the Cold War, the greater part of extremely useful SIGINT came not from any successor to the great break of German machine codes in the Second World War, ULTRA, but from the vast quantity of low-grade and *en claire* (open) communication traffic carrying the day-to-day logistical and battlefield messages of field radios and unscrambled telephones (Bamford, 1983; Burrows, 1988; Laqueur, 1985). It would likewise be naïve to suggest that logistical and low-security information is not of intelligence value, especially when an adversary is gauging one's capabilities as much as one's intentions.

An interesting and often overlooked feature in discussions of information warfare techniques is the physical security of information systems, not just in terms of their location and accessibility, but also the monitoring and interpretation of their electromagnetic emissions, or van Eck radiations (Schwartau, 1996). The capability of intercepting cathode ray tube (CRT) emissions by reading and interpreting their electromagnetic signals is well established. The technique has long been used by the Television Licensing Authority in Britain, and is one of the main reasons that passwords are not echoed verbatim on screen but are replaced with generic "securicons" such as dots or asterisks. But perhaps the most disturbing feature is the very strength and interception-potential of the electromagnetic field created by central processors themselves. Within NATO's defense and intelligence communities, the practice of physically shielding or hardening information systems to forestall this risk is know as TEMPESTing. But outside these communities, the practice is rare, not least because TEMPESTing a PC can cost an order of magnitude more than the computer itself. Even within the intelligence community TEMPESTing has, on occasion, been imperfectly observed, as in the case when the British Secret Intelligence Service (SIS) reportedly purchased a supply of CIA-recommended Wang secure terminals. Only after installation did they discover, through a routine check by the Communications Electronics Security Group (CESG), that the equipment did not live up to its advertising (Urban, 1996).

HAM and the interception of hardware emissions may not have been network-based forms of information system attack, but clandestine computer access is as much a matter of human and physical security as one of network security. Libicki (1995, p. 53) has suggested that "even though many computer systems run with insufficient regard for network security, computer systems can nevertheless be made secure. They can be (not counting traitors on the inside), in ways that, say, neither a building nor a tank can be." And that, of course, raises the question of the role of human intelligence in the new world disorder, and in due course the counterintelligence problems of personnel and physical security as well.

HUMINT and SIGINT

Intelligence discussion since the end of the Cold War has been characterized by a running debate over the relative effectiveness of human and technical methods, intensified by the impact of ICTs. From the outset of the post-Cold War era there was an awareness that intelligence in the old Cold War model was unlikely to suit the new security needs. Without a global nuclear standoff to dominate the world stage, national security requirements shifted fairly uniformly, and almost simultaneously, on both sides of the former Iron Curtain. They shifted away from monitoring the strategic and tactical capabilities of multinational blocs to smaller-scale but often more pervasive and pernicious threats such as terrorism, transnational serious crime (particularly narcotics and its side effect, money laundering), the proliferation of weapons of mass destruction (WMDs) and advanced conventional weapons, and a renewed concern about economic security and, therefore, economic and industrial espionage (Adams, 1994; Boren, 1992; May, 1992; Smith, 1996; Urban, 1996). These new requirements share the common characteristics of being based around small groups that are difficult to identify and monitor, and a blurring of the lines between domestic and foreign threats. Former Director of Central Intelligence James Woolsey described the change to Congress as the death of a dragon replaced by a jungle full of snakes (Adams, 1994; Smith, 1996). There since has developed a fairly widespread agreement that these Woolseyan snakes are relatively unamenable to much of the older mass-production technical intelligence, particularly overhead imagery. To be sure, the increased importance of peacekeeping since the collapse of Yugoslavia and the civil wars in African states like Rwanda and Burundi has meant that traditional military operational intelligence is still of great importance. As a result, there remains a firm, if more limited, demand for overhead surveillance and reconnaissance, as well as military SIGINT. However, a number of commentators have concluded that technical intelligence has generally seen its day, and that a new golden age of human intelligence is taking shape (Boren, 1992; Toffler & Toffler, 1995).

ICTs play directly into this HUMINT-TECHINT debate, and particularly the HUMINT-SIGINT relationship. To start with, they have affected many aspects of the process of collecting intelligence. Of the major classes of collection methods, imagery intelligence remains the least affected by information security issues and least relevant to conducting or preventing information technology attack. Even so, continuous satellite uplink/downlink and the development of charge-coupled devices (CCDs) served to revolutionize real-time satellite imagery with the KEYHOLE generation of overhead reconnaissance and surveillance satellites in the 1970s (Burrows, 1988). Before this, satellites had to be launched with a limited supply of film for their cameras, and that film dropped from orbit in diminutive re-entry canisters. Apart from the obvious risks of accidental loss and destruction, this also prevented IMINT production in real time as film canisters were generally not released until the film had been fully exposed. But it is human and communications intelligence that have been most fundamentally transformed. As put by one senior official to U.K. academics in 1997, "in the old days it took you seven days and a camel to get a message from an agent in the deep desert; today all you need is a satellite telephone" (private communication).

Even barring anonymous electronic mail and other deniable forms of Internet communications, the old espionage standard of clandestine radio has been utterly transformed. During the Second World War, European Resistance circuits relied on collapsible radios that, unpacked, could occupy the entire floor of a room and were acutely vulnerable to Axis direction-finding efforts (Foot, 1984). In the Cold War, Soviet illegals and their subagents concealed sizeable and powerful radios in their homes, and the squirt transmitter that sent prerecorded messages at high speed and in short bursts made counter-clandestine (counter-clan) interception profoundly difficult. But by the 1980s, Western counter-clan intercept operators found their work made far more difficult by the fact that illegals no longer required long-range, high-power transmitters. As long as the transmitters lay within the ground footprint of Soviet military communications satellites, they needed only to be strong enough to be detected by that satellite. The satellite would then store the information for transmittal back to Earth once within range of a Soviet receiving station (Frost & Gratton, 1994). Likewise, the explosion of global communications has potentially created vast new possibilities for communications intelligence. However, if there is one common lesson from the information revolution, it is that ICTs "giveth" with one hand even as they "taketh away" with the other. In principle, they *should* be creating new opportunities for SIGINT, and in some respects they are. But the situation is far less straightforward than it might initially appear.

Undoubtedly, the now widespread use of satellite communications has created an entirely new and highly productive field of SIGINT work, intercepting satellite uplinks/downlinks (Hagar, 1996). During a 1998 briefing to U.K. academics, a senior British official was queried about whether signal intelligence had indeed waned since the Cold War, as so many had expected. The response was that, contrary to such expectations, SIGINT had actually increased in significance because more terrorists and drug traffickers were talking to each other over cellular telephones and the Internet than ever before. On the other hand, there have been real concerns that the potential for anonymity (such as through certain e-mail servers, or the current bane of police telephone interception, prepaid mobile phones) and the ready availability of strong encryption machines no more powerful and expensive than the family desktop computer threaten SIGINT's acccess to the *en claire* and weakly encrypted traffic that has traditionally made up the lion's share of its raw intelligence take. Likewise, the fact that information conveyed over the Internet is broken up into myriad packets sent separately through the world's network of routers means that they cannot be intercepted in real time as one might intercept radio telecommunications. Finally, fiber optic lines are virtually impossible to tap without detection, unlike good, old-fashioned copper cable. As a result, there has been very real concern that the effectiveness of SIGINT can only dwindle as information technology spreads (e.g., Urban, 1996).

It was precisely the fear of wholesale, cheap, and strong encryption that led to the almost panicked efforts in the United States to develop and implement the key-escrow scheme dubbed CLIPPER. U.S. law enforcement agencies (particularly the Federal Bureau of Investigation [FBI]) were acutely concerned that encrypted telecommunications would rob them of one of their most valued sources of both prosecutable evidence and criminal intelligence. America's SIGINT service, the National Security Agency (NSA), was therefore tasked to develop a chip that would provide users with strong encryption sufficient for commercial purposes while providing law enforcement agencies with the ability to access keys that would allow them to read CLIPPER-encrypted traffic. Despite the fact that the agencies would be required to secure a judicial warrant (just as they are required to do even to monitor open traffic), civil libertarians took exception to the policy, claiming it was yet another attempt by Big Government to insinuate itself into the private lives of American citizens (a fairly comprehensive record of the debate can be found at Electronic Frontier Foundation, 2000). By comparison, schemes proposed by the U.K. government for various Trusted Third Party (TTP) key-escrow schemes (e.g., U.K. Department of Trade and Industry, 1997) were rejected as being awkward and impractical (Ward, 1997), while France simply maintained its long-standing ban on strong encryption. In due course, successive demonstrations of the weakness of CLIPPER's design and successively weaker versions of CLIPPER were brought before a resistant Congress until it was so dubious as to be pointless, and the scheme has since lapsed. Likewise, Britain's TTP efforts have been abandoned in favor of the Restriction of Investigatory Powers Act (RIPA), currently before Parliament. RIPA is in many respects an update of the 1985 Interception of Communications Act, with a number of additions. Among these is a provision for police, intelligence, and security services to secure warrants—from the relevant Secretary of State (i.e., senior Cabinet Minister overseeing a Department or Ministry) rather than a judge—that allow them to demand access to the "keys" for a designated body of encrypted data (the definition of keys in the act is broad enough to cover almost any relevant cryptomaterials). The act also allows the agencies to attach so-called black boxes to Internet service provider servers to monitor traffic as it arrives (partially solving the interception problem). France has abandoned its ban on strong encryption, but its final legislative strategy for dealing with the problem has yet to take shape (Segell, 2000).

The problem with most of the various solutions to cheap and strong encryption is that, for the most part, they are really workable only in terms of domestic law enforcement, less suitable for domestic security intelligence operations where one cannot simply be so obvious as to demand cryptographic information from a surveillance subject, and almost completely unsuitable to foreign intelligence collection. This is as important because major contemporary intelligence targets such as terrorist groups and criminal cartels that have traditionally been without strong cryptography can now acquire it with relatively little difficulty, and because their activities are increasingly multinational and transnational. Barring isolated Second World War successes like ULTRA and MAGIC, its American equivalent in the Pacific, or retrospective cryptanalytical successes like VENONA during the Cold War, highly secure national communications systems have rarely been broken. During the Cold War the agencies of the Anglo-American SIGINT alliance, the UK/USA agencies (the NSA, Britain's GCHQ, Australia's Defence Signals Directorate and the Canadian Communications Security Establishment) were forced to rely on low-grade COMINT or information handled by hostile satellite states in the developing world, much of which was handled by the aging and relatively weak Hagelin machine (Bamford, 1983; Laqueur, 1985). The main exceptions occurred when human agents provided consistent and timely access to cryptomaterials, such as GCHQ's Geoffrey Prime (Bamford, 1983; Security Commission, 1983), and John Walker in the United States Navy (Andrew & Gordievsky, 1991; Barron, 1987), all of whom were run by the KGB. Indeed, the early breaks against the Enigma machine were very much due to the French *Deuxième Bureau*'s 1931 walk-in agent Hans Thilo Schmidt (Stengers, 1984). It has also been noted that, for all intents and purposes, hacking intelligence operations have fallen more within the ambit of HUMINT than TECHINT. As a result, it seems likely that human sources will indeed be increasingly important, but not simply because of the relative inaccessibility of Woolseyan snakes to technical methods. Indeed, the human factor is an established piece of the malicious computer cracker's toolkit, accounting for up to 20 percent of the known successful penetrations (Denning, 1999). It would also appear that if SIGINT is to remain the large-scale intelligence producer it has been in the past, it will have to be on the basis of a vanguard of HUMINT. These operations can provide the initial breaks on which SIGINT services will be able to once again tap into communications that would otherwise be denied to them by today's ICTs.

Any account of the failure of key-escrow and the apparent triumph of cheap and strong crytpography must ultimately cope with two very different sets of factors: technical impracticality and civil liberties. On the whole, the failure seems to have been driven more by practical considerations than political or ideological ones, but either way the alternative described above requires some very sober reflection. Prior to the information revolution, any communications intercept required a warrant in Britain, Canada, and the United States. There was some degree of latitude in the warranting procedures involved; in some cases judicial warrants (typically for police intercepts, and in U.S. and Canadian intelligence practice) or, under the British 1985 Interception of Communication Act, a warrant signed by the Home Secretary for a domestic intercept or the Foreign Secretary for one conducted abroad, and then only if justifiable on national security grounds. This was true of communications sent either encrypted or in the clear; and in this respect the key-escrow schemes differed little from what had gone before. But no comparable controls have existed for the recruitment of agents. Of course, the Canadian Security and Intelligence Service must receive approval from the Targeting Approval and Review Committee (TARC), and the SIS's operations must be approved by its Foreign Office Adviser, but there is no equivalent to an interception warrant for recruiting and running an informant. In Canada, where intercepts figure among a family of operations legally described as intrusive measures, a member of the Canadian national security community recently described agent-running as "one of, if not the most intrusive means available" (Whitacker, 1996, pp. 284–285). While this may be of less concern when collecting foreign clandestine information, what of domestic security intelligence operations? America still carries the political legacy of the indiscriminate counter-subversions operations of the 1960s. The FBI's COINTELPRO and the CIA's MHCHAOS conducted against anti-war activists and suspected "radicals" were eventually exposed in court, severely damaging the credibility and legitimacy of those agencies (Mackenzie, 1997); and since the Cold War ended, Westerners have seen the long-term costs of wholesale informant recruitment in the former East Germany. The need for domestic intelligence for counterterrorist, counter-proliferation, and criminal intelligence purposes is not likely to abate in the near future. In all of the hue and cry about the right to private communications and the threat from government control of cryptography, how much attention has really been paid to the civil liberties implications of the alternatives?

Covert Action

The basic principle of covert action in an age of information warfare is that anything the isolated digital thief, vandal, or politico can do, national intelligence services can do on a far larger scale, coupled with and integrated into all of the other instruments of influence and attack traditionally available to the modern state. On the whole, ICT-based espionage has made up the minority of issues and scenarios dealt with in the literature on information warfare. Even when espionage has been the nominal subject, the bulk of attention tends to go to malicious hacking in which information is corrupted or destroyed, rather than simply inspected or downloaded. Peter Sakkas's (1991) relatively early article "Espionage and Sabotage in the Computer World," for example, actually devotes most of its threat assessment to destructive software such as viruses, worms, logic bombs, and trojan horses, and then concerns itself with security methods for preventing such attacks. Indeed, there has been a great deal of discussion of the kind of clandestine sabotage that would fit within the broad category of special operations, involving information system sabotage and larger-scale attacks on critical national information infrastructures (Arquilla, & Ronfeld, 1996; Haeni & Hoffman, 1996; Johnson, 1997; Libicki, 1995; Molander, Riddile, & Wilson, 1996; Schwartau, 1996). The Internet is also a prime medium for both the coordination of terrorism and its implementation (Devost, Houghton, & Pollard, 1997). Arquilla (1998), in particular, has noted the danger of "false flag" operations wherein a party (in his scenario, a political activist-terrorist organization) undertakes an attack they make traceable to a third party, an action that could be used to intentionally exacerbate international, interracial, or inter-sectarian tensions, as well as to conceal one's traces. Typical models have involved terrorist groups and other Woolseyan snakes. What is all too easy to forget is how often national intelligence services have aided, abetted, and funded such snakes both during the Cold War and since, sometimes using them as agents or as intermediaries to attack targets they dare not approach directly, or simply as diversions or political stalking horses. While Sterling (1981) may have exaggerated the reliance of terrorism on state support, the Soviet bloc was indeed highly involved in supporting Euro-Communist and Middle Eastern terrorists (Andrew & Gordievsky, 1991; Koehler, 1999). Throughout the last three decades, intelligence services from the Islamic world such as Syria, Iraq, Libya, and Iran have funded and provided training and equipment to Palestinian extremist groups and, more recently, fundamentalist organizations such as Hamas and Hezbollah (see, for example, Emerson & Del Sesto, 1991; Kinsella, 1992; Leppard & Levy, 1994). And both sides in the Cold War supported amenable guerrilla, partisan, and paramilitary organizations throughout the world. And so, much as intelligence services have found it suitable to recruit hackers for espionage purposes, one might expect the same for covert paramilitary and political actions as well.

With so much attention paid to destructive information system penetration, purely political actions have tended to remain in the background. Special political action is a varied class of covert activity, including, among other things, deceptive actions intended to mislead an enemy (popularly but imprecisely referred to by the Soviet trade term disinformation), disruptive actions intended to set enemies one against the other, gray and black propaganda (propaganda from nominally independent and completely deniable sources, respectively), influence operations (ranging from recruiting persons in key positions in order to propagate particular ideas or policies, to manipulating elections), and even covert diplomatic contacts. Where deceptive and disruptive actions are concerned, one Rand report has already noted the potential of the Internet for falsification of information, such as creating notional documents or the ease of doctoring digitized photographs and documents (Shoben, 1995).

The successful (and embarrassing) hacks of Web sites such as the CIA, the U.S. Justice Department, the U.S. Air Force, and both of Britain's leading Parliamentary parties are also indicative of how clandestine penetration can be used for political purposes. Of course, creating a "Central Incompetence Agency" or "Hacked Labour" site is an exercise in spectacle rather than genuine political effect. However, it would be just as easy to subtly edit existing text for deceptive or disruptive effects, making persons and organizations appear to say things they did not intend, or plant documents on the server that might not be linked to the official pages but could be made available by posting their direct Web addresses (Uniform Resource Locators or URLs) on appropriate Usenet newsgroups, mailing lists, and so forth. Such alterations would be much less likely to be quickly discovered, and by the time they were, considerable damage to the target's credibility or relations with others would already have been done. Of course, the strategic use of information is not confined to deception, and (contrary to popular usage) propaganda is not necessarily deceptive or even acutely spin-doctored. The classic example here would probably be making intelligence information about the Soviet Gulag prison camps, gleaned from secret intelligence, available to the public via journalists provided with the necessary information (Crozier, 1993; Lucas & Morris, 1992). Likewise, as many whistleblowers have discovered (some disaffected members of the intelligence community among them), the Internet is an ideal medium for disseminating apparently factual information. From an operational point of view, with its potential for anonymity and even multiple cyberspace identities, it is also an ideal vehicle for providing various points of dissemination for a particular body of information, factual or deceptive. This allows both the widest dispersal of that information and also the apparent corroboration of one controlled outlet by another, known as false verification, at far less expenditure than bribing journalists or funding front organizations and publications.

Perhaps the most underestimated dimension of ICT-based political action is the potential for influencing operations, ranging from the contact, support, and manipulation of amenable or useful political groups and organizations to the mobilizing of such groups in insurgency campaigns. Virtually from the very beginning, the Internet, in the form of bulletin boards and electronic mail, was a crucial medium of communication and organization for political extremist groups such as European and American neo-Nazis, and this has continued to be the case for emergent groups such as the American militias (Whine, 2000). ICTs are an ideal medium for contacting, coordinating, and organizing useful political groups throughout the world, as well as for the creation of front organizations and notional groups. And of course, it is only a short distance for political groups organized over the Internet and in real life to slip from antipathy to violence, as America has learned with its Patriot movement and Malaysia more recently learned from its "deviationist" Islamic fundamentalist group Al'Maunah.

Much as emission-hardening is a peculiarly underestimated aspect of clandestine information system penetration, so physical information attack is likewise dealt with in far less detail than firewall spoofing, password sniffing, and so forth. Schwartau (1996) has taken up a limited discussion of Electromagnetic Pulse (EMP) bombs and High-Energy Radio Frequency (HERF) guns, and to a very real degree his discussion has been overtaken by events. In the popular imagination, the typical source of an EMP sufficient to disable any but the most hardened information system is a high-altitude nuclear airburst. However, the time of the massively destructive nuclear EMP attack is rapidly waning. While there have been unverified suggestions of microwave weapons being used to disrupt banking systems and police communications in Britain and Russia, the most compelling development from a special operations point of view is the new generation of portable, high-power Marx generators based on conventional explosive charges (Sample, 2000). With designers thinking in terms of briefcase-sized devices, simple, compact Marx generator pulse bombs combine portability and robustness with the maximum of electromagnetic yield for a minimum of physical damage. Weapons of this size could be smuggled in by almost any conventional peacetime access route, dropped offshore or by air in times of hostilities, or buried months or years in advance on the routes of a potential or anticipated enemy advance. The devices could be part of the traditional complement of explosives, small arms, and communications equipment laid down by and for "stay-behind" networks (such as those recruited by the British SIS and the CIA in Germany, Austria, and elsewhere during the Cold War [Smith, 1996]). During the colder days of the Kruschev administration, penetration agent Oleg Penkovsky, run jointly by the SIS and CIA in Soviet military intelligence (the GRU, *Glavniye Razvedivatelniye Upravleniye*), offered to plant small demolition nuclear devices under the Kremlin and defense ministry headquarters on behalf of his SIS and CIA controllers (Schechter & Deriabin, 1992). Cooler heads prevailed and no such devices were placed. It is all too easy to imagine a twenty-first century Penkovsky planting and duly setting off a suitcase-sized Marx generator within the effective range (possibly as much as a kilometer) of installations vital to national security. Blowing up a few trains or harassing enemy columns by the French Resistance pale in comparison with the kind of damage resistance partisan and stay-behind cells could wreak in a postmodern, information-intensive, and ICT-dependent conflict. And the consequent fallout, political or otherwise, would almost certainly be more palatable to those deciding such actions.

Counterintelligence and Security

It is the task of counterintelligence to intercept and interdict the kinds of operations that we have discussed being directed against oneself. The very possibilities for ICT-oriented clandestine collection constitute precisely the challenges faced by agencies seeking to counter espionage activities at the beginning of the new century. We already know something of the counterintelligence problems of information security posed by HACKINT and by "cyber-sabotage." One of the most significant conclusions must be that, just as human intelligence is likely to prove essential to effective signals and hacking intelligence collection, personnel and physical security must also acquire a comparable degree of importance in counterintelligence thinking. Most of what has so far been discussed has dealt with national intelligence work, but it is important to keep in mind that many of the post-Cold War intelligence requirements deal less with direct threats from individual nation-states than from national, multinational, and transnational substate actors such as terrorists, criminal cartels, and arms proliferators. In many cases, counterintelligence needs overlap and intersect with foreign intelligence needs; hence one commonly sees more of a distinction drawn between foreign and security intelligence than offensive and counterintelligence, at least where agency jurisdictions are typically concerned. ICTs intensify those overlaps and intersections as much as they intensify the other dilemmas and distinctions already examined. But the implications for counterintelligence and security policy are deeper and more disturbing than these operational issues.

If HUMINT and social engineering are to become the vanguard of HACKINT, SIGINT, and disruptive actions alike, this means ensuring close attention to conventional personnel and physical security in addition to traditional counterintelligence to detect and intercept such human operations, as well as counterespionage activities to penetrate agencies and nonstate actors such as terrorist groups that might wish to mount combined HUMINT-HACKINT operations. Effective counterintelligence management is a persistent problem in intelligence. Divisions between SIS and MI 5 (the British Directoral of Military Intelligence) are often blamed for the long successful run of a penetration agent like Kim Philby in the early days of the Cold War (see, for example, Brown, 1987). Likewise, balkanization of the counterintelligence system required the formation of a centralized National Counterintelligence Center after the exposure of penetration agent Aldrich Ames in the CIA (see, for example, Adams, 1995), and arguably led to the escape of Edward Lee Howard some years earlier (Wise, 1989). Matters have not improved much with the successive discovery of the compromise of U.S. Department of Energy security by Peter Lee and Wen Ho Lee (Cox, 1999; Rudman, 1999), and still more recently by the discovery of Robert Hanssen in the FBI (Macintyre, 2001). As one recent commentator writing on the security of information operations in the CIA journal *Studies in Intelligence* warned "most articles about the U.S. information superhighway have concentrated on the need for better physical security ... few address what possibly is the most vulnerable element—the human operators—and the inability of those operators to practice good operational security (OPSEC)" (Magnan, 2000, pp. 97–104). In an increasingly networked world, effective institutional integration of intelligence, counterintelligence, and operational security remains an unrealized goal.

Information technology and the tools of information warfare tend to slide slipshod across the conventional, internal distinctions of the intelligence world. Part of the problem Stoll (1991) encountered in dealing with Hess's attacks on networked Department of Defense (DOD) systems was that the problem did not fall neatly into the jurisdiction of the FBI because it involved telecommunications, or the CIA, because it was domestic. Even the NSA, charged with governmental communications and information security, was slow to take up the matter because the sensitivity of the information housed on the penetrated systems was relatively low. As a general rule, effective counterintelligence requires some willingness to combine poacher and gamekeeper roles, either in the same agency or via close inter-agency cooperation. In SIGINT and communications security (COMSEC), this has generally been a successful strategy, with most of the agencies in the Anglo-American UK/USA SIGINT alliance combining both functions under a single roof. Since the collapse of the Soviet Union, the Russian federal intelligence establishment's efforts appear to be emulating the Western model. One feature of this has been the carving out of the SIGINT, COMSEC, and information security (INFOSEC) functions of the old KGB and GRU and consolidating them in a new agency, FAPSI (*Federalnoye Agentsvo Praveitelstvennoy Sviazi I Informatsii*, the Federal Agency for Government Communication and Information), supported by enabling legislation explicitly modeled on that grounding the NSA (Waller, 1994). FAPSI's powers are radically more extensive than the NSA's, however, as it controls not only SIGINT, COMSEC, and the security of the Russian government "information space," but also the national microwave communications network.

INFOSEC and offensive intelligence gathering do appear at first glance to combine poacher and gamekeeper. But this does not describe the whole situation. By contrast, conventional espionage and counterintelligence work have generally been conducted by separate agencies, chiefly because of legal and constitutional divisions between *domestic* security and *foreign* espionage. Hence, inter-agency cooperation has typically been both crucial and fraught with tensions, as between Britain's SIS and MI 5, or between the CIA and the FBI in the U.S. One would imagine that information security would fall neatly into the SIGINT/COMSEC model of practice and management, but it does not for two reasons. Firstly, true ICT-based espionage dovetails more neatly with the human and local technical operations of agencies like SIS, MI 5, or the CIA. Secondly, information warfare itself seems likely to fracture the traditional unity of SIGINT and COMSEC (which has subsumed INFOSEC, although perhaps the reverse is increasingly the case) because, as almost all the assorted threat assessments of information warfare end up concluding, *national* information security no longer means simply *government* information security. Instead, national INFOSEC means the security of the entire critical national information infrastructure, of which the state is only a fragment.

The first problem with trying to combine offensive and defensive information warfare efforts under a single institutional roof is that the body of activities that has been termed HACKINT does not readily fall within the ambit of signals intelligence nor the agencies responsible for it. SIGINT legislation (e.g., the 1994 Intelligence Services Act) tends to empower SIGINT and serves to monitor electromagnetic, acoustic, and "other emanations." The clandestine penetration of information systems is not, however, really a matter of intercepting and monitoring emanations except insofar as one might monitor satellite traffic or tap routers and servers. In practical terms, access to and inspection (let alone alteration, disruption, or corruption) of data held on computers are more compatible with conventional HUMINT services. One might have one's own intelligence officers trained to try to hack into systems, but, on the whole, it is often easier to recruit skilled and experienced individuals to do the work. Hence, from an operational point of view, the attack on DOD computers by Hess and the Chaos Computer Club was technically a *human intelligence* job, with Hess the main agent, his fellow club members subagents under him, and Hess controlled (recruited, paid and tasked) by a KGB case officer. Likewise, physical access operations such as HAM also fall into the domain of HUMINT agencies that routinely maintain clandestine entry and inspection abilities like bypassing alarm systems, defeating locks, and cracking safes. There is an inevitable overlap with classic SIGINT techniques, especially where the target data are encrypted, but the actual work of HACKINT tends to be the work of conventional espionage services. It is not surprising, therefore, that the SIS has included a small section concerned with penetrating computer systems during the last decade (British Broadcasting Corporation, 1993), a decision hardly likely to be unique in the intelligence world. Overlaps between SIGINT and HUMINT operations are not new, as observed here. But this does not do away with the basic problem that the people doing HACKINT are unlikely to be the same people doing INFOSEC, and any effective national information security strategy will depend on the quality and consistency of inter-agency cooperation (and be hampered by any tendency toward parochialism and turf wars).

The second problem is that even within the realm of combined SIGINT/COMSEC/INFOSEC agencies, information warfare has characteristics that could very easily cause a schism between intelligence and security functions and force the separation of the two. Traditionally, SIGINT services have been the most secretive arms of the intelligence world.

As early as the 1960s, people like David Wise and Thomas Ross (1964) and Harry Howe Ransom (1970) could write about the CIA and John Bulloch (1963) about MI 5. Kim Philby could publish his memoirs of SIS work in 1968 (Philby, 1983); and Hugh Trevor-Roper (1968) and the *Sunday Times* team led by Philip Knightley wrote their versions of the Cambridge spy ring in the same year (Page, Knightley, & Leitch, 1979). But apart from a brief appearance in David Kahn's seminal *Codebreakers* in 1967 (Kahn, 1973), the NSA and GCHQ were almost unknown until well into the late 1970s (Bamford, 1983). Allied successes against Axis machine codes, surprisingly, remained completely secret until Frederick Winterbotham's (1974) revelations in *Ultra Secret*. The ability to penetrate communications systems depends on the targets being unaware of the penetration, otherwise they will change systems, which can mean their traffic becomes inaccessible quite literally for decades (see, for example, Soviet diplomatic traffic after Parliamentary statements acknowledging the role of SIGINT in the controversial raid on the All-Russian Cooperative Society [ARCOS] in 1923 [Andrew, 1987]).

Obviously a similar degree of secretiveness is necessary for COMSEC, as states may employ the same cryptosystem, or versions of it, for years or decades. Although the NSA, Canada's Communications Security Establishment (CSE), and Australia's Defence Signals Directorate (DSD) all included COMSEC within their briefs virtually from inception, Britain's London Communications Security Agency (CSA) was not consolidated with its offensive SIGINT service GCHQ until 1969 (Bamford, 1983), even though there had been a close relationship between the two since at least the Second World War (Denniston, 1986). Almost immediately after the consolidation, certainly by 1971 at the latest, computer security research and development were included within the work of GCHQ's COMSEC side (Benjamin, 1994). Today, INFOSEC evaluation and implementation are handled by a semi-autonomous branch of GCHQ, the Communications Electronics Security Group (CESG). CESG has included INFOSEC advice and evaluation for firms undertaking government defense and security contracts ("X-list" firms) for years (U.K. Cabinet Office, 1993); and the other British and American agencies have traditionally done much the same in their own countries as well. However, the need for a more comprehensive INFOSEC capability has meant that these components of the national SIGINT services have had to take on increasingly visible, public roles. The CESG was the first element of GCHQ to have a permanent presence on the Web (U.K. Communications Electronics Security Group, 1997), and both the NSA and CSE have begun to develop publicly oriented INFOSEC outreach programs (U.S. National Security Agency, 1998). The dangers of information attack are increasing the need for national INFOSEC divisions to have an active public role and, ultimately, this cannot sit well with the firm need for extremely tight secrecy where offensive SIGINT is concerned. How is this to be resolved? There are really two choices. Either the INFOSEC divisions will have to be hived off from the SIGINT services as separate, national information infrastructure security organizations, or they will have to be increasingly institutionally separate within SIGINT organizations. The result is the same: whether the separation is *de jure* or *de facto*, it may no longer be possible to combine poacher and gamekeeper, and this can only detract from the effective development of both sides of the equation.

Tasking, Dissemination, and Analysis: The Consumer Side

The demand side of the intelligence market has been affected as much as the operational supply side, and in ways both as promising and as problematic. Communications between intelligence producers and consumers are being revolutionized by electronic mail and networked databases. In Britain, this has had a palpable impact on institutional structures. With information technology, it has become possible to bind producers and consumers more closely than ever through secure faxes and fiber optic electronic mail networks. Langley is now linked to Washington by the highly secure InteLink (Martin, 1998; U.S. Central Intelligence Agency, 1996), and, since 1997, SIS and GCHQ are linked to their consumers by the U.K. Intelligence Messaging Network (UKIMN) (Dorril, 2000; U.K. Intelligence and Security Committee, 2000). In the British case, this has changed the internal organization of the SIS. Since the end of the First World War, the SIS's main consumers have attached liaison or "requirements" sections to SIS headquarters to articulate their home departments' intelligence needs to the service, grouped together as the Requirements Directorate under a single director of their own

(Davies, 2000). With the advent of conduits like the UKIMN, consumer liaison has become a much more direct affair, and the requirements sections have since been subordinated to the various operational heads or area controllers (private communication).

In the case of the CIA, InteLink and its ilk promise to ease the age-old complaint about the relative isolation of the agency from its main customers (private communication). However, some have even higher hopes for an essential transformation in the producer-consumer relationship. As noted above, the essentially demand-driven intelligence cycle has always been something of an abstraction and an aspiration rather than a script followed in practice. This is particularly the case because the CIA provides chiefly finished intelligence analyses rather than raw information, meaning that CIA operational assets tend to be tasked according to CIA analytical requirements rather than those of its Washington consumers. With electronic mail, government intranets, and networked databases, Peter Sharfman (1994) has suggested that a genuinely demand-driven system, or pull architecture, is at last a possibility. The CIA's own Directorate of Intelligence (DI) has also claimed that InteLink is a vital part of an improved ability to identify and satisfy consumer requirements (U.S. Central Intelligence Agency, 1996). However, given that both Scharfman and the DI still visualize the process in terms of the dissemination of finished analyses, it seems unlikely that the basic difficulties of the U.S. intelligence producer-consumer relationship will be resolved by improved communications technologies alone.

Indeed, the use of data networks to disseminate intelligence information has been around for a while. In recent years there has been a great deal of *Sturm und Drang* about the British and American system known as ECHELON, a computer network used to disseminate SIGINT intercepts. For the most part, this discussion has been conducted on profoundly false and misleading premises, especially where the European Union report (Campbell, 1999) and statements by the French government have detailed European concerns about British and American penetration of civilian and commercial communications. In point of fact, it was clearly established when the existence of ECHELON was first publicized by New Zealand antinuclear activist Nicki Hagar (1996) that ECHELON, as such, was simply a system for searching intercepts for keywords and then disseminating them on that basis. The ECHELON system basically runs a string search of intercepted traffic, looking for keywords in the watch lists generated by the UK/USA member services. For example, an intercept station run by the Australians might identify traffic containing keywords that suggest a message deals with Republican or Loyalist terrorists traveling in the Asia-Pacific region and then automatically pass the intercept containing the keyword to GCHQs either directly or via U.K. liaison staff. When originally published, Hagar expressed concern that the NSA consumed the lion's share of New Zealand product, but it should be remembered that the NSA also produces the lion's share of common product available to the member services. A secondary issue raised by Hagar, and that taken up chiefly by the European reports, was the process of intercepting civilian, especially commercial, satellite streams. This has been taken by critics of the British and American alliance in general, and of SIGINT in particular, as yet another example of economic spying by *les Anglo-Saxons*. However, intercepting commercial lines is hardly new. It was commercial cable operators who provided SIGINT services in the 1930s and early in the Cold War with the bulk of their intercepts (see, for example, Denniston, 1986; Snider, 1999). This was not so much an abuse of commercial confidentiality, but done simply because most diplomatic traffic traveled over commercial lines. Likewise, even today, as a Rand report (Shoben, 1995) on information warfare warned, 90 percent of all military traffic travels over commercial lines—and presumably nearly 100 percent of all terrorist or organized criminal traffic as well. Certainly it is a straightforward matter for a system like ECHELON to read and disseminate traffic traveling *en claire* over satellite networks, but prior to the current era of encryption, most legitimate intelligence information in areas like terrorism, serious crime, and arms proliferation has also been free of strong encryption. The problem with these types of targets—none of which is new or unique to the post-Cold War era—is less penetration of their traffic than lifting useful messages out from the background noise of innocuous communications. And that is what information technologies like ECHELON are designed to do.

UKIMS, IntelNet, and ECHELON are part of the dissemination phase of the intelligence cycle, where the notion of dissemination is relatively common and uniform. Issues of intelligence analysis, such as its role and locus, are much less clear, as mentioned earlier. Scharfman's (1994) argument is not as much about the conduct of analysis as about making analytical products available when they are needed, to the people who need them. The impact of information warfare on analysis is less apparent; that is, until one factors in the recent notion of open-source intelligence or OSINT.

In principle, OSINT may be considered an aspect of the collection phase of the intelligence cycle, although by definition it does not fall into the domain of covert collection. Where Godson's (1979) narrower notion of clandestine or covert collection is the point of reference, or the British sense of intelligence as secretly learning secrets, as in this discussion, the main role of open source intelligence is in the analytical phase, where information from special and open sources is combined in what is known as "all source analysis." In the British approach, OSINT is hardly intelligence at all as, also by definition, it is *not* concerned with secrets. However, where one employs the American approach to intelligence as analytically finished product, OSINT has become a central item of concern. Indeed, discussions of the relative merits of OSINT as being against national proprietary assets have developed as an almost specifically American debate. There has even been an increasing tendency in some quarters to suggest that OSINT collection may substitute for the relatively covert work of national intelligence services.

The leading advocate of OSINT is probably David Steele, head of his own OSINT firm Open Source Solutions (OSS). Steele is quick to point out that the primary role of the CIA under the 1947 National Security Act is *analysis* (Steele, 1996). He is equally quick to suggest that its historical emphasis on secret and technology-intensive proprietary collection systems has increasingly diverted it from that original *raison d'être*. An organization like OSS acts as an agent to collect information from publicly available sources such as private research firms, commercial providers of satellite imagery, and even the Internet. Steele is fond of citing a benchmarking exercise in 1995 during the deliberations of the Aspin-Brown Commission (Commission on the Roles and Capabilities of the U.S. Intelligence Community, 1996) as an illustration of the speed and productivity of open sources against national proprietary means. Over a four-day interval, OSS and the intelligence community were tasked to provide information about the troubled country of Burundi, where tribal differences were leading to a domestic collapse comparable to that in neighboring

Rwanda. In his account of the exercise, Steele reports how he acquired political and economic appraisals from Oxford Analytica, order of battle information on the different tribal forces from Jane's Information Services, former Soviet military maps from East View Press, and satellite imagery from SPOT Image Corporation, among others. By comparison, he trumpets that "the U.S. intelligence community had nothing of substance, because Burundi was at the bottom of its priority list and capabilities were not suited for surge coverage of this obscure and remote area that previously had been irrelevant to U.S. interests" (Steele, 1999, p. 95). His account would appear to suggest an unambiguous advantage of OSINT, a form of collection and analysis far more easily devolved to the private sector than agent running and "national technical means" such as SIGINT and SATINT (satellite intelligence).

Very serious questions have been raised about Steele's account of the benchmarking exercise, and these in turn have implications for how OSINT's role in intelligence analysis and policy making should be considered. Loch K. Johnson (2000, p. 24), an experienced commentator on intelligence and a staffer on the Aspin-Brown Commission, remarked of the same exercise that "contrary to some reports, the U.S. intelligence community shined [sic] as well. The CIA generated up-to-date information on the growing political polarization in the country and the high likelihood that violence would erupt. The CIA also presented comprehensive data on regional ethnic populations, illustrated with impressive four-color maps, along with facts on Burundi's acquisition of arms in the international marketplace (which led to U.S. pressure to halt the shipments)." Johnson (2000, p. 22) also remarked on the issue of OSINT in general that

> during the Cold War, about 85 percent of the information contained in espionage reports came from the public domain. Today, in light of the greater openness of governments around the world, that figure is more like 90 to 95 percent. Within this figure, though, are not just well known newspapers and magazines but grey sources that are not secret but are nonetheless hard to find (for example, remarks by Libyan leader Col. Muammar el-Qaddafi at a political rally in Tripoli). The acquisition of such open information may require a covert agent in the right place.

This description almost directly parallels Hibbert's (1990) proportionate breakdown in intelligence, and his distinction between confidential sources and secret sources, strictly understood. Interestingly, both Johnson and Steele go to some pains to assure their readers that OSINT cannot effectively substitute for the specialized work of secret sources where actively concealed or protected information must be acquired. Most significantly, the Steele-Johnson debate serves to remind us of the importance of differing national concepts of intelligence. After all, much of their discussion concerns the kind of information one would expect departments and ministries of state to acquire in the ordinary business of government in the British model; not really intelligence at all in that context. Thus, in their discussions we find the Americans forced into a definition of intelligence closer to the British. Johnson (2000, p. 24) even quotes former CIA Deputy Director of Intelligence Ray Cline that "espionage is now the guided search for missing links of information that other sources do not reveal." This is a turn of phrase eerily close to Nicholas Elliott's (1993), apart from the suggestion that this dynamic is somehow new.

There can be no doubt that information technology is indeed bringing producers and consumers closer together, and certainly this can ease many of the problems of dissemination and of *articulating* intelligence requirements to producers. However, there is a very real question mark over the *formulation* of requirements. Information technology literacy is still not as universal as it really should be, and, to be frank, by the time officials are sufficiently senior to task national intelligence systems, they are also almost certainly of such a vintage that their grasp of the rapidly changing world of technology will be tenuous at best. In the last analysis, if the consumers do not understand the security and intelligence implications of the new information and communication technologies, and of information warfare, then there will be very little their intelligence services will be able to do to remedy the situation.

Conclusion

This chapter has covered a portion of the broad realm of intelligence information, focusing primarily on covert activities, secrecy, and national interests. One might add a host of topics to the theme of secret information, including competitive intelligence in the corporate or non-profit sectors (see Bergeron & Hiller's chapter in this volume), the sociology of secret or illicit groups, and so on. Perhaps the above limited review, however, does suggest that information science traditionally has been preoccupied with overt, public information phenomena and the associated systems and services, to the neglect of parallel, covert, and secret information concerns. Accordingly, some limitations of the previous set of information science approaches and paradigms might now emerge as special cases of a more general subject domain.

This discussion began by stating that intelligence, more than almost any other core state function, is about information and therefore there should be a natural continuity between intelligence and information warfare policy, practice, and discussion. But beyond the simple centrality of information, there is another, perhaps more telling and compelling reason information warfare should be central to national intelligence policy, and for national intelligence services to embrace and expand their infowar capabilities aggressively. That reason lies in the problem about information warfare that makes it so hard to predict, intercept, interdict, or prevent, like so many of the post-Cold War intelligence threats. Information warfare is easy to set up, cheap to implement, and singularly flexible in how and where it may be applied. Successful hacks are nearly impossible to detect unless the unauthorized access is detected *in flagrante*, in which case one may know only that one's system has been compromised when any sabotage occurs. And if the clandestine penetration was purely an exercise in covert information collection, one might never know at all. Electronic communications tools such as the Internet or prepaid mobile telephones allow people to communicate with each other with unprecedented degrees of anonymity and minimal traceability. Thus, the danger of information warfare lies precisely in its obscurity, subtlety, and undetectability, and therein lies precisely its value for the state and potential for the intelligence community. Because, as former Deputy-Chief of the SIS John Bruce Lockhart observed in 1987 (p. 46), "the essential skill of a secret intelligence service is to get things done secretly and deniably."

Bibliography

Adams, J. (1994). *The new spies: Exploring the frontiers of espionage*. London: Hutchinson.

Adams, J. (1995). *Sell out: Aldrich Ames and the corruption of the CIA*. New York: Viking.

Andrew, C., & Gordievsky, O. (1991). *KGB: The inside story of its foreign operations*. London: Hodder & Stoughton.

Andrew, C. M. (1987). *Her Majesty's Secret Service: The making of the British intelligence community*. London: Sceptre.

Arquilla, J. (1998). The great cyberwar of 2002. *Wired 6.02*. Retrieved March 6, 2001, from the World Wide Web: http://www.wired.com/archive/6.02/cyberwar.html

Arquilla, J., & Ronfeldt, D. (1996). *Cyberwar is coming*. Retrieved November 15, 1996, from the World Wide Web: http://stl.nps.navy.mil/~jmorale/cyberwar.html

Badsey, S. (1999). *The conceptual origins of information warfare*. London: Global Transformation Research Group.

Bamford, J. (1983). *The puzzle palace: America's National Security Agency and its special relationship with Britain's GCHQ*. London: Sidgwick & Jackson.

Barron, J. (1987). *Breaking the ring: The rise and fall of the Walker family spy network*. New York: Avon.

Bazna, E. (1962). *I was Cicero*. London: Andre Deutsch.

Benjamin, R. (1994). *Five lives in one: An insider's view of the defence and intelligence world*. Tunbridge Wells: Parapress.

Boren, D. L. (1992). The intelligence community: How crucial? *Foreign Affairs, 71*(3), 52–62.

British Broadcasting Corporation. (1993). On Her Majesty's Secret Service. *Panorama* BBC Television, 22 November.

Brock, J. L. (1996). *Information security: Computer attacks at Department of Defense pose increasing risk*. (GAO/T-AIMD-96-92 May 22). Washington, DC: General Accounting Office. Retrieved March 1, 2001, from the World Wide Web: http://www.fas.org/irp/gao/aim96084.htm

Brooks, C. R. (1994). Testimony before the House Science, Space and Technology Committee's Technology, Environment and Aviation Subcommittee. Retrieved December 19, 1998, from the World Wide Web: www.eff.org/pub/Privacy/Clipper/brooks_nsa_clip._dt.testimony

Brown, A. C. (1987). *'C': The secret life of Stewart Graham Menzies, spymaster to Winston Churchill*. New York: Macmillan.

Brown, M. L. (1996). The revolution in military affairs: The information dimension. In A. D. Campen, D. H. Dearth, & R. T. Goodden (Eds.), *Cyberwar: Security, strategy and conflict in the information age* (pp. 31–52). Fairfax, VA: AFCEA International Press.

Bulloch, J. (1963). *MI 5: Origin and history of the British counter-intelligence service*. London: Transworld.

Burrows, W. E. (1988). *Deep black: Space espionage and national security.* NewYork: Berkley Books.

Campbell, D. (1997, November 27). More naked gun than top gun. *The Guardian*, 2. Retrieved March 16, 2001, from the World Wide Web: http://www.gn.apc. org/duncan/880564579-fumble.html

Campbell, D. (1999). *Development of surveillance technology and risk of abuse of economic information.* PE 168/184/Part 3/4. Luxembourg: European Parliament.

Campen, A. D., Dearth, D. H., & Goodden, R. T. (1996). *Cyberwar: Security, strategy and conflict in the information age.* Fairfax, VA: AFCEA International Press.

Commission of Inquiry Concerning Certain Activities of the Royal Canadian Mounted Police (1981). *Certain R.C.M.P. activities and the question of governmental knowledge: Third report.* Ottawa: Canadian Government Publishing Centre.

Commission on the Roles and Capabilities of the United States Intelligence Community (1996). *Preparing for the 21st century: An appraisal of U.S. intelligence.* Washington, DC: U.S. Government Printing Office.

Cox, C. (1999). *U.S. national security and military/commercial concerns with the People's Republic of China.* Report 105-81. Washington, DC: U.S. Government Printing Office.

Crozier, B. (1993). *Free agent: The unseen war, 1941–1991.* London: HarperCollins.

Davies, P. H. J. (1999). Information warfare and the future of the spy. *Information, Communication and Society, 2*(2), 115–133.

Davies P. H. J. (2000). MI 6's Requirements Directorate: Integrating intelligence into the machinery of British central government. *Public Administration, 78*(1), 29–49.

Denning, D. (1999). *Information warfare and security.* Harlow, U.K.: Addison Wesley.

Denniston, A. G. (1986). The Government Code and Cipher School between the wars. *Intelligence and National Security, 1*, 48–70.

Devost, M. G., Houghton, B. K., & Pollard, N. A. (1997). Information terrorism: Political violence in the information age. *Terrorism and Political Violence, 9*, 72–83.

Dilks, D., & Andrew, C. M. (1984). *The missing dimension: Governments and intelligence communities in the twentieth century.* London: Macmillan.

Dorril, S. (2000). *MI 6: Fifty years of special operations.* London: Fourth Estate.

Electronic Frontier Foundation. (2000). *EFF clipper-key escrow archive.* Retrieved December 19, 1995, from the World Wide Web: http://www.eff.org/ pub/Privacy/Clipper

Elliott, N. (1993). *I spy with my little eye.* Wilton, U.K.: Michael Joseph.

Emerson, S. A., & Del Sesto, C. (1991). *Terrorist: The inside story of the highest-ranking Iraqi terrorist ever to defect to the west.* New York: Villard.

Foot, M. R. D. (1984). *SOE: The outline of the Special Operations Executive 1940–46*. London: BBC.

Frost, M., & Gratton, M. (1994). *Spyworld: Inside the Canadian and American intelligence establishments*. Toronto: Doubleday.

Gill, P. (1994). *Policing politics: Security intelligence and the liberal democratic state*. London: Frank Cass.

Godson, R. (1979). *Intelligence requirements for the 1980s: Elements of intelligence*. Washington, DC: National Strategy Information Center.

Godson, R. (1980a). *Intelligence requirements for the 1980s: Analysis and estimates*. Washington, DC: National Strategy Information Center.

Godson, R. (1980b). *Intelligence requirements for the 1980s: Counter-intelligence*. Washington, DC: National Strategy Information Center.

Godson, R. (1981). *Intelligence requirements for the 1980s: Covert action*. Washington, DC: National Strategy Information Center.

Godson, R. (1982). *Intelligence requirements for the 1980s: Clandestine collection*. Washington, DC: National Strategy Information Center.

Godson, R. (1986a). *Intelligence requirements for the 1980s: Domestic intelligence*. Washington, DC: National Strategy Information Center.

Godson, R. (1986b). *Intelligence requirements for the 1980s: Intelligence and policy*. Washington, DC: National Strategy Information Center.

Haeni, R. E., & Hoffman, L. J. (1996). *An introduction to information warfare*. Retrieved November 11, 1996, from the World Wide Web: http://www.seas.gwu.edu/student/reto/infowar/info-war.html

Hager, N. (1996). *Secret power*. Nelson, NZ: Craig Potton.

Herman, M. (1995). Assessment machinery: British and American models. *Intelligence and National Security, 10* (4), 13–33.

Herman, M. (1996). *Intelligence power in peace and war*. Cambridge: Cambridge University Press.

Hibbert, R. (1990). Intelligence and policy. *Intelligence and National Security, 5,* 110–128.

Hughes-Wilson, J. (1999). *Military intelligence blunders*. London: Robinson.

Johnson, L. K. (2000). SPIES. *Foreign Policy, 120,* 18–24.

Johnson, L. S. (1997). Toward a functional model of information warfare. *Studies in Intelligence, 1* (unclassified ed.), 49–56.

Kahn, D. (1973). *The codebreakers: The story of secret writing*. New York: New American Library.

Kent, S. (1949). *Strategic intelligence for American world policy*. Princeton, NJ: Princeton University Press.

Kinsella, W. (1992). *Unholy alliances: Terrorists, extremists, front companies, and the Libyan connection to Canada*. Toronto: Lester.

Koehler, J. O. (1999). *STASI: The untold story of the East German secret police*. Boulder, CO: Westview.

Laqueur, W. (1985). *A world of secrets: The uses and limits of intelligence*. New York: Basic.

Leppard, D., & Levy, A. (1994, July 31). The black widow. *The Sunday Times* (London), p. 13.

Libicki, M. (1995). *What is information warfare?* Washington, DC: National Defense University, Institute for National Strategic Studies. Retrieved November 19, 1995, from the World Wide Web: http://www.ndu.edu/inss/actpubs

Lockhart, J. B. L. (1987). Intelligence: A British view. In K. G. Robertson (Ed.), *British and American approaches to intelligence* (pp. 37–51). Basingstroke: MacMillan.

Lucas, W. S., & Morris, C. J. (1992). A very British crusade: The Information Research Department and the beginning of the cold war. In R. J. Aldrich (Ed.), *British intelligence, strategy and the cold war 1945-51* (pp. 85–107). London: Routlege.

Macintyre, B. (2001, February 21). Russia's FBI spy "inspired by Kim Philby." *The Times* (London), p. 1.

Mackenzie, A. (1997). *Secrets: The CIA's war at home.* Berkeley, CA: University of California Press.

Madsen, W. (1993). Intelligence agency threats to computer security. *International Journal of Intelligence and CounterIntelligence, 6,* 413–488.

Magnan, S. W. (2000). Safeguarding information operations. *Studies in Intelligence, 9,* Retrieved June 4, 2001, from the World Wide Web: http://www.cia.gov/csi/studies/summer00/art08.html

Martin, F. T. (1998). *Top secret intranet: How U.S. intelligence built InteLink— the world's largest, most secure network.* New York: Prentice-Hall.

May, E. R. (1992). Intelligence: Backing into the future. *Foreign Affairs, 71* (3), 63–72.

Molander, R., Riddile, A., & Wilson, P. (1996). *Strategic information warfare: A new face of war.* Santa Monica: Rand.

Moyzisch, L. C. (1952). *Operation Cicero* (C. Fitzgibbon & H. Fraenkel, Trans.). London: Pocket Book.

Page, B., Knightley, P., & Leitch, D. (1979). *Philby: The spy who betrayed a generation.* London: Sphere.

Philby, K. (1983). *My silent war.* New York: Ballantine.

Phillips, D. A. (1977). *The night watch.* New York: Atheneum.

Ransom, H. H. (1970). *The intelligence establishment.* Cambridge, MA: Harvard University Press.

Rathmell, A. (2000). Information warfare and sub-state actors: An organizational approach. In D. Thomas & B. D. Loader (Eds.), *Cybercrime: Law enforcement, security and surveillance in the information age* (pp. 221–233). London: Routlege.

Richelson, J. T. (1989). *The U.S. intelligence community.* New York: Ballinger.

Richelson, J. T. (1999). *The U.S. intelligence community* (4th ed.). Boulder, CO: Westview Press.

Robertson, K. G. (1987a). Editorial comment: An agenda for intelligence research. *Defence Analysis, 3,* 95–102.

Robertson, K. G. (1987b). Intelligence, terrorism and civil liberties. *Conflict Quarterly, 7*(2), 43–62.

Rudman, G. (1999). *Science at its best, security at its worst: Hearing before the Committee on Commerce, House of Representatives, One Hundred Sixth Congress, First Session, June 22, 1999.* Washington, DC: U.S. Government Printing Office.

Sakkas, P. (1991). Espionage and sabotage in the computer world. *International Journal of Intelligence and Counterintelligence, 5*(2), 155–202.

Sample, I. (2000, July 1). Just a normal town. *New Scientist 167*, 20–24.

Sawatsky, J. (1980). *The men in the shadows: The RCMP Security Service.* Toronto: Totem.

Schechter, J., & Deriabin, P. (1992). *The spy who saved the world: How a Soviet colonel changed the course of the cold war.* New York: Charles Scribner.

Schlesinger, S., & Kinzer, S. (1983). *Bitter fruit: The untold story of the American coup in Guatemala.* New York: Anchor.

Schwartau, W. (1996). *Information warfare: Cyberterrorism-protecting your personal security in the electronic age.* New York: Thunder's Mouth.

Segell, G., (2000). French cryptography policy: The turnabout of 1999. *International Journal of Intelligence and CounterIntelligence, 13*, 345–358.

Sharfman, P. (1994). Intelligence analysis in an age of electronic dissemination. *Intelligence and National Security, 10*(4), 201–211.

Shoben, A. (1995). Information warfare: A two-edged sword. *Rand Research Review: Information Warfare and Cyberspace Security.* Retrieved May 20, 2001, from the World Wide Web: http://www.rand.org/publications/randreview/issues/RRR.fall95.cyber/infor_war.html

Smith, M. (1996). *New cloak, old dagger: How Britain's spies came in from the cold.* London: Gollancz.

Snider, L. B. (1999). Unlucky SHAMROCK: Recollections from the Church Committee's Investigation of NSA. *Studies in Intelligence, 43*, 43–51.

Steele, R. D. (1996). Creating a smart nation: Information strategy, virtual intelligence, and information warfare. In A. D. Campen, D. H. Dearth, & R. T. Goodden (Eds.), *Cyberwar: Security, strategy and conflict in the information age* (pp. 77–88). Fairfax, VA: AFCEA International Press.

Steele, R. D. (1999). Virtual intelligence: Conflict avoidance and resolution through information peacekeeping. *Journal of Conflict Studies, 29*, 69–105.

Stengers, J. (1984). The French, the British, the Poles and Enigma. In C. Andrew & D. Dilks (Eds.), *The missing dimension: Governments and intelligence communities in the twentieth century* (pp. 126–137). Urbana, IL: University of Illinois Press.

Sterling, C. (1981). *The terror network: The secret war of international terrorism.* New York: Rinehart & Winston.

Stoll, C. (1991). *The cuckoo's egg.* London: Bodley Head.

Toffler, A., & Toffler, H. (1995). *War and anti-war.* New York: Warner.

Trevor-Roper, H. (1968). *The Philby affair: Espionage, treason, and secret service.* London: Kimber.

U.K. Cabinet Office. (1993). *Central intelligence machinery.* London: The Stationery Office.

U.K. Communications Electronics Security Group. (1997). CESG Home Page. Retrieved August 5, 1997, from the World Wide Web: http://www.cesg.gov.uk

U.K. Department of Trade and Industry. (1997). *Licensing of trusted third parties for the provision of encryption services.* Retrieved August 5, 1997, from the World Wide Web: http://dtiinfo1.dti.gov.org.uk/pubs

U.K. Intelligence and Security Committee. (2000). *Intelligence and Security Committee: Annual Report 1999–2000.* Cm. 4897. London: The Stationery Office.

U.K. Security Commission. (1983). *Report of the Security Commission.* Cm. 1381. London: The Stationery Office.

U.S. Central Intelligence Agency. (1996). *Analysis: Directorate of Intelligence in the 21st century: Strategic plan.* Washington, DC: CIA.

U.S. Joint Chiefs of Staff. (1998). *Joint doctrine for information operations.* Joint Pub. 3-13. Washington, DC: Department of Defense.

U.S. National Security Agency. (1998). The NSA/CSS INFOSEC Page. Retrieved May 1, 1998, from the World Wide Web: http://www.nsa.gov/isso

Urban, M. (1996). *U.K. eyes Alpha: Inside British intelligence.* London: Faber & Faber.

Walker, M. (1996, May 24). Datastream cowboy fixes Pentagon in his sights. *The Guardian* (London), pp. 1, 2.

Waller, J. M. (1994). *Secret empire: The KGB in Russia today.* Boulder, CO: Westview Press.

Ward, M. (1997, April 26). Coded message plan "too complex." *New Scientist, 154,* 7.

Wark, W. (1987). Great investigations: The public debate on intelligence in the U.S. after 1945. *Defence Analysis, 3,* 119–132.

Whine, M. (2000). Far-right extremists on the Internet. In D. Thomas & B. D. Loader (Eds.), *Cybercrime: Law enforcement, surveillance and security in the information age* (pp. 234–250). London: Routledge.

Whitacker, R. (1996). The "Bristow Affair:" A crisis of accountability in Canadian security intelligence. *Intelligence and National Security, 11,* 279–305.

Winterbotham, F. W. (1974). *The Ultra secret.* New York: Dell.

Wise, D. (1989). *The spy who got away: The inside story of the CIA agent who betrayed his country.* London: Fontana.

Wise, D., & Ross, T. B. (1964). *The invisible government.* New York: Random House.

Wright, P. (1987). *Spycatcher: The candid autobiography of a senior intelligence officer.* Toronto: Stoddart.

CHAPTER 8

Competitive Intelligence

Pierrette Bergeron
Christine A. Hiller
Université de Montréal

Introduction

The practice of competitive intelligence (CI) is not new. The current shift from the industrial age toward an information- and networking-based economy, however, has led to a strong, renewed interest in the topic. In the digital economy (Brynjolfsson & Kahin, 2000), organizations' and societies' frames of references are disrupted. Concepts such as "globalization," "glocalization," "competition," and "co-opetition" (Brandenburger & Nalebuff, 1997; Salmon & de Linares, 1999) are daily realities for citizens of many countries and for organizations of any size in this "planetary civilization in the intelligence revolution" (Dedijer, 1999, p. 67). Organizations, even "mom and pop stores," cannot limit the boundaries of their worlds to their immediate neighborhoods or they run the risk of being surprised (Cronin & Crawford, 1999a, 1999b). What was true in Napoléon's time still holds true: "to be defeated is excusable, but to be surprised is unforgettable" (Rouach, 1996, p. 8).

The concept of competition itself is being redefined (Cronin & Crawford, 1999a, 1999b; Shapiro & Varian, 1999; von Krogh, Ichijo & Nonaka, 2000) with competitor-focused strategies becoming increasingly viewed as essential for survival. A focus on only the competitive environment might be perceived as a straitjacket hampering an organization's capacity to develop advanced strategies based on creativity and innovation (von Krogh et al., 2000). This new context forces organizations to revise their business paradigms and create new strategic models—what von Krogh et al. (2000, p. 74) call advancement strategies—whereby organizationally unique knowledge creation and exploitation turn organizational *survival* into organizational *advancement*. An organization must therefore develop and sustain effective information and knowledge management processes, such as CI, in order to foster interaction between the various forces it must negotiate to achieve its strategic aims.

Sound CI practice is presented as a key element in providing organizations with appropriate "corporate radar" (Pollard, 1999) and actionable intelligence (Fuld, 1995). As this chapter will demonstrate, a common thread running through the wide range of CI definitions is that CI is the collection, transmission, analysis, and dissemination of publicly available, ethically and legally obtained relevant information as a means of producing actionable knowledge. Further, CI is the production of actionable knowledge for the improvement of corporate decision making and action.

The topic of CI is not new to *ARIST* readers, having been introduced by Cronin and Davenport (1993) in their chapter on social intelligence. Choo and Auster's (1993) chapter on environmental scanning and Bergeron's (1996) chapter on information resources management were also related to CI.

This chapter, the first devoted entirely to the topic of CI, reviews the evolution of competitive intelligence since 1994. Online searches have been conducted in ABI/Inform, Applied Science and Technology, Canadian Business and Current Affairs, Computer Index, Current Contents, Dissertation Abstracts, Dow Jones Interactive, EconLit, Global Books in Print, Inspec, LISA, Library Literature, LexisNexis, Repère, Ulrich's, and Web of Science; in addition to WorldCat and various libraries' OPACs; the Internet, using various search engines; and the "snowball technique." This review is limited to English-language documentation plus selected sources in French. Readers should be aware that a substantive body of literature exists in non-English sources, and that CI is discussed somewhat differently in American literature than in the literature of other countries. For example, in Québec and in France there is much interest in small and medium enterprises (SMEs) and CI, economic intelligence and regional development, and government roles in fostering CI in organizational practice—themes that are almost absent from American reports.

This review first presents the terminology in use and defines CI. It then discusses the evolution of CI, describes the CI process, examines common analytical techniques, and explores how information technologies support the CI process. Key players in its implementation and practice are also discussed, with an emphasis on information specialists and the organizational aspects of a CI unit. It then delineates the various milieux where CI has been implemented and addresses the issue of ethics. Finally, the chapter presents CI education and training activities and concludes with suggestions for further explorations of the topic.

Terminology and Definitions

There is no generally agreed-upon terminology, with the most common terms found in English being *competitive intelligence*, *business intelligence*, *competitor intelligence*, and *environmental scanning*. The only effort geared toward standardization is the publication of an experimental standard by the French standards association (Association française de normalisation [AFNOR], 1998) defining the word "veille," which loosely corresponds to *competitive intelligence*. This standard builds upon the work of the Groupe Intelligence économique et stratégie des entreprises (1994), which brought specialists in the field of economic intelligence together in an effort to build consensus concerning the various concepts that came to be embedded within the standard.

The concept of *competitive intelligence* is multifaceted and fuzzy. CI is variously presented as a process, a function, a product, or a mix of all three (Gilad & Gilad, 1988). Adding to the confusion is the multitude of terms and varying definitions of the same terms (for examples of definitions see Fahey, 1999, p. 5; Fuld, 1995, p. 23; Fuld, 2000a; McGonagle & Vella, 1998, p. 149; Pollard, 1999, p. 205; Society of Competitive Intelligence Professionals [http://www.scip.org]; and Westney & Ghoshal, 1994, p. 430).

The wide use of the term *competitive intelligence* as an operational generic may be a result of The Society of Competitive Intelligence Professionals' (SCIP) aggressive promotion of the field. After a few years of using the term *competitor intelligence*, SCIP decided to foreground *competitive intelligence* (Barndt, 2000). ABI/Inform uses *competitive intelligence* as a subject heading; including the term *business intelligence* within the rubric of CI. The Library of Congress Subject Headings uses *business intelligence* to index works "on the systematic accumulation of information regarding business competitors and their products, including trade secrets" (Library of Congress, 1991; also noted in Walker, 1994a, p. 150); thus suggesting a conflation of espionage with CI. Online research using the phrase *business intelligence* retrieves records that are essentially related to information systems and techniques such as data mining, online analytical processing (OLAP), and data warehousing (for more on data mining, see Benoît's chapter in this volume of *ARIST*)—likely influenced by IBM's use of the term *business intelligence* to describe their various data warehousing and mining mechanisms and tools (Whitehorn & Whitehorn, 1999).

While interesting and useful conceptually, the various distinctions expressed in the definitions are difficult to maintain, with important overlaps existing between the various concepts (Choo, 1998a). In practice, they are used indiscriminately to identify the same areas and practices. Choo (1998a, p.76) proposes a conceptual map of the various concepts based on their scope of information gathering; placing them along a continuum of "narrow to broad" and "short-term to long-term." From the narrower and more short-term to the broadest and longer-term lie *competitor intelligence*, *competitive intelligence*, *business intelligence*, *environmental scanning*, and *social intelligence*, with each concept being embedded within the following one and with *issues management* covering business intelligence, environmental scanning, and social intelligence. For Prescott (1995, p.77), these are "stages," rather than the entire scope of practice. He identifies four stages in the evolution of competitive intelligence: (1) competitive data gathering (pre-1980); (2) industry and competitor analysis (1980–1987); (3) competitive intelligence (1988 to present); and (4), a final stage, called "competitive intelligence as a core capability," lying somewhere in the future.

Competitive intelligence covers numerous "sectors" of intelligence: competitor, technology, product/service, environment (ecology), economy, legislation/regulation, acquisition/merger, customer, supplier, market, partner/collaborator, social/historical/political environment, and an organization's internal environment (Baumard, 1991; Fahey, 1999; Nolan, 1999; Vedder & Vanecek, 1998). Together, these sectors create "total intelligence" (Pollard, 1999). This is illustrated by the L'Oréal group's CI process, which covers the following sectors: social, competition, geopolitics, technology, market, legislation, and geographical (Salmon & de Linares, 1999, p. 110).

While all of these sectors contribute to "total intelligence," the technology sector receives particular attention as a result of writings on competitive technological intelligence, or CTI (e.g., Ashton & Klavans, 1997; Coburn, 1999; Dou, 1997; see also the *International Journal of Technology Management*, *10*[1], 1995, which devotes an entire issue to this sector). CTI focuses on scientific and technological developments by identifying, analyzing, and tracking technical and scientific assets or innovations by competitors in order to assess technological developments and enhancements, identify potential collaborative partnerships between for-profit and not-for-profit organizations, and forecast future technological threats and opportunities (Ashton & Klavans, 1997; Coburn, 1999).

Sometimes CI applies to national-level activities related to security, the development of intelligence (or economic intelligence) communities, foresight studies, national competitiveness analysis, and information warfare. Readers interested in these important, but peripheral topics as they apply to CI, should consult Davis's chapter on intelligence, information technology, and information warfare in this volume, as well as authors such as Baumard (1991, 1998), Bonthous (1994), Clerc (1997/1998), Cronin (2000), Cronin and Crawford (1999a, 1999b), Denning (1999), Evans (1994), Groupe Intelligence économique et stratégie des entreprises (1994), Hendrick (1996), Nolan (1999), Porter (1990), Steele-Vivas (1996), and the U.S. House of Representatives 104th Congress Permanent Select Committee on Intelligence (1996).

CI's goal is to provide "actionable intelligence" (e.g., Fahey, 1999; Fuld, 1995, 2000a; Nolan, 1999; Porter, cited in Rouach, 1996); namely, information that has been synthesized, analyzed, evaluated, and contextualized. It is part of the strategic information management that is aligned with an organization's strategy (Bergeron, 1996; Davenport, 1997; Kennedy, 1996; Moon, 2000). CI should stimulate an organization's creativeness, innovativeness, and willingness to change (Salmon & de Linares, 1999), in a continuing quest to create an evolving and intelligent organization (Choo, 1998a, 1998b).

Evolution of Competitive Intelligence

Interest in CI has been growing since 1994, as witnessed by various indicators such as (1) the number of publications on the topic; (2) the flurry of conferences, one-day seminars and workshops; (3) the rapid growth in the number of consultants in the field; (4) government efforts to foster CI practice, particularly in SMEs; and (5) the emergence of university-level CI courses and programs, often offered at the graduate level. Michael Porter's work on strategic management is presented as the catalyst that fostered renewed interest in CI as a concept and practice in the 1980s (Prescott, 1995; Sutton, 1988), leading to, for example, the creation of the then-called Society of Competitor Intelligence Professionals in 1986—now called The Society of Competitive Intelligence Professionals—and the publication of *Competitive Intelligence Review*'s first issue in the summer of 1990.

For the period between January 1987 and June 1994, Walker (1994b) reports that a search in ABI/Inform retrieved 212 records with the subject term "competitive intelligence." For comparison purposes, the same term was searched for during the period between 1994 and April 2000, retrieving 831 records in ABI/Inform. For the year 1999 alone, there are more records (249) than there were in the entire seven-year period covered by Walker (1994b). As was the case in 1994, most of the CI literature is still published outside the field of library and information science.

In the mid-1960s, Wilensky (1967, p. 7) noted that "[T]he obvious significance of the intelligence function in government and industry has not resulted in the long bibliographies of solid sociological studies typical of other areas of organizational theory and practice." This lack of a solid body of theoretical knowledge does not appear to have been rectified as Lesca (1994), Pinkerton (1996), and Prescott (1995) all note that scholarly and empirically based work in CI is rare. Existing empirical research related to CI has concentrated on (1) decision makers' environmental scanning behaviors, the most-studied area, (2) typologies of CI practice, (3) the CI process, (4) critical success factors, (5) the CI function, (6) the impact of CI on organizations, and (7) the role of governments in fostering CI within organizations and society.

In a review of writings on CI and its use in marketing, Pinkerton (1996) claims that researchers and scholars primarily published on this topic during the 1959–1980 period, and that consultants' books and trade publications dominated the 1980–1993 period. Consultants' books and trade publications still prevail during the years 1994–2000. The current literature is mostly conceptual, prescriptive, anecdotal, or "how-to" in nature, with a lack of research to examine the validity of these prescriptions. There is a great deal of redundant material, which has added little of value over the years. New developments related to CI are mostly practical. These include changes in information technologies, use of the Internet, the wealth of secondary sources, and the application and fine tuning of analytical techniques borrowed from the marketing, management, economics, and library and information science disciplines.

CI is increasingly associating itself with knowledge management (KM) (see Davenport and Hall's chapter on organizational knowledge in this volume). Barclay and Kaye (2000) claim that CI has a "symbiotic relationship" with KM. For example, SCIP's *Competitive Intelligence Review* is subtitled *The Journal of Knowledge Management and Insight* ("Insight" having been added in 2000). SCIP also claims that it is "the premier online community for knowledge professionals all around the globe" (http://www.scip.org), signaling its desire to position itself within this broader framework (Kalb, 1999).

This chapter posits that CI is a praxis, part of organizational strategic information management. Its boundaries are somewhat indistinct since there is overlap between CI and other information management components of an organization. CI is neither an independent business unit nor a process that can "live" in economic self-sufficiency removed from other organizational information processes and functions. CI is a micro-organizational learning process involving the transformation of seemingly disparate morsels of data and information via sense-making, knowledge-creating, and decision-making activities into an organizationally unique, ever-evolving view of the world (Choo, 1998b).

The Competitive Intelligence Process

CI is a value-adding information process (Taylor, 1986; Westney & Ghoshal, 1994), which requires creating, implementing, and maintaining formalized activities, products, and services, as well as nurturing, incorporating, and utilizing informal processes in order to be fully and effectively exploited (Miller, 2000a; Prescott, 1995).

CI fulfills both short- and long-term needs, as it has a mixed orientation toward both tactical and strategic management: (1) in a continuing mode, to identify weak signals from the environment and build sense out of them in a strategic approach (akin to environmental scanning [Aguilar, 1967; Choo, 1998a] and issues management [Lancaster & Loescher, 1994]); and (2) in an ad hoc, tactical, short-term approach to answer immediate questions and/or to help in solving a problem that has arisen (Baumard, 1991; Fahey, 1999; Fuld, 1995; Gilad & Gilad, 1988; Miller, 2000a; Moon, 2000; Pollard, 1999; Prescott, 1995; Villain, 1990; Westney & Ghoshal, 1994). Thus, CI is readily adapted to the various types, lifespans, and goals of organizations.

Cartwright, Boughton, and Miller (1995) classify CI practices into four categories: ad hoc, continuous-comprehensive, continuous-focused, and project-based. Their study of seventy-four American firms indicates that all types of CI practices are used, but that ad hoc is the most common. The strategic orientation of the organization affects the perceived usefulness and type of CI practiced (Cartwright et al., 1995; Julien, Lachance, Raymond, Jacob, & Ramangalahy, 1995; Julien, Raymond, Jacob, & Ramangalahy, 1997; Martinet & Marti, 1995).

The CI process can be represented by four broad phases: (1) planning/identifying CI needs; (2) data collection; (3) organization and analysis; and (4) dissemination. While specific authors may divide the process into three phases (Westney & Ghoshal, 1994), or seven (The Society of Management Accountants of Canada, 1996), all cover essentially the same elements with more or less detail in the descriptions of the basic components. Some authors (e.g., Fuld, 2000b; The Society of Management Accountants of Canada, 1996) add "evaluation" to the process as a feedback loop. Even if CI is presented as a series of phases within the process, it is not straightforward and linear. Rather, it is a series of loops both within and between each phase.

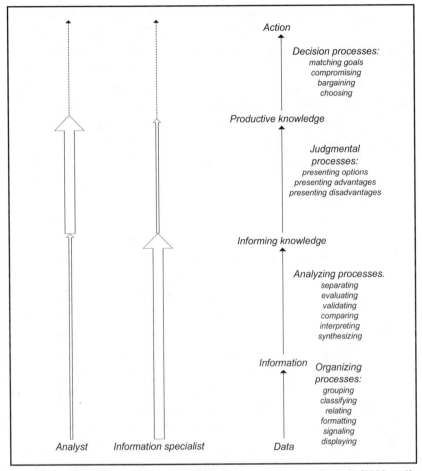

Figure 8.1 Roles of information specialists and analysts along Taylor's (1986, p. 6) value-added spectrum

From an empirical study of CI implementation, Westney and Ghoshal (1994) identify four phases: data management (what do we know?), analysis (what does it mean?), implication (how should we respond?), and action. These phases are akin to Taylor's value-added spectrum of organizing, analyzing, judgmental, and decision processes (Figure 8.1) (Taylor, 1986, p. 6). Westney and Ghoshal divide data management into ten processes: acquisition, classification, storage, retrieval, editing, verification and quality control, presentation (choice of format), aggregation, distribution, and assessment. They separate the analysis phase into three processes: (1) synthesis, (2) hypothesis, and (3) assumption building and testing (Westney & Ghoshal, 1994, p. 433). Their study found that data management was the least preferred activity of the analysts, but it was the activity with which they spent most of their time, often to the detriment of analysis and evaluation activities. Westney and Ghoshal (1994) suggest that, to maximize the processes within the data management phase, organizations should either use powerful and appropriate information technologies or leave this phase to secretaries. These authors appear to downplay the complexity and importance of the entire information management process, a basic underpinning of CI (Romagni & Wild, 1998), upon which the quality of analysis and implications depend.

The CI process uses both primary and secondary, and internal and external, sources (Choo, 1998a; Davenport & Cronin, 1994; Fuld, 1995; Kassler & Sandman, 2000; Nolan, 1999; Westney & Ghoshal, 1994). Primary data sources include human intelligence networks, observations, participation in trade shows, and reverse engineering. Human intelligence networks can include a multitude of contacts such as clients, employees, experts, competitors, market analysts, journalists, university professors, government officials, shareholders, and suppliers. There is a particular need to identify the organizational boundary spanners/gatekeepers (Choo, 1998b; Klobas & McGill, 1995) whose collaboration will be formally embedded within the organizational CI process. France Télécom R&D's strategic and technical intelligence network is an example of a CI process formalizing the use of a human network (Boucher, 1998; Boucher & Henry, 2000). Examples of techniques for tapping the primary data sources are provided by Fuld (1995), Klobas and McGill (1995), Vezmar (1996), and Wheaton (2000). Secondary data sources include online databases, Internet sources, journals, monographs, and internal documents (Choo, 1998a; Davenport & Cronin, 1994; Fuld, 1995; Hall, 2000; Kassler, 2000).

Any of these sources may aim at disinformation, which is "the creation and/or diffusion of false information, with the intent to release the false information for purposes of deception" (Dishman & Nitse, 1999, p. 23). Active disinformation techniques include releasing false information or true information that misleads, while passive techniques encompass concealment, nonreaction, or silence (Dishman & Nitse, 1999, p. 22). Baumard (1996) describes the Perrier affair, where disinformation was used as a tool for strategic destabilization within an information warfare perspective. The data collection phase must therefore be sensitive to and able to detect disinformation.

CI is also concerned with protecting the organization against potential or perceived information threats. This is often referred to as counterintelligence—aimed at protecting the organization against other organizations' CI (Gilad & Gilad, 1988; Nolan, 1999). To date, counterintelligence is not part of the mainstream definitions of CI. Counterintelligence shares common ground with telecommunications and computer security measures, records management applications, and general corporate information policies related to confidentiality and security. In an "information warfare (IW) era" (Cronin & Crawford, 1999a, b), where IW is defined as "offensive and defensive operations against information resources of a 'win-lose' nature" (Denning, 1999, p. 21), counterintelligence and defensive intelligence strategies may well become more mainstream. Readers interested in this issue may consult Cronin (2000), Cronin and Crawford (1999a, 1999b), Gilad and Gilad (1988), McGonagle and Vella (1998), Nolan (1999), Nolan and Quinn (2000), Shaker and Gembicki (1999), and Winkler (1997).

This review has shown that there is a consensus as to what constitutes a generic CI process, and that there is really no debate around this well-covered theme. There is now a need to move forward in order to better understand how to tailor this generic CI process to the specifics of each organization—moving from the current one-size-fits-all model to one that is both user- and organization-centered so as to increase the likelihood of a strong fit between an organization and CI. The general model of information use proposed by Choo (1998b) stands as a useful starting point for further exploration.

Competitive Intelligence: Analytical Techniques

The analysis phase is at the heart of the CI process. Analysis is the value-adding process whereby information is transformed into actionable intelligence (Fuld, 1995; Herring, 1998) or productive knowledge (Figure 8.1). Competitive intelligence, which, to some extent, has its roots in military strategy (Cronin, 2000; Nolan, 1999; Prescott, 1995), freely borrows techniques and insights from many other disciplines; particularly management, marketing, economics, and information studies—notably Porter's Five Forces Model (Porter, 1980); Volume, Value, Growth (VVG) (Davis, 1999); Competing Hypothesis Analysis (Sawka, 1999b); scenario planning (Fahey, 1999; Fink & Schlake, 2000; Tessun, 1997); bibliometrics (Dou, 1995; Watts, Porter, & Newman, 1998; Zhu & Porter, 1999); and patent analysis (Breitzman, 2000; Castells, Salvador, & Bosch, 2000; Fernandez, Montes, Perez-Bustamante, & Vazquez, 1999; Kline, 2000; Mogee, 1994). Herring (1998) claims that few analytical techniques have been created by CI professionals to respond specifically to competitive intelligence needs—the most notable example being Gilad's (1994) business blindspots, which challenges the competitive assumptions hampering executives and their organizations. Fuld (1995) and Fleischer and Bensoussan (2000) provide frameworks for selecting appropriate analytical techniques for a variety of CI problems.

Newer techniques—often drawn from other disciplines—regularly appear on the CI horizon. Two such examples are the military world's war gaming model (Kurtz, 2000; Treat, Thibault, & Asin, 1996) and Macroeconomic Uncertainty Strategy (MUST) analysis (Oxelheim, 1999). Business war gaming is an intense simulation activity that often requires several days and incorporates scenario planning techniques (Kurtz, 2000; Treat et al., 1996). MUST provides a model aimed at identifying the impact of macroeconomics and political risk on a business's competitive environment (Oxelheim, 1999).

While some analytical frameworks and techniques wax and wane in terms of popularity, others have proven their long-term applicability in a variety of CI situations. Over the last decade, a body of CI-oriented analytical techniques literature has appeared. See, for example, the Society of Competitive Intelligence Professionals' *Competitive Intelligence Review* and *Competitive Intelligence Magazine*, both of which regularly feature practical articles describing a wide variety of analytical methods and models. The literature review reveals that some of the most enduringly popular techniques and models include SWOT analysis (Strength and Weaknesses of an organization in light of the Opportunities and Threats in its environment), benchmarking, environmental analysis (STEEP—Sociological, Technological, Economic, Ecological, Political), and scenario planning.

A SWOT analyst's goal is to examine an organization's competitive environment identifying where it stands vis-à-vis its competitors (Fuld, 1995). Examples of SWOT analyses in competitive intelligence are provided by Elston (2000) and Fuld (1995).

Benchmarking is a best-practices measurement tool that permits an organization to rate its performance against identified competitors or best-in-class organizations to determine fruitful areas for improvement (American Productivity & Quality Center, 1995). Finnigan (1996) discusses three types of benchmarking within the area of competitive intelligence: internal, competitive, and functional (generic) benchmarking. Vezmar (1996) describes its application at Xerox.

Scenario planning is a favored forecasting model that aims to match a series of specific options with a range of potential, plausible situations, outcomes, or scenarios (Georgantzas & Acar, 1995; Fink & Schlake, 2000). The series of methodologies and techniques used in scenario planning, such as VVG (Volume Value Growth) Analysis (Davis, 1999) and Competing Hypothesis Analysis (Sawka, 1999b), permits executives to discuss and weight the relative importance of future possible events, create what-if scenarios that may or may not occur at some future time (Georgantzas & Arcar, 1995), and enhance managerial insight into future possibilities (Tessun, 1997). Scenario planning—when combined with early warning systems or weak signals identification (Fahey, 1999)—forms a part of a process of strategic foresight (Fink & Schlake, 2000). Tessun (1997) describes the application of scenario planning at Daimler-Benz Aerospace, and Fink and Schlake (2000) describe its use within the German pump industry.

Patent analysis and bibliometrics are key to competitive technological intelligence (CTI). Patent analysis is used to explore the complex interrelationship between patents and markets in order to discover, analyze, and capitalize on technological interdependencies and trends that can be discerned, and the barriers to imitation that are often deliberately placed in the way of corporations tracking their competitors' technological advances (Castells et al., 2000; Fernandez et al., 1999; Kline, 2000; Mogee, 1994). Breitzman (2000) provides a streamlined methodology for patent analysis. Davis and Livny (1994) and Hoetker (1999) focus on the practical techniques of using commercial databases to monitor scientific and technical information and in understanding the types of competitive intelligence to be gleaned from patents. Specialized analytical patent asset management tools such as Aurigin Systems' IPAM (Intellectual Property Asset Management) (Powell, 1999) and Manning & Napier Information Services' MAPIT (http://www.mnis.net/mpt.html) have appeared to aid in the effort of identifying patterns, in explaining relationships in technology, and in visualizing these patterns and relationships. An example of the results of a patent analysis is provided by Industry Canada (1998). Finally, bibliometrics and technology mapping are used to manage the huge mass of patent activity in any given industry sector and to determine innovation trends (Dou, 1995; Watts et al., 1998; Zhu & Porter, 1999).

To be truly value-adding, CI analysis must go beyond informing knowledge which, in Taylor's (1986) value-added spectrum (Figure 8.1), means validating, synthesizing, comparing, evaluating, separating, and interpreting data as a means of providing productive knowledge. This is a judgmental process in which the task is to present options, advantages, disadvantages, or implications for decision making and action.

Competitive Intelligence Systems

There is no system that automates the entire CI process. The data collection, information dissemination, and analysis processes are supported by many business information technology tools such as online databases, intelligent agents, and push technology, Web information systems (e.g., intranets, extranets, Internet), enterprise resource planning systems (ERPs), groupware, document management systems, text analysis tools, and data warehousing systems. Hohhof (1994, 2000) describes the use of these technologies within the CI context.

Much interest has been stirred by the possibilities offered by the Internet for CI purposes. One early article (Cronin et al., 1994) details the results of an exploratory study of the use of the Internet by commercial enterprises and provides a framework explicitly linking the types of documents found on the Internet and the typical activities performed with those documents relating to CI practices. Others have tackled the Internet's importance within the CI community, outlining potential uses of the Internet (Chu, 1999; Ives, 1995), delineating the benefits for-profit enterprises may derive from the Internet (Graef,

1996), detailing the wealth of sources available (Burwell, 1999; Kassler, 1997, 2000), providing technical tips for identifying experts (da Silva, Mannina, Quoniam, & Rostaing, 2000), retrieving and exploiting both the structure and the information available on a competitor's Web site (Chase, 1998), and concentrating on using accepted CI analytical techniques within the context of the Internet (Vibert, 2000). The Internet has evolved so much that it has become a virtual environment of strategic importance requiring its own surveillance and has resulted in the development of a new information market niche for specialized monitoring services (e.g., Cyveillance [http://www.cyveillance.com]).

Many software products exist to streamline increasingly onerous data collection and organization activities. Intelligence agents—while not specifically created for CI purposes—typically find and filter text according to predefined rules (Bui & Lee, 1999), and are frequently used for continuous monitoring of changes and updates on key Web pages and sites (Fuld, 1999), continuous filtering for weak signals, tracking competitors, and for automating research activities (Boureston, 2000).

Push technology is also a key tool at the data collection and information management levels. Electronic clipping services—analogous to the older, often paper-based selective dissemination of information (SDI) services—have arisen to deliver preselected information directly to the desktop; supporting both data collection and internal information/report dissemination activities within the context of CI (Fuld, 1999; Herther, 1998; Berkman, 1999a, b; Johnson, 1999; Notess, 1999).

Analytical techniques have benefited greatly from the growth in business intelligence tools. Data warehousing technology, with its variety of sophisticated, statistically oriented data mining software including OLAP, neural networks, and advanced data visualization techniques, is particularly useful for CI.

Systems that support knowledge and information sharing within an organization are also important to CI (Shaker & Gembicki, 1999). The literature indicates that employees often hear rumors and see documents that would help in understanding a phenomenon or could be used to start an inquiry, but may not realize the importance of this information to the organization; or, if they do, they do not know how, where, or to whom it should be relayed (Davenport, 1997; Martinet & Marti, 1995; O'Dell & Grayson, 1998). Thus, employees need a virtual learning and sharing space to facilitate information exchange and dissemination. Systems supporting this process are variously presented as part of CI (Shaker & Gembicki, 1999), knowledge management (O'Dell & Grayson, 1998), or information management (e.g., Davenport, 1997). For example, an internal database of organizational expertise is presented as a CI tool (Fuld, 1995), a knowledge management tool (O'Dell & Grayson, 1998), or an information management tool (Davenport, 1997). These systems can be computer-based or utilize more traditional technologies, such as the telephone. Xerox's Competitive Hot Line is an example of a system that permits its sales representatives to quickly share competitive information (Vezmar, 1996).

The purpose of CI is to provide context and meaning to seemingly disparate facts, suppositions, and deductions surrounding a particular topic. Despite software producers' claims to the contrary, no tool yet provides automated competitive intelligence. Existing tools support capturing, assessing, organizing, and displaying of relationships between data elements, but CI still requires human intervention in order to transform information into practicable knowledge.

Key Actors in Competitive Intelligence

There are three groups of key actors: the CI specialists whose main mandate is to manage the formal CI process, the decision makers who use actionable intelligence produced by CI activities (for more on decision makers' use of information see Choo & Auster [1993] and Katzer & Fletcher [1992]), and all members of an organization who, together, form the human intelligence network that contributes to a fully fledged, organizationally integrated CI activity (Fuld, 1995; Martinet & Marti, 1995; Villain, 1990; Weston, 1991). Weston (1991) predicted that, by the end of the 1990s, successful organizations would be those in which CI permeated the organizational culture and the duties of collecting and sharing intelligence were included in each job description. While, in 2000, the number of organizations that have reached this point might not be great, anecdotal evidence suggests that organizations are moving in that direction; blending CI and KM in their information strategies.

Studies of CI specialists' competencies, skills, and personal traits (Chochrek, 2000; Hohhof & Chitwood, 2000; St-Jacques, 1996) show that there are two categories of information workers necessary in a formal CI process: information managers and analysts. While the information specialists, managers, and analysts each have their own areas of expertise, it is important to recognize that, in practice, the nonlinear nature of the CI process means that each of the key actors is present, to a greater or lesser degree, depending on their mandates, skill sets, and organizational requirements, in each step of the process (Bergeron, 1995b). Figure 8.1 illustrates this overlapping of roles throughout the value-added CI processes.

Information specialists should be primarily responsible for the information management phase (Fuld, 1995; Moon, 2000). However, they must increase their capacity to create and use primary data effectively in addition to tapping into secondary sources (Walker, 1994a). They should also master the various technologies and systems that not only support retrieval, analysis, and dissemination of information and intelligence, but also support the development of the organization's social intelligence (Davenport, 2000).

While information specialists' main responsibilities in CI lie within the information management phase, these specialists ought to be involved throughout the entire analytical process (Figure 8.1). Information specialists can also become analysts in their own right even though anecdotal evidence suggests that few of them already are in such positions (Hohhof & Chitwood, 2000). An example of an information specialist providing actionable intelligence to a decision maker using a mode of communication appropriate for her end-user is illustrated by Buchanan (1999), who reports how Highsmith Inc.'s chief librarian works with that organization's CEO in identifying future trends that may affect the company in the short and long term on a project entitled "Life, the Universe and Everything."

Analysts are, generally speaking, subject or business specialists such as economists, engineers, or financial analysts. Their core activities include synthesis, hypothesis creation, and assumption building and testing aimed at providing actionable intelligence (Westney & Ghoshal, 1994), which implies that they are able to develop and maintain their ability to make credible recommendations (Hovis, 2000). While their general mandate concerns analysis, these specialists are also necessarily involved in information management activities (Figure 8.1).

For both groups of CI specialists, key skill sets and attitudes required include creativity; curiosity; innovativeness; risk taking; high tolerance for ambiguity and uncertainty; political acumen; the ability to build and nurture internal and external, formal and informal networks of people; and the ability to identify within those networks the gatekeepers/information boundary spanners who are key organizational players (American Productivity & Quality Center, 2000; Choo, 1998a; Coburn, 1999; Davenport, 1997; Davenport & Prusak, 1998; Fuld, 1995; Martinet & Marti, 1995; Villain, 1990; Weston, 1991). They must also master data collection skills and techniques similar to those of a qualitative researcher in field research or of an investigative journalist.

There is strong agreement that the head of a CI unit must have high credibility within the organization and in the eyes of senior management (Bernhardt, 1999; Fuld, 1995; Villain, 1990). This is in line with the literature on managerial information-seeking behaviors and use, which suggests a link between the credibility of the source and receptivity to the message transmitted (Katzer & Fletcher, 1992; Choo & Auster, 1993; Choo, 1998a, b).

The model based on the presence of CI specialists is more adapted to large organizations. Small and medium-sized organizations will generally not have dedicated CI specialists. The decision makers and other key employees will undertake these activities (Chapus & Lesca, 1997; Julien, 1995, 1996; Julien et al., 1995; Julien et al., 1997).

There are no clear-cut guidelines regarding the optimal mix of personnel, skill sets, and assigned roles within CI, which are dependent upon a specific organization's culture, size, span of operations, and short- and/or long-term needs. Research is needed to better understand this issue. Also, while the literature calls for the participation of all employees within an organization's CI process, little is known about the appropriate mechanisms that need to be put in place to foster, maintain, and enhance their ongoing involvement.

Organizing Competitive Intelligence

Baumard and Benvenuti (1998) posit that organizations that tend to have formal CI units also view their environments as analyzable. Studies have shown a positive relationship between the degree of uncertainty in the environment and the amount of scanning done by a decision maker (Choo & Auster, 1993), suggesting that the perceived increase of environmental uncertainty within an organization will lead to an increase of environmental scanning activities from its organizational members. Case studies of implementations of CI practices in organizations indicate that they are often initiated in reaction to a critical incident, thus following an emergent, rather than a structured approach (American Productivity & Quality Center, 2000; Bergeron, 1995a).

Davenport's (1997) information politics model, with its four categories of feudalism, monarchy, federalism, and anarchy, can be used to evaluate the impact of an organization's choice of CI structure. An organization may choose to create one or more CI units, bringing together information specialists and analysts working in partnership with a network of key informants (Villain, 1990) in a parallel, yet interconnected, CI process (Gibbons & Prescott, 1996). An organization might decide to adopt a decentralized approach whereby information specialists and analysts are scattered throughout various business units, working in a more or less close relationship. Alternatively, an organization might have no formal unit devoted to CI and therefore work on a more ad hoc, project-driven basis (Vedder, Vanecek, Guynes, & Cappel, 1999). Gibbons and Prescott's (1996) study of parallel CI processes in organizations reports that business units also conduct their own informal CI— activities that run the risk of being duplicative rather than complementary and collaborative with formal CI units. Whatever the configuration, there is a need for strong links between the various CI units, be they formal or "ghost" (parallel) CI activities in business units. Otherwise, the organization risks developing a piecemeal CI approach, resulting in an overall lack of strategic intelligence (Bergeron, 1995a).

The CI unit's position within the corporate structure varies depending on whether the organization has a unit-specific or an organizationwide mission. Wherever it is placed, however, a CI unit must maintain a delicate balance between tactical and strategic requirements. For those CI units having an organizationwide focus and impact, Sutton (1988) suggests that the most appropriate reporting levels are the CEO or the highest-level manager responsible for strategy development. Miller (2000a) claims that the criteria of choice for CI unit placement should be the need for intelligence and the support provided by senior management. Surveys of CI units indicate that they generally report to corporate planning, marketing, research and development, or economic analysis departments (Fuld, 1995; Westney & Ghoshal, 1994). For example, if the organizational focus is on competitive technological intelligence, then the R&D vice-presidency might be the most appropriate reporting line for the CI unit (Westney & Ghoshal, 1994). In a 1995 survey of CI practices, Prescott and Bhardwaj (1995) found that 40 percent of the respondents reported to marketing or marketing research, 32 percent to planning, and 8 percent to research and development. Nine percent were independent CI units with the rest scattered among various units such as libraries and sales departments. Lackman, Saban, and Lanasa (2000) recommend a CI structure composed of three building blocks: research, intelligence library, and strategic marketing intelligence. An example of this configuration is found in Matteo and Dykman (1996).

Fuld (1995) and Villain (1990) estimate that it takes from three to five years to firmly embed a CI function within the strategic decision-making processes of an organization, during which time decision makers' views of CI and its usefulness will evolve from mistrust to interest to support, and, finally, to enthusiasm. Among the critical factors for a successful CI implementation within an organization is an informational culture favoring sharing and learning, including learning from decision mistakes (Daft, 1998, p. 429), so as to make sense of the organization's environment (Weick, 1995) and incorporate learning into its common knowledge base (Choo, 1998b). Another critical success factor is an organization's willingness to regularly question what it is thinking and doing so as to minimize the "not-invented-here" syndrome, which is defined as "the tendency of a project group of stable composition to believe it possesses a monopoly of knowledge of its field, which leads it to reject new ideas from outsiders to the likely detriment of its performance" (Katz & Allen, 1992, cited in Choo, 1998b, p. 151), a willingness that leads an organization to the recognition and support of the need to monitor its environment (Baumard & Benvenuti, 1998; Fahey, 1999; Pollard, 1999; Prescott, 1995; Salmon & de Linares, 1999; Westney & Ghoshal, 1994). This critical success factor is illustrated by Salmon, whose mission, as Vice-President and Director of L'Oréal's future scanning unit, was to "cultivate the art of stirring things up" (Salmon & de Linares, 1999, back cover). The support of top management and champions at all levels of the organization is also critical (American Productivity & Quality Center, 1997, 2000; Fuld, 1995; Hussey & Jenster, 1999).

Measuring CI's impact on an organization, particularly on its bottom line, has proven difficult (Lackman et al., 2000; Pollard, 1999; Salmon & de Linares, 1999). CI's impact is related to the information absorption capacity of the organization and the willingness of decision makers to act on the intelligence provided (Herring, 1996; for reviews of decision-making processes in organizations see Katzer & Fletcher, 1992; Choo & Auster, 1993). Herring (1996) proposes four basic measures to evaluate CI's impact: cost avoidance, time saving, cost saving, and revenue increase. Additionally, he supplements an overall measure of value added to the organization. Herring (1996) suggests evaluating the CI unit from the perspective of senior managers as well as the degree to which CI outputs are aligned with the organizational strategy. Bonthous (1995) proposes nine indicators with Likert-type measures in order to evaluate CI's contribution to organizational intelligence and learning. Quality measures, such as the ISO 9001 certification, which France's Agence régionale d'information scientifique et technologique (ARIST) Haute-Normandie received for its CI products and services, can also be employed (Urso, 1997–1998).

It is still a challenge to measure the impact of any information function on an organization, and CI is no exception. Various impact models have been developed within library and information science (e.g., Griffiths & King, 1993; Marshall, 1993; Taylor, 1986), which CI may fruitfully borrow. More research is needed, however, to better assess the impact of competitive intelligence on various components—including, but not limited to the bottom line—information and knowledge management within an organization. There is also a lack of validated guidelines that an enterprise can use to most effectively organize a CI process in terms of structure, placement, human resources, and managerial and organizational expectations, avoiding costly trial and error.

Competitive Intelligence: Implementation

Surveys conducted of CI practice indicate that it is only infrequently implemented as a formal activity (American Productivity & Quality

Center, 1997; Bergeron, 2000a, c; Calof & Breakspar, 1999; Julien et al., 1995; Lesca, 1994; Sawka, 1996). Anecdotal evidence suggests that organizations still do not have a sound understanding of what CI is (e.g., Fuld, 2000b), that they have a piecemeal approach to CI (Hussey & Jenster, 1999), and that those with some formal CI practice are often dissatisfied with their performance (Harkleroad, 1996; Hussey & Jenster, 1999; Sawka, 1996). Formal CI practice is mostly found in very large organizations (American Productivity & Quality Center, 1997; Choo, 1998a; The Futures Group, 1997; Harkleroad, 1996) such as Microsoft, Motorola, General Electric, 3M, IBM, Eastman-Kodak, Procter & Gamble, or Xerox (Ettorre, 1995; The Futures Group, 1997; Galvin, 1997; Pepper, 1999; Vezmar, 1996). This is not surprising, since large organizations are more likely to invest in formal information processes due to factors such as their greater capacity to absorb information, their strategic orientation, and their access to greater financial resources (Baumard & Benvenuti, 1998; Bergeron, 1996). The Futures Group (1997) study of CI practice found that 60 percent of its respondents had a formal CI practice. The sample was limited to 101 American companies, 66 percent of which had annual revenues of more than $1 billion and 28 percent of which had annual revenues of over $10 billion. These companies are certainly not representative of the corporate world in general; particularly when one considers that, in developed countries, SMEs represent the vast majority of firms (Bergeron, 2000c).

There are very few studies and examples of CI in SMEs, and American literature on this topic is rare (e.g., Brandau & Young, 2000; Miller, 2000c). Most studies of SMEs have been conducted in France (Chapus & Lesca, 1997; Clerc, 1998; CRCI Midi-Pyrénées Service ARIST, 2000; Dou, 2000; Hassid, Jacques-Gustave, & Moinet, 1997), in Québec (Bergeron, 2000c; Julien et al., 1995; Julien et al., 1997), and in Canada as a whole (Calof & Breakspar, 1999), where government involvement has been key to the dissemination of the CI concept and the study of its implementation in SMEs (Bergeron, 2000a, b, c). Studies show that the presence of formal CI practice in SMEs is related to the presence of entrepreneurs with a strategic vision and to the level of adoption of new technology. The CI process in such organizations is influenced by the presence of and the participation in high-quality formal and informal networks, and by the level of environmental turbulence (CRCI Midi-Pyrénées Service ARIST,

2000; Julien, 1995, 1996; Julien et al., 1995; Julien et al., 1997; Lesca & Raymond, 1993).

Governments of many countries consider information and knowledge management (I&KM) to be a key success factor within a competitive economy, implementing measures to help organizations, particularly SMEs, develop effective I&KM practices including competitive intelligence. For example, the Department of Industry, Trade, Science and Technology of Québec supported the creation of fourteen competitive intelligence centers specializing in various industrial sectors such as chemistry, environment, light metals, textiles, and fashion to provide CI to SMEs (Bergeron, 2000c). In France, the report of the Groupe Intelligence économique et stratégie des entreprises (1994) acted as a catalyst for a flurry of CI publications, conferences, and activities, such as the development of education in CI, the consultancy market, guidelines for hiring or contracting CI work (for the guidelines, see Association des professionnels de l'information et de la documentation, Association pour la promotion de l'intelligence économique, & Syndicat national des prestataires et conseils en information, 1996), and the creation of agencies and programs in both the public and private sectors (Bergeron, 2000a, c). A comparative study of government approaches covering initiatives undertaken by the European Union, France, Germany, Japan, Québec, Sweden, United Kingdom, and the United States to promote the development of CI in SMEs finds that governments typically support a range of mechanisms, with one of the most common being the use of regional, local, or industrial networks of partners to implement a program designed and managed by a government agency (Bergeron, 2000a, c). In these cases, government agencies more frequently act as catalysts, stimulators, and coordinators, while the network of partners deals with the actual creation and offering of products and services directly to the SMEs. Examples of these products and services include reference services, publications such as SDIs and market research reports, and training programs. Three primary financing sources are employed, often in a mixed approach: government funding, cost recovery, and partner contribution. The majority of these initiatives are on a partial cost-recovery basis and receive a government subsidy for an indeterminate period of time (Bergeron, 2000a, c). While the study did not find one "best model" of government intervention, it did suggest that governments do, indeed, have a role to play in fostering CI and economic intelligence activities in SMEs, in local and regional areas, and in society in general.

Although examples of CI implementations are mostly found in for-profit organizations, the concept of CI has also been adapted and implemented within the public and not-for-profit sectors such as national, provincial, and municipal government departments, public research centers, and museums (for examples see Bergeron, 2000b, c; Hassid et al., 1997). This suggests that CI is, therefore, a value-adding process applicable to any type, style, or size of organization.

Ethics and Competitive Intelligence

As stated earlier, CI is based on ethically and legally obtained information. However, what, exactly, constitutes an ethical practice is not clear-cut, with shifting gray zones of CI activities within industrial sectors from country to country, as illustrated in Paine and Santoro's (1993) case study of United Technologies. To clarify their stance on what constitutes legal and ethical behaviors regarding competitive information gathering, various organizations have adopted their own codes of conduct to which organizational members must adhere (e.g., the Society of Competitive Intelligence Professionals' [SCIP] code of ethics [http://www.scip.org]; United Technologies' "Gathering Competitive Information" policy circular [http://utc.mondosearch.com/cgi-bin/MsmGo.exe?site_id=11&page_id=204]). Readers interested in legal and ethical issues are referred to Duffey (2000), Fuld (1995), Kalb (2000), Paine and Santoro (1993), Pooley and Halligan (2000), Rangan and Porter (1992), and Schultz, Collins, and McCulloch (1994).

Within the context of CI, it is impossible to ignore the issue of industrial espionage. In the literature, authors insist on the ethical and legal aspects of CI in order to clearly distance CI from industrial espionage (e.g., Gilad & Gilad, 1988; Nolan, 1999). These two concepts are readily, but wrongly, conflated by the media, the layperson, and even the Library of Congress' subject headings (see the section on definitions). When covering CI, the popular press readily resorts to using the "spy" metaphor which makes for attention-grabbing headlines (Friedman, Friedman, Chapman, & Baker, 1997; Miller, 2000a). Adding to the confusion is the visible presence of former intelligence agents on the CI scene as SCIP members—a group initially composed of librarians and MBAs (Nolan, 1999)—or as influential writers. Government cuts and layoffs at national intelligence agencies have led to what Sigurdson and Tågerud (1992) refer to as the privatization of intelligence, with former agents turning their skills to "civil" intelligence—not always successfully, according to Baumard (1998).

Economic espionage, which is considered to be on the rise, is seen as the new form of "foreign intelligence" against which nations such as the U.S. have to fight (Fialka, 1997; Fraumann, 1997; Schweizer, 1996; Winkler, 1997). In response to this perceived threat, the U.S. adopted the Economic Espionage Act of 1996 (18 U.S.C. §1831-1839 1996). Interested readers are referred to a special issue of the *Competitive Intelligence Review* (8[3], 1997) as well as to Fraumann (1997), Grosso (2000) and Horowitz (1999).

There is no doubt that there will always be gray areas in the collection of competitive information. As a sound business practice, organizations should include within their portfolios of policies a formal code of ethics that is both well-communicated and clearly understood at all levels of the organization. The code of ethics should take into account the values, culture, and environment of the organization.

Education and Training

In response to the heightened interest in CI, educational opportunities are growing. Efforts have been made to identify the core competencies, skills, and attitudes required for CI. An example is SCIP's 1996 proposal of curriculum modules for educational programs in CI (Society of Competitive Intelligence Professionals Education Committee, 1996). Miller (1994, 2000b), St-Jacques (1996), Sawka (1999a), and Shelfer and Goodrum (2000) also examine CI education from the viewpoint of required competencies.

A broad range of CI-related courses is generally found in the fields of management (e.g., strategy, marketing), economics, communications, and library and information science. These courses are offered primarily within graduate-level business and library and information science degree programs. Three educational tracks exist: special courses within an existing degree program, focused CI degrees/certificates, and continuing education opportunities (noncredit courses or seminars). Some of these courses/programs aim at training CI specialists while others seek to raise awareness and build basic skills and competencies for nonspecialists. For these nonspecialists, the acquired skills and competencies can represent a competitive advantage in the marketplace (Davenport & Cronin, 1994). At the Ph.D. level, various universities accept CI-related research topics, as evidenced by the dissertations found in Dissertation Abstracts and on France's TheseNet (http://thesenet.abes.fr/). A nonexhaustive list of CI-related courses and programs can be found on SCIP's Web site (http://www.scip.org/education/degrees.html).

Consultancies, various international, national, and regional professional associations, and governmental and nonprofit organizations also offer a varied mix of activities, such as internal training to corporate staff, off-the-shelf training, and e-learning modules. Some of them target particular audiences (e.g., SMEs by the Centre de recherche industrielle du Québec [http://www.criq.qc.ca]).

The trend toward distance education and online learning has also fueled the growth in CI seminars and courses available via the World Wide Web by all of these above-noted groups. Examples come from universities (e.g., Drexel University's CI certificate program (http://www.cis.drexel.edu/grad.ci.html); Shelfer & Goodrum, 2000), electronic information clearinghouses (e.g., headlight.com and click2learn.com), and consultancies (e.g., Iron Horse Multimedia's The Fuld War Room [http://www.ironhorsemultimedia.com]). There are also several CI forums allowing the creation of virtual CI communities (e.g., Competia [http://www.competia.com]; Multimedium [http://www.mmedium.com/forum]).

The development of education and training, especially within universities at the graduate level, is one of the factors that may support the professionalization of CI. Some claim that CI is a "growing and mature discipline" (McGonagle & Vella, 1998, p. 149), while others posit that CI is not a discipline, but an area of expertise (Rouach, 1996). Still others state that CI is a profession (Friedman et al., 1997; Nolan, 1999, p.109), although Walker's (1994a) review suggests that CI does not yet meet the criteria to be considered a profession. Interested readers can find a discussion of the CI profession in Walker (1994a, p. 154) and of the information professions in Abbott (1988, chapter 8).

Conclusion

This chapter has reviewed the evolution of CI between 1994 and 2000. The picture that emerges shows that there are areas of consensus related to what constitutes CI, its processes, its tools, and its enabling technologies. It also shows that CI implementation is spreading in every type of organization, with mixed results. Much of the literature available on CI is prescriptive and anecdotal with a high level of redundancy; signaling that perhaps a saturation level has been reached for this type of work. There is growing evidence of the need for a convergent approach to organizational information and knowledge management—within which CI is embedded—among organizations to develop an "organizational intelligence" framework.

This review suggests that CI is expert- and system-driven, with little attention being paid in the professional literature to understanding CI needs and uses. Rather, the literature abounds with advice on data collection and analysis, but is deficient in understanding and developing user-driven CI products and services.

CI research can draw upon both information science's and management studies' theoretical frameworks in order to create useful and valid models upon which to build a better understanding of the transformation of data analysis into an actionable intelligence process from a user-driven perspective, to develop valid and organizationally useful performance measures, and to evaluate the impact and benefits of CI for people and organizations. There is also a need to improve understanding about the appropriate degree of formalization regarding the organizational characteristics, and which informational configurations—within which CI is situated—an organization ought to develop.

The development of CI is at a crossroads. To grow, it requires the development of sound, multidisciplinary research from which results can be appropriately transferred and applied within training programs and practices. Areas of exploration presented throughout this review could contribute to validating and strengthening CI's theoretical base and practice. When frames of reference are disrupted, organizations, more than ever, need this lens that is CI to provide a clearer way of thinking and analyzing, and to focus on near and distant objects in order to create a semblance of order out of a turbulent, ever-evolving world.

Acknowledgments

The authors express their appreciation to Blaise Cronin and Debora Shaw and to the anonymous reviewers for their valuable comments. They also thank Johanne Mongrain and Denise Bernard for their help in document provision and bibliography preparation.

Bibliography

Abbott, A. (1988). *The system of professions: An essay on the division of expert labor*. Chicago: University of Chicago Press.

Aguilar, F. J. (1967). *Scanning the business environment*. New York: Macmillan.

American Productivity & Quality Center. (1995). *Benchmarking: Leveraging best-practice strategies*. Houston, TX: APQC. (Consortium Benchmarking Study Best-Practice Report).

American Productivity & Quality Center. (1997). *Competitive and business intelligence: Leveraging information for action*. Houston, TX: APQC. (Consortium Benchmarking Study Best-Practice Report).

American Productivity & Quality Center. (2000). *Developing a successful competitive intelligence program: Enabling action, realizing results*. Houston, TX: APQC. (Consortium Benchmarking Study Best-Practice Report).

Ashton, W. B., & Klavans, R. (1997). *Keeping abreast of science and technology: Technical intelligence for business*. Columbus, OH: Battelle Press.

Association des professionnels de l'information et de la documentation, Association pour la promotion de l'intelligence économique, & Syndicat national des prestataires et conseils en information. (1996). *Intelligence économique: prestations de veille: Spécifications et exigences contractuelles minimales*. Paris: ADBS.

Association française de normalisation (AFNOR). (1998). *Prestations de veille et prestations de mise en place d'un système de veille. Norme XPX 50-053. Norme expérimentale*. Paris: AFNOR.

Barclay, R. O., & Kaye, S. E. (2000). Knowledge management and intelligence functions—a symbiotic relationship. In J. P. Miller (Ed.), *Millennium intelligence* (pp. 155–170). Medford, NJ: CyberAge Books.

Barndt, Jr., W. D. (2000). SCIP at the crossroads: A response to the President's message. *Competitive Intelligence Magazine, 3*(3), 39–42.

Baumard, P. (1991). *Stratégie et surveillance des environnements concurrentiels*. Paris: Masson.

Baumard, P. (1996). From infowar to knowledge warfare: Preparing for the paradigm shift. In A. D. Campen, et al. (Eds.), *Cyberwar: Security, strategy and conflict in the information age* (pp. 147–160). Fairfax, VA: AFCEA International Press.

Baumard, P. (1998). *Stratégies comparées d'intelligence économique en France et aux États-Unis/A comparison of economic intelligence strategies in France and in the United States.* Retrieved February 1, 2001, from the World Wide Web: http://www.idt.fr/fich_idt97/fr_idt97/F_congres/Abstracts/D4.html

Baumard, P., & Benvenuti, J.-A. (1998). *Compétitivité et systèmes d'information: De l'outil d'analyse au management stratégique.* Paris: InterEditions.

Bergeron, P. (1995a). *An examination of the perceptions and practices of information resources management in large organizations from the Canadian private sector.* Unpublished doctoral dissertation, Syracuse University, NY. (University Microfilms International No96-16298).

Bergeron, P. (1995b). Observations sur le processus de veille et les obstacles à sa pratique dans les organisations. *Argus, 24*(3), 17–22.

Bergeron, P. (1996). Information resources management. *Annual Review of Information Science and Technology, 31,* 263–300.

Bergeron, P. (2000a). Government approaches to foster competitive intelligence practice in SMEs: A comparative study of eight governments. *Proceedings of the 63rd ASIS Annual Meeting,* 301–308.

Bergeron, P. (2000b). Regional business intelligence: the view from Canada. *Journal of Information Science, 26,* 153–160.

Bergeron, P. (2000c). *Veille stratégique et PME: Comparaison des politiques gouvernementales de soutien.* Sainte-Foy, Québec: Presses de l'Université du Québec.

Berkman, R. (1999a). Comparing news alert services—part 1. *The Information Advisor, 11*(10), 1–8.

Berkman, R. (1999b). Choosing a business news alert service—part 2. *The Information Advisor, 11*(11), 1–8.

Bernhardt, D. C. (1999). Consumer versus producer: Overcoming the disconnect between management and competitive intelligence. *Competitive Intelligence Review, 10*(3), 19–26.

Bonthous, J.-M. (1994). Understanding intelligence across cultures. *International Journal of Intelligence and Counterintelligence, 7,* 275–311.

Bonthous, J.-M. (1995). Intelligence as learning. *Competitive Intelligence Review, 6*(1), 4–14.

Boucher, D. (1998). Processus de veille dans un centre de recherche. In P. Bergeron, & S. Tellier (Eds.). *Actes du colloque sur la veille technologique et stratégique. Pour des organisations intelligentes: Méthodes et outils de veille* (pp. 93–101). Montréal: Université de Montréal, École de bibliothéconomie et des sciences de l'information et Centre de recherche informatique de Montréal.

Boucher, D., & Henry, V. (2000). Intelligence technique et stratégique dans un centre de recherche et développement: organisation, méthodes et outils, perspectives de développement - le cas de France Télécom R&D. *Revue d'intelligence économique, 6–7,* 53–60.

Boureston, J. (2000). Using intelligent search agents for CI. *Competitive Intelligence Magazine, 3*(1), 32–36.

Brandau, J., & Young, A. (2000). Competitive intelligence in entrepreneurial and start-up businesses. *Competitive Intelligence Review, 11*(1), 74–84.

Brandenburger, A. M., & Nalebuff, B. J. (1997). *Co-opetition.* New York: Doubleday.

Breitzman, A. F. (2000). Assessing an industry's R&D focus rapidly: A case study using data-driven categorization in a consumer products area. *Competitive Intelligence Review, 11*(1), 58–64.

Brynjolfsson, E., & Kahin, B. (2000). *Understanding the digital economy: Data, tools, and research.* Cambridge, MA: MIT Press.

Buchanan, L. (1999). The smartest little company in America. *Inc., 21*(1), 42–54.

Bui, T., & Lee, J. (1999). An agent-based framework for building decision support systems. *Decision Support Systems, 25,* 225–237.

Burwell, H.P. (1999). *Online competitive intelligence: Increase your profits using cyber-intelligence.* Tempe, AZ: Facts on Demand.

Calof, J., & Breakspear, A. (1999). *Survey of Canadian R&D companies: Awareness and use of competitive technical intelligence in Canadian technology-intensive industry. CI Survey for NRC/CISTI. Phase 2 Report: Interview and Final Results.* Unpublished report, Canadian Institute for Science and Technology, Ottawa, 1999. Retrieved February 1, 2001, from the World Wide Web: http://www.nrc.ca/cisti/ref/nrcci_e.html

Cartwright, D. L., Boughton, P. D., & Miller, S. W. (1995). Competitive intelligence systems: Relationships to strategic orientation and perceived usefulness. *Journal of Managerial Issues, 6,* 420-434.

Castells, P. E., Salvador, M. R., & Bosch, R. M. (2000). Technology mapping, business strategy, and market opportunities. *Competitive Intelligence Review, 11*(1), 46–57.

Chapus, E., & Lesca, H. (1997). Implantation d'une veille stratégique en coopération en milieu de PMI. *Systèmes d'information et management, 2,* 31–62.

Chase, L. (1998). *Essential business tactics for the Net.* New York: Wiley.

Chochrek, D. (2000). Market the value of your competitive intelligence: An added role for the information center. *Information Outlook, 4,* 32–35.

Choo, C. W. (1998a). *Information management for the intelligent organization: The art of scanning the environment.* 2nd ed. Medford, NJ: Information Today.

Choo, C. W. (1998b). *The knowing organization: How organizations use information to construct meaning, create knowledge, and make decisions.* New York: Oxford University Press.

Choo, C. W., & Auster, E. (1993). Environmental scanning: Acquisition and use of information by managers. *Annual Review of Information Science and Technology, 28,* 279–314.

Chu, S. (1999). Competitive intelligence on the World Wide Web. In *Communication jazz: Improvising the new international communication culture* (pp. 237–243). Piscataway, NJ: IEEE.

Clerc, P. (1997/1998). Economic intelligence. In Y. Courrier & A. Large (Eds.), *World information report* (pp. 304–317). Paris: UNESCO.

Clerc, P. (1998). Les PME et l'intelligence économique. *Athéna, 5*, 1er semestre, 181–188.

Coburn, M. M. (1999). *Competitive technical intelligence: A guide to design, analysis, and action.* Washington, D.C./New York: American Chemical Society/ Oxford University Press.

CRCI Midi-Pyrénées Service ARIST. (2000). Les pratiques des PMI de la région Midi-Pyrénées en matière d'information stratégique et d'intelligence économique. *Revue d'intelligence économique, 6-7*, 29–35.

Cronin, B. (2000). Strategic intelligence and networked business. *Journal of Information Science, 26*, 133–138.

Cronin, B., & Crawford, H. (1999a). Information warfare: Its application in military and civilian contexts. *The Information Society, 15*, 257–263.

Cronin, B., & Crawford, H. (1999b). Raising the intelligence stakes: Corporate information warfare and strategic surprise. *Competitive Intelligence Review, 10*(3), 58–66.

Cronin, B., & Davenport, E. (1993). Social intelligence. *Annual Review of Information Science and Technology, 28*, 3–44.

Cronin, B., Overfelt, K., Fouchereaux, K., Manzvanzvike, T., Cha, M., & Sona, E. (1994). The Internet and competitive intelligence: A survey of current practice. *International Journal of Information Management, 14*, 204–222.

Daft, R. L. (1998). *Organization theory and design.* 6th ed. Cincinnati, OH: South-Western College Publishing.

da Silva, A., Mannina, B., Quoniam, L., & Rostaing, H. (2000). Searching for experts on the Internet. *Competitive Intelligence Review, 11*(4), 38–46.

Davenport, E. (2000). Social intelligence in the age of networks. *Journal of Information Science, 26*, 145–152.

Davenport, E., & Cronin, B. (1994). Competitive intelligence and social advantage. *Library Trends, 43*, 239–252.

Davenport, T. H. (1997). *Information ecology: Mastering the information and knowledge environment.* New York: Oxford University Press.

Davenport, T. H., & Prusak, L. (1998). *Working knowledge: How organizations manage what they know.* Boston: Harvard Business School Press.

Davis, J. C. (1999). How volume, value, growth (VVG) analysis can work for you. *Competitive Intelligence Review, 10*, 41–54.

Davis, J. L., & Livny, E. (1994). Monitoring Japanese scientific and technical information using JICST databases. *Database, 17*(3), 33–42.

Dedijer, S. (1999). Doing business in a changed world: The intelligence revolution and our planetary civilization. *Competitive Intelligence Review, 10*(3), 67–78.

Denning, D. E. (1999). *Information warfare and security.* Reading, MA: Addison-Wesley; ACM Press.

Dishman, P., & Nitse, P. (1999). Disinformation usage in corporate communications: CI'ers beware. *Competitive Intelligence Review, 10*(4), 20–29.

Dou, H. (1995). *Veille technologique et compétitivité*. Paris: Dunod.

Dou, H. (2000). Competitive intelligence for SMEs. From intellectual concepts to actionable CI. Rules and good practices. *Proceedings of the 63rd ASIS Annual Meeting*, 301–308.

Dou, H. J.-M. (1997). Technology watch and competitive intelligence: The European way. *Competitive Intelligence Review, 8*(1), 78–84.

Duffey, W. S. (2000). Competitive information collection: Avoiding legal land mines. *Competitive Intelligence Review, 11*(3), 37–53.

Elston, G. (2000). Great analysis to impress your CEO: The SWOT analysis. *Competia. 5*. Retrieved February 1, 2001, from the World Wide Web: http://www.competia.com

Ettorre, B. (1995). Managing competitive intelligence. *Management Review, 84*, 15–19.

Evans, J. C. (1994). U. S. business competitiveness and the intelligence community. *International Journal of Intelligence and Counterintelligence, 7*, 353–361.

Fahey, L. (1999). *Competitors: Outwitting, outmaneuvering, outperforming*. New York: Wiley.

Fernandez, E., Montes, J. M., Perez-Bustamante, G. O., & Vazquez, C. J. (1999). Competitive strategy in technological knowledge imitation. *International Journal of Technology Management, 18*, 535–548.

Fialka, J. J. (1997). *War by other means: Economic espionage in America*. New York: W.W. Norton.

Fink, A., & Schlake, O. (2000). Scenario management - An approach for strategic foresight. *Competitive Intelligence Review, 11*(1), 37–45.

Finnigan, J. P. (1996). *The manager's guide to benchmarking: Essential skills for the new competitive-cooperative economy*. San Francisco: Jossey-Bass.

Fleischer, C. S., & Bensoussan, B. (2000). A FAROUT© way to manage the CI analysis process. *Competia, 9*. Retrieved February 1, 2001, from the World Wide Web: http://www.competia.com

Fraumann, E. (1997). Economic espionage: Security missions redefined. *Public Administration Review, 57*, 303–308.

Friedman, G., Friedman, M., Chapman, C., & Baker, J. S., Jr. (1997). *The intelligence edge: How to profit in the information age*. New York: Crown.

Fuld, L. (1999). Competitive intelligence on the Web: Finding true net worth. *EContent, 22*(4), 16–24.

Fuld, L. M. (1995). *The new competitor intelligence: The complete resource for finding, analyzing, and using information about your competitors*. New York: Wiley.

Fuld, L. M. (2000a). Foreword. In J. P. Miller (Ed.), *Millennium intelligence* (pp. 1–2). Medford, NJ: CyberAge Books.

Fuld, L. M. (2000b). *What competitive intelligence is and is not!* Retrieved February 1, 2001, from the World Wide Web: http://www.fuld.com/whatCI. html

The Futures Group. (1997). *Ostriches & Eagles 1997.* Retrieved February 1, 2001, from the World Wide Web: http://www.tfg.com/pubs/docs/O_EIII-97. html

Galvin, R. W. (1997). Competitive intelligence at Motorola. *Competitive Intelligence Review, 8*(1), 3–6.

Georgantzas, N. C., & Acar, W. (1995). *Scenario-driven planning: Learning to manage strategic uncertainty.* Westport, CT: Quorum Books.

Gibbons, P. T., & Prescott, J. E. (1996). Parallel competitive intelligence processes in organisations. *International Journal of Technology Management, 11,* 162–178.

Gilad, B. (1994). *Business blindspots: Replacing your company's entrenched and outdated myths, beliefs, and assumptions with the realities of today's markets.* Chicago: Probus.

Gilad, B., & Gilad, T. (1988). *The business intelligence system: A new tool for competitive advantage.* New York: Amacom.

Graef, J. (1996). Sharing business intelligence on the World Wide Web. *Competitive Intelligence Review, 7*(1), 52–61.

Griffiths, J.-M., & King, D. W.(1993). *Special libraries: Increasing the information edge.* Washington, DC: Special Libraries Association.

Grosso, A. (2000). The economic espionage act: Touring the minefields. *Communications of the ACM, 43*(8), 15–18.

Groupe Intelligence économique et stratégie des entreprises. (1994). *Intelligence économique et stratégie des enterprises* (pp. 3, 26). Paris: La Documentation française.

Hall, H. (2000). Online information sources: Tools of business intelligence? *Journal of Information Science, 26*(3), 139–143.

Harkleroad, D. (1996). Too many ostriches, not enough eagles. *Competitive Intelligence Review, 7*(1), 23–27.

Hassid, L., Jacques-Gustave, P., & Moinet, N. (1997). *Les PME face au défi de l'intelligence économique: Le renseignement sans complexe.* Paris: DUNOD.

Hendrick, L. G. J. (1996). Is competitive intelligence getting the proper attention? *Security Management, 40,* 149–150.

Herring, J. P. (1996). *Measuring the effectiveness of competitive intelligence: Assessing & communicating CI's value to your organization.* Alexandria, VA: Society of Competitive Intelligence Professionals.

Herring, J. P. (1998). What is intelligence analysis? *Competitive Intelligence Magazine, 1*(2),13–16.

Herther, N. K. (1998). Push and the politics of the Internet. *The Electronic Library, 16,* 109–116.

Hoetker, G. (1999). Patterns in patents: Searching the forest not the trees. *EContent, 22*(5), 37–45.

Hohhof, B. (1994). Developing information systems for competitive intelligence support. *Library Trends, 43,* 226–238.

Hohhof, B. (2000). The information technology marketplace. In J. P. Miller (Ed.), *Millennium intelligence* (pp. 133–154). Medford, NJ: CyberAge Books.

Hohhof, B., & Chitwood, L. (2000). At a crossroads: Information professional to intelligence analyst. *Information Outlook, 4*(2), 22–25.

Horowitz, R. (1999). SCIP policy analysis: Competitive intelligence and the economic espionage act. *Competitive Intelligence Review, 10*(3), 84–89.

Hovis, J. H. (2000). CI at Avnet: A bottom-line impact. *Competitive Intelligence Review, 11*(3), 5–15.

Hussey, D., & Jenster, P. (1999). *Competitor intelligence.* Chichester, U.K.: John Wiley.

Industry Canada. Research Publications Program (1998). *Recent jumps in patenting activities: Comparative innovative performance of major industrial countries, patterns and explanations.* Working Paper number 27. Ottawa, Canada: Industry Canada.

Ives, T. (1995). An overview of the Internet for competitive intelligence professionals. *Competitive Intelligence Review, 6*(1), 28–36.

Johnson, A.R. (1999). When knowing news is good news. *Limra's Marketfacts, 18*(4), 14–15.

Julien, P.-A. (1995). New technologies and technological information in small business. *Journal of Business Venturing, 10,* 459–475.

Julien, P.-A. (1996). Information control: A key factor in small business development. In *International Council on Small Business 41st World Conference.* Retrieved February 1, 2001, from the World Wide Web: http://www.sbaer.uca.edu/docs/proceedings/96ICSW129.txt

Julien, P.-A., Lachance, R., Raymond, L., Jacob, R., & Ramangalahy, C. (1995). *La veille technologique dans les PME manufacturières québécoises.* (Report No. 95-05). Trois-Rivières: UQTR: Groupe de recherche en économie et gestion des PME.

Julien, P.-A., Raymond, L., Jacob, R., & Ramangalahy, C. (1997). Information, stratégies et pratiques de veille technologique dans les PME. *Systèmes d'information et management, 2,* 63–83.

Kalb, C. C. (1999). Beyond competitive intelligence: Repositioning SCIP. *Competitive Intelligence Review, 10*(4), 1–2.

Kalb, C. C. (2000). Conducting intelligence ethically. In J. P. Miller (Ed.), *Millennium intelligence* (pp. 189–202). Medford, NJ: CyberAge Books.

Kassler, H. S. (1997). Mining the Internet for competitive intelligence: How to track and sift for golden nuggets. *Online, 21*(5), 34–64.

Kassler, H. S. (2000). Competitive intelligence on the Internet: Going for the gold. *Information Outlook, 4*(2), 37–42.

Kassler, H. S., & Sandman, M. A. (2000). Information resources for intelligence. In J. P. Miller (Ed.), *Millennium intelligence* (pp. 97–132). Medford, NJ: CyberAge Books.

Katzer, J., & Fletcher, P. T. (1992). The information environment of managers. *Annual Review of Information Science and Technology, 27,* 227–263.

Kennedy, M. L. (1996). Positioning strategic information: Partnering for the information age. *Special Libraries, 87,* 120–131.

Kline, D. (2000). Discovering new value in intellectual property. *Harvard Business Review, 78,* 54–66.

Klobas, J. E., & McGill, T. (1995). Identification of technological gatekeepers in the information technology profession. *Journal of the American Society for Information Science, 46,* 581–589.

Kurtz, C. J. (2000). Business wargaming. *Kappa White Paper.* Laguna Hills, CA: KappaWest.

Lackman, C. L., Saban, K., & Lanasa, J. M. (2000). Organizing the competitive intelligence function: A benchmarking study. *Competitive Intelligence Review, 11*(1), 17–27.

Lancaster, F. W., & Loescher, J. (1994). The corporate library and issues management. *Library Trends, 43,* 159–169.

Lesca, H. (1994). Veille stratégique pour le management stratégique: État de la question et axes de recherche. *Économies et sociétés, 28*(5), 31–50.

Lesca, H., & Raymond, L. (1993). Expérimentation d'un système-expert pour l'évaluation de la veille stratégique dans les PME. *Revue internationale PME, 6,* 49–65.

Library of Congress. (1991). *Library of Congress Subject Headings.* Washington, D.C.: Library of Congress.

Marshall, J. G. (1993). *The impact of the special library on corporate decision-making.* Washington, DC: Special Libraries Association.

Martinet, B., & Marti, Y.-M. (1995). *L'intelligence économique: Les yeux et les oreilles de l'entreprise.* Paris: Éditions d'Organisation.

Matteo, M. A., & Dykman, E. H. (1996). Building credibility, champions, and a mandate for competitive assessment. *Competitive Intelligence Review, 7*(Supplement 1), S19–S23.

McGonagle, J. J., & Vella, C. M. (1998). *Protecting your company against competitive intelligence.* Westport, CT: Quorum Books.

Miller, J. P. (1994). Educational advantage for intelligence professionals. *Library Trends, 43,* 253–270.

Miller, J. P. (2000a). The intelligence process—what it is, its benefits, and current status. In J. P. Miller (Ed.), *Millennium intelligence* (pp. 9–30). Medford, NJ: CyberAge Books.

Miller, J. P. (2000b). Skills and training for intelligence. In J. P. Miller (Ed.), *Millennium intelligence* (pp. 55–68). Medford, NJ: CyberAge Books.

Miller, J. P. (2000c). Small business intelligence—people make it happen. In J. P. Miller (Ed.), *Millennium intelligence* (pp. 225–238). Medford, NJ: CyberAge Books.

Mogee, M. E. (1994). Patent analysis for strategic advantage: Using international patent records. *Competitive Intelligence Review, 5*(1), 27–35.

Moon, M. D. (2000). Effective use of information & competitive intelligence. *Information Outlook, 4*(2), 17–20.

Nolan, J. (1999). *Confidential: Uncover your competitor's secrets legally and quickly and protect your own.* New York: Harper Business.

Nolan, J. A., & Quinn, J. F. (2000). Intelligence and security. In J. P. Miller (Ed.), *Millennium intelligence* (pp. 203–224). Medford, NJ: CyberAge Books.

Notess, G. R. (1999). On the Net: Searching for current news. *Database, 22,* 57–60.

O'Dell, C., & Grayson, C. J., Jr. (1998). *If only we knew what we know: The transfer of internal knowledge and best practice.* New York: Free Press.

Oxelheim, L. (1999). Applying "MUST" analysis and the role of government in CI. *Competitive Intelligence Review, 10*(4), 65–73.

Paine, L. S., & Santoro, M. (1993). *Competitive information policy at United Technologies.* Boston: Harvard Business School. (Case study no. 9-392-091).

Pepper, J. E. (1999). Competitive intelligence at Procter & Gamble. *Competitive Intelligence Review, 10*(4), 4–9.

Pinkerton, R. L. (1996). Competitive intelligence revisited: A history and assessment of its use in marketing. *Competitive Intelligence Review, 7*(Supplement 1), S127–S135.

Pollard, A. (1999). *Competitor intelligence: Strategy, tools and techniques for competitive advantage.* New York: Pitman.

Pooley, J., & Halligan, M. R. (2000). Intelligence and the law. In J. P. Miller (Ed.), *Millennium intelligence* (pp. 171–188). Medford, NJ: CyberAge Books.

Porter, M. E. (1980). *Competitive strategy: Techniques for analyzing industries and competitors.* New York: Free Press.

Porter, M. E. (1990). *The competitive advantage of nations.* New York: Free Press.

Powell, Tim (1999). Tracking patents with 'IPAM.' *Competitive Intelligence Magazine, 2*(2), 33–34.

Prescott, J. E. (1995). The evolution of competitive intelligence. *International Review of Strategic Management, 6,* 71–90.

Prescott, J. E., & Bhardwaj, G. (1995). Competitive intelligence practices: A survey. *Competitive Intelligence Review, 6*(2), 4–14.

Rangan, U. S., & Porter, M. E. (1992). *Ethical dimensions of competitive analysis.* Boston: Harvard Business School.

Romagni, P., & Wild, V. (1998). *L'intelligence économique au service de l'entreprise.* Paris: Les presses du management.

Rouach, D. (1996). *La veille technologique et l'intelligence économique.* Paris: Presses universitaires de France. (Que sais-je? 3086)

Salmon, R., & de Linares, Y. (1999). *Competitive intelligence: Scanning the global environment.* London: Economica.

Sawka, K. (1999a). The analyst's corner: It's the analysis, stupid! *Competitive Intelligence Magazine, 2*(4), 43–44.

Sawka, K. (1999b). Competing [sic] hypothesis analysis. *Competitive Intelligence Magazine, 2*(3), 37–38.

Sawka, K. A. (1996). Demystifying business intelligence. *Management Review, 85*(10), 47–51.

Schultz, N. O., Collins, A. B., & McCulloch, M. (1994). The ethics of business intelligence. *Journal of Business Ethics, 13,* 305–314.

Schweizer, P. (1996). The growth of economic espionage. *Foreign Affairs, 75,* 9–14.

Shaker, S. M., & Gembicki, M. P. (1999). *The warroom guide to competitive intelligence.* New York: McGraw-Hill.

Shapiro, C., & Varian, H. R. (1999). *Information rules: A strategic guide to the network economy.* Boston: Harvard Business School.

Shelfer, K., & Goodrum, A. (2000). Competitive intelligence as an extension of library education. *Journal of Education for Library and Information Science, 41,* 353–361.

Sigurdson, J., & Tågerud, Y. (Eds). (1992). *The intelligent corporation: The privatisation of intelligence.* London: Taylor Graham.

Society of Competitive Intelligence Professionals. Education Committee. (1996). *Curriculum modules for education programs in competitive intelligence for use by academics and professional trainers.* Arlington, VA: Society of Competitive Intelligence Professionals.

Society of Management Accountants of Canada. (1996). *Developing comprehensive competitive intelligence. Management Accounting Practices Handbook.* Toronto: The Society. [Management accounting guideline 39].

Steele-Vivas, R. D. (1996). Creating a smart nation: Strategy, policy, intelligence, and information. *Government Information Quarterly, 13,* 159–173.

St-Jacques, N. (1996). Profession veilleur. *Argus, 25*(3), 23–29.

Sutton, H. (1988). *Competitive intelligence.* New York: The Conference Board.

Taylor, R. S. (1986). *Value-added processes in information systems.* Norwood, NJ: Ablex.

Tessun, F. (1997). Scenario analysis and early warning systems at Daimler-Benz Aerospace. *Competitive Intelligence Review, 8*(4), 30–40.

Treat, J. E., Thibault, G. E., & Asin, A. (1996). Dynamic competitive simulation: Wargaming as a strategic tool. *Strategy & Business.* Retrieved February 1, 2001, from the World Wide Web: http://www.strategy-business.com/strategy/96204

Urso, P. (1997-1998). Les services de veille peuvent être certifiés. *Technologies internationales, 40,* 24–27.

U.S. House of Representatives. 104th Congress. Permanent Select Committee on Intelligence. (1996). *IC21: The intelligence community in the 21st century. Staff study.* U.S. GPO. Retrieved February 1, 2001, from the World Wide Web: http://www.access.gpo.gov/congress/house/intel/ic21_toc.html

Vedder, R. G., & Vanececk, M. T. (1998). Competitive intelligence for IT resource planning: Some lessons learned. *Information Strategy, 15*(1), 29–36.

Vedder, R. G., Vanecek, M. T., Guynes, C. S., & Cappel, J. J. (1999). CEO and CIO perspectives on competitive intelligence. *Communications of the ACM, 42*(8), 109–116.

Vezmar, J. M. (1996). Competitive intelligence at Xerox. *Competitive Intelligence Review, 7*(3), 15–19.

Vibert, C. (2000). *Web-based analysis for competitive intelligence.* Westport, CT: Quorum Books.

Villain, J. (1990). *L'entreprise aux aguets: Information, surveillance de l'environ-nement, propriété et protection industrielles, espionnage et contre-espionnage au service de la compétitivité.* Paris: Masson.

von Krogh, G., Ichijo, K., & Nonaka, I. (2000). *Enabling knowledge creation: How to unlock the mystery of tacit knowledge and release the power of innovation.* New York: Oxford University Press.

Walker, T. D. (1994a). Introduction: The library in corporate intelligence activities. *Library Trends, 43,* 149–158.

Walker, T. D. (1994b). The literature of competitive intelligence. *Library Trends, 43,* 271–284.

Watts, R. J., Porter, A. L., & Newman, N. C. (1998). Innovation forecasting using bibliometrics. *Competitive Intelligence Review, 9*(4), 11–19.

Weick, K. E. (1995). *Sensemaking in organizations.* Thousand Oaks, CA: Sage.

Westney, E., & Ghoshal, S. (1994). *Building a competitor intelligence organiza-tion: Adding value in an information function.* In T. J. Allen & M. S. Scott Morton (Eds.), *Information technology and the corporation of the 1990s: Research studies* (pp. 430–453). New York: Oxford University Press.

Weston, D. M. (1991). *Best practices in competitive analysis: Managing CA as a business.* Princeton: Stanford Research Institute. (Report 801).

Wheaton, K. J. (2000). How to make an embassy work for you. *Competitive Intelligence Magazine, 3*(1): 14–17.

Whitehorn, M., & Whitehorn, M. (1999). *Business intelligence: The IBM solution: Data warehousing and OLAP.* London: Springer-Verlag.

Wilensky, H. L. (1967). *Organizational intelligence: Knowledge and policy in gov-ernment and industry.* New York: Basic Books.

Winkler, I. (1997). *Corporate espionage.* Roseville, CA: Prima Publishing.

Zhu, D., & Porter, A. (1999). *Technology mapping—an application on the Internet domain. TPAC.* Retrieved February 1, 2001, from the World Wide Web: http://www.tpac.gatech.edu/Examples/internet/internet.html

Information Theory

CHAPTER 9

Theorizing Information for Information Science

Ian Cornelius
University College Dublin

Introduction

Does information science have a theory of information? There seems to be a tendency within information science to seek a theory of information, but the search is apparently unproductive (Hjørland, 1998; Saracevic, 1999). This review brings together work from inside and outside the field of information science, showing that other perspectives on information theory could be of assistance. Constructivist claims that emphasize the uniqueness of the individual experience of information, maintaining that there is no information independent of our social practices (Cornelius, 1996a), are also mentioned. Such a position would be echoed in a symbolic interactionist approach.

Conventionally, the history of attempts to develop a theory of information date from the publication of Claude Shannon's work in 1948, and his joint publication of that work with an essay by Warren Weaver in 1949 (Shannon & Weaver, 1949/1963). Information science found itself alongside many other disciplines attempting to develop a theory of information (Machlup & Mansfield, 1983). From Weaver's essay stems the claim that the basic concepts of Shannon's *mathematical theory of communication*, which Shannon later referred to as a *theory of information*, can be applied in disciplines outside electrical engineering, even in the social sciences.

Shannon provides a model whereby an information source selects a desired message, out of a set of possible messages, that is then formed into a signal. The signal is sent over the communication channel to a receiver, which then transforms the signal back to a message that is relayed to its destination (Shannon & Weaver, 1949/1963, p. 7). Problems connected with this model have remained with us. Some of the concepts are ambiguous; the identification of information with a process has spancelled the debate; the problems of measuring the amount of information, the relation of information to meaning, and questions about the truth value of information have remained. Balancing attention between the process and the act of receiving information, and determining the character of the receiver, has also been the focus of work and debate. Information science has mined work from other disciplines involving information theory and has also produced its own theory. The desire for theory remains (Hjørland, 1998; Saracevic, 1999), but what theory will deliver is unclear.

The distinction between data and information, or communication and information, is not of concern here. The convention that data, at some point of use, become information, and that information is transferred in a process of communication suffices for this discussion. Substitution of any of these terms is not a problem. More problematic is the relationship between information and knowledge. It seems accepted that at some point the data by perception, or selection, become information, which feeds and alters knowledge structures in a human recipient. What that process of alteration is, and its implications, remain problematic. This review considers the following questions:

1. What can be gleaned from the history of reviews of information in information science?
2. What current maps, guides, and surveys are available to elaborate our understanding of the issues?
3. Is there a parallel development of work outside information science on information theory of use to us?
4. Is there a dominant view of information within information science?

5. What can we say about issues like measurement, meaning, and misinformation?

6. Is there other current work of relevance that can assist attempts, in information science, to develop a theory of information?

The Reviews: Information Theory in Information Science

Information is not under-theorized. Although Hjørland (1998, p. 607) maintains that information science in itself lacks explicit theories, it can be claimed that theory in information science is implicit in its practices (Cornelius, 1996b). Independent of this debate there is a body of work on information theory in information science. Authors from disciplines outside information science, with technical or conceptual interests in information, have produced a wide range of definitions, theories, and metaphors for information (Machlup & Mansfield, 1983). Within information science the lack of a theory of information has become a perennial lament. Previous *ARIST* chapters have given some attention to this issue. Shera and Cleveland (1977) include a section on the theoretical foundations of information science in which the work of Shannon and Weaver is cited as a logical place to begin. They note Schramm's (1955) attempt to apply information theory to the study of language, indicative of efforts to "fit Shannon's quantitative measure on to qualitative subject areas" (Shera & Cleveland, 1977, p. 261), and Fairthorne's (1967) counter-observation of the adverse effects of an attempt to apply Shannon's theory beyond its valid scope. Fairthorne felt information theory necessary but not sufficient, and that it needed to be set in a framework of a theory of information science. Shera and Cleveland (1977, p. 262) also note Artandi's (1975) call for strict use of Shannon's work to be allied with work in semiotics to produce "a better understanding of information in the context of information systems." Semiotics has attracted recent attention (Cronin, 2000; Gluck, 1997), but Blair's (1990) objections to the use of semiotics remain unanswered.

Zunde and Gehl (1979) also give an account of information, emphasizing the extension of Shannon's theory; the development of modeling and measures of information; the relation between semiotic form and information content; and the problem of relating information to knowledge. They explicitly limit the range of enquiry to information legitimate to information science, saying, "information science as an empirical discipline is *not* concerned with what information is in an ontological or metaphysical sense.... The subject of concern to information science is the phenomena through which the nature of information is revealed and embodied" (Zunde & Gehl, 1979, p. 68).

Boyce and Kraft (1985) redressed this empirical restriction, basing their comments on information theory very firmly in the tradition set by Shannon and Weaver, but extending the range to include work on ignorance (Levi, 1984) and the need to consider the human capacity to process information (Baird, 1984). They conclude that "information theory has not had the impact on information science, at least as yet, that some theoretical works have had in other disciplines" (Boyce & Kraft, 1985, p. 157), and that the "role of information theory as the underlying mathematical model of communication has not to date had a parallel role in information science" (Boyce & Kraft, 1985, p. 157). Moving away from the strict lineage of the Shannon model, Boyce and Kraft drew attention to new work by Harmon (1984) that attempted to find a unitary measure of information, the "inform," work that would be echoed in the later writings of Debons (1992). Devlin (1991) subsequently developed the concept of an "infon" as a unitary measure. Boyce and Kraft cited Kochen (1984), and, balancing disappointment with hope, concluded that "in terms of communication, adaptive information processing, scaling of data, and modeling information flow that information theory may have an important role to play, either directly in terms of aiding modelers or indirectly as a theoretical underpinning" (Boyce & Kraft, 1985, p. 158).

Finally, Heilprin (1989, p. 343) reported on the foundations of information science. In an article that was more substantive than a literature review, he reported a "consensus of opinion that, although many laws, theories, hypotheses and speculations about information have been proposed, adequate scientific and epistemic foundations for a general science of information have not yet appeared." He offered a model framework into which a synthesis of the many fields concerned with information could fit a multidisciplinary foundation for information science. His focus was information processing.

Despite good recent work, the situation seems unchanged. From earlier *ARIST* reviews, we can identify central concerns in developing theories of information. Modeling information flow and processes, measuring information quantity, exploring relationships with knowledge, applying metaphorical extensions of the Shannon model, and developing alternatives to the Shannon model have received the most attention. These efforts may have been driven by the desire for general theory. Saracevic (1970, p. xiv) complained that there was still lacking "an intellectual framework into which a variety of theoretical, experimental, philosophical and practical works from various fields on the general subject of information behavior and communication processes may be fitted." By 1999 Saracevic felt no better.

> We can and do provide various lexical definitions of information, and we have an intuitive understanding of its meaning that we apply daily and widely. Thus, we do understand the message-sense in which we deal with information in information science. But that does not provide for a deeper and more formal understanding and explanation. (Saracevic 1999, p. 1054)

Saracevic indicates the movement that has been made by changing from direct descriptions of information to place the search for information in the wider context of scientific enquiry into all basic phenomena. The investigation focuses on the manifestations, behavior, and effects of the phenomena under question. In a three-tier hierarchy of information interpretations as narrow, broader, and broadest, Saracevic considers information as signals or messages for decisions (narrow); involving cognitive processing and understanding resulting from the interaction of mind and text (broader); and, in a situation, connected to the social context (broadest). This is a retreat from some earlier research to a concern with technical mechanisms for understanding information that explicitly recognize different domains of enquiry. The sciences are limited to the phenomena appropriate to them, a point that Vickery (1997, p. 458) reinforces in saying, "What we are concerned with is a consideration of what particular phenomena are to be *called* information." Agre (1995,

p. 225) recognized the ideological dimensions of this: "Information is an object of certain professional ideologies, most particularly librarianship and computing, and cannot be understood except through the practices within which it is constructed by the members of those professions in their work." For Saracevic (1999, p. 1054), information science is concerned with the broadest sense of information, "because information is used in a context and in relation to some reasons."

This review considers theories of information that focus directly on information. Associated areas such as information seeking are excluded, for that theory has seeking rather than information as its focus. Similarly, other high-level theories that use an unexplored notion of information are omitted from this review. So, too, some aspects of information in business, or information in the sense in which it is discussed in the information society debate, are not proper to this discussion. Also excluded are discussions of the economic value of information, for information is its own value. In the sense in which information is covered here, all that can be attempted is measurement. Therefore, *inter alia,* otherwise interesting and useful works by Introna (1997) and Casson (1997) on information in organizations and business are excluded, as is the useful introduction by Liebenau and Backhouse (1990).

Maps, Surveys, Guides

Three general guides to information and its theory serve to position any current discussion. Zhang (1988) gives a general schema that shows the position of human information processing in relation to other types of information, such as machine-machine communication, that are the foci of other areas of study. Wersig, in various works, but in particular in his *Information Theory* (Wersig, 1997), gives a review and description of various approaches to the information theory problem over the last fifty years. Going into a wider range of social sciences, Qvortrup (1993) reviews Shannon's traditional theory and compares it with Wiener's (1961) work to uncover a fundamental dichotomy in approaches to information. He then goes further to consider contributions in psychology and sociology. Other useful reviews of information theory are in Belkin (1978) and Ingwersen (1995), who discuss current approaches to the information problem within information science. Machlup and

Mansfield (1983), who perceive a range of disciplines using the concept of information as in some way related, discuss, contrary to the stance of Vickery (1997), cultural diversity within the broad range of information sciences. My concern here is with two points which Qvortrup raised.

First, Qvortrup points to the ambiguity in Shannonian approaches to information theory. Cole (1993), too, has worked on this issue. The position of the sender in relation to information is ambiguous in the Shannon model of communication. The sender selects from a possible range of messages; hence some meaning is attached to the decision regarding which message to select, because each message represents a different meaning. The model then cannot be merely technical. The position of the receiver is also ambiguous in the Shannon model of communication: as sender and receiver must be able to understand the message sent, they must be in some kind of social system. Moreover, the existence of any kind of closed system presupposes something outside it—an environment. Qvortrup emphasizes claims made about autopoiesis and introduces claims of Luhmann to the effect that information is an internal change of state, not something that exists in the external environment. Externally there is only data; it is the system that makes it information. This approach moves away from the limitation on the possible range of signals, an important restraint in Shannon's model, in a variation of systems theory. It is meaning, implicit in Shannon's model, says Qvortrup, which is the device used by observers for coping with external complexity. This approach, a constructivist approach, has also been identified from within information science by Wersig (1997).

The second point Qvortrup makes is in the different accounts of information from Shannon (Shannon & Weaver, 1949/1963) and Wiener (1961). For Shannon, information is, in one sense, the reduction of uncertainty; it is associated with disturbance from the normal. The less likely (or probable) the message, the greater the information. Wiener (1961, p. 11) takes the opposite view: "The amount of information in a system is a measure of its degree of organization." For Wiener, information is negative entropy; in this account of Shannon it is entropy. This ambiguity has persisted in information science: The practical work of information science is concerned with the imposition of order to produce information, and also with the lack of order, the natural state of disorganization in the universe of information objects (documents), which can be contrasted with the implicit potential order of their contents. What we can take from Qvortrup is this ambiguity about the nature of information and also, importantly, two other questions of relationships: first, of information in relation to social environments; and second, the relationship to the mind of the receiver.

Wersig (1997) includes, in addition to the constructivist approach that Qvortrup emphasizes, several other traditions in information theory. Up to the 1970s, Wersig sees thinking dominated by work stemming from Shannon's model. He calls this the Shannon and Weaver phase. There were, in summary, six different types of meaning attached to the term *information*. In Wersig's formulation they were:

1. Structures: structures of the world are information;
2. Knowledge: knowledge developed from perception is information;
3. Message: information is the message itself;
4. Meaning: meaning assigned to data is the information;
5. Effect: information is the effect of a specific process— reducing uncertainty, or a change of knowledge, or resolution of an anomalous state of knowledge in the mind of a recipient.
6. Process: information is a process; commonly a process of transfer.

Developments of the "effects" approach became established, from a cognitive viewpoint, as the dominant approach to the problem of information theory from the 1970s to the present—especially in information retrieval research. Attempts to displace it have been centered, according to Wersig, on three approaches: a version of systems theory, most recently manifested in the work of Luhmann (1995) on social systems; action theory, in which information is the value of knowledge in action, and which stems from work on the concept of "information man" (Roberts, 1982); and constructivism (Cole, 1994). Wersig also mentions a fourth: modernization theory, which he says requires a (as yet unavailable) postmodern theory of science, in which information provides order for orientation in a complex modern world (Wersig, 1993). Wersig attempts to integrate all these into a theory that focuses on information as the reduction of complexity: "information is the amount of complexity to be reduced or that has been reduced" (Wersig, 1997, p. 225).

Constructivism is represented by Wersig as either radical or moderate. Moderate constructivists in this account allow that, as all humans perceive and develop knowledge in much the same way, then not all perception or knowledge is entirely subjective because, under the same conditions, we come to the same conclusions (Wersig, 1997, p. 223). Radical constructivists do not allow this. They argue that, as even with the same information people can come to different conclusions and embark on different actions, that all knowledge and information is intersubjective, a product of our social practices (Cornelius, 1996a). Constructivism seems to have secured enough support to diminish in significance claims that information is a "thing," and has some reified existence; or that of Stonier (1989), who proposes that information is a physical property of the universe. Buckland (1981) attempts to recover some sense of information as thing—something that might have informational value—but admits that being informative is situational and potentially unknowable (Buckland, 1991, p. 52). Stonier's recent comment (1997, p. 14) that "information is the raw material which, when information-processed, may yield a message" is also challenged by constructivist claims. In information science, calls for a constructivist approach sometimes appear within work on sociocognitivism (Jacob & Shaw, 1998). Constructivists in information science contribute to the current move away from the cognitive viewpoint, or toward a significant revision of it. We will return to the topic of constructivism after considering the development of other work on information outside the field of information science.

Information Outside Information Science: Process Theories

Fiske (1990) separates process theories of information from all others. Fiske treats the Shannon theory as the prime process theory, and one of the main seeds out of which communication studies has grown. Most references are to the book published by Shannon and Weaver (1949/1963), and not to Shannon's own mathematical work but to Weaver's interpretation and explication of it, which forms the first part of that book. There were other competing theories of information extant at the time

(MacKay, 1969), but Shannon's work quickly came to dominate and define discussion. Three aspects of the work draw attention: first, the claim that the work had application outside the field of mathematical modeling in electrical engineering, even as far outside as the social sciences; second, not so much the formulae as the concepts and the linear model that Shannon produced; and third, Shannon's tripartite division of information into technical, semantic, and influential (what Weaver calls the effectiveness problem) aspects of information. Shannon's claim to be concerned only with the technical aspects has been challenged by Qvortrup (1993), and others, who observe that there are semantic aspects to his model. Practicing information scientists are as likely to be interested in the influential aspects of information. Weaver's statement that communication is "all the procedures by which one mind may affect another" (Shannon & Weaver, 1963, p. 3) seems to suggest that, whatever the mathematical limitations of Shannon's work, his model could legitimately be discussed by those with interests outside the mere technical transfer of information. Tribus (1983) has indicated some of the areas in which Shannon's theory has been applied. Concern has been fixed from this time on information as a measure of something transferred. The theory of information has been restricted to being a model of information transfer. The difficulties of using Weaver's interpretation are described in Ritchie (1986, 1991). Shannon (1956, p. 3) drew attention to the difficulties of transferring his concepts to other domains. His warning that "many of the concepts of information theory will prove useful in these other fields ... but the establishing of such applications is not a trivial matter of translating words to a new domain, but rather the slow tedious process of hypothesis and experimental verification" has not always been heeded.

That work of hypothesis and experimental verification proceeded, but mainly with probabilistic measures of information content. At the 1952 London symposium on Applications of Information Theory, MacKay (1953) indicated the concentration on the "selection made from the ensemble of expected probabilities" as the operational index of information content. He continued,

> selective information content does not measure a "stuff" like water, or electric charge, but a relation (selective power) between a signal and a particular ensemble of representational

acts of response. "*S* is a source of information" is thus an incomplete sentence. It must always be completed (even if sometimes implicitly) in the form, "*S* is a source of information to receiver *R*." (MacKay, 1953, p. 477)

This point, that sender and receiver must be in some form of social relationship for there to be information, is reinforced by Gabor (1953), who points out also that incomplete knowledge of the future is a requirement for information transfer. It is only if a message is not predictable from data previously received that there can be information. So, following Gabor, we can say that if there is perfect knowledge there can be no information. This seems to remove any possibility of conflating the concepts of knowledge and information, at least within information theory. It also provides a basis for later formulations by Brookes (1980). Gabor continues, "on the other hand, complete ignorance also precludes communication; a common language is required, that is to say an agreement between the transmitter and the receiver regarding the elements used in the communication process" (Gabor, 1953, p. 2). Communication of information presupposes a social system based on a shared language. Except in the most artificially constructed of machine-machine environments, it seems that information must require a prenegotiated social environment and language and an imperfect state of knowledge.

Mandelbrot (1953) extended the claims connected to information theory by working on the statistical structure of language. This structure, entirely independent of meaning, underlies meaningful written languages. Such a statistical structure, Mandelbrot hoped, would give a quantitative justification to the assumption that the theory of communication (Shannon's) applies also to the brain. Moving information theory away from its limitation to messages chosen from a finite set of symbols would allow the extension of information theory to analysis of messages in ordinary language.

Moving information theory away from a statistical basis to a semantic basis was the aim of Bar-Hillel and Carnap (1953). They offered one claim and one warning. First, the working premise that a semantic concept of information will serve as a "better approximation for some future explication of a psychological concept of information, than the statistical concept of present day theory" (Bar-Hillel & Carnap, 1953, p. 503). The limitations of their claim should be marked. Second, they observed that the application of the terms and theorems of statistical information theory to fields in which the term "information" was used in a semantic sense "may at best have had some heuristic stimulating value but at worst [would] be absolutely misleading" (Bar-Hillel & Carnap 1953, p. 503). In other words, statistical aspects of information theory should not be used in the social sciences as the basis for a theory of information; and although semantic theories of information may offer more, they were not yet (in 1952) fully available.

These points are emphasized in MacKay (1969). MacKay charted various efforts to deal with the problems of semantic information, its communication, and its effect upon a recipient. Significantly, he drew attention to the complex web or hierarchy of goals in which any human being is at any time enmeshed. The process of communication can alter the goal complex of any one; and in interaction two people might alter one another's goal complexes, as is common in ordinary dialogue. As the goal complex includes both a representation of what is currently the case as well as the goals pursued, there are two kinds of change: change in the "map" of current representations, and changes in the goals. MacKay (1969, p. 108) points toward an essentially relative concept of information, and he claims the concept of information is inseparable from meaning. In this representation, any generator of a message must discover the complex hierarchy of goals of an intended recipient if a message is to be transferred successfully. The message has meaning only when there is agreement about the circumstances—language game, rules of the game, etc. Meaning is a subjective element, dependent upon the state of the recipient, but not solely dependent upon the recipient. When we are dealing with the semantic content of messages—and this is what we deal with in information science—we are in a social situation, as identified by MacKay. In this situation the conditions of the transfer of information, and the effects of that transfer on the recipient, are significant elements in the theory of information. We cannot reduce information theory to some social or human analogy of technical aspects of information transfer. It is much more complex than that. The conditions that determine how a theory of information will be formulated in communication sciences in general should not differ greatly from the conditions in information science.

Summarizing some aspects of his own later work, MacKay (1983) wanted to play down the significance of Shannon's work on measuring the amount of information, when dealing with human subjects, and to substitute a measure of a different property:

> The recipient at any given time has (1) a store of factual information, (2) a repertoire of skills, (3) a hierarchy (or heterarchy) of criteria of evaluation and priorities. These three interlock in a complex manner so as to set up at any given time a certain total state of conditional readiness (SCR) for all possible action, including planning and evaluating action. It is this SCR that can be thought of as the operational target of a communication.

> The meaning (intended, received, or conventional) of a particular communication can now be defined as its readying function on the SCR of the recipient. (MacKay, 1983, p. 491)

MacKay claimed that by quantifying the degrees of freedom of the SCR it would be possible to find a numerical measure for the transfer of information between cognitive agents. This is an interesting proposition. Obviously, the kind of measurement of information we get from Shannon regarding the information content of a message is really of little interest in information science. But information retrieval does have an obvious operational interest in measures of the value of information retrieved (hence the development of user-indicated values in relevance feedback measures). Whether MacKay's measure of SCR can be made operational, however, is another question. Cole (1993) returned to this problem of operability. What we can take from MacKay's work is his emphasis on the recipient as the determinant of information received and meaning, and his identification of the hierarchy of the recipient's goal complex as a crucial element in determining how information is received. Although he seeks to measure the meaning, the impact on the SCR of the recipient, it seems that he is setting up a subjective definition of meaning. This would be familiar to constructivists and inimical to common definitions as accepted by Dretske (1981), whereby the meaning of an utterance seems to be stable.

Since approximately 1980, divisions in the approach to information have become more apparent. Information science was developing its own approach, known as the cognitive turn, from the mid-1970s onwards. Other fields were already independently establishing their own technical and instrumental definitions and models of information (Machlup & Mansfield, 1983), and Dretske's, and Barwise and Perry's works appeared, in 1981 and 1983, as new seminal lines of enquiry in a related but separate field. This review turns next to accounts of the work in information science.

Information and Information Science: The Cognitive Turn

The long development of the cognitive viewpoint in information science is generally believed to have started with De Mey (1977), and has been influenced by several authors since; notably Brookes, Belkin, Wersig, and Ingwersen. The influence of the cognitive viewpoint is reviewed by Belkin (1990). The cognitive viewpoint moves away from claims about the brain as an information-processing machine, and distances information science from mechanistic accounts of the brain (Brier, 1992). Ingwersen (1992) gives a thorough review of the cognitive viewpoint, its relation to cognitivism, and its history in information science. Meadow and Yuan (1997) give a brief history and review of the progress in defining information in information science, including an account of progress toward the cognitive viewpoint and highlighting difficulties about terms and concepts. The critical component in this cognitive viewpoint is that information is mediated by a potential recipient's state of knowledge. A recipient in this argument is a human user. Other previously generated models, for example Otten (1975), had allowed recipients to be human or machine.

Brookes and the Cognitive Viewpoint

The cognitive viewpoint served to swing the research in information transfer away from information systems and toward the state of mind of the user. This viewpoint is distinguished from straightforward cognitivism by its emphasis on modeling the processing of information on conscious mental states, implying meaning rather than simple symbol manipulation (Ingwersen, 1992, p. 21), and by its recognition of individual cognitive states. This emphasis on meaning is now commonplace in discussions of information, though there is disagreement on how meaning can be inferred, whether it can be measured, and how its nature is to be defined. Blair (1990) has worked this out most fully in his comparison of semiotics and Wittgenstein's work on use. As already noted, semiotics has received recent attention in the literature (Cronin, 2000; Gluck, 1997), but the problems that Blair identifies with semiotic approaches have not yet been tackled successfully.

The cognitive viewpoint uses and adapts a model of information transfer that has exercised a hegemony in information retrieval research. The model has been rendered as an equation, or function, by Brookes (1980), as the "fundamental equation of information science."

$$K(S) + \Delta I = K(S + \Delta S)$$

The fundamental claim represented in the equation is that information I (for which we must understand structured information ΔI), when operating on a knowledge structure $K(S)$, produces an effect whereby that knowledge structure is changed; the effect of which change is shown as ΔS. The change from structured information (ΔI) to structured knowledge (ΔS) is to show that the information affects the recipient's state of knowledge according to his or her state of mind. This equation has been amended by Ingwersen (1992, p. 32) to allow for potential information pI, perhaps in the form of a document. In this variation, information ΔI is perceived from potential information pI, and is then mediated by the knowledge state.

$$pI \rightarrow \Delta I + K(S) \rightarrow K(S + \Delta S) \rightarrow pI'$$

The same information may affect different knowledge structures in different ways. Ingwersen (1992) has also added another modification, or rather a transformation, to represent the process of information transfer from the perspective of an information system that is being interrogated.

Zunde and Gehl (1977) rejected this equation as "unoperational." It may have been unoperational in information systems, but it has remained operational as a general consideration, even if not in experimental design, within information retrieval theory and within information science's theorizing of information. It also remains a perennial topic of inquiry and continues to attract academic comment (Todd, 1999). The equation, or expression, has remained in discussion, but it has not gained ground as was intended. It has not been accepted universally as the fundamental equation of information science, and research can proceed without reference to it. We can observe three characteristic problems with the equation. First, discussion has tended to remove the equation from the context from which it emerged in Brookes's thought. Second, Brookes was creating a tool for the understanding of information within information science: Those using the equation have tended to apply it as a guide to understanding pragmatic problems within information retrieval. Third, although, as Ingwersen points out, Brookes's equation does allow for subjectivity—that is, individual perceptions and states of knowledge—the theorizing of this aspect of information theory has always been weak within information science, and the remaining weakness in the Brookes equation symbolizes and reflects this problem. We can also say that the formulation of the individual's state of knowledge lacks social context.

The Cognitive View: Objections and Developments

The Brookesian equation, by which I mean Brookes's original formula and subsequent modifications that are extensions retaining the structure and intentions of the original, is not in itself a complete theory of information. It suffers in respect to measurement. It is difficult to understand how the transformation of structured information into structured knowledge can be considered to take place if no measure of the change is available. Designers of systems need to know if such a transformation has taken place if the efficacy of systems is to be assessed. The Brookesian equation also suffers in underdevelopment of the concept of structure. Knowledge structures are amended, and structured information is transformed into structured knowledge according to a particular structured knowledge state. What is unclear is how the information is structured. The "water into wine" effect of changing information into knowledge is not sufficiently explained. The implication is that it is structured by the recipient's mind. This requires the source and the recipient to be in a common social practice whereby each recognizes the other's use of terms, and so on.

This reiterates MacKay's (1969, p. 108) claim that all parties must be in the same language game—substantially a similar point to one made by Blair. Reviewing Blair's work, Jacob and Shaw conclude that it shows support for a sociocognitive perspective and for the socially constructed nature of cognition itself (Jacob & Shaw, 1998, p. 146). Blair (1990, p. 134) demonstrates the difficulty in constructing any theory on the basis of semiotics: "The problems with an ideational theory of signification means that there can be no clear definition of the contents/signifieds." He also demonstrates that Wittgenstein's attribution of meanings of terms to their common use is the most fruitful approach (Wittgenstein, 1953).

> Without a satisfactory and realistic definition of contents/signifieds, it would be virtually impossible to argue convincingly for their existence. Consequently, further inquiry into the nature of signs and signification is contingent upon the formulation of a new fundamental question—one which does not have implicit assumptions and is not beset by the same mentalistic or referential problems, yet would be useful in the investigation of signs and signification. Instead of asking "what does an expression mean/signify" we shall now ask "how is an expression used?" (Blair, 1990, pp. 135–136)

This point is also recognized by Fox (1983) in his identification of propositions for information, whereby information "that P" is conveyed only if the recipient is in a position to know "that P." Fox's position is similar to Dretske (1981) on this point. This is a crude formulation that needs refinement to be useful. The requirement that the recipient be in a position to know "that P" (that is, effectively, the truth value of the proposition), cannot be sustained when we talk of information transfer in educational situations. Schoolchildren are not in a position to know the structure of Latin verb endings, the periodic table, the longest river in Africa, or the form of quadratic equations. They take these on trust. What is required is that they be in a position to eventually know or possess the capability of knowing. They take part in one of Wittgenstein's "Forms of Life," with its own language game. This again implies that they are participants in the same social practice and are learning the constitutive rules of that practice. This also suggests the utility of a symbolic interactionist approach to the study of information. Symbolic interactionism works from the premise that society is interaction (Brittan, 1998; Fontenot, 1995; Stryker, 1992).

The effect of the amended requirement (that we possess the capability of knowing) is that the Brookesian formula does not give sufficient attention to the "subjective" element it recognizes in information transfer. Brookes claimed that information in documents was the reified and objective instance of Popper's "World 3" (Popper, 1972); a world separate from the mental and physical worlds that was the world of all shared human mental products, such as mathematics or music. This world, and, for Brookes, the documents, could be apprehended by all humans similarly, as if it (World 3) had an objective existence. This is similar to, but not the same as, saying that recipients must share the same social practice as sources, but it is not clear that Brookes's version of World 3 as an environmental structural component of his formula has been accepted or adopted in subsequent work. World 3 itself remains a problematic concept; one that, although frequently addressed and readdressed by Popper (Stokes, 1998, pp. 112–116), remains more a working assumption than a conjecture. Two problems are that, first, in Popper's account, World 3 contains all the knowledge and theories of the world, both true and false. We must thus include some account of misinformation, or account for false information—a point that has not been resolved. Second, Popper's World 3 contains not only known aspects of, for example, mathematics, but also those properties of mathematics not yet discovered by humans. World 3 is thus autonomous and seems to be independent of a human knowing subject—which sets it apart from most current work on information in information science. Neill (1992) takes a more sympathetic approach to World 3.

Brookes set the practical task of information science as the collection and organization for use of all the records of World 3. The "theoretical task is to study the interaction between Worlds 2 and 3, to describe and explain them if they can, and so help in organizing knowledge rather than documents for more effective use" (Brookes, 1980, p. 128). His seeming conflation of information as a part of knowledge (Brookes, 1980, p. 131) creates difficulties for a theory of information, and his extension of knowledge to include unrecorded knowledge, although consistent with Popper's World 3, seems to conflict with other work that emphasizes recorded knowledge (Ingwersen, 1992, p. 34).

The requirement of taking into account the effect of information on the recipient is made clear in Belkin's (1978) criteria for a concept of information. Belkin's list of requirements set a standard for assessing candidate theories of information that has not yet been met or superseded. This is an alternative formulation to Brookes's that offers another model of the communication system; in this case motivated by a potential recipient's state of knowledge. A recipient instigates a query to resolve some anomaly in his or her state of knowledge. Belkin's concept requires that it is possible to measure the effect on the recipient of the transfer of information. Information is what reduces the level of uncertainty in the recipient, whose initial anomalous state of knowledge has led to the search for information. The advantage of this model is that it shifts attention more toward the recipient—in line with the demands of the cognitive viewpoint—but still includes the generator of information. A sympathetic statement of the advantages of the cognitive viewpoint (Ingwersen, 1995, pp. 162–164) claims that it differentiates between information transmitted from the mind of a generator, and that information as it affects the cognitive structure of a recipient. A concept of information thus has a dual requirement, but admitting the first, the information transmitted, is only data without the second, and allowing the second only as sense-data without the first.

The claims of the cognitive view of information have come under strenuous attack. Frohmann (1992) has assaulted the whole cognitive approach and its claims and assumptions. In respect to a theory of information he observed that:

> The reduction of the complexities of real practices, conduct, accomplishments and actions of information seeking, information use, and "information processing" in a stratified social world, to a narrative of mental events, delivers LIS theory to specific interests with a large stake in the construction of human identity as essentially interior. (Frohmann, 1992, p. 375)

This movement toward taking more account of the social construction of reality, identity, and information, rather than relying on the image of an atomistic individual, was continued by Vakkari (1994) and Hjørland (1997). Vakkari reiterated Frohmann's comments and added the observation of Rudd (1983) that the failure of Popper's World 3 to take into account the social context of information should be a warning to information scientists. The claim by Ingwersen (1995, p. 164) that collective cognitive structures, "which imply a sharing of world views among groups of people in a domain" equate to the social impact on individuals, is not worked out. It remains only a conjecture that is at variance with constructivist claims that the individual world view and identity itself are negotiated in the social world and practices in which the individual participates. The importance of this sociocultural context, and the importance of the social in the construction of information, which has been so laboriously established by critics of the cognitive viewpoint, attests to the hold of that viewpoint on the information science consciousness. A similar point had already been made or conceded by MacKay (1953, 1969), albeit in different language. However, the contribution to a theory of information made by the cognitive viewpoint should not be undervalued; at the very least it moved the attention of information science away from a preoccupation with systems and back to the perceiving human subject.

Measurement, Meaning, and Misinformation

All these models and equations seem to require a means of measuring information. They all suppose some measure of meaning, and they raise questions of misinformation, especially where a definition of information requires it to be truthful if it is to be knowledge.

Meaning and Information

Conventionally, following Dretske (1981), debate insists that information extends beyond meaning in any message. The information is the meaning of the message together with any relevant contextual information available to the recipient. This is partly convention, which takes the position that messages in any context are meaningfully stable but that the information content is a subjective construction of the recipient. Dretske (1981) instances bids in a game of bridge, where the meaning of a bid indicates the cards in the hand of one player. The rules require the meaning of the bid to be disclosed to opponents, but the information flows to one player by comparing that meaning with the cards in his (or her) own hand. In this example, the information conveys some competitive advantage. It is debatable whether the artificial constraints of any card game, played by a determined set of rules with a limited range of message possibilities, corresponds more closely to Shannon's requirements for signal transmission, where a message is selected from a finite set of possible signals, or whether such a situation can be seen as an example of Wittgenstein's language games. A radical constructivist argument, to use Wersig's term (Wersig, 1993), would insist that the card game example is too constrained to fit within arguments about language games, except in the simplest sense; and that it does not correspond with normal information searching activity.

Meaning, in a constructivist argument, is negotiated in interaction in relation to other meanings (Cornelius, 1996b, p. 27), just as one learns the language of forms of life by interaction, experience, and use. The meaning of a word is a function of the rules governing its employment (Putnam, 1975). These establish understanding; so in communication the process of communicating any one piece of information is wrapped in a net of meanings, all of which are socially negotiated and which combine to influence or determine what constitutes the information and what the information content is. This is similar to MacKay's (1969) observation that information is inseparable from meaning, and must be perceived within a hierarchy, or heterarchy, of complex goals. In this view (Cornelius, 1996a), there is no separate entity of information to discover independent of our practices. Hjørland (1997) and Hjørland and Albrechtsen (1995) put forward a view similar to this claim about social practices, but they impose a constraint of principles specific to a particular domain, usually a subject domain. Arguments about the importance and role of language games and forms of life are best worked out by Blair (1990).

Measurement

The question of measurement, which is common to all approaches to information theory, poses difficulties when we consider the different types of measurement that can concern us. In the basic Shannon model of communication, what is measured is either the amount of information, which relates to channel capacity, or the extent to which the information reduces uncertainty, which is a probabilistic function. Weaver represents the amount of information sent as the logarithm (to base 2) of the available choices (Shannon & Weaver, 1949/1963, p. 9). This presumes a finite set of possible messages, which does not mirror normal social discourse. Clearly, what is of greater interest to information science is the measurement not of the amount of information sent, but either the amount received or the amount of influence (effect) it has upon a receiver. In constructivist accounts, measures of both amount received and effect would be difficult to derive. In nonquantitative terms, the effect could be expressed as either positive or negative. How can the effect of information be negative? If information is related to knowledge structure, as, for example, the Brookesian account has it, then information that undermines confidence in that knowledge structure will have a negative effect. For example, if a theory that satisfactorily explains most significant things known about the universe is confounded by a new observation, then we do not have an explanation for the universe and our knowledge structure is impaired. It would be difficult to say that no information had been received, or that the information was merely data—for the arguments available suggest that it is when sense-data is incorporated into knowledge structures that it becomes information. There is a special case about misinformation; and another case is where good information, perfectly recognizable to the recipient, is rejected. Measurement in these cases becomes difficult, because conventional methods do not explain the effect.

Another approach to this, adopted by Tague-Sutcliffe, was to measure the informativeness of a document, measured by what the user takes from a document (reported in Frické, 1998). Tague-Sutcliffe and Frické are concerned about the actual supply of documents. In this formulation, a response to a query is the supply of a series of documents, the informativeness of which can be quantified. This is a measure of information service, not of information, and lies outside our concerns here. Cole (1997) has attempted to marry Brookes's fundamental equation to quantitative measures adapted from Shannon to measure the information content of an information process. Cole claims this can measure the effects of new information on a knowledge structure and not the size of the evidence or information. Debons (1992) preferred another approach and developed the notion of an "inform" as a unit of measure of information content.

(This "inform" is not to be confused with the "infon," developed by Devlin [1991] as an item of information, an artifact of a theory.)

A completely different approach to measurement was taken by Sillince (1995), who sought a measure of information value by measuring organizational information channels. This really lies outside the limits placed in this review, having more to do with theories of organizations. Hayes (1993, p. 276) also proposed a quantitative measure. He recognized that "measurement of information is a complicated and as yet unresolved problem," but proposed a four-stage measure of information founded on the Shannon model of data transfer. Hayes added a generalization of Shannon's measure to cope with entropy, and then offered mathematical formulae for the calculation of data analysis and data reduction, his final stages of the information process. To the constructivist, all these measures lack resonance because they reduce the information to a quantitative measure, which does not seem to reflect the need to consider the impact on the recipient, given the recipient's unique state of knowledge. The constructivist requires that we be able to account for the differing effects of the same information on different people in the same social context, such as judges (Cornelius, 1996a).

Misinformation

The problem of misinformation can be represented at both philosophical and pragmatic levels. Godfrey-Smith (1989), tackling a slightly different problem, indicates that this problem of misinformation, or error, may be unresolvable. With misinformation there are, transparently, problems regarding measurement and meaning. Buckland (1991, pp. 111–112) introduces a complication by associating misinformation with harm and distress, and therefore with some social and moral values. Fox formulates misinformation as a falsehood, but maintains that misinformation remains a species of information (Fox, 1983, p. 193). Information may not be true, but misinformation must be false. Dretske (1981, p. 45) opposes this, claiming that, as information to be information must have a truth value, then misinformation cannot be information. Losee (1997) works through this case.

How can we measure this? The only sure method is within Shannon's original formulation of the process by which he accounts for noise within a system (noise will distort a signal, thereby distorting its message, possibly but not necessarily to the point of falsehood). Levi's work on information deprivation, a form of misinformation, concluded that "we need to give up the notion that concepts of belief and information can be handled entirely in probabilistic and entropic terms" (Levi, 1984, p. 361). A constructivist would say that measurement takes place within the context of a continuing exchange of information, within which statements and messages are assessed for truth value and verifiability in a process that is as much about forming identity and theorizing context and situation as it is about transferring information. Within this general sense of information processes, the case of interrogation of systems to disclose documents is no different. As MacKay indicated in his formulation of a hierarchy of complex goals, we are always negotiating a number of objectives in any process of information exchange.

Other Contributions: Dretske, Barwise and Perry, Devlin, Evans

I refer to these authors not for alternative theories of information but as sources of insight on information in social situations and for aspects of information theory that are not treated adequately in current information science approaches to information theory. There is no attempt here to review *in toto* the contributions from these authors to information problems.

Much of the recent literature on information outside information science centers on Dretske's (1981) work. Dretske, coming from philosophy, is far more ambitious about defining information than anyone in information science. He attempts to develop a genuine semantic theory of information and to develop from that an information-based definition of knowledge. This goes further than any claim made in information science. To do this, he criticizes the view that sensory data are informationally barren until invested with meaning by some agent. He claims this is false because it confuses information with meaning. In establishing his semantic theory of information he concludes that his theory of information content, consistent with the quantitative demands of information theory, sits well with our intuitive notion of information. He emphasizes the connection between information and truth, and that "the information one receives is a function of what one already knows"

(Dretske, 1981, pp. 81–82). This, too, is intuitively true, and corresponds with all that has been said previously about senders and receivers being in the same social practice and understanding the same language games. If I interrogate an information system, I will reach a point where I conclude that I have the answer to my question. How do I know when that can be? It must be that, before I begin the interrogation, the formulation of my enquiry reveals to me what would constitute an answer. Information is a function of what I already know. In building his picture of knowledge, Dretske claims that we know something by virtue of having information about it, placing a condition on information that it be true. He also, importantly, brings in the notion of learning. We are able to build knowledge and to infer certain facts by the recursive nature of information exchanges: We learn from previous requests for information. The role of learning in building knowledge, whereby accretions of information are worked upon in a learning process to produce inferences that constitute knowledge, is also dealt with by Barnes (1981).

Barwise and Perry (1983) also tackle the problem of meaning. For them, meaning arises out of recurring relations between situations. Information can only be information about a structured reality, and is relative to the constraints holding between types of situations. Information is provided only if the perceiving organism is attuned to those constraints (Barwise & Perry, 1983, p. 120). The primary function of language, they say, is to convey information; but that requires one to have some information to convey. It is the meaning of expressions that allows them to convey the information that they convey. Possessing information is like knowing or believing; and is therefore what they call an attitude. Having information comes, rather as Dretske claims, before language; before any expression of the information. The deep analysis of situations and attitudes offers a means to investigate and understand the process of transferring information to another person—to give him or her certain knowledge. This offers a more convincing approach to the elements in the information models used in information science that deal with the concept of transforming information offered to someone into knowledge for that person—a process that will amend his or her knowledge structure. This work has something to offer information science in its construction of information theory. Green (1991) noted, from an analysis of information science's own linguistic usage, that the field lacked a coherent model of information transfer and that "we should be more concerned with learning and knowledge" (Green, 1984, p. 143). Devlin (1991) takes the ideas further, partly in pursuit of a mathematics of information; but he also harks back to a theme of Vickery (1997) about the construction of a science of information, to investigate the nature of information flow and the mechanisms that give rise to such flow.

Luhmann (1995) posits a similar operation to learning. His view of information, taken from work by Bateson and from the Shannon and Weaver model, is that information is an event that selects system states. With Luhmann we are back with Qvortrup's social perspective on information and we move into the analysis of social systems, or rather the position of a "system" within a social world. Events are temporal, and if messages are repeated they lose their information value, even though they retain their meaning. The information is not lost, but it has already had its effect in changing the structure of the system. Information presupposes structure. The distinction between information and meaning is made possible by changes in system states. These claims are analogous to some of the claims made by Dretske and also those of Barwise and Perry. Luhmann attempts to proceed further in his characterization of systems, whereby the system is distinguished from its environment, and takes in information from the environment without automatic and predictable alteration of the system. The system is self-referential, autopoietic, and retains self-determination. External information is not like a simple stimulus-response mechanism: "Information is an event that constrains entropy, without thereby pinning down the system" (Luhmann, 1995, p. 68). Luhmann is explaining the operation of information in a system in a way similar to the Brookesian model, but with the sophistication of discrimination between information and meaning. This lacks, however, the depth of analysis of information handling proposed by Barwise and Perry.

Before moving on from these points we should also mention Evans (1982), who conceives our information handling activities as being part of an information system that is a substratum of our cognitive lives. Evans contrasts traditional epistemology, where a human subject would receive data, "intrinsically without information content, into which he was supposed to read the appropriate objective significance by means of an (extremely shaky) inference" (Evans, 1982, pp. 122–123). Inference in this view leads to information, following the subject's beliefs about the world. Evans (1982, p. 23) prefers the notion of "being in an informational state with such-and-such a content," to explain the data that, for any reasoning subject, are already imbued with objective significance and have a propensity to influence our actions. The informational states do not require us to believe the truth of the information—we can listen to a story without necessarily believing it to be true. This seems to be an objection to the requirement that information be true.

These additional comments on information from outside the field of information science show that there is significant work, relevant to some of the operations that are a central concern to information science, that could advance our understanding of information and help refine any theory of information we might have. To relate theoretical work on information to this external work would also link us more closely to general academic enquiry. What might have hampered such development is the practical orientation of information science, particularly in information retrieval research. Our disinclination, as a field of study, to become heavily involved with mathematics should not deter us from continued use of logic. The practical work in information retrieval being done by, for example, van Rijsbergen (1996), or van Rijsbergen and Lalmas (1996), with its orientation to solving system problems, should not conceal the fact that the foundation for such work is an analysis of information informed by the best logical and epistemological commentary. We should not be afraid to add to that work done in the social sciences that emphasizes socially situated decision making, and the unique situation of any recipient of information.

Conclusion

Theories are tools of enquiry. They are good as long as they are useful. Their use is measured by the extent to which they can explain or predict: A good theory will explain or predict more things for a longer period. Theory development is part of the working apparatus of a field of study, and the facility to develop theory must itself be kept in good order. Constructivists will argue that theorizing is part of any practice (Cornelius, 1996b). In this view, theories can be an implicit part of the practice, rather than some explicit formulation external to the inevitable reflection of any practitioner. A discipline may feel the need for, or want of, theory, both for behavioral and scholarly reasons. The scholarly or scientific desire to have a theory that explains basic concepts in the field, establishes conventional definitions, and addresses central problems is understandable. The behavioral need for theory in order to establish a field's claim to academic status, or to support the endeavors of its practitioners, is equally understandable but less productive. Information science should be clear regarding why it seeks a theory of information.

There is apparently little problem about information theory in information science. The challenge to the dominance of the cognitive viewpoint is essentially to seek a revision of that theory. Calls for more radical departures, like the development of a hermeneutic theory of information, have as yet no realization. An apparent tendency to concentrate on problems associated with the issue of representation (Hjørland, 1997; Jacob & Shaw, 1998) merely mirrors the computer science, or systems, tendency to concentrate on what can be realized within systems. However, attempts to build information contexts into information retrieval programs are disadvantaged by a limited view on what constitutes context. The efforts to attach information theory to wider social communication processes are hampered by a failure to show how systems can be appropriately amended. The two main problems within information science are structural. First, a failure to establish the framework for information theory that will serve information science as a whole: It is as if we do not really need a theory of information. Second, a failure to establish a convincing relationship between information, knowledge, and models of learning: It seems as if we are concentrating upon the technical and pragmatic tasks. It may be simply a feature of the practice of information science that we need to express our regret at the absence of grand theory of information, but are content to operate at the level of our own isolated technical problems.

This review shows a concentration in information science on modeling operations, rather than constructing and analyzing grand theory. We can build on the more vertically integrated analyses of data-information-knowledge and use more sophisticated explanations of the "water into wine" moment of information ingestion. If we build better representations of the knowledge that we claim to organize and retrieve for all users, we will improve our professional claim to resources from our society to do the job. However, as we make further attempts to tether the ass of information to the tree of knowledge, we should reflect that, until we know what it is that we cannot do without a theory of information, we will be unlikely to get one.

Acknowledgments

The author wishes to thank the editors and anonymous reviewers for their helpful and constructive comments, and to acknowledge the significant contribution they have made to this paper.

Bibliography

Agre, P. E. (1995). Institutional circuitry: Thinking about the forms and uses of information. *Information Technology and Libraries, 14,* 225–230.

Artandi, S. (1975). Theories of information. In N. R. Stevens (Ed.), *Essays for Ralph Shaw* (pp. 157–169). Metuchen, NJ: Scarecrow Press.

Baird, J. C. (1984). Information theory and information processing. *Information Processing & Management, 20,* 373–381.

Bar-Hillel, Y., & Carnap, R. (1953). Semantic information. In W. Jackson (Ed.), *Communication theory: Papers read at a symposium on "Applications of Communication Theory" held at the Institute of Electrical Engineers* (pp. 503–512). London: Butterworths.

Barnes, B. (1981). On the conventional character of knowledge and cognition. *Philosophy of the Social Sciences, 11,* 303–333.

Barwise, J., & Perry, J. (1983). *Situations and attitudes.* Cambridge, MA: MIT Press.

Belkin, N. J. (1978). Information concepts for information science. *Journal of Documentation, 34,* 55–85.

Belkin, N. J. (1990). The cognitive viewpoint in information science. *Journal of Information Science, 16,* 11–15.

Blair, D. C. (1990). *Language and representation in information retrieval.* New York: Elsevier.

Boyce, B. R., & Kraft, D. H. (1985). Principles and theories in information science. *Annual Review of Information Science and Technology, 20,* 153–178.

Brier, S. (1992). Information and consciousness: A critique of the mechanistic concept of information. *Cybernetics and Human Knowing, 1*(2/3), 71–94.

Brittan, A. (1998). Symbolic interactionism. In E. Craig (Ed.), *Routledge Encyclopedia of Philosophy,* pp. 243–245. London: Routledge.

Brookes, B. C. (1980). The foundations of information science. Part I. Philosophical aspects. *Journal of Information Science, 2,* 125–133.

Buckland, M. (1991). *Information and information systems.* New York: Praeger.

Casson, M. (1997). *Information and organization: A new perspective on the theory of the firm*. Oxford: Clarendon.

Cole, C. (1993). Shannon revisited: Information in terms of uncertainty. *Journal of the American Society for Information Science, 44*, 204–211.

Cole, C. (1994). Operationalizing the notion of information as a subjective construct. *Journal of the American Society for Information Science, 45*, 465–476.

Cole, C. (1997). Calculating the information content of an information process for a domain expert using Shannon's mathematical theory of communication: A preliminary analysis. *Information Processing & Management, 33*, 715–726.

Cornelius, I. (1996a). Information and interpretation. In P. Ingwersen & N. O. Pors (Eds.), *CoLIS 2: Second International Conference on Conceptions of Library and Information Science: Integration in perspective* (pp. 11–21). Copenhagen: Royal School of Librarianship.

Cornelius, I. (1996b). *Meaning and method in information studies*. Norwood, NJ: Ablex.

Cronin, B. (2000). Semiotics and evaluative bibliometrics. *Journal of Documentation, 56*, 440–453.

Debons, A. (1992). The measurement of knowledge. In T. Kinney (Ed.), *Proceedings of the 55th ASIS Annual Meeting*. (pp. 212–215). Medford, NJ: Learned Information.

De Mey, M. (1977). The cognitive viewpoint: Its development and scope. *CC 77: International Workshop on the Cognitive Viewpoint* (pp. xvi–xxxii). Ghent, Belgium: Ghent University.

Devlin, K. (1991). *Logic and information*. Cambridge: Cambridge University Press.

Dretske, F. I. (1981). *Knowledge and the flow of information*. Oxford: Basil Blackwell.

Evans, G. (1982). *Varieties of reference*. Oxford: Clarendon.

Fairthorne, R. (1967). Morphology of information flow. *Journal of the Association for Computing Machinery, 14*, 710–719.

Fiske, J. (1990). *Introduction to communication studies*. 2nd ed. London: Routledge.

Fontenot, K. A. (1995). Symbolic interactionism. In F. Magill (Ed.), *International encyclopedia of sociology* (Vol. 2, pp. 1399–1403). London: Fitzroy Dearborn.

Fox, C. J. (1983). *Information and misinformation*. Westport, CT: Greenwood Press.

Frické, M. (1998). Jean Tague-Sutcliffe on measuring information. *Information Processing & Management, 34*, 385–394.

Frohmann, B. (1992). The power of images: A discourse analysis of the cognitive viewpoint. *Journal of Documentation, 48*, 365–386.

Gabor, D. (1953). A summary of communication theory. In W. Jackson (Ed.), *Communication theory: Papers read at a symposium on "Applications of Communication Theory" held at the Institute of Electrical Engineers* (pp. 1–24). London: Butterworths.

Gluck, M. (1997). Making sense of semiotics: Privileging respondents in revealing contextual geographic syntax and semantic codes. In P. Vakkari, R. Savolainen, & B. Dervin, (Eds.), *Information seeking in context: Proceedings of an international conference on research in information needs, seeking, and use in different contexts, 14–16 August, 1996, Tampere, Finland* (pp. 53–66). London: Taylor Graham.

Godfrey-Smith, P. (1989). Misinformation. *Canadian Journal of Philosophy, 19*, 532–550.

Green, R. (1991). The profession's models of information: A cognitive linguistic analysis. *Journal of Documentation, 47*, 130–148.

Harmon, G. (1984). The measurement of information. *Information Processing & Management, 20*, 193–198.

Hayes, R. M. (1992). Measurement of information. In P. Vakkari & B. Cronin (Eds.), *Conceptions of library and information science: Historical, empirical and theoretical perspectives* (pp. 268–285). London: Taylor Graham.

Heilprin, L. B. (1989). Foundation of information science reexamined. *Annual Review of Information Science and Technology, 24*, 343–372.

Hjørland, B. (1997). *Information seeking and subject representation*. New York: Greenwood.

Hjørland, B. (1998). Theory and metatheory of information science: a new interpretation. *Journal of Documentation, 54*, 606–621.

Hjørland, B., & Albrechtsen, H. (1995). Towards a new horizon in information retrieval: Domain analysis. *Journal of the American Society for Information Science, 46*, 400–425.

Ingwersen, P. (1992). *Information retrieval interaction*. London: Taylor Graham.

Ingwersen, P. (1995). Information and information science. *Encyclopedia of library and information science* (Vol. 56, pp. 137–174). New York: Dekker.

Introna, L. D. (1997). *Management, information and power: A narrative of the involved manager*. London: Macmillan.

Jacob, E. K. & Shaw, D. (1998). Sociocognitive perspectives on representation. *Annual Review of Information Science and Technology, 33*, 131–185.

Kochen, M. (1984). Coding for recording and recall of information. *Information Processing & Management, 20*, 343–354.

Levi, I. (1984). Information and ignorance. *Information Processing & Management, 20*, 355–362.

Liebenau, J., & Backhouse, J. (1990). *Understanding information: An introduction*. London: Macmillan.

Losee, R. M. (1997). A discipline independent definition of information. *Journal of the American Society for Information Science, 48*, 254–269.

Luhmann, N. (1995). *Social systems*. Stanford, CA: Stanford University Press.

Machlup, F., & Mansfield, U. (1983). *The study of information: Interdisciplinary messages*. New York: Wiley.

MacKay, D. M. (1953). Generators of information. In W. Jackson (Ed.), *Communication theory: Papers read at a symposium on "Applications of*

Communication Theory" held at the Institute of Electrical Engineers (pp. 475–485). London: Butterworths.

MacKay, D. M. (1969). *Information, mechanism, and meaning*. Cambridge, MA: MIT Press.

MacKay, D. M. (1983). The wider scope of information theory. In F. Machlup & U. Mansfield (Eds.), *The study of information* (pp. 485–492). New York: Wiley.

Mandelbrot, B. (1953). An informational theory of the statistical structure of language. In W. Jackson (Ed.), *Communication theory: Papers read at a symposium on "Applications of Communication Theory"* held at the Institute of Electrical Engineers (pp. 486–502). London: Butterworths.

Meadow, C. T., & Yuan, W. (1997). Measuring the impact of information: Defining the concepts. *Information Processing & Management, 33*, 697–714.

Neill, S. D. (1992). *Dilemmas in the study of information: Exploring the boundaries of information science*. New York: Greenwood Press.

Otten, C. (1975). Information and communication: A conceptual model as framework for development of theories of information. In A. Debons, & W. J. Cameron (Eds.), *Perspectives in information science* (pp. 127–148). Leyden, Netherlands: Nordhoff.

Popper, K. (1972). *Objective knowledge: An evolutionary approach*. Oxford: Clarendon Press.

Putnam, H. (1975). How not to talk about meaning. In H. Putnam (Ed.), *Mind, language, and reality: Philosophical papers, volume 2* (pp. 117–131). Cambridge: Cambridge University Press.

Qvortrup, L. (1993). The controversy over the concept of information: An overview and a selected and annotated bibliography. *Cybernetics and Human Knowing, 1*(4), 3–24.

Ritchie, L. D. (1986). Shannon and Weaver: Unravelling the paradox of information. *Communication Research, 13*(2), 278–298.

Ritchie, L. D. (1991). *Information*. Newbury Park, CA: Sage.

Roberts, N. (1982). A search for information man. *Social Science Information Studies, 2*, 93–104.

Rudd, D. (1983). Do we really need World 3? Information science with or without Popper. *Journal of Information Science, 7*, 99–105.

Saracevic, T. (Ed.). (1970). *Introduction to information science*. New York: Bowker.

Saracevic, T. (1999). Information science. *Journal of the American Society for Information Science, 50*, 1051–1063.

Schramm, W. (1955). Information theory and mass communication. *Journalism Quarterly, 32*, 131–146.

Shannon, C. (1956). The bandwagon. *IRE Transactions on Information Theory, 2*(1), 3.

Shannon, C. E., & Weaver, W. (1949/1963). *The mathematical theory of communication*. Urbana-Champaign, IL: University of Illinois Press.

Shera, J. H., & Cleveland, D. B. (1977). History and foundation of information science. *Annual Review of Information Science and Technology, 12*, 249–275.

Sillince, J. A. A. (1995). A stochastic model of information value. *Information Processing & Management, 31,* 543–554.

Stokes, G. (1998). *Popper: Philosophy, politics and scientific method.* Oxford: Polity Press.

Stonier, T. (1997). *Information and meaning, an evolutionary perspective.* Berlin: Springer-Verlag.

Stonier, T. (1989). Towards a general theory of information II: Information and entropy. *Aslib Proceedings, 41*(2), 41–55.

Stryker, S. (1992). Symbolic interaction theory. In E. F. Borgatta & M. L Borgatta (Eds.), *Encyclopedia of sociology* (Vol. 4, pp. 2127–2134). New York: Macmillan.

Todd, R. J. (1999). Back to our beginnings: Information utilization, Bertram Brookes and the fundamental equation of information science. *Information Processing & Management, 35,* 851–870.

Tribus, M. (1983). Thirty years of information theory. In F. Machlup & U. Mansfield (Eds.), *The study of information* (pp. 475–484). New York: Wiley.

Vakkari, P. (1994). Library and information science: Its content and scope. *Advances in Librarianship, 18,* 1–55.

van Rijsbergen, C. J. (1996). Information, logic, and uncertainty in information science. In P. Ingwersen & N. O. Pors (Eds.), *CoLIS 2: Second International Conference on Conceptions of Library and Information Science: Integration in Perspective* (pp. 1–10). Copenhagen: Royal School of Librarianship.

van Rijsbergen, C. J., & Lalmas, M. (1996). Information calculus for information retrieval. *Journal of the American Society for Information Science, 47,* 385–398.

Vickery, B. C. (1997). Metatheory and information science. *Journal of Documentation, 53,* 457–476.

Wersig, G. (1993). Information science: The study of postmodern knowledge usage. *Information Processing & Management, 29,* 229–240.

Wersig, G. (1997). Information theory. In J. Feather & P. Sturges (Eds.), *Encyclopaedic Dictionary of Library and Information Science,* pp. 220–227. London: Routledge.

Wiener, N. (1961). *Cybernetics.* Cambridge, MA: MIT Press.

Wittgenstein, L. (1953). *Philosophical investigations.* (G. E. M. Anscombe, Trans.) New York: Macmillan.

Zhang Y. (1988). Definitions and sciences of information. *Information Processing & Management, 24,* 479–491.

Zunde, P., & Gehl, J. (1979). Empirical foundations of information science. *Annual Review of Information Science and Technology, 14,* 67–92.

CHAPTER 10

Social Informatics: Perspectives, Examples, and Trends

Steve Sawyer
Pennsylvania State University

Kristin R. Eschenfelder
University of Wisconsin-Madison

Introduction

What is social informatics? What are the problems, methods, and domains that help define social informatics research? What are the common findings that arise from this work? What does social informatics research provide for those who participate in the practice and conduct of research in the various fields that are information science? In this chapter, and responding to questions posed above, we do the following:

1. Define and explain what we, and others, mean by the term "social informatics" (Kling, 1999; 2000; Sawyer & Rosenbaum, 2000; Kling, Crawford, Rosenbaum, Sawyer, & Weisband, 2001).

2. Survey recent social informatics literature. This is an analytic survey, organized both by several common findings and by levels of analysis. In this survey we also expand on the work of Bishop and Star (1996) in *ARIST*, moving from the focal area of digital libraries to showcase the broad array of computing domains where social informatics inquiry is being pursued.

3. Discuss emerging trends, opportunities, and unexplored issues that social informatics highlights for curriculum development, practice, and research.

Thus, this chapter serves as an introduction to social informatics, as an illustrative survey of current trends and relevant contemporary research, and as a discussion of emerging trends. As we discuss here, social informatics is neither a theory nor a single domain. Social informatics research spans disciplines and research domains. Our particular interest in the relationships between uses of information and communication technologies (ICTs) and organizational effects determines the literatures we cite and examples we present.

What Is Social Informatics?

Social informatics is the term we use to represent a field of research focusing on the relationships between information and communications technologies and the larger social context in which these ICTs exist. Contemporary social informatics work spans issues of design, implementation, and use of ICTs in a wide range of social and organizational settings. This body of research includes analyses of the impacts of the social and organizational settings on the design, implementation, and uses of ICT; including the intended and unintended social and organizational consequences of ICT-enabled change and change efforts. Thus, social informatics research focuses on exploring, explaining, and theorizing about the socio-technical contexts of ICTs.

We use social informatics as a descriptor to represent research that shares a common perspective (and often common findings), but that is found in a range of disciplinary literatures. In this way, social informatics helps to give voice to common findings dispersed in various fields of research. By way of example, we present here three studies, each drawn from a different literature, focusing on different social settings and using different ICTs to showcase the commonalities of social informatics research.

First, Davis (1997) identifies and analyzes the key actors who influence digital library usage rates. She conceptualizes context as the organization surrounding and supporting the system. In her analysis she identifies players both inside and outside the university who shape the digital library system and its use. Further, she analyzes the relationships between these players in terms of the directions of influence between various people and entities. This approach highlights the wide range of actors and relationships that define system usability and use.

In another example, Walsham and Sahay (1999) draw on three years of field-based data collection, framed by contextualism, to explore the implementation and use of a geographic information system (GIS) in local government. Their analysis uses actor-network theory to show that, despite a relatively mature technology (the GIS package), reasonable project management, and organizational commitment, the implementation failed. The analysis demonstrates that this failure is driven by a set of events and factors that mutually shape, and are shaped by, the social milieu in which the GIS implementation took place.

In the third example, Etzioni and Etzioni (1999) focus on computer-mediated communication (CMC) and report that the creation of sustainable (stable) communities of participants (stakeholders) is critical to a CMC system. They explore the role of community and extend observations of behavior in face-to-face communities to their import for computer-mediated interactions. Their analysis maps aspects of community with features of ICTs that support computer-supported communities. In doing this they raise issues of both ICT design and ICT use, reflect on the ways that the social context formed by these communities shapes CMC use, and suggest several hybridized CMC designs that would better meet the needs of virtual communities.

The Davis (1997), Walsham and Sahay (1999), and Etzioni and Etzioni (1999) papers focus on different types of problems, look at different types of ICTs, draw on different literatures, use different theories, and are set in different contexts. However, these studies highlight similar conceptual issues, and their findings have much in common. For example, these studies suggest that ICT use leads to multiple and sometimes paradoxical effects. All three studies describe how ICT use shapes thought and action in ways that benefit some groups more than others and have differential effects. In addition, all three studies depict a reciprocal relationship between ICTs and their context. We return to each of these points in the section on social informatics themes.

In the rest of this section we outline common traits of social informatics research, present overviews of ways to conceptualize this work, and conclude with an explanation of what social informatics is not. In section two we discuss two important principles of social informatics in more depth: the importance of context and methodological pluralism. In section three we provide an overview of recent social informatics literature arranged by both the common findings introduced here and by levels of analysis. In section four we describe current trends in the social informatics literature, including theory use and development. We also suggest opportunities for extending social informatics principles into teaching and professional practice.

The Problem-Oriented Nature of Social Informatics

Social informatics work is problem oriented. Just as the human-computer interaction (HCI) literature reflects the problematic relationships between individuals and computers, and the computer-supported cooperative work (CSCW) literature reflects the problematic relationships between groups of people and computers, the social informatics literature reflects the problems that arise from the bidirectional relationship between social context and ICT design, implementation, and use. Social informatics research spans levels of analysis, often by making explicit links between particular levels of social analysis and the larger social milieu in which computing takes place. In this way, social informatics is similar to other areas of study, such as gerontology, software engineering, or urban studies, that are defined by domain-specific problems.

Empirical and Theory-Based Focus

Social informatics research is empirically focused, and is carried out to help make sense of the vexing issues people face when they work and live with computing. This work is set within the context of social milieux such as work groups, communities, cultural units, societies, and/or organizations, in which use of ICTs is increasingly important and pervasive. This orientation toward context helps to distinguish social informatics from other information science work that focuses on individual behaviors and/or draws on theories rooted in, for example, economics, computer science, or psychology.

Social informatics research is often characterized by its use of a wide range of social theories to engage context in a holistic manner. By using the term "social theory," we invoke a spectrum of perspectives that seeks to represent, define, and predict how humans enact and maintain social order, social structures, and social interaction (e.g., Ritzer, 1996; Sica, 1998, p. 10). The forms and meanings of social theory are, themselves, a field of vigorous inquiry, and there is not space in this chapter to engage in a detailed discussion of what social theory is. For those interested in exploring some of the most widely used social theories, see Ritzer (1996). For those interested in discussions of the roles, meanings, and roots of social theory, see Sica (1998).

To date, contemporary social theory has had a modest presence in studies of computing in organizations. Jones (2000) found that 4 percent of published research in information systems cited social theorists, with a large concentration of this work arising from scholarship in one particular community of scholars. However, social theory has a somewhat larger presence in the conceptualizations underlying studies of societal-level impacts of computing (e.g., Nardi & O'Day, 1999). Additionally, Pettigrew and McKechnie (2001) found that more than 45 percent of the library and information science literature cites social theories. However, many of the studies in this literature do not explicitly focus on the roles of ICTs and thus are not considered social informatics work. More broadly, ethno-methodologic approaches to the study of ICT use, such as ethnography, rely on social theory to ground the research.

A Means of Linking

Research into the bidirectional relationship between ICTs and their contexts spans many disciplines, including information science, communications, sociology, anthropology, information systems, management science, and library science. Often scholars work in one domain (such as hospital emergency rooms) without the knowledge that similar work, often leading to similar findings, is being done in another domain (such as software development groups). In this way, social informatics is an interdiscipline: its literature both spans and links some of the research from these dispersed fields. Further, while the term "social informatics" may be new, social informatics research is not new; researchers from these various fields have been studying the social and organizational aspects of ICTs for more than twenty years (Kling, 1980). This work falls under a range of conceptual labels including (but not limited to) the "social analysis of computing or technology," the "social impacts of computing or technology," "information policy," "computers/technology and society," and, more recently, "computer-mediated communication" (Kling, 1999, p. 1; Bishop & Star, 1996, p. 309). The sheer number of related fields, as well as the wide range of terms, means that the research findings and insights have been difficult for scholars and teachers to access (Kling et al., 2001, p. 12). Moreover, given this dispersion, it is possible for a scholar to contribute to the social informatics literature without ever having considered his work to be a part of this (or any larger) corpus of similar findings.

Ties to Informatics

The meaning of the term "social informatics" rests in part on the broad, evolving, and contested definition of informatics. By informatics we mean the study of information content, representation, technology, and the methods and strategies associated with its use (see Brookes, 1980). Informatics is a term commonly used outside North America to refer to a variety of computing research. While there is an ever-growing number of informatics research areas (e.g., medical informatics, legal informatics, and archive and museum informatics), this chapter focuses on social and organizational informatics.

Organizational informatics refers to those social informatics studies whose level of analysis is tied to formalized organizational or group boundaries. (We consider organizational informatics a subset of social informatics. For convenience, in the rest of this paper we use social informatics to denote *both* social and organizational informatics.) Social informatics arose as a descriptor through a series of discussions among like-minded researchers in the early 1990s. Often these conversations were led by, or included, Rob Kling, who maintains one of the most comprehensive social informatics sites on the Web, and whose work has been instrumental in coalescing social informatics into the interdiscipline we describe in this chapter. See www.slis.indiana.edu/SI for more discussion of informatics. This site, maintained by Rob Kling, contains a brief history on the emergence of the term and some key contributors. A link to a 1997, National Science Foundation (NSF)-sponsored workshop on social informatics points to a partial list of additional contributors who attended, commented on, or whose work directly shaped the workshop report. This workshop report can also be found at the Social Informatics Web site.

What, then, is social informatics? According to Kling (1999, p. 1), "A serviceable working conception of 'social informatics' is that it identifies a body of research that examines the social aspects of computerization. A more formal definition is the interdisciplinary study of the design, uses and consequences of information technologies that takes into account their interaction with institutional and cultural contexts."

What Social Informatics Is Not

Many fields besides social informatics provide insight into, and/or commentary on, the relationships between ICT use and the human condition. In this section, we highlight some of these approaches and explain how they differ from our conceptualization of the inclusive literature we represent as social informatics.

A theory. Like HCI and CSCW, social informatics is best seen as a large and growing federation of scholars focused on common problems. There is no single theory of social informatics and there is no claim being made that the research in this field is pursuing one particular theoretical notion. Currently, there are many theories being used by social informaticians, and we return to this point in section two. In section four we point to some contemporary work oriented toward theory building. However, even from the most charitable perspective, social informatics is not a theory.

Information without technology. Studies that investigate the information contexts of people are certainly relevant to social informaticians. But, without the explicit recognition and analysis of the roles of ICTs in these information worlds, they do not fall within the broad boundaries we draw for the social informatics field. For example, Chatman's (1996, 1999) studies of the information world of the working poor and prisoners explored how social status affects information seeking and sharing between the information-poor "outsiders" and information "insiders." However, the absence of explicit insights into the roles (or lack of roles) of ICTs in these information-seeking social contexts puts her work on the soft and permeable "boundary space" that we use to help define social informatics research. In placing this work outside the boundaries of social informatics, we do not suggest that it is not valuable; social informaticians and other researchers will both draw on and enjoy such work. Our point is simply that there is a difference between social informatics research and other forms of research that explicitly involve context.

Cognitive psychology. Studies that address the individual/psychological or cognitive processes of people using ICTs are not likely to be seen as social informatics research. For instance, Kuhlthau (1991) focuses on the impact of affective factors on an individual's information search process. This work treats social context as peripheral and downplays the importance of levels of analysis beyond the individual. However, in many studies, particularly those that focus on nonexperimental settings, the importance of context becomes more central and the levels of analysis are blurred. For example, in his research on HCI issues in digital library use, Dillon (2000) draws on cognitive science but makes explicit links to the roles of both other individuals and the larger context. Nosek and McNeese (1997), in their research on CSCW among pilots, take a similar approach to make explicit links to the role of context.

Economics. Most contemporary economic analyses of computing decontextualize the uses of ICTs, and in doing so cannot contribute to the social informatics literature. However, there are exceptions. For instance, Schmitz (2000) argues for the importance of context in theories of disintermediation. And, as Swedberg (1994) argues, markets must both arise from, and exist in, social contexts: People choose to have a market and through their informal and formal interactions these exist.

Direct effects (or tool) approach. Direct effects models underlay the earliest and often most simplistic efforts to anticipate the social consequences of computerization in organizations (see, for example, Negroponte, 1997). Laudon and Marr (1996) argue that the direct effects model has a strong appeal to researchers because of the seemingly "natural" causality implied by the effects of computerization on organizational structure and process. They point to researchers who have argued that, for example, the introduction of computers into organizations will lead directly to the elimination of middle management jobs because their information handling roles will be taken over by the machines. However, these studies have little to offer social informatics, given their relatively simple view of how people interact with the ICTs.

Punditry and futurizing. In addition, social informatics differs from other nonacademic commentary about ICTs and society. One of the more common forms is futurizing: glossy conceptualizations of the future impacts of ICTs on society with little (or only anectdotal) support (e.g., Toffler, 1991). This, and other forms of futurizing, may often be both thought-provoking and popular, but their prophesies are rarely validated by empirical study and may be misleading. For example, the rapid rise of the Internet's use has led to many predictions of sweeping social and industrial change. However, empirical studies challenge the simple notion that information easily available on the Internet will lead to rampant disintermediation in many industries, and especially those that are "information intensive" (Crowston, Sawyer & Wigand, in press; Sarkar, Butler & Steinfield, 1995). Perhaps the clearest way to distinguish social informatics from futurizing and punditry is that the former has a clearly articulated conceptual basis, uses rigorous research methods, and supports findings by presenting empirical data.

The Foundations of Social Informatics

In this section we outline two principles of social informatics: the importance of social context and methodological pluralism. Social informatics researchers begin by acknowledging the complex and mutually interdependent set of relationships among ICT uses and social contexts (Abbott, 1995; Argyres, 1999; Kling, 1980). Therefore, understanding ICTs requires that social informatics researchers conduct in-depth analysis of the larger social and/or organizational context. To conduct these analyses, social informatics researchers draw on different empirical approaches, acknowledging that this plurality of perspectives will yield rich understandings of ICTs' roles in work and life. Thus, a broad range of epistemological orientations (in terms of both research purpose and method), can contribute to this literature.

The Roles of the Social Context

The mutual interdependence of ICTs and social context frames social informatics research. By social context we mean a holistic sense of interaction among levels of social analysis, and the particular characteristics that help to define any given level of analysis. These characteristics act as forces on the various levels of analysis and provide the backdrop and perspective from which an understanding of the problem of interest can be developed. The exact nature of the social context is intimately related to the problem of interest: studies focused on regional implementation patterns of GIS (Walsham & Sahay, 1999) will depict context differently from studies that explore ways to improve specific work processes with information technology (Bostrom & Heinen, 1978a, 1978b). This suggests that the characterization of, and factors of interest within, context will vary and the researcher must set out the levels of analysis and factors through either *a priori* depiction or *post hoc* description.

Some theorists have conceptualized context as comprised of interdependent and multilevel networks of socio-technical links (Castells, 1991; MacKenzie & Wajcman, 1999). Others characterize context differently; for example, Covi's (1999) "material mastery" focuses on sets of institutionalized beliefs, values, and practices. However, all social informatics research will represent social context. We return to this issue in the section on social informatics themes.

Research that reduces the larger social context to one or two variables, such as level of uncertainty in the environment or some other surrogate, is not typically considered social informatics. For example, Berthon, Pitt, and Morris's (1998) study of problem perception analyzed the impact of individual and organizational variables on managers' perceptions of different types of problems. Organizational variables included a dichotomous job function variable and a dichotomous level of management variable. While the narrow operational definition of these variables may have aided parsimony (one of the study's goals), it limited the degree to which the study could provide insight about the context of the managers. However, factor-based studies that provide a richer picture of context can contribute to social informatics.

As stated above, social informatics researchers explicitly acknowledge that ICTs are conceived, developed, configured, and/or used within a nuanced and interdependent socio-technical system (Lamb & Kling, in press). Thus, ICTs are in a relationship of mutual shaping with context (Bijker, 1995; Orlikowski & Baroudi, 1991). For example, the embedded nature of ICTs influences the ways people develop them, the kinds of workable configurations they propose, and how they implement and use ICTs. Further, the presence of ICTs influences the ways people interact, how they structure their work and activities, and how they construct or imagine their worlds. We return to this point in the section on social informatics themes.

Methodological Pluralism

Social informatics research is characterized by a pluralistic approach to the conduct of inquiry. It is pluralistic in that it is not method specific. Social informatics researchers employ a variety of methods, ranging from the observational studies of Suchman (1996), to secondary data analysis (Kling, 1980), surveys (Attewell & Battle, 1999), and multiple methods (Crowston et al., in press). In this way social informatics differs from fields such as operations research or linguistic analysis that are defined by their methodologies. Still, while there is no prescribed method, much of the research draws on qualitative approaches including participant observation, interviews, ethnography, archival record collection, and other forms of fieldwork.

Social informatics research is further characterized by the inclusion of normative, analytical, and critical orientations. The *normative orientation* refers to research that aims to recommend alternatives for professionals who design, implement, use, or make policy about ICTs. This type of research has an explicit goal of influencing practice by providing empirical evidence illustrating the varied outcomes that occur as people work with ICTs. The normative orientation is evident in a wide range of organizational and social contexts. For example, much of the work in participatory design focuses on identifying the nuanced ways in which users come to understand and adapt how they work through complex sociotechnical relationships (e.g., Beyer & Holtzblatt, 1997; Wynn, 1979).

The *analytical orientation* refers to studies that develop theories about ICTs in institutional and cultural contexts, or to empirical studies that are designed to contribute to such theorizing. This type of research seeks to contribute to a deeper understanding of how the evolution of ICT use in a particular setting can be generalized to other ICTs and other settings. One example is Kling's (1980) depiction of various perspectives on ICT use in organizations. The previously discussed Walsham and Sahay (1999) study of an Indian government ministry's problems in adopting GIS technology is another.

The *critical orientation* means examining ICTs from perspectives that do not automatically and uncritically adopt the goals and beliefs of the groups that commission, design, or implement specific ICTs. The critical orientation is possibly the most novel (Agre & Schuler, 1997). It encourages information professionals and researchers to examine ICTs from multiple perspectives, such as those of the various people who use them, as well as people who design, implement, or maintain them. The critical orientation also advocates examination of possible failure modes and service losses. As an example, Suchman (1996) examined the failure of an expert system designed to completely automate the task of coding documents used as evidence in civil litigation. She examined the work of clerks who carried out this coding work and learned that it often required more complex judgments than could be made by rule-based expert systems. She recommended that the new information systems be designed to help the clerks with their work rather than to replace them. This critical orientation often challenges commonly held assumptions about the roles, values, and design features embedded into ICTs.

Social Informatics Themes

In this section we review contemporary literature organized around several common findings that arise from social informatics work:

1. ICT uses lead to multiple and sometimes paradoxical effects.
2. ICT uses shape thought and action in ways that benefit some groups more than others and these differential effects often have moral and ethical consequences.
3. A reciprocal relationship exists between ICT design, implementation, use and the context in which these occur.

These items are organized to reflect the way the social contexts are developed (in Table 10.1 on p. 447). The articles surveyed in this section showcase social informatics inquiry across a range of research streams including scientific/scholarly communications, museum informatics, ICT implementation, ICT use, and information/IT policy studies. As a basis for this review, we begin with, and expand upon, Bishop and Star's work on the social informatics of digital libraries (Bishop & Star, 1996; Bishop, Buttenfield & Van House, in press).

We chose articles to include in the survey from the following journals from the years 1996–2000: *Communications of the ACM, D-Lib Magazine, Information Processing & Management, The Information Society, Information Systems Research, Information Technology & People, Journal of the American Society for Information Science, Library & Information Science Research*, and *MIS Quarterly*. As Ellis, Allen, and Wilson (1999) note, the topics, approaches, and concepts in information science and in information systems overlap, although the literature often does not. Clearly, social informatics research appears in a wide range of journals outside this list: We opted to limit our search to journals that (a) regularly carry social informatics-related research, (b) reflect our own particular research domains (as discussed in the introduction to this chapter), and (c) are widely recognized across the diverse fields that comprise the information sciences. There are a number of books and anthologies that serve to both collect and represent the social informatics literature that did not fall within the boundaries of our literature sampling frame. Additional pertinent references include: Agre and Schuler (1997); Borgman (2000); Brown and Duguid (2000); Davenport (1997); Kling (1996); Kling, Rosenbaum, and Hert (1998); those listed in the appendix of Kling et al. (in press); MacKenzie and Wajcman (1999); and Nardi and O'Day (1999).

We first selected articles based on abstract and index searches for key terms such as social informatics, social context, social impacts, contextual factors, and social factors. (In selecting these papers we did not require that the articles made explicit use of a sociological theory.) We narrowed the results of these searches by removing those articles that dealt with context in a peripheral or overly narrow manner (see sections above on "What Social Informatics is Not" and "The Roles of the Social Context" for more explanation). From this subset of articles, we present examples from different journals, subject areas, and authors that help us to illuminate the breadth and value of social informatics research. We want to emphasize that this review does not include all possible examples of social informatics research that appear in these journals. Inclusion and discussion of all articles were not possible given space constraints. Further, the very nature of social informatics as an interdiscipline suggests that, at this stage of our awareness of the linkages between the various contributing literatures, an exhaustive summary is not possible.

Common Finding #1: ICT uses lead to multiple and sometimes paradoxical effects

Social informatics studies highlight the complex outcomes of ICT use in two ways. First, they show that a particular ICT's impacts are rarely isolated to a targeted area, but rather spread to a much larger number of people through the socio-technical links that constitute context. Second, these studies typically highlight unforeseen and unintended outcomes, which, in many cases, may be contrary to the original intentions for the adoption of the ICT. One example of the far-reaching and unintended effects of ICT practice is Adams and Sasse's (1999) investigation of work practices and environments that contribute to improper use of passwords. Their findings challenge the idea that organizations can achieve greater system security through use of strict security regulations such as periodic forced password changes, multiple unique passwords for different systems, and requirements for non-dictionary-word-based passwords. They suggest that more strenuous security measures may in fact decrease overall security. In explaining their thesis, they describe both contextual and cognitive factors leading to password misuse. For instance, they explain how certain types of work tasks encourage group sharing of passwords, e.g., if a workgroup is sharing access to a particular set of files. In these instances, the security mechanisms interfered with the group-based nature of their work. That is, required use of individual passwords interfered with the work done by the employees. The study suggests that security applications developers and departments need to improve their understanding of work practices in order to develop applications and processes that comport with work practices.

In a second example of the far-reaching and unintended consequences of ICTs, Walsham (1998) reports how the use of groupware, ostensibly designed to improve communication, may actually harm group interactions. Participating pharmaceutical sales representatives reported that the software did help to achieve one of the intended goals: use lessened the need for face-to-face communications as certain interactions could be done electronically. Through analysis of the social context surrounding the system, Walsham also reports that reduction in face-to-face time harmed overall group communication by removing opportunities for social networking and relationship building.

Attewell and Battle's (1999) study of the impact of home computer use on academic test scores shows how ICT use does not automatically lead to desired outcomes. Their study challenges the assumption that increasing home computer ownership rates will decrease education score discrepancies between different socio-economic groups. Their findings suggest that home PC ownership may in fact lead to increasing gaps between the academic test scores of a number of groups including boys and girls, affluent and poor children, and whites and ethnic minorities. Given the limitations of the data used in the analysis, Attewell and Battle cannot fully explain the resulting academic test score differences. They speculate, however, that contextual issues such as parental involvement play a role.

In a fourth example of the far-reaching and unintended impacts of ICTs, Frissen (2000) reports how actual and perceived use of ICTs differs within busy, dual-career Dutch families. She reports that while marketers promote ICTs as time and coordination problem solvers, Dutch families do not perceive them as such, even though data show that some ICTs are used by the participants for these purposes. Frissen explores the micro-social context of these families and her analysis shows how the family context shapes both ICT use and perceptions of ICT value. While Frissen reports that her participants did use ICTs for coordination purposes (e.g., calling the day care center via cell phone while in a traffic jam to inform them of delay), most of the participants saw the main values of ICTs as preparing children for the future and appearing modern.

Frissen's study also illustrates the pervasiveness of ICT impacts. Participants feared ICT intrusion upon "caring time" or time spent in family or social activities. Uses of ICTs intruded on this time by blurring work and home (e.g., clients calling on weekends, faxes at home, checking e-mail at home). The use of ICTs also led to social *faux pas* by interrupting social events (e.g., cell phone ringing during lunch with friends). Participants also reported a social stigma attached to ICTs, as some considered it embarrassing to own an "expensive toy." Based on this study, Frissen suggests that marketing schemes to promote the family coordination view of ICT use are misguided, as family members do not perceive ICTs as coordination tools.

Similar findings arise in studies of coordination within formal organizations. Eschenfelder, Heckman, and Sawyer (1998) report on how a group listserv, originally designed to promote sharing of information, became a social testing ground. Instead of freely sharing knowledge with other members across the listserv, members used the listserv to informally evaluate each other by judging the astuteness and appropriateness of posted questions and answers. This evaluation led to the development of cliques, as members chose with whom they wished to share information, and the concentration of knowledge-sharing among members of a clique instead of across all members of the list.

At the societal level of analysis, Larsen (1999) examined the role of context in the failed adoption of electronic voting systems in the United States and Norway. In the Norwegian case study, use of an electronic voting system, instead of leading to more speedy and accurate returns, resulted in a disputed election outcome. Quite simply, ICT use did not reduce voting turmoil. Such empirical evidence stands in stark contrast to the claims of many pundits who seek to promote new voting technologies in the U.S. in response to poor system performance in the 2000 presidential elections.

While most research articles tend to focus on the unexpected, negative consequences of ICT use, several studies have documented positive, unintended consequences. For instance, Curry and Curtis (2000) report that increased branch library connectivity to the Internet has decreased reference service discrepancies between high-resource and low-resource branches (as all librarians have access to online reference sources). Connectivity has also improved inter-library loan services as branches have been able to communicate with each other more effectively to coordinate material loans. In another example, Marty (2000) documents how the creation of a museum collections database to facilitate curator/exhibit designer communication during construction of a new building led to the development of a Web-based virtual museum. And, the pervasiveness of the new ICTs also positively influenced other staff members' work. For instance, Web media created new opportunities and avenues for the museum's education office.

In summary, these examples serve to illustrate the first common finding of social informatics research: ICT uses have both far-reaching and unexpected outcomes. This implies that we should not assume that it is possible to fully understand the impacts of a particular ICT application. It is likely that any given ICT will shape elements not immediately adjacent to it through connections of socio-technical links. Further, we cannot always expect that ICTs will have the (positive *or* negative) effect we might predict.

Common Finding #2: ICTs shape thought and action in ways that benefit some groups more than others and these differential effects often have moral and ethical consequences

The basis of our second common finding is that ICTs act as socio-cognitive structures that shape thought and action. Following Ritzer (1996), we understand structure to include both large-scale social structures that shape interaction and micro-structures involved in individual human interaction. Some social informatics researchers have found that these structures shape thought and action in ways that benefit some groups over others, and that this structural favoritism often has moral and/or ethical consequences.

For example, Introna and Nissenbaum (2000) challenge the assumption that search engines are unbiased indexers and deliverers of Web page links and that all relevant pages have an equal chance of appearing as the result of a search. Through a review of commercial search engine architectures, Introna and Nissenbaum show how the then-current configuration of Internet search engines favored some Web pages over others. They explain how search engines and Web indexes include only a portion of all possible pages on the Web. They assert that the index/selection process is largely governed by market-like forces. For instance, robot-based search engines may index only pages linked to by a large number of already-indexed Web pages. This limits results to very popular (frequently linked) sites. In another example, manually indexed, or expert-based Web indexes (e.g., Yahoo!), may agree to index pages faster for a fee. Thus, organizations able to pay the fee can arrange to have their material readily accessible more quickly.

Introna and Nissenbaum further note that more financially established organizations are better able to purchase the design expertise required to shape Web pages in order to maximize their likelihood of being indexed. The search engines' subsequent biased indexing of Web resources shapes the types of information that searchers retrieve and use in favor of large organizations, commercial organizations, and other mainstream information resources. The search engine designs also place grassroots, small-scale, alternative, and/or controversial Web pages at a disadvantage. Recognizing the potential political consequences of search engines as social structures, Introna and Nissenbaum argue that society should not rely on market mechanisms to shape development of search engines and Web indexes.

As an example of organizational-level structures, Boudreau and Robey (1996) use meta-analysis to support their critical analysis of literature about business process re-engineering (BPR). The resulting findings challenge many of the technological-deterministic assumptions about BPR and its results. Most relevant to this discussion, they investigate the assumption that BPR empowers employees. Their analysis suggests that BPR typically subjects employees to greater surveillance or oversight. Often BPR efforts manipulate employee attitudes and beliefs in order to develop cultural conformity within the organization. Further, BPR often legitimizes layoffs and other staff reductions. Also, BPR efforts tend to decrease the job security of those who remain employed. Moreover, BPR efforts attack employees' sense of self-worth by changing the ways they are evaluated, rewarded, and supervised. This suggests that BPR acts as a structure to legitimize organizational activities that are likely to penalize certain groups.

In another example using organization as context, Curry and Curtis (2000) review how the structural configuration of the Canadian provincial government telecommunications systems penalized certain rural branch libraries attempting to obtain and maintain Internet access services. They note that libraries in regions with highly centralized governments and library administrations typically enjoyed access to government-sponsored Internet service providers (ISPs). Libraries in regions with decentralized governments and library administrations did not, and therefore had to receive service from available private ISPs. Libraries in isolated areas did not have a large selection of ISPs.

Consequently, these libraries sometimes suffered poor service including busy signals, server outages, and unexpected losses of service when a provider went out of business without notification. Their findings illustrated how provincial government telecommunications resources structured the libraries' access to ISP services, and subsequently the level of service they were able to offer their patrons. Similar findings arise in studies of informal communities' ICT use. For instance, Goerwitz (1997) describes the dilemma of building a nondenominational Web-based index to the Bible. He reports that certain index terms or arrangements are ideologically loaded, and thus their inclusion or exclusion may be offensive to one religious group or another.

Clement and Halonen (1998) show how ICT practice can advantage one group over another. They use a Social Construction of Technology (SCOT) approach to examine how user groups and information systems specialists in a large utility company differed in their conceptualizations of a "good" system and good systems development practice. According to Clement and Halonen, for the users, a good system was customized for different offices such that use required minimum knowledge of office-specific codes. Good development practice required code customization for each office; resulting in the existence of multiple unique versions of the software and a great deal of ad hoc programming. From the information systems perspective, good systems development practice required standardization, version control, and minimal code changes. This approach led to the creation of a less user-friendly system that required more end-user expertise.

Clement and Halonen's study also showcases the ways in which different conceptualizations of a good system, and good systems development practices, benefit one group more than another. User groups favored the ad hoc, customized development practices because they resulted in a more flexible, customizable, user-friendly system. The information systems group preferred a more structured, systematized approach to development because it resulted in a more easily manageable software product.

What is common across the ICTs, levels of analysis, and context/problem domains in these studies is the differential effects that ICTs have on existing social groups. Such findings suggest that researchers should be sensitive to the fact that ICTs are part of an evolving social world. New ICTs do not arrive in a vacuum, and existing ICTs are often used to reinforce, not reduce, existing differences in social status, power, and structure.

Common Finding #3: A reciprocal relationship exists between ICTs/ICT practice and context

The third common finding that arises from contemporary social informatics literature is that there is a reciprocal (bidirectional) shaping between ICTs and socio-technical context. That is, social informatics research often leads to discussion of how context shapes ICTs or ICT uses, and how these ICTs and ICT uses shape their contexts. In this section, we examine how the selected articles address the reciprocal shaping between ICTs and their contexts. In Table 10.1 we summarize the treatment of reciprocal shaping in the reviewed literature. From this it is clear that few studies have examined how ICTs shape context, and even fewer studies have used a bidirectional analysis.

The works cited provide an analysis of the treatment of context and shaping in the sampled social informatics literature. Since we could not include every possible social informatics article in this review, the contents of Table 10.1 provide a necessarily limited analysis. We determined directionality by assessing whether the article addressed shaping in one direction or another, or both in a significant manner. For instance, we did not count articles as bidirectional if the vast majority of the article discussed one direction of shaping and one small paragraph addressed the other. The articles we cite as bidirectional had both a significant discussion of context's shaping of ICTs and significant discussion of the impacts of ICTs on context.

This simple analysis shows that the current social informatics literature tends to emphasize context's shaping of ICT design, implementation, and use. We posit three explanations for this pattern. First, the emphasis on context's shaping of ICTs may stem from the theories used by the authors. Some theories contain a tacit "impacts OF context" directionality emphasis. For instance, the SCOT (Social Construction of Technology) approach aims to understand how social groups create facts or truths, and how technology gains its meaning through social interactions (Clement & Halonen, 1998). Similarly, the Social Shaping of Technology

**Table 10.1 The treatment of shaping directionality
in the social informatics literature**

Contexts Shape ICT Design, Implementation, and Use	ICT Design, Implementation, and Use Shape Context	Bidirectional Shaping between Context and ICT Design, Implementation, and Use
Adams & Sasse, 1999	Martin, 1998	Attewell & Battle, 1999
Boudreau & Robey, 1996	Watson et al., 1999	Barrett & Walsham, 1999
Clement & Halonen, 1998		Introna & Nissenbaum, 2000
Covi, 1999		Larsen, 1999
Curry & Curtis, 2000		Marty, 2000
Eschenfelder et al., 1998		Walsham, 1998
Frissen, 2000		
Goerwitz, 1997		
Kling & McKim, 2000		
Kumar et al., 1998		
Soloway et al., 2000		
Walsham & Sahay, 1999		
Ward et al., 2000		

(SST) approach challenges the technologically determinist assumption that technology and technological change "exist as an independent factor, impacting on society from outside of society" (MacKenzie & Wajcman, 1999, p. 5). Instead, it explores how context shapes creation and use of technology. At this point however, it is important to note that many of the studies in the "impacts OF context" use theories other than SCOT and SST. Therefore, theoretical influence is not a complete explanation of the observed patterns of shaping directionality in the literature.

The pattern may also be an artifact of what Talja, Keso, and Pietiläinen (1999) call the behaviorist approach to representing context. This tradition, strong in both library and information science and information systems work, uses context, traditionally described in terms of contextual factors, to explain some desired phenomenon. The research tradition of using context to explain a desired phenomenon, such as ICT implementation success or ICT use, may shape how information science researchers think about shaping and directionality.

Finally, the greater number of "impacts OF context" articles may, to some extent, stem from self-reinforcement. Because of the large number of impacts on context articles, researchers have fewer "impacts ON context" or bidirectional context articles to draw on as examples.

Context Shapes ICT Design, Implementation, and Use

As indicated in Table 10.1, the vast majority of the sampled literature focused on impacts of context on ICTs. For example, Walsham and Sahay's (1999) study of GIS system implementation makes clear how social context complicated implementation within Indian regional government agencies. They discuss how Indian culture, regional government organization, and academic traditions discouraged adoption of the designed GIS. Walsham and Sahay's analysis highlights how the information-oriented/rational decision making that is built into the GIS system ("the scientific") clashes with the intuitive/relationship-based decision making traditional to India ("the political"). They further note a lack of spatial/map traditions in India. Thus, the presentation of diverse data sets on one map clashes with the tradition of separateness and project independence of Indian regional government offices. Further, the frequent movement of district-level administrators complicated efforts to gain support for the GIS project. As one administrator would become interested, he or she would be transferred somewhere else. Additionally, while Indian scientific institutions were quite interested in being involved in GIS development, they were not interested in assisting with project implementation.

Kling and McKim (2000) use an SST perspective to examine electronic scientific communications fora such as preprint servers and online publishing sites. The authors' analysis challenges the popular cultural assumption that all scientific communications will inevitably move to electronic media. Through a comparison of three scholarly fields (high energy physics, molecular biology, and information systems) they explore how the heterogeneity of communications practices within these disciplines shapes the development and use of their electronic media. Analysis reveals four important and overlapping contextual influences on scientific electronic media development and use: research project costs, mutual visibility of ongoing work in the field, degree of industrial integration, and degree of concentration of communications channels (especially journals).

Soloway et al. (2000) explain teachers' nonadoption of computing into their curricula and lesson plans in terms of contextual factors. For example, teachers are hesitant to make their lesson plans dependent on technologies that are currently unstable. Soloway et al. paint a picture of educational computer use where, in any given school, computers might not be working on any given day. The instability occurs because the schools cannot provide sufficient IT support to keep classroom or class lab personal computers (PCs) up and running. The researchers explain this lack of support in terms of the historical emphasis on administrative computing support. The authors suggest that schools employ more stable, thin client PCs that allow children access only to keyboards and monitors, and that schools configure computers so that students cannot change the settings.

Covi (1999) investigates how the social characteristics of scholarly research shape the use of materials in a digital library. Drawing from her analysis of the uses of digital library resources by academics from four different fields (molecular biology, sociology, computer science, and literary theory), Covi highlights differences in scholars' uses of resources in terms of a "material mastery" framework with three components: search strategies, selection skills, and field integration. Findings indicate that differences in digital library resource use are due to differences in work characteristics across the four fields. For example, she compares the search strategies of the different academic groups and how they shape the use of digital resources. The emphasis on priority of discovery in biology, leads the molecular biologists to use digital library resources routinely to scan databases of key journals for relevant articles. In contrast, literary theorists rarely made use of online databases, but would use the online catalog for library collections. Analysis indicates that literary theorists do not use online databases for several reasons. First, the databases do not make use of the highly specialized vocabularies developed in literary theory and thus cannot produce very precise search results. Second, many literary theorists rely on mainly well-known primary texts for their work and thus do not need to search journals. Third, literary theorists tended to purchase the books most relevant for their information needs, thus reducing their use of library materials.

These findings suggest that increasing digital library usage will require greater understanding of the search strategies, selection skills, and field integration techniques of different user groups. Covi (1999, p. 312), states "digital libraries will be used only when workers can readily integrate them into social legitimated and legitimate-able ways of working." Her research illustrates how the structuring of the ICT affects its use. In other words, depending on how the digital library is structured, different groups may find it more or less helpful, and may use it more or less frequently. Covi's suggestion that we incorporate the socially legitimated material mastery skills of major user groups into digital library design shows how the social context of an ICT may, in turn, shape the structure of that ICT.

Ward, Wamsley, Schroeder, and Robins (2000) investigate the assumption that ICT use promotes autonomy, organizational change, and greater government responsiveness. In an historical analysis of ICT implementation and use at the U.S. Federal Emergency Management Administration (FEMA), they explain how existing control structures within the agency shape ICT budgeting. The resulting systems reinforce existing power structures in the organization. The article explains that the Reagan/Bush administration's emphasis on national security led to the allocation of most FEMA ICT resources to civilian defense-related projects and the location of the agency IRM (information resources management) office under the civilian defense division. Analysis highlights how this allocation process left other parts of the agency, including the disaster planning division, suffering for lack of IT resources and unable to deal effectively with major U.S. natural disasters such as hurricane Hugo, hurricane Andrew, or the Loma Prieta earthquake. Ward et al. conclude that government investment in ICTs does not automatically produce greater responsiveness, as the larger social context shapes the programs in which the ICTs are used.

Finally, Kumar, van Dissel, and Bielli (1998) challenge the assumption that commonly espoused theories such as rational systems theory and segmented institutionalism can fully explain ICT-related phenomena in distinctly different cultures. They argue that cultural values such as trust, the role of history, and social connections shape interactions with ICTs in ways that Northern European and North American theories cannot explain. The authors examine the failed implementation of an inter-organizational communications and coordination system designed for the textile industry in Prato, Italy. Kumar et al. posit that the system failed because it offered no new value to the organizations. The authors explain that the system was designed to reduce transaction costs and facilitate communications. But transaction costs between organizations were already very low due to high levels of trust between the organizations. Further, traditional communications patterns, such as face-to-face visits and informal meetings during evening strolls in town, offered much higher media richness than the communications mechanisms the new system provided.

ICT Design, Implementation, and Use Shapes Context

As Table 10.1 indicates, we found few examples of studies that emphasized how ICTs shape context. One such example is the Watson, Akselsen, Evjemo, and Aarsæther (1999) study of how a new, communications-oriented information system, used by thirty-three locally elected officials in Norway, undermined the authority of the most senior and powerful representatives. Prior to the implementation of the information systems, senior elected officials had largely controlled communication between political party members and across party lines. The authors describe how the new information dissemination tools allowed marginalized or less powerful representatives to use the systems' e-mail and electronic discussions to disseminate their views. Further, using the new system, members began to establish contacts across party lines independent of the party leadership. Thus, use of the new system threatened existing power structures as senior members no longer controlled communication paths. The researchers note that the project was cancelled, in spite of its being labeled a success by those involved, so long-term impacts are not observable.

Martin (1998) examines the impact of investments in ICTs (specifically computing and communications equipment) on the information technology workforce. Drawing on U.S. census data, Martin shows that employment in the IT sector is experiencing much slower growth, and may have reached the peak of its growth curve. Martin draws on three related "technological underemployment" theories to explain this. The three theories—productivity increases, hierarchical reduction, and polarization—explain how ICTs shape the job market. For instance, productivity increases theory would suggest that, while ICT use may increase worker efficiency such that fewer workers are needed, product demand may also increase; thereby maintaining or increasing the overall need for workers. Hierarchical reduction theory posits that ICTs replace many middle management data collection, manipulation, and reporting functions, flattening the organization. Polarization theory suggests that ICT use may increase demand for highly skilled nonroutine information manipulation workers, but reduce demand for low-skilled routine information workers. This combination of job expansion and contraction would result in the observed slower growth rate.

Bidirectional Shaping Between Context and ICT Design, Implementation, and Use

Table 10.1 indicates that fewer studies employed a significant bidirectional analysis of shaping between context and ICT design, implementation, and use. In one example, Barrett and Walsham (1999), and Walsham (1998) examine ICTs and professional work identity, especially within the insurance brokerage industry. From the ICT-shapes-context side, they examined how an online bidding system would change insurance brokerage work. In particular, they looked at how the ICT uses changed the nature of the interactions between insurance brokers and some other party. The system was designed to replace face-to-face negotiations between brokers and underwriters, with parties bidding on projects through the system. From the context-shapes-ICT perspective, Barrett and Walsham analyzed how the traditions of the brokerage industry eventually led to the reconfiguration of the system such that it did not replace the face-to-face negotiations, but rather served as a record-keeping system for the results of these negotiations. The brokers rejected the online bidding system because they needed to have visual and voice contact with the other parties involved in the negotiations.

Several previously discussed studies also use a bidirectional approach. For instance, Introna and Nissenbaum (2000) discuss how Web-indexing norms shape the information that the public receives through commercial search engines. They also, however, critique the market assumptions that currently shape search engine design, while Marty's (2000) study of a digital museum discusses both how the context of constructing a museum database shaped the creation of a virtual museum and how the new digital environment changed the work of some of the museum's staff. Finally, Larsen (1999) analyzed how the failure of an electronic voting system had an impact on the perceived level of legitimacy of an election and how voters' expectations about voting and traditional voting system configurations shaped their willingness to accept electronic voting systems. For instance, Larsen tells of how one voter's dissatisfaction with the limited level of privacy provided by a new system led him to use an umbrella to shield himself while voting.

Context and Levels of Analysis in the Social Informatics Literature

In this final section we seek to further characterize how the current social informatics literature treats context by examining the levels of analysis at which authors conceptualize context (see Table 10.2). The cited literature reflects the diverse range of contexts in which social informatics research is found.

As noted earlier in this chapter, social informatics scholars conceptualize context as socio-technical networks of influences. They recognize that these networks exist at what Klein, Dansereau, and Hall (1994, p. 198) call different levels of theory or the "target level[s] at which the researcher aims to depict and explain." In social informatics work, this typically includes formal and informal work groups; departments; formal organizations; formal and informal social units like communities or professional occupations or associations; groups of organizations and/or industries; and nations, cultural groups, and even whole societies (Castells, 1991; MacKenzie & Wajcman, 1999). Thus, one way of understanding context is to focus on the level of theory and analysis that social informatics scholars portray in their research. In Table 10.2 we organize the examples used in this section by level of analysis working from small units of social aggregation (such as work groups) to larger collections (such as U.S. school children or all Internet search engine users).

Social informatics research, ideally, investigates how the influencers and nodes in a socio-technical network shape each other. Further, social

Table 10.2 Levels of context and theory

Conceptualization of Context (organized from smaller to larger social contexts)	Citation
A workgroup	Adams & Sasse, 1999
Technical support workers in a distributed workgroup within one organization	Eschenfelder et al., 1998
The personal networks of busy, dual career families in the Netherlands	Frissen, 2000
Traditional power holders and marginalized group members within a group of local politicians	Watson et al., 1999
School teachers and the IT infrastructures within the schools	Soloway et al., 2000
A U.S. federal government agency	Ward et al., 2000
User groups and the information systems staff in one organization	Clement & Halonen, 1998
A museum organization	Marty, 2000
An organization undergoing a BPR effort	Boudreau & Robey, 1996
Canadian provincial governments and private Canadian ISPs	Curry & Curtis, 2000
Companies in the textile business in the Prato region of Italy	Kumar et al., 1998
Insurance brokers and underwriters in the London insurance market	Barrett & Walsham, 1999
Work practices of three professional occupations	Walsham, 1998
Work practices of three scholarly disciplines	Kling & McKim, 2000
Work practices of four scholarly disciplines	Covi, 1999
An electorate in a particular region of one country	Larsen, 1999
Indian societal traditions and information norms in one region	Walsham & Sahay, 1999
Those people who would access and use a Web index to the Bible	Goerwitz, 1997
Home and school environments of elementary school children in the United States	Attewell & Battle, 1999
U.S. information sector workforce in the period 1970–1995	Martin, 1998
The mass of Internet accessible Web pages that the public could possibly access and the content contained on those pages	Introna & Nissenbaum, 2000

informatics work should investigate how influencers and nodes at different levels in the network shape each other. In this vein, Walsham (1998) specifically calls for more research that explicitly links these different levels of theory, for instance, illustrating how societal trends influence individual and group-level theoretical issues. He explains: "We need to consider IT and social transformation as taking place at multiple and interconnected levels of analysis" (Walsham, 1998, p. 1087).

Trends in Social Informatics Research

Throughout this chapter we have outlined what it means to be doing research in the field of social informatics. We have also commented on the range of problems, methods, and domains that help to define social informatics research. We have highlighted the problem orientation, the methodologic pluralism, and the centrality of social context that help to frame social informatics research. This chapter stands as testimony to the growing awareness of scholars of the emergence of the interdiscipline we call social informatics.

In their *ARIST* chapter, Bishop and Star (1996) discussed social informatics concepts in the context of digital libraries. Much has happened in the years since that publication. A simple measure of activity is the number of published studies, representing the expanded range of problems being studied by social informatics researchers. The increased activity in social informatics is further highlighted by the work of an ever-growing number of scholars, from a range of traditional and emerging disciplines (Kling, 2000; Sawyer & Rosenbaum, 2000). Moreover, funding agencies such as the National Science Foundation (NSF) have begun to announce calls for research into the social and behavioral aspects of ICT development, implementation, and use. See, for example, the NSF's Information Technology Research call for proposals (www.itr.nsf.gov).

In the previous section, we surveyed contemporary research to help illustrate many of the common findings from social informatics investigations. The examples are drawn from different literatures and theories, set in different social contexts, focused on different ICTs, and use different analytic methods. This work showcases a range of approaches to analyzing the complex social milieu in which any computing is embedded and illustrates the deeply intertwined relationships between what is technical and what is social (Agre, 1997; Markus & Robey, 1988; Truex, Baskerville, & Klein, 1999).

When Bishop and Star (1996) wrote about the social informatics of digital libraries, they were helping to orient information science scholars to these inter-disciplinary concepts by linking them to digital library use. In the ensuing years, the scholars who contributed to social informatics (and the research traditions, intellectual disciplines, and domains of interest they represent) have developed a more coherent and accessible body of literature. This literature is united by its empirical and conceptual foundations and, as we show, provides an increasingly insightful collection of findings, theories, and opportunities for further research. In the remainder of this section we highlight some of these opportunities, organized by their focus on education, professional use, and research.

Educational Opportunities

Two of the educational opportunities confronting social informatics scholars are, first, to increase student exposure to the concepts, findings, analytic techniques, and issues that help to define this area; and, second, to help students develop a more critical orientation toward ICT use. Considering the first, and as outlined in Kling et al. (2001), there are a number of practical and ideological issues that, together, limit the exposure students have to the social informatics literature. One serious limitation is that there is no introductory social informatics text. While there are excellent anthologies (such as Kling, 1996), there is no coherent entry point to the literature. Given the dispersed nature of the research literature and the discipline-specific discourse of these research texts, it is very difficult to acquaint students with a survey of the issues, concepts, and analytic techniques that define social informatics. An introductory text would help to reduce this problem.

The second challenge is that most information science/information technology curricula do not cover social informatics concepts and analytic techniques. For example, the underlying principles of social informatics imply a tension between the positive and negative effects of new ICTs. This suggests that the best way to characterize these core issues is to develop an ability to think critically about the roles and values of ICTs. By critical thinking, we mean developing in students the ability to examine ICTs from perspectives that do not automatically and implicitly endorse the goals and beliefs of the groups that commission, design, or implement specific ICTs. Such a critical orientation entails developing an ability to reflect on issues at a number of levels and from more than one perspective. This is a difficult and lofty goal; one that is central to most curricular reform efforts in scientific, mathematics, engineering, and technology education (Abraham & Hoagland, 1996). Further, since an informed critical perspective means being able to draw on the research and theories used to develop the findings, this approach further implies that high quality research must be synthesized for use by members of the broader information science/information technology community.

Professional Opportunities

The commercial value and economic contributions of ICTs are often constrained by the large numbers of failed ICT-oriented projects, limitations of under-used systems, and the added social costs due to the enormous workforce adaptations that are often needed. Social-analysis-of-computing techniques exist, and these should be better infused into professional practices. Paradoxically, many of the analysts and employers who need them most are least aware that these techniques exist.

Currently, there are various means to help information science/information technology professionals develop frameworks to expose the value conflicts embedded in the design of ICTs and to explore different perspectives (such as soft systems analysis, Checkland & Scholes, 1990). However, these are not widely practiced, especially in the United States (Chatzoglou, 1997; Fitzgerald, 1997). Further, these socially sensitive techniques may require a significant commitment of resources and time, which may preclude their inclusion in project plans. Thus, there is a growing need to develop straightforward, low-cost, analytic techniques usable in budget- and time-constrained environments.

Research Opportunities

The findings from the contemporary social informatics literature provide a set of concepts based on rigorous empirical research into ICTs and their uses. In this section we point to three emerging research trends.

First, social informatics researchers are drawing upon contextually focused social theory to explain the ways ICTs are both shaped by, and used in, social contexts. Second, social informatics researchers are beginning to develop their own theoretical frameworks for ICTs, and in doing so, extending existing social theories. Third, social informatics researchers are using new and existing context-sensitive theories to challenge existing conceptions of ICTs and their impacts.

First, the explicit articulation of contextual concepts related to ICT use is both conceptually and empirically promising. Several of the articles reviewed for this chapter use sociological theories to frame their investigations or results. For instance, Frissen (2000) and Kling and McKim (2000) draw on the Social Shaping of Technology (SST) approach. Walsham has employed two different approaches: Latour's Actor Network Theory (ANT), and the theorizing of Anthony Giddens (Barrett & Walsham, 1999; Walsham, 1998; Walsham & Sahay, 1999). Finally, Clement and Halonen (1998) use a Social Construction of Technology (SCOT)-based approach.

According to two recent reviews of the information systems and library and information science literatures, there is only a small number of social theorists whose works are used in studies of ICTs (see Jones, 2000; Pettigrew & McKechnie, 2001). There are two additional approaches that, while not appearing in either Pettigrew and McKechnie's or Jones's literature reviews, serve as important theoretical underpinnings for social informatics research. The first is SST, which has arisen from work in the social studies of science and technology (e.g., Williams & Edge, 1996). The second approach stems from the Tavistock Institute's STS (Socio-Technical Systems) tradition, based on the analysis of work and its organization (e.g., Mumford, 2000). Social shaping of technology research often focuses on the ways in which social arrangements shape emergent technologies. For example, Bijker (1995) develops a socio-technical framework to discuss the development of a wide range of dissimilar technologies such as bicycles, the origin of plastic (bakelite), and other industrial innovations.

Returning to our second point, another emerging trend in the social informatics literature is the development of theories and models that draw upon, and/or extend, social theory to more fully account for the effects of ICTs. For instance, Kumar et al. (1998) present their theory of

"Third Rationality" that extends Kling's dichotomy of system rationalism and segmented institutionalism approaches (Kling, 1980; Kling & Scacchi, 1982). Kling has been the source of one stream of ICT-focused social theorizing. His "Socio-Technical Interaction Networks" (STIN) approach presents a framework for the investigation of the socio-technical networks surrounding ICTs, and the reciprocal shaping between ICTs and their contexts (Kling & McKim, 2000). Another example is Covi's (1999) "Material Mastery," which offers a socially sensitive framework for examining use of digital libraries and other ICTs. Further examples of this trend include recent publications by Orlikowski (2000) and Suchman (2000). Orlikowski continues to advance our understanding of the dual nature of organizational structure and uses of ICTs, while Suchman extends the insight and theorizing presented in her 1987 work on plans and situated actions.

The third emerging trend is that social informatics research increasingly provides an alternative perspective on current debates regarding the uses and values of various ICTs. For example, Kling (2000) analyzes the use of computers in education to broaden the meaning of access to the Internet. Crowston et al. (in press) analyze ICT-enabled process disintermediation in residential real estate. They pose this as a contrast of "socially thin" (transaction cost) with "socially rich" (social capital) views of ICT use and discuss how the socially rich view provides different and often contradictory insights.

In summary, the context dependence, methodological pluralism, problem orientation, and trans-disciplinary character of social informatics research lead to creative and wide-ranging research programs. These broad-scale, contextually based endeavors help both to increase our awareness of ICTs' varied influences and to provide us with a means of engaging in larger-scale discussions of these influences. In this way, social informatics research provides a means of educating practitioners and of extending the scope of research within information science.

Acknowledgments

This chapter has benefited from discussions with, and/or comments by Sharon Ahlers, Angie Barnhill, Ann Bishop, Ed Cortez, Blaise Cronin,

Shaoyi He, Rob Kling, Chuck McClure, Louise Robbins, Howard Rosenbaum, Wayne Wiegand, and three anonymous reviewers.

Bibliography

Abbott, A. (1995). Sequence analysis: New methods for old ideas. *Annual Review of Sociology, 21,* 91–113.

Abraham, N., & Hoagland, K. E. (1996) *Shaping the future: New expectations for undergraduate education in science, mathematics, engineering and technology elaborating on the recommendations to and for SME&T faculty.* Arlington, VA: National Science Foundation, Council on Undergraduate Research.

Ackerman, M. (2000). The intellectual challenge of CSCW: The gap between social requirements and technical feasibility. *Human Computer Interaction, 15,* 69–74.

Adams, A., & Sasse, M. A. (1999). Users are not the enemy. *Communications of the ACM, 42*(12), 40–46.

Agre, P. (1997). *Computation and human experience.* Cambridge: Cambridge University Press.

Agre, P., & Schuler, D. (1997). *Reinventing technology, rediscovering community: Critical explorations of computing as a social practice.* New York: Ablex.

Argyres, N. (1999). The impact of information technology on coordination: Evidence from the B-2 "Stealth" Bomber. *Organization Science, 10,* 162–179.

Attewell, P., & Battle, J. (1999). Home computers and school performance. *The Information Society, 15,* 1–10.

Barrett, M., & Walsham, G. (1999). Electronic trading and work transformation in the London Insurance Market. *Information Systems Research, 10*(1), 1–22.

Berthon, P., Pitt, L., & Morris, M. (1998). The impact of individual and organizational factors on problem perception: Theory and empirical evidence from the marketing-technical dyad. *Journal of Business Research, 42,* 25–38.

Beyer, H., & Holtzblatt, K. (1997). *Contextual design: A customer-centered approach to systems designs.* New York: Morgan Kaufmann.

Bijker, W. E. (1995). *Of bicycles, bakelites, and bulbs: Toward a theory of sociotechnical change.* Cambridge, MA: MIT Press.

Bishop, A. P., Buttenfield, B., & Van House, N. A. (Eds.), (in press). *Digital library use: Social practice in design and evaluation.* Cambridge, MA: MIT Press.

Bishop, A. P., & Star, S. L. (1996). Social informatics of digital library use and infrastructure. *Annual Review of Information Science and Technology, 31,* 301–401.

Borgman, C. (2000). *From Gutenberg to the global information infrastructure: Access to information in the networked world.* Cambridge, MA: MIT Press.

Bostrom, R., & Heinen, S. (1978a). MIS problems and failures: A socio-technical perspective part 1: The causes. *MIS Quarterly, 1*(3), 17–32.

Bostrom, R., & Heinen, S. (1978b). MIS problems and failures: A socio-technical perspective part 2: The application of socio-technical theory. *MIS Quarterly, 1*(4), 11–27.

Boudreau, M., & Robey, D. (1996). Coping with contradictions in business process re-engineering. *Information Technology & People, 9*(4), 40–57.

Brookes, B. C. (1980). Informatics as the fundamental social science. In P. J. Taylor (Ed.), *Proceedings of the 39th FID Congress: FID Publication 566. New Trends in Documentation and Information* (pp. 19–29). London: ASLIB.

Brown, J., & Duguid, P. (2000). *The social life of information*. Boston: Harvard Business School Press.

Castells, M. (1991). The information city: A new framework for social change. In B. Wellman & J. K. Bell (Eds.), *The city in the 1990s series*, (Research Paper 184). Toronto: Centre for Urban and Community Studies, University of Toronto.

Chatman, E. A. (1999). A theory of life in the round. *Journal of the American Society for Information Science, 50*, 207–217.

Chatman, E. A. (1996). The impoverished life-world of outsiders. *Journal of the American Society for Information Science, 47*, 193–206.

Chatzoglou, P. (1997). Use of methodologies: An empirical analysis of their impact on the economics of the development process. *European Journal of Information Systems, 6*, 256–270.

Checkland, P., & Scholes, J. (1990). *Soft systems methodology in action*. New York: Wiley.

Clement, A., & Halonen, C. (1998). Collaboration and conflict in the development of a computerized dispatch facility. *Journal of the American Society for Information Science, 49*, 1090–1100.

Covi, L. (1999). Material mastery: Situating digital library use in university research practices. *Information Processing & Management, 35*, 293–316.

Crowston, K., Sawyer, S., & Wigand, R. (in press). The interplay between structure and technology: Investigating the roles of information technologies in the residential real estate industry. *Information Technology & People*.

Curry, A., & Curtis, A. (2000). Connecting to the Internet: The challenges for Canada's county and regional libraries. *Library & Information Science Research, 22*, 77–103.

Davenport, T. (1996, March). Software as socialware. *CIO Magazine*, 25–30. Retrieved February 12, 2001, from the World Wide Web: http://www.cio.com/archive/030196_dave.html

Davenport, T. (1997). *Information ecology: Mastering the information and knowledge environment*. New York: Oxford University Press.

Davis, C. (1997). Organizational influences on the university electronic library. *Information Processing & Management, 22*, 377–392.

Dillon, A. (2000). Group dynamics meet cognition: Applying socio-technical concepts in the design of information systems. In E. Coakes, D. Willis, & R. Lloyd-Jones (Eds.), *The new sociotech: Graffiti on the long wall* (pp. 119–125). London: Springer.

Ellis, D., Allen, D., & Wilson, T. (1999). Information science and information systems: Conjunct subjects, disjunct disciplines. *Journal of the American Society for Information Science, 50*, 1095–1107.

Eschenfelder, K. R., Heckman, R., & Sawyer, S. (1998). The distribution of computing: Cooperation among technical specialists in a distributed computing environment. *Information Technology & People, 11,* 84–103.

Etzioni, A., & Etzioni, O. (1999). Face-to-face and computer-mediated communication: A comparative analysis. *The Information Society, 15,* 241–248.

Fitzgerald, B. (1997). The use of systems development methodologies in practice: A field study. *Information Systems Journal, 7,* 201–212.

Frissen, V. (2000). ICTs in the rush hour of life. *The Information Society, 16,* 65–77.

Goerwitz, R. (1997, April). Fear of offending: A note on educators, the Internet, and the Bible Browser. *D-Lib Magazine.* Retrieved February 12, 2000, from the World Wide Web: http://www.dlib.org/dlib/april97/04goerwitz.html

Introna, L. D., & Nissenbaum, H. (2000). Shaping the Web: Why the politics of search engines matters. *The Information Society, 16,* 169–186.

Jones, M. (2000). The moving finger: The use of social theory in WG8.2 conference papers, 1975–1999. In R. Baskerville, J. Stage, & J. DeGross (Eds.), *Organizational and social perspectives on information technology* (pp. 15–32). New York: Kluwer.

Klein, K., Dansereau, F., & Hall, R. J. (1994). Level issues in theory development, data collection, and analysis. *Academy of Management Review, 19,* 195–229.

Kling, R. (1980). Social analysis of computing: Theoretical perspectives in recent empirical research. *ACM Computing Surveys, 12*(1), 61–110.

Kling, R. (1996). *Computerization and controversy: Value conflicts and social choices* (2nd ed.). San Diego, CA: Academic Press.

Kling, R. (1999). What is social informatics, and why does it matter? *D-Lib Magazine, 5*(1) Retrieved February 12, 2001, from the World Wide Web: http://www.dlib.org:80/dlib/january99/kling/01kling.html

Kling, R. (2000). Learning about information technologies and social change: The contribution of social informatics. *The Information Society, 16,* 217–232.

Kling, R., Crawford, H., Rosenbaum, H., Sawyer, S., & Weisband, S. (2001). *Information technologies in human contexts: Learning from organizational and social informatics.* Bloomington, IN: Center for Social Informatics. Retrieved February 12, 2001 from the World Wide Web: http://www.slis.indiana.edu/CSI/report.html

Kling, R., & McKim, G. (2000). Not just a matter of time: Field differences and the shaping of electronic media in supporting scientific communication. *Journal of the American Society for Information Science, 51,* 1306–1320.

Kling, R., Rosenbaum, H., & Hert, C. (Eds.). (1998). Social informatics in information science [Special Issue]. *Journal of the American Society for Information Science, 49.*

Kling, R., & Scacchi, W. (1982). The Web of computing: Computer technology as social organization. *Advances in Computers, 21,* 1–90.

Kuhlthau, C. (1991). Inside the search process: Information seeking from the user's perspective. *Journal of the American Society for Information Science, 42,* 361–37.

Kumar, K., van Dissel, H., & Bielli, P. (1998). The merchant of Prato—revisited: Toward a third rationality of information systems. *MIS Quarterly, 22,* 199–226.

Lamb, R., & Kling, R. (in press). Socially rich interaction through information and communications technology: Moving beyond the concept of users. In R. Zmud (Ed.), *Proceedings of the MIS Quarterly Workshop.*

Larsen, K. R. T. (1999). Voting technology implementation. *Communications of the ACM, 42*(12), 55–57.

Laudon, K. C., & Marr, K. L. (1995). Information technology and occupational structure. In M. Ahuja, D. Galletta, & H. Watson (Eds.), *Proceedings of the Association of Information Systems Americas Conference on Information Systems* (pp. 261–270). Pittsburgh, PA: Association of Information Systems. Retrieved February 12, 2001, from the World Wide Web: http://hsb.baylor.edu/ramsower/acis/papers/laudon.htm

MacKenzie, D., & Wajcman, J. (1999). *The social shaping of technology* (2nd ed.). Philadelphia: Open University Press.

Markus, M., & Robey, D. (1988). Information technology and organizational change: Causal structure in theory and research. *Management Science, 34,* 583–598.

Martin, S. B. (1998). Information technology, employment, and the information sector: Trends in information employment 1970–1995. *Journal of the American Society for Information Science, 49,* 1053–1069.

Marty, P. F. (2000). Online exhibit design: The sociotechnical impact of building a museum over the World Wide Web. *Journal of the American Society for Information Science, 51,* 24–32.

Mumford, E. (2000). Socio-technical design: An unfulfilled promise or future opportunity? In R. Baskerville, J. Stage, & J. deGross (Eds.), *Organizational and social perspectives on information technology* (pp. 33–46). Boston: Kluwer.

Nardi, B., & O'Day, V. (1999). *Information ecologies.* Cambridge, MA: MIT Press.

Negroponte, N. (1997). *Being digital.* New York: Vintage Books.

Nosek, J., & McNeese, M. (1997). Augmenting group sense-making in ill-defined, emerging situations: Experiences, lessons learned and issues for future development. *Information Technology & People, 10,* 241–252.

Orlikowski, W. (1993). Learning from notes: Organizational issues in groupware implementation. *The Information Society, 9,* 237–250.

Orlikowski, W. (1996). Improvising organizational transformation over time: A situated change perspective. *Information Systems Research, 7,* 63–92.

Orlikowski, W. (2000). Using technology and constituting structures: A practice lens for studying technology in organizations. *Organization Science, 11,* 404–428.

Orlikowski, W., & Baroudi, J. J. (1991). Studying information technology in organizations: Research approaches and assumptions. *Information Systems Research, 2,* 1–28.

Pettigrew, K. E., & McKechnie, L. E. F. (2001). The use of theory in information science research. *Journal of the American Society for Information Science, 52,* 62–73.

President's Information Technology Advisory Committee. (1999). *Report to the President: Information technology research: Investing in our future.* Washington DC: National Coordination Office for Information Technology Research and Development. Retrieved February 12, 2001, from the World Wide Web: http://www.itrd.gov/ac/report

Ritzer, G. (1996). *Modern sociological theory* (4th ed.). New York: McGraw-Hill.

Robey, D., & Sahay, S. (1996). Transforming work through information technology: A comparative case study of geographic information systems in county government. *Information Systems Research, 7,* 93–111.

Sarkar, M. B., Butler, B., & Steinfield, C. (1995). Intermediaries and cybermediaries: A continuing role for mediating players in the electronic market place. *Journal of Computer-Mediated Communication, 1.* Retrieved February 12, 2001, from the World Wide Web: http://www.ascusc.org/jcmc/vol3/issue1/sarker.html

Sawyer, S., Crowston, K., Wigand, R., & Allbritton, M. (in press). The social embeddedness of transactions: Evidence from the residential real estate industry. *The Information Society.*

Sawyer, S., & Rosenbaum, H. (2000). Social informatics in the information sciences: Current activities and emerging directions. *Informing Science, 3,* 89–96. Retrieved February 12, 2001, from the World Wide Web: http://inform.nu/Articles/Vol3/V3n2p89-96r.pdf

Schement, J. R., & Forbes, S. C. (2000). Identifying temporary and permanent gaps in universal service. *The Information Society, 16,* 117–126.

Schmitz, S. (2000). The effects of electronic commerce on the structure of intermediation. *Journal of Computer Mediated Communication, 5.* Retrieved February 12, 2001, from the World Wide Web: http://www.ascusc.org/jcmc/vol5/issue3/schmitz.html

Sica, A. (Ed.). (1998). *What is social theory?: The philosophical debates.* Malden, MA: Blackwell.

Soloway, E., Norris, C., Blumenfeld, P., Fishman, B., Krajcik, J., & Marx, R. (2000). Log on education: K-12 and the Internet. *Communications of the ACM, 43*(1), 19–23.

Strum, S., & Latour, B. (1987). Redefining the social link: From baboons to humans. In D. MacKenzie & J. Wajcman (Eds.), *The social shaping of technology* (pp. 116–125). Philadelphia: Open University Press.

Suchman, L. (1987). *Plans and situated actions: The problem of human / machine communication.* New York: Cambridge University Press.

Suchman, L. (1996). Supporting articulation work: Aspects of a feminist practice office technology production. In R. Kling (Ed.), *Computerization and controversy: Value conflicts and social choices* (2nd ed.) (pp. 407–423). San Diego, CA: Academic Press.

Suchman, L. (2000). *Human / machine reconsidered.* Unpublished manuscript. Retrieved February 12, 2001, from the World Wide Web: http://www.comp.lancaster.ac.uk/sociology

Swedberg, R. (1994). Markets as social structures. In R. Smelsen & R. Swedberg (Eds.), *The handbook of economic sociology* (pp. 255–282). Princeton, NJ: Russell Sage Foundation.

Talja, S., Keso, H., & Pietiläinen, T. (1999). The production of "context" in information seeking research: A metatheoretical overview. *Information Processing & Management, 35,* 751–763.

Toffler, A. (1991). *The third wave.* New York: Bantam Books.

Trauth, E. M., & Jessup, L. M. (2000). Understanding computer-mediated discussions: Positivist and interpretive analyses of group support system use. *MIS Quarterly, 24*(1), 54–91.

Truex, D. P., Baskerville, R., & Klein, H. (1999). Growing systems in emergent organizations. *Communications of the ACM, 42*(8), 117–123.

U. S. Advisory Council on the National Information Infrastructure. (1993). A Nation of Opportunity: A Final Report of the United States Advisory Council on the National Information Infrastructure. Retrieved February 12, 2001, from the World Wide Web: http://www.benton.org/Library/KickStart/nation. home.html

Walsham, G. (1998). IT and changing professional identity: Micro-studies and macro-theory. *Journal of the American Society for Information Science, 49,* 1081–1089.

Walsham, G., & Sahay, S. (1999). Technology adoption GIS for district-level administration in India: Problems and opportunities. *MIS Quarterly, 23*(1), 39–65.

Ward, R., Wamsley, G., Schroeder, A., & Robins, D. B. (2000). Network organization development in the public sector: A case study of the Federal Emergency Management Administration (FEMA). *Journal of the American Society for Information Science, 51,* 1018–1032.

Watson, R. T., Akselsen, S., Evjemo, B., & Aarsæther, N. (1999). Teledemocracy in local government. *Communications of the ACM, 42*(12), 58–63.

Williams, R., & Edge, D. (1996). The social shaping of technology. *Research Policy, 25,* 865–899.

Wynn, E. (1979). *Office conversation as an information medium.* Unpublished doctoral dissertation, University of California, Berkeley.

CHAPTER 11

Intellectual Capital

Herbert W. Snyder
Fort Lewis College

Jennifer Burek Pierce
Catholic University of America

Introduction

Companies are increasingly valued by the market at amounts far in excess of the assets recorded on their balance sheets. Microsoft, Coca-Cola, Intel, and Merck (to name only a few) record assets that amount to less than 15 percent of their market values. Some of the disparity is undoubtedly attributable to market vagaries, stock options, and other factors unrelated to the firms' performance. It is equally clear, however, that the differences between their book values and their market values are made up of such knowledge assets as research and development, employee know-how, customer relations, and trademarks—assets that simply do not appear in their financial records (Bontis, Dragonetti, Jacobsen, & Roos, 1999; Brooking, 1996; Stewart, 1997a, 1997b). Why do these differences exist, what significance do they have for managers and investors, and why might they have a bearing on thinking and practice in information science?

In his analysis of "post-capitalist" society, Peter Drucker (1993) predicted the advent of a "knowledge society." In it, knowledge would be not only a factor of production on an equal footing with capital or labor, but the only resource of consequence. Whether this prediction has been borne out or not, Microsoft, Coca-Cola, and Merck are compelling examples of organizations whose success is based on intangible, intellectual assets. Wealth creation now relies more often on knowledge than it does on physical assets.

These intangible assets are frequently described as intellectual capital (IC). The term was originally coined in 1969 by the economist John Kenneth Galbraith (cited in Hudson, 1993), and it came into wide circulation after a series of articles and books on the subject by Thomas Stewart (1997a, 1997b; Stewart & Kirsch, 1991). According to Stewart, IC rather than physical assets has become the principal means for the creation of wealth, while the ability to manage knowledge has become the critical skill for success in modern management (Brooking, 1996; Quinn, 1992). Yet, as the examples of Microsoft and others demonstrate, almost none of this value appears in the financial records of the companies that own and rely on IC.

Corporate balance sheets are riddled with lacunae where instead there should be figures showing the value of various kinds of intellectual capital, and that peculiar state of affairs is not merely a curiosity of accounting practice (Skyrme, 1998). A common management axiom is "What can be measured can be managed." It is not enough simply to discuss how to manage intellectual capital; implicit in the very concept of management is the ability to track assets rigorously and to relate them in some way to financial performance. Although IC nearly always represents a competitive advantage, most companies are seemingly unaware both of its value and of how to manage it effectively (Collis, 1996). Even in those firms that recognize the value of IC, managers frequently complain of dissatisfaction with the range of IC measures that are currently available (Waterhouse & Svendsen, 1998). If IC is essential to establishing and maintaining a competitive advantage, then those managers who do not both literally and figuratively take IC into account run the risk of making poorly informed decisions, ones that could damage or diminish the firm's stock of IC assets (Bontis et al., 1999, p. 2).

As more and more managers become aware of the value of IC and the need to include it in their financial accounting, they are also coming to recognize that developing useful measures of it in its various forms is a thorny problem. The dawning awareness of the importance of IC and of the need to devise good measures of it has important implications for information professionals. First, it signals a potential change in managerial practice:

The skills and experience of information specialists may be viewed as assets of the firm and actually counted as such rather than as a drain on resources. Second, although the IC debate originated in finance and accounting, it represents new career opportunities for the information professions. Knowledge management (KM), particularly that part of it concerned with organizing information and making it available to the personnel of a particular enterprise, is already recognized as the province of information professionals. The growing recognition of the importance of KM means that the place of information professionals within an organization is being reconceptualized. Their work is coming to be considered "a core function like financial management or operations management" (Albert, 2000, p. 74). Last, while valuing IC is certainly a technical accounting issue, it is also part of a wider debate about the intersection of two knowledge domains, information science/information management and accounting, and the acceptance by one discipline of expertise from another. At the heart of that wider debate is the debate over credible valuation methodologies for IC. Information professionals have advanced a variety of valuation schemes for IC (e.g., Hall, Jaffe, & Trajtenberg, 2000), but accountants have been reluctant to embrace any of them.

It is not the purpose of this review to increase controversy: We do not advocate one definition or valuation method over another. Instead, the review explores the context of the debate. It considers the principles of asset recognition, the history of the term *intellectual capital* and the definitions of it, and the various methods of calculating the value of IC. It concludes with a discussion of the relationship between IC and knowledge management.

Assets and Recognition

Defining Assets

Since much of the argument in the world of IC revolves around if and how IC can be valued and placed in a set of financial records, it will be useful to understand how accountants treat assets. An asset can be thought of as a prior cost that has a future benefit. Traditional accounting defines assets as (1) probable future economic benefits (2) obtained or controlled by a particular entity (3) as a result of past transactions or events (Johnson, 1994). An intangible asset (of which IC is one type) exhibits all three characteristics and has the additional characteristic of not possessing physical substance. Since physical substance is no guarantee of value, there is no theoretical reason why an asset, if it has probable future value and is controlled by the entity, cannot be intangible (Egginton, 1990).

Many of the proposals for capitalizing IC run afoul of this definition because the value resides in the expertise of employees or arises as a result of relationships outside the firm (Bontis, 1998; Sveiby, 2000). Human or relation capital (according to traditional accounting theory), while it carries the expectation of future benefit, does so without ownership.

Recognizing Assets

Meeting the definition of an asset does not guarantee that an item will appear on an organization's balance sheet. Organizations regularly invest in items with the expectation of future benefits without recognizing these items in their financial records. Recognition is the process of formally incorporating an item into the financial statements of an entity. It requires depiction of the item in both words (a description of the item) and numbers (a value to the item) (Sterling, 1988). The decision to incorporate an item carries a high degree of judgment, but there are general guidelines for the criteria needed for recognition. An item should be recognized as an asset if (1) "it conforms to the definition of an asset," (2) "its magnitude as specified by the accounting model being used can be measured with reasonable certainty," and (3) "the magnitude so arrived at is material in amount" (Solomons, 1997, p. 58). It is with the application of this definition that traditional accounting practitioners fall out with many IC proponents. The conflict arises from fundamental differences between the accepted practices of the accounting profession and the intangible nature of IC and financial reporting. Neither faction questions the significance of IC in creating wealth, but they cannot agree on the validity and reliability of the empirical tests available to identify and value IC nor have they achieved a consensus on whether the materiality of omitting IC assets outweighs the need to own them outright (Miles, Miles, Perrone, & Edvinsson, 1998).

Expressed this way, the recognition of IC appears to be an exclusively technical question involving measurement. What is less apparent is that the determination of what is acceptably reliable and valid arises out of a consensus of practitioners and is not a property of the tests themselves.

Power (1992, p. 49) has observed (in the context of brand valuation), "The calculative practices which become regarded as technical, neutral and self-evident themselves depend upon an elaborate network of tacit support which becomes fully visible only when challenged." In accounting, technical standards rely on professional consensus, which is not invariant across time or geography. According to Sterling (1988), a compelling argument can be made that the calculative tests employed by accountants are supported only by convention rather than correspondence to observation. Or, as Egginton (1990, p. 194) has characterized the debate over intangible assets: "recognition ... depends more on what accountants are currently prepared to recognise than unambiguous criteria."

The implications of this for IC are significant. Recognition of IC as an asset has heretofore been pushed aside due to perceived difficulties in identification, valuation, and determination of future benefits. However, if IC has been excluded from accounting recognition because professional accounting consensus has so decreed and if consensus can change, then methodological room may be found to account for that which has formerly been perceived to be uncountable. Although the acceptance of IC as a theoretical asset is far from universal (Rutledge, 1997), there has been some movement by professional accountants toward recognizing intangible assets, particularly goodwill and R&D (Anonymous, 1999; Hussey & Ong, 2000), and there has also been considerable study of IC accounting by a variety of professional accounting bodies (e.g., Condon, 1999; McDougall, 1999; Osborne, 1998; Petty, 1999; Van Buren, 1999; Weatherholt & Cornell, 1998).

National Practices and the Acceptance of Intellectual Capital

Although there is evidence that a number of firms worldwide monitor IC in various ways and consider it a key issue in corporate success (Arthur Andersen, 1998; Dzinkowski, 1999), officially accepted practices (that is, those prescribed either by law or by national professional bodies such as the Financial Accounting Standards Board in the United States, the Canadian Institute of Chartered Accountants, or the Accounting Standards Board in the United Kingdom) vary widely from country to country. The oldest and most widely accepted initiatives are found in Sweden with what has become known as the "Swedish Community of Practice" (Sveiby, 1996). The use of nonmonetary indicators for IC began informally in Sweden during the late 1980s and gained prominence during the early 1990s when two large Swedish firms—WM-Data and Skandia AFS—adopted nonmonetary IC valuation schemes. Skandia's scheme, known as *Navigator* has since been adopted by a number of firms worldwide.

In 1993 the Swedish Council for Service Industries issued official recommendations for the use of nonmonetary indicators, and by the mid-1990s, more than forty Swedish companies reported at least some of their company data in the form of nonmonetary IC indicators (Sveiby, 1998). To date, Sweden continues to have the widest official acceptance of nonmonetary indicators of IC in companies.

Outside the Swedish Community of Practice, the most widely accepted system of nonmonetary performance indicators is the Balanced Scorecard (BSC). It was first developed by Kaplan and Norton (1992), and it has been officially adopted by a number of entities, including the federal government of the United States (Balanced Scorecard Institute, 2000). Although the BSC considers a variety of nonmonetary factors such as customers and employees, it has come under criticism from many IC proponents for aggregating employee knowledge with information technology (IT) and limiting external factors to employees (Bontis et al., 1999; Sveiby, 1999; see subsequent sections on IC measurement for a more detailed discussion).

Apart from the BSC, IC valuation schemes have been given relatively little official recognition as a whole, although professional bodies have examined, or are examining, selected aspects of IC in various bodies. Among these are the valuation of goodwill and intangible assets in the United Kingdom (Financial Reporting Standard 10, 1998) and in-process R&D in the United States (Anonymous, 1999). To date, despite the voiced support for improved accounting practices for IC from professional accounting bodies, most of the research and recommendations for IC valuation have come from private or academic research institutes (e.g., Blair & Wallman, 2000; Institute for Capital

Research, 2000; Intangibles Research Project, 2000). As Dzinkowski (2000) has noted, the growing support that international accounting professional bodies have given to efforts to achieve a better grasp of the complexities of IC valuation is accompanied by an understanding that there is a long way to go before rigorous and approved practices are ready to be put in place.

A Short History of Intellectual Capital

Beginning in the 1960s, it became apparent that the creation of wealth primarily through physical assets was shifting to include greater amounts of input in the form of knowledge and employee expertise. As the importance of employee input to the success of a firm grew, so too did the pressure to account for people in the financial records of a company. It is widely held that the first concerted effort to account for the value of people in the workplace is found in the work of Hermanson in the mid-1960s. Hermanson (1964) coined the term "human asset accounting" to describe the process of bringing the human element of companies formally onto their balance sheets. Hermanson is notable for breaking with the tradition of not accounting for employee assets, but his work dealt with the mechanics of actually valuing human assets largely in the realm of speculation.

During the 1970s and later, the more concrete aspects of accounting for employees as assets were addressed in the works of Flamholtz and his associates (Brummet, Flamholtz, & Pyle, 1968; Flamholtz, 1989, 1999; Flamholtz & Main, 1999). They coined the term "human resource accounting" to describe their methods. According to Flamholtz, human resource had greater potential value for managers than for investors, and for that reason, his work has a strong management (i.e., internal reporting) accounting focus.

According to Roselender (2000), at no time since its inception has human resource accounting had a significant presence in mainstream accounting practices, and accounting for knowledge remained largely dormant until the 1990s, despite a growing awareness of the importance of employee knowledge in organizational success and the recognition that managerial decision making could be improved if measures of intangible assets were made part of their financial accounting (Eccles, 1991; Kaplan & Norton, 1992, 1996).

Thomas Stewart is generally credited with providing the impetus behind the current interest in IC; his 1991 cover story for *Fortune* magazine, "Brainpower: How Intellectual Capital Is Becoming America's Most Valuable Asset," was followed in 1997 by an expanded article in the same magazine and a widely read book (Stewart, 1997a, 1997b; Stewart & Kirsch1991). During the same year in which Stewart's first article was published, Skandia (a Swedish insurance and financial firm) appointed its first director of intellectual capital and subsequently went on to become the first major firm to supplement its annual report with an evaluation of its intellectual capital assets (Skandia, 1994).

Since the early 1990s, IC has gone on to spawn a number of professional evaluating organizations and products (Skandia, 2000; Sveiby, 2000; Technology Broker, 2000) and research institutes (e.g., Institute for Intellectual Capital Research, 2000) as well as a variety of scholarly researchers. In addition to IC's scholarly and practitioner affiliations, managers have begun to attach more importance to its measurement and reporting. Studies conducted by Arthur Andersen (1998), Waterhouse and Svendsen (1998), and Huseman and Goodman (1999) indicate that a majority of managers surveyed felt that IC would improve organizational performance and that a majority of managers surveyed already tracked one or more nonfinancial metrics.

To date, despite the interest of managers in IC, it has not been widely accepted as a standard addition to financial statements. Some of this is probably attributable to the lack of acceptance by professional accounting bodies. Bontis (1998, 1999, 2000) also reflects that it may be due to the untested nature of many IC measures. According to Bontis and others (e.g., Van Buren, 1999), IC measurement is currently in an experimental phase: Many approaches are being examined, but as yet there are few, if any, actual findings that would support the adoption of one over another. Whether, indeed, a single set of IC measures is possible or desirable continues to be a matter of debate.

Definitions of Intellectual Capital

To facilitate planning and investment in knowledge, some way of conceptualizing intellectual capital is necessary. Managers can then work with it and plan for its use as they do with financial capital. IC is usually assumed to reside somewhere in the difference between a firm's market value (the collective value placed on its stock) and its book value (the total value of its assets as shown in its financial records). In other words, since there is a large difference between what investors have paid for the firm and what the firm officially says that it is worth, that difference must be attributable to some collection of assets that do not appear on the balance sheet. That logical deduction does not constitute a usable, useful definition of IC. Some schema that is both specific and practical is needed. As Miles, Miles, Perrone, and Edvinsson (1998) have noted, no coherent framework has yet emerged for conceptualizing and defining IC, and the many differing opinions as to just what it is militate against widespread acceptance of its use by managers. Their wariness is intensified by the highly speculative nature of many of the proposed measures of IC.

Among the best-known definitions is that by Stewart (1997b); he states that IC is "intellectual material—knowledge, intellectual property, experience—that can be put to use to create wealth." Similar definitions have been proposed by Lynn (1998a), who describes IC as knowledge transformed into something of value to the organization, and Dzinkowski (2000), who characterizes IC as the total stock of knowledge-based equity that the firm possesses. What all three definitions imply is that IC can be both the end result of a knowledge transformation process and the knowledge itself that is transformed into intellectual property or assets. (It is the latter over which the firm normally has property rights and which is already regularly recognized by accountants.)

While writers acknowledge the diverse elements of organizational structure and performance that are used to assess IC, they often describe the divergent approaches rather than identifying the relationships between those elements. Bassi (1997) lists twelve strategies for measuring IC, including both financial and nonfinancial approaches. Relative value, associated with Skandia, emphasizes progress toward objectives, such as the percentage of employees involved in meeting a particular company goal, and the BSC, associated with the Harvard Business School, supplements accounting measures. Other approaches include competency models, in which a dollar value is placed on employee knowledge; subsystem performance, where a quantitative value is assigned to one dimension of an organization's intellectual capital; benchmarking, which uses interorganization comparisons; business worth, which is reflected in the "cost of missed or underutilized business opportunities" (The Montague Institute, 1998, p. 2, cited in Bassi, 1997); business-process auditing, which tracks the way information is used; knowledge bank, which reverses selected conventional accounting practices regarding expenses and assets; brand-equity valuation, which involves monetary gains created by a brand; calculated intangible value, which compares return-on-assets to industry averages; microlending, which is a process of exchanging "tangible assets with intangible collateral" (The Montague Institute, 1998, p. 2, cited in Bassi, 1997); and colorized reporting, which uses contextual measures of organizational success in addition to standard financial data.

Similarly, Martin (2000, p. 22) offers an overview of IC measurement methods. This survey includes a critique of the recent accounting practice of "immediately expensing intangible items ... rather than capitalizing them in the manner of traditional tangible assets," which "produces serious distortions in reported earnings ... and frustrates managers in their efforts at managing their investments in intellectual capital." The contention is that IC indicators are selected according to their relevance to an individual organization rather than for the purpose of creating a generic standard for measurement. Nonfinancial indicators are intended to supplement rather than to replace financial data reporting an organization's assets.

Elsewhere, the emphasis is on the adaptation of accounting practices to create purely quantitative measures of intellectual capital. The advantage of quantitative approaches lies largely in the ability to make comparisons between organizations. Dzinkowski (2000, p. 34) states that "the need to make general comparisons of the intellectual capital stock between firms has led to the development of three broad indicators that are (1) derived from the audited financial statements of the firm and (2) independent of which definitions of intellectual capital are adopted by the firm." These indicators are market-to-book value, Tobin's q, and calculated intangible value (CIV). Dzinkowski (2000) observes that while market-to-book value, the best-known measure, and Tobin's q are useful primarily for comparisons between like organizations, CIV can be used for analysis both within and across industries.

King and Henry (1999) describe the need to assign value to intangible assets in order to assess intellectual capital. There are three standard appraisal or valuation methods, which are in some respects similar to quantitative techniques for assessing intellectual capital: The cost approach is based on determining the dollar amount to acquire assets, particularly tangible assets; the market comparable approach uses current market costs, primarily for items with an established market; and the income approach assigns value based on projected future income. King and Henry contend that these valuation and appraisal techniques used in the banking industry are applicable to the problem of assigning value to intangible assets in accounting and investment realms.

Another pattern of intellectual capital measurement is to focus on nonfinancial indicators. Sveiby (2000, online) is among those who criticize the limitations of using purely financial measures of intellectual capital: "It is tempting to try to design a measuring system equivalent of double entry bookkeeping with money as the common denominator ... As of today, there exists no comprehensive system that uses money as the common denominator and at the same time is useful for managers ... Knowledge flows and intangible assets are essentially non-monetary. We need new proxies."

The best known and most widely used model that incorporates both financial and nonfinancial measures of IC has been developed following the combined work of Bontis (1996, 1998); Edvinsson and Malone (1997); Edvinsson and Sullivan (1996); Roos, Roos, Dragonetti, and Edvinsson (1998); Saint-Onge (1996); and Sveiby (1997). In an effort to tie the intellectual capital of a firm to actual strategic objectives, these models move beyond simple definitions to create an IC management framework. In general these models (Skandia uses the term "value platform") divide IC into three interrelated types: human capital, customer (or relational) capital, and organizational capital.

> Human capital is the accumulated value of competence, training, skills and knowledge residing within organizational members. It is the most problematic aspect of IC because it does not conform to the traditional model of asset ownership used in conventional accounting (Lynn, 1998a). However, although competence cannot be owned by the firm, a case can be made for its inclusion since it is impossible to conceive of an organization without people (Sveiby, 1997).

Customer (relational) capital is the value derived from connections outside the organization; it includes reliable suppliers and loyal customers. Much has been written about the role of the external environment on corporate success (e.g., Dzinkowski, 2000; Huang, 1998), and a variety of such techniques as customer value maps and market-perceived quality profiles have been developed to understand the value of customers and their perceptions.

Organizational capital subsumes all the other measures of IC and includes all forms of intellectual property as well as the knowledge embedded in the routines of the company, such as organizational or operating systems.

In some versions of the model (particularly in Skandia's value platform), a further distinction is made: Organizational capital and relationship capital are gathered under the umbrella of structural capital. The distinction in these cases is between the knowledge contained in individual employees (human capital) and structural capital that is internal to the firm but external to the employees—that is, "everything that remains in the company after 5 o'clock" (Bontis, 1998, p. 12).

Under these models, both relational and human capital are transient and do not have the permanence of organizational capital. Since these two types of IC can be lost, a major challenge of managing IC is the transformation of human and relational capital into organizational capital. Thus transformed, the organizational capital can be retained and improved over time (Lynn, 1998a; Saint-Onge, 1996). Indeed, organizational capital is notable for being an asset that appreciates in value over time rather than depreciating (Urich, 1998).

The several elements of IC also interact with each other, and the exact nature of IC is affected both by the mix of IC types and by the culture of the organization in which the elements have evolved (Dzinkowski, 2000: Lynn, 1998a; Skandia, 2000). The propensity for complexity argues against a single set of standard reporting measures (Dzinkowski, 2000; Edvinsson & Malone, 1997; Lynn, 1998a) with the result that firms are less likely to measure their IC in traditional dollar terms and will instead rely on a variety of customized metrics presented as supplements to traditional accounting statements (Bontis, 1998; Booth, 1998).

Whether to include intellectual property in definitions of IC also continues to be a matter of debate among some IC scholars and practitioners. Intellectual property consists of such assets as patents, trademarks, and copyrights—assets that establish property rights. Definitions such as those proposed by Stewart and Brooking explicitly include intellectual property, while those such as Skandia's value platform imply that intellectual property is included in their use. Some scholars, such as Bontis (1998), argue for the exclusion of intellectual property on the basis that, while intellectual property can be considered the output of IC, it has value only when examined in the larger context of its potential to the organization, rather than as an independent asset.

Measuring Intellectual Capital

Intellectual capital is recognized as adding significantly to both the financial success and the dollar value of companies and organizations. Because this intangible resource has the ability to significantly increase an organization's worth, there are numerous efforts to measure and account for IC. These efforts result from the inability to use extant finance and accounting methods to precisely determine an organization's intellectual capital, and the resulting literature focuses on several quantitative and qualitative indicators.

The inability of conventional accounting methods to register IC's contribution to the wealth of an organization drives ongoing attempts to find ways to quantify or otherwise describe the value of IC. Generally, it is held that "traditional financial reporting is rendered inappropriate [for measuring intellectual capital] by factors which include its emphasis on historical events, its inability to adequately capture intangible assets, its focus on costs and its concentration around regular statements" (Bradley, 1997b, p. 35). One complaint against existing accounting methods is that they have failed to change as business models have changed and, as a result, are designed to account for the accumulation and the use of physical assets rather than the intangible assets such as IC that play a significant role in organizational success in the contemporary economy (Barsky & Marchant, 2000; Bradley, 1997a, p. 55; Lynn, 2000). In recent years, this emphasis on commodities has created a discrepancy between an organization's value as reflected by accounting data and that implied by stock prices and revenues (Bradley, 1997b, p. 55). Generally, it is held that the failure to account for IC means that the value of nearly every organization has been underreported; specifically, it is contended that 40 percent or more of the market value of any public corporation is not accounted for on its balance sheet (Bradley, 1997b, p. 55; Dzinkowski, 2000, p. 32; Handy, 1989). While some (e.g., Martin, 2000) contend that admittedly imperfect but still viable techniques of measuring IC are available, others (Dzinkowski, 2000; Sveiby, 2000; Van Buren, 1999) argue that fully viable accounting practices have yet to be developed. Given the role of IC in producing higher financial returns, these discrepancies concern those who measure and manage organizations' resources.

Indicators of Intellectual Capital

Practices for measuring intellectual capital range widely, as do efforts to categorize the tools and techniques designed to capture this information about intangible assets. The accounting profession has not produced standards that can be reliably applied to compare one organization with another, and the efforts of individual companies to measure their IC resources have yet to result in widely accepted, comparable, or standard measures (Dzinkowski, 2000, p. 36; Van Buren, 1999, p. 72). In response to the growing need to value IC, a number of measurement schemes have been developed. They can be broadly grouped into two categories: multiple variable schemes that include both monetary and nonmonetary measures and aggregate, single indicators. Widely used indicators of both types are discussed here.

Multiple Variable Measures

Multiple measurement schemes are characterized by the underlying theory that money is only one of many possible proxies for measuring human action; such schemes either use a preponderance of nonfinancial indicators to monitor and present their intangible assets or combine traditional financial indicators with nonfinancial ones (Skandia, 2000; Kaplan & Norton, 1996). Many authors observe the need to use multiple measures to assess intellectual capital accurately (Dzinkowski, 2000, p. 34; Martin, 2000, p. 22; Van Buren, 1999). Unlike valuation schemes that rely on accepted accounting principles, multiple variable measurement IC schemes are usually specifically tailored to individual companies.

Intangible Assets Monitor

The Intangible Assets Monitor (IAM) is a system based on Sveiby's concept of the knowledge organization, which has few tangible assets and intangible assets that can only be valued indirectly since they cannot be displayed in normal market transactions. Valuation of such a firm involves not only the creation of a visible balance sheet concerned with material assets but an additional "invisible" balance sheet of intangible assets. According to Sveiby (1997), it is possible to develop a coherent set of valuation measures for a company only if money is dropped as the sole indicator of value and replaced with a system of new, nonfinancial proxies for intangible assets. Sveiby recommends an accounting perspective in which traditional financial statements (measuring visible assets) are used in combination with nonfinancial measures for intangible assets to provide management and shareholders with a complete picture of a firm's worth (Bontis, 2000; Sveiby, 1997).

Sveiby (1997) proposes a model in which there are three families of intangible assets:

1. Internal structure. This includes patents, concepts, models, computer systems and administrative systems that are created by the employees and are thus generally "owned" by the organization. The "culture," or "spirit," of the organization also belongs to the internal structure.

2. External structure. This includes relationships with customers and suppliers, brand names, trademarks, and reputation, or "image."

3. Professional competence. This includes skill, education, experience, values, and social skills.

Sveiby notes that, while most companies measure at least some of their intangible assets and have used some measure of internal efficiency as part of their traditional accounting systems, the use of individual competence and external structure are not monitored on a regular basis. The difficulty, according to Sveiby, is not that intangible systems are difficult to design but rather that the outcomes are difficult to interpret.

In order to measure intangible assets, Sveiby identifies three indicators—growth and renewal, efficiency, and stability—each of which is applied to each class of assets. Each has a specific set of indices for use in measuring a class of asset. For example, the growth and renewal dimension of professional competence is measured using indicators such as years in the profession, education level, and education expenses. The stability of internal structures is evaluated using the age of the organization, seniority of staff, and the proportion of new employees ("rookie ratio"), and so on. The selection and use of specific indices depend on the company's strategy. Simplicity of presentation is stressed, with a recommended length of one page and selection of only one or two key indicators for each intangible asset (Sveiby, 1997, 1998).

A number of firms have adopted Sveiby's system as an adjunct to their financial reports (Celemi Corporation, 2000; WM-Data, 2000), but they have not attempted to place a financial value on their IC assets. An underlying assumption of the valuation scheme is that effective management of IC assets produces a concomitant financial gain. Both Bontis (2000) and Lynn (1998b) have observed, however, that without tying in some system of appropriate financial feedback, it may not be possible to make a business case for the inclusion of IAM in many firms.

Skandia Navigator

Bontis (1996, 2000), Dzinkowski (2000), and others (e.g., Huseman & Goodman, 1999; Stewart, 1997b) have identified Skandia as the first major corporation to attempt a systematic evaluation of their intangible assets and to make such information available to the public as part of their regular financial reports (Skandia, 1994). The system used by Skandia is currently embodied in their IC reporting model, Navigator (Skandia, 2000).

Navigator is based on the Skandia valuation scheme (see Definitions of IC) which divides market value between financial capital and IC and then breaks IC down into customer capital, organizational capital, and human capital. The valuation of a firm includes both financial and non-financial reporting measures and focuses on five areas: financial, customer, process, renewal and development, and human capital (Bontis, 2000; Skandia, 2000).

Navigator uses as many as ninety-one new IC metrics and seventy-three traditional metrics to measure the five focus areas. These metrics include such measures as PCs/employee, staff turnover, revenue/ employee, average patent age, and managers' education level. The authors of the system (Edvinsson & Malone, 1997) acknowledge that some of the measures may be redundant or unnecessary but still recommend the use of all of them to arrive at a universal IC reporting scheme.

The measures use a variety of methods for data collection including direct counts, ratios, dollar amounts, and survey results. Edvinsson and Malone recommend that direct counts be combined with other direct counts to form ratios, leaving only two measurement types: ratios and monetary values. They further recommend combining all monetary values using a predetermined weighting scheme to achieve an overall IC value (C) and all ratios to achieve a coefficient of IC efficiency (i). By this process an organization's total IC is calculated by multiplying the two, where IC= i*C (Edvinsson & Malone, 1997).

Balanced Scorecard

The balanced scorecard is a system of monetary and nonmonetary metrics based on the works of Kaplan and Norton. It appeared first as an article in the *Harvard Business Review* (1992) and was subsequently republished as a book (1996). The original works were part of an accounting movement known informally as the "new management accounting," which advocated reporting schemes that included quality measures as well as financial information.

In addition to the normally reported financial statements, the BSC advocates that it is desirable to report information from three additional perspectives: customer, internal business process, and learning and growth. Within each area of the BSC, it becomes the responsibility of the firm's management team to select those performance measures that best constitute a useful management information system for the firm. The system is intended to be dynamic, with the portfolio of measures changing to fit the evolving needs of the organization. Kaplan and Norton are also at pains to point out that the BSC is intended as a management system rather than a system of measures. The BSC has been widely adopted in a variety of organizational settings, including for-profit, nonprofit, and government (Balanced Scorecard, 2000).

Despite the wide acceptance and intuitive appeal of BSC, IC proponents are not universally accepting of the system. Bontis, Dragonetti, Jacobsen, and Roos (1999) find that the BSC limits the external factors it considers to customers (ignoring the value of supplier relationships) and for aggregating the intellectual contribution of employees with IT under the sole category of learning and growth, thus understating the challenges of managing the creativity of employees. Sveiby (1999) also notes that the BSC is conceptually different from schemes such as his IAM because it fails to mention people's knowledge as a source of wealth and simply adds three nonfinancial perspectives to traditional management information systems.

Technology Broker

Technology Broker is a proprietary IC valuation method offered by Intellectual Capital Services (Technology Broker, 2000); it is based on the work of Annie Brooking (1996). Brooking identifies four categories of intangible assets:

1. Human-centered assets—the collective expertise, creative capability, leadership, entrepreneurial, and managerial skills embodied by the employees of the organization
2. Intellectual property—know-how, copyrights, patents, trademarks
3. Infrastructure assets—technologies, methodologies, and processes that enable the organization to function, including methodologies for assessing risk, methods of managing a sales force, databases of information on the market or customers, communication
4. Market assets—the potential an organization has because of market-related intangibles (examples include repeat business percentage; value associated with goodwill such as branding; and market dominance due to the market strategy, including positioning strategies that have commercial value)

Together, these four components make up the intellectual capital of an organization.

Using the Brooking method, companies answer a series of diagnostic questions that comprise the IC indicator and give an overall rating for the company's level of IC. Each of the four classes of intangible assets is then addressed via separate, proprietary audit questionnaires. Valuation of IC assets using the Technology Broker/Brooking method is unique to a specific organization and time of valuation (Lynn, 1998b) and dependent upon the goals of the organization and the state of the market (Technology Broker, 2000). Once Technology Broker completes the audit, it offers three methods for calculating the value of its IC assets: replacement cost, market value, net present value of the revenue stream produced by the assets (Brooking, 1996).

The Technology Broker approach has received praise for its accessibility and for the widespread marketing of the instrument and conceptual framework (Bontis, 2000). A major criticism of the method, however, is that there is little direct connection, except for expert opinion, between the dollar value placed on the IC assets and the qualitative data in the IC audit questionnaires (Bontis, 2000).

Single Variable Measures

Because multiple variable measures are usually individually tailored to a particular organization, accurate comparisons between firms may be problematic. Single variable measures have the advantage of being standard measures that can be applied across multiple firms and industries (Dzinkowski, 2000), but they are widely criticized for lumping together diverse kinds of assets, each kind of which may require a different management strategy (Brooking, 1996).

Goodwill

The price paid to acquire a going business concern is frequently higher than the value of the business's physical assets if they were purchased separately. The difference the buyer pays includes a number of intangible assets, some or all of which fall into the category of IC. Traditionally, such premiums have been subsumed under the rubric of goodwill or going concern value. Goodwill is defined as "the difference between the cost of an acquired entity and the aggregate of the fair values of that entity's identifiable assets and liabilities" (Financial Reporting Standard 10, 1998, p. 1). As Pollack (1997) has noted, goodwill and going concern value have no "real" meaning outside the financial records of a specific organization, but they exist as a means of recording a premium that a buyer pays.

Until recently, goodwill was treated as a period expense under most accounting schemes. That is, despite the fact that a goodwill premium may have been composed of many items that could be expected to provide future value, buyers were required to write off the entire cost of goodwill as an expense in a single accounting period. Since 1997, however, a number of major accounting standards organizations have made changes that require companies to recognize purchased goodwill as an asset and to amortize it over a period of years (Gowthorpe, 1999; Weatherholt & Cornell, 1998).

Although the recognition of purchased goodwill is a step toward the official recognition of IC, goodwill alone has always been a troublesome method for dealing with intangibles (Osborne, 1998; Schroeder & Clark, 1997). However, the use of a single, undifferentiated account as catchall for most intangible assets has become increasingly problematic, as industries have come to rely on intangible, intellectual assets (Brooking, 1996; Osborne, 1998). Among the most significant problems that have been identified are those of undervaluing firms, of reducing the ability of firms to raise capital based on their recorded assets, and of homogenizing many classes of unrelated assets.

Market Value and Expert Valuation

Market value and expert valuation are related methods for arriving at what is known as exit cost. They refer to the amount of cash (or equivalents) that could be realized by the sale of an asset (Egginton, 1990). There are a variety of conditions under which sales could occur, but the norm for valuation is the orderly liquidation of the asset. The presence of both an active market and a separately marketable IC asset are necessary for recognition under this model (Financial Reporting Standard 10, 1998; Holgate & Ghosh, 1999; Reilly & Rabe, 1997).

Since most IC assets are unique, or at least uncommon, it is unusual to find markets that deal in similar types of assets. However, Power (1992) asserts that the singular nature of IC assets does not necessarily preclude establishing a market value. A variety of IC assets such as brands and trademarks are regularly traded, albeit after a lengthy negotiation. A market valuation could theoretically be placed on them in the same manner as real estate, art, or brands. Expert valuation is recognized for a variety of other assets. The larger issue is the acceptance of the expert valuation of IC by the accounting community, not whether a value could be placed on IC.

A frequent criticism of market-based valuation models is the potential for abuse by management (Condon, 1999; Egginton, 1990). It could be possible, for example, to selectively change the value of assets to manipulate an organization's performance. In order to avoid manipulation, Egginton (1990) suggests the use of some recognized testing procedure as well as an accepted period between valuations.

Market-to-Book

This is the simplest valuation technique and the one that is usually suggested as evidence that much of what makes a company valuable to the market is not reflected in its accounting records (Brooking, 1996; Stewart, 1997b). The measure rests on the claim that the value of a firm's intellectual capital is found in the difference between the assets recorded in a firm's official financial records and the market value of its stock. For example, if a firm's financial records list assets of $100 million and the aggregate price of its stock is $1 billion, it can be said to have market-to-book value of 10:1. The company's book assets are valued separately according to some accounting standard used in the company's resident country, while the market values the firm as a going concern. This difference, it may be argued, can be defined as intellectual capital (Dzinkowski, 2000; Egginton, 1990; Van Buren, 1999).

Although simple to calculate, the method has come under criticism for aggregating IC assets that, because they are severable and capable of being valued separately, are also capable of being adversely affected should management decide to use accelerated depreciation methods that undervalue assets for tax purposes (Dzinkowski, 2000; Financial Reporting Standard 10, 1998).

Historical Costs of Investment

One of the difficulties of valuing intellectual capital is that such assets are frequently created and used solely for internal purposes by the owning firm. In such cases, the assets are never placed on the market, even if they are capable of being severed from the creating firm. In the case of tangible assets, this is not a material difference. Internally created tangible assets are valued as the sum of the costs of the components used to create them, including labor.

In theory, nothing prevents a similar valuation for internally created assets such as software programs from being carried in a firm's financial records as an asset. However, to date no governing financial organization has recognized such a method of capitalization. Financial Reporting Standard 10 (1998) allows for the reporting of internally created intangible assets only where "they have a readily ascertainable market value."

The conventional wisdom for not treating investments in areas such as research and development, advertising, or database design is that there is no guarantee that such investments will ever show a return. There is no guarantee, for example, that an increase in advertising will generate a concomitant increase in sales. Critics of such arguments note that research has demonstrated a connection between increased investment in R&D or advertising and profits (Couretas, 1985; Reekie & Bhoyrub, 1981; Szewczyk, Tsetsekos, & Zantout, 1993). Such research does not necessarily provide proof of profitability for any specific investment. However, the same situation also holds for investments in specific physical assets (Egginton, 1990).

Historical costing still fails to deal with the value created by synergy among the elements of a firm. Nor does it concern itself with nontraditional IC assets such as employee expertise, over which the firm has no legal ownership (Brooking, 1996). The use of historical costs for internally created intangible assets would, however, allow for the capitalization of at least some items of IC while still keeping their valuation methods within the scope of currently accepted accounting principles (Dzinkowski, 2000).

The advantages of recognizing internally generated assets include better accountability for managers using such measures as return on investment, a more realistic reporting of company values (Brooking, 1996; Condon, 1999) and performance, and a general recognition by accounting standards of practices that are already being used by investors to value firms.

Calculated Intangible Value

Calculated Intangible Value (CIV) is a method of calculating the fair market value of intangible assets of a firm developed by NO Research (Stewart, 1997b). CIV begins by calculating the return on hard assets and then uses this as the basis for determining the proportion that can be assigned to intangible assets. Knowledge of a firm's cost of capital is necessary in order to use the technique, and that limits its usefulness for comparing firms within and between industries. When such comparisons are made, it becomes necessary to use the average cost of capital for the industry (Dzinkowski, 2000; Stewart, 1997b).

Tobin's q

Tobin's q is a measure developed by James Tobin, the Nobel-laureate economist, as a method of predicting investment behavior (White, Sondhi, & Fried, 1994). It was first proposed as a possible measure of IC by Stewart (1997b) and has subsequently been used to examine the effects of investment in various types of intangible assets (Brynjolfsson & Yang, 1999; Hall, Jaffe, & Trajtenberg, 2000; Megna & Klock, 1993). The ratio (i.e., the q) measures the relationship between a company's market value (share cost x number of shares) and the replacement costs of its assets. Tobin's q is usually proposed as a method of avoiding the depreciation issue mentioned in CIV.

If the ratio is significantly greater than 1, then the firm is receiving monopoly rents or higher than normal returns on its investments. In the long run, the ratio tends toward zero, but in companies where IC is abundant, such as software firms, the q may be significantly higher (Sveiby, 1997). The measure is subject to the same external factors as those found for market-to-book evaluations. Generally, Tobin's q is most useful in making comparisons between firms that are in the same industry and have similar levels of hard assets. In such cases, the differences in the q-levels may be attributed to different levels of IC within the firms (Dzinkowski, 2000).

Patent-Citation Weighting

For the last forty years, various forms of citation analysis have been successfully used as proxies for valuing research contributions and importance. However, they can also serve as a method for valuing the innovative activity and the creation and use of IC by firms. Using patent citation data from more than 4,800 companies, Hall et al. (2000) have demonstrated that patent citation measures are better predictors for explaining market value than either R&D spending or simple citation counts.

Multiple measure schemes for evaluating patents have also been created. At Dow Chemical, which tracks such R&D measures as number of patents, income/R&D expense, and cost of patent maintenance per sales dollar, the measures are decided on and tracked by representatives from marketing and R&D who arrive at a "technology factor" to value investments in R&D. (Inasmuch as the measure is the result of a changing combination of factors, it might more properly be included in the multimeasure section.)

Managing Intellectual Capital/Knowledge Management

Frequently, measurement and management of intellectual capital are described as interconnected. There are two main rationales for this assertion. First is the familiar contention that an organization's resources must be measured in order to be managed; unless IC assets are identified, described, and accounted for, their value cannot be increased or fully utilized. Second, since IC is an intangible asset, some assert it should be accounted for through the application of managerial principles. Together these issues have resulted in a small body of literature on managing IC that refers alternately to the management of IC or to knowledge management (KM). This distinction, as well as the concepts and practices involved in management of workers' brainpower, is discussed here.

Some proponents of intellectual capital criticize efforts to quantify organizational capital. Mouritsen (1998, p. 462) is among those who argue that IC is best conceptualized as a management tool. She states:

> IC is ... focused on mobilizing internal, foundational capacities and competencies useful for growth in a long-term perspective ... Growth and value creation are not a matter of particular products and markets but of the broad organizational knowledge, unique to a firm, which allows it constantly to adapt to changing conditions.

Noting that this focus requires "strategic management of employee and customer relations," Mouritsen (1998, pp. 470–471) describes the way IC is concerned with "organizational learning" and "competence enhancement" because it directs attention to areas "beyond the realm of financial management ... which cannot be constructed (easily) as a bottom line figure."

While other writers indicate more interest in bottom-line figures, they likewise acknowledge that the use of intellectual capital in an organizational setting involves much more than financial principles. Bradley (1997a, p. 55) poses and responds to a rhetorical question: "Do we have the tools to manage these hidden assets [associated with intellectual capital]? The simple answer is 'no.' Management tools are dominated by finance and accounting and management often amounts to little more than the translation of accounting numbers into behaviour." Instead, Bradley contends that management practices must shift from a focus on physical commodities to intangible ones, with organizations developing a common vocabulary for describing and naming resources and practices associated with the abstract and complex concept of IC. Roos et al. (1998, p. 151) comment that while IC is still concerned with "the continuous growth in sales and the value creation for ... shareholders,"

> the deeper purpose of an IC approach is to change people's *behaviour* [emphasis original], not least through changing the corporate language. The concept of IC brings with it a whole new set of values about what is good and bad management, what is the right and the wrong thing to do in corporations.

Those management practices involve evaluation of strategic resources whether tangible or intangible, re-examination of internal divisions, and continued development of knowledge-based practices (Roos et al., 1998). Similarly, Davies and Waddington (1999, p. 34) contend that considering intellectual capital from a purely financial perspective is "incomplete" and should be done "in the context of a changing model of management and organisation structures." Thus, there is great interest in IC not for its ability to label dimensions of financial worth but for its use in developing employee competence and organizational practices intended to produce growth and leadership.

The name sometimes given to this thrust is knowledge management. The following definition of knowledge management, taken from a 1999 Gartner Group report, is often cited: "Knowledge management is a discipline that promotes an integrated approach to the creation, capture, organization, access and use of an enterprise's information assets. These assets may include databases, documents, policies, procedures, and previously uncaptured expertise and experience in individual workers" (Jones & Abram, 1999, p. 5; Srikantaiah & Koenig, 2000, p. 3).

Elsewhere and more simply, knowledge management is described as the process of "helping [to] make sense of ... information, sifting out what is valuable knowledge, then sharing it" for the purpose of increasing an organization's revenues (Stamps, 1999, p. 42). Wiig (1997, pp. 401–402) operationalizes knowledge management as involving monitoring knowledge activities, creating a "knowledge infrastructure," structuring knowledge, and using knowledge to produce "value." In any of these definitions, the transformation of information or tacit knowledge into organizational assets is central. Bontis (1996) describes the aim of the transformation as the conversion of individual knowledge into group or organizational knowledge.

At the same time, there are numerous additional concepts of knowledge management that adopt a somewhat more skeptical or critical stance toward the concept, particularly as it relates to the information professions. The terminology explored by Davenport and Cronin (2000), Albert (2000), and Broadbent (1998) serves to illustrate this critique. Davenport and Cronin (2000) put forth a three-part conceptualization of knowledge management; KM is variously defined as being much like information management, as being essentially a process engineering model, and ultimately as being a relational concept referring to interactions of knowledge. Likewise, Albert (2000) observes a three-part model of knowledge management in which she distinguishes between the implications for information science in light of technical and cultural/managerial views of the concept. Broadbent (1998, p. 23) cautions against translating the "familiar terms" associated with knowledge management into information science practices, arguing instead that "knowledge management is a form of expertise centered management which draws out people's tacit knowledge, making it accessible for specific purposes to improve the performance of organizations." These explanations of knowledge management, which see it as something other than a straightforward way that information professionals become involved with managing an organization's intellectual capital, indicate the need for still further engagement on this front.

Nonetheless, these definitions bear many similarities to descriptions of the use of intellectual capital. Edvinsson (1996) argues that the use of IC depends on the development of policies, procedures, and processes that allow productive use of an organization's intangible resources. Information sharing plays an important role in this kind of endeavor. Other writers highlight this link more directly. Knowledge management is defined as "the processes by which a firm creates and leverages intellectual capital" (Bassi, 1997, p. 25), and Hermans (1999, p. 161) notes that "KM revolves around the concept of 'intellectual capital,' best described as the knowledge, expertise, 'know how,' and best practices of the corporation's individual employees." Yet another writer lists a series of core knowledge management activities: defining, creating, capturing, sharing, and using intellectual capital (Van Buren, 1999, p. 78). As Wiig (1997, p. 400) observes, "There is considerable overlap in the scope of intellectual capital management and knowledge management." Chiefly, the comparable areas revolve around concern with an organization's ability to make the best use of intellectual assets (Wiig, 1997, p. 401).

At the same time, it should be recognized that there is disagreement over the extent to which intellectual capital and knowledge management may be conflated. This is evident in the work of Albert (2000), Davenport and Cronin (2000), and Broadbent (1998). Additionally, Wiig (1997) notes that despite similarities, there are significant differences as well. Likewise, Srikantaiah and Koenig (2000) distinguish between intellectual capital and knowledge management, describing intellectual capital as a narrower—and now outdated—precursor of knowledge management. In describing knowledge management as different from intellectual capital, Srikantaiah and Koenig (2000, pp. 30–31) cite the importance of technology in bringing about the means of managing knowledge and ultimately refer to knowledge management as "a portmanteau term intended to include all of the positive aspects of management fads of the last decade and a half, while avoiding the excesses."

Three recent compilations further identify and collect articles and monographs on this subject (Hermans, 1999; Liebowitz, 1999; Srikantaiah & Koenig, 2000). Together, these titles offer access to a significant body of literature on knowledge management. Rather than repeat those efforts to comprehensively cover this subject, we turn to the nature of the connections between intellectual capital, knowledge management, and information science.

Libraries and information centers have the potential to play a significant role in managing knowledge or intellectual capital. Albert

(2000, p. 66) writes: "as mediated researchers we have a great deal of tacit knowledge about how our organizations employ information, even if the end product we hand out and measure is explicit information. Depending on our level of involvement with how our research is used, we may even have the best view in our organizations of how information is really employed." Koenig (1996, p. 299) argues that those familiar with information science connect the job skills and tasks associated with knowledge management with those possessed by professionals in this discipline: "We would of course recognize 'knowledge management' and 'knowledge integration' as librarianship, or at least as an extension of librarianship." According to Stamps (1999, p. 39), knowledge management practices are implemented by corporate librarians or specialists in the context of competitive intelligence. An article highlighting competencies for special librarians of the twenty-first century argues that librarians and information specialists are uniquely qualified to take on knowledge management responsibilities because of their proficiency with information technology and their ability to identify, collect, and disseminate information to members of their organizations (Latham, 1999). Peters (1997) also describes the connection between the functions of libraries and information centers and the demands of knowledge management, noting that information professionals' skills are central to efforts to supply information strategically in order to increase decision-making efficiency and to reduce costs. Likewise, Martin (2000, p. 26) observes that knowledge management is "a field rich in opportunities for information professionals of all kinds." Finally, Koenig (1996) pinpoints those opportunities as revolving around the creation and maintenance of resources and structures that collect and organize knowledge and facilitate its use.

Intellectual capital, then, is a significant development for information professionals because it signals that organizations are beginning to account for, often in concrete and financial terms, the very skills and intellectual assets that information scientists and information managers use in the workplace. While the concepts of intellectual capital and knowledge management will not suddenly cause libraries, information centers, and those who work in them to rise in status in any organization that does not already highly value them, they do provide tools and vocabularies that can facilitate change. Libraries and information centers are too often perceived as expenses rather than as central to an organization's work. Models of doing business that both literally and figuratively take IC and KM into account have the potential to alter that mistaken perception. IC represents a systematic effort to value the use of knowledge and information. In particular, KM, when linked with efforts to organize information and make it available to people throughout the organization, can involve the work of information professionals. Although efforts to define and understand IC originate in accounting and finance, in the end the concept is significant for information science as well.

Bibliography

Albert, J. (2000). Is knowledge management really the future for information professionals? In T. Srikantaiah & M. Koenig (Eds.), *Knowledge management for the information professional* (pp. 63–76). Medford, NJ: Information Today, Inc.

Anonymous. (1999). FASB to reexamine in-process R&D. *Financial Executive, 15*(3), 59.

Arthur Andersen. (1998). *Knowledge measurement* (Next Generation Research Group Paper 99-1029). Chicago: Arthur Andersen.

Balanced Scorecard Institute. (2000). Retrieved October 2, 2000, from the World Wide Web: http://www.balancedscorecard.org

Barsky, N., & Marchant, G. (2000, February). The most valuable resource—measuring and managing intellectual capital. *Strategic Finance, 81,* 58–62.

Bassi, L. (1997). Harnessing the power of intellectual capital. *Training & Development, 51*(12), 25–30.

Blair, M., & Wallman, S. (2000). *Unseen wealth: Report of the Brookings Task Force on understanding intangible sources of value.* Washington, DC: Brookings Institution Press.

Bontis, N. (1996, Summer). There's a price on your head: Managing intellectual capital strategically. *Business Quarterly, 60,* 41–47.

Bontis, N. (1998). Managing organizational knowledge by diagnosing intellectual capital: Framing and advancing the state of the field. *International Journal of Technology Management, 18,* 433–462.

Bontis, N. (1999). Intellectual capital: An exploratory study that develops measures and models. *Management Decision, 36*(2), 63–76.

Bontis, N. (2000). *Assessing knowledge assets: A review of the models used to measure intellectual capital.* Retrieved October 5, 2000, from the World Wide Web: http://www.business.mcmaster.ca/mktg/nbontis/ic

Bontis, N., Dragonetti, N., Jacobsen, K., & Roos, G. (1999). The knowledge toolbox: A review of the tools available to measure and manage intangible resources. *European Management Journal, 17,* 391–402.

Booth, R. (1998). The measurement of intellectual capital. *Management Accounting, 76*(10), 26–28.

Bradley, K. (1997a). Intellectual capital and the new wealth of nations. *Business Strategy Review, 8*(1), 53–62.

Bradley, K. (1997b). Intellectual capital and the new wealth of nations II. *Business Strategy Review, 8*(4), 33–44.

Broadbent, M. (1998). The phenomenon of knowledge management: What does it mean for the information professional? *Information Outlook, 2*(5), 23–26.

Brooking, A. (1996). *Intellectual capital: Core assets for the third millennium enterprise*. London: Thomson Business Press.

Brummet, R., Flamholtz, E., & Pyle W. (1968). Human resource measurement: A challenge for accountants. *The Accounting Review, 45*, 217–224.

Brynjolfsson, E., & Yang, S. (1999). *The intangibles costs and benefits of computer investments: Evidence from the financial markets*. Retrieved October 11, 2000, from the World Wide Web: http://ecommerce.mit.edu/erik/ITQ99-12-25.html

Celemi Corporation. (2000). *Celemi intangible assets monitor*. Retrieved December 26, 2000, from the World Wide Web: http://www.celemi.com/company/ia.asp?sidnr=500200000000

Collis, D. (1996). Organizational capability as a source of profit. In B. Moingeon & A. Edmondson (Eds.), *Organizational learning and competitive advantage* (pp.139–163). Thousand Oaks, CA: Sage Publications.

Condon, B. (1999). Gaps in GAAP. *Forbes, 163*(2), 76–80.

Couretas, J. (1985). Study links advertising to increased profit. *Business Marketing, 70*, 42–43.

Cronin, B. (1998). Information professionals in the digital age. *International Information & Library Review, 30*, 37–51.

Davenport, E., & Cronin, B. (2000). Knowledge management: Semantic drift or conceptual shift? *Journal of Education for Library and Information Science, 41*, 294–306.

Davies, J., & Waddington, A. (1999). The management and measurement of intellectual capital. *Management Accounting, 77*(8), 34–35.

Drucker, P. (1993). *Post-capitalist society*. New York: HarperCollins.

Dzinkowski, R. (1999). Managing the brain trust. *CMA Management, 73*(8), 14–18.

Dzinkowski, R. (2000). The measurement and management of intellectual capital: An introduction. *Management Accounting, 78*(2), 32–36.

Eccles, R. (1991). The performance measurement manifesto. *Harvard Business Review, 69*, 131–137.

Edvinsson, L. (1992). Service leadership—some critical roles. *International Journal of Service Industry Management, 3*(2), 33–36.

Edvinsson, L. (1997). Developing intellectual capital at Skandia. *Long Range Planning 30*, 366–373.

Edvinsson, L., & Malone, M. (1997). *Intellectual capital: Realizing your company's true value by finding its hidden brain power*. New York: HarperCollins.

Edvinsson, L., & Sullivan, P. (1996). Developing a model for managing intellectual capital. *European Management Journal, 14,* 356–364.

Egginton, D. (1990). Towards some principles for intangible asset accounting. *Accounting and Business Research, 20,* 193–205.

Financial Reporting Standard 10. (1998, February). Goodwill and intangible assets. *Accountancy, 121,* 105–119.

Flamholtz, E. (1989). Human resource accounting: An overview. In C. Stacat & H. Ramananskas-Marconi (Eds.), *Behavioral accounting* (pp.110–137). Cincinnati, OH: Southwestern Publishing.

Flamholtz, E. (1999). *Human resource accounting* (3rd ed.). Boston: Kluwer Academic Publishers.

Flamholtz, E., & Main, E. (1999). Current issues, recent advancements and future directions in human resource accounting. *Journal of Human Resource Costing and Accounting, 4*(1), 1–20.

Gowthorpe, C. (1999). Goodwill hunting? *Management Accounting, 77,* 74–75.

Hall, B., Jaffe, A., & Trajtenberg, M. (2000). *Market value and patent citations: A first look* (National Bureau of Economic Research Working Paper No. W7741). Cambridge, MA: NBER.

Handy, C. (1989). *The age of unreason.* Boston: Harvard Business School Press.

Havens, C., & Knapp, E. (1999). Easing into knowledge management. *Strategy & Leadership, 27*(2), 4–9.

Hermans, J.A. (1999). Catch the knowledge management wave. *Library Journal, 124*(14), 161–163.

Hermanson, R. (1964). *Accounting for human assets* (Occasional Paper No. 14). East Lansing, MI: Bureau of Business and Economic Research, Michigan State University.

Holgate, P., & Ghosh, J. (1999, February). Internally generated database. *Accountancy, 123,* 83.

Huang, K-T. (1998). Capitalizing on intellectual assets. *IBM Systems Journal, 37,* 578–583.

Hudson, W. (1993). *Intellectual capital: How to build it, enhance it, use it.* New York: John Wiley & Sons.

Huseman, R., & Goodman, J. (1999). *Leading with knowledge.* Thousand Oaks, CA: Sage Publications.

Hussey, R., & Ong, A. (2000). Can we put a value on a name: The problem of accounting for goodwill and brands. *Credit Control, 21*(1/2), 32–33.

Institute for Intellectual Capital Research. (2000). Retrieved September 23, 2000, from the World Wide Web: http://www.business.mcmaster.ca/mktg/nbontis/ic

Intangibles Research Project (IRC). (2000). Retrieved September 21, 2000, from the World Wide Web: http://www.stern.nyu.edu/ross/ProjectInt

Johnson, T. (1994). *Future events: A conceptual study of their significance for recognition and measurement.* Norwalk, CT: Financial Accounting Standards Board.

Jones, R., & Abram, S. (1999, March). *Knowledge management: Cases, complexities & competencies*. Paper presented at the Computers in Libraries conference, Washington, DC.

Kaplan, R., & Norton, D. (1992). The balanced scorecard measures that drive performance. *Harvard Business Review, 70*(1), 71–79.

Kaplan, R., & Norton, D. (1996). *The balanced scorecard—translating strategy into action*. Boston: Harvard Business School.

King, A., & Henry, J. (1999). Valuing intangible assets through appraisals. *Strategic Finance, 81*(5), 32–37.

Knight, D. (1999). Performance measures for increasing intellectual capital. *Strategy & Leadership, 27*(2), 22–27.

Koenig, M. (1996). Intellectual capital and knowledge management. *IFLA Journal, 22,* 299–301.

Latham, J. (1999). Knowledge leaders: Yes, but don't wait for it to happen. *Information Outlook, 2*(5), 52.

Liebowitz, J. (1999). *Knowledge management handbook*. Washington, DC: CRC Press.

Lynn, B. (1998a). Intellectual capital. *CMA Magazine, 72*(1), 10–15.

Lynn, B. (1998b). *The management of intellectual capital: The issues and the practice* (SMAC Issues Paper 16). Hamilton, Ontario: Society of Management Accountants of Canada.

Lynn, B. (2000, January/February). Intellectual capital: Unearthing hidden value by managing intellectual assets. *Ivey Business Journal, 79,* 48–52.

Martin, W. (2000). Approaches to the measurement of the impact of knowledge management programmes. *Journal of Information Science, 26,* 21–27.

McDougall, D. (1999). Managing intellectual capital. *CMA Magazine, 72*(10), 4–5.

Megna, P., & Klock, M. (1993). The impact of intangible capital on Tobin's q in the semiconductor industry. *American Economic Review, 83,* 265–269.

Miles, G., Miles, R., Perrone, V., & Edvinsson, L. (1998). Some conceptual and research barriers to the utilization of knowledge. *California Management Review, 40,* 281–288.

Miller, M. (1999). Leveraging your hardwired intellectual capital. *Strategy & Leadership, 27*(2), 28–32.

Mouritsen, J. (1998). Driving growth: Economic value added versus intellectual capital. *Management Accounting Research, 9,* 461–482.

Osborne, A. (1998). Measuring intellectual capital: The real value of companies. *Ohio CPA Journal, 57*(4), 37–38.

Peters, R. (1997). Information partnerships: Marketing opportunities for information professionals. *Information Outlook, 1*(7), 14–16.

Petty, R. (1999). Managing intellectual capital from theory to practice. *Australian CPA, 69*(7), 18–21.

Pollack, S. (1997). Amortization of intangible assets in a business acquisition. *Taxation for Accountants, 58,* 336–343.

Power, M. (1992). The politics of brand accounting in the United Kingdom. *European Accounting Review, 1,* 39–68.

Quinn, J. (1992). *Intelligent enterprise.* New York: Free Press.

Reekie, W., & Bhoyrub, P. (1981, Summer). Profitability and intangible assets. *Advertising,* 13–18.

Reilly, R., & Rabe, J. (1997). The valuation of health care intangible assets. *Health Care Management Review, 22*(2), 55–64.

Roos, J., Roos, G., Dragonetti, N., & Edvinsson, L. (1998). *Intellectual capital: Navigating in the new business landscape.* New York: New York University Press.

Roselender, R. (2000). Accounting for intellectual capital: A contemporary management accounting perspective. *Management Accounting, 78,* 34–37.

Rossett, A. (1999). Knowledge management meets analysis. *Training and Development, 53*(5), 63–68.

Rutledge, J. (1997, April 7). You're a fool if you buy into this. *Forbes ASAP Supplement, 159*(7), 42–46.

Saint-Onge, H. (1996). Tacit knowledge: The key to the strategic alignment of intellectual capital. *Strategy & Leadership, 24*(2), 10–14.

Schroeder, R., & Clark, M. (1997). *Accounting theory* (6th ed.). New York: John Wiley & Sons.

Skandia. (1994).*Visualizing intellectual capital in Skandia* (Supplement to Skandia Annual Report 1994). Stockholm, Sweden: Skandia.

Skandia. (2000). *About Skandia: Intellectual capital.* Retrieved September 26, 2000, from the World Wide Web: http://www.skandia.com/capital/idx_ic.htm

Skyrme, D. (1998). Valuing knowledge: Is it worth it? *Managing Information, 5,* 24–26.

Solomons, D. (1997). *Guidelines for financial reporting standards.* New York: Garland Publishers.

Srikantaiah, T., & Koenig, M. (Eds.), (2000). *Knowledge management for the information professional.* Medford, NJ: Information Today, Inc.

Stamps, D. (1999, March). Is knowledge management a fad? *Training, 36*(3), 36–42.

Sterling, R. (1988). Confessions of a failed empiricist. *Advances in Accounting, 6,* 3–35.

Stewart, T. (1997a, March 17). Brain power: Who owns it ... how they profit from it. *Fortune, 135*(5), 104–110.

Stewart, T. (1997b). *Intellectual capital: The new wealth of organizations.* New York: Doubleday.

Stewart, T., & Kirsch, S.L. (1991). Brainpower: How intellectual capital is becoming America's most valuable asset. *Fortune, 123*(11), 44–50.

Sveiby, K. (1997). *The new organizational wealth: Managing and measuring knowledge-based assets.* San Francisco: Barrett-Kohler.

Sveiby, K. (1998). *The knowledge organization.* Retrieved September 29, 2000, from the World Wide Web: http://www.montague.com/le/le1096.html

Sveiby, K. (1999). *The Balanced Score Card (BSC) and the Intangible Assets Monitor*. Retrieved October 1, 2000, from the World Wide Web: http://www.sveiby.com.au/BSCandIAM.html

Sveiby, K. (2000). *Sveiby knowledge management*. Retrieved September 22, 2000, from the World Wide Web: http://www.sveiby.com.au

Szewczyk, S., Tsetsekos, G., & Zantout, Z. (1993). The valuation of corporate R&D expenditures: Evidence from investment opportunities and free cash flow. *Financial Management, 25*(1), 105–110.

Technology Broker. (2000). Retrieved October 2, 2000, from the World Wide Web: http://www.tbroker.co.uk

Urich, D. (1998). Intellectual capital equals competence x commitment. *Sloan Management Review, 39*, 15–26.

Van Buren, M. (1999). A yardstick for knowledge management. *Training & Development, 53*, 71–78.

Waterhouse, J., & Svendsen, A. (1998). *Strategic performance monitoring and management*. Toronto: Canadian Institute of Chartered Accountants.

Weatherbolt, N., & Cornell, D. (1998). Accounting for goodwill revisited. *Ohio CPA Journal, 57*(4), 46–48.

White, G., Sondhi, A., & Fried, D. (1994). *The analysis and use of financial statements*. New York: John Wiley & Sons.

Wiig, K. (1997). Integrating intellectual capital and knowledge management. *Long Range Planning, 30*(3), 399–405.

WM-Data. (2000). *Corporate website: Latest report*. Retrieved December 26, 2000, from the World Wide Web: http://www.wm-data.com/wmwebb/Menu3/LatestReport

Technology and Service Delivery

CHAPTER 12

Digital Libraries

Edward A. Fox
Virginia Polytechnic University

Shalini R. Urs
University of Mysore

Introduction

ARIST *and Digital Libraries*

The emergence of digital libraries (DLs), at the interface of library and information science with computer and communication technologies, helped to expand significantly the literature in all of these areas during the late 1990s. The pace of development is reflected by the number of special issues of major journals in information science and computer science, and the increasing number of workshops and conferences on digital libraries. For example, starting in 1995, the *Communications of the ACM* has devoted three special issues to the topic (Fox, Akscyn, Furuta, & Leggett, 1995; Fox & Marchionini, 1998, 2001). The *Journal of the American Society for Information Science* devoted two issues to digital libraries (H. Chen, 2000; Fox & Lunin, 1993); *Information Processing & Management* and the *Journal of Visual Communication and Image Representation* each had one special issue (Chen & Fox, 1996; Marchionini & Fox, 1999). The domain of digital libraries, though still evolving, has matured over the last decade, as demonstrated by coverage through *D-Lib* (http://www.dlib.org), the *International Journal on Digital Libraries* (http://link.springer.de/link/service/journals/00799), and two overview works (W. Y. Arms, 2000; Lesk, 1997; both of which have also served as textbooks). Sun Microsystems published a small book to guide those planning a digital library (Noerr, 2000), and IBM has been developing commercial products for digital libraries since 1994 (IBM, 2000). A number of Web sites have extensive sets of pointers to information on DLs (D-Lib Forum, 2001; Fox, 1998a; Habing, 1998; Hein, 2000; Schwartz, 2001a, 2001b). Further, the field has attracted the attention of diverse academics, research groups, and practitioners— many of whom have attended tutorials, workshops, or conferences, e.g., the Joint Conference on Digital Libraries, which is a sequel to a separate series run by ACM and IEEE-CS. Therefore, it is timely that *ARIST* publishes this first review focusing specifically on digital libraries. There has been no *ARIST* chapter to date directly dealing with the area of DLs, though some related domains have been covered—particularly: information retrieval, user interfaces (Marchionini & Komlodi, 1998), social informatics of DLs (Bishop & Star, 1996), and scholarly communication (see Borgman and Furner's chapter in this volume).

This chapter provides an overview of the diverse aspects and dimensions of DL research, practice, and literature, identifying trends and delineating research directions.

The Concept and the Dream: Early Visions

The concept of a world repository of knowledge has fascinated visionaries. H. G. Wells' (1938) notion of a World Encyclopedia propelled numerous attempts to develop a global repository of knowledge. In an elegantly articulated, highly cited, and now classic paper, Vannevar Bush (1945) outlined his idea of "memex," a device to help manage scholarly communication problems. In the 1950s, Englebart (1963) envisioned electronic technology augmenting human intellect. In the 1960s, Licklider (1965) imagined the "library of the future" and outlined the characteristics of such a library.

The roots of present day digital libraries may be traced to the information retrieval systems of the 1960s and the hypertext systems of the 1980s. Digital libraries have evolved from the techniques and principles developed by early information retrieval researchers (Mooers, 1950; Perry, 1951; Taube & Associates, 1955). Automatic indexing and search systems were pioneered in the 1960s (Salton, 1968); and today's digital libraries build on the solid foundations of more than three decades of research in information retrieval. However, digital libraries as we know them today have been conceived and developed only since the 1990s. Sometimes called "electronic libraries," they changed from the relatively obscure concern of a few people in computer science and the library profession to become popular among a variety of research groups (Fox, 1993). Commercial, academic, and public interest was fueled by U.S. government support, including that of former Vice President Al Gore, under the rubric of the National Information Infrastructure (Gladney et al., 1994). The last decade has been marked by an explosion of interest, research, and development in digital libraries. Much of the impetus for this surge of interest stems from the large-scale funding made available by the federal government's Digital Library Initiative, Phases 1 and 2 (http://www.dli2.nsf.gov) (Fox, 1999a; Lesk, 1999b).

Technologies that Help Translate the Visions to Realities

Over the last three decades a number of technologies has helped the early visions of digital libraries become reality. These may be usefully grouped into computational, networking, and presentation technologies.

Computational Technologies: Digital computers and digital storage are the key technologies that have made digital libraries feasible and viable. The tremendous increase in the power of computers; their multimedia capabilities (helped by compression techniques); the advances in software, secure languages, databases, and interfaces—have all contributed to the evolution of DLs. Continually increasing processing power helps handle the large volumes of data; at the same time multimedia capabilities not only enable computers to store, manipulate, and display images, sound, and video, but also make digital library content more expressive and rich with regard to human-computer interaction. The secure languages have enabled transactions that maintain privacy and security. Advances in database management have resulted in multiple, alternative approaches to the design and development of DLs (Buyya, 1999; Dan & Sitaram, 1999; Gates, 1995; Lee, 1999; Moore, Prince, & Ellisman, 1998; Rasmussen, 1992; Sterling, Messina, & Smith, 1995).

Networking technologies: Before the days of networking, information stored in individual computers was available only to those with direct access to the systems. Computer networking and distributed applications have helped dissolve barriers limiting access to the information stored in the millions of computers around the world. Coupled with advances in computational technologies, the evolution of high-speed networking, the birth and development of the Internet, open protocols, and the ubiquity of TCP/IP (Transmission Control Protocol/Internet Protocol) have all contributed enormously to advancing global access to information (Maurer, 1996). But for networking, digital libraries would have remained site-specific, just like physical libraries. The "site neutrality" of content and collections of digital libraries is possible because of networking.

Presentation technologies: The content of digital libraries—the text, images, videos, and sounds—are encoded streams of ideas. The flexibility of presenting information to the user in myriad ways is perhaps what makes digital libraries popular, usable, and user friendly. Compared with the uppercase English text (limited to Roman characters) in the early days of computing, the rich variety in languages, display, and "look and feel" of computer typography today is extraordinary. The array of alternatives available for the structuring and presentation of not only text, but other media as well, has turned many talented creators of digital media into artists. We have seen major changes in how ideas, information, and images are encoded and presented to the user. These changes also relate to developments in mark-up languages, e.g., Standard Generalized Markup Language (SGML), Hypertext Markup Language (HTML), and Extensible Mark-up Language (XML); as well as their presentation methods, e.g., hypertext, virtual reality, graphics, sonification, multimedia, document interchange, word processing, desktop publishing, and scholarly publishing (Akscyn, 1991, 1994; Hunter, 1999; Moving Picture Expert Group, Description Definition Language Group, 1999; Salembier, 2000; Zhang & Smith, 2001).

Organizational support: Technologies evolve, thrive, or die. Without the support of an institutional or organizational framework, the best technologies will not survive. Advances in digital library technologies have been strengthened by very broad-based support. While the World Wide Web Consortium (W3C) has been largely responsible for steering the development of the World Wide Web (including some aspects helpful for DLs), other agencies have shaped the course of development of DLs: the Council on Library and Information Resources (CLIR, http://www.clir.org), Corporation for National Research Initiatives (CNRI, http://www.cnri.reston.va.us), Digital Library Federation (DLF, http://www.clir.org/diglib), Coalition for Networked Information (CNI, http://www.cni.org), and the Online Computer Library Center (OCLC, http://www.oclc.org). A large community of DL researchers and practitioners exists today, as evidenced by the popularity of *D-Lib Magazine* (http://www.dlib.org) as well as regional publications (Institute of the Information Society, 2000).

The synergistic effects of technologies, along with societal response and support, have helped the emergence, accelerated growth, and continued support of DLs. The synergy, mutual interdependence, and complementarities of the science, engineering, and management of DLs is shown in Figure 12.1. The results have been not only institutionalization, but also the discovery of scientific generalizations, increases in knowledge and understanding, construction of numerous systems, funding of

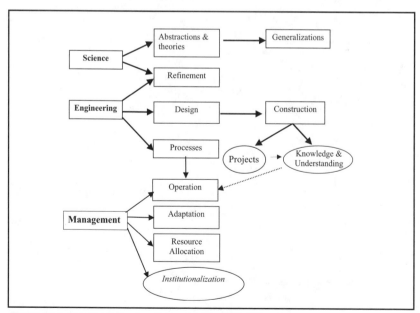

Figure 12.1 The three facets of developing digital libraries

many projects, and employment of personnel in digital library laboratories and departments.

The emergence of digital libraries and related technologies is presented in Figure 12.2 as a timeline. At the top, because of its prominent position, is the emergence of the Web (World Wide Web Consortium, 2000) around 1993. The next row identifies key efforts related to scholarly communication and archives (Davis & Lagoze, 2000; Ginsparg, 2000; Lagoze, 1999; Van de Sompel, 2000). These are partly supported by the standards listed in the following row, such as MPEG (from the Moving Picture Experts Group) and XML (Bray, Paoli, & Sperberg-McQueen, 1998; Hunter, 1999; Moving Picture Experts Group, Description Definition Language Group, 1999; Salembier, 2000; XML.ORG, 2000). As a point of comparison, recall that personal computers became popular in the early 1980s. Next, note that digital libraries were advanced by a sequence of National Science Foundation (NSF)-supported workshops and funding initiatives (Fox, 1993; Friedlander, 1996; Lesk, 1999b; National Science Foundation, 2000a, 2000b). Farther down we see that in 1987, not only was there significant expansion of work on hypertext (Association for Computing Machinery,

DL – Related Timeline

1985	1990	1995	2000
	WWW		
Electronic	arXive		OAI
Publishing in	CSTR	NCSTRL	CoRR
Universities			
SGML	PDF		XML
	JPEG, MPEG		MPEG-7
PCs			
	Proposed	DLI1	DLI2
	Undergrad DL		NSDL
TEI			
HyperCard		Java	
Hypertext Conf.		Dublin Core	RDF
Electronic Theses and Dissertations		NDLTD	

Figure 12.2 DL-related technologies timeline

1988), but also application of SGML to the humanities in the Text Encoding Initiative (TEI) (Burnard, 2000; Willett, 1999) and the first discussion of electronic theses and dissertations that led to the Networked Digital Library of Theses and Dissertations (Fox, 1997, 1998b, 1999b, 1999d, 2000; Fox et al., 1997). In the later part of the 1990s, standards important for DLs, like the Dublin Core (DC) and Resource Description Framework (RDF) for metadata, were launched (Brickley & Guha, 2000a, 2000b; Dublin Core Metadata Initiative, 1999; Lassila & Swick, 1999).

Goals for Digital Libraries

The goals for digital libraries were captured in the 1996 mission statement of the Digital Library Initiative Interagency Coordinating Committee (http://dli.grainger.uiuc.edu/national.htm), which was monitoring the progress of six major projects funded by the U.S. government: "The broad goal of the Digital Libraries Initiative is to dramatically advance the means to collect, store, organize, and use widely distributed knowledge resources containing diverse types of information and content stored in a variety of electronic forms."

To make this clearer, consider the distinguishing features of a digital library:

- Site Neutrality: Ubiquitous anytime, anywhere access paradigm—There is a library wherever there is a personal computer with a network connection (W. Y. Arms, 2000).
- Open Access: Powerful search and browse capabilities facilitate serendipitous discovery of information (Borgman, 2000; Rao et al., 1995).
- Greater variety and granularity of information: Information is not limited to metadata, bibliographic information, text, or discursive information. All objects that can be digitized are potential DL content.
- Sharing of information: Digital libraries enhance the traditional library concept of sharable resources. Marchionini (2000b) captures this feature aptly in his concept of the "sharium."

- Up-to-date-ness: Currency of information, with no time lag between creation and availability (Harnad, 2000b).
- Always available: No library hours—One of the main constraints of a physical library, that it is closed at least for some periods, has given way to "24/7" libraries (McMillan, 1999b).
- New forms of rendering: Information is not limited to "text," or any one kind of symbols. Many disciplines, in traditional sciences, social sciences, and the humanities, have been liberated from the restrictions of the text mode of rendering. For example, in mathematics, formulae can be presented in more imaginative and cognitively appealing ways. Authors in chemistry, architecture, or sociology, for example, also employ digital library technologies as alternative ways of presenting information (Hauptmann & Witbrock, 1996; Mönch & Drobnik, 1998; Weisstein, 2000).

Differing Perspectives

The concept of a DL has different connotations for different professional groups (Marchionini & Komlodi, 1998). For the information technology professional it is a powerful tool and mechanism for managing distributed databases. To the business community it represents a new market. To the information science community it represents a new means of extending and enhancing access to distributed, or remote, information resources. The evolution of the DLs has spanned many disciplines, bringing in not only different expertise but also differing perspectives. Fox (1993) reported on some of the early contributors. The Information Infrastructure Technology and Applications (IITA) workshop of 1995 prepared summaries of a variety of perspectives (Lynch & Garcia-Molina, 1995).

Computer science (CS) community: The CS community views DLs as an extension of networked computing systems (Marchionini & Fox, 1999). For the computer scientist, a digital library connotes a computer system offering library capabilities and facilities. The information retrieval (IR) community perceives the DL as another extension of information retrieval systems. While traditionally IR focused on retrieving document surrogates, what has changed today is the nature of "documents" and their "surrogates" (Belkin & Croft, 1992; Association for Computing Machinery, Special Interest Group on Information Retrieval, 1996). For the multimedia/hypermedia community, DL is another application area (Akscyn, 1994; Snyder, 1996). For the database community DLs are large databases (Fayyad, Piatetsky-Shapiro, & Smyth, 1996).

Library and Information Science (LIS) Community: The LIS community views a DL more as an institution than as a machine. DLs are "libraries without walls" (http://www.benton.org/Library/Kellog/chapter1.html). They are a logical extension of what libraries have been doing since time immemorial—acquiring, organizing, and disseminating information with the use of contemporary technologies (Garfield, 2000; Thorin & Sorkin, 1997). Thus, DLs are augmenting resources and enlarging the services and audiences of libraries (Marchionini & Fox, 1999; McMillan, 2000).

The stakeholders—the different communities of people who use and benefit from digital libraries—have differing views of what DLs are and what they can do.

Politicians / Governments: The debate continues as to whether digital libraries help bridge the gap between information-rich and -poor—"haves" and "have nots"—or widen the so-called digital divide (Witten, Loots, Trujillo, & Bainbridge, 2001). Many governments around the world have positive views about the ability of digital libraries to enhance equity of access to information: They perceive DLs as a means of overcoming the digital divide (Lynch & Garcia-Molina, 1995). Much of the digital library movement has stemmed from governmental initiative and drive. In the U.S., networks have been developed and strengthened to support the building of the National Information Infrastructure.

Publishers: The roles of and boundaries between authors, publishers, and others have evolved partly around technology (W. Y. Arms, 1995a). Since the Gutenburg revolution, publishers have played a significant role—however controversial—in facilitating the production and distribution of information. The new medium of digital libraries is approached with ambivalence by the publishing industry, where digital libraries are both new modes of distribution and also a new competitive challenge. In view of the threat—perceived or real—to their traditional roles and markets, publishers are adapting the new paradigm of electronic publishing through integration of media and new partnerships with other agencies and institutions, e.g., The University Licensing Program (TULIP) Project (Borghuis et al., 1996; Dougherty & Fox, 1995; Lynch, 1995).

Teachers: The symbiotic relationship between libraries and educators is a classic case of collaboration. DLs have further amplified and augmented this relationship (Marchionini & Maurer, 1995). For educators and teachers, digital libraries represent new learning resources, supported by a broadening of media centers and multimedia content. Many projects and initiatives have been undertaken to further the cause of education through digital library development (ARIADNE, 2000; École polytechnique fédérale de Lausanne, Katolicki Uniwersytet Lubelski, & ARIADNE, 1999). Governments, educational institutions, and other agencies and individuals, encouraged by the potential benefits of digital libraries, have vigorously pursued their development. Examples of such initiatives abound (e.g., MathForum, 2000).

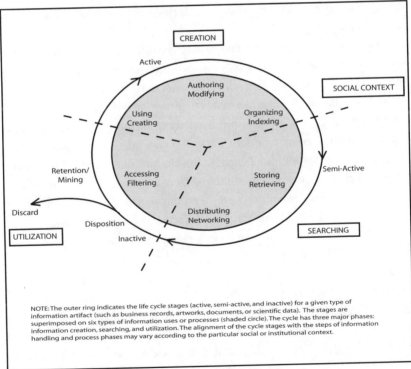

NOTE: The outer ring indicates the life cycle stages (active, semi-active, and inactive) for a given type of information artifact (such as business records, artworks, documents, or scientific data). The stages are superimposed on six types of information uses or processes (shaded circle). The cycle has three major phases: information creation, searching, and utilization. The alignment of the cycle stages with the steps of information handling and process phases may vary according to the particular social or institutional context.

Figure 12.3 Information life cycle (Borgman et al., 1996)

Librarians: To the library community, digital libraries are the next step in the evolution of new publishing media, as well as technological and organizational frameworks for revitalizing their mission of accessing and disseminating information and knowledge. The library community has embraced and adapted itself to changing technologies. Today, librarians look to DLs as a means for more direct involvement in the dissemination of information (McMillan, 1999c). This is illustrated in Figure 12.3, which summarizes much of the discussion at an NSF-funded workshop on *Social Aspects of Digital Libraries* (Borgman et al., 1996). It is particularly important to simplify the authoring and creation processes so that wider populations can participate; adding all types of multimedia content directly into digital libraries. In addition, authors can enter metadata (Severiens, 2000) about the digital objects they submit into open archives (Van de Sompel & Lagoze, 2000).

The end result is that digital libraries shorten the chain from author to reader (see Figure 12.4a). For example, with the Computer Science Teaching Center (Knox, Grissom, Fox, Heller, & Watkins, 2000), all of the players shown in Figure 12.4b connect to the same DL, using role-specific interfaces; this reduces costs and delays in author-reader

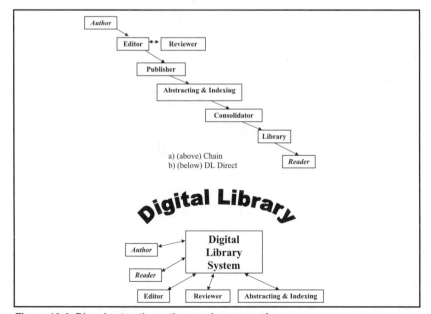

Figure 12.4 DLs shorten the author-reader connection

(teacher-student) communication. The changes underway in scholarly communication and dissemination of information have the potential to create radical economic shifts and to re-engineer publication processes (Buck, Flagan, & Coles, 1999; Flanders & Mylonas, 2000; Harnad, 1991, 2000b; Hitchcock et al., 2000; Kaplan & Nelson, 2000; McMillan, 1999a).

Archivists: For the archival community, digital libraries are a means of preserving heritage: national, cultural, literary, and other (Tibbo, 2001). Digitization is seen as an alternative to traditional microfilming and as a means of preserving and enhancing access to fragile materials. Many programs have been launched, with the Library of Congress' National Digital Library Program (http://memory.loc.gov/ammem/dli2/html/lcndlp.html#Overview), and UNESCO's Memory of the World Programme (http://www.unesco.org/webworld/mdm/en/index) exemplifying such trends.

Researchers and Developers: Collaboration is the key to research and development. Faster transfer of information, the sharable nature of digital collections, and the enriched forms of representation that the new medium offers have helped researchers perceive DLs as dynamic spaces for creating, sharing, and disseminating knowledge. Collaboration is no longer location-specific: research data can now be made accessible to a worldwide community of investigators. This feature of DLs has contributed to the concept of *collaboratory*—laboratories for (potentially) geographically dispersed collaborators (see Finholt's chapter in this volume). Initiatives such as the Human Genome Project, based on international sharing of research data and analysis, are good examples (Agrawala et al., 1997; Duderstadt et al., 2001; Fernandez, Sanchez, & Garcia, 2000; Kaplan & Nelson, 2000; Moxley, 1995; Phanouriou, Kipp, Sornil, Mather, & Fox, 1999).

Commercial enterprises: Many developers of digital libraries have consciously incorporated pricing and economic models into the architecture of DLs (Cousins et al., 1995; Gladney & Cantu, 2001; Ketchpel, Garcia-Molina, & Paepcke, 1996; Sistla, Wolfson, Yesha, & Sloan, 1998), prompting commercial organizations to view DLs as a new global marketplace. Some argue that digital libraries are in fact a specific case of an information economy, e.g., brokering environment (Schaube & Smeaton, 1998).

Multilingual communities: Developments in encoding, software, and other technologies have resulted in an enormous increase in non-English-language material in digital form (Dartois et al., 1997). DLs help transcend language barriers (Bian & Chen, 2000), spurring interest among multilingual communities in tools and techniques for multilingual information retrieval, in addition to developing language resources (Hull & Grefenstette, 1996; Kapidakis, Mavroidis, & Tsalapata, 1999; Klavans & Schauble, 1998; Powell & Fox, 1998).

Definitions

A digital library is not merely a collection of electronic information. It is an organized and digitized system of data that can serve as a rich resource for its user community. Defining a digital library has proved to be a vexing problem. Although there have been many attempts to anchor the concept, consensus is hard to come by. We present a selection of definitions.

The Association of Research Libraries identified the common elements of digital library definitions as (Association of Research Libraries, 1995, online):

- The digital library is not a single entity;
- The digital library requires technology to link the resources of many;
- The linkages between many digital libraries and information services are transparent to the end users;
- Universal access to digital libraries is a goal;
- Digital library collections are not limited to document surrogates; they extend to digital artifacts that cannot be represented or distributed in printed formats.

The D-Lib Working Group on Digital Library Metrics' (http://www. dlib.org/metrics/public) scope definition reads, "The Digital Library is the collection of services and the collection of information objects that support users in dealing with information objects available directly or indirectly via electronic/digital means."

The Digital Library Federation (http://clir.org/diglib/dldefinition.htm) proposes, "Digital libraries are organizations that provide the resources, including the specialized staff, to select, structure, offer intellectual access to, interpret, distribute, preserve the integrity of, and ensure the persistence over time of collections of digital works so that they are readily available for use by a defined community or set of communities."

The definitions range from the simple, "a collection of information which is both digitized and organized" (Lesk, 1997, p. 1), to the elaborate, "Digital Libraries are a set of electronic resources and associated technical capabilities for creating, searching, and using information ... they are an extension and enhancement of information storage and retrieval systems that manipulate digital data in any medium (text, images, sounds, and static or dynamic images) and exist in distributed networks" (Borgman et al., 1996, online). Borgman (1999) presents a well-documented and insightful discussion of definitions in the special issue on digital libraries of *Information Processing & Management.*

Redefining Roles: Interdependence and Relationships

DLs offer interesting possibilities for new kinds of alliances and partnerships between publishers, libraries, and scholarly communities. The roles of each are being redefined, with the players jockeying for position as the value chain linking the creators and users of scholarly knowledge is reengineered. Such efforts to redefine roles and relationships are evident in the various initiatives that aim to bring forth alternative institutional and organizational arrangements for scholarly publishing (Johnson, 2000; MacKie-Mason, Riveros, Bonn, & Lougee, 1999). New partnerships and alliances are forming between the three key players: professional societies, universities and other academic institutions, and other agencies, sometimes including commercial publishers. Good examples of such emerging organizational frameworks include the Scholarly Publishing and Academic Resources Coalition (SPARC, http://www.arl.org/sparc), BioOne (http://www.bioone.org), Pricing Electronic Access to Knowledge (PEAK, http://www.lib.umich.edu/libhome/peak), HighWire Press (http://highwire.stanford.edu), and OhioLINK (http://www.ohiolink.edu).

The assertion that information is free has evoked intense debate and shadowboxing between the players. Harnad (2000b) has been a strident voice for unfettered access, arguing vehemently for freeing scholarship from the clutches of commercial publishers. On the other side of the debate, publishing industry representatives have been equally forceful in challenging the view that information is without cost (Kaser, 2000).

Reinventing Libraries: What Is New vs. Old?

What, then, are the changes in the library world resulting from the emergence of DLs? While the fundamental mission of libraries—to facilitate access to knowledge and information—has remained unchanged, the processes, tools, and techniques employed have undergone profound transformation. These include:

- A shift from mediator to participatory role in the publication and communication processes
- The increase in user-direct publication channels
- Library processes and tools becoming invisible (or less visible) to the user
- Intensified use of iteration in resource discovery
- Increased granularity of content and access
- A wider range of document types (digital objects)
- Decreased dependence on static, as opposed to dynamic (rendered from databases) objects

D. Atkins (1999) presents a succinct and lucid summary of the major differences between DLs and traditional libraries. His analysis is the basis for Table 12.1.

Digital Libraries: Conceptual and Theoretical Underpinnings

Despite the rapid growth in DL research and development, the theoretical underpinnings of digital libraries remain elusive. Attempts to develop formal models or abstractions of digital libraries are conspicuously few. The multidisciplinary roots of the field, the differing perceptions, and the lack of definitional consensus have rendered understanding of underlying concepts and functionalities difficult. Lacking a formal theory of DLs, the field continues to be characterized by uncertain identity, disciplinary tensions, and differing views. The need for a formal theory for DLs has been perceived and advocated—notably in the Joint NSF-EU (European Union) Working Group on Future

**Table 12.1: Distinctions between traditional and
digital libraries (based on D. Atkin's [1999] summary)**

Traditional Libraries	Digital Libraries
Stable, evolving slowly	Highly dynamic, ephemeral, and versioned
Content is mostly individual objects of text and print, generally well defined and categorized, and not dynamically or directly linked with each other	Digital objects are multimedia, multi-sized, not well defined, and fractal
Organization and structuring of content is flat and contextual metadata is minimal	Data structures include significant internal scaffolding and richer contextual metadata
Content is more scholarly, the result of vigorous pre-publication review	Not limited to scholarly content, allow credentialling through prior review or through use
Limited access points and centralized management of content and collections	Virtually unlimited access points, with distributed collections, control, and content management
The physical and logical organization is usually directly controlled and correlated	The physical and logical organization can be separated, allowing virtual collections
Slow and usually one-way interactions	Two-way communication with real-time and rich interactions
The tradition supports free and universal access	DLs can support alternative philosophies: free as well as fee based

Directions of Digital Library Research recommendation that new models and theories be developed in order to understand the complex interactions between the various components in a globally distributed library (Schaube & Smeaton, 1998). The few attempts to develop a formalism began with Wang (1999). More recently Gonçalves, Kipp, Fox, and Watson (2001) have encapsulated the 5S framework (Fox, Gonçalves, & Kipp, 2001; Fox, Kipp, & Mather, 1998) into formal mathematical notation to define and explicate the components of a digital library. The formalism has been developed within the fundamental abstractions of the 5S framework—streams, structures, spaces, scenarios, and societies. Together these abstractions relate and unify concepts of documents, metadata, services, interfaces, and information warehouses required to formalize and elucidate digital libraries. A brief description of the 5S formalism follows.

Streams: Streams are sequences of elements of an arbitrary type. In this sense they can model both static content, as textual material, and dynamic content, as in temporal presentation of dynamic video. Formally, a stream is a sequence whose co-domain is a nonempty set.

Structures: A structure specifies the way in which parts of a whole are arranged or organized. In digital libraries, structures can be represented by hypertext, taxonomies, system connections, user relationships, containment, data flow, and workflow. Structuring orients readers within a document's information space. For example, markup languages are used to structure text, data are structured rigidly using schema in relational and object-oriented databases, indexing for information retrieval purposes helps cluster or classify documents and generates organizational structure for the document space. Structures are defined as labeled graphs, which impose organization.

Spaces: A space is any set of objects together with operations on those objects that obey certain rules. The operations and rules associated with a space define its properties. Spaces are distinguished by the operations on their objects. Digital libraries can use many types of spaces for indexing, visualizing, and other services that they perform. The most prominent of these spaces are measure spaces, probability spaces, and vector spaces.

Scenarios: Scenarios are events or actions that modify states of a computation in order to accomplish a functional requirement. To the library community, scenarios can be thought of as services.

Societies: Societies comprehend entities and the relationships between and among them. Societies allow an emphasis on communities as well as individual users. They help define the target audience of DL systems and facilitate collaboration that builds upon a shared framework of artifacts.

Figure 12.5d shows the 5S layers. The 5S framework is richer than the three- or four-part schemes shown in Figures 12.5b (adapted from a slide used by Stephen Griffin at NSF) and 12.5c (adapted from Marchionini & Fox, 1999). On the other hand, the model in Figure 12.5a, while unsuitable for formalization, is richer in showing six aspects of digital libraries. It also emphasizes which parts are "digital" versus "library," as well as highlighting that "content" relates (more strongly than the other aspects) to both terms.

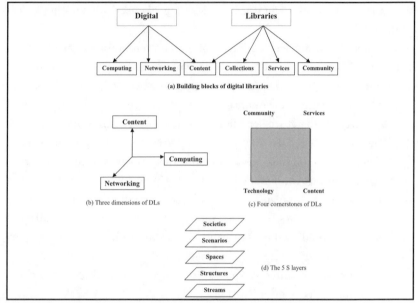

Figure 12.5 Viewpoints on digital libraries and their terminologies

History: Birth and Evolution of Digital Libraries

Digital libraries, in the sense they are perceived today, are sometimes viewed only as a post-Web phenomenon. Yet, both DLs and the Web trace their origins (as explained above) to the 1940s and 1950s. Among the earliest examples of pre-Web DL efforts were Carnegie Mellon University's Project Mercury (1989–1992), the TULIP Project (1993–1995) (Borghuis et al., 1996; Lynch, 1995), the Chemistry Online Retrieval Experiment (CORE) (Entlich et al., 1995), and the Envision Project (Fox, Hix et al., 1993; Heath et al., 1995; Nowell & Hix, 1992, 1993).

Digital Libraries Initiative, Phase 1: Conceptually digital libraries predate the Digital Libraries Initiative (DLI, 1994–1998) (Fox, 1999a) (funded at $24M by NSF, the Defense Advanced Research Projects Agency [DARPA], and the National Aeronautics and Space Administration [NASA]). A major impetus for DL research and development came from the first six major DLI–funded projects (Schatz & Chen, 1996). These projects, initiated in the early and mid-nineties in the U.S., and now referred to as DLI-1, have helped to:

- Clarify conceptualizations and definitions of digital libraries;
- Focus global attention on the promise, possibilities, and potential of DL technologies;
- Advance the design and development of search interfaces for diverse digital library objects;
- Promote standards for digital libraries;
- Bring together diverse professional groups belonging to different disciplines ranging from humanities to science and engineering;
- Increase in the volume of digital content and resources;
- Steer the course of digital library research.

DLI-1 advanced research on, and improved practice of, digital librarianship. It also generated interest among the academic community, policy makers, and the public at large. DLI-1, in turn, stimulated similar initiatives in other countries, e.g., the ELINOR Electronic Library project and eLib programme in the U.K. (Rusbridge, 1995), the Australian Digital Library initiatives (Iannella, 1996), and the Canadian Initiative on Digital Libraries (Haigh, 1998).

Digital Library Initiatives Phase II: The considerable success of DLI-1 encouraged continued and accelerated support, leading to DLI-2 (Fox, 1999a)—a much broader and larger effort. DLI-2 is an expansion in terms of the:

- Kinds of media covered, including sound recordings, music, economic data, software, images, video, and textual material;
- Diversity of the content, including such objects as anthropological models and images, literary manuscripts, and patient records;
- New technological issues being explored such as interoperability, security, automatic classification, and data provenance;
- Widening of efforts as a result of the increase in the number and diversity of agencies sponsoring and participating in the programs.

DLI-2 is a multiagency initiative involving NSF, DARPA, NASA, the Library of Congress, and other U.S. groups, seeking to provide leadership in research fundamental to the development of next generation digital libraries. Unfortunately, politics and funding issues have led DARPA and NASA to play a smaller role in DLI-2 than originally planned; on the other hand, activities in the DL area are now supported through a broad range of initiatives and programs, which may provide a more secure foundation for expansion of the field.

Trends: Differing Contexts and Approaches

The spread of interest in digital libraries has not only ensured rapid growth of the field, but also introduced differing contexts, approaches, emphases, practices, and views. These vary from one country or context to another.

In the U.S., early DL efforts were dominated by research—developing new architectures, organizations, and tools—perhaps a natural consequence of the considerable involvement of the computer science community. Many efforts centered around designing and developing architectures for various digital library systems, demonstrating applications of those systems, developing interfaces, and enhancing search facilities. Since 1999, however, DL projects have proliferated, and the U.S. library community has engaged in the deployment and refinement of systems as well as expansion of collections and services.

In the U.K., many of the digital library efforts have been initiated by the library and information science community, and have tended to focus on enhancing information services offered by traditional libraries, or what is referred to as hybrid libraries (Rusbridge, 1995). In 2001 it appears that further work will emphasize evaluation and identification of best practices.

Europe presents a different model, focusing on digitization efforts, collection building, preservation of heritage materials, and language issues. There has not been a great deal of support for research, except through multinational efforts linked to the DELOS (Network of Excellence on Digital Libraries) initiative (Boehm, Croft, & Schek, 2000; Day & Beagrie, 1998; European Research Consortium for Informatics and Mathematics, 1998; Schaube & Smeaton, 1998).

DL work in Australia is more broad-based. The direction of efforts and initiatives has been wide-ranging, from collection building to metadata initiatives (Iannella, 1996). Two areas of particular concern are geospatial information (Coddington et al., 1998) and subject gateways

(Campbell, 1999). These are also popular in Singapore and many other small nations that are "net importers" of content.

Content: Digital Objects and Their Creation

As can be seen in Figure 12.5a, content has moved to center stage in the DL field. Creating content—the information that users seek and libraries help to provide—is at the heart of designing, developing, and building digital libraries. For a good introduction, see the overview based on experiences at the Library of Congress (American Memory, 2000). The various stakeholders—authors, publishers, users, librarians, and others—are tied together through content. Authors have content to disseminate and distribute, while publishers and librarians add value to the information and facilitate its distribution. Communication through content creation and delivery relies upon supporting technology and techniques. The effectiveness of the message depends upon the representation and rendering of the information.

Figure 12.6 highlights the diversity of DL content, which may be text, images, audio, video, computer programs, or other forms. Newly created content is often born digital, while older resources are typically digitized through a conversion process. Both must be represented digitally, so such attendant issues as character encoding, formats, and files have dominated the discussion of digital libraries content. Although in their details these

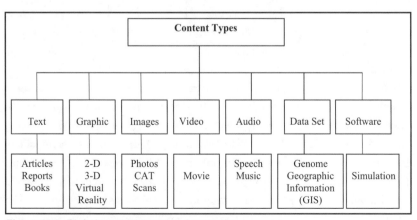

Figure 12.6 Digital content types and examples

depend on the particular forms involved (see upcoming sections), the high-level situation is roughly the same, encompassing creation, capture, conversion, storage, organization, search, retrieval, presentation, and re-use.

Creating Digital Content: Born Digital

One perspective on DLs is that they provide dynamic spaces for knowledge creation. The digital medium offers authors immense flexibility in representing and rendering their ideas. Today it is possible to think of content or information beyond the traditional text, largely due to this capability. New genres of document are evolving (Fox, McMillan, & Eaton, 1999), as text is enriched with still images, sound, and movies, and hypertext and hypermedia make alternative sequences of presentation possible.

Electronic publishing and multimedia: Since the 1960s, when text editors and time-sharing systems (later followed by personal computers) enabled authors to create documents on computers, electronic publishing has emerged as a key application of computers. Beginning in the 1980s, multimedia development gradually shifted to personal computers (initially largely to Macintosh systems, but then also to Windows environments). With the advent of fast networks and the Web, plug-ins and other tools that enable rendering on client machines have made the handling of multimedia commonplace. By the late 1990s, streams of audio and even video (Dan & Sitaram, 1999) could be delivered in scalable fashion, and relatively inexpensive authoring systems supporting such high-end multimedia content became available. Powerful DL systems were demonstrated to handle digital video (Hauptmann & Wactlar, 1997; Hauptmann & Witbrock, 1996; Hauptmann, Witbrock, & Christel, 1997). With the cost of multimegapixel digital cameras and high-resolution digital camcorders dropping rapidly, it appears certain that almost all publishing, even involving complex multimedia, will be electronic, making it feasible for such content to be directly entered into digital libraries.

Text: Text, however, continues to have a special place (W. Y. Arms, 2000). Character encoding, markup, and page description are some of the concerns in creating digital textual materials. Encoding is of special interest with respect to multilingual texts. Unicode provides a standard scheme suitable for all natural languages (Unicode Consortium, 2001); another approach to handling multilingual materials (especially with rarely used characters) is downloading special fonts as needed (Dartois et al., 1997). Digital library development is expected to produce an increase in multilingual content as more nations and societies perceive DLs as a means of preserving and providing access to their language, cultural, and national resources (Witten et al., 2001). There is strong interest in this area worldwide, especially in Europe and Asia (Oard, 1997a).

Markup languages: Any text has two dimensions: structure and form (i.e., the appearance or look). Markup languages—SGML, HTML, XML, and others—enable the creation of digital text in which structure is made clear. They specify what markup is allowed or required and how markup is distinguished from content strings. SGML, developed in 1985, is an international standard (ISO 8879) and is considered a meta-language (in which to specify schemes, like HTML, for describing various types of data or information). SGML, HTML, and XML constitute a family of standards supporting electronic publishing as well as (both the current practice and the future evolution of) the Web (Abiteboul, Buneman, & Suciu, 2000; Biron & Malhotra, 2001; Bray et al., 1998; Burnard, 2000; Connolly & Thompson, 2000; Willett, 1999; XML.ORG, 2000). They support authoring, transmitting (i.e., interchange), archiving, processing, transforming, rendering, and presenting in various ways (e.g., on paper or on screen).

Creating Digital Content: Conversion

Tens of millions of content objects (speeches, music, poems, articles, books, sculptures, paintings, movies, etc.) have been created throughout history. Surrogates for, or representations of, many of them are being entered into digital libraries. This requires capture and conversion to a digital representation suitable for the relevant media form, at a level of quality adequate to support both current and planned requirements, including preservation (Day & Beagrie, 1998). Lesk (1997) discusses suitable formats and conversions for text, page images, and multimedia content. Noerr (2000) explains alternatives, as well as plans, resource requirements, capturing, pitfalls, and vendors.

Content that is not in digital form requires analog-to-digital conversion (e.g., from paper to electronic document). Analysis at the time of conversion can add value by recognizing patterns and other characteristics, for example through optical character recognition (OCR) of texts, or feature extraction from video (Hunter, 1999). Speech can be recognized and represented as text (Witbrock & Hauptmann, 1998). When allowable, the digital form may be compressed to save space and reduce storage and transmission requirements. Editing, filtering, enhancing, combining, and other transformations related to communication and presentation often can proceed on digital materials without loss, moving from electronic to enriched electronic form.

More complex conversions can be undertaken, usually through multi-step processing. Automation can help speed the conversion, and can make possible handling of very large volumes of data. Ideally, raw materials can be converted with little human intervention, to create refined and valuable forms, such as when papers are converted to hypertexts (Myka & Guntzer, 1995).

Digital Objects: Range of and Diversities in Digital Objects

The result of such conversions is a broad range of digital objects. For example, in creating a digital library of music, one may have facsimile images of scores, Musical Instrument Digital Interface (MIDI) files, digital audio recordings, and textual metadata (Bainbridge, Nevill-Manning, Witten, Smith, & McNab, 1999).

Specific application areas can require or facilitate diversity in digital objects. For example, digital libraries of educational resources (ARIADNE, 2000; National Science Foundation, 2000a; Project Kaleidoscope Alliance, 2000; SMETE.ORG Alliance, 2000; Wattenberg, 1998) deal with demonstrations, exercises, images, laboratory activities, lesson plans, metadata, movies, presentations, quizzes, and simulations.

Diversity is evident in the variety of mechanisms for accomplishing a particular goal. As scholarly communication expands to incorporate a range of forms and digital libraries, there are calls for rethinking key concepts such as "document" (Schamber, 1996). For biomedical researchers, handling heterogeneous online data collections seamlessly is important (Davidson, Overton, Tannen, & Wong, 1997). For graduate education, theses are crucial (Eaton, Fox, & McMillan, 1998), and can have added value when they are used to stimulate collaboration (Fernandez, Sánchez, & Flores, 2000). These are examples of the "grey literature" encompassing theses, dissertations, reports, and other materials that serve niche requirements with greater speed than commercial publishing. It is likely that digital libraries will accentuate the importance and increase the coverage of grey literature. In addition, authors are learning how to include not only text but also color figures and images, movies, audio, datasets, and other special objects used in their research when they electronically archive their dissertations (Fox, McMillan, & Eaton, 1999).

In general, digital libraries store digital objects representing diverse types of information, from atomic to composite, from small to large, in original or processed form, in raw form or compressed, ready for presentation or tuned for archiving. Whenever possible, processing of content should not involve loss, and should use international standards, so that the heavy investment required for digitization, and the labor of authors creating documents "born digital," can have maximal long-term effect.

Content: Collections and Processes

While in the previous section content was viewed in terms of individual digital objects, in this section the focus is on sets or aggregations of digital objects, along with the processes for managing such collections, at their various levels of aggregation. At the lowest level is the pairing of a digital object with a metadata object. At the next level are large numbers of these pairs, organized into repositories. At the highest level are distributed DLs, made up of sufficient numbers of repositories to warrant employing resource discovery to identify which repositories are suitable for detailed search.

Thus, based on an appropriate design, DLs can be implemented along the lines of promising architectures, and can support desired services (see next section), with good performance, scalability, and functionality.

Design Issues

Networking and interoperability are two major factors affecting DL design and organization. Conceptually, these issues always have been central to librarianship; and library networking predates computer networking. Libraries committed to the philosophy of resource sharing have traditionally undertaken programs of a collaborative nature and these collaborative networks have raised issues of standardization and interoperability. The methods and means of evolving common standards and practices have remained central to the library and information science community. Thus, since the beginning of the twentieth century, many attempts have been made to resolve interoperability issues, as exemplified by the efforts to develop international cataloging codes (Furrie, 2000). The birth of the *Anglo American Cataloguing Rules* is one such case.

W. Y. Arms (1995b, online) identified eight general principles regarding the design of DLs:

- The technical framework exists within a legal and social framework
- Understanding of digital library concepts is hampered by terminology
- The underlying architecture should be separate from the content stored in the library
- Names and identifiers are the basic building block [sic] for the digital library
- Digital library objects are more than collections of bits
- The digital library object that is used is different from the stored object
- Repositories must look after the information they hold
- Users want intellectual works, not digital objects

Metadata

Until very recently, storage and processing limitations made it necessary for librarians to spend time managing terse descriptions of information, in addition to information artifacts themselves. Even today, when digital objects can be machine-processed in their entirety, there are benefits to working with descriptions, summaries, and other surrogates. So when considering metadata, we first turn to library and information science for general guidance (International Federation of Library Associations and Institutions, 2000). Then, we seek a framework (e.g., from the Warwick workshop) through which to integrate the various types of metadata (e.g., structural versus descriptive) and digital objects, along with their cross links and groupings (Daniel & Lagoze, 1997; Lagoze, 1996). Such a perspective is important in real-life applications, such as when describing diverse categories of educational resources. Thus, several similar schemes have come into widespread use (École polytechnique fédérale de Lausanne, Katolicki Uniwersytet Lubelski, & ARIADNE, 1999; IEEE Learning Technology Standards Committee, 2000; Instructional Management System, 1999), but, fortunately, planning has been adequate to ensure that mappings allow automatic transformation among them.

Invoking Occam's razor, there has been a strong push to simplify metadata schemes so that it is possible for all digital objects to have associated metadata. This makes it feasible to consider producing metadata for large portions of the Web (Hickey, 1999). The result of a global initiative with this intent is the Dublin Core (Dublin Core Metadata Initiative, 1999; Weibel, 1999; Weibel, Kunze, Lagoze, & Wolf, 1998b), which in its basic form requires only fifteen attributes to describe a digital object. This is in sharp contrast with the ubiquitous Machine Readable Cataloging (MARC) standard (Furrie, 2000), with its myriad fields and subfields. Nevertheless, crosswalks exist between these two and other schemes, such as for government information (Library of Congress, 1999).

As metadata applications proliferate to handle the diverse content in DLs, it may become necessary to have richer representations; XML illustrates one approach, supporting re-use of components from one metadata scheme in another application (Brin & Malhotra, 2001). To support such schemes, some have argued that DLs should be based on ontologies (Shum, Motta, & Domingue, 2000). This was one of the themes of the DLI-1 project at the University of Michigan (Weinstein & Alloway, 1997; Weinstein & Birmingham, 1998), but the problems are so difficult that progress has been slow. Research has shown that it is possible to help drive browsing with classification hierarchies (Geffner, Agrawal, Abbadi, & Smith, 1999), and work continues to enhance interoperability on the semantic level (Ouksel & Sheth, 1999).

Powerful tools, like neural networks, can help with automatic construction of topic hierarchies in DLs (Rauber, Dittenbach, & Merkl, 2000). Yet, somewhat simpler tools can help build structure maps in domains (Delcambre, Maier, & Reddy, 1997). Fortunately, very simple tools, like My Meta Maker (Severiens, 2000), can be used by large numbers of authors to apply human intelligence in producing useful metadata descriptions.

Organizing Digital Resources: Collections and Repositories

At the next level of aggregation we address the concept of "collection." This is elegantly built into systems like Hyper-G, now called Hyperwave (Andrews, Kappe, & Maurer, 1995; Pam & Vermeer, 1995), which aims to correct some of the omissions in the design of the World Wide Web. That is, authors and users can benefit from groupings of objects; for example, in a multimedia application it is possible to specify that a three-object collection, made of video and two channels of audio, should be synchronized when presented. Similar capabilities may develop from the set construct that is built into Open Archives (Van de Sompel, 2000).

Considering descriptions across domains, and interoperability (which is quite important in an educational setting), P. Miller (2000a, 2000b) also emphasizes collection-level issues. On the other hand, Moore et al. (2000) emphasize persistence in the context of collections.

If one focuses on a DL as a collection, it is sometimes useful to employ a new term, namely "repository." At this level we have diverse applications with differing content types, ranging from newspapers (Aramburu & Berlanga, 1997) to videos (Geisler & Marchionini, 2000). We must deal with issues of scalability (Hawking, 1997), reliability (Cooper, Crespo, & Molina, 1999), and archivability (Crespo & Garcia-Molina, 1999). These have architectural implications, considered in the next subsection.

Architecture

The architecture of a conventional library can greatly influence its popularity and use. So, too, the architecture of a DL can have great effect (Nürnberg, Furuta, Leggett, Marshall & Shipman, 1995). For example, if a DL system is to be deployed to serve widely varying sizes of user communities, it should be scalable (Andresen, Yang, Egecioglu, Ibarra, & Smith, 1996; Cheng et al., 1998). Due to network bandwidth requirements, this may be difficult when multimedia content is involved (Christodoulakis & Triantafillou, 1995). Further, scalability in terms of numbers of DLs that work together for a common aim (e.g., to support federated searching), may lead to particular architectures for such heterogeneous resources (Dolin, Agrawal, & Abbadi, 1999).

DL architecture may depend on other types of requirements as well. For example, DLs may be built with an emphasis on flexible user interaction, if a user-centered approach is adopted (Theng, Duncker, Mohd-Nasir, Buchanan, & Thimbleby, 1999; Theng, Mohd-Nasir, Thimbleby, Buchanan, & Jones, 2000), or if personalization is required (Wolff & Cremers, 1999). This flexibility can be extended further, including across space, to support collaboration (Wilensky, 2000). Thus, key considerations of DL architecture are modularity, scalability, and extensibility (W. Y. Arms, 1998). But to understand the effects of such requirements on DLs, it is imperative to look inside DL systems and their architectures.

One of the main technical issues at the heart of digital library development efforts is identifying the building blocks of a DL. What are the software components? How are they configured and orchestrated to carry out all the functions that are expected of a library? What software properly connects the repository, mechanisms for identifying and organizing the digital objects, access and search tools, interfaces, and other pieces? To address these questions we note two basic approaches to the development of digital libraries:

1. Defining a universal protocol for all libraries to follow
2. Developing mechanisms to translate between protocols

Most designers of DL architectures have followed the second approach, though the Open Archives Initiative leans more toward the first (Van de Sompel, 2000).

Interoperability: For heterogeneous DLs with distributed collections of digital objects, the key issues become openness and interoperability (Paepcke et al., 1996). Collections and services are provided by different organizations on many different computer systems. Information comes from diverse sources, is processed in various ways, and is managed according to very different quality standards (W. Y. Arms, 1995b). The distributed environment and heterogeneity introduce complexity into the design, as each collection is characterized by its own informational content, its own vocabulary in terms of metadata, its own presentation formats, and its own processing functions. Interoperability has been a vexing problem, and means different things to different people. P. Miller (2000b) discusses the almost all-pervasive term, and looks at what it really means to be interoperable from a very broad perspective. He identifies the different "flavors" of interoperability: technical interoperability; semantic interoperability; political/human interoperability; inter-community interoperability; legal interoperability; and international interoperability. Paepcke, Chang, Garcia-Molina, and Winograd (1998) earlier provided a related and influential overview of the topic.

Technical and semantic interoperability are two important concerns that have dominated the literature. It is technical interoperability that has received greater attention from the designers of DL systems, especially from the programming and computing point of view. An open, interoperable environment is required in order to help users traverse multiple, disparate data sets. Certain key issues must be addressed in creating such an interoperable environment (Maamar, Moulin, Bédard, & Babin, 1997, online):

- The disparities between multiple elements, like hardware platforms, software technologies, users' knowledge about the analyzed domain, etc.
- The complexity of operations that require information from distributed and heterogeneous systems
- The scarcity of design methods and tools for interoperable environments

Kahn-Wilensky: One very important framework for the architectural design of DLs was specified in connection with the DARPA-sponsored Computer Science Technical Reports (CSTR) project. This is a general purpose framework for a DL in which very large numbers of objects, comprising all types of material, are made accessible via networks. Kahn and Wilensky (1995) define the basic entities found in such distributed digital information services, in which information in the form of digital objects is stored, accessed, disseminated, and managed. One important contribution of this framework has been the introduction of naming conventions for identifying and locating digital objects. The most important schemes in this regard are "handles" (globally unique digital object identifiers, specified by CNRI) (W. Y. Arms, 1995b), persistent URLs (PURLs), developed by OCLC, and digital object identifiers (DOIs) (Bearman, Miller, Rust, Trant, & Weibel, 1999; Paskin, 1999; Powell, 1998).

According to the Kahn-Wilensky architecture, a DL has four components:

- A digital object
- A repository
- A Repository Access Protocol (RAP)
- Dissemination

A digital object is an instance of an abstract data type having two components: data and key metadata (including a handle). A repository is a network-accessible storage system in which digital objects may be stored for subsequent access and retrieval. A mechanism for adding new digital objects and making them accessible is the function of the Repository Access Protocol (RAP), while dissemination is the result of an access service request.

Z39.50: Another scheme for interoperability is based on the Z39.50 protocol (also ISO 23950) (American National Standards Institute, 1995; International Standard Maintenance Agency, 2000; Lynch, 1997; P. Miller, 1999; National Information Standards Organization, 1995; Payette & Rieger, 1997). Z39.50 was developed originally for client-server access to collections managed by information retrieval systems. The basic architectural model of Z39.50 is as follows: A server houses one or more databases containing records; associated with each database is a set of access points (indices) that can be used for searching.

This is a much more abstract view of a database than one finds with Structured Query Language (SQL), for example. Details are hidden regarding specific database implementations, relatively arbitrary server-specific decisions are allowed about how to segment logical data into relations, and how to name the columns in the relations. One deals only with logical entities based on the kind of information that is stored in the database (Lynch, 1997). Although the term "semistructured" that is used to describe such information may sound condescending, in reality the documents found in actual DLs are sufficiently rich and complex (recall the 5S framework discussed earlier) to require powerful semantic network representation (Christophides, Durr, & Fundulaki, 1997).

Based on Z39.50, a variety of heterogeneous DLs have been constructed, routing suitable queries to servers that are likely to help satisfy an information need (Lin, Xu, Lim, & Ng, 1999). Because Z39.50 is a rich protocol, with powerful capabilities, DL collections can be well-described and software can "wrap" the content with appropriate mediation support (Christophides, Cluet, & Simeon, 2000; Melnik, Garcia-Molina, &

Paepcke, 2000; Velegrakis, Christophides, & Constantopoulos, 2000; Velegrakis, Christophides, & Vonstanopoulos, 1999). MARIAN (France, 2000b), a digital library system (Zhao, 1999) that grew out of earlier work on information retrieval and library catalogs (Fox, France, Sahle, Daoud, & Cline, 1993), has been extended with wrappers to support not only Z39.50 but also the Dienst and Open Archives Initiative (OAI) protocols discussed here (Gonçalves, France et al., 2001).

Dienst: The Dienst (German for "server") system has been under development at Cornell since the advent of the Web, to support federated information access (Davis, Krafft, & Lagoze, 1995; Lagoze & Davis, 1995). At its heart is a protocol built upon Hyper Text Transfer Protocol (HTTP), and modified repeatedly (Kapidakis et al., 1999; Nelson, Maly, & Shen, 1997). The Networked Computer Science Technical Reference Library (NCSTRL) system (Lagoze, 1999) and approach (Leiner, 1998) has been a key driver of developments for Dienst (Davis & Lagoze, 2000; Lagoze, 1995, 1997, 1999; Lagoze & Fielding, 1998; Lagoze, Fielding, & Payette, 1998; Lagoze & Payette, 1998). The operation and performance of NCSTRL has been analyzed and simulated (Balci & Nance, 1992; Payette, Blanchi, Lagoze, & Overly, 1999). Various later systems have been adaptations of Dienst.

One early extension, Inter-operable Secure Object Stores (ISOS), focused on security (Lagoze, 1995). NASA services were built upon NCSTRL and led to the TRSkit toolkit and NCSTRL+ system (Kaplan & Nelson, 2000; Nelson & Bianco, 1995; Nelson & Esler, 1997; Nelson, Maly, & Shen, 1997; Nelson, Maly, Shen, & Zubair, 1998; Nelson, Maly, & Zubair, 1998). Work at NASA and Old Dominion University continued, adding support for "buckets" (Nelson, Maly, Zubair, & Shen, 1998) as part of the Smart Objects, Dumb Archives (SODA) approach (Maly, Nelson, & Zubair, 1999; Nelson, Maly, Zubair, & Shen, 1999), later applied to educational resources (Maly, Zubair, Liu, Nelson, & Zeil, 1999) and aeronautics (Nelson, 1999). At Cornell, as well as other sites including the University of Virginia, work has extended into the Flexible Extensible Digital Object Repository Architecture (FEDORA) system (Staples & Wayland, 2000).

Other approaches—agents, mediators: Quite distinct from NCSTRL-related schemes is the agent approach. This was emphasized in the University of Michigan DLI-1 effort (Birmingham, 1995a, 1995b). Other examples include the CARROT system (Nicholas, Crowder, & Soboroff, 2000), the Chrysalis environment (Sánchez, Lopez, & Schnase, 1998), and agent-based document retrieval for European physicists (Borghoff et al., 1997). In short, DLs are decomposed into many, smaller modules, each operating relatively autonomously. Schemes for knowledge transfer, scheduling of agents (since they require computation and so may become bottlenecks), and managing registries are among the most important aspects of such systems.

As mentioned earlier, heterogeneous DLs can be integrated using wrappers or mediators, sometimes based on formal schemes and with automatic generation of code (Ashish & Knoblock, 1997; Melnik et al., 2000; Wiederhold & Genesereth, 1997). At Stanford, this led to The Stanford-IBM Manager of Multiple Information Sources (TSIMMIS) approach (Garcia-Molina et al., 1997), the Stanford Protocol Proposal for Internet Retrieval and Search (STARTS) (Gravano, Chang, Garca-Molina, & Paepcke, 1996, 1997), and the Simple Digital Library Interoperability Protocol (SDLIP) (Paepcke et al., 2000). As one of the DLI-1 sites, Stanford made extensive use of mediators as it developed software around its InfoBus architecture (Paepcke, 1999) and metadata architecture (Baldonado, Chang, Gravano, & Paepcke, 1997a, b).

The core of the problems with architecture and interoperability is not engineering but rather consensus building and organizational arrangements. These issues and the role of W3C in that context were summarized succinctly by J. S. Miller (1996, online): "But the hardest problems to be solved are not technological: They are problems of our social and institutional structure that can only be solved by cooperation and agreement within the Digital Library community itself. And these processes are well underway."

Resource Discovery Through Metadata

Key among the processes dealing with collections of content is resource discovery. It is a complex, multidimensional, multi-threaded, and iterative process. It may be viewed as a series of movements between two phases or states—the location and the examination—or as movement along an information granularity spectrum. Alternatively it can be looked at using the metaphor of a digital tourist (Lagoze, 1997).

As was predicted in the 1960s (Licklider, 1965); as became feasible with the emergence of Web technology; and because of political, economic, social, and technical considerations, the world is faced with myriad distributed content collections. Further, since metadata can be separated from the data described, we often have collections of metadata, designed to help with resource discovery (Weibel, 1995; Weibel, Kunze, Lagoze, & Wolf, 1998a, 1998b), in addition to the collections of content (or integrated with them according to various philosophies). This situation presents a rich design space for organizing global information resources, drawing upon the potential of architectures discussed in the previous subsection. It is in this context that the import of resource discovery can best be seen.

The fundamental task of resource discovery includes identifying what a resource is. At the atomistic level, supported by the Resource Description Framework (RDF) (Brickley & Guha, 2000a, 2000b; Lassila & Swick, 1999), we may seek an identifier representing some object, perhaps an authority record, or a name or string designating that object. At the semantic network level, we may navigate through interrelationships among low-level resources (Voorhees, 1994).

But most digital library work views either metadata or documents as the desired resource for discovery. The key question, then, relates to the overall architecture (Roszkowski & Lukas, 1998). At this higher level, there are a number of popular options. First consider the federated search scheme, where content from disparate DLs is brought together when a user searches. Sometimes this aggregation is drawn only from DLs selected as most promising to serve the user's information need (Xu, Cao, Lim, & Ng, 1998), made possible when data demonstrate the property of locality (Viles & French, 1999). Demanding the least cooperation among those developing DLs is the federated-heterogeneous approach where, for example, a central site characterizes, adjusts for, and searches each DL according to its capabilities (Powell & Fox, 1998), often through mediator or wrapper schemes as discussed above. Simpler and more effective on the technical side, but requiring greater cooperation among DL implementers, is the federated-homogeneous approach, where each DL at least uses the same protocol (Gravano et al., 1996), or better yet, runs the same software (as discussed above in connection with Dienst and NCSTRL).

Alternatively, consider the harvesting approach, where content is aggregated in preparation for search, for example, of a combined historical collection (Sanz, Berlanga, & Aramburu, 1998). Then resource discovery is co-managed by those aggregating information, those providing services, and those searching in harvested collections. Harvesting was popularized by the Harvest system (Bowman, Danzig, Hardy, Manber, & Schwartz, 1995; Bowman et al., 1994). It is still used in certain DL applications (Severiens, Hohlfeld, Zimmermann, & Hilf, 2000), although many of those are shifting to the Open Archives approach. This scheme builds upon Harvest, some of the technology used in NCSTRL, and other efforts. First applied to support archives and related types of resources, the Open Archives Initiative was launched in October 1999 (Van de Sompel, 2000; Van de Sompel & Lagoze, 2000). The Open Archives Initiative Protocol for Metadata Harvesting (Van de Sompel & Lagoze, 2001), specified through this initiative, lowers the barriers for information providers to make their content available. As the DL field moves toward componentized approaches to building DLs, where the parts are integrated through protocols, OAI encourages separating data providers and service providers. In analogous fashion to running a Web server, it is quite simple for any individual or group wishing to make a collection of metadata available to run an open archive. As software becomes available, services will support harvesting from (parts of) remote archives, improving quality (Suleman, Fox, & Abrams, 2000), adding value to the aggregation, and exposing new, tailored open archives. Further software development will provide a broad range of services for accessing and using one or more open archives.

Finally, to meet the needs of current DL users, rather sophisticated systems are being built to combine these approaches. Thus, the MARIAN system supports federated search using a variety of protocols, as well as harvesting through both Harvest and OAI (Gonçalves, France et al., 2001). DL managers can thus balance the need for up-to-date information (as from federated search) with requirements for rapid response and higher-quality information resources (as from harvested collections to which post-processing adds value). Ultimately, though, the various schemes for managing content collections aim to support services, as discussed in the next section.

Services

Libraries provide services (i.e., support a variety of scenarios as in the 5S framework). In this section we seek to define DLs by considering the services they supply.

Some DL services are not typical in conventional libraries. For example, DLs may support plagiarism detection. This is particularly important to combat the often-voiced concern that making information available through digital libraries will promote plagiarism. The Stanford Copy Analysis Mechanism (SCAM) was one of the first systems for copy detection among digital documents (Brin, Davis, & Garcia-Molina, 1995). Subsequent efforts have demonstrated scalable and accurate copy detection mechanisms (Shivakumar & Garcia-Molina, 1995a, 1995b, 1996). Parallel computers can help in this process, and allow even more fine-grained control, where the more general problem of document overlap detection is addressed (Monostori, Zaslavsky, & Schmidt, 2000).

Another class of services in DLs involves analysis and processing of digital information. In some cases that can occur using the representation scheme in which data were captured. Thus, when a DL has document page images, it is possible to identify important regions or otherwise construct summaries without employing optical character recognition (OCR) methods (Chen & Bloomberg, 1998). On the other hand, it is often appropriate to load databases from documents; for example, through top-down extraction with semi-structured data (Ribeiro-Neto, Laender, & da Silva, 1999). In a similar vein, it is possible to build a type of document road map through analysis (Wang & Liu, 1998) or to process images sufficiently well to locate and OCR text found therein (Wu, Manmatha, & Riseman, 1997).

Specifically, in dealing with text, various types of analysis may be needed. Because of the problems with limited vocabulary control (Furnas, Landauer, Gomez, & Dumais, 1987), it may not be easy for a searcher to think of the terms to use in a query to match the terms in relevant documents. Accordingly, for concept-based document retrieval, developing a suitable thesaurus may be helpful (Chen, Lynch, Basu, & Ng, 1993). Similarly, having a thesaurus may be useful for retrieving multimedia content (van Doorn, 1999). With modern computers, it is possible to build an adequate thesaurus for a DL covering a particular subject discipline automatically through semantic indexing (Chung, He, Powell, & Schatz, 1999). Approaches such as latent semantic indexing (LSI) show promise in this regard, and also facilitate subsequent retrieval (Dumais, Furnas, Landauer, & Deerwester, 1988).

Since people who use DLs often have unique needs, another type of valuable service is personalization. French (1999) has developed personalized information environments for distributed DLs. Similarly, the MiBiblio system supports personalization (Fernandez, Sánchez, & Garcia, 2000). One approach employs agents to interact directly with DL users (Sánchez & Leggett, 1997).

Some services depend on the type of content involved; for example, geo-referenced information provides interesting opportunities (Zhu, Ramsey, Ng, Chen, & Schatz, 1999). Other services are of a more general nature. Thus, DLs may support filtering or routing, such as through the Stanford Information Filtering Tool (SIFT) (Yan & Garcia-Molina, 1999). Filtering is closely related to information retrieval (Belkin & Croft, 1992), which is discussed in the next subsection.

Access: Information Retrieval

Information retrieval (IR) services are at the heart of DLs. Many of these applications are based on inverted files, which can be efficiently built and deployed on parallel computers if the workload warrants (Sornil, 2000). Developing advanced methods for networked information collections such as DLs has been discussed in various workshops (Association for Computing Machinery, Special Interest Group on Information Retrieval, 1996). Mechanisms to assess retrieval effectiveness in such distributed DLs (French & Viles, 1996) and devices such as query mediators allow almost any remote DL to be included in searches (Dushay, French, & Lagoze, 1999).

Extensions to these services may be appropriate for DLs. One possibility is to support cooperative work on IR problems (Salampasis, Tait, & Bloor, 1996). Another approach is to apply powerful IR methods to archives as well as libraries (Tsinaraki, Christodoulakis, Anestis, & Moumoutzis, 1998). A broad range of retrieval methods exists for content in particular media, such as maps (Samet & Soffer,

1996), musical tunes (McNab, Smith, Witten, & Henderson, 2000), and speech (Oard, 1997b).

Searching: Query Languages, Natural Language Processing

Search services should be designed to support the information seeking needs of DL users, as Marchionini and Komlodi (1998) explain in their recent *ARIST* chapter. Further detail can be found in articles or books (Marchionini, 1995) on this topic. For example, Bates (1989) used berrypicking as an analogy to train users on effective techniques.

Artificial intelligence (AI) approaches to improve searching can provide predictive models that consider information seeking in context (Ennis & Sutcliffe, 1998), or dynamic searching aided by intelligent personal spiders (Chen, Chung, Ramsey, & Yang, 1998). Natural language processing can improve retrieval effectiveness, and logic-based methods have been shown to support retrieval of complex documents that include multimedia elements (Fuhr, Govert, & Rolleke, 1998). Ongoing work in this area by researchers in Europe and the U.S. was the theme of a DELOS workshop at the end of 2000 (Boehm et al., 2000). Related efforts are discussed in the next subsections.

Cross Language Retrieval

Since DLs cover content in many languages, and since many users cannot communicate effectively in all the languages in which relevant documents are written, cross-language IR (CLIR) is an important service (Oard, 1997a). Bilingual dictionaries can translate queries into each of the languages in which relevant documents may be found (Hull & Grefenstette, 1996). Corpus linguistics techniques have also been applied to enhance query translation, such as between Korean and English (Jang & Myaeng, 1998). These schemes continue to be refined; they are promising areas for Europe-U.S. collaboration to better support CLIR (Klavans & Schauble, 1998).

Hypertext and Citation Services

Other important approaches employ hypertext techniques and/or citation information. While many people make extensive use of hypertext, without help it can be like an electronic labyrinth (Snyder, 1996). Hypertext systems have been around for decades. Some, like Knowledge Management System (KMS), readily support collaboration and rapid handling of knowledge resources (Yoder, Akscyn, & McCracken, 1989). While progress was made to support interoperability among hypertext systems prior to the advent of the Web (Leggett, Schnase, Smith, & Fox, 1993), today that need is felt even more urgently in the context of DLs.

One important hypertext service is to build links automatically among the works in a DL (Kellogg, Subhas, & Fox, 1995). This can be a challenge, especially if highly effective links are desired among full-text documents (Ellis, Furner, & Willett, 1996). Ideally, those links will be typed or labeled, for greater specificity, and the hypermedia collections involved will be open, not tied to proprietary systems (Hansen, Yndigegn, & Grnbk, 1999). An important project in which these issues have been explored is Microcosm (Hall, 1999).

Tremendous value can be found in DLs that have large numbers of links, such as the *Web of Science* (H. Atkins, 1999), which builds upon ISI's citation databases. *CiteSeer/ResearchIndex* (Giles, Bollacker, & Lawrence, 1998) behaves similarly, but operates largely autonomously, using citation indexing as well as AI methods to analyze documents (Lawrence, Giles, & Bollacker, 1999). Rule-based methods also are built into the Special Effects (SFX) technology, which supports dynamic link resolution, so that users can link to the least expensive and best available target (Van de Sompel & Hochstenbach, 1999). By analyzing a hyperbase to count in-degree (links to an item), it assists in finding authoritative sources (Kleinberg, 1999). When a DL includes extensive link information, it can be employed to improve retrieval effectiveness (Joo & Myaeng, 1998).

Hypertexts may also have trails or paths (Bush, 1945); Walden's Paths provide a valuable example of tailored routes on the World Wide Web (Furuta, 2000). Implementation and testing of this concept have shown that guided paths may indeed be a helpful service (Shipman, Furuta, Brenner, Chung, & Hsieh, 2000).

Visualization

Progressing from paths to even more complex representations, we next consider DL services that involve presentation and/or interaction using visual representations. These relate in the 5S framework to spaces, typically 2-D or 3-D, as well as to related styles of interaction (scenarios).

First, we note that many visualization schemes involve analysis of collections in order to highlight useful clusterings, groupings, or partitionings. One of the more popular approaches began with an exploration of self-organizing maps (SOMs) to support IR (Lin & Soergel, 1991). This early study led to schemes for dealing with order (Kaski, Honkela, Lagus, & Kohonen, 1996) and to support browsing (Lagus, Kaski, Honkela, & Kohonen, 1996). Neural network methods may help in building DLs around SOMs (Rauber & Merkl, 1999). Tree Maps can provide somewhat similar capabilities (Shneiderman, 1992). In general, it is helpful to personalize DLs through exploration of information spaces (Sugimoto, Katayama, & Takasu, 1998).

Second, there is the matter of visualizing classification schemes to aid searching (Liu et al., 2000). The cat-a-cone approach supports category hierarchies (Hearst & Karadi, 1997). Another scheme involves 3-D trees, demonstrated for the Floristic Digital Library (Amavizca, Sánchez, & Abascal, 1999). While it is natural to try to manage complex classification schemes through interfaces that are as powerful as possible, it is a matter for study whether 3-D methods are best (Sutcliffe & Patel, 1996).

Third, it should be noted that there are many formats for presenting visualizations of DLs. Graphs can be used to represent many aspects. Previews and overviews can be of great value to users, particularly in supporting visual information seeking (Greene, Marchionini, Plaisant, & Shneiderman, 2000). Similarly, since metadata includes date information (and may have time coverage as well), support for timelines is beneficial (Kumar, Furuta, & Allen, 1998). When geospatial information is involved, particularly when it includes multimedia content, it is important to have suitable analysis and representation (Chen, Smith, Larsgaard, Hill, & Ramsey, 1997) to support visual interaction in this regard as well (Jung, 1999).

Fourth, a variety of schemes have been developed to help users work with search results sets. Tilebars help with displaying where the various concepts of a query occur in large documents, making it easier to spot locations where several appear together (Hearst, 1995). The ENVISION interface pioneered a 2-D grid representation, with users choosing what characteristics to portray (e.g., concept *vs.* year, author *vs.* estimated relevance) for each axis (Heath et al., 1995; Nowell, Hix, France, Heath, & Fox, 1996). Such resulting visualization methods can be extended by using categorical and hierarchical axes and by zooming in and out (Shneiderman, Feldman, Rose, & Grau, 2000).

Work on information visualization applied to DLs shows particular promise. One helpful sign is the broadening of this work to consider multiuser situations in suitable social contexts (Jaen & Rigas, 1998). A general need for contextualizing information spaces exists, especially with regard to federated DLs (Papazoglou & Hoppenbrouwers, 1999). This leads us to a more general discussion of human-computer interaction (HCI) and interface issues with regard to DL services.

Human-Computer Interaction: Interfaces

Developing novel interfaces to DLs has been a popular line of research, building upon the related field of user interface design (Hix & Hartson, 1993). One productive approach is user-centered design, addressing, for example, information exploration (Baldonado, 2000) and handling of multimedia content (Sutcliffe, 1999). Typically, an iterative design approach is required (Plaisant, Marchionini, Bruns, Komlodi, & Campbell, 1997), such as that used to develop interfaces and tools for DL work with the Library of Congress (Marchionini, Plaisant, & Komlodi, 1998).

DLs provide opportunities for exploring novel interfaces. The SortTables approach (Wake & Fox, 1995) emphasized rapid interaction supported by tailored indices to facilitate narrowing result sets based on attribute values fitting into suitable ranges. A good deal more work is needed for DLs to support collaborative activities (Nichols et al., 2000). Similarly, more work is needed on suitable frameworks for interacting with geographic DLs (Oliveira, Gonçalves, & Medeiros, 1999). Likewise, undertaking analysis and building interfaces to support browsing in digital video collections (Lee et al., 2000) requires more study and may necessitate using AI methods (Hauptmann et al., 1997). Other difficult interface problems relate to managing conceptual knowledge (Kent & Bowman, 1995), and devising architectures to support advanced queries and complex interaction (Kovcs, Micsik, Pataki, & Zsámboki, 2000).

With such complexity, it becomes essential to study usability and refine user interfaces accordingly.

Usability and Use Studies

Don Waters (1998), former Director of the Digital Library Federation, noted the importance of understanding how users interact with systems, how user needs relate to new types of information, and the functionality required of these information types in the DLs. Fortunately, now that there is a variety of DL systems in use, some deployed for a number of years, there have been careful evaluation efforts. Notable among these is the study of the Perseus Digital Library (Crane, 2000), which emphasized hypermedia concerns and effects on learning (Marchionini & Crane, 1994).

Other studies have tended to be more focused. It is important to evaluate visual navigation, for example (Leouski & Allan, 1998). For multimedia content, evaluation including cognitive issues is especially important (van Doorn & de Vries, 2000). Similarly, we are just beginning to explore how to interact with DLs when a fully immersive virtual environment can be employed (Das Neves & Fox, 2000). Comparative studies are particularly helpful, but experience with DLs is still rather limited, making it difficult for users to assess functionality and utility (Kengeri, Seals, Harley, Reddy, & Fox, 1999). We must compare use across genres (Bishop, 1999), but at the same time, it is important to situate use in today's changing information infrastructure (Bishop et al., 2000). We need good measures of perceived usefulness and perceived ease of use (Doll, Hendrickson, & Deng, 1998), and need to apply them to predict acceptance of Web and DL approaches (Fenech, 1998). We also need longitudinal studies that consider cognitive, individual, and social aspects of DL use (Compeau, Higgins, & Huff, 1999). One promising approach is to build comprehensive logs of DL use, and to analyze them to study user behavior (Abdulla, Liu, & Fox, 1998). This requires models of users' successive searches so that sessions can be identified (Spink, Wilson, Ellis, & Ford, 1998), as well as integration of log analysis with other approaches to assessing usability. While we need more such efforts, we also need to integrate them with DL software and tools so that needed data is automatically captured in standard ways to facilitate comparative studies.

Digital Library Software and Tools

As has been pointed out in discussions at NSF-sponsored workshops (Korfhage, Rasmussen, Belkin, & Harman, 1999), there is great need for readily available software and tools to support research, teaching, and learning in the DL field. Fortunately, some commercial DL systems (IBM, 2000) are now available, although most are rather complex and not easily integrated into research programs.

Simpler software systems are also available, many openly distributed. Ted Nelson, who coined the terms "hypertext" and "hypermedia," has a modern implementation of some of his early ideas (Nelson & Pam, 1998). In addition to the Dienst package (Lagoze & Davis, 1995), there are small kits for developing DLs (Nelson & Esler, 1997). Another set of tools relates to work on compression and scalability suitable for managing gigabytes (Witten, Moffat, & Bell, 1999). For example, Phronesis builds upon the MG software, supporting Spanish as well as English content (Garza-Salazar, 2000; Garza-Salazar, Sordia-Salinas, & Martinez-Trevino, 1999). The Greenstone system, a spinoff of the MG work, is a high quality, open source DL system for making content broadly available; and it is relatively easy to deploy (Witten, McNab, Boddie, & Bainbridge, 2000).

Today, most research on DLs is done with locally developed software. To better support flexible and cooperative programs of DL research, there is need for powerful, well-documented, modular software that can be made readily available. It is hoped that the MARIAN system, developed in connection with a number of research studies over the last decade (e.g., France, 2000a; Zhao, 1999) will advance to the stage where it can help fill this need.

Digital library systems are most often thought of in terms of users and their support. However, library content must be managed as well. Thus, we consider support for content management in DLs in the next section.

Content Management

DLs will succeed only if their content is well managed. This requires proper collection maintenance (Ackerman & Fielding, 1995). Issues of content management and knowledge management have significant overlap, whether one deals with digital libraries or digital museums (Yeh, Chang, & Oyang, 2000). Administratively, managing DL content has typically been the concern of individual projects at universities or other institutions, e.g., Virginia Tech's Scholarly Communications Project (McMillan, 1999a), but in many cases this is now the responsibility of a department in the library, or may even have been more tightly integrated into library planning and activities. As organizations work to address their needs for content management, two issues have attracted great attention: preservation and evaluation. These are considered in the next subsections.

Preservation

Preservation of digital information has been one of the dominant concerns raised over DL efforts. Although awareness of the issue arose in the 1970s, the 1980s and 1990s saw more concern due to the proliferation of electronic publications. The U.S. Commission on Archiving and Access (now part of CLIR, see www.clir.org) encouraged significant research in this area. The CLIR and Research Libraries Group (RLG) Joint Task Force on Archiving of Digital Information published what is considered a seminal report on preservation (Waters & Garrett, 1996). The reports of the Technology Advisory Committee to the Commission on Preservation and Access are also available at the same site (Lesk, 1998). The problems of format migration and technology obsolescence have dominated the discussions. For the library community, traditionally charged with the responsibility of maintaining the scholarly record for posterity, digital objects and their preservation have been major concerns in the movement toward electronic-only genres of documents.

A series of publications made available by CLIR provides a rich background for studying these issues. One report recommends digital image formats that can support preservation (Lesk, 1990). That is supplemented by a later survey of preservation science with regard to paper, film, photos, and magnetic tape (Porck & Teygeler, 2000). Another argues that emulation is necessary for preservation so that the processing that is now supported can extend into the future (Rothenberg, 1999); this is more fully explained in an IBM proposal for using a universal virtual computer (Lorie, 2000). The report of a workshop on access management identifies requirements for privacy, authorization, and authentication (C. Arms, 1999). A discussion of the Making of America II testbed highlights preservation concerns (Hurley, Price-Wilkin, Proffitt, & Besser, 1999). A panel of experts provides broad perspectives on document authenticity (Cullen, Hirtle, Levy, Lynch, & Rothenberg, 2000), a key quality desired for DLs. Another report addresses the risks involved in migrating digital information (Lawrence, Kehoe, Rieger, Walters, & Kenney, 2000), one of the steps required for effective preservation.

Other groups have also worked in this area. Interest extends internationally, with preservation one of the key topics of discussion regarding E.U.–U.S. collaboration on DLs (European Research Consortium for Informatics and Mathematics, 1998). IBM has been active in safeguarding important collections and DL content (Gladney, 1998). We are now at the stage where best practices can be identified in some areas, in the context of an information life cycle approach (recall Figure 12.3) (Hodge, 2000). Regarding technical aspects of archiving, there has been a series of studies, in some cases suggesting possible practice, undertaken at Stanford (Cooper et al., 1999; Crespo & Garcia-Molina, 1998, 1999). One key question is whether it is possible to preserve digital information forever (Waugh, Wilkinson, Hills, & Dell'oro, 2000).

Evaluation

Evaluation of DLs is an important but difficult problem. Some aspects have been discussed in the context of usability, and others will be considered in the next section. As is highlighted in the study mentioned earlier of the Perseus DL (Marchionini, 2000a), it is ultimately necessary to evaluate systems and services, as well as content—all are tightly coupled. Other notable studies relate to the Alexandria DL (Hill et al., 2000) and its use by undergraduate students (Leazer, Gilliland-Swetland, & Borgman, 2000).

Another aspect of evaluation relates to social construction, best approached through case studies (Kilker & Gay, 1998). This naturally leads to the discussion in the next section, which addresses DLs from social, economic, and legal perspectives.

Social, Economic, and Legal Issues

The most difficult problems related to DLs involve social, economic, and legal issues. These fit into the broad set of issues related to information technology adoption (Agarwal & Prasad, 1998). Both Lesk (1997) and W. Y. Arms (2000), in their DL books, give particular attention to these matters. Bishop and Star's (1996) recent *ARIST* chapter on social informatics and DL use is a particularly helpful source. For a gentle introduction to the topic see the overview in *D-Lib Magazine* (Kling, 1999).

Bishop (1995, 1996) ran two workshops in connection with DLI-1 at the Allerton Institute. The first emphasized user-centered design and evaluation while the second was more broadly based. Borgman chaired an important workshop on social aspects of DLs (Borgman et al., 1996). There is strong need for more follow-up meetings on these topics. In the following subsections we focus on some of the key areas.

Human Factors: Acceptance by People

For DLs to be used and useful, they must be accepted. Attitudes, satisfaction, and usage are crucial for such acceptance by those involved (recall "societies" from the 5S framework) (Al-Gahtani & King, 1999). For example, groups of people involved in social interaction that is mediated by collections of artifacts (managed by DLs) should be pleased with DL support of their collaboration (Ackerman, 1994). At a slightly higher level we consider organizational effects of DL use and how they can be modeled and managed (Covi & Kling, 1996).

While these factors are important, in many cases today there is only one DL that handles any given content object. Users may have no choice in satisfying a given information need other than through paper publications or an online DL run by a particular publisher or organization. Thus, there is strong dependence on decisions made based on economic, legal, or content collection issues.

Economic Factors

Many concerns have been voiced regarding economic issues related to DLs. While there is hope that DL-based communication will be significantly cheaper than paper-based approaches, this matter is confounded by a number of considerations, including the following.

- Since DLs are novel, new investment is required to get them working, which somehow must be budgeted. This may lead to higher rather than lower prices.
- Since many of those offering DL services have related services involving paper-based approaches, there are marketing concerns regarding changes in total revenue.
- Although it may be clear that many users will move from old practices to new practices, it is not clear how rapidly that will occur, or how best to encourage the change.

In the DL community, various investigations have explored these and other concerns. There is the matter of handling payment and shopping in a reliable and secure fashion (Cousins et al., 1995). This has led to shopping models, as well as supporting architectures, to enable information commerce (Ketchpel, Garcia-Molina, Paepcke, Hassan, & Cousins, 1996; Ketchpel, Garcia-Molina, & Paepcke, 1996). IBM's Safe Deals approach provides an elegant solution to many of these problems (Gladney & Cantu, 2001).

On the implementation side, various approaches are possible. At the University of Michigan, agents were used for strategy and for managing markets (Park, Durfee, & Birmingham, 1998). In the database community, managing costs and e-commerce may have a theoretical foundation (Sistla et al., 1998). One technique is to work with active views (Abiteboul et al., 1999).

An economic framework in which to arrange pricing and charging is required, as well (Sairamesh, Nikolaou, Ferguson, & Yemini, 1996). In the world of scholarly communication in particular, there is an urgent need for business and cost models (Breu & Weber, 1997). Although funds are likely to continue to support R&D activities in the DL area, commercial DLs must pay their way (Ferguson & Wooldridge, 1997). But how that happens must fit as well into a proper legal framework.

Legal Issues

Laws often provide protection, and serve to guarantee rights of individuals or groups. They help organize the actions of a society (recall the 5S framework, especially considering societies and scenarios). Although extensive discussion is not possible in this chapter, we note that DLs can help enforce copyright, support protection of intellectual property, ensure privacy, and make sure that users benefit from their purchases, subscriptions, license agreement, and other arrangements in which they directly or indirectly engage. When contracts or licenses (Flanders & Mylonas, 2000) are involved, content creators expect that the terms and conditions of the agreement are enforced, and that suitable payments are made.

The readers or users of content that is intermediated by a DL have other concerns. They expect the DL to protect their privacy, so that others may not analyze their patterns of DL use. They expect the DL either to respect their anonymity, or, if they are authenticated, to facilitate any actions for which they are authorized (Ching, Jones, & Winslett, 1996).

The DL serves as a type of middleman in these situations, and it is important that the DL provide suitable services. In some cases it can be absolved from any liability regarding appropriateness of content, if suitable policies are announced and followed. Typically, the DL should ensure authenticity (Cullen et al., 2000) and manage authorization and other aspects of access management (C. Arms, 1999; Ching et al., 1996; Gladney & Cantu, 2001). Creating trust in digital libraries will facilitate their extension into the areas discussed in the next section, and beyond.

Applications and Examples

Digital libraries can be viewed as high-end information systems, containing any type of digital object and/or metadata object. Thus, they may handle almost any type of content, and may be used by large numbers of people in widely varying contexts. In this section we briefly review some of the best-studied application domains.

The Digital Libraries Initiative

As discussed above, the Digital Libraries Initiative helped make clear the potential of work on DLs. The plans of the six original projects were carefully documented (Schatz & Chen, 1996). Phase I alone produced hundreds of publications (Habing, 1998). For an overview of those six projects, see the special issue of *D-Lib Magazine* that discusses their progress at the halfway mark (Friedlander, 1996). Further details are given in the NSF Web page for DLI-1 activities (http://www.dli2.nsf.gov/dlione).

By 1999, DLI Phase 2 was underway. An overview of the awards and funding appeared (Lesk, 1999b) as part of a special section of the *Bulletin of the American Society for Information Science* (Fox, 1999a). Principal investigators met at Cornell late in 1999, during the summer of 2000 in England, and in connection the Joint Conference on Digital Libraries in 2001. The projects vary widely regarding application domain, content, technology, and user community. Topics range from antiquities and humanities (Crane, 2000) to concerns of modern scholarly communication.

Scholarly Communication

Scholarly communication is a key application domain for DLs; readers are referred again to the chapter by Borgman and Furner in this volume for a more extensive discussion. Key results have been published, for example, in the final report of the TULIP Project (Borghuis et al., 1996), in which Elsevier Science worked with nine universities to explore services and usage of electronic as opposed to paper-based resources.

The high-energy physics preprint service, arXiv (Ginsparg, 2000), led the way in terms of shifting control of communication among scholars forward in time (from journals articles to preprints) and away from commercial publishers (to community-controlled, freely accessible services). The computer science DL, NCSTRL, began with a federated approach, which gradually collapsed into a more regionally centralized scheme (Leiner, 1998); integration of diverse archives also moved us closer to centralization (Van de Sompel et al., 1999, 2000).

Current developments favor distributed archives, with harvesting methods to allow aggregation and centralization along political, topical, or economic lines (Van de Sompel, 2000). We expect that the Open Archives Initiative will dramatically change scholarly communication, through the growth of large numbers of archives, through diverse harvesting enterprises, and through a wide variety of services built atop open archives (Hitchcock et al., 2000). These also will have a strong influence on education, as is considered in the next subsection.

Education: NSDL, NDLTD

One of the prime uses of libraries is to support teaching and learning. So, it is expected that DLs will be applied to education, at all levels (Marchionini & Maurer, 1995). For example, in the field of computing, the Computer Science Teaching Center (Knox et al., 2000) supports submission, review, editing, approval, browsing, and search of educational resources. As an extension of this effort, the *ACM Journal of Educational Resources in Computing* (Cassel & Fox, 2000), made accessible through the ACM DL, supports archival works in the field.

The PhysNet service assists with educational resources for physics departments in universities, especially in Europe (Hilf, 2000b). The Maxwell project in Brazil (Pavani & Lukowiecki, 1999), for sharing university course content, deals with a broad range of disciplines but has narrower geographic coverage. In Baltimore, there is DL support to help build an electronic learning community involving the University of Maryland in collaboration with city residents; The Baltimore Learning Community spans age, educational levels, and civil boundaries in a less formal, more open environment (http://www.learn.umd). Since there are so many such efforts, we focus on two case studies in the remainder of this subsection: NSDL and NDLTD.

NSDL: In 1991, a call for the NSF to help develop a national digital library to support undergraduate education appeared in chapter one of an edited report (Fox, 1993). Many other activities prompted thinking along these lines as well. The National Research Council (1997) critique on this topic generated extensive commentary and discussion (Wattenberg, 1998, 1999). The NSF's Division of Undergraduate Education moved forward with well over $50 million in funding, in stages, to build the National Science, mathematics, engineering, and technology education Digital Library (NSDL) (National Science Foundation, 2000a, 2000b). This carefully organized effort aims to leverage NSF support with community and commercial activity to transform undergraduate education in the nation. Funded projects are to focus on core integration, collections, services, and supporting research (Zia, 2001). Some of the support extends efforts like the Computer Science Teaching Center (CSTC) (see previous discussion), the National Engineering Education Delivery System (NEEDS) (Muramatsu & Agogino, 1999), the Science, Math, Engineering and Technology

Education (SMETE) digital library (www.smete.org) efforts focused around engineering, and the BioQUEST Curriculum Consortium (http://www.bioquest.org). The NSF plans to extend NSDL to other communities and disciplines.

NDLTD: In 1987, shortly after the SGML standard was promulgated, discussions began regarding electronic documents replacing paper forms as the primary representation of theses and dissertations. As is shown in Figure 12.2, a variety of standards and technologies has emerged in the intervening years, allowing this vision to become reality in universities scattered around the globe. The Networked Digital Library of Theses and Dissertations (Fox, 1997, 1998b, 1999b, 1999d, 2000; Fox et al., 1997) has evolved to include well over a hundred universities, and national (e.g., Australia, Germany, South Africa) as well as international (e.g., involving UNESCO and the Organization of American States) initiatives. There is work at individual universities (Sharretts, Shieh, & French, 1999), for nations (Zimmermann, 2000), for disciplines (Hilf, 2000a), and for developing nations (Plathe, 1999).

Fundamentally this is an educational initiative. On one hand it aims for students to develop knowledge and skills to create electronic documents that they place into DLs. This learning-by-doing is not difficult and has side benefits, including greatly extending the number of readers of a thesis or dissertation, if the electronic document is made freely available. Further, to the degree that time permits, it is hoped that students will learn about many of the issues considered in this chapter, so that their works will be easy to use and easy to preserve.

On the other hand, students should be prepared to use DLs. While graduate students' understanding of information seeking processes is advancing, there is still a great deal that can be learned regarding search strategies, query reformulation, use of classification schemes, work with advanced interfaces, integration of citation data, and both multimedia and multilingual searching.

Finally, NDLTD serves as a DL case study (Fox, 1999c). The Association of Research Libraries (Soete, 1998) has published a short work identifying the many issues. Although at any given university the collection grows slowly, policies and practices eventually affect all graduate students and, gradually, faculty advisors. In many universities, participation in NDLTD is the first campus DL activity, and stimulates discussion on preservation, copy detection, intellectual property rights, privacy, scholarly communication, research collaboration, research support of education, and other important issues. As NDLTD activities spread, this initiative will introduce new technologies onto campuses, as exemplified by current work regarding XML documents, XML schema, RDF, authority control, open archives, cross-language IR, wrappers, and metadata standards. In addition, there will be benefits with regard to preserving cultural heritage and supporting national DL agendas.

Cultural Heritage and National Content

Part of the worldwide appeal for DLs is their potential to preserve cultural heritage, expand access to national content collections, and promote deeper understanding among peoples and societies. IBM has supported a number of DL efforts to expand access to antiquities (Gladney, Mintzer, Schiattarella, Bescos, & Treu, 1998). This has applied not only to texts, but also to museum collections (Moen, 1998).

In some cases, tailored DL systems have been developed to suit national needs. In Mexico, Phronesis supports Spanish language use (Garza-Salazar et al., 1999). In Korea, supporting the Korean language and providing particular assistance for educational content, is Mirage (Myaeng, 1996). In the U.S., the Library of Congress continues its work on American Memory interfaces, content, and systems (Marchionini, Plaisant, & Komlodi, 1998), and is working to develop an even broader digital strategy (Computer Science and Telecommunications Board, 2000).

In the U.K., there have been various initiatives, including the Electronic Libraries Programme (Rusbridge, 1995). One popular philosophy is to develop hybrid libraries (Rusbridge, 1998). In Portugal, the ArquiTec project rests atop NCSTRL (Borbinha, Jorge, Ferreira, & Delgado, 1998). In Germany, a variety of efforts is underway, including the Global Info program (Schmiede, 1999). There are also various DL initiatives in Australia (Iannella, 1996); including gateway activities (Campbell, 1999), which are important for small countries, like Singapore.

In New Zealand there is the Greenstone system (Witten et al., 2000), which has also been applied to help in a variety of developing countries (Witten et al., 2001). In terms of content, there are various full-text collections, with resources harvested from around the globe (Witten,

Nevill-Manning, McNab, & Cunningham, 1998). On the multimedia side, there are interesting collections of music, supported by specialized services such as tune retrieval (McNab, Smith, Witten, Henderson, & Cunningham, 1996) and a melody index (McNab, Smith, Bainbridge, & Witten, 1997). Many other DL efforts are emerging around the globe, and their number is likely to grow rapidly.

The Future

It is likely that there will be continuing expansion of DL activities, covering the science, engineering, and management of DLs (recall Figure 12.1). Computer, library, and information scientists face myriad related challenges that will no doubt lead to improved systems. Engineering efforts to tune the performance and effectiveness of those systems and to scale them to meet worldwide demand will draw upon new theories and their refinements. More and more libraries will have departments and programs in the DL arena, so that improved technology and practices permeate institutional understanding.

If we view DLs as high-end information systems, we can see that they will build upon the wide range of exploration underway in the information and data management area (Cardenas, Chu, & Fox, 1999). Information retrieval, hypertext, electronic publishing, distributed computing, artificial intelligence, human-computer interaction, visualization, and other fields will have direct applications.

Vast content collections (Lesk, 1999a) will become available, mostly as a result of capturing materials born digital, but also because of expanding digitization efforts. Preservation methods will improve and cover more of the human record. We will move closer to the early visions of global information systems.

Yet, many challenges remain. Referring again to Figure 12.1, we mention only the highest-level needs. First, we must seek a unified and comprehensive theory for the DL field. Second, we need a clear methodology to allow specification, development, and refinement of digital libraries for particular user communities. Finally, we need guidelines for managing DLs, that:

- balance economic, social, and legal considerations;
- adjust to advances in technology and standards (Figure 12.2);

- consider the full information life cycle (Figure 12.3);
- fit into changing contexts of stakeholders (Figure 12.4);
- encompass the diversity of viewpoints regarding DLs (Figure 12.5); and
- cover the wide range of content types and forms (Figure 12.6) that has been devised.

Bibliography

Abdulla, G., Liu, B., & Fox, E. A. (1998). Searching the World Wide Web: Implications from studying different user behavior. *Proceedings of the WebNet98 Conference.* Retrieved March 1, 2001, from the World Wide Web: http://video.cs.vt.edu:90/~abdulla/webnet98/query2.html

Abiteboul, S., Amann, B., Cluet, S., Eyal, A., Mignet, L., & Milo, T. (1999). Active views for electronic commerce. *International Conference on Very Large DataBases.* Retrieved March 1, 2001, from the World Wide Web: http://www-rocq.inria.fr/~abitebou/COMMERCELEC/ACTIVEVIEWS/activeviews.2.html

Abiteboul, S., Buneman, P., & Suciu, D. (2000). *Data on the Web: From relations to semistructured data and XML.* San Francisco: Morgan Kaufmann.

Ackerman, M. S. (1994). Providing social interaction in the digital library. *Proceedings of the First Annual Conference on the Theory and Practice of Digital Libraries.* Retrieved March 1, 2001, from the World Wide Web: http://www.csdl.tamu.edu/DL94/position/ackerman.html

Ackerman, M. S., & Fielding, R. T. (1995). Collection maintenance in the digital library. *Proceedings of Digital Libraries 95, 39–48.* Retrieved March 1, 2001, from the World Wide Web: http://csdl.tamu.edu/DL95

Agarwal, R., & Prasad, J. (1998). The antecedents and consequents of user perceptions in information technology adoption. *Decision Support Systems, 22*(1), 15–29.

Agrawala, M., Beers, A. C., Frohlich, B., McDowall, I., Hanrahan, P., & Bolas, M. (1997). The two-user reponsive workbench: Support for collaboration through individual views of a shared space. *Proceedings of the 24th Annual Conference on Computer Graphics and Interactive Techniques, 327–332.*

Akscyn, R. M. (1991). The ACM hypertext compendium: Lessons in hypertext publishing. *Hypertext '91, Proceedings of the Third Annual ACM Conference on Hypertext, 403.*

Akscyn, R. M. (1993, November). *Reengineering the field: Hypertext in the 21st century.* Paper presented at the Hypermedia '93 conference, Seattle, WA.

Al-Gahtani, S. S., & King, M. (1999). Attitudes, satisfaction and usage: Factors contributing to each in the acceptance of information technology. *Behaviour & Information Technology, 18,* 277–297.

Amavizca, M., Sánchez, J. A., & Abascal, R. (1999, September). *3DTree: Visualization of large and complex information spaces in the Floristic Digital*

Library. Paper presented at Segundo Encuentro de Computación (ENC'99), Pachuca, Hidalgo, Mexico.

American Memory. (2000). Building digital collections: Technical information and background papers. Washington, DC: Library of Congress. Retrieved March 1, 2001, from the World Wide Web: http://memory.loc.gov/ammem/ftpfiles.html

American National Standards Institute. (1995). *Information retrieval (Z39.50): Application service definition and protocol specification: The Z39.50 maintenance agency official text for Z39.50-1995*. Washington, DC: Library of Congress.

Andresen, D., Yang, T., Egecioglu, O., Ibarra, O. H., & Smith, T. R. (1996). Scalability issues for high performance digital libraries on the World Wide Web. *Proceedings of the 3rd Forum on Research and Technology Advances in Digital Libraries*, 139–148.

Andrews, K., Kappe, F., & Maurer, H. (1995). The Hyper-G network information system. *Journal of Universal Computer Science, 1*(4). Retrieved March 1, 2001, from the World Wide Web: http://www.jucs.org/jucs_1_4/the_hyper_g_network

Aramburu, M., & Berlanga, R. (1997). An approach to a digital library of newspapers. *Information Processing & Management, 33*, 645–661.

ARIADNE. (2000). Alliance of Remote Instructional Authoring and Distribution Networks for Europe. Retrieved March 1, 2001, from the World Wide Web: http://ariadne.unil.ch

Arms, C. (1999). *Enabling access in digital libraries: A report on a workshop on access management*. Washington, DC: Council on Library and Information Resources. Retrieved March 1, 2001, from the World Wide Web: http://www.clir.org/pubs/reports/arms-79/contents.html

Arms, W. Y. (1995a). Report of the publishing perspective working group, IITA Digital Libraries Workshop. Retrieved March 1, 2001, from the World Wide Web: http://www-diglib.stanford.edu/diglib/pub/reports/iita-dlw/part1.html

Arms, W. Y. (1995b). Key concepts in the architecture of the digital library. *D-Lib Magazine, 1* (7). Retrieved March 1, 2001, from the World Wide Web: http://www.dlib.org/dlib/July95/07arms.html

Arms, W. Y. (1998). Implementing policies for access management. *D-Lib Magazine, 4*(2). Retrieved March 1, 2001, from the World Wide Web: http://www.dlib.org/dlib/february98/arms/02arms.html

Arms, W. Y. (2000). *Digital libraries*. Cambridge, MA: MIT Press.

Ashish, N., & Knoblock, C. A. (1997). Semi-Automatic wrapper generation for Internet information sources. *Proceedings of the Second IFCIS International Conference on Cooperative Information Systems*, 160–169.

Association for Computing Machinery. (1988). *Hypertext on hypertext*. New York: ACM Press.

Association for Computer Machinery. Special Interest Group on Information Retrieval. (1996). *Workshop on networked information retrieval*: ACM SIGIR. Retrieved March 1, 2001, from the World Wide Web: http://ciir.cs.umass.edu/nir96

Association of Research Libraries. (1995). Definition and purposes of a digital library. Retrieved June 26, 2001, from the World Wide Web: http://sunsite.berkeley.edu/ARL/definition.html

Atkins, D. (1999). Visions for digital libraries. In *Summary report of the series of joint NSF-EU working groups on future directions for digital libraries research*. Washington, DC: National Science Foundation. Retrieved June 13, 2001, from the World Wide Web: http://www.dli2.nsf.gov/eu123.html

Atkins, H. (1999). The ISI® Web of Science®—Links and electronic journals: How links work today in the Web of Science, and the challenges posed by electronic journals. *D-Lib Magazine, 5*(9). Retrieved March 1, 2001, from the World Wide Web: http://www.dlib.org/dlib/september99/atkins/09atkins.html

Bainbridge, D., Nevill-Manning, C. G., Witten, I. H., Smith, L. A., & McNab, R. J. (1999). Towards a digital library of popular music. *Proceedings of the Fourth ACM Conference on Digital Libraries*, 161–169. Retrieved March 1, 2001, from the World Wide Web: http://www.acm.org/pubs/citations/proceedings/dl/313238/p161-bainbridge

Balci, O., & Nance, R. E. (1992). The simulation model development environment: An overview. *Proceedings of the 1992 Winter Simulation Conference*, 726–736.

Baldonado, M., Chang, C.-C., Gravano, L., & Paepcke, A. (1997a). Metadata for digital libraries: Architecture and design rationale. *Proceedings of the 2nd ACM International Conference on Digital Libraries*, 47–56.

Baldonado, M., Chang, C.-C. K., Gravano, L., & Paepcke, A. (1997b). The Stanford digital library metadata architecture. *International Journal on Digital Libraries, 1*(2), 108–121. Retrieved March 1, 2001, from the World Wide Web: http://www-diglib.stanford.edu/cgi-bin/-WP/get/SIDL-WP-1996-0051

Baldonado, M. Q. W. (2000). A user-centered interface for information exploration in a heterogeneous digital library. *Journal of the American Society for Information Science, 51*, 297–310.

Bates, M. J. (1989). The design of browsing and berrypicking techniques for the online interface. *Online Review, 13*, 407–424.

Bearman, D., Miller, E., Rust, G., Trant, J., & Weibel, S. (1999). A common model to support interoperable metadata: Progress report on reconciling metadata requirements from the Dublin Core and INDECS/DOI communities. *D-Lib Magazine, 5*(1). Retrieved March 1, 2001, from the World Wide Web: http://www.dlib.org/dlib/january99/bearman/01bearman.html

Belkin, N. J., & Croft, W. B. (1992). Information filtering and information retrieval: Two sides of the same coin? *Communications of the ACM, 35*(12), 29–38. Retrieved March 1, 2001, from the World Wide Web: http://www.acm.org/pubs/citations/journals/cacm/1992-35-12/p29-belkin

Bian, G.-W., & Chen, H.-H. (2000). Cross-language information access to multilingual collections on the Internet. *Journal of the American Society for Information Science, 51*, 281–296.

Birmingham, W. P. (1995a). University of Michigan Digital Library Project. Retrieved March 1, 2001, from the World Wide Web: http://http2.sils.umich.edu/UMDL

Birmingham, W. P. (1995b). An agent-based architecture for digital libraries. *D-Lib Magazine, 1*(7). Retrieved March 1, 2001, from the World Wide Web: http://www.dlib.org/dlib/July95/07birmingham.html

Biron, P. V., & Malhotra, A. (Eds.). (2001). *XML schema part 2: Datatypes.* Cambridge, MA: World Wide Web Consortium. Retrieved June 1, 2001, from the World Wide Web: http://www.w3.org/TR/xmlschema-2

Bishop, A. P. (1995). *37th Allerton Institute: How we do user-centered design and evaluation of digital libraries: A methodological forum.* Urbana-Champaign, IL: Graduate School of Library and Information Science, University of Illinois at Urbana-Champaign.

Bishop, A. P. (1996). *38th Allerton Institute: Libraries, people, and change: A research forum on digital libraries.* Urbana-Champaign, IL: Graduate School of Library and Information Science, University of Illinois at Urbana-Champaign.

Bishop, A. P. (1999). Making digital libraries go: Comparing use across genres. *Proceedings of the Fourth ACM Conference on Digital Libraries, 94*–103. Retrieved March 1, 2001, from the World Wide Web: http://www.acm.org/pubs/citations/proceedings/dl/313238/p94-bishop

Bishop, A. P., Neumann, L. J., Star, S. L., Merkel, C., Ignacio, E., & Sandusky, R. J. (2000). Digital libraries: Situating use in changing information infrastructure. *Journal of the American Society for Information Science, 51,* 394–413.

Bishop, A. P., & Star, S. L. (1996). Social informatics of digital library use and infrastructure. *Annual Review of Information Science and Technology, 31,* 301–401.

Boehm, K., Croft, W. B., & Schek, H. (2000). *Proceedings of the First DELOS Network of Excellence Workshop on Information Seeking, Searching and Querying in Digital Libraries, December 11–12.* Zurich, Switzerland: ETH Zurich. (European Research Consortium for Informatics and Mathematics Workshop Proceedings No. 1/W001). Retrieved March 1, 2001, from the World Wide Web: http://www.ercim.org/publication/workshop_reports.html/DelNoe01

Borbinha, J. L., Jorge, J., Ferreira, J., & Delgado, J. (1998). A digital library for a virtual organization. *Proceedings of the 31st Hawaii International Conference on Systems Science, 7.* Retrieved March 1, 2001, from the World Wide Web: http://bruxelas.inesc.pt/~jlb/publica/hicss31/hicss31c.ps.gz http://www.computer.org/proceedings/hicss/8236/82360121abs.htm

Borghoff, U. M., Hilf, E. R., Pareschi, R., Severiens, T., Stamerjohanns, H., & Willamowski, J. (1997). Agent-Based document retrieval for the European physicists: A project overview. *Proceedings of the Second International Conference on the Practical Application of Intelligent Agents and Multi-Agents,* 271–285.

Borghuis, M., Brinckman, H., Fischer, A., Hunter, K., van der Loo, E., ter Mors, R., Mostert, P., & Zijlstra, J. (1996). *TULIP: Final report*. New York: Elsevier Science.

Borgman, C. L. (1999). What are digital libraries? Competing visions. *Information Processing & Management, 35*, 227–243.

Borgman, C. L. (2000). *From Gutenberg to the global information infrastructure: Access to information in the networked world*. Cambridge, MA: MIT Press.

Borgman, C. L., Bates, M. J., Cloonan, M. V., Efthimiadis, E. N., Gilliland-Swetland, A., Kafai, Y., Leazer, G. L., & Maddox, A. (1996). *Social aspects of digital libraries: Final report to the National Science Foundation*. Graduate School of Library & Information Studies, Los Angeles: UCLA. Retrieved March 1, 2001, from the World Wide Web: http://dlis.gseis.ucla.edu/DL/UCLA_DL_Report.html

Bowman, C. M., Danzig, P. B., Hardy, D. R., Manber, U., & Schwartz, M. F. (1995). The Harvest information discovery and access system. *Computer Networks and ISDN Systems, 28*(1), 119–126.

Bowman, C. M., Danzig, P. B., Hardy, D. R., Manber, U., Schwartz, M. F., & Wessels, D. P. (1994). *Harvest: A scalable, customizable discovery and access system* (Technical Report CU-CS-732-94). Boulder, CO: Department of Computer Science, University of Colorado, Boulder. Retrieved March 1, 2001, from the World Wide Web: http://harvest.transarc.com

Bray, T., Paoli, J., & Sperberg-McQueen, C. M. (Eds.). (1998). Extensible Markup Language (XML) 1.0 (W3C Recommendation). Retrieved March 1, 2001, from the World Wide Web: http://www.w3.org/TR/REC-xml

Breu, M., & Weber, R. (1997). Charging for a digital library: The business model and the cost models of the MeDoc digital library. In C. Peters & C. Thanos (Eds.), *Proceedings of the First European Conference on Research and Advanced Technology for Digital Libraries, Lecture Notes in Computer Science, 1324* (pp. 375–385). Heidelberg: Springer-Verlag. Retrieved March 1, 2001, from the World Wide Web: http://fast.fast.de/~breu/pisa97.ps

Brickley, D., & Guha, R. V. (Eds.). (2000a). Resource Description Framework (RDF) schema specification 1.0. Cambridge, MA: W3C. Retrieved March 1, 2001, from the World Wide Web: http://www.w3.org/TR/rdf-schema

Brickley, D., & Guha, R. V. (Eds.). (2000b). Resource Description Framework (RDF) schema specification 1.0: W3C Candidate Recommendation 27 March 2000. Cambridge, MA: World Wide Web Consortium. Retrieved March 1, 2001, from the World Wide Web: http://www.w3.org/TR/2000/CR-rdf-schema-20000327

Brin, S., Davis, J., & Garcia-Molina, H. (1995). Copy detection mechanisms for digital documents. *Proceedings of the ACM SIGMOD Annual Conference, 24*(2), 398–409.

Buck, A. M., Flagan, R. C., & Coles, B. (1999). Scholar's forum: A new model for scholarly communication. Pasadena, CA: California Institute of Technology. Retrieved March 1, 2001, from the World Wide Web: http://library.caltech.edu/publications/ScholarsForum

Burnard, L. (2000). Text encoding for interchange: A new consortium. *Ariadne, 24*. Retrieved March 1, 2001, from the World Wide Web: http://www.ariadne. ac.uk/issue24/tei

Bush, V. (1945). As we may think. *Atlantic Monthly, 176*(1), 101–108.

Buyya, R. (1999). *High performance cluster computing: Programming and applications: 2*. Upper Saddle River, NJ: Prentice-Hall.

Campbell, D. (1999). An overview of subject gateway activities in Australia. *Ariadne, 21*. Retrieved March 1, 2001, from the World Wide Web: http://www.ariadne.ac.uk/issue21/subject-gateways

Cardenas, A. F., Chu, W. W., & Fox, E. A. (1999). *Proceedings of the NSF Information and Data Management Workshop*. Los Angeles, CA: Sponsored by National Science Foundation Information and Data Management Program.

Cassel, L., & Fox, E. A. (2000). ACM Journal on Education Resources in Computing. Retrieved March 1, 2001, from the World Wide Web: http://purl.org/net/JERIC

Chen, F. R., & Bloomberg, D. S. (1998). Summarization of imaged documents without OCR. *Computer Vision and Image Understanding, 70*(3), 307–320. Retrieved March 1, 2001, from the World Wide Web: http://www.parc.xerox. com/istl/members/fchen/cviu98.abs.htmlb

Chen, H. (2000). Introduction to the special topic issue [Digital Libraries: Part 2]. *Journal of the American Society for Information Science, 51*, 311–312. Retrieved March 1, 2001, from the World Wide Web: http://bubl.ac.uk/journals/ lis/fj/jasis/v51n0400.htm

Chen, H., Chung, Y. M., Ramsey, M., & Yang, C. C. (1998). An intelligent personal spider (agent) for dynamic Internet/intranet searching. *Decision Support Systems, 23*(1), 41–58.

Chen, H., Lynch, K., Basu, K., & Ng, T. (1993). Generating, integrating, and activating thesauri for concept based document retrieval. *IEEE Expert: Special Series on Artificial Intelligence in Text-Based Information Systems, 8*(2), 25–34.

Chen, H., Smith, T. R., Larsgaard, M. L., Hill, L. L., & Ramsey, M. (1997). A geographic knowledge representation system (GKRS) for multimedia geospatial retrieval and analysis. *International Journal of Digital Libraries, 1*, 132–152.

Chen, S., & Fox, E. A. (1996). Guest editors' introduction to special issue on digital libraries. *Journal of Visual Communication and Image Representation, 7*(1), 1–2.

Cheng, X., Dolin, R., Neary, M., Prabhakar, S., Kanth, K. R., Wu, D., Agrawal, D., Abbadi, A. E., Freeston, M., Singh, A., Smith, T., & Su, J. (1998). Scalable access within the context of digital libraries. *International Journal on Digital Libraries, 1*, 358–376.

Ching, N., Jones, V., & Winslett, M. (1996). Authorization in the digital library: Secure access to services across enterprise boundaries. *Proceedings of the Third Forum on Research and Technology Advances in Digital Libraries*, 110–119. Retrieved March 1, 2001, from the World Wide Web: http://drl.cs.uiuc.edu/security/pubs.html

Christodoulakis, S., & Triantafillou, P. (1995). Research and development issues for large-scale multimedia information systems. *ACM Computing Surveys, 27,* 75–79.

Christophides, V., Cluet, S., & Simeon, J. (2000). On wrapping query languages and efficient XML integration. *Proceedings of the 2000 ACM SIGMOD International Conference on Management of Data,* 141–152.

Christophides, V., Durr, M., & Fundulaki, I. (1997). A semantic network approach to semistructured documents repositories. In C. Peters & C. Thanos (Eds.), *Proceedings of the 1st European Conference on Research and Advanced Technology for Digital Libraries, Pisa, Italy, Lecture Notes in Computer Science 1324* (pp. 305–324). Berlin: Springer-Verlag.

Chung, Y.-M., He, Q., Powell, K., & Schatz, B. (1999). Semantic indexing for a complete subject discipline. *Proceedings of the Fourth ACM Conference on Digital Libraries,* 39–48. Retrieved March 1, 2001, from the World Wide Web: http://www.acm.org/pubs/citations/proceedings/dl/313238/p39-chung

Coddington, P. D., Hawick, K. A., Kerry, K. E., Mathew, J. A., Silis, A. J., Webb, D. L., Whitbread, P. J., Irving, C. G., Grigg, M. W., Jana, R., & Tang, K. (1998). Implementation of a geospatial imagery digital library using Java and CORBA. In J. Chen et al. (Eds.), *Proceedings of the 27th Technology of Object-Oriented Languages and Systems.* Los Alamitos, CA: IEEE. Retrieved March 1, 2001, from the World Wide Web: http://www.dhpc.adelaide.edu.au/reports/047/abs-047.html

Compeau, D., Higgins, C. A., & Huff, S. (1999). Social cognitive theory and individual reactions to computing technology: A longitudinal study. *MIS Quarterly, 23,* 145–158.

Computer Science and Telecommunications Board. (2000). *LC21: A digital strategy for the Library of Congress.* Washington, DC: National Academy Press.

Connolly, D., & Thompson, H. (Eds.). (2000). XML Schema. Cambridge, MA: World Wide Web Consortium. Retrieved March 1, 2001, from the World Wide Web: http://www.w3.org/XML/Schema

Cooper, B., Crespo, A., & Molina, H. G. (1999). Implementing a reliable digital object archive. Retrieved March 1, 2001, from the World Wide Web: http://www-db.stanford.edu/pub/papers/arpaperext.ps

Cousins, S. B., Ketchpel, S. P., Paepcke, A., Garcia-Molina, H., Hassan, S. W., & Röscheisen, M. (1995). InterPay: Managing multiple payment mechanisms in digital libraries. *Proceedings of the ACM Conference on Digital Libraries.* Retrieved March 1, 2001, from the World Wide Web: http://www.csdl.tamu.edu/DL95/papers/cousins/cousins.html

Covi, L., & Kling, R. (1996). Organizational dimensions of effective digital library use: Closed rational and open natural systems models. *Journal of the American Society for Information Science, 47,* 672–689.

Crane, G. (2000). The Perseus digital library. Retrieved March 1, 2001, from the World Wide Web: http://www.perseus.tufts.edu

Crespo, A., & Garcia-Molina, H. (1998). Archival storage for digital libraries. *Proceedings of the Third ACM International Conference on Digital Libraries.*

Retrieved March 1, 2001, from the World Wide Web: http://www-diglib.
stanford.edu/cgi-bin/WP/get/SIDL-WP-1998-0082

Crespo, A., & Garcia-Molina, H. (1999). Modeling archival repositories for digital
libraries. *Proceedings of the Third ACM Conference on Digital Libraries,*
769–778. Retrieved March 1, 2001, from the World Wide Web: http://www-
db.stanford.edu/crespo /papers/ArchSimFull.ps

Cullen, C. T., Hirtle, P. B., Levy, D., Lynch, C. A., & Rothenberg, J. (2000).
Authenticity in a digital environment. Washington, DC: Council on Library
and Information Resources (CLIR). Retrieved March 1, 2001, from the World
Wide Web: http://www.clir.org/pubs/reports/pub92/contents.html

Dan, A., & Sitaram, D. (1999). *Video servers.* San Francisco: Morgan Kaufmann.

Daniel, R., & Lagoze, C. (1997). Extending the Warwick Framework: From metadata containers to active digital objects. *D-Lib Magazine, 3*(11). Retrieved
March 1, 2001, from the World Wide Web: http://www.dlib.org/dlib/november97/
daniel/11daniel.html

Dartois, M., Maeda, A., Sakaguchi, T., Fujita, T., Sugimoto, S., & Tabata, K.
(1997). A multilingual electronic text collection of folk tales for casual users
using off-the-shelf browsers. *D-Lib Magazine, 3*(10). Retrieved March 1, 2001,
from the World Wide Web: http://www.dlib.org/dlib/october97/sugimoto/
10sugimoto.html

Das Neves, F. A., & Fox, E. A. (2000). A study of user behavior in an immersive
virtual environment for digital libraries. *Proceedings of the Fifth ACM
Conference on Digital Libraries,* 103–111.

Davidson, S., Overton, C., Tannen, V., & Wong, L. (1997). BioKleisli: A digital
library for biomedical researchers. *International Journal of Digital Libraries,
1*(1), 36–53.

Davis, J. R., Krafft, D., & Lagoze, C. (1995). Dienst: Building a production technical report server. *Advances in Digital Libraries '95,* 211–222.

Davis, J. R., & Lagoze, C. (2000). NCSTRL: Design and deployment of a globally
distributed digital library. *Journal of the American Society for Information
Science, 51,* 273–280.

Day, M., & Beagrie, N. (1998). DELOS6: Preservation of digital information.
Ariadne, 16. Retrieved March 1, 2001, from the World Wide Web:
http://www.ariadne.ac.uk/issue16/delos/

Delcambre, L., Maier, D., & Reddy, R. (1997). Structured maps: Modeling explicit
semantics over a universe of information. *International Journal of Digital
Libraries, 1,* 20–35.

D-Lib Forum. (2001). Ready Reference: A collection of links to other digital
library sites. Reston, VA: Corporation for Research Initiatives. Retrieved
March 1, 2001, from the World Wide Web: http://www.dlib.org/reference.html

Dolin, R., Agrawal, D., & Abbadi, E. E. (1999). Scalable collection summarization
and selection. *Proceedings of the Fourth ACM Conference on Digital Libraries,*
49–58. Retrieved March 1, 2001, from the World Wide Web: http://www.acm.
org/pubs/citations/proceedings/dl/313238/p49-dolin/http://pharos.alexandria.
ucsb.edu/publications/dl99.ps

Doll, W. J., Hendrickson, A., & Deng, X. D. (1998). Using Davis's perceived use-fulness and ease-of-use instruments for decision making: A confirmatory and multigroup invariance analysis. *Decision Sciences, 29,* 839–869.

Dougherty, W. C., & Fox, E. A. (1995). TULIP at Virginia Tech. *Library Hi Tech, 13*(4), 54–60.

Dublin Core Metadata Initiative. (1999). The Dublin Core: A simple content description model for electronic resources. Dublin, OH: OCLC. Retrieved March 1, 2001, from the World Wide Web: http://purl.org/dc

Duderstadt, J. J., Arms, W., Messina, P., Ellisman, M. H., Atkins, D. E., Fox, E. A., Shneiderman, B., Nissenbaum, H., & Lederberg, J. (2001). *Becoming a scholar in the digital age.* Washington, DC: National Research Council.

Dumais, S. T., Furnas, G. W., Landauer, T. K., & Deerwester, S. (1988). Using latent semantic analysis to improve information retrieval. *Proceedings of the CHI '88 Conference on Human Factors in Computing,* 281–285.

Dushay, N., French, J. C., & Lagoze, C. (1999). Using query mediators for distributed searching in federated digital libraries. *Proceedings of the Fourth ACM Conference on Digital Libraries,* 171–178. Retrieved March 1, 2001, from the World Wide Web: http://www.acm.org/pubs/citations/proceedings/dl/313238/p171-dushay

Eaton, J. L., Fox, E. A., & McMillan, G. (1998). The role of electronic theses and dissertations in graduate education. *The Council of Graduate Schools Communicator, 31*(1), 1.

École polytechnique fédérale de Lausanne, Katolicki Uniwersytet Lubelski, & ARIADNE projects. (1999). ARIADNE Educational Metadata Recommendation,Version 3.0 . Retrieved March 1, 2001, from the World Wide Web: http://ariadne.unil.ch/Metadata

Ellis, D., Furner, J., & Willett, P. (1996). On the creation of hypertext links in full-text documents: Measurement of retrieval effectiveness. *Journal of the American Society for Information Science, 47,* 287–300.

Engelbart, D. C. (1963). Conceptual framework for the augmentation of man's intellect. In P.W. Howerton & D. C. Weeks (Eds.), *Vistas in information handling* (pp. 1–29). Washington, DC: Spartan Books.

Ennis, M., & Sutcliffe, A. G. (1998). Towards a predictive model of information seeking: Information seeking in context. *Proceedings of the International Conference on Research in Information Needs,* 76–82.

Entlich, R., Garson, L., Lesk, M., Normore, L., Olsen, J., & Weibel, S. (1995). Making a digital library: The chemistry online retrieval experiment: A summary of the CORE project (1991–1995). *D-Lib Magazine, 1*(12). Retrieved March 1, 2001, from the World Wide Web: http://www.dlib.org/dlib/december95/briefings/12core.html

European Research Consortium for Informatics and Mathematics. (1998). Sixth DELOS Workshop: Preservation of Digital Information. Tomar, Portugal. *ERCIM Workshop Proceedings,* 98-W003. Retrieved March 1, 2001, from the World Wide Web: http://www.ercim.org/publications/ws-proceedings/DELOS6/index.html

Fayyad, U. M., Piatetsky-Shapiro, G., & Smyth, P. (1996). Data mining and knowledge discovery in databases: An overview. *Communications of the ACM, 39*(11). Retrieved March 1, 2001, from the World Wide Web: http://www. acm.org/pubs/contents/journals/cacm/1996-39/#11

Fenech, T. (1998). Using perceived ease of use and perceived usefulness to predict acceptance of the World Wide Web. *Computer Networks, 30,* 629–630.

Ferguson, I. A., & Wooldridge, M. (1997). Paying their way: Commercial digitallibraries for the 21st century. *D-Lib Magazine, 3*(6). Retrieved March 1, 2001, from the World Wide Web: http://www.dlib.org/dlib/june97/zuno/06ferguson.html

Fernandez, L., Sánchez, J. A., & Flores, A. (2000, October). *An environment for the collaborative revision of digital theses.* Paper presented at the Sixth International Workshop on Groupware, Madeira, Portugal.

Fernandez, L., Sanchez, J. A., & Garcia, A. (2000). MiBiblio: Personal spaces in a digital library universe. *Proceedings of the Fifth ACM Conference on Digital Libraries,* 232–233.

Flanders, J., & Mylonas, E. (2000). A licensing model for scholarly textbases. *Proceedings of the Fifth ACM Conference on Digital Libraries,* 256–257. Retrieved March 1, 2001, from the World Wide Web: http://www.wwp. brown.edu/encoding

Fox, E. A. (1993). Sourcebook on digital libraries: Report for the National Science Foundation. (Technical Report TR-93-35). Blacksburg, VA: Deptartment of Computer Science, Virginia Polytechnic Institute and State University. Available by FTP from directory pub/DigitalLibrary on fox.cs.vt.edu

Fox, E. A. (1997). Networked digital library of theses and dissertations: An international collaboration promoting scholarship. *ICSTI Forum, Quarterly Newsletter of the International Council for Scientific and Technical Information, 26,* 8–9. Retrieved March 1, 2001, from the World Wide Web: http://www.icsti.org/icsti/forum/fo9711.html#ndltd

Fox, E. A. (1998a). Digital library courseware. Blacksburg, VA: Virginia Polytechnic Institute and State University, Department of Computer Science. Retrieved March 1, 2001, from the World Wide Web: http://ei.cs.vt.edu/~dlib

Fox, E. A. (1998b). Networked digital library of theses and dissertations. *European Research Consortium for Informatics and Mathematics (ERCIM) News, 35,* 16–21. Retrieved March 1, 2001, from the World Wide Web: http://www.ercim.org/publication/Ercim_News/enw35/fox.html

Fox, E. A. (1999a). The digital libraries initiative: Update and discussion: [Guest editor's introduction to special section]. *Bulletin of the American Society of Information Science, 26*(1), 7–11.

Fox, E. A. (1999b). Networked digital library of theses and dissertations. *Nature Web Matters.* Retrieved March 1, 2001, from the World Wide Web: http://helix.nature.com/webmatters/library/library.html

Fox, E. A. (1999c). The 5S framework for digital libraries and two case studies: NDLTD and CSTC. *Proceedings of the New Information Technology Conference, 11.* Retrieved March 1, 2001, from the World Wide Web: http://www.ndltd.org/pubs/nit99fox.doc

Fox, E. A. (1999d, August). *Networked digital library of theses and dissertations.* Paper presented at Digital Library Workshop, 15, Nara, Japan. Retrieved March 1, 2001, from the World Wide Web: http://www.ndltd.org/pubs/dlw15.doc

Fox, E. A. (2000). NDLTD: Networked Digital Library of Theses and Dissertations. Retrieved March 1, 2001, from the World Wide Web: http://www.ndltd.org

Fox, E. A., Akscyn, R., Furuta, R., & Leggett, J. (Eds.). (1995). Digital libraries. *Communications of the ACM, 38*(4). Retrieved March 1, 2001, from the World Wide Web: http://www.acm.org/pubs/contents/journals/cacm/1995-38/#4

Fox, E. A., Eaton, J. L., McMillan, G., Kipp, N., Mather, P., McGonigle, T., Schweiker, W., & DeVane, B. (1997). Networked digital library of theses and dissertations: An international effort unlocking university resources. *D-Lib Magazine, 3*(8). Retrieved March 1, 2001, from the World Wide Web: http://www.dlib.org/dlib/september97/theses/09fox.html

Fox, E. A., France, R., Sahle, E., Daoud, A., & Cline, B. (1993). Development of a modern OPAC: From REVTOLC to MARIAN. *Proceedings of the 16th Annual International ACM SIGIR Conference on Research and Development in Information Retrieval,* 248–259.

Fox, E. A., Gonçalves, M. A., & Kipp, N. A. (2001). Digital libraries in education: Background, theory, and prospects. In H. Adelsberger, B. Collis, & J. Pawlowski (Eds.), *Handbook on information systems.* Berlin: Springer-Verlag.

Fox, E. A., Hix, D., Nowell, L., Brueni, D., Wake, W., Heath, L., & Rao, D. (1993). Users, user interfaces, and objects: Envision, a digital library. *Journal of the American Society for Information Science, 44,* 480–491.

Fox, E. A., Kipp, N., & Mather, P. (1998). How digital libraries will save civilization. *Database Programming & Design, 11*(8), 60–65.

Fox, E. A., & Lunin, L. (1993). Introduction and overview to perspectives on digital libraries [Guest editors' introduction to special issue]. *Journal of the American Society for Information Science, 44,* 441–443.

Fox, E. A., & Marchionini, G. (1998). Toward a worldwide digital library [Guest editors' introduction to special section on digital libraries: Global scope, unlimited access]. *Communications of the ACM, 41*(4), 28–32. Retrieved March 1, 2001, from the World Wide Web: http://purl.lib.vt.edu/dlib/pubs/CACM199804

Fox, E. A., & Marchionini, G. (2001). Digital libraries: Beyond traditional values [Guest editors' introduction]. *Communications of the ACM, 41*(5), 1–2.

Fox, E. A., McMillan, G., & Eaton, J. (1999, January 5–8). *The evolving genre of electronic theses and dissertations.* Paper presented at the Digital Documents Track of the Thirty-Second Annual Hawaii International Conference on Systems Sciences (HICSS). Retrieved March 1, 2001, from the World Wide Web: http://scholar.lib.vt.edu/theses/presentations/Hawaii/ETDgenreALL.pdf

France, R. K. (2000a). *Efficient, effective retrieval in a network of digital information objects.* Unpublished doctoral dissertation draft, Blacksburg, VA: Virginia Polytechnic Institute and State University.

France, R. K. (2000b). MARIAN digital library information system. Blacksburg, VA: Virginia Polytechnic Institute and State University. Retrieved March 1, 2001, from the World Wide Web: http://www.dlib.vt.edu/products/marian.html

French, J. C. (1999). Personalized information environments: An architecture for customizable access to distributed digital libraries. *D-Lib Magazine, 5*(6). Retrieved March 1, 2001, from the World Wide Web: http://www.dlib.org/dlib/june99/french/06french.html

French, J. C., & Viles, C. L. (1996). Ensuring retrieval effectiveness in distributed digital libraries. *Journal of Visual Communication and Image Representation, 7,* 61–73.

Friedlander, A. (1996). From the Editor: In this issue. *D-Lib Magazine, 2*(7/8). Retrieved March 1, 2001, from the World Wide Web: http://www.dlib.org/dlib/july96/07editorial.html

Fuhr, N., Govert, N., & Rolleke, T. (1998). DOLORES: A system for logic-based retrieval of multimedia objects. *Proceedings of the 21st Annual International ACM SIGIR Conference on Research and Development in Information Retrieval,* 257–265.

Furnas, G. W., Landauer, T. K., Gomez, L. M., & Dumais, S. T. (1987). The vocabulary problem in human-system communication. *Communications of the ACM, 30*(11), 964–971. Retrieved March 1, 2001, from the World Wide Web: http://www.acm.org/pubs/citations/journals/cacm/1987-30-11/p964-furnas

Furrie, B. (2000). Understanding MARC bibliographic: Machine-readable cataloging. Washington, DC: Cataloging Distribution Service, Library of Congress. Retrieved March 1, 2001, from the World Wide Web: http://lcweb.loc.gov/marc/umb

Furuta, R. (2000). Walden's Paths. Retrieved March 1, 2001, from the World Wide Web: http://www.csdl.tamu.edu/walden

Garcia-Molina, H., Papakonstantinou, Y., Quass, D., Rajaraman, A., Sagiv, Y., Ullman, J., Vassalos, V., & Widom, J. (1997). The TSIMMIS approach to mediation: Data models and languages. *Journal of Intelligent Information Systems, 8,* 117–132.

Garfield, E. (2000). From 1950s documentalists to 20th century information scientists—and beyond: ASIS enters the year 2000 facing remarkable advances and challenges in harnessing the information technology revolution: Dr. Eugene Garfield's Inaugural Address. *Bulletin of the American Society for Information Science, 26*(2), 26–29. Retrieved March 1, 2001, from the World Wide Web: http://www.asis.org/Bulletin/Oct-00/president_s_page.html

Garza-Salazar, D. (2000). Phronesis Project Web site: ITESM-Campus. Retrieved March 1, 2001, from the World Wide Web: http://copernico.mty.itesm.mx/~tempo/Proyectos

Garza-Salazar, D., Sordia-Salinas, M., & Martinez-Trevino, Y. (1999). *The Phronesis system: A practical and efficient tool for the creation of distributed digital libraries on the Internet.* Monterey: ITESM-Campus Monterrey. Retrieved March 1, 2001, from the World Wide Web: http://copernico.mty.itesm.mx/~tempo/Projects/report

Gates, B. (1995). *The road ahead*. New York: Viking Penguin.

Geffner, S., Agrawal, D., Abbadi, A. E., & Smith, T. R. (1999). Browsing large digital library collections using classification hierarchies. *Proceedings of the Eighth International Conference on Information and Knowledge Management*, 195–201. Retrieved March 1, 2001, from the World Wide Web: http://www. acm.org/pubs/citations/proceedings/cikm/319950/p195-geffner

Geisler, G., & Marchionini, G. (2000). The open video project: A research-oriented digital video repository. *Proceedings of the Fifth ACM Conference on Digital Libraries*, 258–259. Retrieved March 1, 2001, from the World Wide Web: http://openvideo.dsi.internet2.edu

Giles, C. L., Bollacker, K., & Lawrence, S. (1998). CiteSeer: An automatic citation indexing system. *Proceedings of the Third ACM Conference on Digital Libraries*, 89–98. Retrieved March 1, 2001, from the World Wide Web: http://www.neci.nj.nec.com/homepages/lawrence/papers/cs-dl98

Ginsparg, P. (2000). arXiv.org e-Print archive. New Mexico: LANL. Retrieved March 1, 2001, from the World Wide Web: http://xxx.lanl.gov

Gladney, H., Fox, E. A., Ahmed, Z., Ashany, R., Belkin, N., & Zemankova, M. (1994). Digital library: Gross structure and requirements: Report from a March 1994 Workshop. In J. Schnase, J. Leggett, R. Furuta, & T. Metcalfe (Eds.), *Digital Libraries '94* (pp. 101–107). College Station, TX: Texas A&M University.

Gladney, H. M. (1998). Safeguarding digital library contents and users: Interim retrospect and prospects. *D-Lib Magazine*, *4*(7). Retrieved March 1, 2001, from the World Wide Web: http://www.dlib.org/dlib/july98/gladney/07gladney. html

Gladney, H. M., & Cantu, A. (2001). Safe deals with strangers: Authorization management for digital libraries. *Communications of the ACM, 44*(5). Retrieved March 1, 2001, from the World Wide Web: http://acm.org/pubs/ contents/journals/cacm/2001-44/#5

Gladney, H. M., Mintzer, F., Schiattarella, F., Bescos, J., & Treu, M. (1998). Digital access to antiquities. *Communications of the ACM, 41*(4), 49–57.

Glanz, J. (1991). Cut the communication fog, say physicists and editors. *Science, 277*, 895–899.

Gonçalves, M. A., France, R. K., Fox, E. A., Hilf, E. R., Zimmermann, K., & Severiens, T. (2001). Flexible interoperability in a federated digital library of theses and dissertations. *Proceedings of the 20th World Conference on Open Learning and Distance Education*. Retrieved March 1, 2001, from the World Wide Web: http://www.fernuni-hagen.de/ICDE/D-2001

Gonçalves, M. A., Kipp, N., Fox, E. A., & Watson, L. T. (2001). Streams, structures, spaces, scenarios, societies (5S): A formal model for digital libraries. Blacksburg, VA: Virginia Polytechnic Institute and State University, Department of Computer Science.

Gravano, L., Chang, C.-C. K., Garcia-Molina, H., & Paepcke, A. (1996). *STARTS: Stanford protocol proposal for Internet retrieval and search* (Technical Report SIDL-WP-19960043). Stanford: Stanford University. Retrieved March 1, 2001, from the World Wide Web: http://www-diglib.stanford.edu/cgi-bin/-WP/get/ SIDL-WP-1996-0043

Gravano, L., Chang, C.-C. K., Garcia-Molina, H., & Paepcke, A. (1997). STARTS: Stanford proposal for Internet meta-searching. *Proceedings of the 1997 ACM SIGMOD Conference,* 207–218.

Greene, S., Marchionini, G., Plaisant, C., & Shneiderman, B. (2000). Previews and overviews in digital libraries: Designing surrogates to support visual information seeking. *Journal of the American Society for Information Science, 51,* 380–393.

Gutwin, C., Paynter, G., Witten, I., Nevill-Manning, C., & Frank, E. (1998). *Improving browsing in digital libraries with keyphrase indexes.* Saskatchewan, Canada: Department of Computer Science, University of Saskatchewan.

Habing, T. (1998). DLI-wide publications: Site for publications from all six Digital Libraries Initiative projects. Urbana-Champaign, Illinois: University of Illinois, Ubana-Champaign. Retrieved March 1, 2001, from the World Wide Web: http://dli.grainger.uiuc.edu/pubsnatsynch.htm

Haigh, S. (1998). Canadian initiative on digital libraries: Looking towards libraries' digital future. *National Library News, 30*(6), 11–13.

Hall, W. (1999). *The history of the microcosm project.* University of Southampton. Retrieved March 1, 2001, from the World Wide Web: http://www.mmrg.ecs. soton.ac.uk/projects/microcosm.html.

Hansen, K. M., Yndigegn, C., & Grnbk, K. (1999). Dynamic use of digital library material - supporting users with typed links in open hypermedia. *Proceedings of the Third European Conference on Digital Libraries, Lecture Notes in Computer Science, 1696,* 254–273.

Harnad, S. (1991). Post-Gutenberg galaxy: The fourth revolution in the means of production of knowledge. *Public-Access Computer Systems Review, 2*(1), 39–53. Retrieved March 1, 2001, from the World Wide Web: http://www.cogsci. soton.ac.uk/~harnad/Papers/Harnad/harnad91.postgutenberg.html

Harnad, S. (2000a). CogPrints. Retrieved March 1, 2001, from the World Wide Web: http://cogprints.soton.ac.uk

Harnad, S. (2000b). E-knowledge: Freeing the refereed journal corpus online. *Computer Law & Security Report, 16*(2), 78–87. Retrieved March 1, 2001, from the World Wide Web: http://www.cogsci.soton.ac.uk/~harnad/Papers/ Harnad/harnad00.scinejm.htm

Hauptmann, A. G., & Wactlar, H. D. (1997). Indexing and search of multimodal information. *Proceedings of the 1997 IEEE International Conference on Acoustics, Speech, and Signal Processing,* 195–198.

Hauptmann, A. G., & Witbrock, M. J. (1996). Informedia news on demand: Multimedia information acquisition and retrieval. In M. T. Maybury (Ed.), *Intelligent multimedia information retrieval.* Menlo Park, CA: AAAI Press/MIT Press.

Hauptmann, A. G., Witbrock, M. J., & Christel, M. G. (1997). Artificial intelligence techniques in the interface to a digital video library. *Conference on Human Factors in Computing Systems, CHI '97*, 2–3.

Hawking, D. (1997). Scalable text retrieval for large digital libraries. In C. Peters & C. Thanos (Eds.), *Proceedings of the First European Conference on Digital Libraries, Lecture Notes in Computer Science, 1324*, 124–146. Heidelberg: Springer-Verlag.

Hearst, M. A. (1995). Tilebars: Visualization of term distribution information in full text information access. *Conference on Human Factors in Computing Systems, CHI '95*, 59–66.

Hearst, M. A., & Karadi, C. (1997). Cat-a-cone: An interactive interface for specifying searches and viewing retrieval results using a large category hierarchy. *Proceedings of the 20th Annual International ACM SIGIR Conference on Research and Development in Information Retrieval*, 246–255.

Heath, L., Hix, D., Nowell, L., Wake, W., Averboch, G., & Fox, E. A. (1995). Envision: A user-centered database from the computer science literature. *Communications of the ACM, 38*(4), 52–53.

Hein, K. K. (2000). Project DL [home page]. Columbia, Missouri: University of Missouri-Columbia, School of Information Science and Learning Technologies. Retrieved March 1, 2001, from the World Wide Web: http://www.coe.missouri. edu/~is334/projects/Project_DL

Hickey, T. B. (1999). CORC—Cooperative Online Resource Catalog. Dublin, OH: OCLC Office of Research. Retrieved March 1, 2001, from the World Wide Web: http://www.oclc.org/oclc/research/projects/corc/ and http://corc.oclc.org

Hilf, E. R. (2000a). PhysDis: Physics theses in Europe, Part of Dissertationen Online. Retrieved March 1, 2001, from the World Wide Web: http://elfikom. physik.uni-oldenburg.de/dissonline/PhysDis/dis_europe.html

Hilf, E. R. (2000b). PhysNet: Educational resources on physics: University of Oldenburg. Retrieved March 1, 2001, from the World Wide Web: http://www.physik.uni-oldenburg.de/EPS/PhysNet/education.html

Hill, L. L., Carver, L., Larsgaard, M., Dolin, R., Smith, T. R., Frew, J., & Rae, M.-A. (2000). Alexandria digital library: User evaluation studies and system design. *Journal of the American Society for Information Science, 51*, 246–259.

Hitchcock, S., Carr, L., Jiao, Z., Bergmark, D., Hall, W., Lagoze, C., & Harnad, S. (2000). Developing services for open e-print archives: Globalisation, integration and the impact of links. *Proceedings of the Fifth ACM Conference on Digital Libraries*, 143–151.

Hix, D., & Hartson, H. R. (1993). *User interface development: Ensuring usability through product and process*. New York: Wiley.

Hodge, G. M. (2000). Best practices for digital archiving: An information life cycle approach. *D-Lib Magazine, 6*(1). Retrieved March 1, 2001, from the World Wide Web: http://www.dlib.org/dlib/january00/01hodge.html

Hull, D. A., & Grefenstette, G. (1996). Querying across languages: A dictionary-based approach to multilingual information retrieval. *Proceedings of the 19th Annual International ACM SIGIR Conference on Research and Development in Information Retrieval,* 49–57. Retrieved March 1, 2001, from the World Wide Web: http://www.acm.org/pubs/citations/proceedings/ir/243199/p49-hull

Hunter, J. (1999). MPEG-7 behind the scenes. *D-Lib Magazine, 5*(9). Retrieved March 1, 2001, from the World Wide Web: http://www.dlib.org/dlib/september99/hunter/09hunter.html

Hurley, B. J., Price-Wilkin, J., Proffitt, M., & Besser, H. (1999). *The making of America II testbed project: A digital library service model.* Washington, DC: Council on Library and Information Resources.

Iannella, R. (1996). Australian digital library initiatives. *D-Lib Magazine, 2*(12). Retrieved March 1, 2001, from the World Wide Web: http://www.dlib.org/dlib/december96/12iannella.html

IBM. (2000). IBM DB2 digital library. Retrieved March 1, 2001, from the World Wide Web: http://www.ibm.com/software/is/dig-libSeptember 9.

IEEE Learning Technology Standards Committee. (2000). IEEE P1484.12 Learning Object Metadata Working Group. Retrieved March 1, 2001, from the World Wide Web: http://ltsc.ieee.org/wg12

Institute of the Information Society [Russia]. (2000). *Russian digital libraries journal.* Moscow: Institute of the Information Society.

Instructional Management System. (1999). IMS (Instructional Management System home page). Retrieved March 1, 2001, from the World Wide Web: http://www.imsproject.org

International Federation of Library Associations and Institutions. (2000). Digital libraries: Metadata resources. Retrieved March 1, 2001, from the World Wide Web: http://www.ifla.org/II/metadata.htm

International Standard Maintenance Agency. (2000). *Z39.50.* Washington, DC: Library of Congress Network Development and MARC Standards Office. Retrieved March 1, 2001, from the World Wide Web: http://lcweb.loc.gov/z3950/agency/September 9, 2000].

Jaen, J., & Rigas, L. (1998). Social engineering: Towards a new paradigm for developing multi-user visualization systems. *Workshop on New Paradigms in Information Visualization and Manipulation Conference on Information and Knowledge Management, CIKM 98,* 55–61.

Jang, M. G., & Myaeng, S. H. (1998). Use of corpus based linguistics for query translation in Korean-English cross-language IR. *Proceedings of Joint Workshop on Cross-Language Issues in Artificial Intelligence and Issues in Cross Cultural Communication,* 43–51.

Johnson, R. K. (2000). A question of access: SPARC, BioOne, and society-driven electronic publishing. *D-Lib Magazine, 6*(5). Retrieved March 1, 2001, from the World Wide Web: http://www.dlib.org/dlib/may00/johnson/05johnson.html

Joo, W. K., & Myaeng, S. H. (1998, October). *Improving retrieval effectiveness with hyperlink information.* Paper presented at the 3rd International Workshop on Information Retrieval with Asian Languages, Singapore.

Jung, V. (1999). *MetaViz: Visual interaction with geospatial digital libraries* [Technical report TR-99-017]. Berkeley, CA: International Computer Science Institute, University of California, Berkeley. Retrieved March 1, 2001, from the World Wide Web: ftp://ftp.icsi.berkeley.edu/pub/techreports/1999/tr-99-017.pdf

Kahn, R., & Wilensky, R. (1995). A framework for distributed digital object services. Reston, VA: Corporation for National Research Initiatives.

Kapidakis, S., Mavroidis, I., & Tsalapata, H. (1999). *Multilingual extensions to DIENST* (TR-248). Heraklion, Crete: Institute of Computer Science, Foundation for Research and Technology-Hellas (ICS- FORTH).

Kaplan, N. R., & Nelson, M. L. (2000). Determining the publication impact of a digital library. *Journal of the American Society for Information Science, 51*, 324–339. Retrieved March 1, 2001, from the World Wide Web: http://techreports.larc.nasa.gov/ltrs/PDF/2000/jp/NASA-2000-jasis-nrk.pdf

Kaser, R. T. (2000). If information wants to be free ... then who's going to pay for it? *D-Lib Magazine, 6* (5). Retrieved March 1, 2001, from the World Wide Web: http://www.dlib.org/dlib/may00/kaser/05kaser.html

Kaski, S., Honkela, T., Lagus, K., & Kohonen, T. (1996). Creating an order in digital libraries with self-organizing maps. *Proceeding of the World Conference on Neural Networks, 1996*, 814–817.

Kellogg, R. B., Subhas, M., & Fox, E. A. (1995). Automatic building of hypertext links in digital libraries. Demonstration presented at the 18th Annual International ACM SIGIR Conference on Research and Development in Information Retrieval, Seattle, WA. Retrieved March 1, 2001, from the World Wide Web: http://pixel.cs.ut.edu/ri/prog3.phf

Kengeri, R., Seals, C. D., Harley, H. D., Reddy, H. P., & Fox, E. A. (1999). Usability study of digital libraries: ACM, IEEE-CS, NCSTRL, NDLTD. *International Journal on Digital Libraries, 2*(2/3), 157–169. Retrieved March 1, 2001, from the World Wide Web: http://link.springer.de/link/service/journals/00799/bibs/9002002/90020157.htm

Kent, R., & Bowman, M. (1995). *Digital libraries, conceptual knowledge systems, and the nebula interface: Transarc ARPA project goal description*. Pittsburgh, PA: Transarc Corporation. Retrieved March 1, 2001, from the World Wide Web: http://www.transarc.ibm.com/~trg/papers/techrep0495.ps

Ketchpel, S., Garcia-Molina, H., Paepcke, A., Hassan, S., & Cousins, S. (1996). U-PAI: A universal payment application interface. *Proceedings of The Second USENIX Workshop on Electronic Commerce*, 105–121. Retrieved March 1, 2001, from the World Wide Web: http://dbpubs.stanford.edu/pub/1996-8

Ketchpel, S. P., Garcia-Molina, H., & Paepcke, A. (1996). *Shopping models: A flexible architecture for information commerce* [Working Paper SIDL-WP-19960052]. Stanford, CA: Stanford Digital Library Project. Retrieved March 1, 2001, from the World Wide Web: http://www-diglib.stanford.edu/cgibin/WP/get/SIDL-WP-1996-0052

Kilker, J., & Gay, G. (1998). The social construction of a digital library: A case study examining implications for evaluation. *Information Technology and Libraries, 17*, 60–70. Retrieved March 1, 2001, from the World Wide Web: http://www.lita.org/ital/ital1702.htm

Klavans, J. L., & Schauble, P. (1998). NSF-EU multilingual information access. *Communications of the ACM, 41*(4), 69.

Kleinberg, J. M. (1999). Authoritative sources in a hyperlinked environment. *Journal of the ACM, 46,* 604–632.

Kling, R. (1999). What is social informatics and why does it matter? *D-Lib Magazine, 5*(1). Retrieved March 1, 2001, from the World Wide Web: http://www.dlib.org/dlib/january99/kling/01kling.html

Knox, D., Grissom, S., Fox, E. A., Heller, R., & Watkins, D. (2000). CSTC: Computer Science Teaching Center. Retrieved March 1, 2001, from the World Wide Web: htttp://www.cstc.org

Korfhage, R. R., Rasmussen, E. M., Belkin, N., & Harman, D. (1999). *Invitational Workshop on Information Retrieval Tools, University of Pittsburgh, March 19–21, 1998 Final Report* (NSF Grant No. IRI-9610070). Pittsburgh, PA: University of Pittsburgh.

Kovcs, L., Micsik, A., Pataki, B., & Zsámboki, I. (2000). AQUA (Advanced Query User Interface Architecture). In J. Borbinha & T. Baker (Eds.), *Proceedings of the 4th European Conference on Digital Libraries, Lecture Notes in Computer Science Volume 1923* (pp. 372–375). Lisbon, Portugal: Springer. Retrieved March 1, 2001, from the World Wide Web: http://www.sztaki.hu/sztaki/aszi/dsd/aqua

Kumar, V., Furuta, R., & Allen, R. B. (1998). Metadata visualization for digital libraries: Interactive timeline editing and review. *Proceedings of the Third ACM Conference on Digital Libraries,* 126–133.

Lagoze, C. (1995). Secure repository design for digital libraries. *D-Lib Magazine, 1.* Retrieved March 1, 2001, from the World Wide Web: http://www.dlib.org/dlib/december95/12lagoze.html

Lagoze, C. (1996). The Warwick framework: A container architecture for diverse sets of metadata. *D-Lib Magazine, 2*(7/8). Retrieved March 1, 2001, from the World Wide Web: http://www.dlib.org/dlib/july96/lagoze/07lagoze.html

Lagoze, C. (1997). From static to dynamic surrogates: Resource discovery in the digital age. *D-Lib Magazine, 3*(6). Retrieved March 1, 2001, from the World Wide Web: http://www.dlib.org/dlib/june97/06lagoze.html

Lagoze, C. (1999). NCSTRL: Networked Computer Science Technical Reference Library. Ithaca, NY: Cornell University. Retrieved March 1, 2001, from the World Wide Web: http://www.ncstrl.org

Lagoze, C., & Davis, J. R. (1995). Dienst: An architecture for distributed document libraries. *Communications of the ACM, 38*(4), 47.

Lagoze, C., & Fielding, D. (1998). Defining collections in distributed digital libraries. *D-Lib Magazine, 4*(11). Retrieved March 1, 2001, from the World Wide Web: http://www.dlib.org/dlib/november98/lagoze/11lagoze.html

Lagoze, C., Fielding, D., & Payette, S. (1998). Making global digital libraries work: Collection services, connectivity regions, and collection views. *Proceedings of the 3rd ACM International Conference on Digital Libraries,* 134–143. Retrieved March 1, 2001, from the World Wide Web: http://www.acm.org/pubs/citations/proceedings/dl/276675/p134-lagoze

Lagoze, C., & Payette, S. (1998). *An infrastructure for open-architecture digital libraries* (TR98-1690). Ithaca, NY: Cornell University, Computer Science Department.

Lagus, K., Kaski, S., Honkela, T., & Kohonen, T. (1996). Browsing digital libraries with the aid of self-organizing maps. *Proceedings of the Fifth International World Wide Web Conference.* 71–79.

Lassila, O., & Swick, R. R. (Eds.). (1999). Resource Description Framework (RDF) model and syntax specification (Recommendation 22 February 1999 REC-rdf-syntax-19990222). Cambridge, MA: World Wide Web Consortium. Retrieved March 1, 2001, from the World Wide Web: http://www.w3.org/TR/REC-rdf-syntax

Lawrence, G. W., Kehoe, W. R., Rieger, O. Y., Walters, W. H., & Kenney, A. R. (2000). *Risk management of digital information: A file format investigation.* Washington, DC: Council on Library and Information Resources.

Lawrence, S., Giles, C. L., & Bollacker, K. (1999). Digital libraries and autonomous citation indexing. *IEEE Computer, 32*(6), 67–71.

Leazer, G. H., Gilliland-Swetland, A. J., & Borgman, C. L. (2000). Evaluating the use of a geographic digital library in undergraduate classrooms: ADEPT. *Proceedings of the Fifth ACM Conference on Digital Libraries,* 248–249.

Lee, H., Smeaton, A. F., Berrut, C., Murphy, N., Marlow, S., & O'Connor, N. (2000). Implementation and analysis of several keyframe-based browsing interfaces to digital video. *Proceedings of the Fourth European Conference on Digital Libraries,* 206–218.

Lee, J. A. N. (1999). The history of computing. Blacksburg, VA: Virginia Polytechnic Institute and State University, Department of Computer Science. Retrieved March 1, 2001, from the World Wide Web: http://ei.cs.vt.edu/~history

Leggett, J., Schnase, J., Smith, J., & Fox, E. (1993). *Final report of the NSF workshop on hyperbase systems, Oct. 15–16, 1992, Washington, DC* (Report TAMU-HRL 93-002). College Station, TX: Texas A&M University, Department of Computer Science, Hypermedia Research Lab.

Leiner, B. M. (1998). The NCSTRL approach to open architecture for the confederated digital library. *D-Lib Magazine, 4*(11). Retrieved March 1, 2001, from the World Wide Web: http://www.dlib.org/dlib/december98/leiner/12leiner.html

Leouski, A., & Allan, J. (1998). Evaluating a visual navigation system for a digital library. *Proceedings of the Second European Conference on Digital Libraries,* 535–554.

Lesk, M. (1990). *Image formats for preservation and access: A report of the Technology Assessment Advisory Committee.* Washington, DC: Council on Library and Information Resources.

Lesk, M. (1997). *Practical digital libraries: Books, bytes and bucks.* San Francisco: Morgan Kaufmann.

Lesk, M. (1998). *Preserving digital objects: Recurrent needs and challenges.* Retrieved March 1, 2001, from the World Wide Web: http://www.lesk.com/mlesk/auspres/aus.html

Lesk, M. (1999a). *How much information is there in the world?* Retrieved September 9, 1999, from the World Wide Web: http://www.lesk.com/mlesk/ksg97/ksg.html

Lesk, M. (1999b). Perspectives on DLI-2—growing the field. *D-Lib Magazine, 5*(7/8). Retrieved March 1, 2001, from the World Wide Web: http://www.dlib.org/dlib/july99/07lesk.html

Library of Congress. (1999). Dublin Core/MARC/GILS crosswalk. Washington, DC: Network Development and MARC Standards Office, Library of Congress. Retrieved March 1, 2001, from the World Wide Web: http://lcweb.loc.gov/marc/dccross.html

Licklider, J. C. R. (1965). *Libraries of the future.* Cambridge, MA: MIT Press.

Lin, X., & Soergel, D. (1991). A self organizing semantic map for information retrieval. *Proceedings of the 14th International ACM SIGIR Conference on Research and Development in Information Retrieval*, 262–269.

Lin, Y., Xu, J., Lim, E.-P., & Ng, W.-K. (1999). ZBroker: A query routing broker for Z39.50 databases. *Proceedings of the Eighth International Conference on Information and Knowledge Management*, 202–209. Retrieved March 1, 2001, from the World Wide Web: http://www.acm.org/pubs/citations/proceedings/cikm/319950/p202-lin

Liu, Y.-H., Dantzig, P., Sachs, M., Corey, J. T., Hinnebusch, M. T., Damashek, M., & Cohen, J. (2000). Visualizing document classification: A search aid for the digital library. *Journal of the American Society for Information Science, 51*, 216–227.

Lorie, R. (2000). *Long-term archiving of digital information* [RJ 10185]. San Jose, CA: IBM Research. Retrieved March 1, 2001, from the World Wide Web: http://www.almaden.ibm.com/u/gladney/Lorie.pdf

Lynch, C. A. (1995). The TULIP project: Context, history, and perpective. *Library Hi-Tech, 13*(4), 8–24.

Lynch, C. A. (1997). The Z39.50 information retrieval standard Part I: A strategic view of its past, present and future. *D-Lib Magazine, 3*(4). Retrieved March 1, 2001, from the World Wide Web: http://www.dlib.org/dlib/april97/04lynch.html

Lynch, C. A., & Garcia-Molina, H. (1995). Interoperability, scaling, and the digital libraries research agenda: A report on the May 18–19, 1995 IITA Digital Libraries Workshop. Reston, VA: IITA. Retrieved March 1, 2001, from the World Wide Web: http://www-diglib.stanford.edu/diglib/pub/reports/iita-dlw/main.html

Maamar, Z., Moulin, B., Bédard, Y., & Babin, G. (1997). Software agent-oriented frameworks meet georeferenced digital library interoperability. *D-Lib Magazine, 3*(9). Retrieved March 1, 2001, from the World Wide Web: http://www.dlib.org/dlib/september97/laval/09laval.html

MacKie-Mason, J. K., Riveros, J. F., Bonn, M. S., & Lougee, W. P. (1999). A report on the PEAK experiment: Usage and economic behavior. *D-Lib Magazine, 5*(7/8). Retrieved March 1, 2001, from the World Wide Web: http://www.dlib.org/dlib/july99/mackie-mason/07mackie-mason.html

Maly, K., Nelson, M. L., & Zubair, M. (1999). Smart objects, dumb archives: A user-centric, layered digital library framework. *D-Lib Magazine, 5*(3). Retrieved March 1, 2001, from the World Wide Web: http://www.dlib.org/dlib/march99/maly/03maly.html

Maly, K., Zubair, M., Liu, X., Nelson, M. L., & Zeil, S. J. (1999). Structured course objects in a digital library. *Proceedings of the Third International Symposium on Digital Libraries,* 89–96. Retrieved March 1, 2001, from the World Wide Web: http://techreports.larc.nasa.gov/ltrs/PDF/1999/mtg/NASA-99-isdl-km.pdf

Marchionini, G. (1995). *Information seeking in electronic environments.* Cambridge: Cambridge University Press.

Marchionini, G. (2000a, June). *Evaluating digital libraries.* Paper presented at Libraries, People and Change, a Research Forum on Digital Libraries, Monticello, IL.

Marchionini, G. (2000b, February 18). *The sharium: A distributed learning space.* Paper presented at the American Association for the Advancement of Science Annual Conference, Washington, DC. Retrieved March 1, 2001, from the World Wide Web: http://www.ils.unc.edu/~march/AAAS/AAAS_slides_files/v3_document.htm

Marchionini, G., & Crane, G. (1994). Evaluating hypermedia and learning: Methods and results from the Perseus project. *ACM Transactions on Information Systems, 12*(1), 5–34.

Marchionini, G., & Fox, E. A. (1999). Progress toward digital libraries: Augmentation through integration [Guest editors' introduction to special issue on digital libraries]. *Information Processing & Management, 35,* 219–225.

Marchionini, G., & Komlodi, A. (1998). Design of interfaces for information seeking. *Annual Review of Information Science and Technology, 33,* 89–130.

Marchionini, G., & Maurer, H. (1995). The roles of digital libraries in teaching and learning. *Communications of the ACM, 38*(4), 67–75.

Marchionini, G., Plaisant, C., & Komlodi, A. (1998). Interfaces and tools for the Library of Congress National Digital Library Program. *Information Processing & Management, 34,* 535–555.

MathForum. (2000). The Math Forum: An Online Math Education Community Center. Retrieved March 1, 2001, from the World Wide Web: http://www.mathforum.org

Maurer, H. (1996). *HyperWave: The next generation web solution.* Harlow, England: Addison-Wesley Longman.

McMillan, G. (1999a). Managing digital content: The scholarly communications project. In L. M. Saunders (Ed.), *The evolving virtual library II: Practical and philosophical perspectives* (pp. 39–60). Medford, NJ: Information Today.

McMillan, G. (1999b, October). *Perspectives on electronic theses and dissertations.* Paper presented at the New Frontiers in Grey Literature: 4th International Conference, Kellogg Center, Gallaudet University, Washington, DC. Retrieved March 1, 2001, from the World Wide Web: http://scholar.lib.

vt.edu/staff/gailmac/presentations/GL99ETDpaper.pdf http://scholar.lib.vt.
edu/staff/gailmac/presentations/GL99ETDslides.pdf

McMillan, G. (1999c, August). *What to expect from ETDs: If you build it, they will use it.* Paper presented at the Digital Library Symposium, Cleveland, OH. Retrieved March 1, 2001, from the World Wide Web: http://scholar.lib.vt.edu/staff/gailmac/presentations/CWRUGMc1.pdf

McMillan, G. (2000, February 17). *The digital library—without a soul can it be a library?* Paper presented at Books and Bytes: Technologies for the Hybrid Library, VALA 2000 Conference, Melbourne, Australia. Retrieved March 1, 2001, from the World Wide Web: http://scholar.lib.vt.edu/staff/gailmac/presentations/VALA.pdf

McNab, R. J., Smith, L. A., Bainbridge, D., & Witten, I. H. (1997). The New Zealand digital library MELody inDEX. *D-Lib Magazine, 3*(5). Retrieved March 1, 2001, from the World Wide Web: http://www.dlib.org/dlib/may97/meldex/05witten.html

McNab, R. J., Smith, L. A., Witten, I. H., & Henderson, C. L. (2000). Tune retrieval in the multimedia library. *Multimedia Tools and Applications, 10*, 113–132.

McNab, R. J., Smith, L. A., Witten, I. H., Henderson, C. L., & Cunningham, S. J. (1996). Towards the digital music library: Tune retrieval from acoustic input. *Proceedings of the 1st ACM International Conference on Digital Libraries, 11–18.* Retrieved March 1, 2001, from the World Wide Web: http://www.acm.org/pubs/citations/proceedings/dl/226931/p11-mcnab/

Melnik, S., Garcia-Molina, H., & Paepcke, A. (2000). A mediation infrastructure for digital library services. In R. Furuta (Ed.), *Proceedings of the Fifth ACM Conference on Digital Libraries* (pp. 123–132). New York: ACM Press.

Miller, J. S. (1996). W3C and digital libraries. *D-Lib Magazine, 2*(11). Retrieved March 1, 2001, from the World Wide Web: http://www.dlib.org/dlib/november96/11miller.html

Miller, P. (1999). Z39.50 for all. *Ariadne, 21.* Retrieved March 1, 2001, from the World Wide Web: http://www.ariadne.ac.uk/issue21/z3950

Miller, P. (2000a). Collected wisdom: Some cross-domain issues of collection level description. *D-Lib Magazine, 6*(9). Retrieved March 1, 2001, from the World Wide Web: http://www.dlib.org/dlib/september00/miller/09miller.html

Miller, P. (2000b). Interoperability. What is it and why should I want it? *Ariadne, 24.* Retrieved March 1, 2001, from the World Wide Web: http://www.ariadne.ac.uk/issue24/interoperability/intro.html

Moen, W. E. (1998). Accessing distributed cultural heritage information. *Communications of the ACM, 41*(4), 45–48.

Mönch, C., & Drobnik, O. (1998). Integrating new document types into digital libraries. *Proceedings of the IEEE Forum on Research and Technology Advances in Digital Libraries, ADL 98,* 56–65. Retrieved March 1, 2001, from the World Wide Web: http://www.tm.informatik.uni-frankfurt.de/Projekte/DigLib/publications/md98.ps

Monostori, K., Zaslavsky, A., & Schmidt, H. (2000). Document overlap detection system for distributed digital libraries. *Proceedings of the Fifth ACM Conference on Digital Libraries,* 226–227.

Mooers, C. S. (1950). Coding information retrieval and the rapid selector. *American Documentation, 1,* 225–29.

Moore, R., Baru, C., Rajasekar, A., Ludascher, B., Marciano, R., Wan, M., Schroeder, W., & Gupta, A. (2000). Collection-based persistent digital archives—Part 1. *D-Lib Magazine, 6*(3). Retrieved March 1, 2001, from the World Wide Web: http://www.dlib.org/dlib/march00/moore/03moore-pt1.html

Moore, R., Prince, T. A., & Ellisman, M. H. (1998). Data-intensive computing and digital libraries. *Communications of the ACM, 41* (11), 56-62. Retrieved March 1, 2001, from the World Wide Web: http://www.acm.org/pubs/articles/journals/cacm/1998-41-11/p56-moore/p56-moore.pdf

Moving Picture Experts Group. Description Definition Language Group. (1999). *MPEG-7 description definition language document 1.0.* Vancouver, BC: ISO/IEC SC29/WG11/N2862.

Moxley, J. (1995). *The politics and processes of scholarship.* Westport, CT: Greenwood.

Muramatsu, B., & Agogino, A. (1999). NEEDS - The national engineering education delivery system: A digital library for engineering education. *D-Lib Magazine, 5*(4). Retrieved March 1, 2001, from the World Wide Web: http://www.dlib.org/dlib/april99/muramatsu/04muramatsu.html

Myaeng, S. H. (1996). MIRAGE: A prototype for a multimedia information retrieval and gathering environment. *Proceedings of the International Conference on Digital Libraries and Information Services for the 21st Century, KOLISS DL '96,* 115–125.

Myka, A., & Guntzer, U. (1995). Automatic hypertext conversion of paper document collections. In N. Adam, B. Bhargava, & Y. Yesha (Eds.), *Advances in Digital Libraries, Lecture Notes in Computer Science, 916,* 65–90. Heidelberg: Springer-Verlag.

National Information Standards Organization. (1995). *Information retrieval (Z39.50): Application service definition and protocol specification (ANSI/NISO Z39.501995).* Bethesda, MD: National Information Standards Organization. Retrieved March 1, 2001, from the World Wide Web: http://lcweb.loc.gov/z3950/agency

National Research Council. (1997). *Developing a digital national library for undergraduate science, mathematics, engineering, and technology education: Report of a workshop.* Washington: National Research Council. Retrieved March 1, 2001, from the World Wide Web: http://books.nap.edu/catalog/5952.html

National Science Foundation. (2000a). National Science, Mathematics, Engineering, and Technology Education Digital Library (NSDL)— Program Information. Arlington, VA: National Science Foundation. Retrieved March 1, 2001, from the World Wide Web: http://www.ehr.nsf.gov/EHR/DUE/programs/nsdl

National Science Foundation. (2000b). National Science, Mathematics, Engineering, and Technology Education Digital Library (NSDL) - Program Solicitation [NSF 00-44]. Arlington, VA: National Science Foundation. Retrieved March 1, 2001, from the World Wide Web: http://www.nsf.gov/cgi-bin/getpub?nsf0044

Nelson, M. L. (1999). *A digital library for the National Advisory Committee for Aeronautics* [NASA/TM-1999-209127]. Hampton, VA: NASA Langley Research Center.

Nelson, M. L., & Bianco, D. J. (1995). Accessing NASA technology with the World Wide Web. *IEEE Aerospace and Electronic Systems Magazine, 10*(5), 7–13. Retrieved March 1, 2001, from the World Wide Web: http://techreports.larc.nasa.gov/ltrs/refer/papers/NASA-IEEE-AES-95p7-13/NASA-IEEE-AES-95p7-13.html

Nelson, M. L., & Esler, S. L. (1997). TRSkit: A simple digital library toolkit. *Journal of Internet Cataloging, 1*(2), 41–55. Retrieved March 1, 2001, from the World Wide Web: http://techreports.larc.nasa.gov/ltrs/PDF/1997/jp/NASA-97-jic-mln.pdf

Nelson, M. L., Maly, K., & Shen, S. N. T. (1997). Building a multi-discipline digital library through extending the Dienst protocol. *Proceedings of the Second ACM International Conference on Digital Libraries, 262–263.*

Nelson, M. L., Maly, K., Shen, S. N. T., & Zubair, M. (1998). NCSTRL+: Adding multi-discipline and multi-genre support to the Dienst protocol using clusters and buckets. *Proceedings of Advances in Digital Libraries 98, 128–136.* Retrieved March 1, 2001, from the World Wide Web: http://techreports.larc.nasa.gov/ltrs/PDF/1998/mtg/NASA-98-ieeedl-mln.pdf

Nelson, M. L., Maly, K., & Zubair, M. (1998). *Interoperable heterogeneous digital libraries* [TR-98-07]. Norfolk, VA: Old Dominion University. Retrieved March 1, 2001, from the World Wide Web: http://www.cs.odu.edu/~techrep/techreports/TR_98_07.ps.Z

Nelson, M. L., Maly, K., Zubair, M., & Shen, S. N. T. (1998). Buckets: Aggregative, intelligent agents for publishing. *Webnet Journal, 1*(1), 58–66.

Nelson, M. L., Maly, K., Zubair, M., & Shen, S. N. T. (1999). SODA: Smart objects, dumb archives. *Proceedings of the Third European Conference on Digital Libraries.* Retrieved March 1, 2001, from the World Wide Web: http://link.springer.de/link/service/series/0558/papers/1696/16960453.pdf

Nelson, T., & Pam, A. (1998). ZigZag[tm] hyperstructure kit: The ZigZag commands, version 0.49 edition. Project Zanadu. Retrieved March 1, 2001, from the World Wide Web: http://www.xanadu.net/zigzag/zzDirectxCondensed.html

Nicholas, C., Crowder, G., & Soboroff, I. (2000). *CARROT: An agent-based architecture for large-scale document information systems* [TR CS-2000-01]. Baltimore: University of Maryland, Baltimore County.

Nichols, D., Pemberton, D., Dalhoumi, S., Larouk, O., Belisle, C., & Twidale, M. (2000). DEBORA: Developing an interface to support collaboration in a digital library. *Proceedings of the Fourth European Conference on Research and Advanced Technology for Digital Libraries, 239-248.* Retrieved March 1, 2001, from the World Wide Web: http://www.comp.lancs.ac.uk/computing/research/cseg/projects/debora/docs/ecdl-submit.pdf

Noerr, P. (Ed.). (2000). *The digital library toolkit* (2nd ed.). Palo Alto, CA: Sun Microsystems.

Nowell, L., & Hix, D. (1992). User interface design for the project Envision database of computer science literature. *Twenty-Second Annual Virginia Computer Users Conference*, 29-33.

Nowell, L., & Hix, D. (1993). Visualizing search results: User interface development for the project Envision database of computer science literature. *Advances in Human Factors/Ergonomics, Proceedings of 5th International Conference on Human Computer Interaction*, 56–61.

Nowell, L., Hix, D., France, R., Heath, L., & Fox, E. A. (1996). Visualizing search results: Some alternatives to query-document similarity. *Proceedings of the 19th International ACM SIGIR Conference on Research and Development in Information Retrieval*, 67–75.

Nürnberg, P. J., Furuta, R., Leggett, J. J., Marshall, C. C., & Shipman, III, F. M., (1995). Digital libraries: Issues and architectures. *The Second Annual Conference on the Theory and Practice of Digital Libraries*. Retrieved March 1, 2001, from the World Wide Web: http://www.csdl.tamu.edu/~leggett/leggettpubs/conferences/dl/dl95-arch.html

Oard, D. W. (1997a). Serving users in many languages: Cross-language information retrieval for digital libraries. *D-Lib Magazine, 3*(12). Retrieved March 1, 2001, from the World Wide Web: http://www.dlib.org/dlib/december97/oard/12oard.html

Oard, D. W. (1997b). *Speech-based information retrieval for digital libraries* [Technical Report CS-TR-3778]. College Park, MD: University of Maryland.

Oliveira, J. L. d., Gonçalves, M. A., & Medeiros, C. B. (1999). A framework for designing and implementing the user interface of a geographic digital library. *International Journal on Digital Libraries, 2*(3), 190–206.

Ouksel, A. M., & Sheth, A. (1999). Semantic interoperability in global information systems. *SIGMOD Record, 28*(1), 5–12.

Paepcke, A. (1999). Using the InfoBus. Palo Alto, CA: Stanford University Digital Libraries Project. Retrieved March 1, 2001, from the World Wide Web: http://www-diglib.stanford.edu/diglib/pub/userinfo.html

Paepcke, A., Brandriff, R., Janee, G., Larson, R., Ludaescher, B., Melnik, S., & Raghavan, S. (2000). Search middleware and the simple digital library interoperability protocol. *D-Lib Magazine, 6*(3). Retrieved March 1, 2001, from the World Wide Web: http://www.dlib.org/dlib/march00/paepcke/03paepcke.html

Paepcke, A., Chang, C.-C. K., Garcia-Molina, H., & Winograd, T. (1998). Interoperability for digital libraries worldwide. *Communications of the ACM, 41*(4), 33–43.

Paepcke, A., Cousins, S. B., Garcia-Molina, H., Hassan, S. W., Ketchpel, S. K., Roscheisen, M., & Winograd, T. (1996). Towards interoperability in digital libraries: Overview and selected highlights of the Stanford digital library project. *IEEE Computer Magazine, 29*(5), 61–68.

Pam, A., & Vermeer, A. (1995). A comparison of WWW and Hyper-G. *Journal of Universal Computer Science, 1,* 744–750.

Papazoglou, M. P., & Hoppenbrouwers, J. (1999). Contextualizing the information space in federated digital libraries. *SIGMOD Record, 28*(1), 40–46.

Park, S., Durfee, E. H., & Birmingham, W. P. (1998). Emergent properties of a market-based digital library with strategic agents. *Fourth International Conference on MultiAgent Systems.* 230–237.

Paskin, N. (1999). DOI: Current status and outlook. *D-Lib Magazine, 5*(5). Retrieved March 1, 2001, from the World Wide Web: http://www.dlib.org/dlib/may99/05paskin.html

Pavani, A. M. B., & Lukowiecki, A. L. S. (1999). Digital libraries and sharing course contents - the Maxwell project. *Proceedings of the International Conference on Engineering and Computer Education, 1999,* 86–98.

Payette, S., Blanchi, C., Lagoze, C., & Overly, E. A. (1999). Interoperability for digital objects and repositories: The Cornell/CNRI experiments. *D-Lib Magazine, 5*(5). Retrieved March 1, 2001, from the World Wide Web: http://www.dlib.org/dlib/may99/payette/05payette.html

Payette, S. D., & Rieger, O. Y. (1997). Z39.50: The user's perspective. *D-Lib Magazine, 3*(4). Retrieved March 1, 2001, from the World Wide Web: http://www.dlib.org/dlib/april97/cornell/04payette.html

Perry, J. W. (1951). Super-imposed punching of numerical codes on hand-sorted punch cards. *American Documentation, 2,* 205–212.

Phanouriou, C., Kipp, N. A., Sornil, O., Mather, P., & Fox, E. A. (1999). A digital library for authors: Recent progress of the networked digital library of theses and dissertations. *Proceedings of the Fourth ACM Conference on Digital Libraries,* 20-27. Retrieved March 1, 2001, from the World Wide Web: http://www.acm.org/pubs/citations/proceedings/dl/313238/p20-phanouriou

Plaisant, C., Marchionini, G., Bruns, T., Komlodi, A., & Campbell, L. (1997). Bringing treasures to the surface: Iterative design for the Library of Congress National Digital Library Program. *Conference on Human Factors in Computing Systems, CHI '97,* 518–525. Retrieved March 1, 2001, from the World Wide Web: ftp://ftp.cs.umd.edu/pub/hcil/Reports-Abstracts-Bibliography/3694html/3694.html

Plathe, A. (1999). Workshop on an international project of electronic dissemination of theses and dissertations. Paris: UNESCO. Retrieved March 1, 2001, from the World Wide Web: http://www.unesco.org/webworld/etd

Porck, H. J., & Teygeler, R. (2000). *Preservation science survey: An overview of recent developments in research on the conservation of selected analog library and archival materials.* Washington, DC: Council on Library and Information Resources.

Powell, A. (1998). Resolving DOI-based URNs using Squid: An experimental system at UKOLN. *D-Lib Magazine, 4*(6). Retrieved March 1, 2001, from the World Wide Web: http://www.dlib.org/dlib/june98/06powell.html

Powell, J., & Fox, E. (1998). Multilingual federated searching across heterogeneous collections. *D-Lib Magazine, 4*(8). Retrieved March 1, 2001, from the World Wide Web: http://www.dlib.org/dlib/september98/powell/09powell.html

Project Kaleidoscope Alliance. (2000). Project Kaleidoscope. Washington, DC: PKAL National Office. Retrieved March 1, 2001, from the World Wide Web: http://www.pkal.org

Rao, R., Pedersen, J. O., Hearst, M. A., Mackinlay, J. D., Card, S. K., Masinter, L., Halvorsen, P.-K., & Robertson, G. G. (1995). Rich interaction in the digital library. *Communications of the ACM, 38*(4), 29–39.

Rasmussen, E. M. (1992). Parallel information processing. *Annual Review of Information Science and Technology, 27,* 99–129.

Rauber, A., Dittenbach, M., & Merkl, D. (2000). Automatically detecting and organizing documents into topic hierarchies: A neural-network based approach to bookshelf creation and arrangement. *Proceedings of the Fourth Annual European Conference on Research and Development for Digital Libraries, Lecture Notes in Computer Science, 1923,* 348–351.

Rauber, A., & Merkl, D. (1999). SOMLib: A digital library system based on neural networks. *Proceedings of the Fourth ACM Conference on Digital Libraries,* 240–241. Retrieved March 1, 2001, from the World Wide Web: http://www.acm.org/pubs/citations/proceedings/dl/313238/p240-rauber/

Ribeiro-Neto, B., Laender, A. H. F., & da Silva, A. S. (1999, September). *Top-down extraction of semi-structured data.* Paper presented at the Sixth String Processing and Information Retrieval Symposium, Cancun, Mexico.

Roszkowski, M., & Lukas, C. (1998). A distributed architecture for resource discovery using metadata. *D-Lib Magazine, 4*(6). Retrieved March 1, 2001, from the World Wide Web: http://www.dlib.org/dlib/june98/scout/06roszkowski.html

Rothenberg, J. (1999). *Avoiding technological quicksand: Finding a viable technical foundation for digital preservation.* Washington, DC: Council on Library and Information Resources.

Rusbridge, C. (1995). The UK electronic libraries programme. *D-Lib Magazine, 1*(12). Retrieved March 1, 2001, from the World Wide Web: http://www.dlib. org/dlib/december95/briefings/12uk.html

Rusbridge, C. (1998). Towards the hybrid library. *D-Lib Magazine, 4*(7/8). Retrieved March 1, 2001, from the World Wide Web: http://www.dlib.org/dlib/july98/rusbridge/07rusbridge.html

Sairamesh, J., Nikolaou, C., Ferguson, D., & Yemini, Y. (1996). Economic framework for pricing and charging in digital libraries. *D-Lib Magazine, 2*(2). Retrieved March 1, 2001, from the World Wide Web: http://www.dlib.org/dlib/february96/forth/02sairamesh.html

Salampasis, M., Tait, J., & Bloor, C. (1996). Co-operative information retrieval in digital libraries. *Proceedings of the 18th BCS IRSG Annual Colloquium on Information Retrieval Research,* 13–26. Retrieved March 1, 2001, from the World Wide Web: http://osiris.sund.ac.uk/~cs0msa/bcsir96.ps

Salembier, P. (2000, September). *Status of MPEG-7: The content description standard.* Paper presented at the International Broadcasting Conference,

Amsterdam. Retrieved March 1, 2001, from the World Wide Web: http://www.cselt.it/mpeg/documents/ibc2000_tutorial/Salembier.htm

Salton, G. (1968). *Automatic information organization and retrieval.* New York: McGraw-Hill.

Samet, H., & Soffer, A. (1996). MARCO: MAp Retrieval by COntent. *IEEE Transactions on Pattern Analysis and Machine Intelligence, 18*(8), 783–798.

Sánchez, J. A., & Leggett, J. L. (1997). Agent services for users of digital libraries. *Journal of Network and Computer Applications, 20,* 45–58.

Sánchez, J. A., Lopez, C. A., & Schnase, J. L. (1998). An agent-based approach to the construction of floristic digital libraries. *Proceedings of the Third ACM International Conference on Digital Libraries,* 210–216.

Sanz, I., Berlanga, R., & Aramburu, M. J. (1998). Gathering metadata from Web-based repositories of historical publications. *Proceedings of the Ninth International Workshop on Database and Expert Systems Applications,* 473–478. Retrieved March 1, 2001, from the World Wide Web: http://ieeexplore. ieee.org/iel4/5718/15304/00707442.pdf

Schamber, L. (1996). What is a document? Rethinking the concept in uneasy times. *Journal of the American Society for Information Science, 47,* 669–671.

Schatz, B., & Chen, H. (1996). Building large-scale digital libraries. *Computer, 29*(5), 1–3. Retrieved March 1, 2001, from the World Wide Web: http://www.computer.org/computer/dli/

Schaube, P., & Smeaton, A. F. (1998). *Summary report of the series of joint NSF-EU working groups on future directions for digital library research: An international agenda for digital libraries.* DELOS. Retrieved March 1, 2001, from the World Wide Web: http://www.dli2.nsf.gov/eu_a.html

Schmiede, R. (1999). Digital library activities in Germany: The German digital library program GLOBAL INFO. *Proceedings of the IEEE Forum on Research and Technology Advances in Digital Libraries,* 73–83. Retrieved March 1, 2001, from the World Wide Web: http://www.computer.org/proceedings/adl/0219/02190073abs.htm

Schwartz, C. (2001a). Digital libraries: Readings. Boston: Simmons College. Retrieved March 1, 2001, from the World Wide Web: http://joan.simmons.edu/~schwartz/mydigital2.html

Schwartz, C. (2001b). Digital libraries: Resources. Boston: Simmons College. Retrieved March 1, 2001, from the World Wide Web: http://joan.simmons.edu/~schwartz/mydigital.html

Severiens, T. (2000). My meta maker, to markup resources in physics using the Dublin-Core-Standard. Oldenburg, GE: University of Oldenburg. Retrieved March 1, 2001, from the World Wide Web: http://www.physik.uni-oldenburg.de/EPS/mmm/b

Severiens, T., Hohlfeld, M., Zimmermann, K., & Hilf, E. R. (2000). PhysDoc—A distributed network of physics institutions documents: Collecting, indexing, and searching high quality documents by using Harvest. *D-Lib Magazine, 6*(12). Retrieved March 1, 2001, from the World Wide Web: http://www.dlib.org/dlib/december00/severiens/12severiens.html

Sharretts, C., Shieh, J., & French, J. C. (1999). Electronic theses and dissertations at the University of Virginia. *Proceedings of the 62nd Annual Meeting of the American Society for Information Science,* 240–255.

Shipman, III, F. M., Furuta, R., Brenner, D., Chung, C.-C., & Hsieh, H.-W. (2000). Guided paths through Web-based collections: Design, experiences, and adaptations. *Journal of the American Society for Information Science, 51,* 260–272.

Shivakumar, N., & Garcia-Molina, H. (1995a). SCAM approach to copy detection in digital libraries. *D-Lib Magazine, 1.* Retrieved March 1, 2001, from the World Wide Web: http://www.dlib.org/dlib/november95/scam/11shivakumar.html

Shivakumar, N., & Garcia-Molina, H. (1995b). SCAM: A copy detection mechanism for digital documents. *Proceedings of the Second International Conference on the Theory and Practice of Digital Libraries,* 13–32.

Shivakumar, N., & Garcia-Molina, H. (1996). Building a scalable and accurate copy detection mechnism. *Proceedings of the First ACM Conference on Digital Libraries,* 160–168.

Shneiderman, B. (1992). Tree visualization with tree maps: A 2-d space filling approach. *ACM Transactions on Graphics, 11*(1), 92–99.

Shneiderman, B., Feldman, D., Rose, A., & Grau, X. F. (2000). Visualizing digital library search results with categorical and hierarchical axes. *Proceedings of the Fifth ACM Conference on Digital Libraries,* 57–66. Retrieved March 1, 2001, from the World Wide Web: http://www.acm.org/pubs/citations/proceedings/dl/336597/p57-shneiderman

Shum, S. B., Motta, E., & Domingue, J. (2000). ScholOnto: An ontology-based digital library server for research documents and discourse. *International Journal on Digital Libraries, 3,* 237–248. Retrieved March 1, 2001, from the World Wide Web: http://link.springer.de/link/service/journals/00799/first/bibs/s007990000034.htm http://kmi.open.ac.uk/projects/scholonto

Sistla, A. P., Wolfson, O., Yesha, Y., & Sloan, R. H. (1998). Towards a theory of cost management for digital libraries and electronic commerce. *ACM Transactions on Database Systems, 23,* 411–452. Retrieved March 1, 2001, from the World Wide Web: http://www.acm.org/pubs/articles/journals/tods/1998-23-4/p411-sistla/p411-sistla.pdf

SMETE.ORG Alliance. (2000). Information portal: A digital library for science, mathematics, engineering, and technology education. Berkeley, CA: NEEDS. Retrieved March 1, 2001, from the World Wide Web: http://www.smete.org

Snyder, I. (1996). *Hypertext: The electronic labyrinth.* Washington Square, N.Y.: New York University Press.

Soete, G. J. (1998). *Transforming libraries: Issues and innovations in electronic theses and dissertations.* (Spec Kit 236). Washington, DC: Association of Research Libraries.

Sornil, O. (2000). *A distributed inverted index for a large-scale, dynamic digital library.* Unpublished doctoral dissertation draft, Virginia Polytechnic Institute and State University, Blacksburg, VA.

Spink, A., Wilson, T., Ellis, D., & Ford, N. (1998). Modeling users' successive searches in digital environments: A National Science Foundation/British

Library funded study. *D-Lib Magazine, 4*(4). Retrieved March 1, 2001, from the World Wide Web: http://www.dlib.org/dlib/april98/04spink.html

Staples, T., & Wayland, R. (2000). Virginia dons FEDORA: A prototype for a digital object repository. *D-Lib Magazine, 6*(7/8). Retrieved March 1, 2001, from the World Wide Web: http://www.dlib.org/dlib/july00/staples/07staples.html

Sterling, T., Messina, P., & Smith, P. H. (1995). *Enabling technologies for petaflops computing.* Cambridge, MA: MIT Press.

Sugimoto, M., Katayama, N., & Takasu, A. (1998). A system for constructing private digital libraries through information space exploration. *International Journal on Digital Libraries, 2,* 54–66.

Suleman, H., Fox, E. A., & Abrams, M. (2000). Building quality into a digital library. *Proceedings of the Fifth ACM Conference on Digital Libraries,* 228–229.

Sutcliffe, A. G. (1999). User-centred design for multimedia applications. *Proceedings of the IEEE International Conference on Multimedia Computing and Systems, 1999.* Retrieved March 1, 2001, from the World Wide Web: http://dlib.computer.org/conferen/icmcs/0253/pdf/02539116.pdf

Sutcliffe, A. G., & Patel, U. (1996). 3-d or not 3-d: Is it nobler in the mind? In M. A. Sasse, R. J. Cunningham, & R. Winder (Eds.), *Proceedings of HCI-96, People and Computers 9* (pp. 79–93). Heidelberg: Springer Verlag.

Taube, M., & Associates (1955). Storage and retrieval of information by means of the association of ideas. *American Documentation, 6,* 1–18.

Theng, Y. L., Duncker, E., Mohd-Nasir, N., Buchanan, G., & Thimbleby, H. W. (1999). Design guidelines and user-centred digital libraries. *Proceedings of the 3rd European Conference on Digital Libraries,* 167–183.

Theng, Y. L., Mohd-Nasir, N., Thimbleby, H., Buchanan, G., & Jones, M. (2000). Designing a children's digital library with and for children. *Proceedings of the Fifth ACM Conference on Digital Libraries,* 266–267.

Thorin, S., & Sorkin, V. D. (1997). *The library of the future: The learning revolution: The challenge of information technology in the academy.* Bolton, MA: Anker.

Tibbo, H. R. (2001). Archival perspectives on the emerging digital library. *Communications of the ACM, 44*(5). Retrieved March 1, 2001, from the World Wide Web: http://www.acm.org/pubs/contents/journals/cacm/2001-44/#5

Tolle, K. M., & Chen, H. (2000). Comparing noun phrasing techniques for use with medical digital library tools. *Journal of the American Society for Information Science, 51,* 352–370.

Tsinaraki, C., Christodoulakis, S., Anestis, G., & Moumoutzis, N. (1998). Implementing powerful retrieval capabilities in a distributed environment for libraries and archives. *Proceedings of the Second European Conference on Digital Libraries, Lecture Notes in Computer Science, 1513,* 653–655.

Unicode consortium. (2001). Unicode home page. Retrieved March 1, 2001, from the World Wide Web: http://www.unicode.org

Van de Sompel, H. (2000). Open Archives Initiative. Ithaca, NY: Cornell University. Retrieved March 1, 2001, from the World Wide Web: http://www. openarchives.org

Van de Sompel, H., Ginsparg, P., & Luce, R. (1999). The universal preprint service initiative. Retrieved March 1, 2001, from the World Wide Web: http://vole.lanl.gov/ups/ups.htm

Van de Sompel, H., & Hochstenbach, P. (1999). Reference linking in a hybrid library environment, part 2: SFX, a generic linking solution. *D-Lib Magazine, 5*(4). Retrieved March 1, 2001, from the World Wide Web: http://www.dlib.org/dlib/april99/van_de_sompel/04van_de_sompel-pt2.html

Van de Sompel, H., Krichel, T., Nelson, M. L., Hochstenbach, P., Lyapunov, V. M., Maly, K., Zubair, M., Kholief, M., Liu, X., & O'Connell, H. (2000). The UPS Prototype: An experimental end-user service across e-print archives. *D-Lib Magazine, 6*(2). Retrieved March 1, 2001, from the World Wide Web: http://www.dlib.org/dlib/february02vandesompel-ups/02vandesompel-ups.html

Van de Sompel, H., & Lagoze, C. (2000). The Santa Fe convention of the open archives initiative. *D-Lib Magazine, 6*(2). Retrieved March 1, 2001, from the World Wide Web: http://www.dlib.org/dlib/february02vandesompel-oai/02vandesompel-oai.html

Van de Sompel, H., & Lagoze, C. (2001). The open archives initiative protocol for metadata harvesting: Protocol version 1.0, document version 2001-01-21. Ithaca, NY: Cornell University. Retrieved March 1, 2001, from the World Wide Web: http://www.openarchives.org/OAI/openarchivesprotocol.htm

van Doorn, M. G. L. M. (1999). *Thesauri and the mirror retrieval model.* Unpublished master's thesis, University of Twente, Database group, Enschede, The Netherlands.

van Doorn, M. G. L. M., & de Vries, A. P. (2000). The psychology of multimedia databases, *Proceedings of the Fifth ACM Conference on Digital Libraries,* 1–9. Retrieved March 1, 2001, from the World Wide Web: http://www.acm.org/pubs/citations/proceedings/dl/336597/p1-van_doorn

Velegrakis, Y., Christophides, V., & Constanopoulos, P. (1999). Declarative specification of Z39.50 wrappers using description logics. *Proceedings of the 3rd European Conference on Digital Libraries, Lecture Notes in Computer Science, 1696,* 383–402.

Velegrakis, Y., Christophides, V., & Constantopoulos, P. (2000). On Z39.50 wrapping and description logics. *International Journal on Digital Libraries, 3*(3), 208–220.

Viles, C. L., & French, J. C. (1999). Content locality in distributed digital libraries. *Information Processing & Management, 35,* 317–336.

Voorhees, E. M. (1994). Query expansion using lexical-semantic relations. *Proceedings of the Seventeenth Annual International ACM-SIGIR Conference on Research and Development in Information Retrieval,* 61–69. Retrieved March 1, 2001, from the World Wide Web: http://www.acm.org/pubs/citations/proceedings/ir/188490/p61-voorhees

Wake, W., & Fox, E. A. (1995). SortTables: A browser for a digital library. *Proceedings of the 4th International Conference Information and Knowledge Management,* 175–181.

Wang, B. (1999). A hybrid system approach for supporting digital libraries. *International Journal on Digital Libraries, 2,* 91–110.

Wang, K., & Liu, H. (1998). Discovering typical structures of documents: A road map approach. *Proceedings of the 21st Annual International ACM SIGIR Conference on Research and Development in Information Retrieval,* 146–154.

Waters, D., & Garrett, J. (1996). *Preserving digital information: Report of the Task Force on Archiving of Digital Information.* Washington, DC: Council on Library and Information Resources.

Waters, D. J. (1998). The Digital Library Federation: Program agenda. Washington, DC: Digital Libraries, a program of the Council on Library and Information Resources.

Wattenberg, F. (1998). A national digital library for science, mathematics, engineering, and technology education. *D-Lib Magazine, 4*(9). Retrieved March 1, 2001, from the World Wide Web: http://www.dlib.org/dlib/october98/wattenberg/ 10wattenberg.html

Wattenberg, F. (1999, June). Stretching the zero sum paradigm with a national digital library for science education. *Information Impacts.* Retrieved March 1, 2001, from the World Wide Web: http://www.cisp.org/imp/june_99/wattenberg/ 06_99wattenberg.htm

Waugh, A., Wilkinson, R., Hills, B., & Dell'oro, J. (2000). Preserving digital information forever. *Proceedings of the Fifth ACM Conference on Digital Libraries,* 175–184.

Weibel, S. (1995). Metadata: The foundations of resource description. *D-Lib Magazine, 1*(1). Retrieved March 1, 2001, from the World Wide Web: http://www.dlib.org/dlib/July95/07weibel.html

Weibel, S. (1999). The state of the Dublin Core Metadata Initiative: April 1999. *D-Lib Magazine, 5*(4). Retrieved March 1, 2001, from the World Wide Web: http://www.dlib.org/dlib/april99/04weibel.html

Weibel, S., Kunze, J., Lagoze, C., & Wolf, M. (1998a). *Dublin core metadata for resource discovery* [Technical Report IETF #2413]: The Internet Society.

Weibel, S., Kunze, J., Lagoze, C., & Wolf, M. (1998b). *RFC 2413, Dublin Core Metadata resource discovery.* Reston, VA: Internet Engineering Task Force. Retrieved March 1, 2001, from the World Wide Web: http://www.ietf.org/rfc/ rfc2413.txt http://community.roxen.com/developers/ idocs/rfc/rfc2413.html

Weinstein, P. C., & Alloway, G. (1997). Seed ontologies: Growing digital libraries as distributed, intelligent systems. *Proceedings of the Second ACM International Conference on Digital Libraries,* 83–90.

Weinstein, P. C., & Birmingham, W. P. (1998). Creating ontological metadata for digital library content and services. *International Journal on Digital Libraries, 2,* 19–36.

Weisstein, E. (2000). Eric Weisstein's World of Mathematics [MathWorld™]. Champaign, IL: Wolfram Research. Retrieved October 1, 2000, from the World Wide Web: http://mathworld.wolfram.com

Wells, H. G. (1938). *World brain*. Garden City, NY: Doubleday.

Wiederhold, G., & Genesereth, M. (1997). The conceptual basis for mediation services. *IEEE Expert, 12*(5), 38–47. Retrieved March 1, 2001, from the World Wide Web: http://dbpubs.stanford.edu/pub/1997-64

Wilensky, R. (2000). Digital library resources as a basis for collaborative work. *Journal of the American Society for Information Science, 51*, 228–245.

Willett, P. (1999). TEI text encoding in libraries: Guidelines for best encoding practices (Version 1.0 [July 30, 1999 ed.]). Washington, DC: Digital Library Federation. Retrieved March 1, 2001, from the World Wide Web: http://www.clir.org/diglib/standards/tei.htm

Witbrock, M. J., & Hauptmann, A. G. (1998). Speech recognition for a digital video library. *Journal of the American Society for Information Science, 49*, 619–632.

Witten, I. H., Loots, M., Trujillo, M. F., & Bainbridge, D. (2001). The promise of DLs in developing countries. *Communications of the ACM, 44* (5). Retrieved March 1, 2001, from the World Wide Web: http://www.acm.org/pubs/contents/journals/cacm/2001-44/#5

Witten, I. H., McNab, R. J., Boddie, S. J., & Bainbridge, D. (2000). Greenstone: A comprehensive open-source digital library software system. *Proceedings of the Fifth ACM Conference on Digital Libraries*, 113–121.

Witten, I. H., Moffat, A., & Bell, T. C. (1999). *Managing gigabytes: Compressing and indexing documents and images* (2nd ed.). San Francisco: Morgan Kaufmann.

Witten, I. H., Nevill-Manning, C., McNab, R., & Cunningham, S. J. (1998). A public digital library based on full-text retrieval: Collections and experience. *Communications of the ACM, 41*(4), 71–75.

Wolff, J. E., & Cremers, A. B. (1999). The MYVIEW project: A data warehousing approach to personalized digital libraries. *Proceedings of the Fourth International Workshop on Next Generation Information Technologies and Systems, Lecture Notes in Computer Science, 1649*, 277–294. Retrieved March 1, 2001, from the World Wide Web: http://www.informatik.uni-bonn.de/~jw/publikationen/NGITS99_short_version.ps.gz

World Wide Web Consortium. (2000). World Wide Web Consortium (W3C). Retrieved March 1, 2001, from the World Wide Web: http://www.w3.org

Wu, V., Manmatha, R., & Riseman, E. M. (1997). Finding text in images. *Proceedings of the 2nd International Conference on Digital Libraries*, 1–10.

XML.ORG. (2000). XML.ORG: The XML industry portal. Retrieved March 1, 2001, from the World Wide Web: http://www.xml.org

Xu, J., Cao, Y. Y., Lim, E. P., & Ng, W. K. (1998). Database selection techniques for routing bibliographic queries. *Proceedings of the 3rd ACM Conference on Digital Libraries*, 264–273.

Yan, T. W., & Garcia-Molina, H. (1999). The SIFT information dissemination system. *ACM Transactions on Database Systems, 24,* 529–565.

Yeh, J., Chang, J., & Oyang, Y. (2000). Content and knowledge management in a digital library and museum. *Journal of the American Society for Information Science, 51,* 371–379.

Yoder, E., Akscyn, R. M., & McCracken, D. (1989). Collaboration in KMS, a shared hypermedia environment. *Proceedings of the SIG CHI Conference on Wings of the Mind, CHI '89,* 231–248.

Zhang, H. J., & Smith, B. C. (Eds.). (2001). *Readings in multimedia computing.* San Francisco: Morgan Kaufmann.

Zhao, J. (1999). *Making digital libraries flexible, scalable, and reliable: Reengineering the MARIAN system in JAVA.* Unpublished master's thesis, Virginia Polytechnic Institute and State University, Blacksburg.

Zhu, B., Ramsey, M., Ng, T. D., Chen, H., & Schatz, B. (1999). Creating a large-scale digital library for georeferenced information. *D-Lib Magazine, 5*(7/8). Retrieved March 1, 2001, from the World Wide Web: http://www.dlib.org/dlib/july99/zhu/07zhu.html

Zia, L. L. (2001). The NSF national science, mathematics, engineering, and technology education digital library (NSDL) program. *Communications of the ACM, 44*(5). Retrieved March 1, 2001, from the World Wide Web: http://www.acm.org/pubs/contents/journals/cacm/2001-44/#5

Zimmermann, K. (2000). Dissertationen online. CvO University of Oldenburg: Department of Physics: Oldenburg, Germany. Retrieved March 1, 2001, from the World Wide Web: http://www.dissonline.org/ http://www.educat.huberlin.de/diss_online/englisch/index1e.html

CHAPTER 13

Health Informatics

Marie Russell
Victoria University of Wellington

J. Michael Brittain
Health Informatics Consultant

Introduction

This chapter is based in part on reviews of health informatics by MacDougall and Brittain (1998), and Brittain, MacDougall, and Gann (1996), and highlights some of the dominant issues in the period 1998–2001. In a wide-ranging discussion, we identify current trends and issues in health informatics with examples of applications, particularly in English-speaking countries.

Health informatics deals with the management of health information and the application of information technology to support health services. The chapter reviews recent literature on a broad range of health information, including informatics relating to healthcare practitioners, patients, scientists, managers, caregivers, and the general public. In general the review does not cover medical informatics, which is considered a separate field, although there is some overlap. Medical informatics concerns the use of information technology for medical and scientific research, clinical diagnosis, and treatment. Where the more inclusive nature of health information is concerned, we prefer the term health informatics, as it embraces many subdisciplines and areas.

At the turn of the century, several forces are at work in health informatics. These are not primarily technological, but, rather, interact with technological developments. Factors at work include financial restrictions and resulting changes in the structures of healthcare, concerns about health outcomes and health service quality, the evidence-based medicine movement, changes in the provider-patient relationship, and expanding popular use of information technology, particularly of the Internet. The latter is of course by no means universal. The "digital divide" between the information technology "haves" and "have-nots," identified in the U.S. by the Department of Commerce's National Telecommunications & Information Administration (2000), affects health and medicine as much as other sectors. Although health informatics has now emerged as a discipline and practice in its own right—with journals, conferences, professional associations, research, and university-level education programs—the field is derived from computer and information sciences, library science, information management, and some of the social sciences (Brittain, 1997).

The chapter reviews developments under three broad headings: health systems, professionals, and patients; evidence-based medicine and its implications; and e-health. The review concludes with a view toward the future.

Health Systems, Professionals, and Patients

At all levels of national health systems, groups and individuals are grappling with the implications of developments in health informatics. In this section, we review health informatics in relation to governments, health professionals and managers, and patients by considering national strategies, management issues, changes in the provider-patient relationship, information about patients and information for them, informatics in primary care and in nursing, privacy and confidentiality issues, and education and training.

National Strategies

Economic restructuring and limits on health spending have led to reforms in health systems in many countries over the last two decades. Prompted both by the need to limit costs and by rapid technological developments, governments have recognized the strategic importance of health information. There has been an increased interest in quality of services and health outcomes; with accountability becoming a pressing issue in the face of scandals in some places, and litigation in others. Where governments provide health services, information technology services at national and local levels have, over the last fifteen years, commonly been outsourced to private companies. A number of national initiatives are being implemented in such countries, but in the U.S. no national approach is discernible, in contrast with many European countries and Australasia.

In Britain, the government's aim in a December 1997 white paper was to build a modern, dependable National Health Service (NHS), with a strong emphasis on quality in the health services. To this end, the concept of clinical governance has been advanced, meaning "a framework through which NHS organizations are accountable for continuously improving the quality of their services and safeguarding high standards of care by creating an environment in which excellence in clinical care will flourish" (U.K. National Health Services Executive, 1999a, p. 6). The concept is underpinned by statutory requirements for accountability and monitoring. These developments follow a period when scandals such as that of the Bristol Royal Infirmary showed some aspects of the British health services to be unreliable and indeed often fatal for patients (Hammond & Mosley, 1999). The publication of tables showing hospital performance has added to pressures for quality improvement. Concern with clinical effectiveness is part of the strategy for best practice using evidence-based medicine.

More directly related to information in the "new NHS" is a seven-year plan (1998–2005) to "provide the right information wherever it is needed in the NHS, from the doctor's surgery to any hospital accident and emergency unit. The strategy will also ensure proper information is available to tackle the causes of ill health and to plan and monitor healthcare" (U.K. National Health Service, 2000c, online). Some areas have their own information strategies, e.g., mental health or cancer. The NHS Information Authority has an interest in "more effective management" and introduction of a National Framework for Assessing Performance. Accurate information for managers and planners is acknowledged as essential to support improvements and monitoring (U.K. National Health Service, 2000b).

A review seeking to identify the factors associated with success in implementing information technology in the National Health Service found that: Most problems relate to human and not technical factors; work processes must adapt as new technology is introduced, expectations and timeframes must be realistic, involving and training users is crucial, and key technical requirements are flexibility and communication capabilities (Bowns, Rotherham, & Paisley, 1999). Outside government circles in the U.K., the King's Fund, a London-based charity, has started an independent quality improvement and accreditation organization: Health Quality Service (King's Fund launches quality service, 1998).

In Canada, the Canadian Institute for Health Information (CIHI) is a federally chartered but independent and not-for-profit organization whose work covers identifying health information needs, collecting and using data, and setting national standards in health information. The CIHI leads the "Roadmap Initiative," a national vision and four-year action plan to modernize Canada's health information system, funded by the federal government from 1999 (Canadian Institute for Health Information, 2000).

In 1999 the Australian Institute of Health and Welfare released a strategy for the development of public health information. "A rapidly-growing need for comprehensive and consistent public health information at national, State, Territory and local levels" is identified, with recommendations (Australian Institute of Health and Welfare and National Public Health Information Working Group, 1999, p. iii). These cover three areas: developing public health information capacity, improving its scope and coverage, and improving the use and delivery of public health information.

Hospital Management and Other Large Systems

The impact of information technology developments in large healthcare ventures, such as hospitals, has been mixed. Introducing information technology into large hospital systems has been dogged by difficulties; delivery is often late, the cost is often higher than predicted, and the system may not deliver the promised functionality. Chandra, Knickrehm, and Miller (1995) identify pitfalls for U.S. healthcare companies when buying information technology: failing to focus on productivity, allowing other players to capture the value created, poor execution, and being tempted to buy pointless gadgetry. Carr (2000) identifies the main reasons for information technology project failures in the health sector as poor management and improper identification of the requirements of the system. This appears to have been the case in a computer project failure in a New Zealand hospital system, at Health Waikato. The project cost over $NZ14 million before being discontinued, with ongoing running costs and system testing expected to cost up to $NZ72 million (New Zealand Health Information Service, 2000). Another example from Australia, and the lessons to be drawn from it, are discussed by Southon, Sauer, and Dampney (1999).

The hospital information system at Geneva University Hospital in Switzerland, DIOGENE, has been under development for over twenty years. It includes four aspects: medico-economic information, patient information, external information (e.g., Medline), and integration of this knowledge in a case-based reasoning format, all available on the provider's desktop (Borst, Appel, Baud, Ligier, & Scherrer, 1999). A successful project at Chang Gung Memorial Hospital in Taiwan is described by Chuang, Tan, Wu, and Kuo (1996). Factors accounting for the success include top-level management commitment, cross-functional teams, training and promotion, system reliability and availability, and the right conversion strategy. The chief executive officer's attitude is also identified as important in a survey of eighty-four Australian hospitals examining the significance of various factors related to the progressive use of information in the hospitals. Hospital size also has a significant positive relationship with the progressive use of information technology (Reeve & Rose, 1999).

Learning from mistakes occurred in a rural community trust in the U.K., where a ten-year-old information management system with hand-held computers required staff to enter data that they rarely found useful and which also had limited use by management (James & Thomas, 1999). The system was to be replaced and a consultative process with staff was used to ensure that a better system could be introduced. Staff participation in the process led them to have a new, more positive, and constructive attitude.

Where individual providers, patients, or smaller healthcare systems lack access to information or technological capacity, a "digital divide" can emerge. One example of an information system addressing a rural-urban digital divide comes from Utah where a medical library outreach program teaches information access skills to rural health professionals (McCloskey, 2000).

There are possible adverse effects from the application of new technologies in healthcare for managers and policy makers, according to Rigby (1999), who discusses how information system developments are radically reshaping organizations. Dependence on unverifiable information is part of the problem (Rigby, 1999). In the U.S., according to McGee (1998), healthcare companies have under-spent on information technology systems. A particular challenge is to keep up with government billing requirements.

Changes in the Provider-Patient Relationship

Changes in social values, including an increased awareness by patients that they are consumers, and the consequences of readily available information technology are bringing about changes in the provider-patient relationship. The *British Medical Journal* has summed up these changes thus: "Patients have grown up—and there's no going back" (Coulter, 1999, p. 719). Three models of doctor-patient interaction are identified: the more traditional paternalistic model, in which the doctor decides what to do; the informed approach, where the patient decides after the doctor has explained the options; and a middle approach, where doctor and patient decide together in a shared partnership model. The partnership approach is currently favored in official policy in the U.K., although it is unclear if patients and doctors are ready to adopt joint decision making.

Some practical issues of involving patients in decisions about healthcare are discussed by Entwistle, Sheldon, Sowden, and Watt (1998), who believe the processes and outcomes of evidence-informed patient choice are poorly understood, and need careful evaluation. They note two arguments in favor of promoting such choice. The first is a moral one in which informed patient choice is seen as desirable, because it is a right.

The second argument rests on hoped-for, but not yet proven, positive outcomes: clinical effectiveness and health gain, improved compliance, reduced expenditure, and reduced litigation. The authors explore the practical and ethical issues that may arise, noting difficulties where patients actively choose ineffective options, refuse to get involved at all, or choose excessively expensive options. Elsewhere, Entwistle, Sowden, and Watt (1998) ask what criteria should be used to judge effectiveness when evaluating interventions to promote patient decision making. They conclude that, when the aim is to improve health status and well being, health outcomes should take priority over process variables such as decision-making behavior and patients' knowledge. A systematic review of randomized trials of patient decision aids finds that they improve knowledge, reduce decisional conflict, and stimulate patients to be more active in decision making without increasing their anxiety (O'Connor et al., 1999). The authors conclude that the effects on outcomes remain uncertain.

In the U.S., the health informatics community has been urged to develop computer-based applications to support the process of integrating patient preferences with scientific knowledge and clinical practice guidelines, given that computer-based tools have proven acceptable to both patients and clinicians (Brennan & Strombom, 1998).

The impact of the Internet on provider-patient relationships is profound (see, for example Eberhart-Phillips et al., 2000; Jadad, 1999). Access to the Internet gives patients an increased level of knowledge, enabling them, if they wish, to participate as partners with providers. But improvements could be made by increasing collaboration between consumer groups and professional organizations; understanding more precisely how patients and doctors use the Internet; making access to the technology easy and fast, with relevant, valid, and engaging information available; balancing electronic and face-to-face interactions; ensuring equitable access; and balancing privacy and connectivity (Jadad, 1999). Quality control of information on the Internet is likely to remain a formidable problem for the foreseeable future.

Consumer Health Information

As patients seek more involvement in their own healthcare and providers thrust more responsibility onto patients, consumer health information has expanded greatly. The sources of consumer health information are many and diverse: medical reference works; articles in medical periodicals; healthcare providers' information on services; leaflets, books, personal advice from consumer and self-help groups; television and radio programs; popular magazines; and Web sites. Some questions that arise are: what services exist and where they are delivered, who is able to access them, and what are the quality of information and its effect on the provider-patient relationship both immediately and in the long term? Finally, there are vexing legal issues regarding responsibility for quality and use of information.

A major concern in the area of healthcare is the question of what happens in the information transfer or exchange between provider and patient. What has been conveyed and what has been understood? Aims of consumer health information include improving patients' understanding and compliance with treatments, and reducing their stress and anxiety. In this section, we discuss some national programs for disseminating consumer health information, ways of evaluating information, and legal implications. In Britain, NHS Direct, a twenty-four-hour nurse-led telephone service for information, gives advice about health, illness, and health services (U.K. National Health Service, 2000a). The New Zealand equivalent, Healthline, started in 2000. Sites like NHS Direct Online in Britain, launched in 1999 as an extension of the NHS telephone advice service, provide a gateway to health information on the Internet. Yet many patients get their information from sources other than the Internet, the most obvious being health professionals. They are not always willing to hand over written information to their patients, however, for various reasons (Entwistle, Sheldon, et al., 1998), although the information might benefit patients (Entwistle & Watt, 1998). Entwistle and her team have also described the experience of the NHS Centre for Reviews and Dissemination in developing information materials for consumers (Entwistle, Watt, et al., 1998).

Sources of consumer health information may be based in public libraries or shopping malls. In the U.S., the National Library of Medicine has tried to work with public libraries to provide health information. An evaluation showed a definite need, as health information was in the top-ten or top-five topics of interest to library users (Wood et al., 2000). A study of a high-street consumer health information shop serving a widely dispersed population in the Scottish Highlands found that most people were looking for information about a specific personal health problem. This service was well used by all social classes (Barker & Polson, 1999).

In the U.S., a public-private partnership has proposed a National Patient Library of evidence-based health information intended to identify and vet information for consumers (Lerner, 1998). Already in existence for many years is Medline Plus, a service of the National Library of Medicine, which provides health topics, drug information, dictionaries and directories, as well as other information (Medline Plus, 2000). Also in the U.S., a Web-based clinical trials register designed for patients became available in 2000 (Clinicaltrials.gov, 2000). The trials listed are primarily those sponsored by the National Institutes of Health, but in the later stages of this new project, trials sponsored by other governmental and private organizations are to be included (McCray & Ide, 2000).

But what of the quality of consumer health information? In Britain several initiatives seek to enhance quality. The Centre for Health Information Quality (ChiQ) was set up in 1997 as part of the National Health Service's Patient Partnership Strategy. Appraisal of consumer health information is only one of its activities; recently it has worked with the National Institute of Clinical Excellence (NICE) on developing patient information to complement clinical guidelines the Institute had developed for professionals. Extensive databases and links to recommended sources are available from the Centre for Health Information Quality. According to ChiQ, good patient information exhibits three elements: It must be clearly communicated, involve patients, and be evidence based (Centre for Health Information, 1999). From the consumer's point of view, more may be needed: According to Oliver (2000), information about the social and emotional aspects of health is often missing in the materials professionals use. An overview of consumer health information services and activities is provided by Gann (1997).

DISCERN, a short instrument enabling patients and information providers to assess the quality of written information about patient choices has been developed by Charnock, Shepperd, Needham, and Gann (1999). The authors claim that DISCERN is the first standardized quality index of consumer health information. The tool also facilitates production of new, high-quality, evidence-based consumer health information. Although some subjectivity is required in ratings, it combines qualitative methods and a statistical measure leading to consensus across raters. Three of the authors elsewhere advise professionals on how they can help patients find good quality information (Shepperd, Charnock, & Gann, 1999), listing recommended tools and offering advice on quality appraisal instruments such as those for readability. Some of the uses of DISCERN (2000), which is available on the Internet, are described by Charnock and Shepperd (2000).

For a specific disease state, Gustafson et al. (1999) have tested an in-home computerized system providing information, decision support, and contact with experts and other patients. The Comprehensive Health Enhancement Support System (CHESS) was tested on HIV-positive patients and shown to improve patients' quality of life and promote more efficient use of healthcare. CHESS has also been used for other conditions, including substance abuse, sexual assault, and for women with breast cancer. Feasibility and pilot studies, and some randomized control trials have been carried out, showing benefits. More information is available about the development and applications of the system (Comprehensive Health Enhancement Support System, 2000).

Healthcare consumers, however, may be seeking information not only about healthcare, but also about health services and providers. A U.S. Internet-based consumer health information service has developed formulae for rating hospitals, physicians, and health plans from publicly available data (Morrissey, 1999). This may concern providers whose livelihoods could be enhanced or threatened by such information.

Also in the U.S., the legal implications of consumer health information on the Internet are explored by Keltner (1998). The Clinton administration promoted networked health information as a means of lowering health costs while improving citizens' health. Managed care organizations and private health information providers use the Internet to convey consumer health information, but the legal standing of providers and consumers concerning the accuracy, timeliness, and integrity of that information is unclear. Law modifications and enforcement to promote standard practices are needed. The area is complex: Who, for instance, is responsible if technical glitches lead to consumer harm? Legal changes need to be accompanied by education about the appropriate use of Internet information. According to Lewis (1999), research is needed regarding cost-benefit analyses of computer-based patient information and the impacts of such technologies on health outcomes over time.

Patient-Generated Data—Electronic Medical Records

Information from a patient's medical records or clinical documentation about a patient may have many forms: textual, numerical, or images such as X-rays. Details included may cover the individual's or family's medical history, symptoms, diseases, diagnoses, therapeutic and drug treatments, and the like. This information is of use both in the treatment of the individual patient and in medical teaching and research in epidemiology and medical audits.

Technology is available to use multimedia electronic medical records containing textual, numeric, imaging, audio, and signal-based components, available across the diverse sites where a patient might use medical services. These sites include the family doctor, hospital specialists, ancillary health providers, residential care, and laboratory or diagnostic services (Lowe, 1999) and encompass clinical, financial, and administrative information (Doyle, 1998).

The potential of electronic medical records includes the possibility of reducing costs while improving quality of care, but after decades of effort developing technology, the use of electronic medical records remains a challenge. In many places, very basic technologies may be in use. In New Zealand, for example, an assessment suggests 30 percent to 40 percent of general practitioners use at least some form of electronic medical record (Schloeffel, 1999). The potential of electronic medical records is by no means fully exploited. A survey of U.S. healthcare executives in 1998 showed that only 2 percent had fully operational electronic patient records systems in place (Serb, 1998). The absence of portable generic electronic patient records is one difficulty, and it illustrates the continuing gap between the potential and the reality of electronic medical records (Lowe, 1999; Retchin & Wenzel, 1999; Terry, 1999).

Other developments in health services await fully implemented electronic medical records systems. Quality-inspired initiatives using integrated care pathways in the U.K. National Health Service may be frustrated by barriers to the implementation of electronic medical records (Norris & Briggs, 1999).

Barriers to widespread use of electronic medical records are legion: software problems of codification and data entry, security and privacy issues, lack of integrated delivery systems, professional reluctance or resistance, and prohibitive costs, especially where there are no economies of scale (Retchin & Wenzel, 1999; Terry, 1999). The slow uptake of electronic medical records systems and consequent inability to access longitudinal patient care information are as frustrating to commercial interests as they are to medicine and healthcare management (Doyle, 1998). In the U.S., the Medical Records Institute has devised a conceptual framework to accelerate the implementation of electronic health records, which requires work on several fronts including information modelling, standards, legal and regulatory issues, policies, the requirements of different medical specialties, and patient issues (Medical Records Institute, 1999). An effort to develop an international code for electronic medical records is reported by the College of American Pathologists, which is working with the U.K.'s National Health Service on a unified computerized coding system (Agreement signals milestone, 1999).

In Australia, a major government-commissioned report on patient records was released in 2000. The report by the National Electronic Health Records Taskforce proposed setting up a national health information network. The necessary building blocks and other issues were fully explored, and the report was endorsed by ministers in July 2000 (Australia National Electronic Health Records Taskforce, 2000).

Primary Care

General practice increasingly entails computer support. In Britain, most general practices have been computerized: over 80 percent in 1998 (Brown, 1998). In New Zealand, 75 percent of all general practitioners use some form of electronic communications on a daily basis (Bowden, 2000). Internet use among New Zealand's general practitioners is frequent: 68 percent of those surveyed said they used the Internet at least monthly, and 71 percent had patients who indicated that they sought medical information from the Internet (Eberhart-Phillips et al., 2000). In Australia, where a general practice computer system was developed in 1997 (More & Clarke, 1999), value may be added to encompass services such as prescription support and tracking; online access to pharmaceutical information; links to international electronic medical libraries; patient advisory services and Web sites, news, and discussion groups; and continuing medical education programmes (Carlile & Sefton, 1998). An Australian survey concluded that there may be a positive relationship between quality, general practice, and computerization (Bolton, Douglas, Booth, & Miller, 1999). Cork, Detmer, and Friedman (1998) have prepared and tested an instrument to assess physicians' use of, knowledge about, and attitudes toward computers.

Quality and accountability in healthcare could be greatly enhanced by using information technology for supporting clinical guidelines, according to Owens (1998). Shiffman, Liaw, Brandt, and Corb (1999) review studies of computer-based guideline implementation systems and find a number of key characteristics. Adherence to guidelines improved in fourteen out of eighteen systems where it was measured, and there are other benefits as well. A trial reported by Lobach and Hammond (1997) finds that clinicians' use of a clinical guideline increases if there is a decision support system generating a customized protocol for the individual patient. From Finland, a descriptive study of how physicians use a computerized collection of guidelines for primary care (Jousimaa, Kunnamo, & Makela, 1998) shows that users average 3.12 searches a day, and that sufficient facts were found in 71 percent of the searches. The average time needed to find and read an article was 4.9 minutes, with the main areas of interest being dermatology, infectious diseases, and cardiology.

Interactive computer technology applications, like multimedia kiosks, the Internet, and handheld digital devices, have the potential to assist in family practice, according to Glasgow, McKay, Boles, and Vogt (1999). Combined with behavioral science principles, these technologies can help with patient self-management, for example, of chronic disease. How general practitioners are to find time to explore the use of new technologies is unclear. The information overload syndrome is outlined by Noone, Warren, and Brittain (1998, p. 287) who see the future challenge as one of presenting the "vast array of information sources to the GP in an acceptable and useable information system interface."

Does general practitioner computing make a difference to patient care? Ellis and May (1999), assessing the use of desktop computing in primary care, suggest that, while there have been advances in primary care administration, the evidence for improvements in patient care is mixed. Kidd and Mazza (2000) point out the potential for incorporating the use of clinical guidelines with the use of electronic patient records in Australia, now that most general practitioners there are using computers. Sullivan and Mitchell (1995) conclude from their review of thirty studies that the impact of the computer system includes lengthening the consultation times, and tends to increase the amount of time doctors speak. Computer systems are associated with more uptake of targeted preventive services, decreased time and costs associated with repeat prescribing, and increased generic prescribing. Patient satisfaction is not affected. In a more recent review on effects of electronic communication in general practice, only a few studies reported improvements over paper communications (van der Kam, Moorman, & Koppejan-Mulder, 2000). An Australian study of discharge communications finds no good evidence to suggest that information technology could improve the quality of these communications between hospitals and primary care (Bolton, 1999).

Nursing Informatics

Nursing informatics is a branch of health informatics that has been recognized since 1992 by the American Nurses Association as a nursing specialty (Simpson, 1998a, 1998b). The broad range of areas addressed in nursing informatics is evidenced by the program of a recent nursing informatics conference (International Nursing Informatics Congress, 2000). The role of an informatics nurse is discussed by O'Reilly (1998), who sees the informatics nurse as equally competent in the clinical and technical languages and acting as an intermediary between the medical and the information technology worlds. Simpson (1998a, p. 22) notes that "computers and technology won't ever truly replace nurses but there's certainly no advantage to nursing without technology."

Reviewing types of nursing record systems, Currell, Wainwright, and Urquhart (2000, p. 2) note that "nurses have long been recognised as key collectors, generators and users of patient/client information ... the exchange and transfer of information is a significant nursing activity."

They ask how different types of nursing record systems affect nursing practice and healthcare outcomes, given that there has been considerable investment in computerized nursing information systems, whose benefit to patients is not established. The review shows no evidence of effects on practice that are attributable to changes in record systems, although the quality of existing research is questioned.

Simpson (1998a, 1998b) identifies reasons why nurses in the U.S. are not "technologically savvy": The health services have focused on cost rather than value of technology; research funding is limited and the educational/training infrastructure is inadequate. Ballard (1999) concludes that nurses need special informatics education and training to meet the requirements of their work.

Privacy and Confidentiality

A perennial concern about the application of information technology in healthcare has been its impact on patient confidentiality and privacy issues. In the U.S., privacy of automated personal health data has been debated since 1974. In a review of that debate, Freeman and Robbins (1999, p. 317) discuss the 1996 law that mandated a unique identifier for each participant in the U.S. medical care system and the use of a uniform data set for all health information transmitted in financial and administrative transactions. The authors believe that anxieties about privacy must be openly addressed "in a time of cynicism about government and discomfort with corporate medicine." The U.S. Congress failed in 1999 to meet its self-imposed deadline to enact comprehensive confidentiality legislation (Tang, 2000). Beyond healthcare, personal medical information is bought and sold on the open market, according to Etzioni (1999) in a recent review. Companies purchase such information for hiring and firing and to identify potential customers.

Some specialties address their own patient privacy issues, both out of concern for patients and to limit their own liability. The American Academy of Pediatrics (1999) lists pediatrician responsibilities and notes the competing interests in the privacy issue: the health needs of the community, the rights of the patient, and the ability of the pediatrician to provide quality care.

Education and Training

The implications of enormous change in healthcare information include a new focus needed in primary and continuing education, according to Carlile and Sefton (1998). The focus should move from delivering content to developing the ability to manage the changes that are occurring. Investment in information technologies is not always accompanied by sufficient education and training of staff for the development, implementation, and operation of new systems (Brittain & Norris, 2000). In Britain, planning for health informatics services has been required as a key component of local information strategies in the government's Information for Health policy since 1998, although it is recognized that the needed skills are in short supply (U.K. National Health Services Executive, 2000a). Norris and Brittain (2000) review the health informatics education and training scene in the U.K. and also note some international activities. In particular, they cite the increasing tendency for providers of health informatics education and training to collaborate internationally, rather than to compete, as they have done in the past.

Evidence-Based Practice and Its Implications

The evidence-based medicine movement is now well established as one of the driving forces in healthcare. "Evidence-based medicine is the conscientious, explicit and judicious use of current best evidence in making decisions about the care of individual patients" (Sackett, Rosenberg, Gray, Haynes, & Richardson, 1996, p. 71). Failure to learn from available evidence has caused delays in the introduction of effective healthcare measures, and allowed the continued use of ineffective or even dangerous measures (Cochrane Collaboration, 2000). The search for evidence involves efficient literature searching, and the systematic review, evaluation, and meta-analysis of the clinical research literature.

A key approach is epitomized by the Cochrane Collaboration. In 1972, Cochrane argued that only findings derived from blind randomized control trials would provide valid evidence for the effectiveness of healthcare procedures (Cochrane Collaboration, 2000). On this basis, the Cochrane Collaboration, an international organization that aims to help people make well-informed decisions about healthcare by preparing, maintaining, and ensuring the accessibility of systematic reviews of the effects of healthcare interventions, was founded in 1992. The Cochrane Collaboration has nine principles:

- Collaboration
- Building on the enthusiasm of individuals
- Avoiding duplication
- Minimising bias
- Keeping up to date
- Ensuring relevance
- Ensuring access
- Continually improving the quality of its work
- Continuity

(Cochrane Collaboration, 2000).

On topics where there is low or little consensus, however, such systematic review may not be helpful. Even where there is plenty of information, the challenge of deriving treatment guidelines may be problematic. Meta-analysis, where the results of earlier studies are pooled and analyzed using various statistical tools, is not straightforward, for example, where there are contextual differences between contributing trials—as there often are (Freemantle, Mason, & Eccles, 1999). Goodman (1998b) cautions against making decisions based on the results of meta-analysis.

Not all providers are comfortable with the current approaches in evidence-based medicine. Buetow and Kenealy (2000) advocate a wider definition of evidence-based medicine through acknowledgment of the multiple dimensions of evidence, including, among others, expert evidence and theoretical evidence. Certainly for nurses, Rolfe (1999) claims evidence-based medicine's promotion of the randomized controlled trial as the "gold standard" of evidence may be too narrow. What counts as evidence should be rethought in light of nursing's distinctive approach. These views questioning the evidence-based medicine approach were foreshadowed by Knotterus and Dinant (1997), who emphasized the importance of clinical reality in the practice of medicine.

Domenighetti, Grilli, and Liberati (1998) propose that pressure should come bottom-up from patients to doctors for evidence-based medicine, and suggest how this consumer demand could be promoted. An aspect of the Cochrane Collaboration that is regrettably uncommon is its stress on consumer involvement. Membership is open to all. The Cochrane Library is an electronic one, and Cochrane reviews online are subject to comment and improvement by means of an iterative system. Both online and manual searching, across all languages, are carried out for Cochrane reviews. Traditionally, the Cochrane approach dealt with reviews of a limited number of treatments, for example, a particular surgical or drug intervention, and limited permissible evidence to randomized control trials. Now, the Cochrane Effective Practice and Organisation of Care Group (EPOC) takes a rather different approach. EPOC is a group under the Cochrane umbrella that works on reviews of organizational healthcare interventions—those that involve a change in the structure or delivery of healthcare (Cochrane Effective Practice and Organisation of Care Group, 2001).

A criticism of the zealotry evident among many proponents of evidence-based medicine was seen at a 1999 conference reported by Bastian (2000, p. 18). A "post-EBM" agenda may involve a "new, widespread, far more critical attitude to the phenomenon on EBM," one that recognizes the varying human values underlying so-called scientific objectivity. Because the movement relies on the "enthusiasm of individuals," values are prominent. One problem, for those with an interest in equity, is that evidence-based medicine's emphasis on effectiveness and efficiency does not help in overcoming social and economic disadvantage.

Finding Information

The evidence-based practice movement places new importance on retrieving information. It is one thing to have information available, and quite another to find it. Allison, Kiefe, Weissman, Carter, and Centor (1999) identify finding information (in this case, from MEDLINE, the excellent database of records of articles from biomedical journals, dating from the 1960s) as both an art and a science. In investigating how well physicians used electronic information retrieval systems, Hersh and Hickam (1998) developed a conceptual framework for assessment. According to Hersh and Hickam, most use of information retrieval systems is with bibliographic, rather than full-text databases, and overall use of such systems averaged from 0.3 to 9 times per month even though physicians had two unanswered questions for every three patients. Moreover, not all information physicians need is published in journals: Hersh and Price (1998) review means of identifying randomized control trials in conference proceedings abstracts.

The Internet provides a rich source for tracking evidence, and tools to guide the searcher are available. The School of Health and Related Research at the University of Sheffield in Britain, for example, offers "Netting the evidence: a ScHARR introduction to evidence-based practice on the Internet," which lists and annotates hundreds of sites, not only in English (Netting the evidence, 2000). Also in Britain, the British Medical Association (2000) suggests sources and the National Electronic Library for Health (NeLH) aims to keep health professionals up to date with the latest clinical research and best practices as these are needed (U.K. National Health Services Executive, 1998, p. 168). The NeLH is organized into four "virtual" floors of information: the patient and public information floor (involving Centre for Health Information Quality [ChiQ, see earlier]); the know-how floor, developed with the National Institute for Clinical Excellence; the knowledge floor, involving the healthcare library community; and the knowledge management floor, developed with British education and training programs and the medical informatics world (National Electronic Library for Health, 2000).

Not all information resources available are textual. The Visible Human project (U.S. National Library of Medicine, 2000), for example, is a digital image library of volumetric data representing complete normal adults, male and female. Indexing images in multimedia medical information poses additional problems. Tang, Haska, and Ip (1999) review intelligent content-based indexing and browsing of medical images and describe the I-Browse project, which aims to develop techniques enabling a physician to search over image archives through a combination of semantic and iconic representations.

Using Information

Identifying evidence is only half of the challenge. Provision of evidence-based medicine and best practice protocols in the workplace at the point of care is being addressed in different ways. Bero et al. (1998) review ways to implement research results in practice, and find that the specific strategies that work best are educational outreach visits, reminders, multifaceted interventions, and interactive educational meetings. Anderson, Burrows, Fennessy, and Shaw (1999) describe an "evidence centre" in an Australian hospital setting. The Centre for Clinical Effectiveness in Melbourne, set up in 1998, finds and evaluates the best available evidence in response to requests from clinicians. Meanwhile, a pilot project in the U.K., e-STABLISH, provides improved access to evidence-based information sources for primary healthcare workers in their workplaces (Farrell, Cunningham, Haigh, Irozuru, & Cuffin, 1999). The major barrier to practicing evidence-based medicine in a survey of British GPs is lack of personal time (McColl, Smith, White, & Field, 1998). A later qualitative study suggests that, in fact, many GPs may not share the central assumptions of the evidence-based medicine paradigm (Tomlin, Humphrey, & Rogers, 1999).

Having information about the patient and other sources of information readily and seamlessly available at the point of healthcare delivery has long been seen as ideal. A clinical workstation that facilitates easy access to these information sources is still not achievable, however, while components such as the electronic patient record are not fully available or in use. Goncalves, Steele, Franks, and Wilson (1999) have tried to develop a ward-based clinical workstation to support evidence-based medicine, using Web-based technology, and their evaluation finds high acceptability both of the user interface and of the concept of a clinical workstation that gives access to patient-specific data and reference sources.

Miller and Goodman (1998) define medical or clinical decision support systems as computer programs that assist healthcare providers in decision making. In studying the ethics of using such tools, the authors ask when and how these systems should be used, and also what their impact is. One of the most common types is reminder systems, where certain events in patient care trigger reminders to the healthcare professional to take particular actions or avoid others. Reminder systems may be on paper (generated manually or by computer) or on-screen; four reminder subtypes are identified by Gorman et al. (2000): cue sheet, checklist, patient profile, and profile checklist. In a review of 98 trials, Balas et al. (1996) find that physician and patient reminders—among other ingredients of computerized information services—could make a significant difference in family medicine. A meta-analysis of trials to evaluate computer-based clinical reminder systems for preventive care in the ambulatory setting finds that the systems are effective in improving preventive care (Shea, DuMouchel, & Bahamonde, 1996). A systematic review by Hunt, Haynes, Hanna, and Smith (1998) supports the finding regarding preventive care, and notes that clinical decision support systems can also enhance performance for drug dosage and other aspects of care, but do not convincingly improve diagnosis.

E-Health

The use of readily available, popular information technology systems is having considerable impact on how consumers and providers relate to each other, and on the ways health services are delivered. This section discusses the Internet, the use of e-mail, and aspects of telemedicine.

Internet

The move to patient responsibility discussed earlier goes hand-in-hand with the development of electronic means of communication, particularly the Internet (McLellan, 1998).

It is estimated that one billion people are connected to the Internet. In countries such as Finland and Norway, approximately one half of the population has Internet access. In the year 2000, the number of people searching for health information seemed to outstrip even those looking for sex information: One assessment suggested that health information was sought 34 percent of the time (Medical Records Institute, 1999). From 36 percent (Kiley, 1998, p. 202), 40 percent (Eberhart-Phillips et al., 2000) to nearly half (McLellan, 1998, p. 39) of Internet users surveyed had recently accessed medical and health sites.

While the amount of erroneous information on medical and health matters available on the Internet is alarming, it is not the only source of poor advice to patients. Popular printed information and hearsay may be similarly unreliable.

Codes of conduct for medical Web sites and guidance on evaluating the quality of health information sites are noted by the Centre for Health Information Quality (CHiQ). A guide to healthcare on the Internet rates top Web sites and directories of online resources (Guide to healthcare on the Internet, 1999). This type of guide has been studied in a review of published criteria for evaluating health-related Web sites

(Kim, Eng, Deering, & Maxfield, 1999). The reviewers found 165 criteria in twenty-nine published rating tools, noting that most of the authors agreed on the key criteria for evaluating health-related Web sites. The most frequently cited criteria dealt with content, design and aesthetics of sites; disclosure of authors, sponsors, or developers; currency of information; authority of source; and ease of use.

An International e-Health Code of Ethics has been developed by the Internet Healthcare Coalition, with guiding principles covering candor and honesty, quality, informed consent, privacy, professionalism, responsible partnering with other sites and organizations, and accountability in healthcare professionals' provision of care via the Internet (Internet Healthcare Coalition, 2000). This organization has now developed a consensus agreement with others who have also worked on Web site accreditation: the Coalition for Health Information Policy and the American Accreditation HealthCare Commission (American Medical Informatics Association, 2000).

De Groen, Barry, and Schaller (1998) describe an unusual research use of the Internet. They have developed a means of studying patients with rare diseases. As trials of rare diseases are almost impossible to conduct, the authors designed a computerized disease tracking system coupled with a database accessible on the Web. This enabled them to track the patients, their symptoms, and treatments. There are applications in clinical research and practice and coordination of multicenter trials.

Patients who seek information that meets social or emotional needs may find much on the Internet. Pathographies or narratives of illness, not subject to editorial scrutiny, are readily available (McLellan, 1998), as are online support groups. Concerning these, Goodman (1998a, p. 12) describes the problem, "not that free people are taking control of their own healthcare; it is that ignorant people or people misled by unrealistic hope will mistake comfort or gossip for skilled medical, nursing, or psychological help."

E-Mail

While the Web allows technology-rich patients to tap into a huge range of health information, e-mail enables two-way communication across distance between doctor and patient. Nearly half of the U.S. patients already using online health information reported in a 1999 survey that they wanted contact with their physicians by e-mail, but only 3 percent were actually doing so, and only 11 percent had their physicians' e-mail addresses (Physician-patient e-mail underused, 1999). The advantages of using e-mail for doctor-patient communication include increased access, advancing patient education, and improving compliance with treatment. Reluctance on the part of doctors to communicate with patients by e-mail is understandable: There are many pitfalls with potentially serious consequences. Doctors may well fear being overwhelmed by e-mail communications from patients, and being unable to respond to requests. In 1998, Mandl and his colleagues identified areas of concern, some of which have been ameliorated by technological advances (Mandl, Kohane, & Brandt, 1998). The inappropriate use of e-mail, as when face-to-face or telephone contact is actually necessary, or in emergencies, is of concern. Security and confidentiality issues, given that "most violations of the confidentiality of electronic data are committed by authenticated persons" (Mandl et al., 1998, p. 497), and medico-legal issues may worry both patients and doctors. E-mail's ability to generate paper copies can be positive for record-keeping, but may increase physicians' liability. Equity in healthcare access and outcomes may be threatened when technology-advantaged patients can contact their doctors by e-mail, while poor, nonnative speakers or illiterate patients cannot.

Attempting to grapple with some of these issues, the American Medical Informatics Association has developed guidelines for the clinical use of electronic mail with patients. The guidelines tackle "two interrelated aspects: effective interaction between the clinician and patient and observance of medicolegal prudence" (Kane & Sands, 1998, p. 104). The guidelines cover negotiation and agreement between patient and provider, handling of messages, medico-legal issues, and other matters.

Telemedicine

Telemedicine is variously defined (Currell, Urquhart, Wainwright, & Lewis, 2000; Goodman, 1998a; Grigsby & Sanders, 1998; Murdoch 1999; Paul, Pearlson, & McDaniel, 1999; Thrall & Boland, 1998; Wallace, Wyatt, & Taylor, 1998; Watts & Monk, 1999). Some prefer the term "distance medicine" (Balas et al., 1997). The definitions suggest a combination of three essential elements: healthcare, distance, and communications technology. Two modes are identified: real-time systems and store-and-forward systems (Wallace, et al., 1998). The American Telemedicine Association's (2001, online) definition of telemedicine is "the use of medical information exchanged from one site to another via electronic communications for the health and education of the patient or healthcare provider and for the purpose of improving patient care." However, as with electronic medical records, there is a gulf between the potential and the reality in telemedicine. The utilization rates for telemedicine projects are "falling well below expectations," even while there is growth in new installations (Paul et al., 1999, p. 279).

Of course, the use of telecommunications in healthcare has a history as long as that of the telephone; currently, interest is in the transmission of images and other information for diagnosis and care. Much is made of the potential for live, interactive telemedicine, such as consulting between the patient and family in one place and healthcare providers in another through videoconferencing, as described by Murdoch, (1999). But in fact, according to Reich-Hale, (1999), most telemedicine is done on a desk-top, and is mostly of the store-and-forward type.

Telemedicine is used in remote areas, by the military, and for screening. It is commonly used in certain of the more visual medical specialties, including radiology, cardiology, dermatology, and ophthalmology. "The only things a doctor can't do with telemedicine is touch and smell. With a trained nurse, this can be taken care of as well" (Reich-Hale, 1999, p. 35). Home healthcare is asserted to be the fastest-growing service in telemedicine. Gaining expert opinion for primary care workers in both developed and developing countries is another application of interest (Murdoch, 1999; Pal, 2000; Thrall & Boland, 1998).

Advantages summarized by Wallace et al. (1998) include equitable access for remote areas, home care for the elderly, cost savings with reduced clinician and patient travel, and reduced professional isolation. Disadvantages include danger of incomplete information and technological failure, demands on clinicians' time, and cost. Examples of applications include Internet-based home monitoring for asthma patients (Finkelstein, Cabrera, & Hripcsak, 2000).

Balas et al. (1997) review eighty trials of computerized communication, telephone follow-up and reminders, and other telephone-based contacts between professionals and patients. These technologies are found to be beneficial in preventative care, and in the management of patients with osteoarthritis, cardiac illness, and diabetes. More continuity of care, improved access, and coordination of care are achieved with the technologies. A recent systematic review finds little evidence of clinical benefits in telemedicine versus face-to-face patient care, and while the authors recommend more research, they caution against increased investment in unevaluated technologies (Currell, Urquhart et al., 2000). The cost-effectiveness of telemedicine has not yet been demonstrated (Balas et al., 1997; Grigsby & Sanders, 1998). The cost benefits for patients must be balanced against increases in costs to providers (Hakansson & Gavelin, 2000).

Norway is among the most advanced countries when it comes to telemedicine, with an emphasis on distance learning. There, recent trends are less toward videoconferencing, focusing more on asynchronous medicine (Murdoch, 1999).

Important considerations to be addressed in telemedicine are quality of the transmission technology, quality of images to be transmitted, changes in provider-patient relations, and technology availability (Murdoch, 1999). Research on video linking in Britain suggests that high quality sound is of prime importance; also, the remote consultant needs to see the faces of the patient, the accompanying consultant, anyone else in the room; all the parties need to work from the same image of the problem; facilities for remote pointing are desirable; and patients feel more confident when they can see and hear the remote consultant (Watts & Monk, 1999). Mair and Whitten's (2000) systematic review of research into patient satisfaction with real-time interactive video was inconclusive. The authors found a paucity of data examining patients' perceptions or the effects of the method on provider-patient interaction.

Online consulting is developing rapidly, according to the founders of Doctor Global in New Zealand. They claim Doctor Global is pioneering e-health, and that the service provides one-on-one Internet medical consultations. "Our doctors and other health professionals practise from virtual 'e-Clinics' which encompass a growing range of medical specialties" (Doctor Global, 2000, online). The advantages for practitioners include working at a time and place they choose.

Telemedicine cannot wisely be promoted in isolation from other uses of healthcare technologies, according to an Australian study (Mitchell,

2000). A 1999 national study of telemedicine there led to promotion of the concept of e-health, the health sector's equivalent of e-commerce. When telemedicine is used as part of an integrated use of telecommunications and information technology, it is more cost effective.

The barriers to telemedicine's development include technological, legal, and social factors:

- Lack of end-user and technical training
- Poor sound quality
- The gap between the sophistication of the technology and the end-users' needs for clinical activity
- Danger that healthcare is technology led
- Medico-legal issues and professionals' liability
- Licensure; this is a particularly serious issue in the U.S., where each state is responsible for licensing healthcare practitioners, and practicing telemedicine from across state borders may be illegal
- Reimbursement; in the U.S., for example, Medicare will reimburse for teleradiology, but generally not for other telemedicine
- Patient confidentiality and privacy
- Cost
- Provider and patient resistance

(Edlin, 1999; Grigsby & Sanders, 1998; Paul et al., 1999; Reich-Hale, 1999; Thrall & Boland, 1998; Wallace et al., 1998)

What Does the Future Hold?

Writing about health information systems in *ARIST* a decade ago, Tilley (1990) noted some of the changes occurring at the time. People expected information to be at their fingertips, and health professionals were starting to do their own online database searching. She wisely predicted that "new discoveries and implementations will accelerate as we approach the year 2000" (Tilley, 1990, p. 355). She could not have foreseen in detail the Internet explosion and its implications.

More recent writers are cautious about predictions, although Fletcher and Fletcher (1998) are prepared to predict that general medical journals, whether paper or online, "will continue to occupy a central place in medicine, despite increasing specialization." The new journals that summarize existing information will rise in importance. Since there were estimated to be about 16,000 serial medical journals in 1997, there is definitely a place for distillation of their information (Rennie, 1998). Kastin and Wexler (1998) foresee the availability of the full text of all journal articles and textbooks online, including images and tables, and more e-journals that have no printed counterpart. There is a price, though, with the loss of serendipity in library stack browsing.

Finding the right information will remain a central activity. According to Payne (2000, p. 16), "much valuable clinical data is unstructured," and tools are being developed to use much more refined and "intelligent" "concept agents," rather than keyword searches for searching unstructured content.

New kinds of information in the health sector are becoming available. Genomic databases are increasingly likely to develop, for example. This has already occurred in Iceland, where there is a genomic database containing genetic profiles of most of the 275,000 inhabitants (Cerberus, 2000).

Technology issues dominated health informatics in the 1980s and early 1990s, and there were many failed systems and disappointments. During the last decade, however, there has been an increasing emphasis on service and conceptual issues; thus widening the horizons and indicating to a greater range of health professionals, governments, and healthcare consumers the relevance of health informatics to the provision of healthcare. Progress has been slow and uneven. The evidence-based medicine movement has taken twenty years to gain a footing in day-to-day practice, and is still unevenly applied across health services. Some conceptual and philosophical issues are still largely ignored; for example, the nature of medical and related knowledge is rarely debated or researched, and although attention was drawn to problems of arriving at consensus in the field (Brittain, 1985), little progress has been made to resolve outstanding and fundamental problems (Brittain, in press).

At the end of the 1990s, information technology-related issues figure strongly in a list of top-ten health trends likely to ride into the coming decade (Pavia, 1999). The American Medical Informatics Association sees three goals: "a virtual healthcare databank, a national healthcare knowledge base, and a personal clinical health record" (Stead, 1999, p. 88). Further predictions made by Collen (1999, p. 4) include informatics continuing as a transforming force in healthcare. "Information technology will penetrate every aspect of professional practice, as very small, inexpensive computers pervade clinicians' offices and examination rooms, nursing stations, procedure rooms, bedsides, clinics and patients' homes."

Mandl et al. (1998, p. 499) believe that "new communication technologies must never replace the crucial interpersonal contacts that are the very basis of the patient-physician relationship." In health informatics' brave new world—long awaited and not yet fully realized—the human element remains central.

Bibliography

Agreement signals milestone. (1999). *Association Management, 51*(8), 27.

Allison, J. J., Kiefe, C. I., Weissman, N. W., Carter, J., & Centor, R. M. (1999). The art and science of searching Medline to answer clinical questions: Finding the right member of articles. *International Journal of Technology Assessment in Healthcare, 15,* 281–296.

American Academy of Pediatrics. Pediatric Practice Action Group and Task Force on Medical Informatics (1999). Privacy protection of health information: Patient rights and pediatrician responsibilities. *Pediatrics, 104,* 973–977.

American Medical Informatics Association. (2000). AMIA Public Policy. Retrieved December 9, 2000, from the World Wide Web: http://www.amia.org/resource/policy/chip/10-16-00.html

American Telemedicine Association. (2001). Retrieved April 14, 2001, from the World Wide Web: http://www.atmeda.org/whatis/defined.html

Anderson, J., Burrows, E., Fennessy, P., & Shaw, S. (1999). An "evidence center" in a general hospital: Finding and evaluating the best available evidence for clinicians. *ACP Journal Club and Best Evidence, 4,* 102–103.

Australia. National Electronic Health Records Taskforce. (2000). Retrieved December 9, 2000, from the World Wide Web: http://www.health.gov.au/healthonline/ehr_rep.htm

Australian Institute of Health and Welfare and National Public Health Information Working Group. (1999). *National public health information development plan: Directions and recommendations.* Canberra: Australian Institute of Health and Welfare.

Balas, E. A., Austin, S. M., Mitchell, J. A., Ewigman, B. G., Bopp, K. D., & Brown, G. D. (1996). The clinical value of computerized information services: A review of 98 randomized clinical trials. *Archives of Family Medicine, 5,* 271–278.

Balas, E. A., Jaffrey, F., Kuperman, G. J., Austin Boren, S., Brown, G. D., Pinciroli, F., & Mitchell, J. A. (1997). Electronic communication with patients—evaluation of distance medicine technology. *Journal of the American Medical Association, 278,* 152–159.

Ballard, E. (1999). Informatics in the NHS: Paving the way for advanced practice. *Learning Curve, 3*(4), 2–4.

Barker, A. L., & Polson, R. G. (1999). Best of health: Evaluation of a high-street consumer health information shop in a rural area. *Journal of Information Science, 25,* 15–26.

Bastian, H. (2000). Values and the EBM movement: Views after Toronto and Rome. *Consumer Network Newsletter, 8,* 18. Retrieved April 12, 2001, from the World Wide Web: http://www.cochraneconsumer.com/News8_18.htm

Bero, L. A., Grilli, R., Grimshaw, J. M., Harvey, E., Oxman, A. D., & Thomson, M. A. (1998). Closing the gap between research and practice: An overview of systematic reviews of interventions to promote implementation of research findings. *British Medical Journal, 317,* 465–468.

Bolton, P. (1999). A review of the role of information technology in discharge communications in Australia. *Australian Health Review, 22,* 56–64.

Bolton, P., Douglas, K., Booth, B., & Miller, G. (1999). A relationship between computerisation and quality in general practice. *Australian Family Physician, 28,* 962–965.

Borst, F., Appel, R., Baud, R., Ligier, Y., & Scherrer, J. R. (1999). Happy birthday DIOGENE: A hospital information system born 20 years ago. *International Journal of Medical Informatics, 53,* 157–167.

Bowden, T. (2000). Healthcare gains new dimension in cyberspace. *New Zealand Family Physician, 27,* 53–54.

Bowns, I. R., Rotherham, G., & Paisley, S. (1999). Factors associated with success in the implementation of information management and technology in the NHS. *Health Informatics Journal, 5,* 136–154.

Brennan, P. F., & Strombom, I. (1998). Improving healthcare by understanding patient preferences. *Journal of the American Medical Informatics Association, 5,* 257–262.

British Medical Association. (2000). Clinical Effectiveness. Retrieved December 9, 2000, from the World Wide Web: http://library.bma.org.uk/html/faqsco.html

Brittain, J. M. (Ed.). (1985). Consensus and penalties for ignorance in the medical sciences: Implications for information transfer. London: Taylor Graham.

Brittain, J. M. (Ed.) (1997). Introduction. In J.M Brittain (Ed.), *Introduction to information management* (pp. 1–6). Wagga Wagga, Australia: Centre for Information Studies.

Brittain, J. M. (in press). Developing consensus: A case history in communication of information about drinking. *New Review of Health Informatics 2001.*

Brittain, J. M., MacDougall, J., & Gann, R. (1996). Health informatics: An overview. *Journal of Documentation, 52,* 421–448.

Brittain, J. M., & Norris, A.C. (2000). Delivery of health informatics education and training. *Health Libraries Review, 17,* 117–128.

Brown, J. (1998). The computer in the general practice consultation: A literature review. *Health Informatics Journal, 4,* 106–108.

Buetow, S., & Kenealy, T. (2000). Evidence-based medicine: The need for a new definition. *Journal of Evaluation and Clinical Practice, 6,* 85–92.

Canadian Institute for Health Information. (2000). Retrieved December 9, 2000, from the World Wide Web: http://www.cihi.ca/eindex.htm

Carlile, S., & Sefton, A. J. (1998). Healthcare and the information age: Implications for medical education. *Medical Journal of Australia, 168,* 340–343.

Carr, J. J. (2000). Requirements management: Keeping your technology acquisition project under control. *Journal of Nursing Administration, 30,* 133–139.

Centre for Health Information Quality. (1999). Topic Bulletin 5. Retrieved December 9, 2000, from the World Wide Web: http://www.hfht.org/downloads/TB5%20final%20version.pdf

Centre for Health Information Quality. (2000). Retrieved December 9, 2000, from the World Wide Web: http://www.hfht.org/chiq

Cerberus. (2000). Genetic privacy: Will it be a pact with the devil? *British Journal of Healthcare Computing & Information Management, 17,* 15.

Chandra, R., Knickrehm, M., & Miller, A. (1995). Healthcare's IT mistake. *The McKinsey Quarterly, 3,* 90–100.

Charnock, D., & Shepperd, S. (2000). DISCERN and its role in the future of consumer health information. *Health Libraries Review, 17,* 56–58.

Charnock, D., Shepperd, S., Needham, G., & Gann, R. (1999). DISCERN: An instrument for judging the quality of written consumer health information on treatment choices. *Journal of Epidemiology and Community Health, 53,* 105–111.

Chuang, Y. C., Tan, R. R., Wu, M. Y., & Kuo, H. H. (1996). Managing information technology: An empirical study of a computerized management system in ambulatory services at Chuang Gung Memorial Hospital in Taiwan. *International Journal of Computer Applications in Technology, 9,* 181–192.

Clinical effectiveness. (2000). Retrieved December 9, 2000, from the World Wide Web: http://www.doh.gov.uk/swro/0401.htm

Clinical governance: In the new NHS. (1999). *Health Service Circular,* HSC 1999/065, 16 March 1999.

Clinicaltrials.gov. A service of the National Institutes of Health. (2000). Retrieved December 9, 2000, from the World Wide Web: http://clinicaltrials.gov/

Cochrane Collaboration. (2000). Retrieved December 9, 2000, from the World Wide Web: http://www.cochrane.org

Cochrane Effective Practice and Organisation of Care Group. (2001). Retrieved March 3, 2001, from the World Wide Web: http://www.abdn.ac.uk/hsru/epoc

Collen, M. F. (1999). A vision of healthcare and informatics in 2008. *Journal of the American Medical Informatics Association, 6,* 1–5.

Comprehensive Health Enhancement Support System. (2000). Retrieved December 9, 2000, from the World Wide Web: http://chess.chsra.wisc.edu/Chess

Cork, R. D., Detmer, W. M., & Friedman, C. P. (1998). Development and initial evaluation of an instrument to measure physicians' use of, knowledge about, and attitudes toward computers. *Journal of the American Medical Informatics Association, 5,* 164–76.

Coulter, A. (1999). Paternalism or partnership? *British Medical Journal, 319,* 719–720.

Currell R., Urquhart, C., Wainwright, P., & Lewis, R. (2000). Telemedicine versus face to face patient care: Effects on professional practice and healthcare outcomes. (Cochrane Review). *The Cochrane Library,* Issue 2. Oxford: Update Software.

Currell, R., Wainwright, P., & Urquhart, C. (2000). Nursing record systems: Effects on nursing practice and healthcare outcomes (Cochrane Review). *The Cochrane Library,* Issue 2. Oxford: Update Software.

de Groen, P. C., Barry, J. A., & Schaller, W. J. (1998). Applying World Wide Web technology to the study of patients with rare diseases. *Annals of Internal Medicine, 129*(2), 107–113.

DISCERN. (2000). Retrieved December 9, 2000, from the World Wide Web: http://www.discern.org.uk

Doctor Global. (2000). Retrieved December 9, 2000, from the World Wide Web: http://www.doctorglobal.com

Domenighetti, G., Grilli, R., & Liberati, A. (1998). Promoting consumers' demand for evidence-based medicine. *International Journal of Technology Assessment in Healthcare, 14,* 97–105.

Doyle, J. J. (1998). Longitudinal patient data - Rx for better decisions. *Medical Marketing & Media, 33,* 86–90.

Eberhart-Phillips, J., Hall, K., Herbison, G. P., Jenkins, S., Lambert, J., Ng, R., Nicholson, M., & Rankin, L. (2000). Internet use amongst New Zealand general practitioners. *New Zealand Medical Journal, 113,* 135–137.

Edlin, M. (1999). Several barriers inhibit telemedicine growth. *Managed Healthcare, 9,* 36.

Ellis, N. T., & May, C. R. (1999). Computers and the general practice consultation. *Health Informatics Journal, 5,* 124–127.

Entwistle, V. A., Sheldon, T. A., Sowden, A., & Watt, I. S. (1998). Evidence-informed patient choice: Practical issues of involving patients in decisions about healthcare technologies. *International Journal of Technology Assessment in Healthcare, 14,* 212–225.

Entwistle, V. A., Sowden, A. J., & Watt, I. S. (1998). Evaluating interventions to promote patient involvement in decision-making: By what criteria should effectiveness be judged? *Journal of Health Services Research Policy, 3,* 100–107.

Entwistle, V. A., & Watt, I. S. (1998). Disseminating information about healthcare effectiveness: A survey of consumer health information services. *Quality in Healthcare, 7,* 124–129.

Entwistle, V. A, Watt, I. S., Davis, H., Dickson, R., Pickard, D., & Rosser, J. (1998). Developing information materials to present the findings of technology assessments to consumers: The experience of the NHS Centre for Reviews and Dissemination. *International Journal of Technology Assessment in Healthcare, 14,* 47–70.

Etzioni, A. (1999). Medical records. Enhancing privacy, preserving the common good. *Hastings Center Report, 29,* 14–23.

Farrell, L., Cunningham, M., Haigh, V., Irozuru, E., & Cuffin, T. R. (1999). Virtual evidence: Helping primary care practitioners access and implement evidence-based information. *Health Informatics Journal, 5,* 188–192.

Finkelstein, J., Cabrera, M. R., & Hripcsak, G. (2000). Internet-based asthma monitoring: Can patients handle the technology? *Chest, 117,* 148–155.

Fletcher, R. H., & Fletcher, S. W. (1998). The future of medical journals in the western world. *Lancet, SII,* 30–33.

Freeman, P., & Robbins, A. (1999). The US health data privacy debate: Will there be comprehension before closure? *International Journal of Technology Assessment in Healthcare, 15,* 316–331.

Freemantle, N., Mason, J., & Eccles, M. (1999). Deriving treatment recommendations from evidence within randomized trials: The role and limitation of meta-analysis. *International Journal of Technology Assessment in Healthcare, 15,* 304–315.

Gann, R. (1997). Consumer health information services. In J. M. Brittain (Ed.), *Introduction to information management* (pp. 261–268). Wagga Wagga, Australia: Centre for Information Studies.

Glasgow, R. E., McKay, G., Boles, S. M., & Vogt T. M. (1999). Interactive computer technology, behavioural science, and family practice. *Journal of Family Practice, 38,* 464–470.

Goncalves, S., Steele, B., Franks, C., & Wilson, A. (1999). Integration of all information sources in a clinical environment. *Health Informatics Journal, 5,* 193–199.

Goodman, K. W. (1998a). Bioethics and health informatics: An introduction. In K. W. Goodman (Ed.), *Ethics, computing, and medicine: Informatics and the transformation of healthcare* (pp. 1–31). Cambridge: Cambridge University Press.

Goodman, K. W. (1998b). Meta-analysis: Conceptual, ethical, and policy issues. In K. W. Goodman (Ed.), *Ethics, computing, and medicine: Informatics and the transformation of healthcare* (pp. 139–167). Cambridge: Cambridge University Press.

Gorman, P. N., Redfern, C., Liaw, T., Mahon, S., Wyatt, J. C., Rowe, R. E., & Grimshaw, J. M. (2000). Computer-generated paper reminders: Effects on professional practice and healthcare outcomes (Protocol for a Cochrane Review). *The Cochrane Library,* Issue 2. Oxford: Update Software.

Grigsby, J. & Sanders, J. H. (1998). Telemedicine: Where it is and where it's going. *Annals of Internal Medicine, 129*(2), 123–127.

Guide to healthcare on the Internet: A comprehensive guide to new Internet technologies and applications, including rating of top Web sites and directories of online resources, 2000 edition (1999). New York: Faulkner & Gray/Thomson Financial.

Gustafson, D. H., Hawkins, R., Boberg, E., Pingree, S., Serlin, R. E., Graziano, F., & Chan, C. L. (1999). Impact of a patient-centred, computer-based health information/support system. *American Journal of Preventive Medicine, 16,* 1–9.

Hakansson, S., & Gavelin, C. (2000). What do we really know about the cost-effectiveness of telemedicine? *Journal of Telemedicine and Telecare,* Supplement 1:S133–S136.

Hammond, P., & Mosley, M. (1999). *Trust me (I'm a doctor): A consumer's guide to how the system works.* London: Metro Books.

Hersh, W., & Price S. (1998). Identifying randomized controlled trials in conference proceedings abstracts. *Abstract Book, Sixth International Cochrane Colloquium,* 52.

Hersh, W. R., & Hickam, D. H. (1998). How well do physicians use electronic information retrieval systems? A framework for investigation and systematic review. *Journal of the American Medical Association, 280,* 1347–1352.

Hunt, D. L., Haynes, R. B., Hanna, S. E., & Smith, K. (1998). Effects of computer-based clinical decision support systems on physician performance and patient outcomes: A systematic review. *Journal of the American Medical Association, 280,* 1339–1346.

International Nursing Informatics Congress Programme. (2000). *One Step Beyond: The Evolution of Technology and Nursing.* Retrieved December 9, 2000, from the World Wide Web: http://www.ninz.org.nz

Internet Healthcare Coalition. (2000). Retrieved December 9, 2000, from the World Wide Web: http://www.ihealthcoalition.org/community/ethics.html

Jadad, A. R. (1999). Promoting partnerships: Challenges for the Internet age. *British Medical Journal, 319,* 761–764.

James, S. D., & Thomas, R. E. (1999). Problems in community healthcare information systems: A case study. *Health Informatics Journal, 5,* 146–153.

Jousimaa, J., Kunnamo, I., & Makela, M. (1998). Physicians' patterns of using a computerized collection of guidelines for primary care. *International Journal of Technology Assessment in Healthcare, 14,* 484–493.

Kane, B., & Sands, D. Z. (1998). Guidelines for the clinical use of electronic mail with patients. *Journal of the American Medical Informatics Association, 5,* 104–111.

Kastin, S., & Wexler, J. (1998). Bioinformatics: Searching the net. *Seminars in Nuclear Medicine, 27,* 177–187.

Keltner, K. B. (1998). Networked health information: Assuring quality control on the Internet. *Federal Communication Law Journal, 50,* 417–439.

Kidd, M., & Mazza, D. (2000). Clinical practice guidelines and the computer on your desk. *Medical Journal of Australia, 173,* 373–375.

Kiley, R. (1998). Consumer health information on the Internet. *Journal of the Royal Society of Medicine, 91,* 202–203.

Kim, P., Eng, T. R., Deering, M. J., & Maxfield, A. (1999). Published criteria for evaluating health related Web sites: Review. *British Medical Journal, 318,* 647–649.

King's Fund launches quality service. (1998). *British Medical Journal, 316,* 1754.

Knotterus, A., & Dinant, G. J. (1997). Medicine based evidence, a prerequisite for evidence based medicine. *British Medical Journal, 315,* 1109–1110.

Lagerlov, P., Loeb, M., Andrew, M., & Hjortdahl, P. (2000). Improving doctors' prescribing behaviour through reflection on guidelines and prescription feedback: A randomised controlled study. *Quality in Healthcare, 9,* 159–165.

Lerner, J. C. (1998). The National Patient Library: Evidence-based information for consumers. *International Journal of Technology Assessment in Healthcare, 14,* 81–96.

Lewis, D. (1999). Computer-based approaches to patient education. *Journal of the American Medical Informatics Association, 6,* 272–282.

Lobach, D., & Hammond, W. (1997). Computerized decision support based on a clinical practice guideline improves compliance with care standard. *American Journal of Medicine, 102,* 89–98.

Lowe, H. J. (1999). Multimedia electronic medical record systems. *Academic Medicine, 74,* 146–152.

MacDougall, J., & Brittain, J. M. (1998). Health services information. In M. Line, G. MacKenzie, & P. Sturges (Eds.), *Librarianship and information work worldwide 1998* (pp. 171–199). London: Bowker Saur.

Mair, F., & Whitten, P. (2000). Systematic review of studies of patient satisfaction with telemedicine. *British Medical Journal, 320,* 1517–1520.

Mandl, K. D., Kohane, I. S., & Brandt, A. M. (1998). Electronic patient-physician communication: Problems and promise. *Annals of Internal Medicine, 129,* 495–500.

McCloskey, K. M. (2000). Library outreach: Addressing Utah's "digital divide." *Bulletin of the Medical Library Association, 88,* 367–373.

McColl, A., Smith, H., White, P., & Field, J. (1998). General Practitioners' perception of the route to evidence based medicine: A questionnaire survey. *British Medical Journal, 316,* 361–365.

McCray, A. T., & Ide, N. C. (2000). Design and implementation of a National Clinical Trials Registry. *Journal of the American Medical Informatics Association, 7,* 313–323.

McGee, M. K. (1998). IT seen preventing cost overruns. *Information Week, 700,* 165–170.

McLellan, F. (1998). "Like hunger, like thirst": Patients, journals, and the Internet *Lancet, SII,* 39–43.

Medical Records Institute. (1999). Retrieved December 4, 2000, from the World Wide Web: http://www.medrecinst.com/index.shtml

Medline plus. (2000). Rockville, MD: National Library of Medicine. Retrieved December 4, 2000, from the World Wide Web: http://www.medlineplus.gov

Miller, R. A., & Goodman, K. W. (1998). Ethical challenges in the use of decision-support software. In K. W. Goodman (Ed.), *Ethics, computing, and medicine:*

Informatics and the transformation of healthcare (pp. 102–115). Cambridge: Cambridge University Press.

Mitchell, J. (2000). Increasing the cost-effectiveness of telemedicine by embracing e-health. *Journal of Telemedicine and Telecare, 6* (Supplement 1) S16–S19.

More, D. G., & Clarke, P. A. (1999). The General Practice computer system project: A doctor's desktop for Australia. *Journal of Medical Informatics, 55,* 65–75.

Morrissey, J. (1999). Internet company rates hospitals. *Modern Healthcare, 29,* 24–25.

Murdoch, I. (1999). Telemedicine. *British Journal of Ophthalmology, 83,* 1254–1256.

National Electronic Library for Health. (2000). Leeds, U.K.: National Health Service. Retrieved December 9, 2000, from the World Wide Web: http://www.doh.gov.uk/nhsinfo/pages/informat/library.htm

Netting the evidence: A ScHARR introduction to evidence based practice on the Internet. (2000). Retrieved December 4, 2000, from the World Wide Web: http://www.shef.ac.uk/~scharr/ir/netting

New Zealand. Health Information Service. (2000). Retrieved December 9, 2000, from the World Wide Web: http://www.nzhis.govt.nz/projects

Noone, J., Warren, J., & Brittain, M. (1998). Information overload: Opportunities and challenges for the GP's desktop. In B. Cesnik, A. T. McCray, & J. R. Scherrer (Eds.), *Proceedings of the Ninth World Congress on Medical Informatics* (pp. 287–291). Amsterdam: IOS.

Norris, A. C., & Briggs, J. S. (1999). Care pathways and the information for health strategy. *Health Informatics Journal, 5,* 202–212.

Norris, A. C., & Brittain, J. M. (2000). Education and the development of health informatics. *Health Informatics Journal, 6,* 189–195.

O'Connor, A. M., Rostom, A., Fiset, V., Tetroe, J., Entwistle, V., Llewellyn-Thomas, H., Holmes-Rovner, M., Barry, M., & Jones, J. (1999). Decision aids for patients facing health treatment or screening decisions: Systematic review. *British Medical Journal, 319,* 731–734.

Oliver, S. (2000). Revolutionizing how we generate new knowledge: A challenge for librarians, health professionals, service users and researchers. *Health Libraries Review, 17,* 22–25.

O'Reilly, K. E. (1998). Nursing Informatics: What can it do for managers? *Nursing Management* (Chicago), *29*(7), 65–66.

Owens, D. K. (1998). Use of medical informatics to implement and develop clinical practice guidelines. *Western Journal of Medicine, 168,* 166–175.

Pal, B. (2000). Internet helps communication between doctors and patients. *British Medical Journal, 320,* 59.

Paul, D. L., Pearlson, K. E., & McDaniel, R. R. (1999). Assessing technological barriers to telemedicine: Technology-management implications. *IEEE Transactions on Engineering Management, 46,* 279–288.

Pavia, L. (1999). Healthcare's top 10 trends that should ride into next decade. *Healthcare Strategic Management, 17,* 12–13.

Payne, W. (2000). Managing unstructured content. *British Journal of Healthcare Computing & Information Management, 17,* 16.

Physician-patient e-mail underused. (1999). *Lancet, 354,* 1654.

Reeve, R., & Rose, G. (1999). The role of top management in supporting the use of information technology in Australian hospitals. *Australian Health Review, 22,* 151–60.

Reich-Hale, D. (1999). Technology gains fuel telemedicine growth. *National Underwriter, 103,* 35.

Rennie, D. (1998). The present state of medical journals. *Lancet, SII,* 8–22.

Retchin, S. M., & Wenzel, R. P. (1999). Electronic medical record systems at academic health centers: Advantages and implementation issues. *Academic Medicine, 74,* 493–498.

Reviewing Health Informatics Services. NHS Executive Full LIS Guidance Annex A. (2000). Retrieved December 9, 2000, from the World Wide Web: http://www.doh.gov.uk/nhsexipu/implemen/flis/guidance/annexes/annexa1.htm

Rigby, M. (1999). The management and policy challenges of the globalisation effect of informatics and telemedicine. *Health Policy, 46,* 97–103.

Rolfe, G. (1999). Insufficient evidence: The problems of evidence based nursing. *Nurse Education Today, 19,* 433–42.

Rose, J. R. (1998). States are still erecting barriers against it. *Medical Economics, 75,* 26–32.

Sackett, D. L., Rosenberg, W. M. C., Gray, J. A. M., Haynes, R. B., & Richardson, W. S. (1996). Evidence based medicine: What it is and what it isn't. *British Medical Journal, 312,* 71–72.

Schaffer, R. A. (1999). The Internet may finally cure what ails America's healthcare system. *Fortune, 140,* 274.

Schloeffel, P. (1999). Good electronic health record. *New Zealand Health Informatics Foundation News Update.* Retrieved December 9, 2000, from the World Wide Web: http://www.nzhis.govt.nz/infostandards/nzhif/news-current.html#gehr

School of Health and Related Research, University of Sheffield. (2000). Retrieved December 4, 2000, from the World Wide Web: http://www.shef.ac.uk/~scharr/ir/def.html

Serb, C. (1998). Tech travails. *Hospitals & Health Networks, 72,* 38–40.

Shea, S., DuMouchel, W., & Bahamonde, L. (1996). A meta-analysis of 16 randomized controlled trials to evaluate computer-based clinical reminder systems for preventive care in the ambulatory setting. *Journal of the American Medical Informatics Association, 3,* 399–409.

Shepperd, S., Charnock, D., & Gann, B. (1999). Helping patients access high quality health information. *British Medical Journal, 319,* 764–766.

Shiffman, R. N., Liaw, Y., Brandt, C. A., & Corb, G. J. (1999). Computer-based Guideline Implementation Systems: A systematic review of functionality and effectiveness. *Journal of the American Medical Informatics Association, 6,* 104–114.

Simpson, R. L. (1998a). The technologic imperative: A new agenda for nursing education and practice. *Nursing Management,* (Chicago), Part 1, *29*(9), 22–24.

Simpson, R. L. (1998b). The technologic imperative: A new agenda for nursing education and practice. *Nursing Management,* (Chicago), Part 2, *29*(10), 22–25.

Simpson, R. L. (1999). Nursing informatics. Changing world, changing systems: Why managed healthcare demands information technology. *Nursing Administration Quarterly, 23,* 86–88.

Simpson, R. L. (2000). Minding the store: How IT impacts outcomes measurement. *Nursing Administration Quarterly, 24,* 87–90.

Southon, G., Sauer, C., & Dampney, K. (1999). Lessons from a failed information system initiative: Issues for complex organisations. *International Journal of Medical Informatics, 55,* 33–46.

Stead, W. W. (1999). The challenge to health informatics for 1999–2000. *Journal of the American Medical Informatics Association, 6,* 88–89.

Sullivan, F., & Mitchell E. (1995). Has general practitioner computing made a difference to patient care? A systematic review of published reports. *General Practice, 311,* 848–852.

Tang, L. H. Y., Haska, R., & Ip, H. H. S. (1999). A review of intelligent content-based indexing and browsing of medical images. *Health Informatics Journal, 5,* 40–49.

Tang, P. C. (2000). An AMIA perspective on proposed regulation and privacy of health information. *Journal of the American Medical Informatics Association, 7,* 205–207.

Tang, P. C., & Newcomb, C. (1998). Informing patients: A guide for providing patient health information. *Journal of the American Medical Informatics Association, 5,* 563–570.

Terry, K. (1999). Electronic medical records make sense—at last. *Medical Economics, 76,* 134–153.

Thrall, J. H., & Boland, G. (1998). Telemedicine in practice. *Seminars in Nuclear Medicine, 27,* 145–157.

Tilley, C. B. (1990). Medical databases and health information systems. *Annual Review of Information Science and Technology, 25,* 313–382.

Tomlin, Z., Humphrey, C., & Rogers, S. (1999). General practitioners' perceptions of effective healthcare. *British Medical Journal, 318,* 1532–1535.

U.K. National Health Services. (2000a). Direct Online. Leeds, U.K.: National Health Service. Retrieved December 9, 2000, from the World Wide Web: http://www.nhsdirect.nhs.uk/main.jhtml

U.K. National Health Services. (2000b). Information Authority. Leeds, U.K.: National Health Service. Retrieved December 4, 2000, from the World Wide Web: http://www.nhsia.nhs.uk

U.K. National Health Services. (2000c). The new NHS. Leeds, U.K.: National Health Service. Retrieved December 4, 2000, from the World Wide Web: http://www.doh.gov.uk/nhsinfo/index.htm

U.K. National Health Services Executive. (1998). Health Service Circular 1998/168 Leeds, U.K.: National Health Service. Retrieved December 9, 2000, from the World Wide Web: http://www.doh.gov.uk/nhsexipu/strategy/hsc/hsc.pdf

U.K. National Health Services Executive. (1999a). Health Service Circular 1999/065. Leeds, U.K.: National Health Service. Retrieved December 9, 2000, from the World Wide Web: http://www.doh.gov.uk/npg/65hsc.pdf

U.K. National Health Services Executive. (1999b). Working together with health information—summary briefing. Leeds, U.K.: National Health Services Executive. Retrieved December 9, 2000, from the World Wide Web: http://www.doh.gov.uk/nhsexipu/develop/nip/together.htm

U.K. National Health Services Executive. (2000a). Information Strategy & Development Leeds, U.K.: National Health Service. Retrieved December 9, 2000, from the World Wide Web: http://www.doh.gov.uk/nhsexipu/strategy/index.htm

U.S. Department of Commerce. National Telecommunications and Information Administration. (2000). Retrieved December 9, 2000, from the World Wide Web: http://www.ntia.doc.gov/ntiahome/digitaldivide/index.html

U.S. National Library of Medicine. (2000). The Visible Human Project. Retrieved December 9, 2000, from the World Wide Web: http://www.nlm.nih.gov/pubs/factsheets/visible_human.html

van der Kam, W. J., Moorman, P. W., & Koppejan-Mulder, M. J. (2000). Effects of electronic communication in general practice. *International Journal of Medical Informatics, 60,* 59–70.

Wallace, S., Wyatt, J., & Taylor, P. (1998). Telemedicine in the NHS for the millennium and beyond. *Postgraduate Medical Journal, 74,* 721–728.

Watts, L. A., & Monk, A. F. (1999). Telemedicine: What happens in remote consultation. *International Journal of Technology Assessment in Healthcare, 15,* 220–235.

Wood, F. B., Lyon, B., Schell, M. B., Kitendaugh, P., Cid, V. H., & Siegel, E. R. (2000). Public library consumer health information pilot project: Results of a National Library of Medicine evaluation. *Bulletin of the Medical Libraries Association, 88,* 314–322.

Index

U

W

X

More Great Books from Information Today, Inc.

ARIST 35: Annual Review of Information Science and Technology

Edited by Martha E. Williams

Contents of Volume 35 include:

♦ *The Concept of Situation in Information Science,* by Colleen Cool

♦ *Conceptual Frameworks in Information Behavior,* by Karen E. Pettigrew, Raya Fidel, and Harry Bruce

♦ *Distributed Information Management,* by William M. Pottenger, Miranda R. Callahan, and Michael A. Padgett

♦ *Digital Privacy: Toward a New Politics and Discursive Practice,* by Philip Doty

♦ *Subject Access Points in Electronic Retrieval,* by Birger Hjorland and Lykke Kyllesbech Nielsen

♦ *Methods of Generating and Evaluating Hypertext,* by James Blustein and Mark S. Staveley

♦ *Digital Preservation,* by Elizabeth Yakel

♦ *Knowledge Management,* by Noreen Mac Morrow

♦ *Library and Information Science Education in the Nineties,* by Elisabeth Logan and Ingrid Hseieh-Yee

2001/600 pp/hardbound/ISBN 1-57387-115-X
ASIST Members $79.95 • Non-Members $99.95

Evaluating Networked Information Services
Techniques, Policy, and Issues

Edited by Charles R. McClure and John Carlo Bertot

As information services and resources are made available in the global networked environment, there is a critical need to evaluate their usefulness, impact, cost, and effectiveness. This new book brings together an introduction and overview of evaluation techniques and methods, information policy issues and initiatives, and other critical issues related to the evaluation of networked information services.

2001/300 pp/hardbound/ISBN 1-57387-118-4
ASIST Members $35.60 • Non-Members $44.50

Historical Information Science

An Emerging Unidiscipline

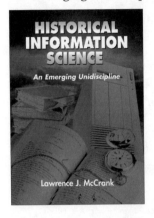

By Lawrence J. McCrank

Here is an extensive review and bibliographic essay, backed by almost 6,000 citations, about developments in information technology since the advent of personal computers and the convergence of several Social Science and Humanities disciplines in historical computing. Its focus is on the access, preservation, and analysis of historical information (primarily in electronic form) and the relationships between new methodology and instructional media, technique, and research trends in library special collections, digital libraries, electronic and data archives, and museums.

2002/1200 pp/hardbound/ISBN 1-57387-071-4
$149.95

Statistical Methods for the Information Professional

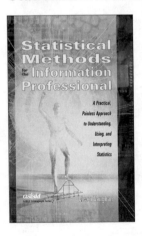

By Liwen Vaughan

For most of us, "painless" is not the word that comes to mind when we think of statistics, but author and educator Liwen Vaughan wants to change that. In this unique and useful book, Vaughan clearly explains the statistical methods used in information science research, focusing on basic logic rather than mathematical intricacies. Her emphasis is on the meaning of statistics, when and how to apply them, and how to interpret the results of statistical analysis. Through the use of real-world examples, she shows how statistics can be used to improve services, make better decisions, and conduct more effective research.

Whether you are doing statistical analysis or simply need to better understand the statistics you encounter in professional literature and the media, this book will be a valuable addition to your personal toolkit. Includes more than 80 helpful figures and tables, 7 appendices, bibliography, and index.

2001/240 pp/hardbound/ISBN 1-57387-110-9
ASIST Members $31.60 • Non-Members $39.50

Editorial Peer Review

Its Strengths and Weaknesses

By Ann C. Weller

This important book is the first to provide an in-depth analysis of the peer review process in scholarly publishing. Author Weller (Associate Professor and Deputy Director at the Library of the Health Sciences, University of Illinois at Chicago) offers a carefully researched, systematic review of published studies of editorial peer review in the following broad categories: general studies of rejection rates, studies of editors, studies of authors, and studies of reviewers. The book concludes with an examination of new models of editorial peer review intended to enhance the scientific communication process as it moves from a print to an electronic environment. *Editorial Peer Review* is an essential monograph for editors, reviewers, publishers, professionals from learned societies, writers, scholars, and librarians who purchase and disseminate scholarly material.

2001/360 pp/hardbound/ISBN 1-57387-100-1
ASIST Members $35.60 • Non-Members $44.50

Introductory Concepts in Information Science

By Melanie J. Norton

Melanie J. Norton presents a unique introduction to the practical and theoretical concepts of information science while examining the impact of the Information Age on society. Drawing on recent research into the field, as well as from scholarly and trade publications, the monograph provides a brief history of information science and coverage of key topics, including communications and cognition, information retrieval, bibliometrics, modeling, economics, information policies, and the impact of information technology on modern management. This is an essential volume for graduate students, practitioners, and any professional who needs a solid grounding in the field of information science.

2000/127 pp/hardbound/ISBN 1-57387-087-0
ASIST Members $31.60 • Non-Members $39.50

The Web of Knowledge

A Festschrift in Honor of Eugene Garfield

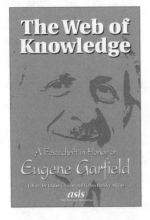

Edited by Blaise Cronin and Helen Barsky Atkins

Dr. Eugene Garfield, the founder of the Institute for Scientific Information (ISI), has devoted his life to the creation and development of the multidisciplinary Science Citation Index. The index, a unique resource for scientists, scholars, and researchers in virtually every field of intellectual endeavor, has been the foundation for a multidisciplinary research community. This ASIS monograph is the first to comprehensively address the history, theory, and practical applications of the Science Citation Index and to examine its impact on scholarly and scientific research 40 years after its inception. In bringing together the analyses, insights, and reflections of more than 35 leading lights, editors Cronin and Atkins have produced both a comprehensive survey of citation indexing and analysis and a beautifully realized tribute to Eugene Garfield and his vision.

2000/544 pp/hardbound/ISBN 1-57387-099-4
ASIST Members $39.60 • Non-Members $49.50

Intelligent Technologies in Library and Information Service Applications

By F.W. Lancaster and Amy Warner

Librarians and library school faculty have been experimenting with artificial intelligence (AI) and expert systems for 30 years, but there has been no comprehensive survey of the results available until now. In this carefully researched monograph, authors Lancaster and Warner report on the applications of AI technologies in library and information services, assessing their effectiveness, reviewing the relevant literature, and offering a clear-eyed forecast of future use and impact. Includes almost 500 bibliographic references.

2001/214 pp/hardbound/ISBN 1-57387-103-6
ASIST Members $31.60 • Non-Members $39.50

Information Management for the Intelligent Organization, 3rd Edition

By Chun Wei Choo

The intelligent organization is one that is skilled at marshalling its information resources and capabilities, transforming information into knowledge, and using this knowledge to sustain and enhance its performance in a restless environment. The objective of this newly updated and expanded book is to develop an understanding of how an organization may manage its information processes more effectively in order to achieve these goals. The third edition features new sections on information culture, information overload, and organizational learning; a new chapter on Knowledge Management (KM) and the role of information professionals; and numerous extended case studies of environmental scanning by organizations in Asia, Europe, and North America. This book is a must-read for senior managers and administrators, information managers, information specialists and practitioners, information technologists, and anyone whose work in an organization involves acquiring, creating, organizing, or using knowledge.

2001/352 pp/hardbound/ISBN 1-57387-125-7
ASIST Members $31.60 • Non-Members $39.50

Historical Studies in Information Science

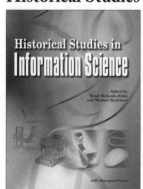

Edited by Trudi Bellardo Hahn and Michael Buckland

The field of information science has a broad history spanning nearly a century. *Historical Studies in Information Science* focuses on the progression of this dynamic and evolving industry by looking at some of its pioneers. This informative volume concentrates on the following areas: Historiography of Information Science; Paul Otlet and His Successors; Techniques, Tools, and Systems; People and Organizations; Theoretical Topics; and Literature.

1998/317 pp/softbound/ISBN 1-57387-062-5
ASIST Members $31.60 • Non-Members $39.50

Knowledge Management for the Information Professional

Edited by T. Kanti Srikantaiah and Michael Koenig

Written from the perspective of the information community, this book examines the business community's recent enthusiasm for Knowledge Management (KM). With contributions from 26 leading KM practitioners, academicians, and information professionals, editors Srikantaiah and Koenig bridge the gap between two distinct perspectives, equipping information professionals with the tools to make a broader and more effective contribution in developing KM systems and creating a Knowledge Management culture within their organizations.

2000/608 pp/hardbound/ISBN 1-57387-079-X
ASIST Members $35.60 • Non-Members $44.50

Knowledge Management: The Bibliography

Compiled by Paul Burden

Knowledge Management (KM) is a holistic process by which an organization may effectively gather, evaluate, share, analyze, integrate, and use information from both internal and external sources. *Knowledge Management: The Bibliography* is the first comprehensive reference to the literature available for the individual interested in KM, and features citations to over 1500 published articles, 150+ Web sites, and more than 400 books. Organized by topic area (i.e., "KM and Intranets," "KM and Training," "KM and eCommerce"), this work is a natural companion volume to the ASIS monograph *Knowledge Management for the Information Professional* and an important new tool for anyone charged with contributing to or managing an organization's intellectual assets.

2000/160 pp/softbound/ISBN: 1-57387-101-X
ASIS Members $18.00 • Non-Members $22.50

For a complete catalog, contact:
Information Today, Inc.
143 Old Marlton Pike, Medford, NJ 08055 • 609/654-6266
email: custserv@infotoday.com • Web site: www.infotoday.com